P9-AFV-075

MONEY
CHANGES
EVERYTHING

PRINCETON UNIVERSITY PRESS
PRINCETON & OXFORD

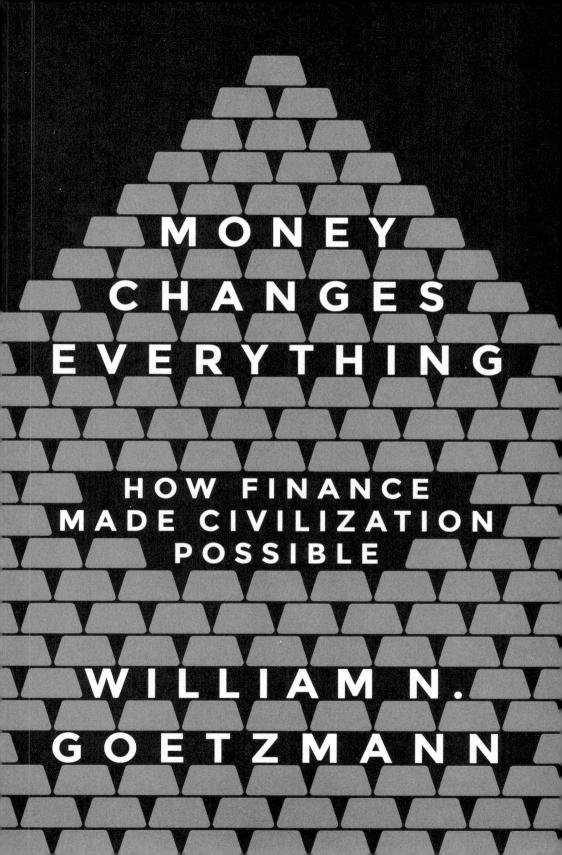

MONEY CHANGES EVERYTHING

HOW FINANCE MADE CIVILIZATION POSSIBLE

WILLIAM N. GOETZMANN

Copyright © 2016 by William N. Goetzmann

Requests for permission to reproduce material from this work
should be sent to Permissions, Princeton University Press

Published by Princeton University Press
41 William Street, Princeton, New Jersey 08540

In the United Kingdom: Princeton University Press
6 Oxford Street, Woodstock, Oxfordshire OX20 1TR

press.princeton.edu

Jacket design by Chris Ferrante

All Rights Reserved

Library of Congress Cataloging-in-Publication Data
Goetzmann, William N., author.
Money changes everything : how finance made civilization possible /
William N. Goetzmann.
pages cm
Includes bibliographical references and index.
ISBN 978-0-691-14378-1 (hardcover : alk. paper)
-- ISBN 0-691-14378-1 (hardcover : alk. paper)
1. Finance--History. 2. Economic history. 3. Civilization--History. I. Title.
HG171.G638 2016
332.09--dc23
2015025879

British Library Cataloging-in-Publication Data is available

This book has been composed in Garamond Premier Pro and Montserrat

Printed on acid-free paper. ∞

Printed in the United States of America

3 5 7 9 10 8 6 4

CONTENTS

ACKNOWLEDGMENTS

Many thanks to everyone who read and commented on drafts of this book—they include friends, colleagues, and coauthors: my editor Seth Ditchik; my colleagues K. Geert Rouwenhorst, Rik Frehen, David Le Bris, Martin Shubik, Zhiwu Chen, Douglas Rae, Valerie Hansen, Henry Hansmann; and three anonymous reviewers. Most of all I acknowledge the support of my late father William H. Goetzmann, whose encouragement and support throughout the project kept me going. He stressed the importance of communicating to broader audiences. I thank Leigh Ann Clark for her help with the practical challenges of key parts of this project. Many thanks to Johanna Palacio for project management and her excellent work on the images for the book. I owe a great debt to Yuan Chen for her thoughtful editing of the sections of the book pertaining to China. Over the years, Ulla Kasten has helped me with access to the Yale Babylonian Collection.

I also thank the many scholars who gave me advice and pointed me in the right direction: Ben Foster, Marc Van De Mieroop, Elisabeth Köll, Robert Shiller, Timothy Young, Catherine Labio, Jonathan Spence, Steven Pincus, and Naomi Lamoreaux. I thank William Fitzhugh and Harvey Weiss for including me in their pathbreaking archaeological expeditions early in my career. And I thank my friend William S. Reese for introducing me to many of the extraordinary documents in financial history that have become part of the narrative of this book.

I particularly acknowledge the support of the Yale School of Management over the years. Yale funding, along with the funding of an anonymous donor to the International Center for Finance, allowed me to visit the important sites in financial history, to collect and study early financial documents, to explore archives throughout the world, to build databases of early capital markets, to bring together the leading scholars in the field for rewarding discussions and the cross-pollination of ideas, and finally to develop cases and a course in financial history. Although not part of the book per se, the cases developed by Jaan Elias, Andrea Nagy-Smith, and Jean Rosenthal deeply enriched my understanding of the past. Most of all, I thank Yale University for creating an intellectually generous environment—and one that consistently celebrates interdisciplinary research.

New Haven, 2015

MONEY
CHANGES
EVERYTHING

INTRODUCTION

Finance is often regarded as an abstract, mathematical subject that occasionally calls attention to itself by dramatic crises or as a symbol of excess. In fact, finance has been an integral part of the development of human society over the past 5,000 years. Finance played a key role in the development of the first cities, the emergence of classical empires, and the exploration of the world.

The history of finance is an exciting story. For example, writing was invented in the ancient Near East specifically for recording financial contracts. Finance was integral to the first complex models of time and risk. The golden age of Athens owes as much to financial litigation as it does to Socrates. Rome's legendary wealth could not have sustained itself over the centuries without complex financial organization. Ancient Chinese civilization developed its own financial tradition that enabled rulers to hold together a vast empire.

In modern Europe, finance stimulated a novel mathematical tradition that quantified and analyzed risk and made possible an unprecedented era of exploration and discovery. A new financial structure—the corporation—emerged as a means to aggregate capital for trade with Asia and the Americas. Finance was an important co-factor in the Industrial Revolution. In the twentieth century, capital markets democratized investing and stimulated novel solutions to major social problems: social security, sovereign funds, and personal savings accounts are all mechanisms intended to reduce household economic risk. They have deep roots in the history of finance.

Along with these important contributions to humankind, finance has also created problems: debt, market bubbles, devastating crises and crashes, exploitative corporations, imperialism, income inequality—to name only a few. The story of finance is the story of a technology: a way of doing things. Like other technologies, it developed through innovations that improved efficiency. It is not intrinsically good or bad.

TIME AND MONEY

The power of finance to effect such important transitions in world history is that it moves economic value forward and backward through time. Think about a mortgage. It converts a homebuyer's promise of thirty years of future monthly payments into a lump sum of money in the present. A mortgage is so commonplace that it is hard to fully appreciate it. A homebuyer can suddenly conjure up a fortune he or she does not have. Where did this great power come from? Why does it work? What can go wrong? These are some of the key issues explored in this book.

A mortgage shifts money to the present, but, for the lender it also moves money into the future. By the same token, a person worried about retirement can actually buy future living money today—usually at a significant discount. The ability to solve the fundamental problem of taking care of your future self is incredibly empowering. It rests on a sophisticated technological structure that is able to express and enforce commitments that extend over decades and in some cases over centuries.

In essence, financial technology is a time machine we have built ourselves. It can't move people through time, but it can move their money. As a result, it alters the economic position of our current and future selves. It also changes the way we think. Finance has stretched the ability of humans to imagine and calculate the future. It has also demanded a deeper understanding and quantification of the past, because history is the fundamental basis for making future predictions. Finance has increasingly made us creatures of time. Financial architecture exists in—and shapes—the possibilities of the temporal dimension.

This book explores key steps in the evolution of finance in world history. My fundamental premise is that civilizations demand sophisticated tools for managing the economics of time and risk. Finance emerged with the first civilizations of the ancient Near East and since then has played a key role in many cultures we recognize as complex societies. Civilizations over the past 5,000 years have faced a common set of problems, and they have either borrowed or invented a similar set of financial tools to solve them.

China is an important part of this book precisely because it faced civilization's complex challenges of economic time and space in its own way. Although certain financial tools and methods diffused across the Eurasian continent by trade and faith, China's financial development took its own course; China developed its own monetary economy, its own accounting and financial control systems, and the first paper securities—printed money that Marco Polo saw and used in China centuries before printing emerged in Europe. The resonance and dissonance between Chinese and European financial development reflects alternative historical paths. From it we learn what is common in the technologies of finance; how parallel innovations can arise; and how new ideas are adopted, altered, and embedded into broader social, political, and cultural frameworks. The comparison between financial developments in China and Europe reflects my personal research interest over the past two decades. With great regret I've left out evidence from many other civilizations.

The extraordinary expansion of humanity and urban society over the five millennia is testimony to the fact that finance has vastly improved our species' ability to reduce existential risks and to allocate resources through time to foster growth. However, civilization's growth has engendered its own problems. The biggest of these is whether the intertemporal balance—the trade-off between current and future generations—can be preserved.

This book is a somewhat personal narrative about the people, places, and things that, in my view, shaped the history of finance as a technology of civilization. It does not pretend to be a comprehensive financial history of the world. That is a vast task that, to some extent is currently under way as a result of collective scholarly efforts. The book reflects not only the specific themes that linked finance and civilization but also my personal, idiosyncratic experiences—both as a financial economist and as a former participant in the worlds of archaeology and filmmaking; both of which provided a different frame of reference with respect to the role of finance in society. These prior experiences took me to some extraordinary locations in the history of finance. I hope the reader will forgive me for personalizing some of them. A "place where" frame of reference sometimes evokes a richer context for discovery. Before launching into the story, however, an overview of financial technology, some definitions of civilization, and the logic of the connection between the two are in order.

Finance has four key elements:

1. It reallocates economic value through time;
2. It reallocates risk;
3. It reallocates capital; and
4. It expands the access to, and the complexity of, these reallocations.

Let me explain each of these.

The example of the mortgage above demonstrates the first key element: reallocation of economic value through time. A mortgage is one kind of financial contract, but there are many others. All of them are promises today about a future action. The contract ties the present and future together in a way that can benefit the contracting parties.

Second, finance reallocates risk. Reallocation through time means that financial contracts must cross the barrier of uncertainty that separates present and future. Some risks we must simply live with—such as the risk of a meteorite striking the earth. Other risks we can take steps to reduce or to restructure. Financial contracts take the exposure to risk that is inherent in the dimension of time, and they allocate it among various parties. For example, life insurance contracts can shift the risk of mortality from a single household to a large institution, which, in turn, can diversify by pooling it together with many other contracts.

Third, finance reallocates capital. The stock market, for example, allows the flow of investment into productive enterprises. Banks, for example, make loans to businesses with the potential for profits. In this way finance is a technology for facilitating economic growth.

Fourth, finance expands the access to and complexity of these reallocations. As it developed through history, finance provided an increasingly richer set of intertemporal contracting possibilities. This richness and complexity mirrored the complexity of the society that engendered it. At times, this complexity challenged the very boundaries of written language's ability to specify them. A modern mortgage-backed securitization contract, for example, can be 900 pages long and can detail an enormous variety of conditions, rights, and responsibilities. The virtue of such complexity is that it expands the contracting "space" between parties—that is, the number of dimensions along which they can negotiate. When you do this, you are able to arrive at agreements that simpler systems might not. The very richness and complexity of the intertemporal agreements finance allows is itself an important contribution of the technology. Without this multidimensional freedom, some fundamental activities of civilization would not be possible.

REALLOCATION THROUGH TIME

Financial contracts are typically struck between someone who wants to shift value to the present and someone who wants to shift value to the future. There are two broad reasons for shifting money to the present: consumption and production. The consumption motive is the need for cash to cover current expenses, to buy food, to pay medical bills, or to deal with some other unforeseen cost.

Consumption loans can be used to reduce risk. In an uncertain world, sudden expenses arise. Financial contracts allow you to borrow or pledge against the future to mitigate negative shocks today. In extreme circumstances, such as crop failure or a sudden illness, an emergency loan is a way to put food on the table and provide medicine to the sick—it smooths out the difference between good times and bad times. Financial contracts can be essential tools for survival. They provide the same potential benefits to governments, by the way. Governments borrow to pay for military defense or a sudden calamity, and then repay the loan with future tax revenues. The economic term for this financial function is "intertemporal smoothing of consumption."

Productive loans are different from consumption loans. They play a special role in the economy, because they are based on the notion of growth. They do not simply smooth economic shocks between the present and future; they make a different kind of future possible. Finance can bring capital together to create an enterprise that will generate higher future value. For example, a farmer can borrow to buy seeds to plant, and the harvest can yield a bounty well beyond the original cost of the seeds. If a farmer could not borrow, the land would not be used productively.

By the same token, finance allows productive use of human ingenuity. Without finance, the only people who could start a business would be those who already had money to do so. Finance removes the prerequisite of wealth from entrepreneurship. It feeds capital to potentially productive projects regardless of whether or not the entrepreneur is rich. In this sense, finance broadly disseminates the economic advantages of wealth—it democratizes access to productive capital and removes the natural constraints to funding productive projects. This is the basic logic connecting finance and economic growth.

The use of finance for consumption and production also has potential problems. Consumption loans have been criticized as promoting profligate behavior and exploiting desperate borrowers. Productive loans can lead capital astray; easy money can fuel foolish projects just as it can fund profitable enterprise.

Shifting money to the present for reasons of consumption and production can be done through different kinds of financial contracts. The simplest is the loan, but there are other kinds of financial promises. A share of stock or a partnership share offers an ownership stake in an enterprise rather than a fixed future payment. Insurance and option contracts offer a future payment depending on the occurrence of a particular event or condition. Throughout history, people have come up with various forms of contracts that allow for broader participation in productive enterprise. We will explore some of these in detail in this book.

INVESTMENT

Consumption and production use current capital; investment provides that capital. It is the basic technology for saving for the future. That is why pension funds hold stocks and bonds and other financial assets.

Investing money rather than spending it requires delaying gratification. No one likes to delay gratification without a good reason. For investors, a key incentive is the expectation of higher future consumption. In the simplest form of a financial contract—a loan—the lender expects to get back the money lent plus some extra amount: interest. The longer the loan is made for, the longer the investor delays personal consumption and thus, typically, the more interest is promised in compensation.

The rate of return on the investment can be thought of as the price of time. It equilibrates the intertemporal supply and demand for money. It balances the needs of investors against those of consumers and producers. For example, if the interest rate is too low, investors may prefer to spend their cash now rather than save it. If the interest rate is too high, producers may forgo projects, because their expected return on borrowed capital is insufficient to repay the loan.

While these trade-offs seem simple, they have global implications. The productivity of capital investment intermediates between the world's consumers, producers, and investors. Investors are connected to today's consumers and producers through financial institutions and markets. The balance is a delicate one. When financial markets crash, investors can curtail the flow of capital to enterprise. Demographics are fundamental to the equation. As the world's life expectancy grows, the need to save grows as well. As the world population ages, the ratio of producers to consumers declines. Finance not only intermediates the present and the future, it also intermediates between the young and the old.

By the same token, the financial equation between the present and the future only works if there is genuine economic growth. This is fine in a world of low-hanging entrepreneurial opportunities, but as the growth of emerging economies slows down to the pace of mature economies, the question of where future growth will come from looms large. The specter of the limits to growth—and the consequent breakdown between present and future economic value—has long concerned economists and planners.

CULTURE VERSUS FINANCE

It is easy to think about finance as an abstraction—after all, the notion of transcending time is fundamentally abstract. However, finance is embedded in human culture and behavior. Society has long struggled with placing finance in a moral and cultural context. While finance can solve great problems, it also can threaten the status quo. It changes who turns to whom in an emergency. It reallocates wealth; it creates the potential for social mobility and social disruption.

In some sense, the most basic intertemporal economic institution is the family. A social compact in which children take care of aging parents, for example, is a retirement plan. Likewise, a reciprocal gifting commitment among family, friends, or members of a community fulfills the same function as a financial loan. Unlike a loan, however, the compensation is a future social obligation rather than interest payments—tightening a social network rather than loosening it.

These arrangements long preceded formal financial contracts. Finance emerged in a cultural context that already addressed intertemporal problems to some extent. In this sense, financial contracts were not entirely new. Rather they substituted for, and often improved upon, traditional intertemporal mechanisms. As such they represented a challenge to the status quo.

At times, culture has lashed back at finance—particularly around financial crises. This response may in part be due to the threat finance poses to tradition social, economic, and political institutions. For example, some of the earliest ad hominem attacks on financiers were by Babylonian political leaders consolidating authority. The first stock market boom in eighteenth-century Britain was criticized in part because female investors were making money in a traditionally male-dominated realm.

Because finance is a potentially destabilizing force, society has often sought to place bounds on it. These constraints are sometimes couched in moral terms. Usury laws were introduced under the guise of protecting borrowers. Britain's Bubble Act restricted the creation of business corporations under the guise of stopping immoral speculation. The Securities and Exchange Commission was created in the 1930s in the United States to regulate the potential misuse of financial techniques and tools. Behind these and other restrictions on financial contracting is the implicit—and reasonable—supposition that rules are needed to prevent the financially adept from exploiting those less sophisticated—and underlying this is the fact that finance reorganizes power. A financially adept mind that can think through trade-offs between present and future is an extraordinary asset in a world with financial instruments and markets—but it can also represent a danger. Finance has the potential for great social change, which is inherently risky.

FINANCE AND CIVILIZATION

Finance offers a rich variety of ways to reconfigure human relationships, particularly because it expands the domain of interaction through time. It can focus economic power, shifting it quickly from place to place. It can be both a weapon of war and an instrument of peace. This complexity and potentiality makes finance a particular tool of civilization. In this book I argue that there are reasons finance emerged in the first civilizations; reasons complex financial instruments are less frequently part of the toolkit of traditional cultures.

The hallmarks of civilization are urbanism; social specialization; sophisticated symbol systems; and complex, multidimensional interactions. Civilizations are also open systems that absorb and synthesize knowledge. As my father, the late historian W. H. Goetzmann once put it:

> Cultures are structures of interrelated institutions, language, ideas, values, myths and symbols. They tend to be exclusive, even tribal. Civilizations, on the other hand, are open to new customs and ideas. They are syncretistic, chaotic, and often confusing societal information systems. They continue to grow in the richness, variety and complexity of societal experience.[1]

Financial systems expand the scope and nature of these social relationships into the realm of time and across both great and very close distances. A dense, urban society creates relationships of all kinds. In a city you not only interact with family and long-term acquaintances. You also interact with people for whom traditional reciprocal relationships do not work. Urban life may demand one-off interactions with foreign visitors or repeated interactions with tradespeople who cannot reciprocate in ways you require.

Such financial tools as coins, loans, and partnership agreements expanded the set of economic interactions to people who may not willingly interact otherwise. Financial markets allow strangers to exchange value through time more efficiently than traditional reciprocity arrangements do. They do not require shared belief systems or cultural norms, simply a structure for documentation and enforcement. Financial instruments expanded the dimensions over which individuals could come to agreements, and this expansion uniquely fits the needs of a complex, multidimensional urban society.

Civilization not only requires contracting among many different types of economic agents, but it also requires flexibility to respond to complex, multidimensional problems. Financial contracts allow an enormous variety of novel payoffs and promises. Even the very first financiers operated in a sophisticated nexus of institutions and commitments; they had deals with institutions such as temples and palaces; with farmers and other producers; and with long-distance traders, who in turn interacted economically with other cultures and civilizations. These first financiers depended on a variety of outcomes and events: political decisions, agricultural output, the fortunes of overseas trade ventures, the fluctuating price of commodities, and the honesty of employees. Complicated lives require interaction, planning, and commitment in many different dimensions over a variety of unknown future outcomes. The development of finance was driven by the demands of civilization's social and economic complexity.

FINANCE AND KNOWLEDGE

Finance also played a role in another key aspect of civilization: the development of knowledge. One important way that humankind learned about the boundaries of the world was through merchant voyages requiring money and time—underwritten by investors hopeful of a future profit. In this way, finance has been a cofactor in civilization's expansion and outreach. Trade routes linked societies from distant parts of the world. These distant connections were not only spatial, they were also temporal. From the outset, long-distance trade created long gaps of time: intervals between investment and return separated by the veil of uncertainty. Columbus had to wait patiently for the funding of his first transatlantic voyage, and then he had to promise the future unknown profits to his benefactors. His contract with the Spanish crown was extraordinarily complex: he received not only political favors but also 10% of future revenues from transatlantic trade. He also negotiated an option to invest up to 1/8 share of any commercial enterprise organized to exploit his discoveries. Without this intertemporal contracting, he might never have set sail.

I will also show how finance has changed the tools humanity uses to develop and preserve knowledge. Financial problems stimulated the development of writing, recording, calculation, and printing. It also directly spurred some of humanity's most important mathematical innovations, including the discovery of logarithms, the mathematics of probability and uncertainty, and the ability of mathematics to express an infinitely long series and to divide time and the process of change into infinitesimally small intervals.

Finance stimulated the development of quantitative models of the future and the maintenance of deep records about the past. Markets taught people about such things as the limitations of the capacity for reason and the dangers of miscalculation. These complex conceptual frameworks augmented and stimulated the development of problem solving, but they also set up a conflict between traditional and quantitative modes of thought. This conflict is heightened during periods of financial innovation and financial disaster. Not only did financial architecture challenge traditional institutions, it also challenged traditional conceptual frameworks for dealing with the unknown. Cultural notions of chance and fortune are embedded in a rich set of symbols, myths, and moral valences. Understanding and managing this conflict remain important challenges to modern society.

HARDWARE AND SOFTWARE

Finance has two different dimensions—what might be thought of as hardware and software. The hardware is constituted by such things as financial contracts, corporations, banks, markets, and monetary and legal systems. I generally refer to this as financial architecture. Finance is also a system of analysis that incorporates counting; recording; algorithmic calculation; and advanced mathematical methods, such as calculus and probability theory. On an even deeper level, finance is a system of thought; a means of framing and solving complex problems about money, time, and value. In essence, this is the software of the technology.

This book highlights historical episodes in the development of both financial hardware and software. Both dimensions are embedded in the broader structures of society. As they evolved, not only did they draw from other fields of work and other technologies, but other technologies also have drawn from finance.

THE OTHER SIDE OF THE COIN

With each advance in the hardware or software of finance, a problem was solved, but new problems appeared. Financial solutions improved the capability of humankind to create cities, to explore new worlds, to expand and equalize economic opportunity, to control risk, and to provide for an uncertain future. But at times financial innovation has created serious disequilibria in and across societies; disruptions that have defined the fundamental conflicts in the modern world and that will continue to shape the development of the world to come. I hope to explore both faces of finance: its capacity to solve problems and its tendency to create them.

PERSPECTIVES

This book is told from a number of perspectives. The first is that of the inventors and users of financial tools. Sometimes we know these people, but often they are anonymous. The invention of the first loan was a great idea, but no one knows who had it. Financiers are not historians; capital markets are not libraries—financial techniques were invented to make money, not to make their inventors famous. In fact, usually when we know a lot about financial innovators, it is due to a disaster. For example, the visionary banker John Law is still known for the collapse of his innovative Mississippi Company designed to rescue France from bankruptcy in the years leading up to the bubble of 1720. However famous, anonymous, or infamous its inventors, keep in mind that finance is by, for, and about people's lives. Each shareholder in John Law's Mississippi Company bought shares for personal reasons—maybe to take a flyer on a risky venture, maybe he or she trusted John Law's scheme, or perhaps just because others were doing it. Whatever the reason, the only way to figure out how a financial tool works is to ask why someone might need it in the first place. Ultimately, finance is personal and concrete, not abstract and theoretical. It is not only about money but also about people and how they use money.

The second perspective is that of the researcher. History is discovery, and historians are explorers. Much of this book unfolds from research by archaeologists, classicists, historians, economists, and mathematicians.

Just as important, however, are those who are devoted to preserving the past—librarians, collectors, and dealers—all of whom treasure the documentary evidence of history. I hope to convey the excitement of all their quests. Some of their views are sparks of insight mixed with years of careful research. For example, we would not understand the birth of finance in the ancient Near East without Professor Denise Schmandt-Besserat of the University of Texas, who discovered the origins of cuneiform writing—along with the origins of financial contracts. We owe a lot to the Shanghai financier and monetary historian Peng Xinwei 彭信威, who devoted his life to Chinese financial history before disappearing in the Cultural Revolution. We might never understand the first inflation-indexed security if not for economist Robert Shiller's personal mission to help people insure themselves against everyday economic risks.

A third perspective is empirical: the world of things and places. Technology requires actual tools and locations. For finance, this means coins, documents, correspondence, and places where these things were made and exchanged. Objects like coins and stock certificates functioned as tools, because they solved such problems as the storing and conveyance of value and the transmission of value through time. They have been made of many different things—clay, metal, and papyrus—and printed on vellum, bark, or paper. It is important to understand the material culture of finance to appreciate how it worked as a technology.

Yet another perspective is cultural. Although this book is not a cultural history of finance—in many instances, artists, writers, moral philosophers, dramatists, and even comedians have interpreted financial markets, and this in turn has influenced the course of these markets' development. The criticism of finance as a tool of exploitation on moral grounds goes back to Babylonian times. The discomfort that society has felt with the complexity and abstraction of financial tools has stimulated rich artistic interpretations that in turn shaped cultural attitudes. We sometimes turn to art for a perspective, and artists' views on finance—from seventeenth-century tulip mania prints to the twentieth-century murals about commerce in New York's Rockefeller Center—depict finance in the context of familiar cultural symbols. The artist's vision is an integral part of the narrative of this book.

Much of my research in finance has been directed toward a scholarly audience; however, one motivation for writing this book is the hope that a broader audience will be curious about the origins of a toolkit that we all share and a mindset that seems at times difficult and perhaps unnatural. As important as it is to live every day in the present, finance challenges us to think hard about the future.

My personal view is that the trajectory of technological innovation has been mostly upward and will continue to be so. The financial solutions we have in the world today are generally life improving. The problems they created have been serious at times, but as a global society, we seem to make progress in dealing with them. Would the world have been a better place without the discovery of loans, banks, bonds, stocks, options, capital markets, insurance, and corporations? Perhaps, but I doubt it. The argument in this book is that financial technology allowed for more complex political institutions, enhanced social mobility, and greater economic growth—in short, all the major indicators of complex society we call civilization. Ultimately, financial relationships have become important means by which economies are knit together into a complex global civilization. As a global civilization, we must continue to face the basic problem posed by finance: how to equilibrate between the needs of the present and those of the future; and how to make the benefits of finance broadly available to everyone in society, wealthy and poor. The historical trajectory of financial innovation may just provide a useful guide.

FROM CUNEIFORM TO
CLASSICAL CIVILIZATION

Finance began with the first cities—and vice versa. This first section focuses on the parallel emergence of urban civilization and finance. The joint emergence of finance and civilization in the ancient Near East teaches an important lesson. Higher levels of political and social development demand complex economic organization and technology. Financial infrastructure made many of the advances of urban society possible—and it still does. Humanity gave up a certain measure of economic innocence on the developmental path to urbanism, but at the same time it began a process of discovery and invention that fundamentally changed human experience.

The first four chapters trace the extraordinary arc of financial development in the ancient Near East. I argue that the invention of a way to express the exchange of value through time created a novel model of thought: a capacity to forecast economic outcomes and to treat past, present, and future values as equally concrete. With the invention of finance, people lived their economic lives in an exquisitely articulated framework of time. Stepping into this quantified temporal framework opened up many new possibilities. Some were ways of mitigating risk. For example, financial thinking was embedded in the earliest agricultural civilizations because of the need to plan farming and husbandry operations, and to record promises of future commodity deliveries. However, financial tools were also part of waging war. The earliest record of a boundary dispute in antiquity includes a demand for reparations with punitive compound interest.

Neither finance nor urban society remained stationary through the first two millennia of their coexistence, and the chapters on the ancient Near East emphasize the way in which financial tools were adapted to trade as well as to agricultural production. Finance became a mecha-

Detail of the Enmetena cone, ca. 2400 BCE. The cone is a Sumerian document commemorating the conquest of the city of Umma by Enmetena, the king of the rival city of Lagash. The ruler's claim for war reparations is the earliest known record of compound interest.

nism for facilitating complex mercantile operations stretching from Anatolia to the Indus.

The chapters on Athens and Rome show how two different cultures adopted and transformed the Near Eastern financial legacy. I argue that financialization in fact made both the Athenian and Roman economies possible. Both were reliant on imported grain. Their financial systems developed, in part, to allocate investment capital to support the commodity trade and to allocate the risk of this trade.

Two aspects of Greek civilization are highlighted: law and money. The simple existence of courts in Athens created enforceable property rights and attracted investors. I claim that the courts also had an important intellectual and perhaps cognitive effect. Trade disputes were regularly argued before juries of hundreds of citizens, and this must have created an intensely financially literate society. The monetization of the Athenian economy was an equally important step. Recently, scholars have argued that it played a central role in the transition to the political phenomenon for which Athens is most famous: democracy. Money became both a tool for sharing the Athenian economic success and an instrument for aligning personal loyalties to the state.

This section finishes with a chapter on Rome and a picture of a fully financialized ancient economy—like Athens, an import society that sustained one of the largest cities in the world via commodity trade. Personal wealth in Rome played a key role in political power, and fortunes were sustained through a variety of direct and indirect investment opportunities. Debt played an important role in the Roman financial system, and it left its trace in a series of financial crises.

One of the Rome's most innovative contributions to finance was the creation of shareholder companies that supplied services to the growing needs of the state. Investors in these companies, called publican societies, participated in profits from tax-farming, public works construction, and provisioning Rome's armies. Publican societies were the world's first large-scale publicly held companies—something like modern corporations. Their shares fluctuated in value and were held broadly by citizens of Rome. I argue that these financial instruments played a crucial role in the political structure of Rome at a certain juncture in its history, because they provided a means to reallocate the economic benefits of Rome's expansion and conquest among key political constituents.

1

FINANCE AND WRITING

This chapter explores the appearance of finance as a technology in the ancient Near East and the role it played in the unique features of the world's first large-scale urban societies. Mesopotamia gave the world its first cities, first written language, first laws, first contracts, and first advanced mathematics. Many of these developments directly or indirectly came from financial technology. Cuneiform writing, for example, is an unintended by-product of ancient accounting systems and contracts. Babylonian mathematics owes its development to arithmetic and calculation demanded by its financial economy. The first mathematical models of business growth and profit appeared 4,000 years ago. The legal system of the Babylonians depended crucially on the use of notarized and witnessed documents and contracts establishing individual rights and obligations, many of which are similar to modern financial instruments and contracts. The first mortgages, deeds, loans, futures contracts, partnership agreements, and letters of credit appear as cuneiform documents dating to the second millennium BCE or earlier. In short, the dramatic development of urban society beginning more than 5,000 years ago involved the simultaneous development of new kinds of institutions and processes, many of which were economic and financial in nature. These financial practices, embedded in larger social and economic institutions, are what I refer to as the hardware of finance in the Introduction.

This chapter also explores how financial tools changed the way people thought. Financial technology made possible not just financial contracts but also financial thinking—conceptual ways of framing economic interactions that use the financial perspective of time. Borrowing, lending, and financial planning shaped a particular conceptualization of time, quantifying it in new ways and simplifying it for purposes of calculation. This way of thinking and specialized knowledge, in turn,

Clay tokens from the ancient Near East symbolizing economic commodities. They are thought to have been used as a system of accounting and are also believed to be the precursors of the world's first written language.

Clay tokens
metal coins
why not crypto?

affected and extended the capabilities of government and enterprise. This conceptual framework is what I refer to as the software of finance in the Introduction.

Finance relies on the ability to quantify and calculate and reason mathematically. Thus, much of this chapter focuses on the development of mathematical tools in ancient times. Another basic ingredient of finance is the dimension of time. Finance requires the measurement and expression of time and this chapter explores time technology in some depth. Finally, it deals with record-keeping, contracting, and the legal framework of finance. This is because finance is mostly about future promises. Promises are meaningless without the capacity to record and enforce them.

The first evidence of financial tools appears in the context of the early urban, agricultural societies of the ancient Near East, roughly contemporaneous with the beginning of the Bronze Age. The prehistoric roots of urban society in the ancient Near East extend back perhaps 7,000 years. By 3600 BCE, the cities of ancient Sumer arose around the confluence of the Tigris and Euphrates rivers in what is now modern Iraq—a location well suited to cultivation of grain and livestock but lacking in other needs, such as timber, copper, and tin. These last two items were especially important, because they are the essential ingredients for making bronze—a metal vital for ancient warfare. Archaeological evidence suggests that Sumerian cities relied on long-distance trade for these key commodities. They also traded for exotic prestige items, such as ivory and precious stones, which played a role in the intensification of social and political hierarchy—likewise a hallmark of civilization.

In short, the economy of ancient Near Eastern civilization required methods for producing and distributing basic foodstuffs locally to a concentrated urban populace and also ways of obtaining goods from afar. The basic unit of finance—a contract that extends through time—addressed both of these economic imperatives. As ancient unban societies of the Near East grew in scale and scope (i.e., density of population and geographical range of trade), they relied increasingly on intertemporal contracting techniques (i.e., finance). Finance first appeared with one of humanity's most remarkable inventions—writing; the ability to memorialize something now that can be interpreted unambiguously in the future. Even writing, however, had its precedents, and these emerged out of a financial imperative.

We begin this chapter with the discovery of an essential piece of financial hardware: counting, accounting, and contracting tools.

TEMPLES AND TOKENS

> He built the town wall of Uruk, (city) of sheepfolds,
> of the sacred precinct of Eanna, the holy storehouse.
> Look at its wall with its frieze like bronze!
> Gaze at its bastions, which none can equal!
> Take the stone stairs that are from times of old,
> Approach Eanna, the seat of Ishtar,
> the like of which no later king—no man—will ever make.[1]

One of the earliest literary works ever written tells the story of Gilgamesh, the hero who traveled to distant lands to obtain timber for building a temple in his city. The passage above is from the epic of Gilgamesh.[2] It sings the praises of the majestic city walls and the Eanna temple of Uruk, the birthplace of Mesopotamian civilization. Although the text is eloquent, the cuneiform script in which the epic was first recorded owes more to merchants and accountants than it does to poets. Cuneiform was not invented for writing poetry but for accounting and business, and Uruk may have been the original site of both. Of course, it is difficult to precisely pinpoint the time and location of the development of any technology, but some of the earliest material remains of writing—and the precursors to writing—have come to light at Uruk. Scholars working on the beginnings of writing believe that it evolved from a peculiar system of symbolic accounting records associated with the Uruk temple economy.

In 1929, the German archaeologist Julius Jordan excavated the heart of the ancient city—Uruk's central temple complex. This Indiana Jones–scale dig revealed Jordan's long-sought prize, the "sacred precinct of Eanna, the holy storehouse," the place where the fertility goddess Inanna was worshipped but also where goods and commodities were distributed to the populace. Near the temple, Jordan and his crew of excavators found the stone steps of the temple—exactly as described in the epic of Gilgamesh. Jordan kept a careful record of all his discoveries—not only the monumental architecture, but even small artifacts and objects that were unearthed in the dig. In his journals, he documented curious little tokens "shaped like commodities of daily life: jars, loaves and animals" that came to light around the temple complex. These little objects went largely unstudied until Professor Denise Schmandt-Besserat, a scholar at the University of Texas at Austin, began to analyze them in systematic fashion.

Born and educated in France, Schmandt-Besserat began her research at Radcliffe in a fellowship program for promising female scholars. She became fascinated with the question of whether clay was used as a technology before the invention of pottery. This puzzle first took her to museum collections to search for early clay objects. She became a research fellow in Near Eastern Archaeology at Harvard's Peabody Museum, and there rediscovered the mystery of Jordan's little tokens. Denise moved to the University of Texas in the 1970s, where she continued her work on the tokens—painstakingly tracking down every recorded mention of them in archaeological digs in the Near East and visiting all the museum collections that contained them.

I first met Denise when I was a graduate student in art history at the University of Texas at Austin, and she was a curator at the University of Texas Art Museum. She was my teacher, and I was able to observe directly her path-breaking work. I had no idea at the time that it would be the finance implicit in the token system—rather than the art of it—that would ultimately capture my interest.

While other scholars of the ancient Near East were studying big problems like the evolution of temple architecture, the political history of ancient city-states, and the question of how the ancient climate affected farming and urbanism, Denise concentrated her efforts on laboratory analysis and documentation of the tokens. She established that tokens predated even the ancient city of Uruk. They appeared in prehistoric sites throughout the Near East as early as 7000 BCE. Whatever these things were—counters, game tokens, or mystical symbols, they were used by many different peoples and cultures long before the invention of writing.

The objects are about the size of game pieces. Their stylization and simplification suggest that they were standardized for easy recognition—abstract and simple rather than realistic. A systematic organization of the tokens by form and place of discovery led Denise to a stunningly novel hypothesis. Her analysis linked them iconographically to the earliest pictographic writing on clay tablets found in the oldest parts of Uruk.

The oldest Uruk tablets were made circa 3100 BCE by scribes who took wet lumps of clay, shaped them into lozenges, and wrote on them with a wooden stylus. The stylus had a sharp end and round end—one end for lines and the other for dots. Laid sideways, the stylus could also make triangular and cylindrical impressions. The combination of these formed a lexicon that scholars have now concluded was the first writing.

What Schmandt-Besserat famously recognized is that the pictographs on these early tablets were essentially pictures of the little clay tokens. For instance, she showed that the pictograph for cloth could be traced to a round, striated token. The symbol for sweet evolved from a token shaped like a honey jar. The symbol for food evolved from a token shaped like a full dish. Most represented commodities from daily life: lambs, sheep, cows, dogs, loaves of bread, jars of oil, honey, beer, milk, clothing, ropes, wool, and rugs, and even such abstract goods as units of work. Apparently, these were the items once contained in the goddess Inanna's "holy storehouse." These beautiful little objects were not about art—they were about economics—commodities in the Sumerian redistribution system.

The connection between the tablets and the tokens helps explain the function of each. Virtually all of the earliest tablets from Uruk were accounting documents recording the transfer of goods and commodities. They were administrative records used by some central governing economic authority—almost certainly the temple.

The tokens evidently were used in the same kind of process, perhaps by the world's first accountants sitting in front of the storehouse door of the temple, keeping track of how much went in and out. In a preliterate society that needed a way to keep track of economic transactions, the tokens were natural symbols that could be matched one-for-one with standardized goods and services. This connection between the symbolic record and the early written record led Schmandt-Besserat to her theory about how writing evolved.[3]

In the classic model of the Sumerian economy, the temple functioned as an administrative authority governing commodity production, collection, and redistribution. The discovery of administrative tablets from these complexes suggests that token use and consequently writing evolved as a tool of centralized economic governance. Given the dearth of archaeological evidence from Uruk-period domestic sites, it is not clear whether individuals also used the system for personal agreements. For that matter, it is not clear how widespread literacy was at its beginnings. The use of identifiable symbols and pictograms on the early tablets is consistent with administrators needing a lexicon that was mutually intelligible by literate and nonliterate parties. As cuneiform script became more abstract, literacy must have become increasingly important to ensure one understood what he or she had agreed to.

The idea of writing certainly spread beyond the immediate zone of the Tigris and Euphrates. Sumerian cities in the fourth millennium traded extensively with Susa immediately to its east in what is now southwestern Iran. In fact, Susa was likely colonized by Uruk as early as the late fifth millennium. It developed its own clay tablet script (called *proto-Elamite*) and used the same token system found at Uruk.[4] Perhaps the accounting system was used not only for local commodity distribution but also for interregional trade agreements.

A key link in the theory of the development of cuneiform writing is yet another enigmatic clay object from the ancient Near East: hollow, round clay envelopes called *bullae*. The French scholar Pierre Amiet found a bulla that had a set of markings on the outside that matched the same number and types of tokens on the inside. Amiet theorized that Uruk accountants made the external marks to show what tokens were contained inside a bulla without opening it up. Schmandt-Besserat built on Amiet's insights to reconstruct the early development of writing. She theorized that the bullae were the forerunners of pictographic tablets, and the tokens representing articles of daily life evolved from three-dimensional models into stylized cuneiform symbols, as the models were themselves abstracted into impressions on a clay surface. Later, the stylized pictographs became even more abstract and evolved from drawing to stylus impressions, now called "cuneiform."

Schmandt-Besserat's theory is not universally accepted—some scholars question the basic idea of a transition from tokens to writing and point out discrepancies in the notion of a temporal evolution from models to signs. For example, tokens were used for thousands of years in the ancient Near East—not just in the preliterate period. Why, for example, did the bullae system survive after the invention of writing? Also puzzling is that the widest variety of tokens appeared after the first writing began, not before—suggesting that the token and bullae system was alive, well, and developing in parallel to cuneiform. While tokens and bullae may have led to the discovery of writing, it appears that this technology continued to respond to needs that were not completely met with the written word.

ANCIENT CONTRACTS

Why would the ancient accountants of Uruk use a cumbersome bullae system for their records—and then keep using it even after they could simply write the information down? Although the bullae were not exactly accounting tools, they may have been contracts. Everything we think of as a financial instrument today is a contract. A government bond, for instance, is a contract between the government and the bondholder to guarantee a series of payments in the future. A share of stock is a contract between the shareholder and the corporation that guarantees participation in the profits of the firm and a right to vote on its management. Although contracts existed before the invention of writing—and even before the invention of bullae—the hollow clay balls and their tokens are arguably the earliest archaeological evidence of contracts.

Each bulla evidently meant that someone made a promise to give some commodity—jars of honey, sheep, cattle, perhaps even days of work—to the temple. The writing on the outside of the bulla allowed the contracting parties to refer to the amount owed over the term of the contract or to the people entering into the contract. The tokens inside tangibly symbolized the obligation. This interpretation may explain other curious features of the bullae as well. Some envelopes are covered entirely in the cylinder seal impressions—the Mesopotamian equivalents of signatures—suggesting that the contracting parties were concerned that the someone might open a small hole and insert or remove tokens.

Cuneiform scholar Stephen Lieberman points out that the key feature of the bullae are not that they recorded information, but rather that they are a conditional verification device that could be examined in case of a dispute over quantity, just like a modern paper contract can be referred to by the parties in case of a disagreement.[5]

If the Uruk tablets are protowriting, perhaps the bullae are protofinancial instruments. Of course, we do not know for certain whether the obligation is a loan, a tax, or tribute to the temple. All we know for sure is that they formalized commitments of future payments. The bullae were contracts that bridged some indeterminate temporal interval between two events—from the moment when the parties entered into an obligation, to the moment when the obligation was discharged and verification was potentially needed.

The bullae and token system appeared in a society that relied crucially on the production and distribution of agricultural commodities but in which not everyone was a farmer. Some people in the ancient city grew grain and made beer; others tended sheep, collected wool, and made textiles. Still others were involved in trading activities to obtain goods from distant lands. While we take it for granted today that we can drop by the market and buy the food we need for dinner, modern urban economies are quite complex and involve countless intermediaries between farm and table. It's inconceivable that the economic chain to supply a city's daily needs could exist without purchase orders, receipts, and reimbursements. And so it was in ancient Uruk.

FINANCIAL ACCOUNTS

Cuneiform writing opened up vast possibilities. Although the exact process of evolution continues to be debated, archaeologists agree that sometime circa 3100 BCE the people of Uruk, as well as those of other places in the Near East—Sumeria and Susa—began to use pictographic clay tablets to record economic transactions. The tablets from Uruk, however, are by far the most plentiful, and it seems likely that Gilgamesh's city was an early and important center of writing.

The tablets are important in their own right in an ancient financial system that was growing to accommodate the needs of the economy. While the bullae typically contained no more than a couple dozen tokens, the pictographic tablets recorded much larger quantities of goods. They did this in an ingenious way—they used a number system.

The numerous pictographic tablets from Uruk are the first evidence for an abstract number system. This was a crucial step in the development of the software of finance. Once economic quantities became large enough, it was difficult to represent them one-for-one with tokens, or even pictographs. The Uruk tablets began to separate the pictographic representations of commodities from the abstract numbers. For instance, on one tablet five sheep were represented by the combination of a sheep symbol (the crossed circle) next to five impressed strokes in the clay (the numeral for five). A round impression represented the numeral for ten. Thus the Uruk accountants could represent thirty-three by three round marks and three strokes. Interestingly enough, even though the quantity and type of good were represented by different symbols, the early Uruk tablets do not have freestanding numbers. A number is always accompanied with the object that is enumerated. The system does not represent the "concept" of the number five, but rather always records five things. This would suggest that the early Mesopotamians were tied at first to concrete notions as opposed to abstract concepts.

MODEL OF TIME

Time is a fundamentally abstract notion, particularly once it is decoupled from the cycle of the seasons and from astronomical phenomena, such as the phases of the moon. Time—more specifically, the notion of a common metric for time—is central to finance. For example, a promise to return something in the future is not useful unless there is a way to agree on when this can happen. The ancient Mesopotamian symbol system abstractly conceptualized time—represented it symbolically, and perhaps most intriguingly, performed arithmetic operations on quantities of time. While Mesopotamians certainly had time before they had finance, their economy seems to have influenced their notion of time.

University of California, Los Angeles, professor Robert Englund is the director of the Cuneiform Digital Library Initiative, which is creating an online visual archive of all the world's cuneiform texts for scholarly research. He has decoded precisely this idealized Sumerian framework for administrative time.[6] Englund studied a series of protocuneiform tablets that apparently document daily grain rations over a span of three years—2½ liters or 5 liters a day meted out on a precisely regular basis. What makes these records interesting is that these payments were not made on a "natural cycle of time [but] an artificial year consisting of 12 months, each month of 30 days."[7] By the late third millennium BCE, the ancient Sumerians had decoupled economic time from astronomical time—they created a year of extraordinary mathematical convenience: 360 is evenly divisible by, for example, 2, 3, 4, 5, 6, 8, 9, 10, 12, 15, 18, 20, 24, 36, 40, 45, 60, 72, 90, 120, and 180. The number 365 is only evenly divisible by 5 and 73. A 360-day year thus allows many different time periods to be thought of as annual ratios: the year can be cut into halves, thirds, quarters, fifths, sixths, eights, ninths, and twelfths, with round numbers of days in each period. Mesopotamians apparently thought in terms of round quantities and neat fractions, and mathematical tools were utilitarian as opposed to philosophical.

A 360-day year also made the calculation of interest very convenient. Indeed, even today, the calculation for corporate and municipal bond interest accruals is based on a 360-day year. It is tempting to think of the Sumerian administrative year as a kind of idealized, cleaner, improved year—a year as mathematicians and administrators might like it, as opposed to time as defined by astronomical reality. In short, the Sumerians invented a model of time that would serve well as a framework for analyzing periodic economic phenomena. It was also a development of remarkable hubris; the assertion of human's time over natural time.

By 3000 BCE, the ancient cities of the Near East had developed the fundamental tools of finance. They had a highly adaptable recording system for economic quantities that developed from symbols to pictographs to script written on clay tablets. The system could be used for contracting through time and for verifying receipt of goods between parties. The most basic unit of finance is an intertemporal contract. The Sumerians created tools for explicitly quantifying intertemporal contracts, eliminating ambiguity or disagreement between the parties through the invention of notation for economic units and a flexible number system. Writing and numbers brought clarity and precision to the economic arrangements demanded by the Near Eastern economic system.

There is also evidence that financial contracting developed alongside and stimulated conceptual development. Increasing urban density in an economy managed by a common authority required a record system—and a conceptual framework—capable of expressing big numbers. Evidence from early cuneiform appears to document this leap in written expression and perhaps an accompanying shift in arithmetic thought. Likewise, scholars have documented an administrative quantification of time that abstracted from natural, astronomical time. Both of these laid a foundation for the development of further abstractions. The expression of immense quantities was limited only by the human imagination, as was the division of time into infinitesimal slices. We can appreciate the roots of modern mathematics as these two great conceptual leaps that owed much to the emergence of financial technology.

While the foundations of finance may well have appeared in cultural contexts other than an urban agricultural society, the specifics of the financial technology of the ancient Near East fit well with its particular social and political structure. Since the special characteristics of the Sumerian economic system are so fundamental to the emergence of finance, it is important to understand it in a broader context. We next turn to a consideration of the social and political milieu in which these financial tools were ultimately developed.

FINANCE AND URBANISM

On June 12, 2003, three men in a red car drove up to the Iraqi national museum and unceremoniously handed the museum guards a piece of stone wrapped in a blanket, somehow managing to make their way past the security checkpoints along the thoroughfare fronting the Tigris River. When the bundle was unwrapped, it turned out to be a large fragment of the Warka Vase, one of the treasures looted from the museum during the Iraq War. Since the tragic pillaging of the museum, no single artifact had been so sorely missed. Although countless other treasures were stolen, no single work of art meant more to the country than this vase. It dates from the beginnings of Mesopotamian civilization and was found in the temple district of Uruk. It had been poorly handled—large pieces of the vase are still missing and are unlikely to ever be found. Fortunately for science, the vase was extensively photographed before the war.

Dating to about 3000 BCE, the Warka Vase was a narrow, three-foot high alabaster cylinder decorated with three bands of carved figures—each band represents a different level of the world. The bottom is water—the wavy lines perhaps depicting the banks of the Euphrates on which Uruk was situated. Above the water is a band depicting domesticated plants, apparently the irrigated fields that once surrounded the ancient city. Above this is a parade of alternating rams and ewes. The world of mankind occupies the central register on the vase. Naked men walk in file—husbandmen—each carrying a basket or an amphora, evidently the commodities collected and processed from the domesticated world below. Their lack of individuality suggests that they themselves are commodities—perhaps symbolizing human labor as opposed to humanity. Finally, at the top of the vase is the world of the temple—a magnificent procession of animals and people with a priest at their head who is presenting gifts to a temple priestess or to the goddess Inanna. In this register is an image of narrow vessels just like the vase itself.

The Warka Vase before its destruction in 2003. This 5,000-year-old ceremonial alabaster vase depicts a religious procession that has been interpreted as a representation of the economic structure of ancient urban life.

FIGURE 1. Aerial photograph of Uruk in 2008.

The vase obviously depicts a religious ceremony, but it is also a picture of the ancient economy. The ruler is the people's representative to the goddess, and he presents to her the fruits of Uruk's labor. Since most of these commodities were perishable, we must presume that the temple redistributed them rapidly in some fashion. Apparently the numbers from the Uruk tablets indicate that this was a big job—taxing people in kind and then redistributing the results. In fact, this economic system—the reliance on a central distribution center, may explain the movement of people into the cities, closer to the temple. Judging by the size of the city in its heyday circa 3000 BCE, Uruk was home to more than 10,000 people. The variety of goods and materials that survive from Uruk suggests that most of its ancient inhabitants had distinct trades. Labor was specialized. Undoubtedly some of its citizens were shepherds; others were farmers, bakers, brewers, weavers, even accountants, scribes, and teachers. The Warka Vase hints at the importance of individual obligation to the temple, which was fundamental to the agricultural production and distribution system.

An economy based on large-scale redistribution of goods cannot function on goodwill. It requires pre-commitment—promises of delivery that allow planning. Without the ability to document an individual's indebtedness to the temple, it would be impossible to keep track of who was working hard and who was shirking; who skipped a grain delivery last season and had to make it up the next season; who had already picked up their ration for the month or how much they were owed. In a centralized system, people become numbers, and accounting has mortal implications. The only thing the Warka Vase is missing is a depiction of the accountants recording the stream of gifts, but the remains of the Uruk tablets and tokens remind us not only that the ancient economy relied on turning civic obligations into a sacred commitment, but also that carefully documenting these obligations and their fulfillment was integral to the emergence of urban life.

Not surprisingly, the oldest known credit obligations are lists of individuals and the amount of barley they owe to the temple.[1] One of these lists from the early twenty-fourth century BCE reads like a narration of the worshippers on the Warka Vase—naming the supplicants and the amount they are expected to supply to the temple: "Lugid, the man of the levy, 864 liters of barley, Kidu, the man from Bagara, 720 liters of barley, Igizi, the blacksmith, 720 liters of barley" and so forth. Thus, with the birth of an economy based on central planning and redistribution came indebtedness and taxes.

A system that relied on these kinds of promises and deliveries to feed 10,000 people also must have required long-range planning over long time periods. For a city to sustain itself, it takes more than a year-by-year distribution system. How will you make sure, for example, that there will be sufficient meat to feed the city next year? To solve a problem like this, the planner needs to balance current consumption against the rate that flocks and herds replenish themselves. This is a financial problem. A flock of sheep left to itself (and with plenty of pasture) will grow exponentially through time, but this growth also depends on how many are slaughtered for consumption. The mathematics of growth can get really complicated.

THE APPEARANCE OF COMPOUND INTEREST

An example of the complexity—and perhaps the logical extreme of the concept of exponential growth—is a document in the Babylonian collection of Yale University, a clay cone about the size and shape of a large pineapple. On it, a Sumerian inscription dating to about 2400 BCE records a border dispute between two ancient cities: Lagash and Umma, two large cities in southern Mesopotamia. One of the rivals, Umma, seized a fertile strip of land from Lagash and held it for two generations. The Lagash ruler, Enmetena, eventually retook the land and demanded reparations in the form of back "rent" plus cumulated interest. The text reads: "The leader of Umma would exploit 1 guru of the barley of Nanshe and the barley of Ningursu as a loan. It bore interest, and 8.64 million guru accrued."[2]

It is not surprising that these Sumerian cities fought for decades over agricultural land, since grain was the foundation of the ancient economy. However, the document is important for understanding the level of conceptual abstraction that had been achieved by this time and the role that financial concepts played in politics.

First, the cone is striking because of the immense numbers it uses. Enmetena invokes the precedence of a barley loan to claim a customary rate of interest on grain of 33⅓%. Converted to modern quantities, the bill submitted to the people of Umma amounted to 4.5 trillion liters of grain. This is about 580 times the annual barley harvest of the United States in recent times—almost certainly more barley than had ever been harvested in Mesopotamia in human history by that time. Interestingly, even the untrained eye can easily identify these giant numbers in the inscription: three round punch marks with smaller punch marks inside of them representing a big number times another big number. The ability to imagine and then to express such vast quantities would not have been possible without the leap of mathematical abstraction in the Uruk period. Now, however, the tablet is not a claim on an individual, it is a claim on an entire city-state.

The second significant thing about the Enmetena cone is that it is the world's first evidence of compound interest. Compounding causes the debt to grow exponentially through time rather than in equal proportion each year, which is what led to the vast numbers.

FIGURE 2. The Enmetena inscription in the Yale Babylonian Collection.

Enmetena's claim of compound interest is based on the premise that the profits from one year can be reinvested in the same productive enterprise the next year. Enmetena's claim is of course logically impossible. Compounding grain yields would require not only an ever-increasing number of seeds, but also an ever-increasing field to plant the new seed. The Lagash ruler must have understood that his compound interest claim was absurd. It was therefore simply a rhetorical device invoking the language of mathematics and finance for demanding heavy reparations from Lagash. In effect, the cone argues that, because the debt was impossible for Lagash to pay, the ruler of Umma "owned" them.

Where did the idea of compound interest come from? One possibility is that it emerged from the inherently exponential nature of the other economic foundation of the Sumerian economy: livestock. Sheep, goats, cattle, and oxen were all important; providing meat, wool, milk, and power.

FINANCIAL PLANNING

A cuneiform document from a slightly later period in the third millennium BCE demonstrates not only the importance of raising livestock as big business, but also the extraordinary level of mathematical sophistication it required. Most interesting from our perspective is that it represents a key development in the software of finance. It is a mathematical model of growth used to formulate a long-term financial plan.

The tablet came from a city called Drehem—a place associated with livestock sales.[3] It was written during the third dynasty of Ur (Ur III), which began circa 2100 BCE—later than the Enmetena cone. Professor Robert Englund, together with a team of other scholars in Berlin, including an archaeologist and a historian of mathematics, deciphered and analyzed a large tablet. It describes the growth of a herd of cattle over a ten-year period and the corresponding quantity of milk and cheese expected from an exponential increase in the herd. It also counts up the economic value of the foodstuffs produced, using units of silver—the currency of the ancient Near East.

Englund points out that the text is not an actual accounting record of a herd, since it makes certain unrealistic assumptions—including the assumption that no cow or bull ever dies and that each mated pair has either a male or female calf each year. Each year, every cow has a calf and then in successive years, female calves themselves reproduce, turning an initial pair into a large herd.

FIGURE 3. The Drehem tablet.

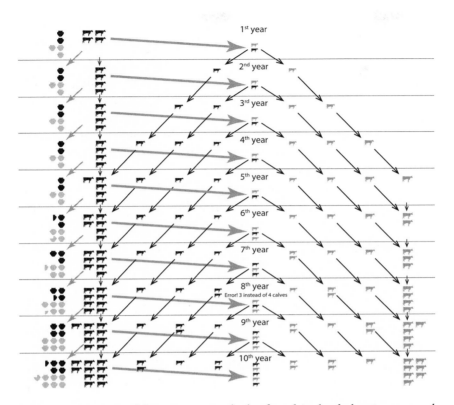

FIGURE 4. Diagram of the ten-year growth plan for a dairy herd, showing expected future profits in dairy products, third millennium BCE.

The text is an abstract model of geometric growth using mathematical tools. It is also a model of investment, since the bottom line translates the result of the process into silver. From a financial perspective, this document is something akin to an earnings growth model of a business enterprise, in which livestock represent the investment and the sale of dairy products represents the annual earnings.

Why would the Drehem accountants need such a model? Was this a theoretical exercise dreamed up by a mathematician curious about exponential growth? It was a benchmark established under ideal conditions in which no animals died, prices never fluctuated, and offspring could be accurately forecast. It reveals the potential profits to buying one breeding pair and managing them under ideal conditions. It could have even served as a business plan.

The Drehem tablet is one of the most exciting of all the documents from the ancient Near East concerning finance, precisely because it reveals the most about the development of a financial way of thinking. It demonstrates that the basic tools for imagining, quantifying, and ultimately valuing a future business enterprise were fully developed at least by the end of the third millennium BCE.

The tablet could not have been produced without the imperative to forecast the future in concrete, numerical terms. It incorporated the fundamental insight that time itself has a price that is based on the underlying economy—the breeding of animals. It is an absolutely stunning work of abstract, financial thought. The "business plan" implicit in the Drehem tablet embodies an expectation of growth and change, not only of the herd, but also of what the herd can support. As cattle multiply, the society that they can support also can grow.

BORROWING AND LENDING

All people, urban as well as rural, tend to lend things to one another. They do this even when the benefits from such helpful behavior are not immediately apparent. In small communities, people lend their tools and their time to one another. While they may expect reciprocity in the future, they do not explicitly write a contract to formalize it. Such cooperation is a form of insurance. You help out when you can afford to do so, and you call on your neighbors when you find yourself in need.

When people started living in large communities like Uruk, they shared their lives with strangers as well as friends. It may have been possible to know everyone in a large farming village, but not in a vast city, such as Uruk. What were once implicit agreements among neighbors now became explicit contractual agreements among strangers. When everyone had the same profession and skills, neighborly help could always be repaid in kind. But when people developed different professions, it must have been difficult to maintain neighborly reciprocity. Urban societies still needed cooperation, but limits to familiarity with fellow inhabitants and difficulty with quantifying the units of such cooperation meant that people required more formal ways to ensure a return on their helpful efforts. Cambridge University's Paul Millett traced this developmental relationship between urbanization and interest loans in ancient Athens. The pattern he identified is clear—urbanism necessitated explicit contracts and gave rise to interest charges. Interest is a sweetener to induce someone to lend you what you need.

Neighborly cooperation appears to be a way for a community to respond to periods of crisis, but loans in which the "gift" is repaid with interest allows a lender to accumulate wealth—to obtain repayment even when he or she isn't in need. This contrast between implicit and explicit contracts embodies civilization's ambivalence toward lending—perhaps it just doesn't feel right to charge a friend or neighbor interest, because reciprocity was our pre-urban method of adapting to crises. The invention of interest, in the very shadow of the gates of Eden—may have been humankind's original fall from grace. Indeed, explicit contracting, record-keeping and documentation of effort and rations that characterize the ancient city states appear to be a departure from the idealistic world of communal life. Yet these tools undoubtedly made larger-scale urbanization and political entities possible.

Private financial contracts also existed in ancient Mesopotamia. A Sumerian record from the mid-twenty-fourth century BCE is a candidate for the first recorded personal loan, as opposed to a contract with a temple. The document reads: "40 grams of silver and 900(?) liters of barley, Ur-garima hold over Puzur-Eshtar."[4]

Although many things are left unspecified, including the date, the required time until the obligation is due, the position and institutional affiliations of the contracting parties, and the names of witnesses, this document is nevertheless a clearly stated obligation that Puzur-Eshtar has made to Ur-garima, and it serves as a record of that commitment. Despite the problems of identifying the most ancient financial records, by this time personal lending and documented debts were undeniably part of the financial architecture of ancient Mesopotamia.

The invention of debt and the emergence of interest to incentivize lending is the most significant of all innovations in the history of finance. Debt allowed borrowers to use money from the future to meet obligations in the present. For example, suppose a farmer suddenly discovered that his or her store of food had spoiled and the harvest was a month away. Without lending and interest, the farmer would have to starve for a month, or depend on the vagaries of charity. However, debt allows the farmer to smooth consumption between the present and the future. In this sense it substitutes for the spoiled grain—it has the effect of moving the future harvest to the present.

Smoothing of consumption is only one possible use for a loan. In fact, the technology of borrowing and lending in ancient Mesopotamia depended on the economic system that prevailed at the time. For example, in settings in which the temple or the ruler demanded tax payments, personal loans might have been used to cover a shortfall. In other settings, such as the acquisition of goods and trade, lending in Mesopotamia was part of a complex chain of intermediaries and played a key role in the supply of goods.

OVERSEER OF MERCHANTS

Steven Garfinkle is a cuneiform scholar at Western Washington University who has made a study of the loan contracts of the late third millennium BCE—the Ur III period. There is an abundance of financial material from this era, which was characterized by an economy based on large institutional households, to which people were bound in various forms. Traditionally this period has been regarded as one that allowed relatively little entrepreneurial activity—most economic activity was in the service of larger institutions rather than the individual.

Garfinkle points out that borrowing extended through all levels of Ur III society—from lowly farmers to prominent officers of government. Contracts were made in both silver and barley, and they ranged from interest-bearing loans to zero-interest loans to *antichretic* loans (loans with the interest paid in labor). As with Puzur-Eshtar's loan mentioned above, these documents were sometimes terse statements for which the context of the contract is lacking and some of the terms must be inferred from broader context. Some loans were sealed in clay envelopes with cylinder-seal impressions and descriptions on the outside—reminiscent of the bullae tradition. Garfinkle believes that the envelopes were destroyed when a loan was repaid, rather than the loan document itself.

A man named Tūran-ilī was the overseer of merchants in the city of Nippur during the Ur III period, and the Yale Babylonian Collection houses part of his business archive. This archive presents a test case to examine the extent to which finance was solely used in service to an institution rather than an individual. More than sixty of Tūran-ilī's tablets have been studied by cuneiform scholars, including Garfinkle and Marc Van De Mieroop of Columbia University. Their analysis demonstrates the fundamental role that borrowing and lending played in the ancient economy in the Ur III period and suggests that even in a highly controlled and hierarchical economy, lending was essential. Tūran-ilī's records date from 2042 to 2031 BCE.[5] They show that he oversaw the accounts of a number of merchants used by a major "households"—such as a temple, a governor's house, or royal palace—to acquire goods. These merchants ran accounts with the household—the merchants were advanced silver and wool, and with these goods the merchants bought and delivered back to the household various other commodities, such as onions, chickpeas, garlic, barley, madder, raisins, dates, wheat, oxen, and goats; as well as other necessities, such as alum, gypsum, alkali, grinding stones, bitumen, and ox hides; and precious items, such as copper boxes, gold, and aromatics.

Merchants, in turn, used their silver advances to make loans, and from time to time they relied on Tūran-ilī for advances on their account or loans to clear their debts. This mercantile credit system not only provided the necessary liquidity for merchants to buy and deliver goods, it also allowed financial profit. The overseer of merchants himself used credit instruments for personal profit. He may have even functioned as a tax farmer of sorts, collecting government taxes, supplying credit when taxpayers came up short, and using the tax revenues as an account to further support merchant activities. The conclusions that Garfinkle and Van De Mieroop draw from these remarkable archives is that even when economic intermediaries served at the pleasure of a larger economic entity, they nevertheless acted as economically motivated agents. By 2000 BCE, roughly a millennium after the appearance of the concept of interest, even highly controlled economies needed a way to manage the complex intertemporal needs. If Ur III was not a market economy per se, it clearly was a financial one. Finance facilitated the complex external intermediation demanded by the city-state.

ORIGIN OF THE WORD FOR INTEREST

What gave the ancient Sumerians the idea of charging one another interest? Linguistic evidence provides a clue. In the Sumerian language, the word for interest, *mash*, was also the term for calves. In ancient Greek, the word for interest, *tokos*, also refers to the offspring of cattle. The Latin term *pecus*, or flock, is the root of our word "pecuniary." The Egyptian word for interest, like the Sumerian word, is *ms*, and means "to give birth." All these terms point to the derivation of interest rates from the natural multiplication of livestock. If you lend someone a herd of thirty cattle for one year, you expect to be repaid with more than thirty cattle. The herd multiplies—the herder's wealth has a natural rate of increase equal to the rate of reproduction of the livestock. If cattle were the standard currency, then loans in all comparable commodities would be expected to "give birth" as well. The idea of interest seems to be a natural one for an agricultural or pastoral society, but not so for hunter-gatherers. Ancient Sumerian society—in particular, Uruk, sometimes referred to as "the city of sheepfolds"—would have been the perfect setting for the evolution of the practice of lending money at interest. The Drehem tablet pictured earlier in the chapter is in fact a detailed expression of this idea.

In this chapter we have seen how the intensification of settlement in ancient cities led to contracting and interest payments. The agricultural economy that supported ancient cities was a logical crucible for the development of increasingly sophisticated financial tools. Farmers have to plan for the next harvest, to decide each year about how much to consume versus how much to save or plant. It is not surprising that the early cities of the Near East developed methods for planning and the concept of a fair yield on assets, and that these became so fundamental to their way of thinking that even political disputes between states were quantified using sophisticated financial calculations.

We also explored the development of financial technology in the first cities and the emergence of financial theory: models of financial growth that were both practical and wildly hypothetical. The Drehem tablet used the reproductive rates of cattle to express a useful theory—a production plan for the future. In contrast, the Enmetena cone used compound interest mathematics to push the boundaries of the imagination beyond any realistic quantity of grain production. The case of Tūran-ilī of Nippur demonstrates that complexity of the economy necessitated a technology to manage the timing of merchant purchases and deliveries of commodities. Even in periods of relatively high levels of control, the economic value of time plays an important role.

FINANCIAL ARCHITECTURE

We saw in Chapter 2 the inhabitants of the first cities in the ancient Near East, the Sumerians, developed not only basic financial tools but also sophisticated modes of financial modeling. However, the Sumerians were just the first in a series of increasingly numerate societies spanning another two and a half millennia that relied on financial contracts, record-keeping, and markets. In this chapter we examine one of these societies in depth, looking at the role that finance played in law, trade, and commerce. We also visit an ancient site where an entire neighborhood of ancient Mesopotamian financiers has come to light, and where one modern scholar has been able to reconstruct their business ventures, legal disputes, loans, and transactions. The letters these ancient financiers left us shed light not only on their business operations but also on their lives and personalities.

The early second millennium was a time of great political turmoil in the ancient Middle East and is generally referred to as the Old Babylonian period. By this time, Semitic speaking peoples in the north had largely replaced Sumerian speakers. The Semitic language, Akkadian, is by far the largest of all the dead languages, in terms of the number of surviving documents as well as extent of known vocabulary. Unless you are an economist, however, most of these texts are of little interest. Nine out of ten tablets are accounting records. Of these, a considerable number are mortgages, land deeds, loan contracts, promissory notes, and partnership contracts.

The most famous ruler of this period was Hammurabi, who lived circa 1792–1750 BCE. He is best known for the Code of Hammurabi—a set of laws inscribed on a black basalt pillar that now stands in the Louvre Museum. Hammurabi's code specifies the rate of interest on silver at 20% and on barley at 33⅓%. What is most important about the code is not what is says but what it represents. The code is a uni-

Detail of the financial district of second millennium Ur,
excavated by Sir Leonard Woolley.

form legal framework for the entire the Babylonian empire. It covered everything from criminal law to family law, commercial practice to property rights. It details a range of punishments for transgressions, methods of dispute resolution, and attributions of fault for various offenses. It specifies the roles of judge, jury, witnesses, plaintiffs, and defendants. It recognizes and elaborates the rights of ownership of property, including rights to lease and rights of eminent domain. It specifies the role of the written document in a contractual obligation, the necessity of receipts, and what should be done if they do not exist. It specifies legal tender. It describes the obligations of merchants, brokers, and agents and their fiduciary duties and limits to their liabilities in case of attack or theft. It places limits on the term of debt indenture (three years). In short, it creates a comprehensive, uniform framework for commerce.

Although the existence of contracts from early Mesopotamian history implied the existence of a legal system, with rules, courts, juries, and witnesses, the Code of Hammurabi is important because it spells out this legal framework in great detail. Without laws—and a court system to adjudicate them—and a government committed to specifying and enforcing them, contracts would have no meaning. It would not matter what someone wrote on the surface of a bulla or on a cuneiform tablet if these documents were not recognized as a promise that, if broken, would be discovered and punished. The Code of Hammurabi is as much a part of the financial architecture of the ancient Near East as loan tablets, mortgage tablets, leases, letters of credit, and the whole range of financial documents that sprung forth during Old Babylonian times. It is the institutional environment that made progressively more detailed contracting possible.

AN ANCIENT FINANCIAL DISTRICT

In the 1920s, Sir Leonard Woolley, while excavating the ancient city of Ur—the fabled birthplace of Abraham—found himself standing in the remains of what must have been an upper middle class neighborhood near the center of the city. His Iraqi excavators uncovered the narrow walls and small rooms that signified domestic architecture—rather than the majestic palace architecture that typically attracted the attention of

Near Eastern archaeologists. In an area separated from the massive temple complex by the main canal running through town, Woolley and his crew uncovered the mud-brick foundations of homes, shops, schools, and chapels. He even found the business district and the waterfront, with piers and docks indicating that Ur was a harbor town—the home of fishermen and maritime traders as well as farmers and herdsmen. Many of these individuals buried their personal financial records, along with their ancestors, in the floors of their houses for safekeeping. These houses were all from the Old Babylonian period of Ur, and their documents were thus written in Akkadian, despite the millennia-long Sumerian heritage of the city.

Professor Marc Van De Mieroop of Columbia University is one of the leading scholars in the world in the study of the ancient Mesopotamian economy. He used Woolley's excavation notes to match the dozens of excavated clay tablets to the homes where they were found. From these, he identified the financial district in the ancient city—the neighborhood of Ur's second-millennium lenders and entrepreneurs. From their records, he reconstructed a fascinating story about this early financial center.

Most of the cuneiform texts found in the financial district date from the early years of the reign of the King Rim-Sin (1822–1763 BCE), who ruled from the capital city of Larsa shortly before Hammurabi's time. During this period, Ur was probably home to 25,000–40,000 people. Woolley's excavations revealed a large neighborhood of houses, large and small, clustered around a central square. Two shrines faced this plaza, and wide thoroughfares and narrow alleys led away from the square to other parts of the densely populated city.

THE MERCHANTS OF UR

No. 3 Niche lane (the names for all of the streets were borrowed by Woolley from the English town of Canterbury) was the home and office of the businessman Dumuzi-gamil. Although he left no personal records, only financial ones, we know something about Dumuzi-gamil's personality. He was educated, self-reliant, and careful with his money, and he kept his own accounts rather than hiring a scribe. Despite his training, however, Dumuzi-gamil avoided lavish prose in favor of what

Marc Van De Mieroop calls "terse phraseology." Benjamin Franklin springs to mind.

The activities of Dumuzi-gamil and other residents of the financial district of Ur reveal much about the role that financiers played in ancient Mesopotamia. In 1796 BCE Dumuzi-gamil and his partner, Shumi-abiya, borrowed 500 grams of silver from the businessman Shumi-abum. Dumuzi-gamil promised to return 297.3 grams on his share of 250 grams after five years. According to the manner in which the Mesopotamians calculated interest, this equaled a 3.78% annual rate. The term of the loan was a relatively long one—five years. Shumi-abum turned around and sold the loan to a couple of well-known merchants, who successfully collected on the debt in 1791.

Marc Van De Mieroop suspects that Dumuzi-gamil was acting as a banker—taking in deposits at low rates of interest, and in the interim, making productive use of the money. Indeed, Dumuzi-gamil tried his hand with great success at a number of business ventures. His principal trade was as a bread distributor. He invested in institutional bakeries that supplied the temple. In fact, he may even have supplied bread to the capital city of Larsa, which lay a day's travel to the north. He was also the "grain supplier to the King"—one of his tablets was a receipt from a monthly issue to Rim-Sin for more than 5,000 liters of grain.[1]

There is little doubt that Dumuzi-gamil's loan represented the productive use of the time value of money. When he borrowed business capital from Shumi-abum, he apparently had a plan for increasing his wealth. Perhaps it was the entrepreneurial idea of setting up institutional bakeries. It appears likely that debt in the hands of Ur's entrepreneurs like Dumuzi-gamil could be a means to social and economic mobility. Without the ability to shift money through time—to borrow against future income—Dumuzi-gamil might not have been able to set up shop. We don't know much about his lender, but, since he charged interest, it must have been more than a neighborly gesture.

Dumuzi-gamil used at least some of the money to make short-term loans. According to Van De Mieroop, Dumuzi-gamil frequently lent silver to fishermen and farmers. On some of these loans he exacted 20% interest for a single month. At that pace, 1 mina of silver (an ancient unit of weight equal to about 1.25 pounds) could grow to 64 in two and a half years. Of the fifteen loan records of Dumuzi-gamil's that survived, most of them were very short term—one, two, or three months. The price of time was high for citizens in debt to the Ur moneylenders.

The difference between the long-term loan of Dumuzi-gamil and the short-term loans to the fishermen is important. The short-term loans were clearly consumption loans, while Dumuzi-gamil's was for productive purposes—for developing the bakery business and for lending activities. In fact, most loans in second millennium Ur were for consumption, not production. Borrowing was more typically a response to emergencies, and Dumuzi-gamil was probably not very popular with his creditors, given the high interest rates he charged.

ABSTRACT WEALTH

The ancient financiers in Ur, like other merchants, kept running accounts. Among Dumuzi-gamil's records are indications that certain payments were credited to individuals. While not as sophisticated as credit cards, these "tabs" at various merchants and financiers minimized the need for hard currency. This accounting system may have mirrored the temple's own method of accounts, but its use in the dealings of individuals is a subtle but important advance in financial thought. It meant that people could recognize "paper profits." You could become wealthy without having the silver hoard to prove it. This was the first stage in the development of intangible wealth, on which our current financial system depends. These intangible gains only existed if people believed that they existed, and if a legal system existed to ensure that creditors had secure rights to their loaned property.

Courts existed in Mesopotamia to adjudicate property disputes, and it was not unheard of for lawsuits to span decades. Evidently, it was part of the function of the local chapels in Dumuzi-gamil's time to notarize or witness the drawing up of important documents like deeds of sale. Such deeds were necessary for even tiny plots of property. Marc Van De Mieroop found one transaction for four square yards. Neighborly lending appears to have been on the decline in second-millennium Ur— sales were recorded even between brothers. Almost all these sales were denominated in silver.

In a world where "clay" profits were counted as real, even the financier's debt could serve as money. As noted above, the Ur documents reveal a remarkably liquid market for personal promissory notes. Shumi-abum, Dumuzi-gamil's lender, sold the note to two other investors—Nur-ilishu and Sin-ashared. Apparently, Dumuzi-gamil and his partner's debt were easily transferable. Several other Ur records indicate that selling loans was a common practice. It appears that Ur had a functioning secondary loan market, in which the promise of a loan repayment could be regarded as currency. Although no broad, macroeconomic records exist to measure the effect of Ur's ancient financiers, it is likely that their moneylending activities encouraged commerce of other kinds.

DEBT AND RISK

Second-millennium Ur may have been an early hothouse of capitalistic enterprise, but what of the borrowers mired in debt? It is interesting to note that Mesopotamian legal codes guaranteed property rights to an even greater extent than they guaranteed what we now call human rights. For instance, a person had the right to sell him- or herself into slavery or pledge his or her liberty as collateral for a loan. This seems cruel and exploitive, but it may have been efficient. A study by the economist M. Darling of the rural economy of the Punjab in modern times suggests a disturbing thing about human nature—people work harder and produce more when they are in debt.[2] Darling found that crop yields for farmers in debt typically exceeded yields from unencumbered farmers. Farmers in the Punjab may have faced foreclosure, but for the ancient inhabitant of Ur, the motivation was even greater. Debtors were often forced to sell themselves into slavery.

It is difficult to escape the conclusion that, while the first loan contracts and the legal system that enforced them may have made the Mesopotamian economy efficient, they made life miserable for the working man and woman. If lending began, as historian Paul Millett believes, as a process of neighborly reciprocity in rural societies, it evolved into something quite different. In Babylonian times, short-term debt was a tool used to extract taxes from the population and to increase the productivity of temple lands. It is almost as though the government had found a way to extract the residual goodwill from the economy by allowing individuals to shift financial obligations into the future.

Although some fraction of lending in ancient Ur was for emergency purposes, where the government in all likelihood created the emergency, the other side of the coin is that certain entrepreneurs, such as Dumuzi-gamil, accrued wealth through borrowing and lending. Thus, although the system could be harsh on the general populace, it encouraged creative and productive enterprise, and it rewarded those with financial skills.

FINANCING TRADE

There is considerable scholarly disagreement about the extent to which the traders and merchants of ancient Mesopotamia were independent agents or worked for the state. Around the corner from Dumuzi-gamil lived Ea-nasir—a like-minded entrepreneur. He made his fortune by organizing and financing maritime expeditions from Ur to Dilmun. Archaeologists believe that Dilmun was the key entrepôt in the Mesopotamian copper trade.

Maritime expeditions to Dilmun and ports south along the coasts of the Persian Gulf and the Indian Ocean appear to have taken place since Sumerian times, but by Ea-nasir's time, Dilmun traders were the key intermediaries between Mesopotamia and points south. Indeed, the Dilmunites may have been the Venetians of their time, establishing commercial communities in remote ports that allowed them to control trade. Their distinctive signatures, found at scattered points in second-millennium levels at Ur, were cylinder seals bearing the stylistic echo of the Indus civilization—including the image of the sacred bull. While there is no direct evidence that Ea-nasir himself was a Dilmunite, he was clearly a major player in the Dilmun trade. For one large expedition, Ea-nasir assembled fifty-one investors, who contributed money in the form of silver, as well as a variety of trade goods, including what were apparently the most desirable crafts of the city: Ur baskets. These were exchanged with the merchants in Dilmun for copper, precious stones, and spices.

Ea-nasir's tablets indicate that considerable diplomacy was required to equitably partition the profits from the Dilmun trade. Unlike Dumuzi-gamil's debt, many of the capital contributions to Dilmun expeditions were equity investments. The contributors expected to gain if the expedition was a success. While bond contracts limited the payoff to the lender to a prescribed amount of interest, there was no limit to the profits that could accrue to Ea-nasir's backers if they got lucky. They shared in the benefits according to the proportions of their investments. Another feature of Ur partnership contracts is also interesting: loss was often limited to the amount of the contribution. In fact, in some expedition charters, this limited liability was a stated condition of the investment.

The exciting thing for financial historians is that these equity contracts represent concrete evidence of a limited partnership—in which the limited partner assumed no liability beyond the value of the paid-in capital. It was a joint venture with silent, but contributing, investors. This is the same way that such risky things as oil-drilling ventures and real estate investments are financed to this day. Presumably, since Ea-nasir was the general partner who took the biggest risk, he made the largest profit.

JOINT VENTURES

Many of the tablets deciphered by Van De Mieroop and other Assyriologists indicate that such financial tools as loans, mortgages, and limited partnerships were collaborative ventures. The involvement of several partners in Ea-nasir's expeditions to buy copper in Dilmun indicates that such enterprises were often beyond the means of a single investor. Financial tools allowed very large projects. Just like the large-scale monumental palace architecture that the Babylonian kings built during this era, these financial projects encompassed the efforts of more than one source of capital.

Interestingly, the palace was itself a contributor to Dilmun expeditions. Governmental participation in the southern maritime ventures was nothing new. The temple of Eanna had been involved in financing the Dilmun trade for at least five centuries before Ea-nasir's time. The interesting thing about his partnership records is that ordinary citizens, some with only small contributions like a bracelet or two, could join in the profits of the venture. Enterprise was not only for the wealthy or the politically powerful. The financial technology of second-millennium Ur made the power of time accessible to a broad spectrum of society.

Like modern-day investors in mutual funds, Ea-nasir's investors did not have to be experts in the copper trade to profit from it. Neither did they have to commit their entire fortunes to a single risky venture. The effect of this business structure on personal fortunes must have been significant. People were able to insure themselves against personal failure—if their own venture collapsed, then the investment in Ea-nasir's might carry them through hard times. By repeatedly investing in one of Ur's key industries—the Dilmun trade—they were able to participate in the general economic growth of their city.

SOMETHING LIKE CAPITALISM

Ea-nasir and the other investors in the Dilmun trade were something like capitalists. In the classical sense of the term, their money was used to make money. Although we do not have statistical information about the prevalence of this kind of capitalism in second-millennium Mesopotamia, it had important implications for the structure of society, and, in particular, the emergence of a stratum of economically independent individuals who were able to rely on invested assets for their future economic security, as opposed to reliance on the state or the family to provide for them in their old age.

Consider the U.S. Social Security system. Millions of citizens rely on this state-administered institution to provide for them after their productive working days are past. In traditional societies, extended families took the place of a government pension. Older people lived with their children and grandchildren. In Mesopotamia during the Old Babylonian period, considerable evidence suggests that people were using investments and financial contracts—and even the legal definitions of the family—to finance their retirement.

Assyriologist Anne Goddeeris has made a comprehensive study of the economic contracts from the major cities in northern Mesopotamia in the Old Babylonian period from 2000 to 1800 BCE. She traced the business activities of a number of women in the Old Babylonian city of Sippar who were financially independent even while being members of a religious cult that regulated their ability to marry and have children— much like Catholic nuns of a later era. These Nadiatum women, as they were called, began their careers earlier than their brothers, who typically worked in the family business before acting as separate economic agents upon inheritance.[3] Nadiatum women owned land and profited from leasing it. At times, they operated in partnerships. The series of cuneiform texts related to a woman named Kumu-silli is typical.

> Kumu-silli inherits a field of 4 iku 31 sar in the middle of Babum, another field of 2 iku in Babum, a slave named Ribatum, and a house plot, after division with Hunnubtum and Ahusina. Witnessed by the cloister officials.

> Kumu-silli leases a field of 4 iku in the Mahana irrigation district to Hattalum, son of Mudadum, for a lease of 4.1.3 kor of barley. Hattalum is responsible for three festivals and a piglet for the elunum festival

> Purchase of a house plot of ½ sar by Kumu-silli, daughter of Ishitia from Innabatum, daughter of Bur-sin and Hussutum, daughter of Qarassumuia. Witnessed by the cloister officials. She sold a house plot of 2/3 sar ½ NE belongs to Hussutum and Innabatum.

> Hunnubtum (sister of Kumu-silli) appoints Lamassi as her heir and adopts her. Hunnubtum gives a field of 8 iku in nagum, a house in Sippar owned by Illabrat-ennam, a house plot in the cloister, as far as it extends, and all of Hunnubtum's possessions. As long as she lives, she will enjoy the usufruct. Ilsu-ibbisu is appointed as Lamassi's heir. Witnessed by the cloister officials.[4]

These documents record a series of transactions at once remarkable and mundane. They are remarkable for demonstrating the property rights of Babylonian women and their activities as real estate entrepreneurs, not only as inheritors and lessors of commercial farmland and residential property but also as partners in property transactions. The last text also shows how one of the Nadiatum women planned for retirement—by adopting an heir in return for a contractual promise of support—in effect, a life annuity based on the yield of the property. They are mundane in the sense that they could easily describe property transactions and partnerships of today. The legal framework of land transactions and leasing was simply part of the technology used by people of that era to support themselves, adjust their investment portfolios, and provide for a comfortable retirement.

In this respect, finance can subtly undermine the state. Investment assets give people the ability to create their own economic future rather than relying on governmental or family institutions. If the investment class in ancient Mesopotamia grew to sufficient size, protected by a legal framework that shielded its property from seizure by the state, it is not hard to see how the reliance on government—and thus the power of the state—might be reduced.

GOVERNMENT REGULATION

Back in Ur, Dumuzi-gamil, Ea-nasir, and their fellow financiers profited through banking and trading activities during the first half of Rim-Sin's reign, but their financial dealings were not without risks. In fact, in 1788 BCE a financial catastrophe occurred. Rim-Sin issued a royal edict declaring all loans null and void. Debtors must have rejoiced, and creditors must have panicked. Dumuzi-gamil and the other lenders appear to have been wiped out. After Rim-Sin's edict, Marc Van De Mieroop finds little evidence of financial dealings—with the exception of lawsuits. A number of parties sued in the wake of the edict to claim property pledged in security for loans. They were evidently unsuccessful.

Loan forgiveness edicts were common both before and after Rim-Sin's reign. A cone tablet in the Middle Eastern galleries of the Louvre represents an edict issued by the populist reformer Urukagina. Circa 1900 BCE, this ruler promised to restore the power of ordinary citizens of the Mesopotamian city-state Lagash, who had suffered under the heavy taxes of the palace and the temple. The proclamation abolishes the tax collector and rids the city of usurers, robbers, and criminals. This not only abolished debts but also demonized financiers—lumping usurers with criminals to be cast out of the city.

Although finance was a fundamental instrument of the state and private lenders were essential to trade and taxation, government of the ancient Near East had an ambiguous relationship with the financial sector. Financiers indirectly provided silver to the temple and the palace, but they did so at a high social cost. The government in effect created a sector that might not have been entirely under its economic control.

Although scholars still do not agree on the extent to which such economic institutions as the copper trade were in the hands of independent entrepreneurs or representatives of the state, there is no doubt that direct personal investment meant that some people did well, others didn't, and their fortunes did not depend entirely on their allegiance to the king or the temple.

The existence of legal limits on the charging of interest shows that Rim-Sin intended to cap the moneylenders' profits and perhaps exert some control over the burgeoning financial sector. He was only partly successful.

Such edicts provided periodic relief to the citizens mired in debt, but across-the-board debt forgiveness was the only kind of risk which loan investors could not protect themselves against by diversifying. Ea-nasir could insure against his Dilmun ship sinking by lending money to Dumuzi-gamil to invest in the bread-making business, for instance, but if all loans were wiped out, this diversification would not help.

Following Ea-nasir, there are virtually no documents relating to the Dilmun trade for another thousand years. Ur apparently ceased to be the flourishing maritime entrepôt it had been in its heyday. While scholars attribute broad political forces to the decline of long-distance maritime trade, perhaps they should look to financial reasons as well. At some point, the gains from long-range trade ventures could not offset the potential loss faced by investors subject to debt forgiveness. In such an economic environment, trade, as well as short-term lending, may grind to a halt.

We can only speculate on Rim-Sin's reason for eliminating all debt by royal decree. Perhaps he himself or those close to him had gotten into debt—or perhaps it was a political move to restore popularity with his subjects. The financial innovations that aided the throne and the temple in procuring silver and copper may suddenly have become more of a liability than an asset. Regardless of his reasons, the effects on the financial district of Ur were permanent. Marc Van De Mieroop conjectures that the golden age of finance in Ur drew to a close as the economic authority shifted to the capital city of Larsa. Perhaps Dumuzi-gamil and his comrades survived the great crash of 1788 BCE and, ever vigilant for financial opportunities, moved to follow them.

A CITY OF MERCHANTS

Loans and investment contracts of the ancient Near East could be denominated in grain and even in units of labor; however, many of them were denominated in silver. This is strange, because silver is not native to Mesopotamia. Where did the silver come from, and how did it become a unit of accounting in the financial system? As discussed near the start of Chapter 1 the natural endowments of ancient Iraq were modest. Basic things like timber and copper had to be obtained through foreign trade. As early as the fourth millennium, Uruk had established trading outposts—perhaps even colonies—in distant lands such as Anatolia in what is now modern Turkey and Susa in what is now modern Iran to import such goods as stone bowls. The beautiful lapis inlaid jewelry of the royal tombs of Ur almost certainly came by trade from the region that is now Afghanistan, and much of Mesopotamia's copper—used to create bronze—came by trade via Dilmun and points south. Ea-nasir and other long-distance maritime traders played a vital role in the economy of Ur. Without copper there is no bronze. Without bronze there are no weapons. Without weapons there is no empire.

Silver, however, is a different story. It is a beautiful, malleable metal, but it has little practical use. Yet in Mesopotamia it was borrowed, lent, invested, used in payment, and collected as taxes. The ancient Mesopotamians regarded it as vital as any other good that they consumed or used in manufacture; however, silver's value was abstract. It was valuable because it was valuable.[5]

Van De Mieroop argues that silver developed as a unit of value and medium of exchange in Mesopotamia because the political structure up until the late second millennium was fragmented into city-states that had to trade with one another and had to trade externally to obtain key goods. Silver was important because it was a broadly accepted currency beyond the relatively limited borders of the early Near Eastern polities. What is particularly interesting is that, while silver was used as a currency, it often may have played this role in a virtual sense as opposed to a concrete one. Values in accounts were written down in silver but not necessarily settled up in silver. Silver became a unit for expressing the value of many different kinds of goods in a single monetary dimension—a tool of thought as much as a tool of transacting.

The ancient Mesopotamian city-states had to obtain silver in trade. In the early second millennium, roughly contemporaneous with the reign of Rim-Sin and the activities of the traders of Ur, one city in the northern part of Mesopotamia—in the region called Assyria (from which the name "Syria" is derived)—became a major trading entrepôt for silver.

The city of Assur is remarkable in the history of the ancient Near East in that, for the first two centuries of the second millennium, it was essentially governed by merchants.[6] The city council operated out of a city hall, and a leader was chosen by lots from leading citizens of Assur, in a political structure that in some ways resembled the medieval Italian trading republics. Historian Klaas Veenhof has spent much of his career documenting the activities of the Assur traders: what they traded, how they organized their trade, and how the city governance fostered Assur dominance in the trade with Anatolia.

A fortuitously preserved cache of documents traces the story of Assur as a merchant city. The documents were discovered in an excavation of Kanesh in central Anatolia, which was Assur's major trading outpost. It was also a major locus of silver production and trade. The relation between Kanesh and Assur was so close that merchant families in Assur sent relatives to live permanently in Kanesh and in small colonies of cities along the caravan route linking the cities. These foreign merchant colonies were called *kārum*. Merchants of Assur were called *timkārum*. Many such kārum districts are documented in this period, and Veenhof notes that commercial disputes that arose in the kārums could be further adjudicated in Assur itself.

The Assur trade was financed by loans as well as sophisticated equity trading partnerships that extended over multiple years. These partnerships were initiated in a ceremony attended by witnesses and were documented by a tablet. The ceremony involved investors placing their contributions in a *naruqqum* (literally, a sack) and entrusting it to a merchant. One such partnership agreement for the Kanesh trade provides a clear example.

> In all: 30 minas of gold, the naruqqum of Amur-Igtar.
> Reckoned from the eponymy Susaja he will conduct trade for twelve years. Of the profit he will enjoy [lit. "eat"] one-third. He will be responsible [lit. "stand"] for one-third.

He who receives his money back before the completion of his term
must take the silver at the exchange-rate 4: 1 for gold and silver.
He will not receive any of the profit.[7]

The quantity of 30 minas of gold is equivalent to about 37½ pounds.
It is entrusted to Amur-Igtar for twelve years, and one-third of this is
for his personal consumption. In addition, he is held responsible for another one-third—evidently meaning that if he loses everything, he personally owes the investors 10 minas of gold. Finally, if any investors pull
out before twelve years, they get no profit, and evidently have to accept
a very high exchange rate of silver to gold.

Like Ea-nasir's Dilmun venture, the naruqqum contract from the
Assur period documents an important development in the financial
hardware of the ancient Near East: investment pools that brought together large amounts of capital from multiple investors. On the one
hand it provided resources to a merchant who otherwise would not
have the means to trade on a large scale, or perhaps to overcome the
fixed costs of outfitting and staffing a caravan. On the other hand, much
like Ea-nasir's Dilmun ventures, it allowed investors to diversify their
risk. Investing in ten ventures like Amur-Igtar's was a good way to avoid
losing everything to one unlucky expedition.

Much of Mesopotamia's silver in this period came from Anatolia,
with Assur serving as the critical intermediary. Assur merchants organized caravans with donkeys laden with Mesopotamian textiles—evidently highly coveted by Anatolians—and moved them north through
the Assyrian plain to the Taurus mountains. Letters from the Kanesh
trove describe stops at prominent cities along the route, where Assurites'
precious cargo would be protected. Assur merchants struck deals with
local rulers and kingdoms along these caravan routes; paying duty on
their goods, and exacting exclusive rights and shutting out other Assyrian competitors. They even pursued gray market exporters from their
own city. When the traders returned—minus most of their donkeys—
they brought silver, the economic lifeblood of Mesopotamia.

A major stop along the Assure trade route was a city in the region
of what is now northeastern Syria, in the valley of the Khabur River.
Documents attest to it having a kārum district.[8] In the late third millennium, the city may have been the capital of the kingdom of Apum,

although the attribution is not certain. As luck would have it, in my pre-professorial days, I joined an expedition to search for this ancient trade outpost.

DIGGING AN ANCIENT CITY

In 1979 I spent several months on an excavation in the northern part of Mesopotamia, living in the remote market town of Qibur-al-baid, working from dawn to dusk on a vast city mound called Tell Leilan with an international crew of archaeologists and Kurdish laborers. Harvey Weiss, a Yale archaeologist and the expedition leader, picked Tell Leilan as a result of studying the records of ancient caravan routes. It is located in a rolling geography cut by wadis and punctuated by mounds—the remains of ancient towns and cities—as far as the eye can see.

Tell Leilan is not the largest of these mounds, but, by Weiss's calculations, it was in a spot where caravans would have stopped on their way north. It had a distinctive feature most other mounds in the Khabur plain lacked—the clearly evident remains of a city wall. Dirt roads leading up to the mound still pass through the slumped but massive remains of the city gate, through the lower town of the ancient city (where its kārum was located), and on to the citadel—a hill that was ancient even in the second millennium BCE. The citadel at Tell Leilan is dominated by a ziggurat and a massive temple complex with over a thousand years of occupation and superposition of palace on palace, a complex of great streets, decorated buildings, and gracefully plastered courtyards.

Work at Leilan in 1979 proceeded on several fronts. Excavations on the citadel focused on uncovering the ancient palace system that dated back to the second millennium. Tablets from these trenches led Weiss and the epigraphers from the project, Ben Foster and Marc Van De Mieroop, to conjecture that Leilan was once Shubat-Enlil, the capital city of one of Hammurabi's rivals, the Assyrian king, Shamshi-Adad (1813–1781 BCE), whose conquest of northern Mesopotamia coincided with an abrupt suspension of the Assur trade. Assyriologists believe that Shamshi-Adad took over the ancient capital of Apum and seized control of its valuable trade concession.

In fact, the really exciting evidence from a financial perspective may have been in the nongovernmental neighborhoods below the citadel;

the kārum where merchants and moneylenders lived and worked. In excavations over a number of years, Weiss and his team uncovered an extensive residential district in the lower town, which was undoubtedly the place where the caravans stopped and traded. In 1987, in the lower town, the Leilan team discovered another monumental structure—this time with extensive diplomatic archives that documented the politics of the Apum kingdom over the late third millennium.[9] Shubat-Enlil was linked to other Mesopotamian cities as much by commerce and finance as by politics and religion. Indeed the latter likely followed the former. The land of Apum where Leilan is located was an important stop on the silver trade—undoubtedly before, during, and after its dominance by the merchants of Assur.

The relevance of the Assur trade and its aftermath is not simply that an extensive trade network existed—or that city politics could be organized around commercial principles, but rather that silver could be regarded as an essential input to economic life. Mesopotamia needed money as much as it needed food, clothing, and shelter. While we tend to think of precious metals as "luxury goods" and perhaps dismiss them as prestige items of the upper class, it is the seemingly arbitrary assignment of prestige to silver and gold that rendered them useful as currency. Silver's particular utility as a currency or unit of account is that it was accepted widely in the ancient Near East as money. Its value was global, not local. It allowed distant cities—even adversaries—to interact economically. Grain was the "coin of the realm" within a household system that produced and distributed subsistence goods locally to its members. In contrast, silver was the medium of exchange that connected Mesopotamian cities with the broader world.

The focus of this chapter has been the remarkable institutional development of financial technology in the second millennium BCE. The survival of an immense amount of rich documentary material, some of it in good archaeological context, allows a detailed understanding of Mesopotamia's financial architecture. Its political organization varied from cities organized around "meta-households," like temples and palaces in which merchants served political masters, to cities virtually run by merchants for the purpose of trade. In both settings, finance served as a crucial factor in the economy. Short-term loans smoothed income and consumption shocks to households both great and small. Lending also solved the problem of the timing of income and expenditure inherent in any kind of trade—merchants were allocated resources in advance that allowed them to trade at opportune times. Individuals accumulated capital through business operations and used this not only to make loans that facilitated trade but also to make loans for the purpose of increasing wealth. Many such loans were short term and had high interest rates, leading to the conjecture by modern scholars that they were predatory in some sense; either a means to draw the needy into debt slavery or as a means to deprive landowners of property. Short-term debt was not the only form of borrowing. Long-term loans at lower interest rates appeared to provide necessary capital for profitable ventures that required time to mature.

Debt was not the only financial tool used in this period. Long-distance trade was financed by the investment of equity capital. We looked at two such partnerships—the first one for a maritime expedition to Dilmun for copper. The second was likely connected to the silver trade with Anatolia. This form of investment allowed the pooling of capital and the diversification of risk. These actions were necessary for large-scale enterprises for which the prospects for profit were highly uncertain. As such, equity partnerships were well suited to risky international trade.

MESOPOTAMIAN TWILIGHT

Finance certainly did not disappear with the passing of the Old Babylonian period, but less is known about Mesopotamian cities over the several centuries that followed. We do know, however, that financial technology survived a succession of political changes in the ancient Near East, and finance later played a salient role in the Persian Empire (626–330 BCE). Some of the Near East's most interesting financial documents date to this time. In this chapter we explore two cases in depth that center on dramatic political changes that took place near the very end of the era in which cuneiform writing was used. These highlight the role finance and markets played in institutional change as well as in stability.

The temple mound of Nippur lies north of the ancient sites of Ur and Uruk, and like these other Mesopotamian cities, it was occupied over the course of several millennia. In 1889, American archaeologists tunneling deep into the Nippur mound recovered a remarkable archive: the records of the financial transactions of three generations of a family engaged in lending and property management. Their contracts, accounts, deeds, and lawsuits extended over the era of the final flourishing of Mesopotamian civilization. Using this rich documentary source, the Assyriologist Matthew Stolper has pieced together the story of a clan called the Murašu family.[1] What he discovered about their role in the finances and politics of late Mesopotamian society reads like a modern mystery story full of intrigue, scandal, and a web of financial deals that ultimately toppled the government from power.

In the period of the Persian Empire, Nippur was a prosperous and productive protectorate of the Persian kings, who built grand royal residences at Susa and Persepolis. The home of the Murašu family was a large private residence overlooking Nippur's temple precinct. Like the financial district in Old Babylonian Ur, it stood across the central city

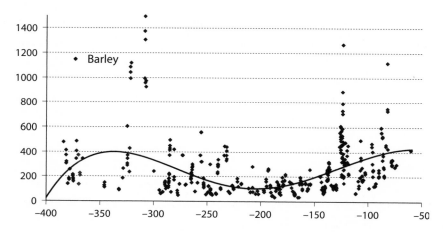

Barley prices in the market of Babylon, 380–60 BCE.

canal from the religious district—perhaps symbolizing the distinction between the sacred and the profane.

Little is known about the patriarch of the Murašu clan, who was born about 500 BCE, but his three sons and three grandsons were landowners, agricultural managers, and active lenders to other landowners of Nippur. Through careful business dealings, they amassed a considerable fortune, and the family business remained under their active control until about 417 BCE. Some years were better than others, but one particular date stands out as important for the Murašu.

The year 423 was a turbulent one for politics. Court intrigue began shortly after the mid-winter death of King Atraxerxes. The eldest son, Xerxes II, seized the throne, only to be murdered 45 days later by his half-brother Sogdianus, who, with one treacherous act suddenly held in his grasp the entire Persian Empire, from the Zagros Mountains to the Mediterranean Sea. While Sogdianus may have had the throne, another son of Atraxerxes had the support and sponsorship of some of Persia's most powerful landowners. Ochus, son of the Babylonian concubine Costmartidus and satrap of lower Mesopotamia, was living in a spacious rented residence in Babylon when his half-brother ascended the throne. One of Sogdianus's first imperial acts was to summon his powerful half-brother to the imperial city of Susa—perhaps to put him under the sword and consolidate his own power.

When the summons came in the form of an official cuneiform tablet delivered by royal messenger, Ochus had to work fast. His supporters urged him to fight, but they could not immediately provide the means for him to do so—they were land rich but cash poor, and the mercenaries and supplies to fight Sogdianus could only be obtained with silver. With Sogdianus pressing for a reply, they turned to the Murašu family for help. Ochus's backers mortgaged their vast property holdings in the Euphrates valley to the Murašu and used the proceeds to hire an army. Deserters from the disaffected Persian regulars soon joined them, and when Ochus rode into the city of Susa, it was not as Sogdianus's prisoner but as his successor. The usurper was usurped. Ochus took the royal title of Darius II.

The overthrow of Sogdianus may be the first war we know of to have been fought on borrowed money, but it certainly was not the last. The Persian rulers following Darius II frequently resorted to tax levies in later years to finance wars. Financial intermediation was a crucial link—some firm or agent that could turn a contractual promise into money in a hurry. In the fifth century BCE, the Murašu firm provided this essential line of credit, and it probably turned the tide of victory. But fate is not always kind. The landholders who supported Ochus remained mired in debt, and many faced foreclosure.

The story of the Murašu is important, because it shows how finance could rapidly and powerfully focus economic assets in one time and place for political gain. Battles were fought not just in the dimension of space—one army against another—but in the temporal domain. Darius II—or at least his political backers—mortgaged the future for military advantage.

PRICES, CYCLES, MARKETS, AND MODELS

The last known document written in cuneiform is a record of the prices in silver of commodities in the city of Babylon in 75 CE—after the birth of Christ. Babylon by this time had long lost its role as the capital of Mesopotamia, but it survived as an important trade center and as a center of astronomical observation. This last cuneiform document is the final one in a sequence of diaries and almanacs that recorded prices and astronomical phenomena over more than 700 years. The Babylonian diaries record prices (actually quantities) for each lunar month for six common commodities in terms of the amount that a shekel of silver will buy in the streets of Babylon. Alice Slotsky is a cuneiform scholar at Brown University. She made the first comprehensive attempt to compile the Babylonian diaries and study them. According to her, the diaries are typically twelve-month compilations of more frequent price and sky observational records.

A typical half-year diary was composed of six or seven units, each spanning one lunar month. A monthly account was filled with day-by-day astronomical and meteorological observations. Concluding every section was a recapitulation of planetary positions, a list of market values of six commodities, statements about the water level of the Euphrates, and, occasionally, some historical notes.[2]

The quoted commodities were barley, dates, mustard, cress (or cardamom), sesame, and wool, and this order of quotation was preserved exactly through the centuries. The diaries do not explain themselves—there is no record of why they were kept. Slotsky hypothesizes that they were "pieces in some mathematical 'grand scheme' of the world."[3] This makes sense in the context of what is known regarding Babylonian models of astronomical phenomena and the long historical precedent for economic modeling in Mesopotamia.

These various ancient price series have recently become the empirical foundation for analysis of the Babylonian economy in late antiquity. Scholars have applied a range of sophisticated mathematical methods to the cuneiform records to examine ancient market forces.

Bert van der Spek, a professor at the University of Amsterdam, has spent a number of years rectifying the data from the Babylonian diaries, identifying problems of interpretation, collating them to other ancient price lists, and then making the data available for many other scholars to study.[4]

He and other teams of economists have analyzed these amazing data. Their efforts have revealed a lot about the nature and role of ancient commodities markets. Prices of commodities—particularly foodstuffs—varied a lot. Predicting the cost of grain in ancient Babylon would have been difficult from month to month because it changed so much. Scholars observe that Mesopotamia was an isolated agricultural zone, where famines could not be mitigated by importing grain from a neighboring region. Even within Mesopotamia, markets of the north and the south did not equilibrate.[5] Although there were common trends through time, agricultural subsistence in late Mesopotamia—as in early Mesopotamia—was local. The early temple-based economy may have adapted to more complex markets and financial mechanisms, but the populace evidently ate what was grown locally. This left Mesopotamia at the mercy of severe climate fluctuations. There were times when barley prices doubled, tripled, and quadrupled. If one of the functions of a market economy and a financial system is to smooth income shocks, the astronomical diaries indicate a system that was still imperfect.

The most painful periods for Babylonian shoppers were actually due to political distress. Alexander the Great died in Babylon in 321 BCE, and his death is noted in one of the astronomical diaries. It was unexpected—Alexander was thirty-two years old—a young, powerful commander in his prime. He fell ill and died within two weeks, leaving no clear successor. Immediately following Alexander's death, food prices in Babylon doubled—and remained high for another generation, as military rivals competed to succeed him. Did prices rise because food was requisitioned for soldiers? Did battling forces destroy crops? Perhaps the supply of food did not change, but a flood of silver money pushed prices higher. One can even imagine rulers opening up the treasury to keep the peace. This period of hardship continued until the establishment of political order with the Seleucid empire, although a correlation between internal armed conflict and price dislocations remained significant.[6] Nonetheless, while markets fluctuated in periods of distress, they continued to function, and the Babylonian diarists patiently tracked them and perhaps even used them for understanding the driving economic factors.

The astronomical diaries appear at the very end of a civilization that invented writing, pioneered the quantitative modeling of natural phenomena, and introduced new modes of thought about the use of numbers in economic and political life. Finance was only one aspect of Mesopotamian society, but throughout its history, finance played a central role. Economic concerns stimulated the need for innovation in calculation, quantitative record-keeping, and contracting. Technological innovation feeds on itself. In a society that mastered the use of numerical symbols and clay counters as symbols of actual goods, the leap to conceptual and detailed mathematical models seems a natural one. The Drehem tablet—the idealized mathematical forecast of the exponential growth of a herd of cattle—suggests that the technology of mathematical calculation, and the abstraction that naturally grows with symbolic representation, may have been a by-product of the development in early Mesopotamia of record-keeping and representation.

Financial tools were not only critical to the development of modes of thought, communication, and contracting, they were also important to the development of the Mesopotamian state. Large-scale central planning could not exist without an accounting technology and a means for individuals to generate money—whether as silver or as grain—to pay their taxes. The legal framework that made short-term loans possible and the specification of individual liabilities and assets are what created individual entrepreneurship. Ultimately, the technology of finance became embedded in politics. Wartime finance appeared in Mesopotamia, and this practice is still with us today.

Financial contracts allowed Mesopotamians to move value through time and to attribute a cost to it. Time was not only a dimension but also a commodity itself, meted out in interest. Even the Drehem tablet modeling the growth of a herd is the recognition of growing expectations—that the future holds more. What might these ancient people have reckoned about the land of Uruk 2,000 years after the final decline of Babylon?

Mesopotamian civilization evolved over more than 3,000 years, and throughout that extraordinary extent of history, a complex array of economic and financial institutions developed—built on a foundation of enumeration, accounting, contracting, and law. Over such a broad scope, no simple model of the relationship between finance and the state is adequate. The technology of finance at times served the interest of the central planner and at other times the interest of the individual entrepreneur, and of course it also served both at once.

The primary goal of Chapters 1–4 is to document the early development of the hardware and software of finance. This includes the first appearance of financial contracts, as well as the development of financial mathematics and financial thought. A secondary goal was to show the integral role these played in Mesopotamian society. Finance developed out of the need for intertemporal contracting, which was the economic foundation of the first cities. It also made possible the organization and intensification of long-distance trade. While such trade existed in societies with less financial architecture, the toolkit in the ancient Near East included a silver-based monetary system, equity-like partnerships, and a legal system of enforcement that was evidently robust and flexible enough to allow even small, combative city-states to access prestige goods and metals from afar. One interesting question is how such know-how could have survived over thousands of years.

Technology is a set of methods and ideas that develops and is maintained by culture. No one is born knowing how to calculate compound interest. It relies on the ability to pass this know-how down through time. One by-product of the clay tablet–based writing system of

Mesopotamia is that texts written in one millennium could be found and read in another. Although sophisticated financial techniques developed over three millennia of civilization in the ancient Near East, there were long stretches when cities were abandoned and knowledge of the past was lost. Fortunately, the ancient scribes wrote on clay rather than paper. Some texts were preserved, like the epic of Gilgamesh, by being copied over and over and stored in ancient libraries. Others must have been lost and rediscovered by Mesopotamian scholars sifting through the remains of ancient cities themselves. In this way an entire array of conceptual technologies—such as mathematics, surveying, astronomy, and financial instruments—could be sustained over centuries of growth and decline.

What scholars have gleaned over the past century from the study of Mesopotamian texts and archaeological excavations is only the merest glimpse of a rich, complex economic existence that emerged from the beginnings of urbanism and long-distance trade. Hundreds of thousands—perhaps even millions—of texts remain to be studied, yet what they have already taught us about the role of finance in civilization is immense.

ATHENIAN FINANCE

Nobody is qualified to become a statesman who is
entirely ignorant of the problem of wheat.

SOCRATES

The classical civilizations of Greece and Rome developed sophisticated
financial economies based on money and markets. The Greeks invented
banking, coinage, and commercial courts. The Romans built on these
innovations and added business corporations, limited liability investments, and a form of central banking. Unlike the ancient cities of Mesopotamia, which were primarily organized around the redistribution of
local produce and secondarily around long-distance trade, Athens and
Rome both outgrew their local agricultural capacity and substituted
overseas trade for it. Athens imported much of her wheat from as far
away as the Black Sea. Rome depended on the rich farmland of the Nile
delta for its grain. To make these audacious economic models work required a novel financial structure. Athens and Rome had to make grain
flow toward the center. The economy had to motivate farmers overseas
to grow grain for export, to motivate sailors and captains to risk their
lives to bring the grain, to motivate investment in ships and trade goods,
and to create a system of payment that was robust to uncertainties of
international commerce. The solutions involved the invisible hand of
the market, financial technologies for dealing with the unpredictability
of the sea, and a monetary economy that relied on universally accepted
measures of value.

Much of what we know about the ancient Athenian financial system comes from surviving judicial orations. The courts themselves
were key elements in the financial system. The Athenian court system
resolved disputes between plaintiffs and defendants through trial by

Electrum coin, 322 BCE, with a portrait of the Athenian
orator Demosthenes on the obverse.

jury. Jurors—typically 500 at a time—were chosen randomly and sat for a day, which was the maximum length of a trial. Plaintiff and defendant represented themselves, although famous orators were sometimes engaged to compose their speeches. Speaking time was regulated by a water-clock. Jurors did not deliberate together; rather they voted, and the ruling was determined by a majority vote.[1] At the end of the day, the matter was settled. The system was widely used for commercial disputes, many involving the Athenian grain trade. Courts specifically for maritime cases were held from September to April, when ships were not at sea and business could be settled in time for the next season. I argue in this chapter that the unique features of the Athenian court system created a financially literate society with a keen sense of abstractions, such as the price of risk, the time value of money, and the negotiability and hypothecation of entire business enterprises.

ATHENS AND GRAIN

In 386 BCE, a group of Athenian grain dealers faced the death penalty. They were on trial for price-fixing and hoarding. Their apparent crime was collusion in negotiating the price of grain with importing merchants. What risk did this economic cooperation represent? Why did it merit the death penalty? By the fourth century BCE, the city had outgrown its local agricultural capacity—the Attic plain and surrounding hills were more suited to cultivation of olive trees and honey rather than wheat and barley. The population was in the hundreds of thousands, and bread was a basic staple.

Athenians addressed this geographical limitation in part with laws. For example, two-thirds of all imported grain was required to go to the city of Athens. Shipping grain to any other port by an Athenian citizen was a capital offense. The law also restricted maritime lending solely to the overseas grain trade. Once grain was brought into Athens, laws constrained the profits allowed on grain dealing. Dealers could only store limited quantities of grain, and their mark-ups on resale were capped. All of these regulations were enforced by official market overseers, and rewards were offered to *sycophants*; informers who sold out grain dealers who skirted the rules.[2] In fact, these constraints raise the question— what were the positive incentives to provide grain to Athens?

One answer was the market price. Grain was sometimes expensive and difficult to obtain—prices to importers rose and fell with supply and demand. Grain prices could suddenly double. Sometimes Athenians paid dearly for the barley to make their morning cakes or the wheat for bread that accompanied dinner. Investors in voyages could expect a solid profit when they brought their cargo ashore at the Athenian port of Piraeus.

The trigger for the grain dealers' trial appears to have been a sudden price shock, perhaps due to a naval blockade of one of Athens' key grain suppliers. The dealers' defense was that they colluded at the behest of the Athenian market regulator, a man named Anytus, to obtain grain from shippers at low prices. Instead of passing the savings on to buyers, they then stored the grain and dribbled it out at high prices, violating laws against hoarding.[3] They colluded against both suppliers and customers.

No doubt Anytus was well meaning—perhaps he expected that the collusion would give the dealers greater leverage in negotiations with importers—however, the prosecutor in the trial recognized that the cartel would have a long-term detrimental effect. Merchants would no longer ship grain to Athens if they could not obtain a fair market price. As the Greek orator Lysias, the author of the prosecutor's closing argument, put it:

> If you condemn them you will do what is just and make corn cheaper; if you acquit them you make it dearer.[4]

His argument was that the crucial flow of grain would shift elsewhere in response to the invisible hand of the market, making corn (i.e., grain) dearer. Investors in the grain trade would no longer make loans on grain voyages if prices at the dock were too low. Captains would have little incentive to brave the risks of sea if they could not sell their cargo at a profit.

The text of the trial is incomplete. We do not know the fate of the grain dealers, but the trial is famous as the earliest evidence of antitrust prosecution. Underlying the argument by Lysias was a deep understanding of the extent to which Athens survived only by creating market incentives. It could not order grain prices to be lower. Laws governing reexport and local price controls could only go so far. Only the market could tempt entrepreneurs into the grain trade by dangling before them economic profits.

FINANCE AND THE SEA

Much of the Black Sea had been Hellenized by the fourth century BCE, and many places—such as the Crimean peninsula—had permanent Greek colonies. Half of Athens' annual grain imports came from the Black Sea kingdoms: roughly 13,000 tons of wheat. Oxford historian Alfonso Moreno calculates that this was enough to feed more than 50,000 people.[5] In fact, by his calculations, at least one-third of the population of Athens relied on imported grain. This means that hundreds of Greek vessels a year must have made the trip through the Aegean.

In 2002, Robert Ballard and a team of National Geographic undersea explorers dropped a probe into the depths of the Black Sea off the coast of Varna, Bulgaria. The researchers' curiosity had been piqued by a large feature on the sea floor. Their unmanned submersible approached the anomaly through the clear, dark water. Rows of amphorae emerged from the gloom: the cargo of an ancient Greek trading vessel. The researchers managed to pick up one of the amphorae for analysis. The shape of the amphora placed its manufacture at Sinope—a Greek trading city on the northern coast of modern Turkey in the region the Greeks called Pontus.

Pontus amphorae were often used for the wine trade, so when scientists unsealed the amphora in the lab, its contents were a surprise. The vessel was packed with the bones of freshwater catfish called sheat and were radiocarbon dated to the middle of the third century BCE. The sheat fillets came from the Dnieper river delta, where they are still regarded as a delicacy—evidently Greek vessels were shipping more than grain around the Black Sea. Assuming the Varna voyage made commercial sense, who put up the money for it? What happened when the ship and cargo were lost? Interestingly enough, we can speculate on the answers to some of these questions using a text from antiquity.

RISKS AT SEA

Preserved among the famous speeches of Athens' great fourth-century orator Demosthenes is a contract for a voyage. The contract, dating from about 352 BCE, is a loan financing a merchant voyage from Athens to the Black Sea and back again—presumably to trade wine for grain to ship back into Athens. The loan went bad, and a lawsuit ensued.

Demosthenes wrote the speech for the plaintiff, who was suing Lacritus, the elder brother of two young traders. The traders, Artemon and Apollodorus, borrowed 3,000 drachmas to finance a voyage from Athens to the Black Sea and north as far as the Dnieper—undoubtedly one of the places the Varna shipwreck visited. The Demosthenes oration spells out in great detail how Athenian sea loans worked; how they treated the risks of the sea voyage; and how they specified, in great detail, the terms demanded by lenders. It is worth quoting at length, because it shows how the Athenians managed the complex set of risks associated with maritime trade.

Androcles of Sphettus and Nausicrates of Carystus lent to Artemon and Apollodorus of Phaselis 3,000 drachma of silver for a voyage from Athens to Mende or Scione, and from there to Bosporus, and if they wished, on the left as far as Borysthes[6] and back to Athens, at 225 a thousand—and if they do not sail after Arcturus out of the Pontus towards Hierum, at 300 a thousand—on security of 3,000 Mendaean jars of wine, which will be shipped from Mende or Scione in the twenty-oared ship skippered by Hyblesius. They pledge these, not owing any money to anyone else on this security; nor will they obtain any further loan on it. They will convey back to Athens in the same boat all the goods from the Pontus purchased with proceeds from the outward cargo.

If they do not enter the Pontus after waiting in the Hellespont for ten days after the Dog-star, they shall unload in any place where Athenians are not liable to seizure of goods and after sailing back from there to Athens they shall pay the amount of interest written in the agreement the previous year. If any ship in which the goods being conveyed suffers irreparable loss but the pledged goods are saved, the lenders shall share what is preserved. On these matters nothing else is to prevail over the written agreement.

Witnesses: Phormion of Piraeus, Cephisodotus of Boeotia, and Heliodorus of Pithus. . . . Archenomides, son of Archedamas, of Anagyrus, deposes that Androcles of Sphettus, Nausicrates of Carystus, and Artemo and Apollodorus, both of Phaselis, deposited articles of agreement with him, and that the agreement is still in custody in his hands.[7]

A key feature of the contract is that the borrower did not have to repay the loan if the ship sank. The lenders—not the borrowers—accepted the risk of a shipwreck. If the brothers' ship met the same fate as the Varna wreck, then they were absolved of debt. A term for this form of lending is "bottomry," in which the ship and cargo are hypothecated to the lender, but repayment was only due if the ship survived.

Notice how this shift in risk from the entrepreneur to the investor made sense for both. Bottomry lenders could diversify the risks of a disaster by lending a little bit on a great number of voyages. Given the scale of the grain trade with the Black Sea region, these opportunities must have been considerable. That way, if a single ship went down, all was not lost.

In contrast, merchants who went to sea quite literally had all of their eggs in one basket. They had every incentive to buy grain cheaply in the Pontus, sell it dearly in Piraeus, and make enough to repay the loan, but could not protect themselves from circumstances—like the weather—beyond their control. Unlike the lenders, they could not diversify across many voyages without partnering with other merchants.

Even though lenders could diversify their investments, they still required compensation for the risk of a shipwreck. The two brothers, Artemon and Apollodorus, pledged to return either 22.5% or 30% interest to the lenders Androcles and Nausicrates on their investment of 3,000 drachmas. The rate was higher if the brothers did not start back through the Bosporus by the rising of Arcturus—around the time of the autumnal equinox, when the weather became stormier. The difference between 22.5% and 30% was an extra risk premium for disaster.

Another key risk control was collateral. The contract specified that the 3,000 drachmas would be used to purchase 3,000 jars of Mendaean wine in a northern Aegean port, not far from modern Thessaloniki. If anything happened to the boat, and some or all of the goods were saved, then these jars became the property of the lenders. This seems prudent. However, the lenders could not monitor the collateral—or even verify whether it existed. In fact, the collateral the brothers purchased was evidently used by the skipper of the boat as security for another loan, once they got to the Black Sea.

The Phaselite skipper wanted to borrow a further sum in the Pontus from a Chian man and because the Chian man refused to lend it unless he was given as security the whole of what the skipper had on board with the consent of the previous lenders, they did consent that this money of ours should become security for the Chian and gave him control of everything.[8]

Demosthenes argued that Artemon and Apollodorus never bought the promised cargo of wine, but instead turned around and lent the money they borrowed. Although they apparently sailed to the Black Sea, they returned to Greece empty handed, with the claim that their cargo of salted fish and wine was lost in a shipwreck between Pantica-peaum and Theodosia, two Greek colonies in Crimea. The description of their cargo echoes the (one century more recent) underwater find by Ballard and his associates.

In the quote above, the Chian lender's claim became more "senior" to the claim of Androcles and Nausicrates, despite a contract to the con-trary. It is difficult to see how the brothers could manage to pay off both loans. In a scheme something like the plot of the Broadway musical *The Producers*, the two young rogues clearly overpromised to investors, and their only hope of getting out of these debts was that the ship and cargo would be lost. Who knows—maybe the Varna ship was also intention-ally scuttled to avoid repaying a bottomry loan.

In a larger sense, the bottomry contract shows that Athens had a commercial code that tied together the economic lives of people from all over the Greek world. The borrowers were from a city in Asia Minor, near Lycia. The lenders were from a city outside Athens, and another Greek city-state in the northeast, Boeotia. Athens served as the legal venue in which the parties contracted. When the deal was broken, the lawsuit was brought under Athenian law. The parties together used a system that provided for adjudication under specific rules. The trans-parent Athenian rules for dispute resolution attracted external as well as internal capital.

The Athenian legal framework can be thought of as a financial technology. The ability of the lenders to sue for compensation over events that occurred in the Black Sea—and the power of Lacritus to defend himself using agreed-on rules of evidence—made the financing of long-distance trade possible. Greek merchant voyages to Ukraine undoubtedly involved great risk. The bottom of the Aegean is littered with shipwrecks of similar voyages, but the legal technology of maritime loans and legal enforcement reduced the uncertainty about simple fraud. The Athenian port of Piraeus had many attractive features—a natural, protected inner harbor surrounded by wharves and markets—but its vital architecture was legal: a tradition of contracting and commercial law.

BANKERS AND INVESTORS

Finance in the Greek world developed out of practices similar to those we saw in ancient Ur: loans and the financing of mercantile voyages. However, the historian Edward Cohen argues that a distinctively Greek mode of thought—a mentality based on dichotomies that pervaded both language and worldview—gave rise to a new kind of financial system.[9] On the one hand, visible wealth such as land was something that could be seen by everyone and was part of the physical world. Abstract wealth, on the other hand, took the form of bank deposits, accounts, and contracts. These assets existed as rights defended in court, contracts between two parties, or accounts held in trust by a banker. While abstract wealth existed before the Greeks—we saw this in the ancient city of Ur, where financiers stored their loan tablets—Cohen argues that Athenian banks conceptually decoupled finance from other enterprises, making it flexible enough to accommodate the needs of distant maritime trade and ultimately the needs of an empire.

The abstraction of financial wealth also makes the archaeology of banking more difficult. The best place to start is the modern port of Piraeus—Athens' seaport, where archaeologists have identified the ancient layout of the harbor. The Emporion, which stretched along the northeast side of the great harbor, was the center of international trade. Marked out in ancient times (like all major Greek spaces) by boundary stones, the Emporion is where merchants, investors, and bankers conducted the Black Sea trade. Archaeologists have uncovered the remains of the Emporion and its *stoas*—shelters where business was conducted. The foundations came to light with the construction of the modern city of Piraeus in the 1880s.[10]

FIGURE 5. Reconstruction of the central harbor of Piraeus as it would have appeared in the fifth century BCE, with a view of Emporion, where the first Greek bankers operated.

The Makra Stoa is the northernmost structure and the likely locus of the ancient grain trade. The central stoa fronting an area called the Deigma was used for display and sale of imported wares. These and fragments of the other three stoas were found near the modern customs house and town hall in Piraeus, suggesting that the modern city and its institutions rests squarely atop the ancient town. Walking the modern streets of Piraeus along the east side of the harbor is essentially a tour around the first Greek banking district.

The Greek term (both ancient and modern) for bank, *trapeza*, refers to a table on which the banker conducted business.[11] The name suggests that banks were not places or buildings but operations that took place over a modest piece of furniture where money was counted out, or more likely, where arithmetic calculations were conducted. True to the Cohen hypothesis about real versus abstract wealth, even the names of the earliest banks referred to the medium through which the activity occurred rather than its location.

We do not know what the Piraean trapezas looked like, but it is tempting to think of them as modeled on the as-yet undiscovered Babylonian counting boards. An artifact known as the Salamis tablet is a possible model for a Greek banker's trapeza. A marble slab five feet long by two and a half feet wide dating to the Roman era was found on the island of Cyprus in the nineteenth century. The surface has two sets of lines orthogonal to the long side of the slab. A banker seated behind one side of the stone table would face vertical columns. Sets of numbers on the sides of the table indicate fractions and multiples corresponding to Greek currency. Presumably the Salamis tablet was used with counters that could be moved on the lines or spaces between the lines to perform arithmetic calculations. This method of reckoning lasted through the Renaissance, virtually until the modern era. An abacus—a Greek, not a Chinese, invention—is nothing more than a portable version of the Salamis tablet, where the counters are strung on wire rather than moved across a board.

The earliest known bankers in Piraeus were the *trapezitai* Antisthenes and Archestratos, who operated at the end of the fifth century. They passed their bank to their freed slave, Pasio, in 394 BCE, who in turn transferred the bank to his freed slave Phormio before his death in 370. Thus, this multigenerational bank must have been the major financial Athenian institution of the fourth century. The fact that it was passed each generation to a freed slave reveals a lot about the way slavery— property rights over human capital—allowed business owners to capitalize on specialized, technical training. Talent was literally captive and transferable through a simple transaction. The business of a bank is to take in deposits and make loans; the true assets are not a stockpile of currency, a grand edifice, or a legion of clerks. Instead it is the business acumen of the banker, the eye for opportunities, the canny assessment of risk, and the reputation for integrity. That combination of human talent—plus a simple calculating table and a careful record-keeping system—constituted a bank in ancient Athens.

Much academic ink has been spilled about whether the Athenian trapezitai precisely fit the standard definition of a bank; that is, an institution that took short deposits and made longer-term loans. In the twenty-first century, this has been recognized as restrictive—today we know that financial services can be bundled and unbundled in a variety of ways. It is best to resist the desire to impose modern institutional notions on the distant past—even though banks in Athens today are called trápezes. Historical evidence makes it clear that Athens' bankers took deposits. There is also evidence that they made loans. Demosthenes claimed that Pasion had 50 talents out on loan, and scholars have estimated the use of bank loans was common among the well-off of the city.[12]

Bank loans could be made for productive purposes, such as sea ventures and business enterprises, but they could also be made of purposes of consumption smoothing. One of the duties of the Athenian elite periodically was to underwrite ceremonial events—liturgies—which were extremely expensive. This form of tax was an unpredictable shock to wealth, and it is no surprise that financial tools—such as loans from other members of the elite class and presumably bank loans, were used to smooth out this peculiar form of intertemporal shock. Indeed it is difficult to treat these shocks as "consumption loans"—a term that would imply that they were nonproductive. Historian Paul Millett, in his study of Greek banking, calls them "prestige expenditures," which recognizes that they were necessary to the maintenance of powerful positions in the Athenian social and political hierarchy.[13]

Bankers were indispensable for maintaining a store of wealth and for smoothing shocks to the wealth of clients, but they may also have been key intermediaries in the process of investment. Not only were they major investors of their own money (Pasion, for example, owned a major shield factory), but they also may have helped oversee and direct investments for their clients. We know Pasion risked his own capital on loans, and he also risked bank capital on loans. Perhaps he also played an intermediary role in matching borrowers and lenders in the economy. A hint of this can be seen in the maritime trade contract.

Notice that the first witness to the bottomry loan to the Black Sea was banker Phormion of Piraeus. Perhaps he was a convenient bystander, but more likely he was the banker for the lenders on the occasion of the loan being paid out. As one of the major financiers in Piraeus, he was in an ideal position to know who was lending to whom, which merchants needed money, and who owned what. Perhaps he used this position to advise clients, or even to syndicate loans—pooling bottomry lenders together. Our modern perspective suggests there are a range of financial services Athenians needed: from a basic institution that took deposits and relieved patrons of keeping their money under the mattress in coin, to an entity that could transfer large sums to and from counterparties in transactions, to a source of temporary cash buffer against economic shocks. Bankers also may have served as facilitators of economic investments—either because they profited economically or because this enhanced their reputations and connections. As business opportunities and personal investment needs scaled up with the Athenian economy, the need for financial intermediation inevitably scaled up as well.

FINANCIAL LITERACY

As a young man, Demosthenes sued his relatives. His uncles were appointed as his guardians after his father's death, and they stole his inheritance. The financial details in the trial were extremely complex. They involved two businesses, inventories, loans, and other assets. The trial, like all others, took place before a randomly selected jury of Athenian citizens. Demosthenes's challenge was not only to convince the jury that he had been deprived of his rightful inheritance, but also to explain exactly what it was worth and why. His approach to financial valuation offers a rare glimpse into how ordinary Athenians thought about finances.

Demosthenes senior was an entrepreneur. His business consisted of a sword factory, which presumably cast and finished weapons for the army, and a furniture factory that made luxury couches. The furniture factory came to him as collateral for a loan—he was holding the factory until the borrower repaid him.

These firms were substantial; the sword factory employed thirty-three slaves, and the couch factory employed twenty-two—more than fifty full-time, skilled laborers. In addition to the businesses, Demosthenes senior had an investment portfolio of deposits and loans. He had 2,400 drachmas with the banker Pasion, 600 drachmas with the banker Pylades, a maritime loan of 7,000 drachmas to Xuthos, 1,600 drachmas loaned to his nephew Demomeles, and about 6,000 drachmas in small loans without interest.[14] In addition, there was a house and such personal items as his wife's jewelry.

In Demosthenes's oration, he values these assets in two ways: first according to market value and then according to the annual net income they generated. Both of these approaches must have been completely familiar to the jury—the brevity of Athenian trials placed a premium on succinctness and clarity.

> My father, men of the jury, left two factories, both doing a large business. One was a sword-manufactory, employing thirty-two or thirty-three slaves, most of them worth five or six minae each and none worth less than three minae. From these my father received a clear income of thirty minae each year. The other was a sofa-manufactory, employing twenty slaves, given to my father as security for a debt of forty minae. These brought him in a clear income of twelve minae. In money he left as much as a talent loaned at the rate of a drachma a month, the interest of which amounted to more than seven minae a year. . . . Now, if you add to this last sum the interest for ten years, reckoned at a drachma only you will find that the whole, principal and interest, amounts to eight talents and four thousand drachmae.[15]

Notice in his last line, he takes into account the time value of income forgone over the ten years before he came of age to reclaim his patrimony at 12% simple interest. Just like the capitalized interest claimed in the Sumerian Enmetena cone (see Chapter 2), Demosthenes wanted compensation for the time that he was deprived of the property.

There are two remarkable things about the valuation. The first is that it shows that an apparently normal investment portfolio of a moderately well-to-do businessman of Athens at the time was quite diversified. Not only was Demosthenes senior invested in his main enterprise, but he was also saving money and investing it at a roughly 12% per year return in other businesses—including bottomry. His portfolio included slaves, equipment, inventory, loans, and bank deposits. Some capital was used for production, and some was deferred to future use. Athens apparently provided ample opportunity for both.

The second and even more striking thing is that Athens must have been filled with people for whom financial calculation and long-term planning were well understood. I wonder how many randomly chosen citizens today would be able to clearly follow Demosthenes' financial logic. The level of financial literacy of the average Athenian man in the fourth century BCE was evidently substantial. Reread the extract above and tell me it's an easy argument to follow!

FINANCE AND THE LAND

Of silver they possess a veritable fountain,
a treasure chest in their soil.[16]

AESCHYLUS, *PERSIANS*

In Aeschylus's famous tragedy about the hubris of the Persian Xerxes, the ruler's mother Atossa asks about the strengths of Athens. The chorus paints a picture of the treasure that awaits. Everyone in the audience in the spectacular theater of Dionysus Eleutheris on the Acropolis in 472 BCE would have known precisely what the play referred to. A few miles southeast of Athens, in an area called Laurion, lay one of the richest silver deposits in the ancient world.

Athenians may not have been endowed with farmland, but they were endowed with silver. Silver had been mined on and off in Laurion since the Bronze Age. Beginning in the sixth century, however, Athens began to intensively exploit the mines there and mint increasingly larger quantities of coins for both domestic and foreign use. The Laurion mines helped make Athens an economic powerhouse. At peak production in the fifth century BCE, 736 talents—20 tons of silver—were generated each year from the mines, and the city of Athens received 1/24 of this in mine taxes—30 talents of silver a year.[17]

Historian Gil Davis argues that even these large annual sums were small compared to the multiplier effect of the flow of silver money to the Athenian economy. Seven hundred talents created 4 million drachmas. A drachma was roughly the price of a day of labor at the time. It is not difficult to see how the fountain of silver in Laurion could have helped finance the magnificent architecture of the Acropolis. The Laurion silver evidently flowed from the mines to private and public coffers, and then, as coinage, it flowed out of the port of Piraeus through the Mediterranean, the Black Sea, and doubtless well beyond. According to Xenophon, Athens' silver gave her a clear advantage in international trade:

at most other ports merchants are compelled to ship a return cargo, because the local currency has no circulation in other states; but at

Athens they have the opportunity of exchanging their cargo and exporting very many classes of goods that are in demand, or, if they
do not want to ship a return cargo of goods, it is sound business to
export silver; for, wherever they sell it, they are sure to make a profit
on the capital invested.[18]

Athenians did not have to have commodities to exchange at other ports.
Their silver was accepted everywhere.

PRIVATIZATION

The Laurion mining operations were not state owned—although the
state got a share. Instead—like the grain trade—they were financed
by private investment. Entrepreneurs leased unexplored or previously
abandoned tracts of land from the state and then invested capital to dig
for silver ore. If successful, they set up local smelting operations that
required even more capital investment. The silver ore contained substantial amounts of lead. Separating the two metals required smashing,
roasting, and re-heating ore and used a lot of water, which was not necessarily close to the mines. The operations were both a technical and a
financial challenge. Investors took great risks in prospecting for ore and
then had to raise more capital once it was discovered.

Research on the Laurion mines reveals how these risky ventures were
licensed and financed.[19] Mining sites were leased out by the Athenian
magistrates called *poletai*, who were in charge of municipal concessions
and auctions. The poletai made up an important body in the Athenian
political system dating back to the seventh century BCE. They were
a council of ten magistrates appointed annually from among Athens'
ten tribes. Their job was to preside over the public auctioning of state
property, such as the Laurion silver leases. Their limited tenure guarded
against corruption, and their broad representation of the people of Athens created a sense of fair dealing. Their decisions were posted publicly,
so they could not be accused of subterfuge.

By a stroke of amazing fortune, archaeology in Athens' Agora has
yielded a number of stone steles with inscribed records of the Laurion
mining concessions. Many of these were discovered in the southwest
corner of the Agora—leading scholars to tentatively identify a modest

trapezoidal building with a central court and adjoining rooms as the *poleterion*.[20] Excavations in 2004 in this building unearthed a hoard of more than 400 Athenian tetradrachms—the largest cache of ancient currency ever found in the Agora digs. The money trove suggests the prominent role that the poleterion played in Athenian civic life.[21]

The Laurion steles revealed something of the complexity of financial arrangements. Leases fell into three broad categories: unexplored, developed, and previously developed but abandoned. Each of these had their own risks and demanded different rates of return in compensation. Scholars note that the prices for each of the three risk classes were different—reflecting again the acute awareness of the trade-off between risk and required return. Just like they did in financing sea voyages, Athenian investors formed partnerships to lease mining rights, as well as to lease the slaves and working equipment necessary to work the mines. These partnerships were evidently a way to share the risks of prospecting and mining as well as put excess capital to productive use. The financial dealings around the Laurion mines were every bit as complicated as the Athenian bottomry loan contracts.

A MINING DEAL

One of the most complex of all Demosthenes's lawsuits was a dispute over the lease of mining operations. In 346 BCE, the entrepreneur Pantaenetus leased a mine and then borrowed 100 minas (10,000 drachmas) to buy into a partnership that owned the slaves and workshop to run the mining operation.

His partnership share of the slaves and workshop served as collateral for his loan. The trouble started when he and his partners sold the slaves and workshop to another consortium with the understanding that Pantaenetus would continue to rent them. Then Pantaenetus failed to meet the rent and to pay the poletai for the lease.

The consortium seized the assets—but discovered that they were already pledged as collateral for Pantaenetus's original loan. The collateral was only a fraction of the enterprise, not the whole. The various creditors argued their claims, and the accusations got personal. Pantaenetus blamed everyone—but particularly the creditors, who were evidently professional financiers.

The lawsuit reveals an amazing institutional framework. Virtually everything in Athens was fungible—anything could be pledged as collateral, even slaves, mining rights, and entire workshops. Investors who knew nothing about how to mine could get into the business by buying expertise in the form of a crew of enslaved miners. Whole businesses could change hands as financial needs and resources shifted.

The financial system of Athens not only facilitated long-distance trade. The technology of financing at sea—the contracts, collateralization, partnerships, and external financing tools—also worked to finance other enterprises. Just like the risks of the sea, the risks of mining were managed by diversification in a financial system of extraordinary fluidity and adaptability. The state profited by this privatization by obtaining the highest returns on its leases through a transparent and cleverly designed public bidding system that, because of its mechanism design, elicited the highest bids. The liquidity of the workshops, and the ability to transfer property rights, encouraged investors to enter the mining business and served the needs of the state as well as their own.

What we can glean from surviving ancient literature and legal records reveals that the Athenian contribution to finance was motivated by the profound reliance of the city on imported grain.

Athens by the fourth century BCE was a private marketplace, where private capital was one of the commodities for sale. The Athenian legal system made this possible, and a novel institution—the private bank—likely emerged as a medium for channeling, monitoring, and accounting for private investments in trade. This development was either the cause or the effect of the Greek capacity to see a dichotomous relationship between tangible and intangible wealth.

If Edward Cohen's thesis about Greek thought is correct, this easy separation allowed finance to move toward increasingly abstract and complex structures. The evidence for this complexity is preserved in Demosthenes's speeches, some of which reflect the apparent legal ambiguities posed by the financial architecture. Whose claim takes precedent in circumstances of failure? What standings did creditors have? What were fiduciary responsibilities? Juries were required to address these questions through reliance on chains of logical argument—legal rather than geometrical proofs. These legal disputes over contracts—some for very large amounts of money—contrast with the meager physical remains of the Athenian banking system. The whole thing operated on a nexus of interpersonal relationships, reliance on law, and trust. The tables used by the trapezitai were simply a means to keep score.

The jury system engaged hundreds of Athenian citizens at a time in disputes over business deals, partnerships, loans, inheritance, and even market collusion. Because the assignment to a jury was random, orators had to communicate clearly to the average Athenian citizen and had to rely on their general knowledge about the disputed issues. Concepts like the time value of money and compensation for risk appear regularly in the surviving trial records. Given that each jury included hundreds of people, a great many Athenians must have circulated through the commercial court system. They must have listened to—and understood—complex financial arguments and then cast their ballots in favor of one side or the other. Perhaps jury duty itself taught the people of Athens about loans, banks, partnerships, trade, income statements, collateral, and fraud. At the very least, a modern reading of the ancient orations makes it clear that the capacity for comprehension of financial issues was surprisingly sophisticated.

A voyage to the Black Sea for grain was risky, and fitting out a galley with oarsmen, merchants, skipper, and crew was expensive. Without state sponsorship, it is a wonder such voyages could be undertaken at all. Those wealthy enough to afford to underwrite the cost might prefer to remain in the safety and comfort of Athens instead of venturing across hundreds of miles of sea. A financial system that could induce investors to give thousands of drachmas to virtual strangers in the hopes of a 20–30% profit from trade was a magnificent innovation. Indeed the economy of Athens was completely dependent on it. Likewise, the Athenian state was able to induce investors into the equally risky venture of prospecting and mining through mechanisms for dispute resolution and the means by which the state fairly and transparently allotted property rights. This incentive structure meant that investors could diversify across not only sea voyages but also industrial ventures and mining operations. Athens had a financial system that facilitated investments and spread risks, and it supported the complex, import-based economy that the great city required.

MONETARY REVOLUTION

Athens is most famous as the birthplace of democracy. Although the development of the Athenian political institutions has long been the subject of study, the economic foundation of democracy has attracted less interest until recently. Democracy is a system of shared governance by the people—a novel organizational structure that demands complex institutions for decision-making and a realignment of individual allegiance away from that of the traditional family, tribe, and monarch. Democracy as it evolved in Athens involved the pooling of common interests and the distribution of control through mechanisms such as the poletai described in Chapter 5. This was accomplished by a process that reached all the way down to the level of *demos*—the common people.

The Athenian system that evolved over a two-century period from the rule of Solon at the end of the seventh century to the era of Pericles in the fifth century BCE fundamentally restructured the relationship between the individual and the state. The basic instrument of this realignment was a system of public finance that had a number of unprecedented elements. Without financial innovation—and unique financial resources—the experiment of democracy in ancient Athens may not have succeeded.

Historian Hans Van Wees, a professor at University College London, is an expert on the development of the archaic Greek state. His thesis is that the first great political reformer of Athens, Solon, created a fiscal structure for Athens based on a central fund, which was used to finance wars and to advance the other collective interests of the people. Solon established a mandatory and explicit tax system to support the fund, and, among other things, he reformed the system of weights and measures—presumably as a necessary step to have a uniform and fair financial system.[1]

Athens, tetradrachm, after 449 BCE.

Solon also outlawed Athenian citizens from being held as slaves, establishing the principal of natural right to freedom (at least insofar as it was selectively applied to Athenian citizens and not the people they enslaved). He did this through a comprehensive mortgage loan forgiveness program that rebalanced the power relationship between the haves and the have-nots and presaged Athenian democracy.

An irony in the development of Athenian democracy is that after Solon, some of the most important financial innovations were made by monarchs. The tyrant Peisistratus ruled intermittently from 561 to 527 BCE, followed by his sons Hippias and Hyparchus, who ruled until 508 BCE. According to Van Wees, during this period Athens was transformed into a monetary economy.

Peisistratus introduced a silver coinage system that was used, among other things, to pay the salaries of a growing municipal workforce, the judiciary, and the military. If you wondered why, for example, the court system required hundreds of jurors selected at random—and mandated a limited number of times any one of them could serve—the answer might lie in the perceived political benefits of salaried compensation by the state. The courts and other institutions were staffed by citizens chosen by lot or appointed for limited spans of time. This was a means by which money was fairly dispensed through Athenian citizenry and allegiance to the state was developed. To pay for this, Athens exacted tribute from its protectorate states and levied a progressive tax on citizens to generate a steady flow of revenues. It was a fiscal system that increasingly engaged citizens in a direct, economic relationship with the state.

MONEY AND THE GREEK MIND

Financial literacy—the ability to calculate costs and benefits—was recognized by the Greeks as an important underpinning of Athens's special political structure. According to the fourth-century Pythagorean philosopher Archytas,

> The discovery of calculation (logismos) ended civil conflict and increased concord. For when there is calculation there is no unfair advantage, and there is equality, for it is by calculation that we come to agreement in our transactions.[2]

Who might have guessed that the roots of democracy lay in financial literacy? The conceptual ability—the *logismos*—to follow Demosthenes as he valued his father's estate was regarded by Archytas as the mental tool on which a political system could be built. The principles of quantitative valuation were the "software" that increased agreement and reduced civil conflict. Athenian numeracy was not simply a skill required for successful business. It was a trait on which the democratic process fundamentally relied. The challenge of democracy is to accommodate a wide diversity of opinion and resolve this cacophony into governance. Even when there is vast disagreement on principles, it is hard to argue with numbers.

Richard Seaford, an expert in Greek literature and author of the insightful book *Money and the Early Greek Mind*, advances the proposition that money played an important role in the mental framework of ancient Athenian society. The monetization of Athens was not only important to the emergence of democracy, it was also a factor in the development of Greek philosophy. In Seaford's view, monetization led to abstract thought. Money could be exchanged for an infinitude of different material things, but the coins themselves did not satisfy basic human needs.

Seaford goes so far as to suggest that the money economy influenced Platonic and Aristotelian notions of the individual. When economic interactions were defined by quantitative measures of potential value, people became more autonomous, less reliant on traditional institutions of social reciprocity, and more reliant on an incentive structure ultimately measured by profit.

Socrates recognized this and did not approve. He was particularly critical of Pericles—the famous fifth-century Athenian statesman who essentially completed the process of democratizing Athens. Pericles increased payment to jurors, further extending their reliance on the public dole and orienting their incentives toward money. In Socrates's view, this monetization amounted to bribery of the soul. Salaried service corrupted incentives. In his words (or at least in Plato's) "Pericles has made the Athenians idle, cowardly, talkative, and avaricious, by starting the system of public fees."[3] The democratic system did not promote personal virtue—at least as Socrates defined it.

THE OWL COINS

Athens first began minting its famous owl coin in the late sixth century BCE, probably under the tyrant Hippias. The Athenian tetradrachm was one of the most widely produced coins in history, with as many as 120 million pieces struck. It was also one of the most long-lived—minted from the fifth to the first centuries BCE.[4]

The coin has Athena's profile on the front and her owl familiar on the back, together with a sprig of an olive tree, and the letters AΘE, for Athens. The Athenian tetradrachm was worth four drachmas—it has a nice heft to it, and the emblems on both sides are bold and clear. The coin pointedly does not bear the portrait or emblem of a particular ruler, even though it first appeared under monarchic rule. The goddess Athena on the front is synonymous with the city, and the coins thus were symbols of the state. Worshipping Athena was equivalent to worshipping her city.

The reverse side of the coin had an equally rich meaning. The particular aspect of the goddess (and thus the city she celebrated) was wisdom, symbolized by the owl; writing; and Athens' primary export good—olive oil. Thus commerce, intelligence, and learning were all depicted on the coin.

The Athenian tetradrachm was a constant advertisement for Athens itself, a reminder that monetary benefits flowed from the goddess and the principles she represented. It must have eventually evoked a Pavlovian response. As citizens rotated through the court systems and other municipal services and received their compensation in coin, just seeing a gleaming Athenian tetradrachm must have caused anticipation of a state-sponsored reward. The challenge of democracy was to reorient individual identity away from traditional institutions like family and tribe toward a larger, collective enterprise. Using emblems of the democratic state—like the Athenian owl coin—was a powerful way to achieve it.

One of the coin's most important functions was to serve as a liquid, ready store of value for the Athenian government. According to Thucydides, one of Athens's great military strengths was her treasure of coined silver, which could pay for soldiers and fleets.

They [the Athenians] were also to keep a tight rein on their allies—
the strength of Athens being derived from the money brought in by
their payments, and success in war depending principally upon conduct and capital . . . there were still six thousand talents of coined
silver in the Acropolis, out of nine thousand seven hundred that
had once been there, from which the money had been taken for the
porch of the Acropolis, the other public buildings, and for Potidaea.[5]

This treasure was kept in the most famous of all buildings in Greece: the
Parthenon. On the eve of the Peloponnesian War, the temple of Athena
on the Acropolis held 36 million drachmas.

A tourist visiting the Acropolis today looks up to the Parthenon and
sees its magnificent pediment and thinks of it as a temple. Ancient Athenians also saw it as their treasury—their great monetary weapon against
invasion. The front door of the Parthenon led to the room with a giant
cult statue of Athena—itself gilded in gold that could be peeled off and
minted if times got desperate. The back door of the Parthenon led to the
treasury. Athena cast a protecting eye over her eponymous city below,
but her protection was backed up with financial might. Coinage was not
only a brilliant economic invention—it was also a great political one.

The Athenian owls spread far beyond Athens. Athenian tetradrachms
have been found throughout the eastern Mediterranean and beyond,
indicating that they were used in long-distance trade. Even more interesting is that imitation owls were minted in Egypt, Arabia, and Babylonia, as well as cities in *Magna Graecia*: Tarentum, Pergamum, and the
Hellenized cities of Asia Minor. The quality of these imitations varied,
but they retained the basic form: Athena on the obverse and the owl on
the reverse. Sometimes—but not always—city names were substituted;
however, owl coins minted in Egypt, Arabia, and Babylonia in the
fifth century BCE retained the AΘE, suggesting that they were passed
off as monetary equivalents to the Athenian tetradrachm.

In fact, the form of the Athenian owl came to symbolize money itself—in the same way that modern brand names like Kleenex and Xerox
came to be used to indicate the entire product category. More importantly, the coin became an international currency for which Athens had
a monopoly—a position that stimulated competition through technical
imitation. The world of the eastern Mediterranean and the Near East

looked to Athens in part to supply the currency of international trade. Like the Nippur silver trade centuries earlier (see Chapters 2 and 4), that money itself became increasingly valuable as a technology for exchanges that could not be handled by repeated accounts and supported by reputation and legal claims. Payment in (legitimate) coin had no counterparty risk; it was immediate and precise. The Athenian owls suited not only the internal political requirements of Athens. They also fit the need of a network of trade among peoples who did not share Athenian government or other institutions.

WHERE DID COINS COME FROM?

Ephesus was once a clamoring seaport, already an ancient city by Roman times and one of the most important harbors on the coast of Asia Minor. It became famous in antiquity for its temple of Artemis, one of the seven wonders of the ancient world; a vast edifice rebuilt in the sixth century BCE after a devastating earthquake. The new temple was funded by the legendary King Croesus of Lydia.

In 1904, British Museum archaeologists digging in the foundations of the temple of Artemis uncovered a cache of tiny coins made of electrum—a natural amalgam of silver and gold. Some of these ancient offerings were stamped with symbols: geometric shapes, cross-hatching, and even the head of a lion. The weights of the electrum offerings were regularly spaced—indicative of monetary units. These objects, dating to the middle of the sixth century BCE, represent one of the most interesting mysteries in financial history—the puzzle of coinage. Subsequent finds and further research have pushed the earliest date for these electrum coins back to the beginning of the sixth century.[6] So electrum coinage appeared a few decades before Athens began to mint its own silver money. With its discovery came the fundamental question: where did money come from?

Aristotle's explanation is international trade:

For when, by importing things that they needed and exporting things of which they had too much, people became dependent upon more distant places, the use of money was invented out of necessity. For not all of the things that are required by nature are easy to transport;

and so for use in exchanges they agreed among themselves to give and take something of a sort that, being itself one of the useful items, was easy to handle for the needs of life, such as iron or silver, or anything else like that. At first it was simply defined by size and weight, but finally they also added an impressed stamp, to free them from measuring it, since the stamp was put on as a sign of the amount.[7]

This explanation is rejected by scholars on the grounds that long-distance trade predated the invention of coinage. Also, the early electrum coins from Ephesus do not appear to have circulated widely, so circulation in international trade could not have been their reason for being.

Modern scholars have instead posed two alternative explanations for the selective emergence of coinage. David Schaps is a classics professor at Bar Ilan University in Israel and an expert on money and the classical economy. He points out that coins appeared in the political context of warring city-states. Whereas the Mesopotamian and Egyptian empires of the sixth century BCE were large-scale economies with efficient distribution systems, Schaps notes that the first coins appeared in quite different circumstances. He argues that the emergence of coinage is connected to the increased reliance of the state on the marketplace and the need of the government to stimulate it.[8] In his view, coinage was a method for local rulers of competing Greek city-states to increase the money supply. Their existence, he suggests, is potential evidence that governments recognized the central role that the marketplace played in the economy. This last assertion is irrefutable and important. Whatever the spark of inspiration for coins, the fact that the government got involved in their production indicates a new role for the government as keeper of the market and as the "tender of the tender."

Another related explanation offered by Alain Bresson of the University of Chicago addresses the particular features of the electrum coins from Lydia.[9] Since they are an amalgam of silver and gold, the precise mixture is unknown to the user. Bresson points out that assaying electrum by weight and volume was a specialized and costly technology. For small denominations of value, the cost of weighing amounted to as much as 10% of the value. The solution to this problem was to weigh the coin once, perhaps under government auspices, then certify it by a stamp and enforce the acceptance of the certification by government decree. This process theorized by Bresson is entirely consistent with Schaps's proposal that coinage signified governmental commitment to maintaining a functional market via support of the money supply. Coinage thus grew out of a demand for small change, and the production process reflected the most efficient means of supply.

These theories can also be reconciled with Aristotle's explanation for the invention of coinage, and they perhaps provide further insight into the evolution of the Aegean economy in the sixth century BCE and the role played by international trade.

Consider again the long time series of market prices in Babylon. At the most basic level, when Babylonians went to the streets to buy cress, grain, or dates, how did they pay? Was it with copper bracelets, or did they carry lumps of silver? Probably neither. Although they used a silver-based pricing system, more than likely they recorded their small payments or obligations in accounts—like running a tab at a local store. They used silver as a "language" of account, but a grocer could not constantly and reliably weigh out shekels of silver while bargaining over barley, cress, and dates.

Payment by account via small-scale extension of credit presupposes a common trust in a record-keeping system, a reputation for honesty, and a setting in which the preponderance of transactions occurred between people who knew each other and interacted with enough frequency to settle accounts. Take away any of these features—records, reputation, or repeat business—and the use of small accounts as money breaks down.

Now consider the picture Aristotle paints of international trade. Imagine wooden ships from Athens, Egypt, Cyprus, the Levant, and the Black Sea moored at Ephesus's stone wharves, loading and unloading cargo: amphorae of oil and grain, housewares, textiles, and other bulk cargo from the far-flung Mediterranean world. The captain, crew, and traders on the ships want to eat, sleep, and enjoy themselves after weeks at sea. They need to re-provision the boat for their onward voyage. How do they pay? Why should a merchant run any of them a tab? The old saying "In God we trust—all others pay cash" comes to mind. The risks of never seeing the crew again are high. At the same time, barter with their cargo of commodities is inconvenient and not necessarily economically efficient. The stakes are way too small to write an official contract.

Instead, trading some goods for local coinage would have been a simple means to allow foreigners to shop in an unknown land. Among the various stalls along the wharves at Ephesus, the money changers must have been the first stop.

Mediterranean trade existed long before the sixth century, of course. The fifteenth-century BCE Mycenaean cities of mainland Greece, for example, traded with Egypt and Crete. The earliest written Greek records are Linear B tablets detailing commodities transactions by palaces. However, such government-sponsored exchange might not have required the same kind of payment technology as independent, small-scale enterprise. Tribute and exchange among polities presumably involved other means of assurance and verification. Trusting a foreign state is different from trusting a foreign skipper and his crew. Coins gave trading power to the individual as opposed to the state.

Had the tradition of coinage stopped with the use of small electrum pellets like the Lydian staters, it might never have emerged to fascinate generations upon generations of scholars. In fact, the deep attraction to Greek coins lies in their role as symbols for the state. By the late sixth century BCE, coinage had developed into a remarkable art form—each city-state had its own distinctive design: Athens had the owl, Aegina had the turtle, and Corinth had a winged horse. These designs were punched into weighed lumps of silver or bronze, leaving the sculpted figures in relief: a token of the city, a certification of monetary value, and a bit of classical art.

The coin is more than a symbol, however. Athens is the first democracy, and the silver Athenian owl is thus our link back to the roots of democratic society. To hold one is a tangible connection to ancient government. Coinage, a financial instrument, became an integral tool of the state; a means of facilitating and regulating commerce; and if Aristotle is correct, a tool particularly useful for international trade.

The two big factors that distinguished Athens from most prior ancient societies were the reliance on maritime trade and the development of a unique governance system. Athens in classical antiquity was quite different from the early Sumerian city-states. Despite its magnificent Acropolis, it was not centered on a temple-based, local, agricultural redistribution system. The overseas grain trade relied in part on the invisible hand to attract risk capital—both wealth and human-risk capital. The invisible hand played an important role in creating an incentive structure to pull grain toward the city to replace the grain it could not produce on its own. That said, Athens was not simply a laissez-faire society. Strict regulatory constraints prevented grain re-exports and the financing of non-Athenian grain trade. The secondary sale and storage of grain were likewise restricted. Legal and regulatory architecture played a key role.

The dispersion of capital investment in trade means that the evidence itself is dispersed and fragmentary. There is no central Athenian state archive that documents economic activity, as has been found for some earlier Mesopotamian cities. No clay tablets survive—only a tiny selection of the most memorable court orations and disputes; archaeological evidence of maritime trade; some references from Greek drama; and of course, coins. It is difficult from these to quantify the extent of financial activity. We are really only able to identify the existence of certain contracts and institutions. Modern researchers who work on ancient finance try hard to connect the dots, because the Athenian economy—stretched as it was across the eastern Mediterranean and Black Sea—was remarkable. It proved that, with a sufficient financial structure, a large and complex society that relied fundamentally on international trade was possible.

Athenian democracy and Athenian finance evolved together, and they embodied a paradox. The trade economy worked by decentralizing capital investment and allowing the invisible hand to allocate capital to the grain trade. Athenian democracy also required a structure for decentralizing governance, but at the same time it also relied on a means to unify its citizens behind an abstract institution—the state—to which citizens would willingly pay taxes and for which they would adhere to the demands of public service. Democracy is more than a political structure. It is also an economic structure. It required a technology that operated on many levels, which sometimes includes religious symbolism. Athenian coinage refocused its citizens' loyalties from such traditional groups as family and tribe to a new structure—the state. It used Athena as the emblem of the state and money as a medium through which the state was constantly experienced. Money was a reward system, a measurement system, and the store of collective treasure.

ROMAN FINANCE

Rome's financial system was more complex than anything that preceded it, and by some accounts it was as sophisticated as anything that appeared until the Industrial Revolution.[1] Rome's financial architecture matched the complexity of the empire's economy. One of its key functions—like that of the Athenian financial system—was to supply food to an urban metropolis that had grown well beyond local agricultural capacity. The Roman trade network encompassed much of what is now modern Europe and North Africa, and its distant connections extended to India and China. This vast matrix did not function without finance: just as in ancient Athens, merchants needed capital, trade credit, and insurance against risks.

Rome became an empire through conquest. The conquest itself was a financial feat. Armies were paid, fed, transported, and garrisoned across three continents. Rome had to develop a monetary economy that could compensate her armies. Once provinces were conquered, they had to be taxed and administered. To address these logistics, Rome privatized various functions of the state, including tax collection, military supply, and construction.

In this chapter we explore the Roman financial system through a few key examples that elucidate the role that finance played in Roman expansion, the role that complex economic institutions played in trade and the Roman food chain, the role that large-scale private enterprises played in Roman growth, and the role that financial intermediation played in the political struggle for power. These examples reveal, in many cases, a strikingly modern set of financial tools to address intertemporal exchange, capital formation, and the control of risk and uncertainty. They also reveal a system that was subject to the familiar modern maladies of financial crises and inflation. The occasional crises of credit contraction and runaway inflation that hit the Roman economy raises

Temple of Castor and Pollux, Roman Forum. At the steps of the temple, contracts were auctioned for Roman companies called *societas publicanorum*. Shares in these firms were also traded here, making this the earliest stock market.

the question of whether a complex financial system—ancient or modern—is inevitably subject to systemic shock.

One feature that set Rome apart in financial history was the development of a financial system to sustain the enormous wealth of its ruling class. In Rome, there was no political power without wealth, and wealth grows through investment. The Roman financial system evolved to provide opportunities for capital investment necessary to sustain the fortunes of Rome's narrow oligopoly. It developed flexible and strategic methods for sharing the economic benefits of conquest among the participants in the upper classes and for resolving complex political power struggles through financial trade-offs.

ROMAN SOCIETY

The salient feature of Roman society throughout its history was a sharp division into classes and the dependence of political rank on wealth. Money was a necessary, although not sufficient, requirement for rising to a position of power. Over the course of Roman history—from monarchy, to republic, to empire—Rome was ruled by a small, self-perpetuating oligarchy defined by heredity and property. At is greatest extent, a group of roughly 10,000 people ruled an empire of 60 million.

Membership in the Senate, Rome's ruling body required a fortune of 250,000 denarii; election by Senate members; and, in imperial times, approval by the emperor. Rome conducted regular censuses during the Republican era that sorted its subjects into ranks—assessing and documenting family status and wealth. Senators who failed to meet the wealth requirement forfeited their positions. Each year senatorial seats opened up, and senatorial families vied with one another to secure these open spots for relatives.

Of the two social ranks that qualified for appointment to the Senate, the most exclusive and privileged was the patrician class; the hereditary descendants of Rome's earliest ruling families. Next came the equestrian class—Rome's knights. Their elevated rank derived from a traditional role of providing cavalry to Rome's army. Membership in the equestrian class had a minimum wealth requirement of 100,000 denarii. The wealth requirement reflected the need to either possess horses (hence the term "equestrian class") or have sufficient resources to pay for horses and soldiers. Although qualification for the equestrian membership was at first hereditary, one could eventually advance into this class by amassing a fortune. Plebeians and freedmen (i.e., former slaves) constituted the lower ranks of Roman society.

Because of this connection between wealth and rank, financial cooperation, competition, and intrigue represented important dimensions of political strategy. This led to legal constraints on entrepreneurial activity by politicians. For example, the Lex Claudia, a law passed by the Senate in 218 BCE, limited the carrying capacity of merchant ships owned by senators. It was intended to prevent senators from exploiting their political advantage for economic gain. A senator was expected to make his money from land; to own large estates that grew wheat, wine, and olives; and to sell these locally. Without large ships, exporting produce from senatorial estates was effectively controlled.

Once a knight achieved the rank of senator, he was theoretically barred from direct participation in the vast and profitable trade of the empire, except through indirect investment, such as lending. Senators not only had to be rich but their active capital was also seriously constrained, even though it was the explicit basis for their eligibility.

In short, senators had to maintain great fortunes without direct involvement in lucrative enterprise. Thus, the ability to delegate financial operations—to have plausible deniability of involvement in business—and to separate ownership and control were essential. As we shall see, the Roman financial system evolved institutions that allowed senators precisely these opportunities.

The next rank down, Roman knights and their families—unlike Roman senators—could engage in commerce. They conducted major business operations and manned important government posts. The equestrian class ultimately developed a form of financial organization much like a modern corporation. The corporate structure gave the equestrian class the ability to make equity investments, but it also preserved Rome's oligopolistic structure—knights who invested in these companies effectively shared the risk and return of enterprise with their co-investors.

Thus, Roman finance cannot be separated from politics. Innovations and sophisticated financial institutions reflect the peculiarities of Roman governance. After all, the most distinctive thing about Rome is that it existed as a political entity for 1,000 years, and at its peak it ruled a significant fraction of the world's population. It was an extraordinary political equilibrium that relied on a unique set of financial tools to support it.

A FINANCIAL CRISIS

This discussion of Roman finance begins with a financial crisis that will dispel any notion that Rome was, in any way, a primitive economy. "Unpacking" the crisis of 33 CE will elucidate many of Rome's financial institutions in the early years of the empire and will also demonstrate how they ultimately derive from the complexities of Roman politics.

Rome's transition from a republic, which was governed by the Senate, to an empire governed by an emperor involved a series of civil wars culminating in the famous battle of Actium in 31 BCE, in which Anthony and Cleopatra's fleet was defeated by Octavian, who became Augustus Caesar. His adopted son, the general Tiberius, ruled Rome from Augustus's death in 14 CE to 37 CE. When he began his rule, he paid lip service to the Senate as the seat of Roman power; however, the final five years of Tiberius's reign were characterized by power struggles, an attempted coup, and subsequent persecutions.

Four years before Tiberius died, Rome was struck by a financial crisis involving mortgages and defaults. Unlike his profligate successor Caligula, Tiberius had been conservative in public expenditures—there was plenty of money in the treasury. The financial crisis of 33 CE arose in the private sector, but it ultimately needed to be resolved by the government through an intervention in the credit markets.

The crisis was preceded by a purge that had begun in 31 CE with the execution of Tiberius's challenger Sejanus. The aging Tiberius famously had many of the coup's supporters killed and pitched into the Tiber River. The financial crisis may have been an extension of the purge following a failed coup attempt.

The crisis was described years later by historians Tacitus, Dio, and Suetonius.[2] It evidently began with the renewed enforcement of laws enacted decades earlier by Julius Caesar regulating loans and defining the terms of holding estates in Italy. Caesar's regulations were themselves a response to a financial crisis that began in the 50s BCE and came to a head after his march on Rome in 49 BCE. At that time, in response to a dearth of credit and declining property values—perhaps also brought on by political uncertainty—the Senate capped interest rates at 12%, which evidently did not solve the credit crisis. Caesar took additional action by allowing debt repayments in land at pre-crisis values; he also canceled interest due on mortgages, forbade cash hoarding, and required lenders to hold a portion of their wealth in real estate.[3]

These same remedies—eighty years later—were applied to solve the credit crisis of 33 CE. The Julian law was invoked by Roman tribunes (the representative of the people), but their action was likely instigated at the behest of Tiberius. In what was evidently an attack on senatorial finances, the tribunes lowered interest rates to 5% and closed loopholes used to evade usury and landholding laws. The powerful senator Nerva reportedly starved himself to death over the conflict with Tiberius and the tribunes—ostensibly because he was convinced that it was a disastrous policy, but perhaps because he suffered catastrophic financial failure.

According to Tacitus, virtually all senators were moneylenders. Cut out of the commercial trades by law, lending was the primary means by which senators maintained their wealth. Research by Roman historian Nathan Rosenstein on the economics of the senatorial estates makes it clear that, at least for most senators, farming was just not profitable enough to sustain them.[4]

The Senate requested and received from Tiberius an eighteen-month reprieve from enforcing the law, but this grace period did not work. What followed was a scarcity of money, as credit disappeared and borrowers desperately tried to raise cash for repayment by selling estates. The crisis in estate prices was likely exacerbated by the emperor liquidating the confiscated estates of Sejanus's supporters.

The Senate next tried to prop up estate prices by requiring three-quarters of all loan capital to be secured on land in Italy—trying to force mortgage credit to landholders. This echoed the earlier Julian proclamations—but apparently did not work. Lenders simply withdrew from the mortgage market, keeping capital on the sidelines until the uncertainty over land values resolved. Tacitus describes the consequences:

many were utterly ruined. The destruction of private wealth precipitated the fall of rank and reputation, till at last the emperor interposed his aid by distributing throughout the banks a hundred million sesterces, and allowing freedom to borrow without interest for three years, provided the borrower gave security to the State in land to double the amount. Credit was thus restored, and gradually private lenders were found.[5]

To get a sense of the scale of the government mortgage bailout in 33 CE, when Tiberius died four years later, he left 2.7 billion sesterces. So the bailout was roughly 4% of government funds and was 100 times the wealth qualification for a senator during the earlier Republican period.[6]

Despite the brevity of the historical account, the crisis of 33 CE tells us an enormous amount about Roman finance. This interrelationship among the major lenders created systemic risk. By 33 CE, Rome already had a legacy of financial crises characterized by credit contractions and mortgage defaults. When a new crisis emerged, its rulers looked back to regulatory responses to earlier crises for guidance. The Roman treasury then functioned in the way the US Treasury traditionally has done when faced with a financial crisis—it relieved the lack of credit through loans and used intermediary institutions to implement the solution.

The crisis of 33 CE also shows the close connection between politics and finance in ancient Rome. The crisis followed a period of political uncertainty. In fact, it has the hallmark of a financial purge that followed a political purge. If so, the vendetta expanded beyond its intended scope. Even though Tiberius may have used the crisis as a weapon against the Senate, he had to open the treasury to prevent a greater financial and perhaps political collapse.

As the power of the Senate declined in the Imperial era, perhaps the financial system was increasingly prone to crises. Some part of the value of a major estate in Italy in the Republican era must have been tied to the value of a seat in the Senate. Perhaps Tiberius's assertion of imperial power and his violent persecution of leading senators contributed to the decline in property value. At the beginning of his reign, he had made a show of deferring to the Senate as Rome's ruling body. At the end of his life, he demonstrated that through the credit system, he held the reins of financial power.

FINANCE IN THE FORUM

In his analysis of the 33 CE crisis, William Harris, one of the leading scholars in the study of the ancient economy, makes a simple but important point. The vast sums of money that changed hands were not exchanged in silver coin. They were transferred within a sophisticated system of financial intermediaries—bankers.[7] Note that Tacitus says the emperor distributed the relief money "throughout the banks." The government used banks *plural*—to make three-year, interest-free mortgages with a loan to value ratio of one-half.[8]

The Basilica Aemilia stood on the east side of the Forum, fronting the Via Sacra. Among other things it housed bankers, *argentarii*, whose shops looked out on the temple of Janus; the Roman god of doorways—the god whose face graced the obverse of Rome's earliest bronze coins. Presumably these are the same banks used by Tiberius as intermediaries in the crisis bailout. Once funds were released by the treasury, these banks must have made the property loans and monitored and serviced them, either in the name of the government or for their own account.

In fact, the actual bailout probably took place right in the Roman Forum. Across from the Basilica Aemilia built right into the monumental foundation of the temple of Saturn was the Roman treasury. Just like the Athenian Parthenon, it held the state's monetary assets as well as its financial accounts. During the financial crisis, Rome's treasurers probably did not open the gate and carry out great bagsful of sesterces across the Forum to the bankers in the shops of the Basilica Aemilia. They likely handled the operations through ledger transfers. Nevertheless, the Basilica Aemilia bankers did handle cash. Visitors can still see stains on the Basilica floor from the sack of Rome in 410 CE, where a bag of bronze money was burned. The bailout operation was almost certainly conducted by an accounting transfer—a government commitment or guarantee to provide the capital on which the banks could then write mortgages. A government guarantee allowing a banker to draw on the treasury for cash was as good as hard money.

FIGURE 6. Balustrade of Trajan depicting debt foregiveness.

A grand piece of sculpture found in the Forum also gives some idea of what the financial crisis and its resolution might have looked like.

The Balustrade of Trajan depicts a later financial bailout—Trajan's forgiveness of tax debt in 101 CE. In that year, Trajan set up a vast system of charitable foundations in Italy—invested in mortgages—to support poor children and to lend to small farmers. He also canceled the tax arrears of the Roman provinces. With these two financial acts, he endeared himself to the Italian populace as well as gained the thanks of provincials, who evidently were suffering at the hands of their tax collectors.

In the sculpture, the emperor is standing before the temple of Saturn, overseeing the destruction of tax records that presumably were stored in the treasury. The accounts are bound in large folding volumes carried on the backs of officials, who have stacked them up to be burned. Significantly, the emperor is not handing out money, he is overseeing accounts—the value is in the contractual tax records. It is a scene of imperial financial generosity with echoes of Tiberius's munificence of seventy years earlier. The role of a government bailout was deemed important enough to memorialize on a public monument.

BANKERS IN ROME AND AFTERWARD

In Chapter 5 we saw that the first banking houses arose in fifth-century Athens as depository institutions and financial intermediaries. Banking was already a centuries-old practice in the Mediterranean world by the time of the financial crisis of 33 CE. In fact, the Macedonian rulers of Egypt set up state banks well before Roman rule to collect taxes. Amazingly, fragments of these financial records have survived.

An Egyptian banker named Python, for example, lived in the city of Crocodilopolis and was active from 255 to 237 BCE. Python's bank was an essential instrument of Greek governance of Egypt. He and other bankers collected and transferred government revenues, as well as provided personal financial services to Egyptians, such as deposit banking, checking, payment by money of account, and provision of letters of credit. Sitta von Reden, one of the leading authorities on Ptolemaic finance, has reconstructed some of the dealings of these bankers. She believes that their services extended to substantial credit activities. In one case she studied, a banker lent money using a tax farming contract as collateral.[9]

In Rome, private bankers were called argentarii, and they appear in Roman history as early as the mid-fourth century BCE. The name "argentarii" suggests they had their origin as money changers, as did, perhaps the Athenian bankers. Argentarii supplied a variety of banking services, including taking deposits, transferring by check or account, advancing money to clients, lending to bidders at auction, and money transfer via bills of exchange.[10] They had their own guild and occupied shops along the Via Sacra in the Forum. As in Athens, bankers may also have operated nearer the wharves of the city—in Rome's case, the cattle market was in the Forum Boarium. A small arch, the Arcus Argentariorum still stands at the entrance to the Forum Boarium. Its inscription says that it was a gift of the moneylenders and merchant guilds and was dedicated to the emperor Septimus Severus circa 203 CE.

On the whole, however, Rome's bankers were not as illustrious as her politicians. Perhaps the most famous was Titus Pomponius Atticus, a member of the equestrian class and a friend of Cicero. His fame derived as much from his publication of Cicero's works as from his financial operations. Bankers did not occupy an important role in Roman society—at least until late antiquity. We know at least some bankers made enough to live in luxury—one of Pompeii's most beautiful houses is the villa of the banker Lucius Caecilius Iucundus. He could afford to keep up with his neighbors in terms of sumptuous wall paintings and floor mosaics. Remarkably, some of his dealings with clients were preserved in the volcanic ash on sealed wax tablets.

The evidence for bankers through Roman antiquity ebbs and flows. Classical references to bankers decline in the third century—just decades after the erection of the Arcus Argentariorum. This has often puzzled financial historians. However, there is undeniable evidence that banking remained a highly profitable and important business even after the sack of Rome in 410 CE.

The landlocked city of Ravenna on Italy's east coast is home to some of the most well-preserved works of Byzantine art. Before its harbor silted up, Ravenna was a seaport and the capital of the Ostragothic kingdom after the fall of Rome. The Basilica of San Vitale, completed in 547 CE, is a soaring octagonal edifice encrusted with brilliant mosaics. Among other things, it celebrated the Byzantine emperor Justinian's establishment of Ravenna as the new western capital of the empire. One mosaic depicts him and his military and ecclesiastical retainers. Just to the emperor's left is a man with a slightly unkempt beard. Scholars generally believe he is the banker Julian Argentarius, who evidently underwrote the construction of San Vitale and several other magnificent churches in Ravenna, which were erected after the Byzantine conquest. San Vitale alone is said to have cost 26,000 gold solidi—roughly 260 pounds of gold.[11]

Not much about Julian's life is known, but his likely inclusion in Justinian's retinue makes the point that the emperor relied on the strength of the army, the legitimacy of the church, the wisdom of his advisors, and the backing of his bankers. Scholars also believe that Julian played a role in the successful military taking of Ravenna—a reasonable speculation, given the critical importance of money in war. Other evidence suggests that Justinian relied heavily on bankers to manage government finances—perhaps as tax farmers. If so, the expansion of the Eastern Empire under Justinian created opportunities for financiers. Who knows how rich Julian was, but no banker since has left such a lasting and magnificent architectural legacy.

DISCOVERY AT THE CROSSROADS

In the spring of 1959, construction on the highway from Naples to Salerno halted, because digging exposed traces of an ancient ruin. The halt was not entirely unexpected, as the route passed half a mile south of Pompeii near the intersection of a Roman road that followed the now-buried pre-eruption coastline. Excavations through the ash revealed a beautifully preserved courtyard surrounded by decorated meeting rooms called *triclinium*—alcoves with built-in banquettes on three sides ringing a low stone table. In one of these rooms archaeologists found a basket filled with folding wooden tablets: an archive of legal documents belonging to a banking family called the Sulpicii, who undoubtedly abandoned them in the confusion of Mount Vesuvius's eruption in 79 CE. The remains of a boat were also found nearby, suggesting that the house was not a Pompeian pleasure villa but instead the site of a business enterprise close to the ancient port. The documents contained years of loans, lawsuits, and other transactions and revealed that the Sulpicii were a family of bankers, and the house, perhaps, was their place of business. The economic historian Peter Temin observes that the Sulpicii likely provided all the services we now associate with a bank and more: they took deposits, made account transfers and payments, made loans, brokered investments, and made advances to successful bidders at auctions.[12]

Although discovered in Pompeii, the archive actually documents the transactions of the Sulpicii in the port city of Puteoli on the other side of the Bay of Naples. Most of the records date from the period right around the financial crisis of 33 CE and a decade or two afterward. The tablets tell of deals struck in the Forum of Puteoli and concern the operations of merchants and traders who did business out of the bustling, ancient port. The business involved Mediterranean trade—in particular the Egyptian grain shipments that fed the Roman populace.

ALEXANDRIAN ARRIVAL

On a mid-summer day, from his house in the port city of Puteoli, the Stoic philosopher Seneca witnessed the arrival of the merchant fleet from Egypt.

Suddenly there came into our view today the "Alexandrian" ships—I mean those which are usually sent ahead to announce the coming of the fleet; they are called "mail-boats." The Companians [citizens of Campania] are glad to see them; all the rabble of Puteoli stand on the docks, and can recognize the "Alexandrian" boats, no matter how great the crowd of vessels, by the very trim of their sails. . . . While everybody was bustling about and hurrying to the water-front, I felt great pleasure in my laziness, because, although I was soon to receive letters from my friends, I was in no hurry to know how my affairs were progressing abroad, or what news the letters were bringing; for some time now I have had no losses, nor gains either.[13]

Puteoli served as Rome's deep-water harbor for much of the late Republican period and early Roman Empire. Situated a few miles up the coast from the Campanian towns of Neapolis, Pompeii, and Herculaneum, Puteoli's natural sheltered harbor was large and deep enough for the great trans-Mediterranean freighters to anchor safely. From there, the grain was shipped in smaller boats to Ostia at the mouth of the Tiber and then upriver to the city of Rome itself. It was eventually unloaded at the bustling wharves and marketplace at the foot of the Palatine Hill near the end of the Circus Maximus.

Even before its formal annexation by Rome in 80 BCE, Egypt played a vital role in the Roman economy. The capital city depended on imported foodstuffs from all over the Mediterranean—and indeed on luxury goods from all over the world. Each year, once the storms of winter broke and the seas calmed, merchant fleets would leave Alexandria laden with sacks of Nile delta wheat, amphorae of wine, textiles, and treasures from India and make their way to Rome. It was a trip of a month or more, depending on the winds. Despite their significance to the Roman economy, the ships in the great fleets from Alexandria were not government owned. Although much of the grain was destined for state coffers, the funding for the entire mercantile operation was provided by the private sector, and the risk and profits from the venture accrued to individual investors. The question is which legal and financial institutions made this large-scale international trade possible.

FIGURE 7. Fresco depicting the ancient harbor of Puteoli, the Roman port of entry for grain shipments from Alexandria. The Sulpicii bankers operated in this port city.

Seneca's portrayal of the arrival of the Alexandrian ships makes it clear that the fleet brought news of his overseas investments, perhaps land he inherited from his aunt when he lived for a time with her in the African provinces. The key element of the passage, however, is risk. Seneca, a statesman whose landed inheritance placed him above commerce, contrasts his stoic calm with the emotions of the crowd. He tells us that he faced neither gain nor loss. Obviously he did not invest in one of the ships—his happiness did not hinge on news of events or the vagaries of fortune. Perhaps he was even fortunate enough to be well diversified. Unlike the serene Seneca, however, the Sulpicii bankers were almost certainly among those clamoring to meet the fleet. Much of their business involved loans to local entrepreneurs tied in some way to Alexandrian trade.

Traces of Puteoli's famous port can still be seen in the shallow waters of the modern city of Pozzuoli. Its ancient sea walls, concrete wharves, portside shops, and brick warehouses are clearly visible under the shallow aquamarine bay. In fact, the submerged city is an underwater national preserve for snorkelers to explore. On land, its amphitheater still stands as evidence of the ancient crowds. In antiquity, it boasted temples, theaters, and a forum. As in the port of ancient Athens, there were also bankers ready at the dockside.

The financial writer and classics scholar David Jones has reconstructed the dealings of the Sulpicii banking house from an in-depth study of the hundreds of tablets recovered.[14] His book paints a rich picture of the firm and the financial markets in which it operated. Jones focuses on a set of five tablets in the Sulpicii archive that show something of the role of business credit and financial intermediaries in the Alexandrian grain trade.[15] Most operations were conducted by freedmen and slaves, not members of the equestrian class. However, the connections to the upper classes are clearly evident.

For example, on June 18, 37 CE, the freedman (i.e., former slave) Gaius Novius Eunus borrows 10,000 sesterces from Evanus Primianus, also a freedman, who executes the agreement via his slave Hesychus. Eunus pledges 7,000 modi (equivalent to 2,142 cubic feet of grain) and 200 sacks of chickpeas, lentils, and other legumes. These goods are stored in the public warehouse, and Eunus accepts the risk of their loss, presumably by spoilage, theft, or nonpayment of warehouse rent. The later document is for another 3,000 sesterces under the same terms. A third document shows Hesychus leasing the storage space in the warehouse from the slave Diognetus; a fourth records the continued indebtedness of Eunus to Hesychus, and a fifth documents what appears to be the interest owed (at 1% per month) for the outstanding loan balance.[16]

Sulpicius Faustus—the Sulpicii banker—witnessed the first two transactions and then later is named a receiver of the loan repayments. He thus served as Hesychus's banker, who in turn extended commercial credit to Eunus, a grain negotiant.

This complex operation shows in exquisite detail how the grain trade was financed. The grain was pledged as collateral, insurance was explicitly contracted, and a banker with ready capital was central to the operation. In fact, by September 39 CE, Hesychus has moved up in the world. He is identified in a tablet as the slave of Gaius Caesar Augustus Germanicus—the Emperor Gaius. The emperor either inherited or purchased Hesychus, and the slave now continued his financial dealings for his new, powerful patron.

Jean Andreau, the leading expert on banking in classical antiquity, points out that the Sulpicii raised capital by borrowing from the upper classes. In particular, one record documents a 94,000 sesterces' loan from a slave of the imperial household.[17] In this period, the Roman equestrian and senatorial classes were lending on much more than Italian real estate. Through specialized intermediaries like Hesychus, they advanced loans on commercial enterprises. The emperor and his retinue were not partners with the Sulpicii; rather they were their ultimate creditors. Small-time financial intermediaries evidently borrowed from lenders farther up the food chain. This arms-length financial architecture allowed senators and emperors to invest in business without getting their hands dirty.

By the same token, the class structure of Roman society that demanded arms-length business operations by politicians also created an architecture by which all financial roads led back to Rome. Rome was where finances were ultimately concentrated—where financial regulations were made and enforced. Rome's oligopoly extended its power through credit markets and created forms of intermediation that protected them from political and, in some cases, financial ruin.

However, it would be wrong to conclude that the Roman financial system was run entirely for the benefit of the ruling class. The network of sophisticated intermediation demonstrated by the Sulpicii archives demonstrates the capability of the Roman commercial world. If capital can be deployed to finance Egyptian grain shipments, it can be deployed for myriad other mercantile activities. Indeed one of the most sophisticated of all financial documents from the Roman era is a contract for financing the shipment of trade goods from India through Egypt by caravan and Nile barge to the port of Alexandria for export to Rome. The loan contract was struck in the Roman trade outpost of Muziris on the west coast of India.[18] It testifies to Rome's vast sphere of trade and the way it was supported by financial contracting.

SLAVERY AND LIMITED LIABILITY

Consider slavery from a purely legal perspective as opposed to a moral one for the moment. If a slave commits a crime, the harmed party will sue the slaveholder. Indeed one could imagine an angry slave getting back at his master by incurring a huge liability—for example, sinking someone's ship. Roman law evolved to address this potential problem by limiting the extent of the slaveholder's liability. The slaveholder was not liable for actions of the slave that were not taken under his or her direction. If the slaveholder could show that he or she never told the slave to sink someone's ship, then the harmed party would have no recourse.

This limited liability extended to financial dealings. If an investor sets up a slave in a business and gives the latter a free hand, then his or her liability was limited to the capital invested with the slave via an account called a *peculium*. A creditor can go after the peculium, but not the assets of the slaveholder, unless the creditor can show that a particular loan was made at the master's direction. This institutional structure is one of the most unusual innovations of Roman law and finance. Investors could take more risk if the potential liability of any single investment was limited to the peculium.

David Jones, along with earlier scholars, interprets Hesychus's grain dealing in the later document of 39 CE as business on his own account, and thus the slave's bank account with the Sulpicii has a natural interpretation as his peculium. The emperor profited from Hesychus's business acumen, but his vast wealth was shielded from the slave's creditors, who could only recover the balance of the peculium. Because of this, creditors would have wanted to know how much money was in the peculium at any given time. The banker holding the deposits *and* the slave's other financial assets, including loans and liabilities, would have been in a perfect position to vouch for his net worth.

The institution of the peculium must have functioned very much like the way limited corporate liability functions today. Limited liability allows the investor not only to limit loss—it also means that the investor no longer has to be closely involved in the business. Investors could substitute diversification for direct oversight. In ancient Rome, by using the peculium structure the investor spread his or her wealth across a number of different enterprises run by slaves, while keeping his or her own hands clean of business. Not only did the law effectively force the slave owner to delegate the management as a condition of limited liability, it also gave peace of mind that no one investment threatened the entirety of savings. No wonder Seneca maintained his serenity prior to receiving news of his Egyptian affairs. More than likely the affairs were managed by slaves, and his exposure to losses was hedged beyond the amount of their peculiums.

The institution of the peculium may also explain the role of freedmen in the Roman economy. The slave labor market must have extended to business acumen and management skill. Although we typically imagine slaves in the Roman economy as manual laborers and household servants, the most valuable slaves were those who could profitably run a business with a minimal amount of oversight and direction. A natural equilibrium in the Roman world would likely be a complete separation of investors from direct business dealings above a certain minimal scale that could keep a slave employed full time.

This separation of ownership and control would be necessary to meet the legal standard for limited liability, however, it would not be sufficient to run a profitable business. A slaveholder would need to find a way to incentivize the slave to generate profits in a setting in which direct oversight was disallowed. The obvious means is through compensation. Just as today's corporate managers are given shares of profits in the firm to align their interests with that of the investors, so too must Roman slaves have been motivated by a carrot as opposed to a stick.

The prevalence of freedmen in business dealings suggests that the motivation was the ability to purchase one's freedom if business went well. Of course this incentive also had the drawback for the slaveholder of losing the manager. However, a regular theme throughout the Sulpicii documents and others from the Roman era is the continued business dealings between former slaves and former masters. Freedmen by law were held to contractual relationships with their former masters. When Hesychus changed hands from one master to another, the transaction was executed in expectation of getting a significant business run by a successful, independent manager and perhaps a future business partner.[19]

Was the legal institution of the peculium investor friendly? It promoted investor risk-taking and thus drew capital into industry and trade. It also clearly worked to promote an efficient allocation of managerial talent, which would be a further boon to the development of trade and economic growth. However, with only some exceptions, it did not aggregate capital from many investors. Shares in a slave with a peculium were not traded on a stock market.

Legal scholarship has typically focused on the limitations of the Roman law of organizations. Roman law evidently only defined partnerships (*societas*) without limited liability. In the history of finance, limited liability has always been regarded as an essential innovation that made modern finance possible. The institution of the peculium, although important and adaptive to the needs of Roman economic development, would seem to be only a half-measure.

Yale Law School professor Henry Hansmann is a leading authority on the law of organizations. He and two colleagues, Reinier Kraakman of Harvard and Richard Squire of Yale, have developed a novel theory of the corporation—one that replaces the focus on limited liability with a different concept, called "entity shielding."[20] Their idea is that the major risk to an investor is not so much that the firm's creditors can come after them. Rather, an investor's biggest worry is that his or her own partner's creditors could pursue the assets of the firm—shutting the business down and demanding liquidation of the assets to satisfy their claims against one of the investors.

Thus, before investing alongside anyone, you would need to assess their financial assets and liabilities. A Roman partnership, a societas, was vulnerable in that way. Thus, partnerships would naturally tend to be limited to a few participants who trusted one another and could share personal financial information. This put an upper bound on the ability to create large pools of capital and to trade shares in a company. Without entity shielding, it really matters who else owns the shares.

The lack of entity shielding also creates problems for lenders to a firm. They would also need to be assured that they stood first in line of claimants to the firm's assets in the event of bankruptcy. The peculium did not solve these problems, because it involved only one investor, and a creditor of the investor could demand the slave's peculium in the event of bankruptcy. For Hesychus, it was preferable to serve the emperor rather than an owner with credit risk.

In contrast to the Roman *societas*, the modern corporation enjoys entity shielding. Creditors to an investor in a corporation can seize the shares but can't lay direct claim to the assets of the firm he or she invests in. Even if an individual investor goes bankrupt, the firm can keep operating as usual. The marketability of shares would thus seem to be another crucial feature that relied upon entity shielding. Hansmann, Kraakman, and Squire delve into Roman law to ask whether entity shielding arose in antiquity. In fact, Rome did develop a marketable share structure something like a modern corporation.

THE SHAREHOLDERS OF ROME

Following the Second Punic War (218–201 BCE), Rome expanded relatively rapidly throughout the Mediterranean world. This expansion created challenges for the Republic. It had to supply a large standing army; build and maintain a vast urban infrastructure; and tax remote, newly conquered provinces. Rather than build a governmental bureaucracy to do all these things, Rome auctioned off government contracts to private consortiums called *societas publicanorum*—publican societies.

Publican societies were essentially business partnerships that had many of the features of modern corporations. They were organized and managed by the equestrian class of Rome, the well-to-do knights. Shareholders were called *publicani*. Unlike senators, members of the equestrian knights were not precluded from direct commercial interests. During the period of Rome's rapid growth after the Second Punic War, the publican societies provided a means for the equestrian families to share in the profitable opportunities that emerged through Rome's expansion, while also solving some of the Republic's logistical and financial problems.

The publican societies bid for government contracts at public auctions—particularly for contracts to collect provincial taxes, but also for other services ranging from construction and maintenance of public monuments to supplying and provisioning the armies. Roman legal historians are convinced that these firms were not only large-scale business enterprises, but that they also had ownership shares that were liquid and tradable.

The publican societies were most active in Rome's Asian provinces—conquests in Anatolia and Syria were followed by the auctioning of tax rights in the Roman Forum for huge financial stakes. Subsequent complaints from the provincial taxpayers about the aggressiveness of the publican tax collectors were not surprising, given that the winning bidders were inevitably the most optimistic about the excess revenues they could wring from the populace. In fact, as mentioned earlier in this chapter, the Balustrade of Trajan actually celebrated the relief of the provinces from excess tax obligations.

The historian Polybius observed that in the second century BCE, virtually every citizen in Rome participated in the business of government contracts, implying that membership in the publican societies was widespread. If it were only true among the equestrian class, it would still be a remarkable fact. Corporate-like institutions owned collectively among hundreds or perhaps thousands of investors offered a novel form of business venture; one in which investors were not directly involved in the activities of the company but instead were passive recipients of profits according to their ownership shares.

We saw earlier how Athenians could own, sell, and hypothecate a range of various businesses (see Chapter 6). The Roman publican society was a step beyond that. Investors could buy and sell fractions of a business without the complicated legal entanglements implied by partnerships. The easier and more widespread trading in publican societies became, the more diversified a Roman investor could be, and the greater the opportunities were to earn profits beyond the limited rates of interest available to lenders.

The pervasiveness of share ownership has two crucial implications. First, these companies must have had a form of entity shielding that prevented them from being disrupted by outside creditors. Second, it suggests that the collective economic burden, benefit, and uncertainty associated with Rome's expansion during this period was shared widely among the equestrian class via an equity stake. This was particularly clear with respect to the collection of provincial taxes. For a time, publican societies were the biggest tax farmers for the Roman state. They assumed the uncertainty of revenue collection in return for the potential to extract excess profits. This was good for the state but perhaps painful for provincial taxpayers.

From a political point of view, the share system was a way of parsing the benefits of Rome's military conquests. The Senate kept the plebeian classes happy with the distribution of free bread—it kept the equestrian class happy by offering it a share of the economic spoils. Although it is tempting to think of the publican companies as private corporate entities pursuing various business opportunities—like modern corporations—it is clear that they were focused primarily—if not exclusively—on government contracts. This inevitably entangled them in government affairs. As the ownership base of the companies expanded, so too did their political influence. This led to power struggles.

For example, the popular reforms of Roman law led by the plebeian tribune Gaius Gracchus in 123 BCE shifted control of the courts overseeing the administration of provincial governors from the Senate to the equestrian class. This was not a mere technicality. Governors of the provinces had to answer to the leading publican shareholders; in particular, governors were now more inclined to stay out of the way of heavy-handed tax collection methods.

In the context of Roman politics, the flexibility of share ownership simply made bribery that much easier. Perhaps this led inevitably to the weakening of the class prohibitions against senatorial participation in business.

A case in point. In the late Republican era, 59 BCE, the orator Cicero, as tribune, accused Julius Caesar's protégé Publius Vatinius of corruption. He argued that Vatinius misused his imperial appointment as financial overseer of Puteoli to extract personal profit, causing a revolt.[21] Among Cicero's accusations is that Vatinius held shares in a publican company and manipulated share prices for profit—a tantalizing passing reference to early securities market fraud.[22]

To the late Harvard classicist Ernst Badian, the case of Vatinius demonstrates how the publican system in the late Republic was adapted to the new political order. In his careful study of the publican societies and their relation to Roman politics, Badian argues that the publican business structure allowed the equestrian class to accrue power and influence—particularly through the late Republican period, when senatorial control weakened and gave way to the imperial model.

Badian believes that both Vatinius and Julius Caesar held shares in publican companies, and in fact, senators themselves—not just knights—were investors.[23] How could they do this? The late Roman Republic was an era when old rules were broken. The Gracchi brothers in the 120s weakened senatorial power, and a generation later, the dictator Sulla eliminated the census. Without an official census, there was no way to document the source of senatorial wealth. Badian believes that, after this time, Romans traded unregistered shares in publican companies, perhaps through intermediaries like bankers.

The broader investor base for publican shares was, of course, good for the companies. The publican system was a way to align the interests of politicians with the interests of shareholders. It was an extraordinarily flexible—and novel—means of combining the interests of government and business. The corporation as a mechanism for sharing the economic benefits of imperialism reappears later in world history—frequently enough to suggest that it addresses a fundamental issue in the military expansion of the state.

The economist Thomas Picketty has suggested that the root of inequality lies in the differential rates of return between financial investment and economic growth. Those with capital to invest are able to grow their wealth at higher rates. Rome's ruling classes seem to be a case in point. Because their power depended crucially on wealth, they needed their capital to grow. They developed ways of investing their capital in both debt and equity securities—and on top of that, they used their political influence to favor investment outcomes. When the Republic broke down, wealth was even more important, because money was required to pay armies. During the Roman civil wars, for example, Julius Caesar raided the Roman treasury. When the keys were not surrendered, he had to break in the door. He carried out "fifteen thousand bars of gold, thirty thousand bars of silver, and fifty million sesterces of coined money."[24]

ROMAN LAW AND COMPANIES

Ulrike Malmendier is a financial economist at the University of California at Berkeley and an expert in behavioral finance—particularly the behavior of CEOs and directors of major corporations. Most of her research is absolutely current, addressing such questions as the potential regulatory failures of the modern financial system. But Ulrike is also a

financial historian; part of her research focuses on the publican societies. She argues that we may be missing an important piece of Roman
law—the law from the Republican era that governed the creation of the
publican societies.

Because publican societies disappeared during the later empire, details about these organizations are rare. Malmendier points out that
most of what is known about Roman law is derived from texts com-
piled at the very end of Roman history, rather than around the time
when publican societies operated. In particular, the Code of Justinian
was assembled many centuries after publican societies—when they were
no more than an historical oddity to Roman scholars. Malmendier has
focused particularly on a text discovered in the ruins of the Basilica of
St. John in Ephesus. A marble slab holds a public inscription detailing
the rights and obligations of the tax collection agency in 62 CE in Ephesus—a publican society.

The inscription makes it clear that the company operated within a
sophisticated legal framework that governed the leasing of tax collection rights: what the company received, what it was obligated to deliver
and how, and what types of collateral or guarantees were required by the
government to ensure the fulfillment of the company duties. It was created right in the middle of the period when publican shares were being
criticized and the Asian companies in particular were being debated.

Malmendier points out that the tax collection firms enjoyed legal
rights unlike normal partnerships. While standard Roman partnerships (*societas*) were limited in duration, dissolving with the death of
any individual members, the publican societies maintained a juridical
"personality" independent from that of their investors, and they could
exist indefinitely.

They also differed from normal Roman partnerships in that they
protected investors from their partners' creditors. This is the early genetic code of the modern corporation that Hansmann, Kraakman, and
Squire are looking for; the moment when the number of investors in
an enterprise could expand beyond a handful of mutually trusting partners. These scholars theorized that entity shielding would allow the
widespread pooling of capital and would also lead to the tradability of
shares. These appear in ancient Rome—governed, evidently, by missing
Roman law.

In the middle of the Roman Forum stand three Corinthian columns linked by a cornice, the remains of the temple of Castor. Situated at the base of the Palatine Hill, near the sacred spring of Lacus Juturnae, the remains of the podium and stairs leading to the temple are still visible today. This is also evidently the place one went to trade for shares in publican societies and to participate in the auctions for government contracts. A reconstruction of the temple shows it with a triangular pedimental frieze—oddly enough, not unlike the facade of the New York Stock Exchange building. Of the millions of visitors to the Roman Forum each year tramping the Via Sacra and marveling at the triumphal arches, few realize that they are also paying a visit to the first stock market.

Why did the publican societies disappear? Malmendier argues that Roman law under the republic must have been a flexible, adaptive system. As Rome expanded rapidly into an empire, its economic needs grew faster than its institutions. The publican societies were a means by which the state could contract out for vital services without building a bureaucracy. This may also explain their decline. In the Roman Empire, imperial bureaucracy replaced publican societies. Although they may have played an important role in the early development of the Roman Empire, the companies faded from existence with the decline of public auctions for contracts.

By the sixth century CE, the laws governing them were not even included in the scope of Justinian's ambitious codification. Law many be important to finance, but it is not sufficient to sustain a financial technology when that technology is no longer needed. Both Roman law and Roman finance reflected the shifting political economy from republic to empire. Ulrike Malmendier's work on these ancient public companies suggests that Roman law—at least in its natural state—served the needs of financial development when it was called on to do so.

MONEY AND WAR

Earlier we saw that access to Laurion silver gave Athens an enormous economic advantage. As Rome rose to power in the Italian peninsula, it had the reverse situation. Its lack of silver put it at an important strategic disadvantage. When Rome began to embark on its overseas conquests, it did not have the same capacity for minting coins as its rivals.

The Greeks had their own silver mines in Attica and Macedonia. The Carthaginians controlled the Iberian trade and thus the rich gold and silver mines of Spain.

The Second Punic War and its aftermath changed all of this. The epic war with Carthage was not only a military struggle, it was also a financial one. It brought Rome to the brink of financial failure. Philip Kay is a London financier and a historian of Rome. His professional perspective on the role of money and financial institutions is useful. In his view, Rome's financial transition at this moment in history was the key ingredient in its later success as an empire. He argues that the Second Punic War represented, for Rome, an economic revolution. In 216 BCE, when Rome could not pay its troops, it reached out to foreign rulers for a loan—it borrowed from Hieron of Syracuse—and then defaulted.[25] It could not pay the publican societies provisioning its army and constructing its state buildings. It raided its widow and orphan funds; it levied a wealth tax; in 210 it simply begged its wealthy citizens for loans, and in 205 it sold off state property in Campania. The Roman government was clearly almost broke. And yet the financial brinksmanship worked. Winning the war flooded Rome's coffers with booty.

With the defeat of Hannibal in 202 BCE, Carthage was stripped of her colonies and settled with a huge tribute—the Carthaginians silver and gold mines of Iberia were transferred to Rome, and Roman carpetbaggers swarmed west to exploit them. The economic consequence was a dramatic increase in the Roman money supply. Access to Iberian silver mines set Rome on its path of domination over the Mediterranean world. It went from being metal poor to metal rich, and just as in the case of ancient Athens, the power of money gave it the power to pay armies and navies, and to create a currency that dominated the global marketplace.

Interestingly enough, there is little evidence that the Iberian mining operations were monopolized by publican societies. It appears that Roman entrepreneurs of all sorts got into the mining trade. Government regulators established rules for how small-scale companies could operate. Surviving examples of these rules suggest that publican societies were not the only corporate form in Roman history. Smaller-scale share companies—evidently with a form of limited liability—also existed. Thus a range of different organizational forms emerged to exploit the mineral wealth of Iberia. This very rapidly led to monetary expansion.

FIGURE 8. An early Roman denarius, ca. 211 BCE.

Beginning in the Second Punic War, Rome began to mint a small and quite convenient silver coin called a denarius. It was a dramatic improvement over its former currency. The denarius would become a pan-Mediterranean monetary standard.

EARLY ROMAN COINAGE

Roman metallic currency began with the use of iron rods—firespits—as coins. Imagine going shopping with three-foot-long iron bars. This early money has been found in archaeological context and must have derived from a standardized—if awkwardly proportioned—household item. Spit money gave way to bronze scrap metal and finally to large bronze disks called *aes grave*, "grave" meaning heavy. The basic *as* weighed a whole Roman pound. A pocketful of pound coins was still an inconvenience. Any contemplated military operation had to include plans to transport not only soldiers to the battlefield but also the *asses* to pay them.

The denarius was worth ten Roman pounds, and weighed a fraction of it. Access to Iberian silver made a huge difference to Rome's ability to maintain armies. A typical soldier's salary during the period of the late Roman Republic (140–37 BCE) was 112 denarii per year—a sum that would comfortably fit in a small purse, as opposed to 1,000 asses of a Roman pound each. Rome's monetary upgrade was a strategic advantage for the expansion of the empire.

FIGURE 9. Roman as, ca. 235 BCE.

As in ancient Athens, a further consequence of Rome's increasing use of coins to pay for government services was a transformation to a monetary economy. Soldiers paid in coin became used to buying in coin. The Roman economy increasingly operated on metallic money, with the denarius as a common monetary standard and the sesterce (worth a quarter of a denarius) as the largest bronze denomination.

Silver money stimulated the economy; gave it liquidity; and fostered trade, market development, and specialization in manufacturing. Before the introduction of these silver coins, a limited supply of money and the frictions caused by a poor monetary technology (e.g., heavy bronze coins) was a drag on the economy. Iberian silver removed these constraints and allowed Rome to flourish economically—not only because it could more easily pay its armies, but also because the Roman monetary system became a valuable technology in and of itself.[26]

William Harris takes this argument a step further. He observes that the expansion of Rome's money supply also took place in the virtual realm, through the rapid growth of credit institutions like banks and investment organizations. The coinage was important, but for an empire that was centered on the sea and dependent on hazardous transportation systems, metallic currency posed a risk of a decline in money supply—in short, money sinks.

The hoards of Roman coins we find today survived mostly because they were lost. Soldiers hid their sacks of denarii in holes before a battle. Families buried their savings in haste when they could not carry it. Coins carried by sailors at sea went down with the ships. Coins that circulate long enough wear down and lose weight. However, coins that remained in circulation were ultimately melted down and used by the next government to mint its own coinage.

Hence the "virtualization" of value through accounting—as long as accounts themselves were safe—removed certain kinds of risk posed by physical coinage. As Roman wealth inequality became more extreme, it is clear that major monetary transactions took place virtually.

Harris points out that banking and lending in the Roman economy expanded the money supply beyond the physical limits of the currency. Without money of account, and without financial institutions facilitating investment and long-distance trade, Rome could not have fielded its vast armies and maintained a geographically extended empire that relied on shipping commodities across the sea. In short, Rome became an empire because of its financial technology—coinage as well as investment and credit institutions. Finance was not a sideshow—it was the lifeblood of Rome.[27]

What military success gives, it can also take away. Kenneth Harl, an authority on the history of Roman currency, has studied Rome's monetary difficulties in the twilight of the empire. He traces Rome's biggest currency crisis to the period after 235 CE, when Roman frontiers were overrun. Germanic tribes cut the empire off from northern European mines, and the Moors disrupted Iberian mining.[28] The consequent contraction in Rome's silver bullion occurred precisely when Rome needed it most to pay its armies.

To address this monetary problem, Rome debased its currency. A new denomination, the antoninianus (nominally worth two denarii) was introduced, but its silver content was not double that of the denarius. This rival unit continued to be debased through the following decades, leaving Romans with two competing units of sliding relative value. The confusion between the two coins and the fluctuation in relative amounts of silver forced markets to resort to an abstract unit of account—a hypothetical *denarii communes* against which actual denarii and antoninianii were quoted.[29] With the loss of Rome's mines came the loss of faith in its currency and its ability to maintain economic power.

Morris Silver, a scholar at City College of New York, has championed the application of economic models to understanding the ancient economy. He theorizes that the debasement of the currency in the late Roman Empire also explains the disappearance of deposit banking after the middle of the third century CE. Scholars have long noted a decline in the classical references to bankers after this period, and a subtle change in the words used to refer to them. In the later empire, the words for "money changer" and "banker" seem to be used interchangeably—as if bankers, such as they existed in that era, dealt mostly in the realm of hard currency (i.e., petty cash). Professor Silver attributes this decline in the visibility and prominence of bankers to the enforcement of caps on interest rates, coupled with the currency debasement. The official rate of interest in Rome was 12%, and attempts to evade this rate with subterfuges, such as disguising higher rates as principal repayment, were evidently enforced. Interestingly enough, this enforcement may have coincided with increased pressures on the early Christian church in Rome to provide for people made indigent—or enslaved—by defaulting on personal loans.[30]

Silver points out that, as the coinage was debased, consumer prices rose. The annual inflation rate for wheat in the Egyptian provinces—for example, during the late third century CE—ranged from 4% to 9%.[31] If a banker loans money at 12% over the long term and gets paid back in cash that is worth 7% less each year, then lending profits are drastically reduced. By the same token, depositors are disinclined to put money in a bank that pays out at 5% when this is about the rate of inflation. In other words, a cap on interest rates—although well meaning as a way to reduce predatory lending—had the same effect at the end of the empire as it did in the financial crisis of 33 CE. It drove investment out of the financial system. Silver speculates that bankers did not entirely go out of business—Egyptian banking is still documented—but they might have gone underground. He even wonders whether a documented shift in the late empire toward contracting in commodities may reflect a rational economic hedge against expected inflation.

ROME AND THE ANCIENT ENVIRONMENT

There is one more curious consequence of Rome's intense mining of the Iberian peninsula after the Second Punic War. It allows us to compare the industrial intensity of the Roman economy to the modern industrial age.

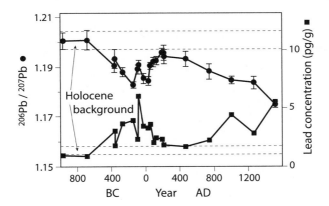

FIGURE 10. Lead ^{206}Pb/^{207}Pb isotopic ratio (upper curve) and concentration (lower curve) in Greenland ice. Historical spikes indicating intensification of copper mining are visible around the beginning of the current era, and around the year 1000 CE.

The Rio Tinto is one of the most polluted rivers in Europe.[32] Its red-brown current flows out of the mineral-rich mountains of southern Iberia, laden with heavy metals. These metals made Iberia one of the most important mining regions in world history. Metal mining in Spain and Portugal extends back at least 5,000 years. Iberian copper, lead, iron, and silver deposits were worked by Tartassians, Phoenicians, Carthaginians, and Romans. Mining continued at a lower level through the Gothic period and revived in the late Middle Ages. In fact, it continues to the present day. The residue of millennia of strip mining and smelting has left its mark in the soil of southern Iberia. Indeed, it has left its mark on the world.

In 1997, a team of environmental scientists found traces of Iberian atmospheric lead pollution in the Greenland ice core.[33] They were able to distinguish between the lead residues from the Rio Tinto and Cartagena mines. Using isotopic analysis, they attributed 70% of the industrial lead pollution in the northern hemisphere between 366 BCE and 36 CE to the Rio Tinto mines. After that, the mines of Cartagena became important contributors. Other production sources, such as Britain, added little to airborne lead pollution in antiquity.

From the perspective of the rise and fall of Rome, the lead signature provides an interesting timeline to track its monetary history. The fraction of industrial (i.e., anthropogenic) lead was elevated—as much as double—over the period 680 BCE to 193 CE, with dramatic peaks in the years 143 BCE and 36 CE—right around the time of the Roman financial crisis. It reached a low point in 473 CE—nearly as low as the pre-metal ages. Anthropogenic lead levels did not climb as high as those in the Roman era until 1200 CE. Roman finance—the mining and smelting of lead-rich ore to mint silver—left a permanent mark on the world in many ways—including on the Greenland ice cap. The airborne lead pollution around the mines in fact left a chemical residue in the bones of the Iberian people.

SUMMARY OF ROMAN FINANCE

Rome adopted many of the existing financial tools of its age: coinage, banks, maritime contracts, collateralization, mortgages, a public treasury, and central banking operations. However, these were put to use in a uniquely Roman context.

Wealth was explicitly a condition for belonging to the ruling class, and the Roman financial system evolved to generate, document, and display this wealth. Laws separating governance from direct economic interests at first created a sophisticated system of credit markets. Senators could lend, but they could not directly engage in business. However, financial intermediation provides an infinite variety of ways to conceal investment or to put it at arm's length.

The legal form of the peculium was one solution to the problem—there were many others. Modern scholarship has recently documented the amazing sophistication of the Roman economy, particularly with respect to financial intermediation. In fact, sometimes the Roman financial system seems shockingly familiar to the modern eye. The degree to which we can actually compare modern institutions like banks to Roman institutions has been regularly debated. However, institutional labels are less important than function. An empire of Rome's extent demanded financial tools like currency, public debt, treasury bailouts, and tax farming to make it possible to conduct commerce, smooth revenues, and deal with crises. The longevity of Rome itself is a testament to the flexibility of its financial architecture. Financial levers existed to address financial and economic failures—from imperial debt forgiveness to currency debasement.

In the context of the long history of Rome, the emergence of the publican societies stands out. Much of Rome's wealth was in the hands of private citizens. Roman conquest made the ruling classes of Rome rich. They had to invest their wealth somewhere, and it certainly trickled down through the credit system. However, credit does not align the interests of the borrower and lender—indeed it can lead to conflicts concerning default. In times of economic downturns, politicians turn to debt forgiveness to maintain stability.

In contrast, a corporate structure puts shareholders on an equal footing. If benefits are paid out on a per-share basis, all investors see their wealth grow proportionately with corporate profits. When these shares are publicly traded, and especially when they can be held anonymously, they become a tool for negotiating among parties that might otherwise be in conflict. In the context of Roman politics, publican company shares offered a means by which power struggles among senators, knights, and emperors could be resolved. It is thus not surprising that, as the emperors consolidated their power, the usefulness of the publican companies declined. It is tempting to draw the conclusion that the corporate form first emerged as a means to negotiate and resolve conflicts between political and economic powers.

The most remarkable thing about finance in the ancient world is that virtually all of the basic financial tools were developed by early societies of the Near East and the eastern Mediterranean before the current era: financial contracts, mortgages, equity and debt instruments, commercial courts, merchant law, private corporations, banks, and banking systems. Even more sophisticated conceptual tools emerged, such as financial planning, models of economic growth, the mathematics of compound interest, and empirical records to memorialize and analyze price trends through history.

Most useful for the purposes of this book is that finance at its origin provides a way to understand the fundamental problems that financial technology emerged to address and the necessary tools that it built on. The foundations of finance included a means to record quantities and to verify promises, an increasing level of numeracy, and the capacity to deal with abstraction in time and space.

As the technology of finance developed, it shaped the way people thought about the future and the past. The mathematics of compound interest made possible a new kind of political discourse. Loans with long-term maturity made the future palpable in a way it may never have been before. Perhaps most importantly, financial tools enabled first the operation of a complex urban economy, and ultimately the creation and support of far-flung empires, in which tribute could be extracted and monetized by bankers operating at the behest of a distant ruling government and by financial entrepreneurs who managed Athens' and then Rome's vital overseas grain trade. Finance played a central role in the emergence of Athenian democracy and a different kind of role in parsing Roman power.

Was the emergence of finance in the ancient world one great accident of history? Could it have happened at another time and place, and if so, would it have played out in similar fashion, facilitating the emergence of cities, expansion of the state, and support of long-distance trade? Would financial technology have led to a sophisticated record-keeping tradition, the capacity for planning, and the necessity of historical documentation of markets? Is a financial system a necessary technology for the emergence of the state? A partial answer to this speculation lies in Part II of this book.

THE FINANCIAL
LEGACY OF CHINA

In this section, I argue that the course of financial development in civilizations does not follow an inevitable path toward the same institutions and contracts. The Chinese experience demonstrates that varieties of solutions are possible to the fundamental problems of time and value. While some tools (like loans) are ubiquitous, others (like government bonds) are not. I propose that these differences in financial technologies shaped a particular relationship between the individual and the state over stretches of Chinese history and set up an encounter between European and Chinese financial systems in the nineteenth century that resulted in an innovative Chinese governance structure for enterprise.

"China would of herself have developed slowly into a capitalist society even without the impact of foreign capitalism," proclaimed Mao Zedong [毛澤東] in 1939.[1] Was Mao correct? Left to its own, without the incursion of Western powers in the nineteenth century, would China ever have become a capitalist power? China has a long history of financial innovation. The Chinese invented metallic coinage, paper money, bills of exchange, transferable rights certificates, sophisticated accounting and management systems, and securitized lending. Examples of wealthy entrepreneurs, financial institutions, private partnerships, and business organizations can be found throughout China's history. Given all these financial innovations, why were the first global corporations European in origin, not Chinese? I argue in Part II of this book that the answer is rooted fundamentally in the relationship between government and private enterprise in Chinese history.

China developed a financial technology that solved many of the same problems encountered in the ancient Mediterranean and the Middle East, including economic contracting and planning through time and space. China was (and remains) a great empire, with vast and complex

Rubbing of the inscription inside the He Zun [何尊], a Chinese ritual bronze
vessel commemorating the Zhou dynasty dating to the reign of King Cheng
(1055–1021 BCE). Its maker was paid thirty strings of cowries.

cities, a vigorous trade economy, and a long history of mathematical thought and application. The financial development of China helps us understand what tools are necessary or unnecessary. For all the similarities in the financial development that this part documents, the differences between East and West are most revealing. While China also created debt instruments and mathematical tools for the calculation of interest, it was distinct in three specific ways.

The first is in its monetary development. The great, unifying financial theme of Chinese finance is money. In the same way that financial technology led, in Mesopotamian civilization, to abstract notions of time, growth, and interest rates, the early emergence of money in China evolved into an extremely sophisticated and abstract technology that touched nearly every aspect of economic life. Just as the existence of financial tools influenced modes of thought in the ancient Near Eastern and Mediterranean worlds, so too did the highly developed tools and theories about money influence Chinese thought and philosophy. China's remarkable contribution to finance was the invention of paper money, but this innovation appeared only after nearly two millennia of experimentation with various forms of payment systems embedded in a network of political and economic obligations that constituted Chinese society.

The second distinctively Chinese financial technology is sophisticated bureaucracy. The vast Chinese empire, first unified in 221 BCE, expanded and contracted through two millennia. China sometimes broke into smaller states or was conquered by its Asian neighbors, but through long stretches of history, China's major challenge was how to manage a political entity of great size and varied cultures. Simple problems like how to collect taxes from distant provinces loomed large and required organizational capabilities that, for the most part, were not needed in other parts of the ancient world. We saw, for example, how a banking system arose in Hellenistic Egypt to deal with this kind of challenge, but the scale of the Chinese empire was much greater. Getting money from the province to the capital and vice versa was a major financial problem. Even bigger problems were managing, motivating, and controlling the vast human bureaucracy necessary to run such a state. This required recognizing and dealing with the dark side of human nature: corruption.

Scale was not the only problem of the Chinese empire. An entity that large inevitably encompasses many and varied regional economies—

some of which may be doing well and others poorly at any given time. Even today, one of the macroeconomic challenges of the European Union is how to manage the ebb and flow of prosperity among very different regional cultures and economies. Without a technology for doing so, China would inevitably have fractured into regional polities. As we shall see, from earliest times, this problem of economic equilibration stimulated creative thinking, a deeper understanding of economic principles, and recognition of the crucial role of money and finance.

The third distinctively Chinese financial development is the role of government in enterprise. When financial innovations occurred in China, they were often appropriated for the benefit of the government, not the individual. Through the lens of modern capitalism, China is a classic example of the grabbing state. However, from the perspective of Chinese history, this expropriation is consistent with the idea of a providing state, in which individualism is subordinated to collectivism. The providing state is a large, powerful, and complex state. The intricate bureaucratic structure that made China the world's longest-lived continuous civilization survived by regularly seizing commercial opportunities from private entrepreneurs and crowding out private enterprise with state-supported monopolies. Even when the state sought to fund private businesses, government officials could not keep themselves out of them. This environment created an additional source of entrepreneurial risk—the risk of success as well as failure.

Besides this crowding-out factor, there is one additional reason China did not develop earlier into a capitalist society (at least in the modern European sense): because of the power of the state, rather than its weakness. It is telling that one key financial innovation appeared in the West long before it appeared in China: government bonds. Weak city-states in Europe, constantly at odds with one another, learned how to borrow from investors by offering them promises of future repayments. Government bonds appeared in Italy in the twelfth century, and full-scale bond markets appeared in the thirteenth century.

China in this same time period had paper money but no bonds. This was not an accident of discovery. Before the unification of China under the Qin [秦] emperor in 221 BCE, individual Chinese states likewise occasionally financed warfare by borrowing. An established technology for a wide variety of financial contracts has long existed in China. Commercial claims and financial property rights were being adjudicated before the turn of the last millennium. Thus, China had the technical capacity for government debt markets. However, up until the nineteenth century, the Chinese state did not issue debt. Indeed, periodically throughout Chinese history, the government provided credit. If anything, it competed with private credit institutions rather than using them to finance government enterprise.

What is so good about a state having to borrow? Doesn't this create long-term problems for its subjects? Aren't government bonds simply claims on future taxes rather than past taxes? Yes, but they are more than this. Financial markets do two things. First, they trade promises about the future. This allows entrepreneurs as well as states to capitalize future anticipated cash flows. Second, they provide a mechanism for individual savings and financial planning. Investors like bonds because this allows them to transfer current wealth into an uncertain future. This technology feeds on itself. Early European government markets, once institutionalized, provided a ready mechanism and built-in demand for future promises of private enterprise.

Only with the opening up of China's treaty ports in the nineteenth century through semi-colonial aggression by Great Britain and other countries did China resort to state debt. It is telling that the first Chinese government bonds were floated on international debt markets rather than in China itself. The domestic demand for debt did not yet exist. China's financial modernization in the nineteenth century was a mixed blessing. Chinese government borrowings not only financed the country's international indemnities, they also helped create a vast rail transportation system, which, in turn, helped modernize the Chinese economy.

The forced encounter with the West in the nineteenth century also introduced share capitalism and fostered an explosion of entrepreneurial growth. By the 1870s, several Chinese corporations had formed on a blended East/West model with private owners and government participation and sponsorship. Despite the social tumult and revolution that created the Chinese Republic in 1912, this number grew into the hundreds. At its apex in the 1920s, Shanghai was one of the great banking centers in the world and had a stock market to rival many in Europe. In fact, these early twentieth-century foundations are the basis on which modern China is rebuilding its financial future. Before speculating about the future, however, there is still much to be learned from China's past.

CHINA'S FIRST
FINANCIAL WORLD

THE RICHES OF A WARRIOR QUEEN

In 1976, Chinese archaeologist Zheng Zhenxiang [鄭振] headed an excavation of the ancient ruins of Yin [殷], the last capital of the Shang [商] civilization (1766–1045 BCE), which was the first great dynasty of China's Bronze Age. The site is located near the modern city of Anyang [安陽] in Henan [河南], north of the Yellow River.

Before Zheng's work, the excavation results at Anyang, though tantalizing, had been scant. Like the Egyptian Valley of the Kings, most of the ancient royal graves had been plundered long ago. Zheng and her crew began digging into an earthen palace foundation—a potentially promising ceremonial site. After fifteen feet of excavation and no artifacts, Zheng's colleagues told her to stop—however, she persevered. In another few feet, the most striking discovery in the history of recent Chinese archaeology came to light: an untouched royal tomb. Inside a wooden chamber of twenty meters square, a lacquered coffin contained the body of a woman. She was surrounded by sixteen human sacrifices. As Zheng and her crew carefully uncovered the coffin, they realized that this striking discovery would change the way the world looked at ancient Chinese civilization. The grave goods themselves were a remarkable find—400 ceremonial bronze vessels came to light, 590 jades, 560 bone carvings, and more than 7,000 cowrie shells. The bronze vessels were characteristic of the art of the Shang era: a massive rectangular *ding* [鼎] stood on four legs decorated with snarling animal heads emerging from every side and corner. A covered wine vessel resembled a fantastic bird with the legs of a dog. Every part of the surface of the vessels had some zoomorphic decoration that brought it to life.

Inscriptions on the amazing bronze grave furnishings reveal this to be the tomb of Fu Hao [婦好], a female general of the Shang era. Fu Hao

Bronze banliang coin, third century BCE, Qin dynasty. China's currency was standardized by Qin shihuangdi, and a round coin with a square central hole became the common currency of the empire.

FIGURE 11. Excavations in 1976 of the Tomb of Lady Fu Hao,
a queen and general of the Shang dynasty.

was a consort of emperor Wu Ding [武丁]—one of the longest reigning
Shang emperors. Fu Hao was also a landed lord, who maintained her
own walled estate outside the capital city. According to Chinese oracle inscriptions from Wu Ding's reign, Fu Hao led a successful military
campaign of 10,000 soldiers against the Qiang [羌]—the Shang's enemies to the west. After her death, Wu Ding honored her with the title
Hou Xin [后辛] (Queen Xin)—one of his three official wives. It was a
rare connection between modern archaeology and a legendary figure
out of earliest Chinese history. "What impressed me most in my life was
finding Fu Hao's tomb," recalls Zheng. Had she not persisted, the final
link between Shang history and archaeology may never have been made.

Archaeologists have been studying the Fu Hao trove since its discovery, but one of the prosaic details of the burial is of great interest to

Chinese financial history—the 7,000 cowrie shells. The warrior queen was buried with all the trappings of dynastic wealth—magnificent animal-shaped bronze vessels decorated with mythical beasts, exquisite figurative jades, even her personal slaves and attendants—why also these simple white shells? In all likelihood, they represented an even purer form of wealth—they were money. What Fu Hao could not take with her into the afterlife, she perhaps intended to buy.

The first great dynasty of China's Bronze Age, the Shang, has long been known from Chinese histories. Until the late nineteenth century, however, the geographical roots of Chinese civilization remained a mystery. Shortly after the turn of the nineteenth century, historians working with inscribed cattle and turtle bones from private collections recognized in the archaic Chinese inscriptions the names of Shang rulers and vassals within the texts. In fact, Lady Fu Hao was known to be an historical figure long before her tomb was discovered.

In 1910, epigrapher Luo Zhenyu [羅振玉] traced the source of these oracle bones to the region of Anyang in northern Henan near the Yellow River—there archaeologists found the ancient capital—a city of more than eighty rammed earth platforms and countless royal tombs. The Anyang ruins have kept Chinese excavators like Zheng Zhenxiang hard at work for generations, looking for traces of its ancient rulers and seeking to understand the basis for the florescence of China's first Bronze Age civilization.

Quite unlike Mesopotamia, the Chinese writing system did not evolve from accounting records. The first Chinese writings of any length are divination texts on cattle scapulae and turtle shells. Shang divination involved exposing animal bones to fire or heated metal. Rulers retained diviners to put their queries to the spirit world. A diviner engraved the date and relevant participants in the bone and future potential events. The random cracks caused by heat were inspected for whether they predicted auspicious or negative outcomes. Some asked whether a given day was right for battle, or whether the harvest would be good. Others recorded ritual events and even celestial phenomena. Inscriptions concerning Fu Hao ranged from anxious inquiries by Wu Ding about whether she was pregnant and whether her delivery would go well, to questions about whether he should direct her to join forces with another general in a crucial battle.[1]

Thus the early use of writing in China reflects the fundamental anxiety people everywhere share about the unknown future and suggests that the ancient Chinese ruler played a key role in moderating between his subjects and the unknown. Along with the diviner and the ruler, however, was the animal world. Chinese ritual art of the Shang and Zhou (周, its successor dynasty) is based on a principle of latent animal spirits. Divination crucially relied on the bones of animals—and perhaps even their departed spirits. The animal figures on Chinese ritual bowls and drinking vessels are a reminder of the constant presence of the spirit world behind the world of the visible. How completely unlike the Warka Vase—itself a ritual vessel representing the world of gods and humans! On the Warka Vase, the god is being honored through the re-distribution of goods; the ruler moderating a system of commodity exchange (see Chapter 2). In the Shang, the bronze vessels were used by the rulers in their ritual intermediation between the natural and the spirit worlds. They did not depict the structure of human society. However, each in its own way indicates an important role of government to address uncertainty.

MONEY IN ANCIENT CHINA

As Fu Hao's tomb so dramatically demonstrates, money was already considered by the Chinese to be the ultimate store of wealth. As early as the Shang civilization, China developed a monetary society quite independently, but, in similar fashion to the civilizations of Greece and Rome, money ultimately played an important role in governance and the economy.

Chapter 3 described how Mesopotamians used silver as a medium of exchange—they paid taxes in silver, made contracts, and even recorded commodity prices in silver weights. Silver fits most of the classic definitions of money: a medium of exchange, store of value, and standard of worth. However, the cowrie shells in Fu Hao's tomb are the telltale sign of a step beyond the Mesopotamian money system—away from a medium of exchange with intrinsic value toward a symbolic system of exchange.

Chapter 6 noted that the first coins known in the Mediterranean world were electrum pellets minted in Lydia sometime in the sixth century BCE. The first bronze coins in China date from perhaps a century earlier or later, although the question of precisely which came first has not clearly been settled. Curiously, coins also appeared in India about this time as well, suggesting a potential transcontinental technological advance. While the Anatolian coinage appears to have evolved as a method of certifying the quality of precious metal, Chinese coins appear to have developed as metallic replacements for the cowrie shells. By the time Lady Fu Hao was buried, cowries had been an important part of central Chinese civilization for thousands of years. The Swedish geologist and archaeological pioneer J. G. Andersson identified both shell cowries and bone imitation cowries in pre-Bronze Age burials in central China.

Were the Neolithic and Bronze Age cowries of China used as coins, or were they simply precious decoration or status items—rarities acquired by distant trade with the peoples of the Indian Ocean? This is an ongoing matter of dispute. There is ample evidence that cowries have been used as money in primitive societies at various times throughout history. Histories of China report that the founder of the Qin dynasty abolished the use of cowries as money—suggesting that at least by 221 BCE, cowries were used as coinage. Despite an official edict, the use of cowries as money persisted in the southwestern province of Yunnan [雲南] until the fourteenth century CE; in 1305, cowries were accepted by the government of Yunnan in payment of taxes, and the importing of shells was punishable as counterfeiting.

Why would something with no apparent intrinsic value—other than a curious shape—be used as coinage? Coinage is a tool for storing, measuring, and transferring value. Storage requires a coin to be nonperishable, measurement requires easily recognized standard units of size and quality, and transferability requires that money be portable. Cowries fit all these requirements. They last thousands of years, they are uniform in size, easily recognized, and portable. However, there is one other important feature that money requires. It must be are hard to come by. To be a store of wealth, it is crucial that money not easily be gathered or made. Anyang is far from the Indian Ocean—the principal source of cowrie shells found in Shang tombs. The rarity of cowrie shells in the Yellow River basin meant that the money supply was relatively fixed. This preserved the value of wealth saved as cowrie strings, but it also limited the capacity of the monetary system of early China to grow with the growth in the economy. Cowries can be gathered, but they cannot be made. When an economy needs more money, not even a queen can create more cowries.

There is some evidence that the Bronze Age Chinese economy expanded beyond the capacity of natural cowrie shells to meet the demand for money. Other Shang graves excavated near Anyang have yielded bronze cowries instead of shells. Apparently, ancient Shang metallurgists of the fourteenth through the eleventh centuries BCE were "minting" cowries for inclusion in royal tombs. The minted cowries have no holes for attachment to garments and no other details that would suggest a decorative use. It is difficult to imagine what purpose these bronze imitations might have had other than as money. As such, they are arguably among the world's first minted metallic coinage. The fact that synthetic cowries appear in ancient archaeological context also suggests that the dramatic emergence of Shang civilization may have been accompanied with an economic expansion as well. The sumptuous graves tell of a powerful feudal society in which the emperor's rule was absolute. The cowries are ultimately only a tantalizing suggestion of an economic system moving toward the use of money in the Shang era. It was not until after the fall of the Shang dynasty in 1045 BCE that the use of shell money is confirmed in historical documents.

A BRONZE VESSEL

An inscription on a bronze wine vessel from the successor to the Shang dynasty, the Zhou dynasty (1045–771 BCE), supplies the final link between cowrie shells and money. The monumental He *zun* [何尊] was found in Shaanxi [陝西] province, and its interior bears the curious story of its manufacture.

> When the king first moved his residence to Cheng Zhou [成周; i.e., Luoyang 洛陽], he resumed the practice of King Wu [武王] and performed rituals seeking blessings from Heaven. In the fourth month, on the day bingxu [丙戌], the king made an address to the junior princes of royal ancestry in the principium hall, speaking as follows: "In past times, when your late fathers, the heads of your noble families, were alive, they ably came to the support of King Wen [文王]; and so King Wen received this great [commission, to rule the world]. When King Wu had conquered the Dayi Shang [大邑商] (Great City Shang), then in the court he made an announcement to Heaven,

FIGURE 12. Picture of the Da Yu Ding in the National Museum of China, Beijing.
Early Western Zhou (ca. eleventh–tenth centuries BCE). The vessel contains an
inscription describing the use of cowrie shells as money.

saying 'I will reside in the middle country, and from this place govern
the people.' Oh, even though you are only junior princes, surely we
can expect that you will emulate [your] princely [fathers] in the noble
status they earned in Heaven's regard, attending dutifully to Heaven's
bidding and caring reverently for the sacrifices! Help [me] the king
to uphold [my] virtue, so that Heaven will make me compliant when
I am not earnest." The king concluded his lecture. I was given thirty
strings of cowrie shells, and with this I made for the Duke this precious zun [尊] vessel—this being the king's fifth cult year.[2]

Created perhaps only a century or two after Fu Hao's burial, the vessel leaves little doubt that cowries were currency—the donor used them to commission the bronze. Similar inscriptions from other monumental bronzes from the early Zhou indicate that cowries paid not only for casting bronzes but also for the salaries of warriors.

If one is willing to take the early Zhou bronze inscriptions as indicative of practices in the preceding era, it is even conceivable that the warrior queen Fu Hao paid her soldiers in cowrie money. Her cowrie shell hoard may have been her war chest for the battles she would face in the afterlife.

There is one more telling piece of evidence suggesting that cowries were the primordial money of ancient China—the word for treasure has the component (or radical) for shell—a vertical rectangle with two horizontal interior lines and two feet (*bei* 貝). The Chinese written language is composed of ideograms that are constructed from 214 standard building blocks called "radicals," many of which can be traced to Shang ideograms. The shell/money radical in the Shang era is clearly a pictographic representation of a shell. It also forms the root of many other Chinese characters associated with commerce, among them treasure (*bao* 寶), collateral (*dai* 貸), wealth (*cai* 財), buy (*gou* 購), sell (*mai* 賣), possession (*zi* 資), redeem (*shu* 贖), and more. As such, it became one of the fundamental building blocks in the Chinese written language representing money, wealth, and value. Because of the special nature of the Chinese written language, we can trace how the fundamental concept of money is embedded in communication and also likely embedded in Chinese thought.

The anthropologist Benjamin Lee Whorf was one of the first scholars to theorize that language affects thought as much as thought affects language—that the mode of expression cannot be separated from the content. Language, like finance, is also technology that serves as a conceptual structure. Each language has its own architecture, and living in these architectures affects one's perspective. We may never know whether queen Fu Hao fully grasped the significance of the new economic medium her grave goods represented. However, writings from later centuries leave little doubt that China's rulers fully recognized the potential of money and the marketplace. The incorporation of the sign of the cowrie shell into the written Chinese language means that finance was, almost by definition, embedded in the architecture of future Chinese thought.

IF THE MYRIAD OF GOODS CAN FLOW UNOBSTRUCTED . . .

The last Shang emperor, King Zhou [紂王], was overthrown by King Wu of the western Zhou dynasty in 1045 BCE. At its apex of power, the rule of the Zhou dynasty stretched a thousand miles from the heart of the Yellow River valley east beyond what is now modern-day Beijing. Although never conquered from the outside, this extended empire ultimately fell to centrifugal forces, breaking up into separate states. At first, these separate powers preserved a symbolic but weakened imperial dynasty, but by 771 BCE, the fiction of a unified Chinese empire was gone. China broke up into smaller states that recognized their origins in the Zhou but were effectively independent, sharing a culture but not a government. The philosopher Confucius lived during this era, which is referred to as the Spring-Autumn period [春秋时代] (771–480 BCE).

The Confucian era was followed by a period of intensified interstate warfare. In a manner reminiscent of Renaissance Italy, the rulers of the Warring States (*Zhanguo* 戰國) period (481–221 BCE) vied constantly for dominance. Also like Renaissance Italy, this competition led perhaps unexpectedly to a remarkable flowering of culture. Many of China's greatest philosophers—Mencius [孟子], Mozi [墨子], Zhuangzi [莊子], and Han Feizi [韓非子]—lived during the Warring States period, seeking patronage and offering guidance to China's ruling dukes. This period also marked the beginning of large-scale urban Chinese civilization and the emergence of Chinese literature.

One of the greatest of all China's Warring States cities was Linzi [臨淄] in the eastern Chinese state of Qi [齊]. Colonized by a Zhou general shortly after the fall of the Shang empire, the state of Qi occupied the Shandong [山東] peninsula and thus had access to shoreline trade routes as well as north–south inland commercial traffic. It was noted in Zhou times for its silks and other textiles, fish, and salt.

According to the Grand Historian Sima Qian [司馬遷], who wrote the first account of the Zhou and Warring States era, the people of Qi were "generous, easy-going, of considerable intelligence, and fond of debate. . . . All five classes of people (scholars, farmers, traveling merchants, artisans, and resident traders) are to be found among them."[3] Note that two of the five classes were directly engaged in commerce. Linzi of the Warring States period was alive with a mercantile energy—enough to bring to Sima Qian's mind the aphorism:

Jostling and joyous,
the whole world comes after profit;
racing and rioting,
After profit the whole world goes.[4]

Linzi was a major commercial center during the late Zhou and Warring States periods. The Grand Historian attributed Qi's first great period of growth to the economic genius of the first Qi ruler Jiang Shang [姜尚], who, when he first came east, found the land of Qi

damp and brackish and the inhabitants few. He encouraged the women workers, developed the craft industries to the highest degree and opened up the trade in fish and salt. As a result, men and goods were reeled into the state like skeins of thread; they converged upon it like spokes about a hub. Soon Qi was supplying caps and sashes, clothes and shoes to the whole empire, and the lords of the area between the sea and Mt. Tai adjusted their sleeves and journeyed to court to pay their respects.[5]

Archaeological work at the famous cosmopolis of Linzi began in the 1930s and continues to this day. Discoveries by Chinese archaeologists have revealed a relatively complete picture of an ancient Chinese city—not just its royal tombs, but also its neighborhoods, industrial areas, roads, and markets. Linzi was a walled city with more than 9½ miles of broad earth embankments protecting the populace from military attack. The Zi River [淄水] flanked the city on the east. The riverside was doubtless crowded by docks and wharves for riverine trade to the east and maritime trade to the west—Linzi was situated so as to control trade in the Bay of Bohai [渤海灣] and beyond to the Yellow Sea. On the other three sides, the city had monumental city gates. Inside, the town was crisscrossed by sixty-foot-wide avenues and channels for drainage and water supply. It was the one of the largest Chinese cities of its kind—probably one of the largest cities in the world. Mere statistics do not do Linzi justice, however. Sima Qian notes that in Linzi's avenues,

Cart hubs bang each other and people rub shoulders; their garments form an [endless] curtain. When people raise their sleeves, it looks as if there were a tent; when they shake off sweat, it feels like rain. Families are rich, individuals are well off, aspirations are high and spirits soar.[6]

The secret of Linzi's success was Jiang Shang's program of economic development. But what was the secret behind that?

LINZI TODAY

The ancient city of Linzi is now a vast cabbage farm (perhaps until modern times a collective farm), but you can still see the grid pattern of the city, with pathways and dirt roads leading west, up from the waterfront and toward the inner walled sanctum and a large platform mound. Most visitors come to Linzi to see the spectacular burials that predate the more famous terra cotta warriors. In one burial mound in the eastern precinct, more than 600 horses were buried with their deceased owner. Even for a state the size of ancient Qi, this must have been a significant economic sacrifice—particularly if the city was at war. Another burial preserved the remains of an ancient chariot and armor. Parts of the 2,500-year-old city walls made of *huang tu* [夯土] (rammed earth used for architecture) still survive, as does the ancient stone drainage system constructed with a baffling screen to prevent attackers from entering the city. Less visible are any traces of the philosophical and economic tradition that is associated with Linzi.

ECONOMIC WARFARE

Qi was ruled by two different families during the Zhou and the Warring States periods, and each had their traditional precinct in Linzi. In 386 BCE, in an act that, in fact, helped define the beginning of the Warring States period, the Tian [田] family—a powerful clan of ministers—overthrew the royal family of Jiang [姜] in a popular uprising that included participation across the five classes. The Tian family precinct is believed to be the walled "city within a city" in the southwest corner of Qi. The thick walls of the precinct face not only outward but also toward the rest of the city, suggesting that it not only provided refuge to Linzi's populace but also occasionally provided refuge from them. Inside these inner walls, the rulers of the Tian family built their palace and kept an iron workshop to make tools and weapons, a bronze workshop for metal vessels, and the royal mint for coining money.

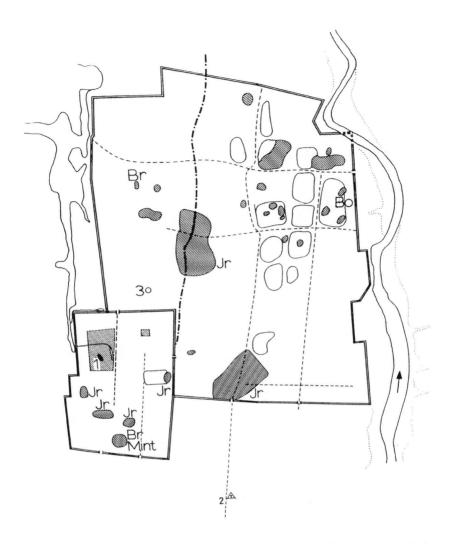

FIGURE 13. Plan of Linzi. The mint where coins were struck is in the lower left, within the duke's precinct. The western gate, Ji Xia, is conjectured to be near the duke's precinct.

Just outside of this inner city, immediately below the western gate of Qi, stood one of the most famous features of the state of Qi—the Jixia Academy [稷下學宮]. Jixia may have been the first historical instance of government-sponsored scholarship on a large scale. Academy may actually be a misnomer, since there is actually no evidence of a formal educational institution—it was apparently not an ancient university. Rather, it might have been a community of scholars serving at the pleasure of the state.

Under the patronage of the dukes of Qi, the Jixia Academy was undoubtedly a lively center of philosophical debate about politics and government. Despite being one of the great centers of thought in the golden age of philosophers, little more about the Jixia Academy is known today, other than that its scholars numbered in the hundreds, perhaps even thousands, by the year 300 BCE. Nothing remains of the vigorous arguments, theories, and dialogues that may have illuminated the Jixia Academy throughout most of the fourth and third centuries BCE. But walking around the site, with the massive city walls still visible nearby, echoes the feeling of walking through the ruins of the Athenian Agora, where Western philosophy was born. Some scholars have argued that the Jixia Academy was fabricated by later historians—that it did not really exist. There is one body of work, however, that suggests that an important and distinct intellectual tradition emerged in some form in ancient Linzi—whether it was organized under royal patronage or not.

GUANZI

The only written work potentially attributable to the Jixia Academy is a collection of essays called the *Guanzi* [管子]. The *Guanzi* is written, in part, as an imaginary dialogue between Duke Huan of Qi [齊桓公] and his prime minister Guan Zhong (管仲; i.e., Master Guan), who lived in the early years of Qi's history. The text itself is commonly believed to have been composed later in the fourth century BCE by Jixia scholars and also written and revised during the Han dynasty 200–400 years later.

The seventy-six chapters in the *Guanzi* range from Daoist geomancy to discourses on politics and education to musical treatises and medical texts—there is even a pre-Galen analysis of the circulation of blood. Although the text is fragmented and wide ranging, an image of Guan Zhong emerges from the chapters. He is more clever than wise. He is a problem solver rather than a paragon of virtue. He understands human nature and is willing, at times, to exploit it for the good of the state.

One account in the book about his financial dealings is particularly telling. Guan Zhong financed the defense of Qi by an emergency surtax on the populace, who in turn raised money by borrowing from wealthy nobles. The war was won, but the people's indebtedness remained, creating unrest. The duke asked if the burden of debt could be relieved. Guan Zhong's response: "Only by the use of subtle devices."

His solution to this financial problem was a political one. He recommended that the ruler thank the nobles for their support of the state in its time of need by awarding each a special jade plaque symbolizing the special favor of the ruler. He called all the nobility together, awarded the plaques, and asked them to forgive the loans. The ploy apparently worked. Guan Zhong could see solutions others could not see—solutions that relied on factors like symbols of imperial favor and the hidden power of the market. Real or a fictional creation of the Jixia scholars, Guan Zhong embodied a distinctively different archetype in the Chinese imagination: a trickster figure remembered for invention, guile, and the understanding of human nature, rather than as a model of ethical behavior or the embodiment of the way to live.

The most important work in the *Guanzi* from a financial perspective are several chapters dealing with economics and money. The most famous of these is a chapter titled "Light and Heavy" [轻重], which has been regarded as the first clear articulation of the economic law of supply and demand. Light and heavy refers to relative prices of goods, which in turn creates incentives for trade and leads to a price equilibrium. Marking up or down prices rather than commanding obedience can achieve the ruler's desired outcome.

Another chapter, "The State Savings" (*Guoxu* 國蓄), articulates a remarkably sophisticated monetary theory. It is often cited as the first expression of the quantity theory of money, but that characterization in no way does justice to its revolutionary economic vision. A careful reading shows why the dukes of Qi may have been willing to sponsor the Jixia scholars. The text not only discusses money as a medium of economic equilibrium, it also details exactly how money can be used as a tool of the state.

Chinese philosophers delighted in paradox, and money provided a fascinating puzzle for the Jixia philosophers to ponder. According to the *Guanzi*,

If you grasp three coins, there is nothing to warm you. If you eat them, there is nothing there to nourish you. [Yet] the former Kings used them to store up goods, to manage men and to pacify the world. That which is used to order things is called a measure.[7]

To the *Guanzi* authors, money—not armies, legal doctrines, piety, or philosophy—was the secret to managing men and bringing peace to the world. Monetary policy was a clever way to bring about desirable change, as opposed to direct imperial decree. In the *Guanzi*, the mint was treated as a crucial instrument of governance. Hence, it is not surprising that the Linzi's mint was located in the inner city, under the watchful eyes of its rulers. The remains of that same mint today are located behind a row of houses in a village that occupies a part of the Tian precinct.

Qi coins are exquisitely cast bronze in the shape of knife blades with a ring at the bottom—presumably for stringing them together. They were not real knives but symbolic forms resembling actual Shang era knives of the type that has been unearthed at Anyang. Sometime between the era of the Shang queen and the emergence of Linzi, coinage in China's northeast had formally developed from actual to vestigial metal commodities. The handles of the Linzi coins typically bear a slogan—"Construct the Nation" (*Jianbang* 建邦)—an optimistic exhortation that tells of a dynamic, practical spirit and explicitly portrays money as an instrument of development. The museum at Linzi contains coins that were found near the site of the city mint.

Consistent with the recognition that warfare embodied economic as well as political conflict, the Warring States had warring currencies. China was effectively divided into four different currency zones. Rival states to the west minted spade-shaped coins and circular bronze rings. States to the south minted so-called ant-nosed coins (*yibiqian* 蟻鼻錢) that presumably developed from bronze cowries. Qi and its neighboring states in the east minted knife coins (*daobi* 刀幣), and their distribution overlaps somewhat with the spade and ring currencies. The prevalence of Warring States currencies through both northern and southern China suggests that a complete monetary economy, albeit with different currencies, linked trade through most of China by this time. Although spade-shaped coins were known from the Spring-Autumn period and the concept of cash dates to the Shang, the Warring States era experienced an unprecedented explosion in the use of money. The economic historian Peng Xinwei [彭信威], comparing twentieth-century prices for Spring-Autumn spade coins versus Warring States spade coins to measure their relative scarcity, figures that the money supply in the latter era expanded by a factor of ten.

Peng Xinwei is himself an interesting and important figure in Chinese scholarship. A banker from Shanghai, he lived through an amazingly turbulent period in his city's history. When he was young, he saw the emergence of Shanghai as a global banking center during the so-called Warlord period, when the country was divided among battling, post-imperial factions. He was a resident when Shanghai became a captive city of the Japanese occupation government. After the Second World War, Shanghai resumed its role as the center of national finance—the place where reconstruction bonds were floated and where the battle against Chinese Communists was financed. Peng Xinwei did not flee Shanghai when the Republican government left for Taiwan. In fact, some of his most valuable work was likely done in the period of the late 1940s and 1950s during the turmoil of Communist accession and the great famines that decimated China. It was then that he wrote his comprehensive study of Chinese monetary and economic thought. Peng Xinwei simply disappeared in 1960, either because of his business career or because of his interest in financial history, during the Cultural Revolution.

His monumental two-volume work, *A Monetary History of China*, is much more than a history of money. It is a comprehensive history of Chinese economic thought. In it, he tackles many of the open questions of Chinese economic history, particularly the appearance and early use of money, as well as the continued role of money in Chinese political history. We can thank Peng Xinwei for the insight that the distinctive "construct the nation" Qi knife coins were minted under the reign of the Tian family, contemporaneous with the *Guanzi* monetary theorists.

The *Guanzi* regards coinage not as the goal of economic policy but only as a medium—an abstraction for which they chose an interesting metaphor. "Knife coins are the channels and ditches," write the *Guanzi* authors. Like channels that guide the flow of water to the field, or like veins and arteries that channel the flow of blood, the *Guanzi* suggests that money is the channel through which economic activity flows. By implication, the ruler who controls that channel controls the entire well-being of the state. The importance of this insight cannot be overstated. It took the philosophers in Europe 2,000 years before they fully understood this.

(a)   (b)

FIGURE 14. Shrine to Guan Zhong. (a) A smaller mound near the tombs of the rulers of Qi is revered today as the tomb of Guan Zhong. (b) An offering on the side of the mound.

During the period in which the *Guanzi* was written, China's political milieu was curiously like the warring city-states era of the Italian Renaissance. Chinese philosophers were not only symbols of the enlightenment of the rulers, but also competitive "weapons" in the battles among the rival states. Sunzi's [孫子] famous *Art of War* was written in this period. Another philosophical school, the Mohists [墨家], offered their services in designing war machines, defensive structures, and battlefield stratagems, while Jixia scholars understood that the struggle between the states took place in the marketplace as well as on battlefields. Perhaps the dukes of Qi were able to hold out against Qin hegemony for so long because they could marshal natural economic forces to their service. When the Qi experienced shortages, prices (ratios of exchange)—naturally or by explicit government policy—led to equilibration. According to the *Guanzi*:

> Now, the price of grain is heavy in our state and light in the world at large. Then the other lords' goods will spontaneously leak out like

water from a spring flowing downhill. Hence, if goods are heavy, they will come; if light they will go.[8]

In this passage, heavy means expensive and light means cheap. The metaphor of a fluid served the scholars well in conceptualizing how the market adjusted spontaneously to price differentials. However, when the invisible hand did not work, the Jixia scholars were not above suggesting explicit price warfare. Since coins do not feed the populace, there are ways to obtain the necessities without seizing them by force: "If the [other] lords' grain is priced at ten, and if we price our grain at twenty, then their grain will flow to our state."[9] The ruler who controls prices does not have to control the flow of goods—price ratios will motivate trade to achieve the desired results. People were motivated by profit.

Despite advocating government control of commodity prices, the *Guanzi* writers also recognized the extraordinary social benefit of the market price system—free trade had the capability of making everyone better off. According to the *Guanzi*, "If the myriad of goods can flow unobstructed, they will be put in motion. If they are put in motion, then they will be cheap."[10] In other words, if there are markets, trade will occur. With free trade come lower prices and the sharing of benefits across regions. The leaders of the modern World Trade Organization could not have put it better.

LOANS AND TAXES

Given the *Guanzi* philosophy about the spontaneous power of the marketplace, it is not surprising that the Warring States period was also an era of the flowering of private enterprise—some of which builds on financial enterprise. Great wealth had been amassed in China before. The Shang tombs tell us that. However, beginning in the fourth century BCE, great wealth was not confined to royal families and their vassals. In the Grand Historian Sima Qian's *The Biographies of the Money-Makers*, he surveys the commoners of earlier times who became wealthy. Great fortunes in the Warring States era were made by smelting iron, trading with barbarians, developing real estate, owning and hiring out slaves, peddling food and other goods, selling grain, farming, robbing graves, sharpening knives, and lending money.

The most famous moneylender of his era was Lord Mengchang [孟嘗君] of Qi, a member of the ruling Tian clan who was famous for his modesty and benevolence. Lord Mengchang lived circa 300 BCE. Among other things, he was a financier whose annual income from lending was reported to be 100,000 strings of cash. The tale we have of him describes exactly how his loans were collected and verified—and how he sometimes failed to collect.

> There was a man of Qi named Feng Xuan [馮諼] who was so poor he could not maintain himself. He sent a servant to ask that he himself be placed under Lord Mengchang. He wished to be lodged and fed as one of the lord's retainers. . . . Later Lord Mengchang put out a request among his retainers asking which of them could keep records, and thus was able to collect his debts in Xue [薛]. Feng Xuan said that he could do so. . . . Thereupon Feng secured a chariot, and rode off carrying the tallies of indebtedness. . . . Feng hurried to Xue, where he had the clerks assemble all those people who owed debts, so that his tallies might be matched against theirs. When the tallies had been matched, Feng brought forth a false order to forgive those debts, and so he burned the tallies. The people all cheered.[11]

A telling aspect of the story that resonates with Mesopotamian finance discussed in Chapter 3 is the theme of debt. It is clear that the problem of indebtedness by the populace existed in ancient China as well as in ancient Mesopotamia and that popular sentiment against creditors was common to both societies. But the prosaic details of the story reveal the level of financial technology that existed in Mengchang's era.

In the story, the tallies burned by Feng Xuan represented obligations—perhaps taxes owed to the lord. He evidently collected the debts from wealthy nobles from Xue but erased those of the common folk. The tale of Lord Mengchang and the stories of the other money makers in early Chinese history are important, because they show that not only did entrepreneurs exist and flourish in the Warring States period in China but also that finance played a significant role. We see in fourth-century China much the same lending practices as we saw throughout Mesopotamian history, but instead of clay tablets, the contracting technology was based on bamboo tallies. These tallies had to function in the same manner as bullae. They had to allow mutual verification and prevent both debtor and creditor from substituting a different contract ex post.

The way this worked is due to the peculiar nature of bamboo. A text could be written on the smooth outer surface of a large piece of bamboo, and then this was split in two, parallel to the grain. The two parts were then able to be uniquely matched against each other when the loan was either paid or disputed. Clay or bamboo—enterprising financiers independently developed a verification technology for financial contracting that derived from the natural resources at hand. Bamboo is more perishable than clay, so the myriad financial documents from ancient China have disappeared. Most of the bamboo slips that have been discovered intact are from ancient tombs that were waterlogged, allowing perishable items to survive. Unfortunately for the financial historian, ancient Chinese moneylenders chose to be buried more often with classical literary texts as opposed to their loan records.

A set of bronze replicas of bamboo tally sticks did come to light in Anhui province in 1957, dating from the Western Zhou period, 1046–770 BCE— centuries earlier than Lord Mengchang. The matching pair is inlaid in gold characters. Their text gives a merchant permission to transport goods and pay tariffs. The metallurgist who cast the two pieces made sure to preserve the joint of the bronze bamboo that divides the text on both halves into a top and bottom portion and served as a unique verification mechanism.

While the Mengchang story does not tell us what interest rates he charged on his loans, just like in Mesopotamia, there are mathematical student texts that provide information on this issue. The *Suanshu shu* [算數書] is a mathematical treatise excavated from a Chinese tomb in Hubei [湖北] province dating to 186 BCE. The government official buried in the tomb served in the Qin dynasty and then in the Han dynasty that followed.[12] This is more than a century after Lord Mengchang and Feng Xuan lived, but the text likely represents the mathematical knowledge that Feng Xuan would be expected to master. Historians of mathematics, like the translator of the text, Christopher Cullen (a fellow of the Needham Institute at the University of Cambridge) are naturally interested in the extent of mathematical knowledge that existed in China at this time. From the perspective of financial history, we are more curious about the role of financial techniques in the *Suanshu shu*. Written on 190 bamboo strips, the text contains a wide range of practical problems and their solutions that an official like Feng Xuan might encounter in his administration of a local district. Typical problems involve the calculation of customs fees, the calculation of the output of manual labor (e.g., weaving and arrow making), the calculation of rations for animals, the measurement and calculation of the value of bolts of silk, even the calculation of the number of bamboo tallies that can be made from a bamboo of a specific length and breadth. It provides techniques for calculating price ratios of such commodities as millet, wastage in various production operations, distances and rates of travel, and some problems pertaining to the construction of earthworks—particularly the volume of earth needed to construct various shapes, such as ramps, cones, and pavilions. Also included are geometric methods for calculating field areas.

The financial problems are few but interesting. One set of them addresses the problem of the division of profits from invested capital. Presumably these are motivated by merchant trade. Another set are interest rate (*xi* 息) calculations. For example: "If the capital is 100 cash, the interest is three a month, now the capital is 60 cash; it is returned when the month has not yet filled 16 days. Calculate how much the interest is." This is equivalent to asking the interest on sixty coins over sixteen days of a thirty-day month when the monthly interest rate is 3%.

This simple problem tells us several things. First, loans might be as small as sixty copper coins for terms as short as sixteen days. It also suggests that those interest rates could be as high as 3% per month. Even not compounded, this rate annualized exceeds Babylonian rates of 33⅓%. No wonder the citizens were pleased that Feng Xuan destroyed the tallies. The rate in China—like the those in ancient Mesopotamia for short-term loans—far exceeded the productive capacity of capital. Finally, we can be sure that the Chinese mathematical tradition, at least as early as the unification of the empire under the Qin, incorporated precise concepts of the time value of money, and loans were being made and paid back in the coin of the realm.

Lord Mengchang almost certainly visited the Tian family precinct and perhaps even climbed the mound that still dominates it today. Although now blanketed by a tangle of bushes and weeds, it is still an impressive structure. A scatter of earthen houses in the village at the ancient crossroads of two of Linzi's avenues only hint at the vibrant domestic life of the Warring States city.

FIGURE 15. Royal tombs of Qi. The four hills on the horizon are the tombs of the Dukes of Qi, third or fourth century BCE(?). Guided by the philosophy of the *Guanzi*, the rulers of Qi used economic theory, including monetary policy, as a tool of the state.

From this vantage point, however, it is clear that Chinese cities exist on a vertical as well as a horizontal plane. Important places are elevated—be they temples or tombs. In fact, the city is still punctuated by dramatic monumental funerary earthworks standing out from the fabric of the fields, walls, and houses laid out below. Who knows—in a city like Linzi, some of these ancient tombs might be the final resting places of merchants and moneylenders rather than government officials. Beyond the city a backdrop of mountains rises still higher to the west, across the Zi River. These hills contain a fascinating modern remnant of the ancient Chinese economic thought.

Across the Zi River, a mile-long earthen boulevard is flanked by four large earthen mounds—royal tombs from the Warring States period. Despite 2,500 years of erosion, the Chinese tumuli are magnificent—seventy-five feet tall, rounded mounds built on square bases. They command a vast perspective over the river plain and the city below. A smaller mound nearby is less conspicuous.

About a mile and a half away, on the outskirts of a small farming village, is a smaller mound believed to be the tomb of Guan Zhong. Only twenty feet high or so, it likewise has a magnificent view of the city of Linzi below. Regardless of whether there is any factual basis for the attribution of Guan Zhong's tomb to this site, it is clear that people in the area regard it to be so. A tree grows out of the back of the mound—countless bits of paper and plastic are tied to its branches, each one a prayer or invocation to Guan Zhong. People still worship at the grave of the inventor of the law of supply and demand.

In this chapter, we traced the development of money in China from its origins as a unit of account in an early urban, military society ruled by elites with great wealth. The first Chinese rulers exercised control through taxation and developed a technology for these obligations. The fundamental concept of money is embedded in the written language of Chinese through its earliest manifestation as a cowrie shell, but Chinese money evolved into different forms—spades and knives—that could be manufactured from metal, rather than having to be collected and traded from the sea coasts. We explored one of these ancient cities in depth—Linzi—the last to fall to Qin Shihuangdi [秦始皇帝] (First Emperor of Qin) in the unification of the Chinese state. Linzi is a particularly interesting example because of the pragmatic economic policies of its rulers. It owed its origins to the insight of economic development based on handicraft and trade, and it was home to one of the greatest philosophers of economic thought, Guan Zhong. Whether *Guanzi* was written by a single person or simply represents a school of thought is not important. The text reflects a level of extraordinary abstraction in the realization of the role of money in the economy. *Guanzi* identified money as the fundamental medium of the equilibration between supply and demand for goods. It recognized it as a tool to achieve the goals of the state. It proposed—and perhaps even implemented—monetarist policies. More subtly, *Guanzi* highlighted the role that profit-seeking incentives play in society. The invisible hand of the market functions because of the profit motive. Most of *Guanzi*'s "subtle" devices make use of this natural human desire.

UNITY AND BUREAUCRACY

The Warring States era came to an abrupt end in 221 BCE, when Qin emerged as the winner of a centuries-long rivalry. The first emperor of Qin fully recognized the power of monetary authority. Not only did he subdue all rival states, he also eliminated all rival currencies—nationalizing and standardizing the production of money. The money he introduced should be familiar to everyone—a round copper coin with a square hole in the middle. This Qin design, perhaps patterned on the round-holed disks current during the Warring States period, remained unchanged until the fall of the last emperor of the Qing [清] dynasty in the early twentieth century. In 1900, the year of the Boxer Rebellion, the province of Guangdong [廣東] minted a round copper coin without a hole in the middle—the first in more than 2,000 years.

The central problem of Chinese government has long been the management of a large bureaucracy. With the unification of the empire after the Warring States period, this problem increased in significance as the new emperor brought together a set of culturally related but politically disparate entities with questionable loyalties. In a sense, much of the philosophical discourse in China before and after the reunification relates in some way to the problem of bureaucracy—a system in which one person works under the direction of another in an organization.

Embedded in large-scale organizational structure is a fundamental issue that is called by modern economists the "principal-agent problem": a principal (boss) must delegate a task to an agent (employee). The problem is that by delegating a task, the principal cannot be sure that it will be done exactly as he or she wishes. The agent might not work hard or might be dishonest. Agency can be thought of as a problem of motivation, but it is also a problem of information. If the principal could always check up on the agent, and reward or punish according to effort and honesty, then the bureaucracy would function perfectly.

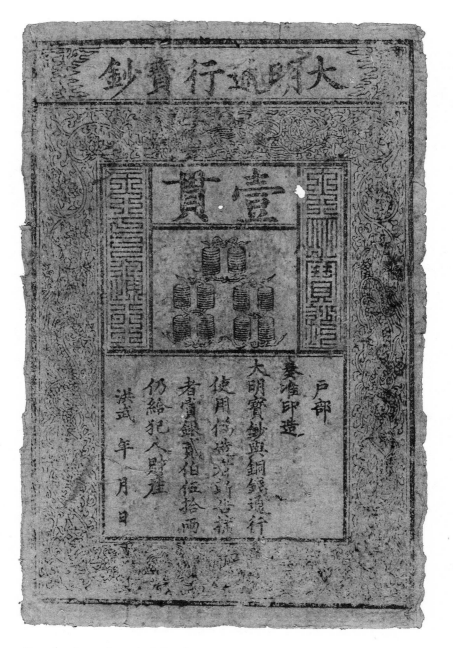

Paper banknote from the Ming dynasty, ca. 1375–1425 CE. Printed on mulberry bark paper with a copper plate, the note depicts the equivalent value in strings of coins. Fiat money that has value by government decree was invented in China.

Unfortunately for the boss, such constant monitoring is expensive and counterproductive. Some element of trust must remain in the system, and whenever you rely on trust, there is the potential for abuse. The problem of agency grows with the scale and scope of the organization— each link in the bureaucracy presents an opportunity for slacking and for dishonesty. Particularly with the unification of previously independent states, the challenge of forcing agents to work in the best interest of the principal is a large one. The best solution to the agency problem is for the agent to be completely devoted to his or her task, and to behave correctly. This, in essence is the solution to the agency problem posed by Confucius [孔子], the most famous philosopher of ancient China.

AGENCY AND HUMAN NATURE

Confucius lived in the second half of the sixth century BCE, just before the Warring States period, but at a time when China was effectively divided into autonomous political states. His writings focus on correct behavior. Confucius exhorts officials to show modesty, compassion, and self-restraint. Frequently hearkening back to a golden age of political unity and righteous leadership in the Zhou period, Confucius invoked historical precedent. Modern echoes of Confucian tradition can be seen in the periodic public prosecution of corrupt bureaucrats who have exploited their position for personal gain. If every public official would only practice Confucian ethics, there would be no need for such purges. An ideal Confucian official would be righteous, generous, and forgiving. The state that resulted from this ideal would be one in which the desires of the official are subjugated to the will of the enlightened ruler, who governs for the good of the populace as a whole. Confucianism appeals to the noblest instincts of humankind and is predicated on the belief that everyone has the potential to behave in a righteous manner and that they should strive throughout life to achieve this goal.

There is, however, a contrary view of human nature; one that presumes the worst in humanity—or at least presupposed that people will act in their own best interests rather than in the interests of their superiors or subordinates. The solution to this problem is not to appeal to their noblest instincts but to patiently explain the severity of the punishment meted out for those who violate the law, and the reward for behaving correctly. The famous scholar Han Feizi was the son of a noble family of the state of Han [韓]. He was trained in a Confucian tradition, but his ideas differed from Confucianism in that he focused on external rather than internal influences on behavior. He advocated the creation of a uniform code of law and uniform punishment for violations. Within the framework of the law, individuals were free to pursue self-interest, and in fact it would be pointless to try and exhort them not to do so. These ideas later came to be referred to as "Legalism," although no such intellectual categorization existed in antiquity.

Han Feizi's ideas came to the attention of the ruler of Qin—later the Qin emperor. Although Han Feizi was assassinated as a result of political intrigue while on an ambassadorial visit to Qin, he was honored and pardoned by his host after his death. It is not surprising that the Qin emperor Qin Shihuangdi admired the ideas of Han Feizi, since he ultimately conquered a series of hostile neighboring states by force. It made little sense for him to presume that the incentives of his subjects would be naturally aligned to his own, or that an appeal to the innate moral sense of the subjects of his far-flung empire would be effectual. More subtly, through much of human history, politics relied on the kinship and family loyalties as the basis for obligations. Marriages between ruling families of competing states were a means to cement a truce, and family ties were the basis for requesting military assistance. With the widespread extension of political control under the Qin, the new emperor could not count on kinship as the basis for authority. Laws and penalties replaced appeals to family ties or to a higher moral sense. According to Han Feizi, "When a sage rules a state he does not count on people doing good on their own but rather takes measures to keep them from doing wrong."[1]

The legalist philosophy has some superficial appeal to laissez-faire economists—after all, law is the basis for property rights and contracts. Hammurabi's code and its predecessors created the institutional framework for the financial infrastructure of ancient Mesopotamia. Surely the creation of a transparent and uniform code with pre-stated punishments would have similar effects in China. If it did, we have no clear evidence of it. Unlike the *Guanzi*, legalist writings appear unconcerned with the benefits of free markets. They seem to focus on the law as a means to maintain political control—they address the agency problem: the problem of governance and management as opposed to economic growth and statecraft.

Confucianism and Legalism—although perhaps anachronistic characterizations of the polarities of ancient Chinese thought—are two of its best-known ancient schools. In contrast, the *Guanzi* is less often discussed, perhaps because it does not fit neatly into the polarity defined around human nature and solutions to the problem of bureaucracy. The role model presented in *Guanzi* is neither that of the exemplary, empathic official nor that of the all-powerful rule giver. Guan Zhong is a bit like Odysseus, an official who devises ingenious solutions, a minister who recognizes that, with the right incentives, the invisible hand can be made to support the state, and that prosperity of the people has benefits for the ruler.

BUREAUCRACY AS FINANCIAL TECHNOLOGY

Modern economic theory poses two solutions to the agency problem: incentives and monitoring. The incentives solution is based on the idea that the agent will behave in the best interest of the principal if their mutual incentives are aligned. An example of this in the *Guanzi* is the control of the economy through adjusting the money supply. Minting more money created incentives to sell grain to the state of Qi. This incentive system is silent on whether those selling the grain were doing so out of high moral purpose or conniving self-interest—the *Guanzi* does not judge the ethics of the market, but looks to use its forces for the good of the state by aligning individual incentives with the ruler's goals.

These philosophical disputes may seem far removed from contemporary financial and governance issues, but they are not. The modern example of the use of incentives to overcome the agency problem is executive compensation for managers of corporations. Incentive theory says that, if the manager has stock options, he or she will take actions that will make them more valuable. These actions will also maximize the price of the stocks and thus increase the wealth of the shareholders of the company. If this happens, the CEO can become fabulously wealthy—but only if the company itself does well. In contrast, a Confucian view of the CEO would question why the leader must be bribed to work in the best interest of the shareholder. Shouldn't the fiduciary responsibility he or she has to shareholders be sufficient to motivate maximum effort? Contemporary society is extraordinarily critical of high CEO compensation.

Does this criticism reflect a deep-seated belief that an ethics-based solution to the agency problem—one that appeals to the nobler aspects of character—is preferable to a positive incentives scheme?

A MYSTERIOUS TEXT

Interestingly enough, another ancient and little-known Chinese text points the way toward the alternative solution to the problem of bureaucracy: monitoring. The *Zhouli* [周禮] (The rites of Zhou) is a remarkably odd document. It does not present itself as the teachings of a philosopher or the account of a wise minister. It is essentially an anonymous but detailed organizational chart of the imperial government of Zhou.

The *Zhouli* dryly details every single office necessary for the state—from the king and prime minister down to the palace cook and kitchen hands. Some of the offices described in the *Zhouli* are strange indeed. For example, there is an official in charge of knocking down the nests of malicious birds, another charged with studying worms and establishing rules for their preservation, and a collector of oysters and clams that are due to the government. The *Zhouli* divides the rule of the state into six departments and lists in detail how these departments are staffed and what their duties should be. These duties include not only governance activities but also religious rituals—the book makes clear that a major function of the state is the maintenance of the relationship between humankind and the supernatural—presumably a reflection of the idea that the Chinese emperor rules with the mandate of heaven. In the *Zhouli*, the emperor is the embodiment of the state:

> the sovereign alone constitutes his domains; determining the four boundaries and fixing the initial positions, he traces the plan of the capital and the countryside; creates the ministries and separates their functions in order to form an administrative center for the people.[2]

The six ministries created by the emperor are the Ministry of the State (Sky, *Tianguan* 天官), the Ministry of the Multitude (Earth, *Diguan* 地官), the Ministry of Cult (Spring, *Chunguan* 春官), the Ministry of War (Summer, *Xiaguan* 夏官), the Ministry of Justice (Autumn, *Qiuguan* 秋官), and the Ministry of Public Works (Winter, *Dongguan* 冬官). The head of the Ministry of State is the prime minister—the second most powerful person in the kingdom. Most interesting are his instruments of power—a corps of accountants and auditors to oversee the financial system of the entire kingdom.

The Department of Accounting was assigned two officials of the second rank—a rank just below the prime minister. The staff of sixty-seven people was charged with conducting monthly and annual audits of all government agencies. Significantly, the rank of the royal treasurer was below that of the ministers in charge of accounts. This hierarchy was intentional, because the accounting office was responsible for overseeing the activities of the royal treasury. The treasury supervised the palace storehouses, the royal collection of jades and precious metals, and the currency of the state. The accounting office made sure that these riches were regularly counted and that all inflows and outflows of the treasury were documented and reviewed on a regular basis. Accounting in general was regularized by the prime minister on a calendar basis. According to the *Zhouli*, at the end of the year, the minister directed his one hundred superior officers to put their administrative activities in order. He received their accounts, examined their reports, and proposed removals and confirmations to the sovereign. Every three years, he undertook a major audit of the administration of all officials. He either punished or rewarded them.

Notice that this administrative process included not only dismissals and confirmations but also rewards and punishments—carrots and sticks. These rewards and punishments were based on audits of accounts on a periodic basis. Significantly, they were not based on assessments of the enlightenment of the official but on facts and figures, measurement and quantitative assessment.

Monitoring can be thought of as accounting: checking the numerical quantities of what goes into a bureaucrat's office and what comes out; making the official sign for goods received and obtain receipts for goods delivered; checking that all the people who work for the official actually show up; checking that the taxes and revenues collected by the official's office are used properly.

Among the many strange things about the *Zhouli* is that there is no clue about who wrote the book, when, or why. How much, if any, of the book was composed in the Zhou period is unknown. One suggestion about the origin of the book is that it may have been fabricated in the early part of the Han [漢] dynasty (206 BCE–220 CE) and used by the so-called usurper Wang Mang [王莽] to justify major political reforms. Wang Mang is sometimes regarded as China's first "socialist," because he freed slaves, stripped wealthy landowners of property, and eliminated debt. Wang justified these reforms by appealing to the golden age of antiquity—the Zhou. Although his rule was short lived, some of his themes resonated through Chinese history. One of the most significant economic events of the Han dynasty was the creation of the salt and iron monopolies—state ownership and control of two of China's most important enterprises. There was great debate in the Han over the role of private enterprise versus state ownership, and state ownership won.

The importance of the *Zhouli* is that it became a paradigm for the management of Chinese government for nearly 2,000 years. Its organizational structure provided a solution to the basic question of what a governing bureaucracy should look like and what checks and balances were needed to incentivize and oversee government officials. It even specified an active financial role for the government. The *Zhouli* is charged with some of the activities described in the *Guanzi*—including price stabilization. It is also the oldest Chinese text to describe government credit. In the *Zhouli*, the government served as lender, not borrower. The treasury ministry was authorized to extend short-term loans to ordinary subjects to cover emergency costs, such as those for funerals. The implication of the *Zhouli* is that the government, not private moneylenders, should be making loans.

PAPER MONEY, PUBLIC GOOD

Given its long tradition of understanding money as a medium of exchange and an instrument of the state, it is not surprising that paper money first appeared in China. However, the most interesting thing about the emergence of paper money is that it was not the first or the only paper security created to transfer value. Not only did China invent paper money, it also developed a complex system of paper instruments used to manage the financial affairs of the central state and its provinces. Paper instruments also played an important role in the economy of the Silk Road, the great mercantile network that linked East and West, and they functioned in a broader institutional context of contracts, contract laws, and property rights that, as we have seen from the ancient civilizations of the Near East and the eastern Mediterranean, were key requirements of a financial system. The story of these developments is the subject of this chapter.

The two great civilizations, Han China and the Roman Empire, were approximate contemporaries. While Rome was expanding east into the Levant, China during the Han expanded west along the Central Asian Silk Road. This growth was spurred as much by economics as by a quest for political control.

Chang'an [長安] and Luoyang [洛陽] were "twin" capitals of China during the Tang [唐] era (618–907 CE), a dynasty that followed the Han by four hundred years. Chang'an—now called Xi'an—was one of the greatest cities in the world at the time. Situated at the terminus of the Silk Road, Chang'an was laid out by the short-lived Sui [隋] dynasty in the late sixth century CE in a classic Chinese city plan—a rectangular walled city, encompassing thirty square miles, divided by 300-foot-wide avenues and crisscrossed by canals. Chang'an's imperial complex stood at the northern axis with a rational administrative structure: a department of state affairs with ministries of personnel administration, finance, religious rites, army, justice, and public works; a chancellery for imperial decrees; a grand secretariat in charge of policy; and a council of state to deal with China's increasing foreign affairs. Its cosmopolitan character was legendary—Muslims, Zoroastrians, and Nestorian Christians all had their own quarters in the capital.

Commerce in the capital city was carried on in two great centers: the eastern and western markets—walled commercial districts where exotic goods from all over the world were imported and sold. The western market was the center of trade for the silk route—thousands of shops lined its edges, and languages and cultures from all of Asia could be heard and seen. Six hundred yards on each side, the western market had more than two hundred licensed merchants. The Western market was Tang China's Wall Street. Financiers pawned goods, took deposits, honored checks, exchanged currencies, and made short-term loans.

While loans earlier in China's history appear to have been usurious, short-term, high-interest contracts, the proximity of the Tang money shops in the western market to commercial traders suggests that they must have made business loans, or at least provided commercial financial services. Commerce in the market was taxed by government officials and regulated by measurement offices and weigh stations.

REDISCOVERY OF THE SILK ROAD

In 1900, a daring scholar led an expedition from India, through the wilds of Afghanistan to "High Tartary," the barren landscapes of the ancient Silk Road. The intrepid Hungarian-born adventurer Aurel Stein is one of the most colorful and controversial figures in Central Asian archaeology. Despite the great political risks occasioned by the Chinese revolt and the shifting alliances of Central Asian states at the height of "The Great Game," Stein was determined to rediscover and excavate the legendary cities of the Silk Road that linked the Roman and Chinese empires. Leading a caravan of camels like the Silk Road entrepreneurs of 2,000 years ago, Stein and his co-adventurers traced the southern route of the ancient track around the Takla Makan Desert, through Khotan [和田] to the deserted ancient city of Dandan-Uiliq [丹丹乌里克], an abandoned metropolis where three great cultures once came together in the mutual pursuit of commerce: Chinese, Indian, and Central Asian.

As hard as it may be to imagine now, this remote city in the heart of Central Asia, perched at the edge of the desert, was once a cosmopolitan, multilingual city. While the outlines of the ancient city were still evident to the excavators, and houses, temples, towers, and walls still survived after millennia, the truly exciting discoveries were documents. Everywhere the excavators looked, they found evidence of written culture: Buddhist religious texts written in Sanskrit, Chinese letters and notes, and what have come to be understood as texts written in the now-dead Tocharian languages of Central Asia. The following year Stein pushed on to the nearby ancient city of Niya [尼雅], where he found even richer and better-preserved documents—rolls of Indian script on parchment, abandoned where they lay nearly two millennia ago.

Stein's expeditions showed that the Silk Road was an information highway as much as it was a commercial one. With merchants traveling great distances, living in foreign cities, taking orders from people who spoke and wrote different languages, and worshipping different gods, the Silk Road became a prime vector in the transmission of knowledge and culture across the continent, including writing systems. Writing—sometimes on wood, parchment, palm leaves, and eventually on paper—served as a primary information medium.

Aurel Stein's greatest discovery was also his most controversial. In 1907, he followed Marco Polo's account of his journey across the great Lop Desert into a region now known as the Tarim Basin. This route proved to be extraordinarily profitable. The expedition trekked its way into the oasis of Dunhuang [敦煌]. From there, Stein went to visit the legendary Caves of 1,000 Buddhas, a sanctuary of elaborately painted shrines cut into the living rock and guarded by giant Tang-era statues of the Buddha. The site itself had been visited by religious pilgrims since the fourth century CE. The true prize for Stein, however, was a hidden and carefully guarded chamber containing the archives of the shine since its inception. Stein suspected that this trove of documents might be the elusive prize of his career—the records of the passage of Buddhism and Indian culture along the ancient Silk Road into China. Stein was able to secure a large number of these documents through bribery—in all, five horse-loads of material. It was everything he could have hoped for: a unique archive of religious texts; the earliest dating from the fifth century CE. Much of Stein's Dunhuang trove is now in the British Library. Later document hunters also managed to buy Dunhuang materials, and now many of these early texts are preserved in museums around the world. It is, of course, a mixed blessing. It is wonderful that they are in the hands of skilled archivists and broadly accessible to scholars, but unfortunate that they are not in their original context, and that one of China's greatest historical treasures has been dispersed. Nevertheless, the tumultuous history of early modern China makes one wonder if Stein's removal of the documents was fortuitous.

Stein returned again to the Silk Road. His 1915 expedition to western China focused on the Turfan [吐魯番] region. The highlight of the expedition was the discovery of the Astana [阿斯塔那] graveyard, a dune-covered city of the dead, where ancient Asian people were buried with elaborate grave goods. Once again, the desiccated atmosphere preserved almost everything—from strange paper-covered coffins to little pastries that the deceased took with them into the afterlife.

Some of the most elaborate of these graves included personal libraries and artwork—beautifully decorated figurines depicting scenes of life from the Tang era: among them, musicians, dancers, and entertainers. Although he excavated large portions of the Astana graveyard, Stein left a lot for archaeologists of later generations. Modern Chinese excavators have been working the Astana site now for decades and have been fortunate to find a number of well-preserved tombs from the Tang era. In one of these, they found a marvelous set of figurines, made partially of ceramics, cloth, and paper. Manufactured in the capital city of Chang'an and apparently shipped out to the frontier, these figurines held a curious secret. Their arms were made of spindled scrap paper, collected in the capital city and later reused by artisans. It is perhaps ironic that the richest woman in China today is entrepreneur Zhang Yin [張茵], who amassed a multibillion-dollar fortune by collecting and reprocessing American scrap paper. The Astana figurines tell us that Chinese entrepreneurs have been making money this way for more than a millennium. The important thing about the Astana figurine paper, however, is what it was first used for. Each separate sheet represents the record of a transaction in a seventh-century Chinese pawnshop.

Yale historian Valerie Hansen, with her student Ana Mata-Fink, made a study of a set of these extraordinary financial documents.[3] Few business records from Chang'an have survived from this early period, because paper is so perishable. Only the chance that these tickets were reused and shipped off to a desert city caused their preservation. Indeed, one fascinating question yet unanswered is how paper first came to be used in China for business records and transactions. We know that bamboo records were the early form of recording contracts, but after its invention, paper at some point became a financial recording medium. Hansen is a world expert on the commerce of the Silk Road. A Yale professor who lives with her family on the Connecticut shore and teaches classes in Chinese history, she specializes in the analysis of ancient Chinese contracts. The pawnshop tickets are interesting because of the concrete links they provide to finance.

Hansen and Mata-Fink were able to trace the origin of the tickets to the capital, Chang'an. Each ticket recorded prosaic records of portable wealth—anything that had value for resale apparently was potentially useful as security for a short-term loan. Most interestingly, the tickets contained three place names actually known from ancient Chang'an: Yanxing gate [延興門], Guanyin Monastery [觀音寺], and the Shengdao quarter [昇道坊]. These addresses would place the pawnshop in a neighborhood near the southeast corner of ancient Chang'an, perhaps one or two miles from the eastern market. The scholars were able to effectively triangulate the location of a loan operation in the ancient Chinese capital and document the way that the pawnshop was used. The pawnbrokers clients were not particularly well off, and most of what they tendered were worn pieces of clothing—an old yellow cloth shirt, a decorated scarf, a purple cape, a silk jacket, the frayed lining of an official's headdress, and ragged sandals. Occasionally there were some precious items: a bolt of silk, a bronze mirror, and four strings of pearls. The borrowers were generally illiterate. Instead of signing these contracts, they marked lines measuring their knuckles. Some tickets tell of interest payments:

> Cui Jin, on the 19th day of the first month of the lunar year received 100 coins. The 7th day of the 6th month of the lunar year he paid 40 coins towards the principal and 9 coins in interest. The silk was given to Cui who took it away. Redeemed, the 18th day of the 7th month of the lunar year. Lives in East head 20 years old.[4]

Who was the young Cui Jin, and why did he need one hundred coins? Was it worth 9% interest over half a year to borrow this amount? The terse receipts do not say, but the rate of interest in the Tang capital city seems somewhat less than 20% per year. This is also borne out by another loan made on the day following Cui's. Wang Shuai received forty coins and paid down fifteen in principal four months later. He also paid two coins in interest, suggesting roughly a 15% annualized discount rate. High, perhaps, but hardly usury. The pawn tickets from Astana tell us that Tang China had a well-functioning system of personal credit with moderate rates of interest. In this system, mobile goods, particularly clothing, represented wealth. When in need, a jacket, shoes, or pearls could be hypothecated and thus converted into hard currency. While it is easy to criticize the emergence of consumerism, a secondary market for status items (and a financial system that takes such items in pledge) reveals another side to materialism—it can be a store of value. Indeed, unlike cash, durable goods when well maintained seem to have served as a hedge against inflation. Pawnshops were a technology that created liquidity—and they relied on paper as the prime medium of record and contracting. Not long after it was created, paper was put to more widespread use in the Chinese financial system.

FLYING MONEY

The Tang dynasty was famous for its canals and highways that facilitated commercial traffic and linked the capital to remote provinces. To maintain strong relations with the central government, Chinese provinces maintained chancelleries, or "memorial offering bureaus," in the capital city. Something like modern lobbying offices, they served the provincial governments' interests and that of their subjects. Under the Tang dynasty, chancelleries began to function like transfer banks. Merchants—like tea merchants from Sichuan [四川]—sold goods in the capital and then deposited their profits with the provincial chancellery, which wrote them receipts termed *feiqian* [飛錢] or "flying money," so called because the money could "fly" back to the province without being carried overland. The *feiqian* consisted of two parts: one half was held by the merchant, and the other matching part was held by the bureau. When both were returned to the province, the merchant would present his half of the receipt to the governmental office for full payment. The chancelleries liked the system, because it provided them with ready cash to meet expenses in the capital. The merchants liked the system, because it relieved them of the risks and expenses of transporting hard currency. It kept copper cash from gravitating to the province; it increased the money supply in the country's commercial center; and perhaps most importantly, it served as an interest-free loan to the provincial agencies. Chancelleries had the use of the cash until the merchant returned to the province to present the certificate—occasionally merchants would find their government reluctant to promptly redeem *feiqian*. Not surprisingly, other government agencies, like the finance ministry and the army, competed to offer similar services.

None of the Tang *feiqian* have survived, so we cannot read them to see whether they were negotiable notes, were dated, came in standard denominations, or had other features that could teach us more about how they were used and the economic and financial role they played in Chinese society. While we do not know whether *feiqian* were negotiable, it is hard to imagine that they were not assigned or transferred by merchants, and in that sense they could have functioned as money. Nevertheless, it is unlikely they were printed as money. There is an interesting story about this, however. The American collector and financial historian Andrew McFarland Davis purchased a number of Tang era bills in the early twentieth century, images of which he published in a book titled *On Certain Chinese Notes, Deposited in the Boston Museum of Fine Art*. Nowhere to be found today, in all likelihood Davis's discoveries were recent forgeries. They did not fit the description of flying money— they looked suspiciously like printed paper notes from a later era.

A PAPER SOCIETY

The Tang dynasty lasted until 907 CE. Once again in Chinese history, a weakened central government fell to centrifugal provincial forces. Some part of the imperial family and its retinue fled to the southwestern province of Sichuan, a mountainous and verdant region at the headwaters of the Yangzi River. Sichuan after the Tang dynasty existed as a separate kingdom called the Shu until it was eventually brought to heel and incorporated into China in the late tenth century with the reunification of the country under the Song [宋] dynasty.

The Song dynasty (960–1279 CE) is one of the most widely admired periods of Chinese history—it is sometimes called the Chinese Renaissance. All the high arts flourished: poetry, theater, painting, calligraphy, gardening, music, and architecture. The low arts also fared well. Song cities abounded in acrobats, circus performers, storytellers, puppeteers, dance troupes, and restaurateurs. Song science was the most advanced in the world for its time, in such fields as metallurgy, botany, astronomy, archaeology, agronomy, and chemistry. Scholars included encyclopedists, historians, and philosophers, some of whom taught in academies and others of whom worked for the government: bureaucrats were expected to be cultured as well as wise. Officials were promoted according to merit and performance on national exams rather than by patronage and contacts. Commerce as well as the arts flourished in the Song. Merchants were a respected class whose activities were no longer confined to market districts as they had been under the Tang. They plied their trade widely through the city. The capital of the Northern Song, Kaifeng [開封], probably numbered a half-million at its peak.

One of the most important developments in the Song was the technological development of paper making and printing. In part because national examinations were the basis for appointment and promotion to government posts, literacy was widespread—books were published and sold in bookstores, and even relatively poor students had access to the Chinese classics of literature and mathematics. In what has been called an "examination hell," students from all over China were tested relentlessly on their memorization of the classics—a task that was estimated by historian Benjamin Elman to have taken six years of memorization at the rate of 200 characters a day.[5]

Today we talk about an evolution toward a paperless society in which information is stored and communicated through electronic media. The revolution in Song China that introduced the pervasive use of paper must have been no less radical a development. Paper culture clearly had its roots in the Tang—as evidenced by the paper pawnshop slips studied by Hansen and Mata-Fink, and the use of flying money certificates. However, the Song was a period of extraordinary invention with respect to the possibilities of paper as a medium to store and cheaply disseminate information.

Paper was adopted as a primary instrument of state finance. Song paper money was the first item ever printed with four-color copper plates—the same technology used today to print color books. Song mulberry bark paper—developed and perfected in Sichuan, where mulberry trees were used in the silk industry—became the first durable medium for bills that could be passed from hand to hand and could circulate for years. Financial innovation relies on the technology of documentation, recording, and contracting. Along with the Mesopotamian invention of clay tablets and the apparently simultaneous Eurasian discovery of metallic coinage, the Chinese development of metal-plate printing on durable paper is one of the most enduring legacies of financial innovation.

HEAVY CASH

Despite being a golden age of Chinese culture, the Song was also a period during which the country fought a constant and ultimately losing battle against rival states, particularly the steppe peoples to the north and west—the Mongols and related groups. This political context is no less important to the evolution of paper currency as printing technology. Even as it flourished culturally, whole regions of the Song were militarized buffer zones, where armies stood on alert, and troops were constantly garrisoned, fed, and supported by local economies. Although the Song was militarily unified by assembling the disjoint earlier provinces of the Tang, its greatest challenge was not holding the new union together but resisting invading forces. The Song dynasty is divided into two eras, Northern Song and Southern Song, because half the country—including the beautiful capital of Kaifeng—fell to invaders in 1126, and the imperial capital moved south.

During the Song, Sichuan was one of China's most important buffer provinces—isolated as it was in the far west, exposed on three sides to invaders, it represented China's main military front. It had a strange feature in its economy, dating to the time it was incorporated into the Chinese state—it used iron money. Sichuan's iron money created problems—it was heavy and difficult to use. Merchants preferred copper currency, but its use was forbidden. Mandated use of iron currency was not a penalty imposed on Sichuan but an attempt by the government dynasty to prevent its precious copper coinage from flowing out to the countries of the west—the states of Jin and Tibet, with whom China was also occasionally at war. Perhaps attempting to use the *Guanzi* principles of light and heavy and allow the invisible hand of the market to attract cash from abroad, the ministers of the Chinese Financial Agency continued to mint coins out of the heavier metal. The only problem was that, while iron had intrinsic value, it was not quite valuable enough. Simple shopping required several pounds of change. Merchants trading in Sichuan had to check their copper currency at the border and exchange it for iron.

The low value of the iron coinage is attributable in part to the low intrinsic value of iron, but it was also likely due to the government issuing too much of it. Chinese imperial coinage in this era was effectively fiat money—government issue coins were legal tender by decree, not because they contained a specific amount of base metal. In effect, it cost the government less to buy the iron and mint the coins than its stated face value. The invisible hand adjusts prices and quantities: in Sichuan at this time, a pound of salt cost a pound and a half of Sichuan iron coins. The problem of iron coinage sparked one of the most important financial innovations in the history of the world: paper money.

In 993 CE, rebels seized Chengdu [成都], the capital of Sichuan, and shut down the mint, creating a shortage of coin but evidently also partly reversing the depreciating value of the currency in circulation. In response to this local monetary crisis, merchants in Chengdu began to issue paper currency. According to the leading historian of Chinese monetary history, Richard Von Glahn, there is little surviving information about this monetary crisis. However, it is tempting to speculate on the economic impetus to substitute paper for iron coinage. With the mint closed, the uncertainty about future metallic money supply would certainly have induced a commercial demand for change and innovative solutions, such as the issuance of paper notes. Such shortages would also have created a motivation to maintain less than 100% reserves to back paper notes. Von Glahn observes that such temptations led to a "proliferation of numerous sundry private bills, many issued by unscrupulous entrepreneurs [which] resulted in widespread abuse and a surge of lawsuits."[6]

After the rebellion was put down, the government stepped in. In 1005, the prefect of Chengdu, Zhang Yong [張詠], took steps to regularize the issue of the notes, limit the merchants authorized to issue them, and resume the minting of iron money. Only sixteen merchant houses were granted a monopoly on the printing of promissory notes called *jiaozi* [交子]. Customers could deposit strings of iron cash and in return received a jiaozi paper receipt that participating merchants would take in payment in lieu of cash. These deposit houses were called *guifang* [櫃坊]. These first receipts were partially printed, with blank slots—like modern checks—that could be filled in with the amount of the deposit. When a customer wanted to get burdensome iron cash back—perhaps to pay taxes—he or she could redeem it from the original merchant, or from any of the participating businesses, since they had all agreed on the rules for these receipts. There were fees for redemptions, and the issuing merchants used some stamp or design to indicate which house issued the bill. Presumably this would allow the redeeming house to demand transfer of specie from the issuing house. The notes were of one uniform design printed in black and red ink from wooden blocks, and, according to Von Glahn, had pictures of people or buildings. None of these private notes have survived from the Song dynasty. However, the intent of the elaborate design is obvious—the government had to stay one step ahead of the counterfeiters. In a society in which the technology of printing was widespread, an ingenious printer could turn mulberry bark into treasure.

A CURRENCY CRISIS

For a time, the private guifang functioned well. With the paper bills, people rarely bothered to redeem their cash, and it sat idle but secure in the storehouses of the Chengdu merchants. Perhaps it sat too idle, because unfortunately, it appears someone cheated. Some merchants were slow about honoring redemptions. We do not know whether one of them gave in to temptation and simply took the cash or whether a counterfeiter presented fake bills for redemption. Whatever triggered it, the private system came down with a crash, requiring a government bailout. In the year 1016, the Chinese government revoked the private monopoly on paper money in Sichuan and nationalized the printing of currency. In 1023, it established a bureau of exchange medium, *Jiaozi wu* [交子務], and began to issue notes with cash reserves equal to about 30%.

If there were profit to be made on the float, it would be government profit. These new issues were standardized according to denomination and were printed in a special government printing office in a suburb of the city. Perhaps the rebellion of the previous generation taught the government the importance of separating the locus of production from densely populated areas. From 1160 on the state monopolized paper money issuance. The jiaozi notes of a few decades later (1111 CE) may have represented the high point in the design and printing of paper bills. Four copper plates were used to print the basic text and denominations, and then two color plates—blue and red—were used to print decorative designs. The issue for the year 1161 carried the aphorism "Attaining wealth also enriches the realm" (*Zhi fu guo cai bing* 至富國財並)—an interesting echo of the Qi knife coin inscription. A golden cock holding an inscription was printed in blue, and the red plate printed an oval device picturing a wisteria—the emblem of long life. A dragon and a tortoise bearing charts and documents also appeared in black ink, and on the reverse of the largest of these denominations, the 500 wen bill, was printed the poetic phrase "Wang Xiaoxiang [王孝祥] is moved by the leaping carp and flying sparrow."

The practice of printing paper money spread slowly from Sichuan to other parts of China. For a time, the use of paper currency was confined to the southern provinces and was forbidden in the north, perhaps because much of China's international commerce took place through the southern provinces. Song notes have not survived; however, money from the successor dynasty, the Yuan [元], has.

As important as paper money was, it should also be understood in the broader context of the Song paper culture. The jiaozi and later notes were by no means the only form of paper certificates, vouchers, and money. China's salt monopoly in particular became a central operation in the new financial configuration of the Chinese state. Rights to purchase and resell salt were licensed by the state in the form of vouchers. Like modern-day baseball tickets, these vouchers were "scalped"—that is, a secondary market developed for salt tickets, and people began to use them like money. Perhaps the best modern analogy to salt vouchers is not baseball tickets, but pollution-rights certificates issued by governments. The US Environmental Protection Agency began a program to auction off allowances for emissions of sulfur dioxide in 1993, and made them tradable. The modern concept of pollution rights is that the government has a monopoly on the legal amount of pollution that a power plant is allowed to emit. Plants get vouchers for these rights, and they can use them or sell them. The plants for which the pollution rights represent the highest economic value eventually buy the most vouchers—thus the market allocates the rights in the most efficient manner. The net amount of pollution in the air is fixed no matter who used them, but the power production per unit of pollution in the issuing country is maximized. In the interim, vouchers can change hands many times. Speculators with no intention of running a power plant can step in and buy them with the expectation of selling them in the future when prices go up. Eventually they are bought and used by companies that need them, but not until the market has conferred on them the marginal economic value of one more unit of pollution.

The same principles applied to the salt monopoly vouchers, only instead of pollution rights, these were salt sale rights. They had value as long as there was a supply of salt to buy and sell. A canny speculator could amass a bunch of the vouchers and hold them in anticipation of salt price increases. However, when floods destroyed the salt pans, the right to sell salt that did not exist was worth little. Despite such risks, the salt business was largely predictable, and profits were regulated to such an extent that the vouchers had a reliable economic value. As a consequence, there were long stretches of time in the Song dynasty when salt vouchers functioned as paper money. In some sense, they were complex commodity futures that functioned as a medium of exchange.

FIGURE 16. A paper certificate from the Song dynasty that functioned as a means of payment for military supplies.

TRAVELING MONEY

Stephen Ross is a finance professor at the Massachusetts Institute of Technology and is one of the creators of modern financial theory. Among many other things, he developed the basic theoretical framework of the principal-agent problem. He is also a good friend of mine who shares an interest in China. One day I was visiting his office and I idly glanced at a document framed on his wall. I realized, to my surprise, that I could read some of the Chinese characters. I could make out the characters for "money" and a couple of characters that seemed to read "Great Song" (i.e., the name of the Song dynasty). Another character in the title read "cash." "Cash" . . . "Song"—"cash Song". . . . Here was a document I had seen on Steve's wall for years but had never paid close attention to. Only after I had begun studying Chinese financial history did I look at the piece more closely. With all of my research into early financial contracts, could it be that right in front of my nose was a previously undiscovered piece of Chinese money from the Song? This launched me on a quest to learn all I could about this ancient document.

I worked closely on the analysis of the document with Elisabeth Köll, a professor of Chinese history. We learned that the piece is another type of voucher; a requisition form used during the Song dynasty by government officials. Like early paper money, not only does it have a stated face value, but it also has blanks for dates and the name of the official spending it. The bill is printed on thin paper—not the durable mulberry bark medium of contemporaneous paper money. Instead of pictures of a string of cash—or even the motifs of golden cocks, dragons, or turtles—it bears an image of a flying horse. It is titled "spending money in the service of the people." Dated to 1208 CE, it carried a cash value of 500 wen [文] (the standard unit of currency in China prior to modern times—equivalent to one copper coin). The government authority that issued it was an army agency stationed in Sichuan.

This curious piece brings home the immediacy of Song China's military crisis in the early thirteenth century. A separate voucher system developed to facilitate the provisioning of the border armies. Procurement officers used vouchers like this to pay for requisitioned goods on the military frontier. The document says that the bill is good for 500 wen, and it is not endorsed to a particular person, so presumably it is a bearer security—a document that could be presented for payment by anyone who held it. The fact that it is printed on thin paper suggests that it was meant to be promptly redeemed rather than change hands repeatedly like paper money. The distinguishing feature of the voucher as a financial tool is the space for the name of the official and the date. Presumably this feature allowed government auditors to review and total up all the expenditures by requisition officers, and to hold these officers accountable for how they spent government money. Thus, the voucher's importance is not simply that it is a surviving financial document from Chinese history, but that is represents an alternative financial technology to freely circulating money or commodity-based instruments like salt monopoly certificates. Elisabeth Köll and I have argued that this voucher represents an alternative payment system to the use of universally circulating paper money, a system depending on a government-controlled economy as opposed to a free market economy. It represented monetary value that could be traced back to specific issuing officials. While the government might subject officials to strenuous examinations and hold them to the highest Confucian moral standards, the requirement that they actually sign and date their checks means that the Chinese bureaucracy functioned on verification as much as on trust.

WANG ANSHI AND GOVERNMENT EXPROPRIATION

Wang Anshi [王安石] is one of the most colorful figures in Chinese history. A product of a Chinese educational system that emphasized erudition as well as bureaucratic competency, Wang is now remembered as one of the Song dynasty's greatest poets as well as one of its most controversial political figures. He was a public-sector entrepreneur who sought to redirect the profits of private enterprise for the good of the state. Serving in the government of the Song, Wang took note of the profiteers who benefited from the country's perpetual state of frontier warfare—with the movement of commodities and the constant demand for such resources as horses for the cavalry, the state found itself at the mercy of the private sector for supplies. When he became the emperor Shenzhong's [神宗] chief advisor in 1069, he promulgated a series of dramatic economic reforms that effectively expropriated large portions of the Chinese economy for the state. In clear reference to the ancient minister Guan Zhong, Wang sought to wrest control of the price system, the ratios of exchange (*qingzhong*) from the private sector, to ensure the smooth flow of resources throughout the empire.

Like his ancient predecessor, Wang also saw the government control of the price system as a means to economically benefit the state. The Tea and Horse Agency (*Cha ma si* 茶馬司) grew to great power under Wang's rule. It exploited the strong demand for tea to finance the constant need to purchase horses from the Tibetan frontier to fight the encroachment of the barbarian armies to the north.[7]

Powerful merchants profited from state privilege and concessions in the tea and horse trade before Wang's reform, but under Wang, the state cut out the intermediary—creating a business in the government to capture profits for the state. Small wonder that Wang's reforms are sometimes interpreted as an early form of socialism. Wang also set up agencies to make loans to peasants at low rates—20%—a move that also put the government in direct competition with the private financial sector. The demands of the state, particularly on the front lines of battle, at times effectively crowded out private commerce. During this period, China was in frequent conflict with the Xi Xia [西夏] state to the west. Chinese soldiers had to be fed and quartered, and horses and transportation had to be purchased, regardless of the state's financial position.

Wang's crusade against private enterprise did not eliminate the quest for profit, but rather it replaced private sector with public sector, maintaining enterprise but channeling its benefits through the central government—the "single source." Rents accrue to the government as the great equalizer and steward of the flow of trade. Enterprise was fine, as long as it was controlled and regulated and validated from above. During this period, a substantial portion of state revenue came from national monopolies on tea, salt, and alcohol. Although Wang was eventually dismissed in 1074 (ironically as a result of overzealous pursuit of bankrupt borrowers from the state), he had a brief return to power but finally resigned in 1076. Some of his visionary plans were scrapped in the next decade. However, the fundamental theme of economic expropriation by the state, legitimized by his clever use of Chinese history and ancient precedent—from invocations of the *Guanzi* to adaptations of the *Zhouli*—became part of the new lexicon of Chinese government rule. He may not have been the first to introduce the use of financial engineering in the service of the central state, but few politicians refined it as well as he did, using timeless and familiar populist rhetoric.

CHINESE INNOVATION THROUGH WESTERN EYES

Although it may be difficult for us today to imagine a world without paper money, we have a rare opportunity to see how wondrous this financial innovation appeared to a contemporary foreign observer. There is some doubt whether the thirteenth-century Venetian trader Marco Polo ever traveled east of the Black Sea. Polo's fabulous account was told to and written down by the medieval novelist Rusticello while both were imprisoned in Genoa. The book relates the tale of Marco Polo's travels to China and of serving the Emperor Genghis Khan. It may have been constructed from stories he heard from other Silk Road traders—a pastiche of anecdotes into which he inserted himself as a great advisor to the emperor, entrusted with the rule of an entire Chinese city. However, the immediacy of one part of the book—his account of how money was made from the bark of trees—directly or indirectly conveys the European amazement at first acquaintance with fiat money. I quote it in full:

How the Great Khan Causes the Bark of Trees, Made into Something Like Paper, to Pass for Money All over His Country.

Now that I have told you in detail of the splendor of this city of the emperor's, I shall proceed to tell you of the mint which he has in the same city, in the which he has his money coined and struck, as I shall relate to you. And in doing so I shall make manifest to you how it is that the great Lord may well be able to accomplish even much more than I have told you, or am going to tell you in this book. For, tell it how I might, you never would be satisfied that I was keeping within truth and reason!

The emperor's mint then is in this same city of Cambaluc, and the way it is wrought is such that you might say he has the secret of alchemy in perfection, and you would be right. For he makes his money after this fashion. He makes them take of the bark of a certain tree, in fact of the mulberry tree, the leaves of which are the food of the silkworms, these trees being so numerous that the whole districts are full of them. What they take is a certain fine white bast or skin which lies between the wood of the tree and the thick outer bark, and this they make into something resembling sheets of paper, but black. When these sheets have been prepared they are cut up into pieces of different sizes.

All these pieces of paper are issued with as much solemnity and authority as if they were of pure gold or silver; and on every piece a variety of officials, whose duty it is, have to write their names, and to put their seals. And when all is prepared duly, the chief officer deputed by the Khan smears the seal entrusted to him with vermilion, and impresses it on the paper, so that the form of the seal remains imprinted upon it in red; the money is then authentic. Anyone forging it would be punished with death. And the Khan causes every year to be made such a vast quantity of this money, which costs him nothing, that it must equal in amount all the treasure of the world.

With these pieces of paper, made as I have described, he causes all payments on his own account to be made; and he makes them to pass current universally over all his kingdoms and provinces and territories, and whithersoever his power and sovereignty extends. And nobody, however important he may think himself, dares to refuse them on pain of death. And indeed everybody takes them readily, for wheresoever a person may go throughout the great Khan's dominions he shall find these pieces of paper current, and shall be able to transact all sales and purchases of goods by means of them just as well as if they were coins of pure gold.

Furthermore all merchants arriving from India or other countries, and bringing with them gold or silver or gems and pearls, are prohibited from selling to anyone but the emperor. He has twelve experts chosen for this business, men of shrewdness and experience in such affairs; these appraise the articles, and the emperor then pays a liberal price for them in those pieces of paper. The merchants accept his price readily, for in the first place they would not get so good a one from anybody else, and secondly they are paid without any delay. And with this paper money they can buy what they like anywhere over the empire, while it is also vastly lighter to carry about on their journeys. . . . So he buys such a quantity of those precious things every year that his treasure is endless, while all the time the money he pays away costs him nothing at all. Moreover, several times in the year proclamation is made through the city that anyone who may have gold or silver or gems or pearls, by taking them to the mint shall get a handsome price for them. And the owners are glad to do this, because they would find no other purchaser gives so large a price. Thus the quantity they bring in is marvelous, though those who do not choose to do so may let it alone. Still, in this way, nearly all the valuables in the country come into the Khan's possession.

When any of those pieces of paper are spoilt—not that they are so very flimsy neither [sic]—the owner carries them to the mint, and by paying three per cent on the value he gets new pieces in exchange. And if any baron, or anyone else soever, hath need of gold or silver or gems or pearls, in order to make plate, or girdles, or the like, he goes to the mint and buys as much as he list, paying in this paper money.

Now that you have heard the ways and means whereby the great Khan may have, and in fact has, more treasure than all the kings in the world; and you know all about it and the reason why.[8]

Marco Polo's account is more than a report on the making of paper money. It describes a monetary system carefully regulated by the central government and used as an economic instrument of policy. By forcing the conversion of precious goods into paper money, the emperor effectively interrupted private commerce. The paper money served not only as a circulating medium of exchange but also as a means to certify and legitimize the capital of foreign merchants operating in China. It was also, obviously, a means to tax commerce. The description of the redemption process of pearls and precious materials by the populace is also instructive. Notice that the government set the redemption price higher than the prevailing market prices to motivate redemption—a ploy straight from the millennium-old *Guanzi*.

By the time of Marco Polo, the glorious, civilized, aesthetically rich Song dynasty had fallen to the barbarian invaders. The new Mongol rulers brought their own system of governance—sometimes including the placement of foreign overlords above local Chinese officials. Genghis Khan saw the benefits, however, of continuing the use of fiat money. He continued to print bills modeled on the Song precedent and continued the practice of inflationary spending. When the Yuan dynasty fell to the Ming in the late fourteenth century, the use—and abuse—of paper money continued.

FINANCIAL DIVERGENCE

Joseph Needham devoted much of his life to the publication of a series of volumes detailing China's extraordinary scientific achievements. *Science and Civilization in China* is unquestionably one of the greatest publications of the twentieth century. Its intent is to systematically document the mathematical, scientific, and engineering achievements of ancient China. From Needham's original volume published in 1956, the series has now grown to seventeen volumes, spanning mathematics, physics, engineering, printing, chemistry, military technology, the technics of textile manufacture, mining, botany and biological sciences, agricultural science, medicine, and logics. The continuing publication of *Science and Civilization in China* is managed by the Needham Institute at Cambridge. Over the half-century of its creation, the series has almost single-handedly caused a re-evaluation of a Western-oriented history of civilization. The sheer volume and detail of Chinese scientific and technical knowledge from the centuries before direct contact with Europe makes it virtually impossible to argue that Western societies were the world's sole source of light and truth. *Science and Civilization in China* demands at the very least a bicultural perspective, and it further implies that whatever may have made European culture special in the second millennium, it was not superior scientific and technical know-how.

Indeed, as the evidence of Chinese scientific knowledge continued to grow with each published volume of the series, Joseph Needham himself began to wonder why the Industrial Revolution occurred in Europe rather than in China. If Song Chinese scientists were so clever and their technologies of production so efficient, why did this not lead to a technological takeoff as witnessed in nineteenth-century Europe and America, in which technical innovations seemed to suddenly compound on themselves? In the span of a single lifetime (the 1820s to the First World War),

Joseph Needham, historian of science. He posed the puzzle of the great divergence between China and the West in the eighteenth and nineteenth centuries.

the transportation system in Europe rapidly evolved from horse-drawn carriages to canals to railroads to automobiles to the beginnings of air transportation. Over the same period, lighting in Europe and America evolved from oil lamps to gaslight to electricity. High-speed communication began as a postal system, developed into a trans-Atlantic telegraph system, then rapidly mutated to a radio and telephonic system. For each one of these amazing technological developments, Needham and the other authors of *Science and Civilization in China* are able to point to some feature of Chinese science that could have led to a similar development. For example, Chinese hydraulic engineers created the world's most extensive system of canals, and they were the world's leaders in iron mining and metallurgy. They understood steam power. Why didn't China develop the world's first steam-powered rail system? Why were James Watt, Robert Fulton, and Alexander Graham Bell not Chinese? How could China have been so far ahead of the rest of the world technologically (and for that matter, as we have seen from this chapter—bureaucratically) and yet have stumbled on the eve of the greatest technical transformation in world history, the Industrial Revolution?

One simple answer is chance. Watt, Fulton, and Bell were rare geniuses. Perhaps the Industrial Revolution was a random confluence of genius at a certain moment of history; a genetic "sport." The counterargument to the chance theory is articulated by Chinese economist Justin Lin.[1] Lin points out that nothing follows the rules of probability like genetic variation. The chance of a towering genius being born is a function of population size, and no country in the world had more people during the Song dynasty than China. An extension of that argument is that genius needs to be nurtured and exposed to interesting problems. The Chinese educational system was nothing if not egalitarian; although one might question whether Thomas Edison would have had time to play with electricity if he had taken six years out of his life to memorize the Chinese classics. Certainly, the density of Chinese cities in the Song would have led to creative knowledge spillover of the sort that would stimulate innovation. So Lin demonstrates that chance alone could not explain the difference.

A number of brilliant scholars have taken a crack at solving what has become known as "the Needham Puzzle." Lin explains it by introduction of the scientific method of experimentation in the West, which, in effect served to systematically speed up, organize, and make optimal use of random processes of discovery. In his view, it was the development of the scientific method that made the difference.

Another is the sustained success of Chinese civilization itself. The financial solutions described in Part II of this book make it clear that China had successfully solved myriad complex problems involving planning, resource allocation, and risk mitigation. It took its own path to monetization and market developments. Historian Mark Elvin argues that Song China fell victim to a "high equilibrium trap." Its agricultural advances around the first millennium were so successful that there was no apparent need for further innovation. In contrast, Europe started from a lower level of development and thus had greater need for radical technological change.

University of California professor Kenneth Pomeranz has proposed yet another particularly radical idea—geographical determinism. He argues that Chinese natural resources were not configured appropriately for efficient exploitation. The great sources of ore in China do not occur near good riverine transportation routes. The landscape itself held China back from intensive industrialization.

What all these explanations ignore is the supporting role of finance in technological development. Technology requires genius, but it also requires capital. Railroads need financing to build tracks and rolling stock. However, if successful, these investments can pay for themselves. Entrepreneurs need motivation to keep experimenting when their peers are working a steady job—patents and legal protection allow the former to capitalize on their innovations. If an entrepreneur faces state expropriation of his or her innovation, it makes little sense to invest in the human capital required. Capital markets and the protection of intellectual property rights can serve as cofactors in sustaining entrepreneurial motivation and capital investment. While the centralized Chinese government had the capacity to reward individuals for creating new technologies, it typically did not simply allow the market to provide financing for new ideas.

There are of course exceptions. Columbia University professor Madeleine Zelin showed that a capital market for shares in salt mining operations emerged in Sichuan province in the late eighteenth and early nineteenth centuries in a form that echoes modern share capitalism.[2]

Kenneth Pomeranz has studied an agricultural company from the same period in Chinese history that brought together the capital from multiple investors.[3] So entrepreneurs in China occasionally found ways of using corporate-like structures and securities trading to finance enterprise. Thus, perhaps the differences in financial development were more a matter of scale and widespread application as opposed to fundamental constraints. In a quest for the solution to the Needham Puzzle, the financial cofactor deserves serious consideration.

At least one leading historian of the Industrial Revolution has argued that the financial system of Europe in the nineteenth century was an essential cofactor. The Industrial Revolution resulted in rising income inequality in Europe and a shift in income toward investors. Robert Allen is one of the leading economic historians of technology. In his 2005 study of rising inequality in the British Industrial Revolution, he writes: "The shift of income to capitalists was necessary in order to provide the savings needed to implement the new factory methods . . . it was the rising share of profits that induced the savings that met the demand for capital and allowed output to expand."[4] In short, a financial system that could reward investors with profits—albeit at the expense of rising inequality—induced further investment and sustained technological development. As will be discussed in Part III, the process to develop a system that rewards investment was a long and complex one and it took place principally in Europe.

The most telling evidence is that the differential in financial development between China and the West preceded the differences in technological advancement. European financial markets did not suddenly spring up with the invention of the steam engine and the mechanization of manufacturing processes. By the time of the Industrial Revolution in Europe, commercial banks and organized securities exchanges had existed for at least two centuries. When nineteenth-century railway companies wanted to raise capital to lay track and build cars, they had access to a pre-existing widespread class of investors who were accustomed to paying good money for future promised cash flows—there was a demand for investment opportunity and the structural know-how to create products that met this demand. In contrast, China had fewer organized means to bring private investors with capital together with enterprises having technological advantage. In short, despite having vast, organized marketplaces for goods and commodities, China had less well-developed capital markets.

If the great industrial divergence between East and West in the nineteenth century was preceded and potentially explained in part by a financial divergence, how, when, and why did this happen? How could Europe develop a paper-based economy that surpassed China's? As we have seen, Song China had a remarkably advanced paper technology for documenting and transferring ownership. It already had extremely abstract concepts of value. Chinese people understood and made use of the notion that a piece of paper could effectively symbolize wealth and function as bearer securities. It would seem to be a short conceptual leap to the development of corporate capitalism, in which business entities—like perhaps the salt monopoly—would have investors who contributed capital and received, in return, a certificate indicating ownership shares.

In fact, China also had a highly developed information management system. Accounting and documentation were fundamental tools used to address problems of moral hazard. Surely these technologies would have led naturally to the successful management of private enterprise: the oversight of corporate managers and agents.

The single missing ingredient in Chinese financial technology was the dimension of time. Weak European governments continually resorted to deficit financing and borrowing through the late Middle Ages and Renaissance. China did not.

We will see one particular example of this in Chapter 12. In 1174, Venice was locked in a battle with Constantinople, and the city needed to build a fleet. It issued bonds to its citizens—promises of future repayment. A market for these bonds developed at the foot of the Rialto Bridge, a few short steps away from Marco Polo's house. In contrast, when the Song government was confronted with a military crisis, it did not issue bonds—it printed more paper money. Inflation was the Chinese solution to financial crises, not shifting the cost into the future. In fact, the Chinese government during Wang Anshi's time in the Song did not borrow, it lent. This has subtle implications for the conception of time and the growth of the state.

State borrowing is, in some sense, a national pyramid scheme. The idea is that money borrowed today is invested in things that can increase the future economic power of the state. In simple terms, a state borrows to invest in activities that increase future tax revenues. Citizens need to believe in economic returns on state investment to trust that future revenues will provide a positive long-term rate of return. In China, the government since the time of the *Guanzi* was seen as providing instead a strategic, economic reserve. Current financial capacity represented a powerful tool—a means to provide for the populace when nature or enemies of the state caused problems. The financial ministry's duty was to husband this reserve. Personal savings and investment effectively separated the interests of the individual from the interests of the state. The mechanism for the divergence in financial systems—at least from the Chinese perspective, was the failure to develop mechanisms for government borrowing in the Song dynasty, just at the moment when European nations were learning of the remarkable demand for their paper promises of future repayment.

Kenneth Pomeranz does not ignore the financial system as the basis for the great divergence, but he argues that China did, in fact, have a private capital market. There exist historical records of domestic interest rates. The private loan market continued well into historical times. As pointed out above, there are even records of private Chinese companies formed in the eighteenth century that appear to draw on the indigenous roots of Chinese property rights, law, and accounting practices. Although private enterprise and capitalism existed in China all the way up to 1949, it rarely was divorced from the involvement and oversight of government officials. State sponsorship and control were the rule in Chinese enterprise rather than the exception.

REFLECTIONS ON CHINA

The vast scope of finance and financial thinking in Chinese history is impossible to summarize. However, there are a few key themes we have explored in Part II. First, although the roots of written language were closely tied to accounting, finance, and urbanism in the Near East, this was not true of China—rather it appears in the context of uncertainty about the future.

Comparing the early financial development of China to that of the ancient Near East and Mediterranean civilizations clearly shows that a financial system of great complexity can develop from very different root stock. Indeed, while it is always possible that the idea of coinage diffused across the Eurasian landmass from West to East, the very different format of the Chinese coins—and their obvious derivation from cowries—suggests independent invention. This means that financial technology is not only robust, but also that certain parallel solutions to basic problems are discovered and rediscovered by clever entrepreneurs or officials time and again, and that certain institutions and techniques can be thought of as stable equilibria, even when they derive from different traditions: coins, loans, accounting systems, contracts, securities—even paper money.

The tools and financial concepts important to the development of Chinese civilization are different from those that were most useful in the West. The scale and scope of China led, early on, to theories about management based on an understanding of economic incentives and oversight. Among these are, on the one hand, the profit motive and on the other hand the control of corruption by oversight, annual accounting, and reporting. The early Chinese mathematical text discussed in Chapter 8 considered many problems of how to measure and account for labor production, as well as problems of how to calculate wastage that occurs in construction and manufacturing. These problems are critical in a bureaucratic system in which each administrator is responsible for reporting accounts to a superior. This system of accounting may not seem extraordinary in the modern era but certainly the problem of accountability of government officials is a perpetual one.

While money was important in both Eastern and Western civilizations, it played a more prominent role in China. Indeed the unification of China in 221 BCE was symbolized by the introduction of a new coinage system. The audacious strategy of unifying an empire under a single currency must have led to the same kind of trade efficiencies enjoyed by the people of the Eurozone in the 1990s when the euro was introduced. However, it must also have created localized economic problems as well, since monetary policy and decisions about the quantity of money in circulation were centrally controlled.

The appearance of paper money in Sichuan resulted from a peculiar monetary problem: the introduction of an iron coin to prevent the flow of bronze cash from a frontier region. Paper money, based as it was on a long history of flying cash and negotiable receipts, was a logical break-through. Once discovered, paper fiat money became a powerful tool of the state, but of course it depended on a powerful absolute ruler. It is impossible to create fiat money without complete fiat. Thus, the value of the currency rose and ultimately collapsed with the state. This is a lesson learned much later in European history.

THE EUROPEAN CRUCIBLE

In this section we track the early history of financial innovation in Europe, up to the beginning of modern globalization. We return from China, where we studied the role of financial technology in maintaining a vast, unified empire. We shift west, where a very different financial system emerged from a fragmented and competitive patchwork of cities and states that only rarely organized themselves into a unified polity. Europe after the year 1000 became the crucible for a financial system that completely reconfigured society's relationship with time and money. There have been countless theories about how and why this happened.

In Part III I argue that the fragmentation of European states was the stimulus for a variety of creative, somewhat independent financial experiments. The fragmented political economy of Europe fostered the development of investment markets; the reinvention of the corporation; extra-governmental banking institutions; complex insurance contracts on lives, property, and trading ventures; and a sophisticated tradition of financial mathematics, reasoning, and analysis. These innovations, in turn, changed human behavior. I argue that they altered attitudes toward risk and chance, leading on the one hand to probabilistic thought and calculation and on the other hand to unbridled speculation that fueled the world's first stock market bubbles. Europeans ultimately turned themselves and the rest of the world into investors.

The key stages in Europe's development are first, the emergence of financial institutions; second, the development of securities markets; third, the emergence of companies; fourth, the sudden explosion of stock markets; fifth, the quantification of risk; and finally, the spillover of this system to the rest of the world. This radical reconfiguration of the financial architecture of Europe following the year 1000 solved

Detail from a print in the Dutch volume, *The Great Mirror of Folly*, printed in 1720 as a warning to future generations about the dangers of stock market speculation. It depicts the frenzy of financial markets as the work of the devil.

many economic problems in stunningly novel ways, but the solutions were subtly challenging and occasionally socially disruptive. As a result, they engendered further innovation and change. Over the course of the second millennium, Europe became a vast laboratory for financial experimentation. As we shall see, the development of modern financial technology was anything but linear. Some new ideas worked well, and some failed spectacularly.

THE TEMPLE AND FINANCE

The Knights Templar might appear to be an unusual subject for a study of financial history. They were a religious order that developed during the Crusades. However, they are an important case of a social institution that repurposed itself as a financial institution. By the fourteenth century, the Templars had become a vast extra-governmental entity that controlled large parts of the European economy and the finances of some of its major kingdoms. They became essential financial intermediaries, despite being sworn to a vow of poverty and to an entirely religious mission. The story of how the Templars became repurposed to serve Europe's financial as opposed to its spiritual needs is instructive. Their downfall and persecution demonstrates the limits of the modern theory of a financial institution being "too big to fail."

LONDON'S FIRST BANK

Getting to Temple Church always feels like a holy quest; a walk through a series of mazelike courtyards; a passage that takes you from the bustle of Fleet Street progressively deeper into London history until you reach the quiet heart of the Inns of Court. There stands a column topped by two Templars astride a single horse. Opposite the monument is a modest Gothic nave appended to an unusual circular chapel—the church of the Knights Templar, the dramatic setting for a scene in Dan Brown's *Da Vinci Code*. The circular chapel was built by the Knights Templar in 1185, echoing the design of the church on Temple Mount in Jerusalem, the origin of their order and the place they swore to protect. The Temple and two of the Inns of Court once formed the convent of the London chapter of the Templars; the place where this monastic order of militant knights lived apart from the secular world of London. It is a place that became, quite improbably, the English branch of an international

Temple Church, London.

financial institution that stretched from the Holy Land to the British Isles, an organization that managed the money and financial affairs of the kings and nobles of Europe through much of the thirteenth century. The institution came to a shocking end with the immolation of the Grand Master Jacques de Molay on the site of the Pont Neuf in Paris in 1314, and the seizure of its vast assets through Europe by its royal debtors and rival mendicant orders. Thus ended one of the most curious experiments in financial history: a nonprofit bank whose agents, sworn to personal poverty, nevertheless amassed a fortune in land and treasure.

The First Crusade captured Jerusalem in 1099 and reopened the city to European pilgrims who streamed in to visit its religious sites. The Templar order was founded twenty years later to protect these Holy Land travelers. The Templars maintained a series of fortresses across the Levant, from which they could defend the pilgrimage routes. When a monk entered the Templar order, he took a vow of poverty and chastity, swore an oath that he was debt free, and made a promise never to spend more than a single night away from the Templar convent. He dedicated his life to the defense of Christian pilgrims.

This mission evolved into insuring the safe transfer of money from Europe to the East. Foreigners with money belts around their waists sufficient to support months of expensive travel must have been easy targets. The Templars created a system by which pilgrims could deposit money with the order in Europe and withdraw it in the Holy Land. This became the European equivalent of Chinese *feiqian* discussed in Chapter 9. Out of this basic economic function—long-distance remittance—a financial institution was born.

The Templar letter of credit used by the pilgrims is lost to history. Of all the financial instruments I've examined in my research, this is the one document I would love to find. Like the Tang remittances and other financial documents of earlier eras, the Templar documents must have had some feature that prevented theft or fraud. Perhaps the traveler carried a particular code or key to verify his or her identity against Templar account records. Historians have speculated that pilgrims carried an encoded document with a cipher known only to the Templar stations along the route. It is more likely, however, that travelers dispatched their money ahead of them as they did in antiquity: by means of letters from one banker to another indicating the amount of transfer or the amount of credit to be extended. The letters may also have included information about the traveler to be verified on demand—just like the personal identification codes we use today for ATM withdrawals. On arriving at a distant destination, the traveler would presumably present a written and sealed document, prepared by the Templar who took the original deposit, then supply some evidence of identity, and then his or her account would be debited. It is a pity that none of these documents have survived. How did the Templars verify the traveler's identity? Were their letters encrypted so that they were useless to a thief who did not know the secret passcode? Put this on the list of the many remaining Templar mysteries.

Not only did the Templars serve as depositories and financial intermediaries, but they also amassed their own fortune. Their wealth, at first, came from charitable gifts by converts to the order and from pious laity. The Templars were one of the prime charities of choice for donors to the Crusades. Gifts to the order took the form of property. For example, their first donation came from Baldwin, the ruler of Jerusalem, who gave them land on the Temple Mount and the Al-Aqsa Mosque. Other donations came in the form of feudal rights and taxes assigned from kings and dukes to the Templars. They even received a "cut" of lands they helped conquer. The kings of Aragon promised the Templars a fifth of all booty and property seized in the wars against the Moors. The Aragonese kings thus employed the Templars as a faith-based mercenary army, deploying them along the Spanish frontier in the twelfth century and favoring them with the grant of castles, royal rents, and effective political control over large swaths of the Aragonese kingdom.

The complexity of Templar financial arrangements—from their transfer system to their records of account to their depository function and finally to their contractual arrangements for ownership of property and the assignment of the yields on these properties—is an important prelude to the development of the first European capital markets. The Templars organization was a technological response to the needs of a European society, which, like its contemporary Chinese society during the Song, had to move assets great distances, across seas and through dangerous terrain in the midst of wars and uncertainty. One contrast with China, however, is that the Templar organization operated in a vastly different political environment. There was no unified European political empire it served. Instead, the Templars responded to the needs of a constellation of European rulers who lacked financial power, who relied chronically on loans to meet military and political needs, and yet at the same time required neutral, nonpolitical entities with whom to entrust their finances. The Templars served the pope and the monarchs of England, France, and the Iberian kingdoms with equal fidelity, even in times when these rulers warred against one another. The needs of European rulers led to the Templars' success and finally to their downfall.

BANKING SERVICES

The most prominent financial services provided by the Templars—after their long-distance remittance business—was a constellation of intermediary activities we now interpret as banking. Templar convents in both London and Paris served as royal treasuries in which kings and nobles deposited their valuables. At one time the crown jewels of England were kept at the Temple rather than in the Tower of London. This made sense in many ways. What could be more secure than a walled stronghold protected by trained warriors who have taken a vow of poverty and who maintain an accounting system to monitor personal deposits and withdrawals?

The Templars also performed myriad other financial intermediary functions. They collected and monitored the payment of taxes for the English crown through the thirteenth century and maintained accounts of royal debt and dues in both England and France. While England had its own Exchequer that maintained the government finances and made extensive use of the services of the Templars, France relied on the order as a de facto royal treasury and accounting office.

The English kings borrowed from the Templar order, using their valuables as collateral. In 1213, for example, King John borrowed 1,000 gold marks for military expenses, as did his successor Henry III.[1] The Templars also functioned as payment intermediaries among the crowned heads of Europe—for example, when Henry III agreed to buy the island of Oleron from the Count of March, he agreed to pay 200 pounds for five years at the Temple in London, and the Templars would then reimburse the count.[2] Indemnities and royal debts due from one king to another could be handled through the Templars.

The Templars played a more subtle financial role, however, in that they managed the intertemporal exchange of value. They served as trust officers—overseeing bequests, guaranteeing the fair settlement of estates, and even selling life annuities. In 1214, for example, King John established a pension and funded it by providing the Templars at La Rochelle a sum sufficient to ensure annual disbursements. He likewise established a dowry of 500 pounds for the countess Alice of Angoulême by advancing 2,500 pounds to the Templars, an arrangement that (conveniently or intentionally for the Templars) ignored the time value of money.[3] The kings of France likewise used the Templars to arrange bond-like instruments which, interestingly enough, could be traded. For example in 1259, Etienne de Mont-Saint-Jean received from Saint Louis (Louis IX of France) a perpetual rent of 300 livres paid through the Temple of Paris in exchange for abandoning his chateau in Ferte-Alais. He sold half of this annual stream in 1270 to Jean Sarrasin.[4] These obligations could also be restructured from perpetual streams to life annuities.[5] The Templars created and serviced a range of what we now would call "financial products." While most records of Templar banking deal with the aristocracy, financial services also extended to merchants and tradespersons. Some accounts suggest that even lowly cooks contracted payments through the Temple.

Were the Knights Templar truly bankers, and if so, how might the bank have worked? First, we should observe that their mission was not to run a bank but instead to protect pilgrims and regain the Holy Land. Their financial activities should be seen in this light. Presumably the assets they acquired, the tools they developed, and the royal privileges they sought were a means to an end. This is not to suggest that they did not deviate from this mission, but individually, the Templars did not profit from their financial activities. When a Templar joined the order, he renounced all personal wealth.

A bank is an organization that takes deposits, makes loans, and offers a range of financial services. Banks do other things as well. Depending on the legal environment in which they operate, some make equity investments, underwrite the issuance of securities, and participate in the governance of corporations. By these criteria, the Templars were almost certainly a bank. This bank was ultimately "owned" by the Catholic Church in that the pope had the right to transfer Templar assets to other orders and ultimately to order the liquidation of the order. This ownership right only became relevant when the order came to an end, however. For most of its existence, the Templars were governed as a kind of partnership, with carefully defined rules of admission into the order and for succession in the governance structure. The assets were managed only by members of the order, and they were intended to further the mission of the organization. The Templars were "chartered" by the pope upon their founding, and this legitimized their right to operate as a unified institution. Presumably, this meant that debts incurred by the Paris Temple would be regarded as debts of the London chapter, for instance.

Banks—whether public, private, or nonprofit—rely on two key advantages. The first is financial expertise and the second is capital. Financial expertise includes the ability to assess borrowers and control default risk; safeguard assets; and evaluate, enumerate, document, and record deposits, withdrawals, income, and outlay. These are skills that the Templars developed from their first forays into pilgrim finance and perfected as the de facto treasurers to the kings of England and France. But they also had capital. Although there is no final record of accounts of Templar assets, they were said to have owned a vast number of properties throughout western Europe. How did they obtain these properties? Some of their wealth came in the form of gifts. Pious donors would give money, land, and treasure to the Templars. Some of this came when a monk joined the order and brought his personal assets with him. Others came in the form of spectacular bequests. For example, Alfonso I of Spain willed a significant portion of his kingdom to the Templars. Only in 1143, after protracted negotiations did the Templars renounce any claims resulting from this grant in exchange for the castles of Monzon, Mongay, Barbera, Chalamera, Belchite, and Remolins; annual dues from Zaragoza and Huesca; and one-fifth of all conquered Moor territory.[6]

Some of the Templar treasure likely came in the form of donations tied to the financial services they performed. While most banks make their money through the charging of interest, there is little direct evidence that this is how the Templars amassed their fortune. Usury laws would have made explicit interest charges difficult for the order, but not impossible. Interest could be hidden as a fee for late payment. However, usury proscriptions would certainly not have prevented gifts in return for the services the Templars provided. In addition, the Templars secured other rights in exchange for financial services to the crown that were just as good as interest payments, including exemption from taxes, franchise rights, or tariff reductions on the sale of such commodities as salt and wine.[7]

TEMPLAR TREASURE

Given what is known about the Templars as bankers, we can hardly doubt that there was a Templar treasure. Although the wealth of the order was put to work in the construction and maintenance of castles, monasteries, and churches and the financing of the Crusades, its vast property holdings in Europe represented a major asset. It is interesting to see how these assets worked. One place where good records of Templar assets have survived is in the Aragonese kingdom of northeastern Spain. These records provide a window into the exact nature of Templar property holdings.

Jerusalem was the eastern front in Christendom's global war with Islam, and the Iberian peninsula was the western front. King Alfonso I—the overly generous donor mentioned above—enlisted the military support of the Templars in the early 1100s by grants of properties to the order. He made a gift of the castle of Granena in 1122, hoping the Templars would defend this frontier fortress. In yet another grant in 1164, the Kingdom of Catalonia borrowed 1,000 morabetins from the Knights Templar for two years and in return, they received the rents from two mills in Barcelona.

These grants to the Templars essentially assigned to them the economic rights pertaining to the property. This included rights to the rents due in the form of money, produce, and labor; rights to take tolls and customs duties; fishing and hunting rights; control of natural resources; oversight of "weights, measures, ovens, mills [and] the office of public notary" and the like.[8] Templars were also assigned "terms and tenements"—that is, the current lease agreements with property occupants and the rights to hold commercial fairs and markets. In cases in which the grant to the Templars was made by the king or a feudal lord, they acquired judicial rights as well, occasionally resulting in dual local court systems.[9]

BAILIWICKS AS FINANCIAL CLAIMS

Just as the king and other lords had the power to assign rents, proceeds, and control of properties under their protection, so too did the Templars have the right to reassign rights. For example, they could grant lordship over a city to someone in exchange for a gift or grant. This assignability was not special to the Templars—it was a standard form of contractual agreement based on feudal property rights.

Thomas Bisson, a professor at the University of California at Berkeley and an expert on medieval contracts and society, was able to study a trove of fiscal archives from the Catalonian count-kings from 1151 to 1213, shortly after the entry of the Templars into northeast Spain. The archives studied by Bisson document royal wheeling and dealing on a grand scale. Royal privileges were like chits in a monopoly game used by the count-kings to borrow money, obtain favors, and drive concessions.[10]

The basis of many royal loans was the bailiwick, the stewardship of a town or region that carried with it the rights to collect dues and taxes. Bailiwicks in the Aragonese kingdom were auctioned for periods of a year or more. A creditor would give the crown money in exchange for the right to take revenues and rights that were due the crown.

Consider, for example, a contract Bisson found and translated, dated May 27, 1205:

> Ramon Batala, the King's procurator and Perfet, bailiff of Barcelona, sells the bailiwick of Moià to Ramon de Passarell and Guerau de Uilar Jouam for the year beginning on 3 May 1205. The King's "five clauses" are reserved. The price is 1000 s.b. [i.e., sous of Barcelona, the Catalan currency] payable in three installments. If the proceeds should be damaged by storms, a revaluation will be made by "good men" of the region. Having named surities for payment, the purchasers pledge their faithful and just administration.[11]

The town of Moià, thirty miles north of Barcelona, is now a tiny village and vacation spot of about 3,800 people in the foothills of the Pyrenees. In 1205, it was a fortified town in the possession of Queen Sancha and was administered by her husband, Alfonso II, hence the sale of the bailiwick by Ramon Batala, his procurator. The bailiff of Moià was entitled to hold a market and fair, which apparently was

operated by the monks of l'Estany, who shared in the profits. Dues
were also collected from households in the town—perhaps in the
form of produce—and from the royal granary. Evidently, the rights
to collect these revenues exceeded 1,000 sous of Barcelona (equal to
3,240 grams of silver). When the contractual obligations were discharged, the parchment was cut with cancellation marks to indicate
that it was no longer valid.

Note what the contract does. It monetizes the feudal rights from a
property over a specific time period. A bailiff gives 1,000 sous of Barcelona and receives an unspecified cash flow, which is evidently connected
to agricultural yield from the bailiwick (since the contract makes an exception for storms). It is akin to a loan to the king that is repaid from
revenues from the king's estate.

The bailiwick was not only a way for the king to raise cash, but also
a way for an investor to use cash to generate future income. Bailiffs did
not bid on these contracts so they could govern a town for a year—after
all, most contracts lasted briefly. This was not about power, it was about
money. Bailiwicks were a financial instrument.

This form of contract was common in the European Middle Ages—
it was also called a "*census*" or a "*rente*," an exchange of money for the
yield on property for a specified time period. Although the Moià contract did not specify a rate of interest, some census contrasts did. For
example, in 1209, Pere I, the king of Spain and count of Barcelona, recognized a debt of 7,500 mazmudins to Gobmau de Ribells, agreeing to
pay 20% in interest until the debt was discharged.[12]

INTERNATIONAL FINANCE IN THE
THIRTEENTH CENTURY

The assignable feudal rights framework provided the foundations for all
later European financial architecture. Municipal and sovereign finance
in the early twelfth century was based on monetizing land-based, feudal income: rent, agricultural yield, tolls, taxes, maritime tariffs, mining
rights, and traditional labor corvées. This financial system allowed lords
and landowners to borrow against, and investors to receive and to reassign profits derived from, a feudal system of obligation. Although it
existed long before the emergence of the Templars, this system of baili-

wicks and census contracts allowed the Templars—as well as any other enterprising lender—to put their capital to use.

One key problem is that these contracts encroached on the power of the sovereign or the lord who assigned them, and this was risky. The result of this financing by counts, dukes, cities, and republics in need of cash was not only the diminishment of sovereign control, but also the threat of default or expropriation. Over the course of roughly a century, the Templar organization amassed thousands of properties and a complex network of contracts that made them a major economic force in Europe and also a target of opportunity for monarchs looking for money.

THE FALL

Tartus is a sunny resort on the Syrian shore, with a wide sand beach. The city extends along the strand in the shadow of hills that must have been covered with vineyards and orchards in Crusader times. Ruad is a tiny island only a mile or so offshore and is easily visible from the town. Its main attraction is the ruined foundations of the last Templar outpost. Even as the Templars became progressively embedded into the European financial system, they were failing in their fundamental mission. Throughout the thirteenth century, the Crusader states gradually lost control of the Holy Land. Jerusalem fell to Muslim control in 1244. The Templars progressively retreated from castle after castle until their last foothold, a castle off the coast of Syria, was taken in 1302.

The Templars survived only a little longer as a financial organization and as a monastic order. Ironically, their downfall came at the swords of a French king, not Islam. The destruction of the Templars in Europe began with a surprise raid in 1307 by King Philip IV on the Paris Temple. The Templar complex stood just outside the old city walls on the site of what is now the Temple stop of the Paris Metro. Their arrest was followed by imprisonment in the dungeons of their own fortress, charges of heresy, and torture to extract confessions. The goal of this persecution was undoubtedly their vast wealth. The Templars had earlier made the mistake of failing to forgive Philip's debts. They should have known better. Just a few years before, the king had expelled his

Jewish and Italian creditors from France for the same sins against the state. Despite generations of mutual dependence between the knights and the French crown, in the years leading up to the arrest, Philip had begun to separate the French fiscal system from the Templar treasury, choosing to receive and make royal payments out of the Louvre rather than the Temple.

The trial of the Templars is one of the most famous inquisitions in the history of the Catholic Church. Hundreds of members of the order were tortured and forced to confess to worshipping false idols, performing secret rites, or engaging in homosexual relations. Contemporary church observers were skeptical about the validity of these extracted confessions, but the stories nevertheless turned popular sentiment against the Templars.

The Templars in London and Spain suffered somewhat less than those in France. Edward I was at first reluctant to arrest them, but finally went along with orders from the pope following Philip's accusations. The Templars in Aragon fought arrest from their fortresses but were finally arrested as well. After the outcome of the trial, they were freed and pensioned. The assets of the Templars—their castles, churches, and properties—were transferred to another religious order, the order of Saint John—the Knights Hospitaller. The remaining Templar monks joined the Hospitallers.

The destruction of the international system of deposit and payment the Templars had created must have been a loss to all of Europe, although the division of their assets and renunciation of their financial claims—seizure or reassignment of their properties, census contracts, royal debts, and other obligations—was probably a temporary salve to the European rulers in need of cash. The fall of the order left an institutional vacuum eventually occupied by Italian bankers.

After the dissolution of the Templars, the Hospitallers maintained the Temple church in London but rented out the living quarters, dining halls, training grounds, storage vaults, and gardens of the urban stronghold to two colleges of lawyers, where it became a center for the training, study, and practice of English common law, a function it serves to this day. Where once knights swore to uphold the defense of Jerusalem, young lawyers now swear allegiance to the law. The Templar precinct still preserves a sense of a sacred mission.

ALTERNATIVE INSTITUTIONS

The argument advanced in the introduction to Part III was that European finance was born out of the political weakness and fragmentation of the continent into city-states, in contrast to the unified governance structure of China. This weakness caused European kings to constantly raise money through assignment of properties and rents and, once they had hocked everything else, to expand their kingdoms militarily to generate other sources of revenues. This need, in turn, engendered financial institutions to meet it.

In short, necessity is the mother of invention. The Templar's societal role as bankers was not envisioned at the creation of the order. It evolved according to need and opportunity. In another trajectory of history, this same role of depository and intermediary might have been played by private bankers—the Lucchese, for example, who lent to Edward I. It might also have been played by a stronger central state—a Holy Roman Empire, which in different circumstances might have maintained control over Europe in the way Chinese emperors maintained central authority and fiscal management.

Financial technology is redundant, adaptive, and sometimes mercurial. The institutions we take to be sacrosanct, inevitable, and indispensable are probably not. Given the random outcome of historical events, another set of institutions might have emerged to solve the same financial problems. Financial innovation is thus a series of accidents of history—the caprice of time, location, and opportunity.

The Templar financial empire is interesting as evidence that different institutional technologies can serve the same function. Another important feature is the feudal foundation of their wealth. The Templar treasure was not the gold and silver stored in their treasuries, but the hundreds of properties they owned under what was essentially a feudal system of fiefs, bailiwicks, and rentes. In the Middle Ages, land was the primary medium of transferring value through time. Farms, vineyards, orchards, flocks, and herds backed the perpetuities, contracts, and money fiefs that kings and lords settled on their vassals and creditors. Feudal rights were the rights of a ruler to assign land or the yield of the land in return for support. While traditionally envisioned as quid pro quo for military support, fiefs were also clearly assignable in return for other support as well—even in return for a monetary gift or loan. Religious institutions like the Templars and Hospitallers became important beneficiaries of fiefs, and a legal system in Europe developed to adjudicate disputes over fiefs and other assignable rights. Although based on the principle of assignment of land and land yields, fief law ultimately became a framework for a system of purely monetary obligations and was the conceptual foundation for Europe's unique financial architecture.

The central argument of this book is that financial innovations emerged to solve economic problems of time and geography, but they inevitably engendered new problems. The Templar organization provided a stable, long-lived institution that made contracting on future payments credible. Its selection of ethical personnel who took a vow of poverty reduced the likelihood of fraud. Its extensive geographical network provided for transfer of money through space as well as time. However, these same characteristics that made the Templar organization ideal as a financial institution also led to its failure. Its wealth made it a political target, and the loss of its original mission rendered it peripheral to the Catholic Church in the early fourteenth century. After the loss of the Holy Land, its former protectors were expendable. In fact, the wealth of the Templars challenged the scale of the possessions of the church itself.

The Templar story is important, because it is an example of an alternative institutional financial structure that emerged and was stable for a time. Unlike modern central banks, it was not accountable to a nation-state—a feature that ultimately led to its downfall. That is what makes the analogy to the European Central Bank interesting.

VENICE

This chapter traces the birth of modern financial securities and markets to Renaissance Venice. It shows how the stage for these innovations was set by the tradition of medieval census contracts and describes how the moment of discovery was precipitated by a political crisis. The creation of a market for financial securities in Venice in the twelfth century represents a watershed in European history. It began the practice of deficit spending by the state, financed by the issuance of liquid debt. Finance became one of Venice's key instruments of power in its rise as a mercantile empire. Its financial architecture was every bit as important as its bricks and mortar.

The invention of bonds in Venice led to a philosophical crisis in Europe. The Catholic Church's proscription against usury put Venetian investors in a morally ambiguous position as lenders to the state. This problem led in turn to a deeper analysis of the use of capital and changed the way Europeans conceptualized and quantified time.

JOHN RUSKIN

The reader will now begin to understand something of the importance of the study of the edifices of a city which includes, within the circuit of some seven or eight miles, the field of contest between the three pre-eminent architectures of the world: —each architecture expressing a condition of religion; each an erroneous condition, yet necessary to the correction of the others, and corrected by them.[1]

JOHN RUSKIN, *THE STONES OF VENICE*

A gondola ride along the Grand Canal today illustrates what the famous critic John Ruskin saw as the great conflict of civilizations—East versus

Rialto Market, Venice. Europe's first bond market and financial center.

West—played out in the decorative designs of the city's aging palazzos. Ruskin's Venice is both a ruin and a puzzle, but above all it is a place where the traces of ancient cultural institutions are miraculously preserved—fitted together into an improbable matrix of stone and water. Armed with a copy of *The Stones of Venice*, a tourist can see Ruskin's famously architectural progression from Roman to Lombard to Arab in the Classical, Gothic, and Middle Eastern decorative motifs on the city's buildings—most notably preserved together in the facade of the Doge's Palace in the Piazza di San Marco.

Curiously enough, the stones of Venice also preserve the remnants of successive stages of the world's financial architecture—beginning, of course, with the fundamental fact that the city emerged, flourished, and declined by its maritime trade—mercantile adventures that risked lives and fortune on the open sea to buy and sell goods across the Mediterranean world and beyond. Embedded in Venetian urban geography are traces of the most important financial institutions that created modern capital markets.

Start your trip at Harry's Bar, for example, where well-heeled tourists and the occasional celebrity are crammed into a tiny room to pay unbelievable amounts of money to eat the—admittedly delicious—cuisine. Just behind Harry's is the Hotel Luna Baglioni in the Calle dell'Ascensione. Luna is Venice's oldest hotel, claiming a heritage back to 1118. In that year, the Knights Templar occupied a "Locanda della Luna" just off Piazza di San Marco. Hotel Luna Baglioni thus stands on the most likely location of the Templar's Venetian convent, occupying, as well, the foundations of a long-demolished Templar church, Santa Maria in Brolo—also known as Santa Maria dell'Ascensione. It is the one hotel in the world here you can sleep in what may once have been a Templar stronghold and perhaps a Templar bank.

Crossing the Piazza di San Marco and walking east along the Grand Canal, you will next find the church of San Giovanni in Bragora, formerly called San Giovanni del Tempio—a church and neighboring hospital acquired by the Templars in 1187 and turned over to the Hospitallers after the dissolution of the order.

The most spectacular, if unproven, remnant of the Templar urban geography in Venice is the Church of the Magdalene in the Cannaregio district: a circular church rebuilt in the eighteenth century in austere, classical style. Over the entrance to the church is a device of an inter-

FIGURE 17. Hotel Luna Baglioni, Venice. The Luna occupies the site of the Templar's convent in Venice.

twined circle and triangle—at its center: the all-seeing eye—the Masonic symbol and the same sign found on the back of the US dollar bill.

The original church was built by the Balbo clan. One of Venice's most heroic crusaders, Ezzelino I fought in the second crusade with Frederick I, Barbarossa. His son, Ezzelino II, also fought valiantly in imperial service, but late in life renounced all worldly goods and joined the Templar order. The Church of the Magdalene in the Cannaregio district of Venice may reflect the family's ancient Templar ties. Did the eighteenth-century architect choose a round plan based on an ancient tradition or on earlier round foundations? The connection is tenuous, but to fans of *The Da Vinci Code*, these coincidences tempt the imagination.

Regardless of whether the Templar order or Templar tradition survived past its dissolution in the early fourteenth century, the few architectural traces of the Templars in Venice are enough to remind us that
the "Serenissima" was integral to the order's broader financial network.
Indeed, given that Venice was a key point of departure for seafaring pilgrims to the Holy Land, it must have been continental Europe's most
important link.

We can still visit their churches and see—more or less—where the
Templars lived. But how did the Venetian branch operate? Where are
the copious accounting records they used to keep track of travelers' deposits? Where are the letters that must have passed from convent to
convent, noting the debits and credits, as pilgrims withdrew funds in
the Holy Land, and their families paid these expenses with deposits
in Paris, London, Barcelona, and Venice? What clever chits and secret
signs did pilgrims carry and present when their boats tied up to the
wharves near the Piazza di San Marco—or perhaps right at the dock of
the modern Hotel Luna? None are to be found—not in the Venetian
government records at least. Perhaps a chance discovery someday in a
church archive or a sunken Crusader galleon will help us piece together
the details of the Templar's financial technology. And maybe there is
some underwater financial archaeology to be done just outside the front
door of Harry's Bar.

If the stones of Venice preserve traces of the ecclesiastical institution
that first served as an international bank in the early Middle Ages, they
also tell the story of a somewhat different financial institution—a secular and governmental network that coexisted in Venice with the Templar
order and eventually superseded it. The story of this institution is best
told from the perspective of one of Venice's most famous citizens—a
character we have already met in our study of financial innovation in
China: Marco Polo. His life in Venice introduces us to yet another element of the city's ancient financial architecture.

Venice in Marco Polo's lifetime—the thirteenth century—was a
maritime colonial empire that stretched down the Dalmatian coast to
Crete and through the Aegean Sea. Venetian armies sacked Byzantium
in 1204 during the Fourth Crusade, looting the ancient city of her treasures. Venetian traders pushed well beyond Constantinople and the
Holy Land, however. Like the ancient Greeks, they established trade

routes through the Bosporus and into the Black Sea—a frontier that gave them access to the ancient Silk Road and trade with the peoples of the north.

Marco Polo was born in Venice in the middle of the thirteenth century and traveled to China with his uncles, who, though Venetians, spent most of their lives as merchants on the eastern frontiers of Christendom—first at a trading port on the Black Sea and later in central Asia. The Polos' adventures—their grand trips to China and back over the course of decades—were memorialized by Marco when he was imprisoned in Genoa. With the help of the writer Rusticello, he penned *Livre des Merveilles du Monde*—which became *Il Milione* in Italian. In fact, the famous account was not written in Latin or Italian but in courtly French. A book in French, written by an Italian about travels in Asia is evidence alone that Marco Polo lived in a period of broadening contact between Italy and the wider world.

By virtue of its close affiliation with Byzantium before and after the Fourth Crusade, Venice had active trade contacts with the eastern Mediterranean. However, the rival city-states of Pisa and Genoa increasingly competed for access to eastern markets. The Crusades represented not only a challenge to Arab control of the Mediterranean and Levant but also became the prime vector by which Italian city-states and traders competed with, and ultimately hastened, the fall of the Byzantine Empire. Even before the First Crusade and the founding of the Templar order, Genoa and Pisa had joined forces to attack Muslim-occupied Sardinia in 1015. Genoa supplied the armies of the First Crusade in Antioch in 1096, thus gaining a foothold in an eastern trade traditionally dominated by Venice. Its rivalry with Venice came to a dramatic peak with a Venetian attack on the Genoese fleet in 1100 near the island of Rhodes, establishing a pattern of naval competition that would continue for centuries.

The emergence of Europe in the Middle Ages was not the reemergence of a unified empire built on the ashes of Rome, but instead the appearance of small, aggressive, trade-oriented mercantile city-states. This period of economic resurgence after the year 1000 has been the subject of much historical study; however, the best way to understand the role of finance in the reawakening of western Europe is to focus on how early urban finance actually worked.

THE RIALTO MARKET

When Marco Polo was finally ransomed in 1298, he returned to his home in Venice. Two courtyards still bear the name of his famous book: Corte Prima del Milion and Seconda del Milion. If the attribution of this as his home is correct, Marco Polo's house was particularly well situated as a merchant's residence—like many well-to-do houses of the time, it was a multistoried building surrounding linked courtyards and connected by a small channel to the Grand Canal just north of the Rialto Bridge. Paintings of the Rialto area show that the bridge in Marco Polo's day was a steeply peaked, palisaded wooden structure spanning the canal. At its middle was an opening though which merchants could lower bundles of merchandise to trade galleys below. Beyond the bridge, the geography of the Rialto neighborhood was important.

The Rialto of Marco Polo's day brought together shipping magnates, entrepreneurs, financiers, investors, speculators, bankers, borrowers, insurance agents, brokers, money changers, tax authorities, government inspectors, and even, perhaps, gossips, gamesters, spectators, and tourists to see the financial heart of the greatest commercial center in Europe. The spatial intensification of various financial services made intermediation easier.

As Marco Polo walked over the Rialto bridge, he would have seen the Venetian customs house where boats could dock and load, and goods could be inspected. To the immediate right at the end of the bridge was soon to be built a loggia for merchants—an arched, open structure that served as a commercial gathering place for the sharing of knowledge and information—a place where, if the Merchant of Venice had actually been a real person, one might imagine Shakespeare's characters visiting each day for words of the missing galleon. The steps from the bridge led to a small square, the Campo San Giacomo di Rialto. The physical organization of the intimate Campo became a model for virtually all subsequent physical financial architecture of Europe: a colonnaded courtyard, around which various financial specialists and functions were stationed. Today this square is surrounded by shops, porticos, and small, covered stands. Among other things, it is the Venetian fresh vegetable market.[2]

Seven centuries ago, the Rialto probably looked much like it does today. Instead of wholesale vegetable vendors, however, one would have seen bankers and money changers with little wooden tables called "*banci*," counting, weighing, and assaying. These bankers took deposits and made loans—secured and unsecured. Part of their business was pawn brokerage, but they undoubtedly made commercial loans for trade, managed accounts for families, and handled brokerage. At the north side of the square, merchants could negotiate maritime insurance for their overseas ventures; beyond them were wharves and markets—a fur and pelt market and a fish market. Most of the Rialto square was lined with commerce, but one side of the square was devoted to God. Overlooking Venice's medieval financial district is the ancient church of Saint Giacomo, perhaps the oldest on the main islands of Venice, whose brick facade is dominated by an oversized clock on a small bell tower—a monument to the passage of time. Around the church is an inscription admonishing merchants to measure fairly. Just before it, across the square, is a small fountain with an Atlas-like figure bearing a heavy load on his shoulders, said to be a warning about the dangers of debt.

Government was also well represented in the Rialto. Fronting the Grand Canal south of the bridge stood the grain office, the wine tax office, and the salt office. Like China, salt was a source of government revenue. There, too, stood the office of tax delinquents and a tax office for brokerage. Of these government offices, one of the most important did not front the square or the Grand Canal directly. In a row of buildings just to the west of the piazza, behind the main row of shops, stood the *Camera degli Imprestiti*: the Venetian loan office. This loan office was the Venetian equivalent of the US Treasury. It was in charge of government debt. Although the decision to finance state budgets through loans was taken in the city's political center, the palace on the Piazza di San Marco, its implementation by Marco Polo's day had moved to the Rialto.

One of Venice's early official forays into public finance was an arrangement in 1164 with a group of twelve prominent Venetians, including Sebastiani Ziani, the future doge. The contract with this investor group exchanged eleven years' worth of rents from the Rialto for a loan of 1,150 silver marks to the commune. As we saw earlier, this pledge was similar to arrangements that other Mediterranean city-states made with lenders, including with the Knights Templar. The Rialto loan was in fact much like a census contract used by the kings of Catalonia to assign the administrative rights and revenues from their domains to creditors.

FIGURE 18. View of the Rialto Market in 1500 from
Jacopo de' Barbari's *View of Venice.*

FIRST PUBLIC FINANCE

Eight years later, however, Venice took a strikingly novel approach to
financing. It issued public debt. It did so through a forced loan, a *prestiti*
settled on Venetian citizens according to their wealth. The loan was a
response to a massive hostage crisis and a bitter struggle with Byzantium
over control of the Adriatic. In the years leading up to the loan, Byzantium had acquired ports on the Adriatic Sea through its victory over the
Hungarian kingdom. This put the empire in direct competition with
Venice. In 1171, on fabricated charges that the Venetians had burned the
Genoese neighborhood in Constantinople, Emperor Emmanuel seized
all Venetian merchants in the capital, locked them away in prisons, and
impounded their goods.[3]

This was as much a fiscal crisis as a political one. Had Doge Vitale II
Michiel been able to hypothecate future government revenues like the
early Rialto loan, government bonds might not have been born. Instead,
he devised a borrowing scheme that shared the financial pain among all
Venetians. For purposes of the loan, the city was divided into six districts—
these same divisions of the city survive to this day: Castello, Cannaregio,

Dorsoduro, Santa Croce, San Polo, and San Marco. Each district assessed the wealth of its citizens through an *estimo* and then collected and forwarded its share to the Grand Council. The key feature of this arrangement was that, although it was mandatory, the loan differed from a tax, in that Venice promised to pay 5% interest until the debt was retired.

The interesting difference between the 1164 and the 1172 financing is that the prestiti, painful as it was to the broader populace, created a lender-borrower relationship between city and citizens, rather than leaving creditor control concentrated in the hands of a few investors. Whether this was by accident or by design is difficult to know; however, it had the immediate effect of making all Venetians both debtors and creditors of the state. The other interesting feature of the 1172 loan was that any rearrangement of the debt was now under the political control of the newly created six divisions in the city. The broad-based roots of the loan served indirectly as a political device for equitable government fiscal decisions.[4]

The loan enabled the doge to raise a massive fleet against the Byzantine Empire. One-hundred twenty ships sailed off to save the hostages and recover Venetian property. The fleet anchored off the coast of Asia Minor. Emperor Emmanuel stalled for time by promising a negotiated resolution. As these negotiations dragged on, the Venetian fleet, waiting to attack, was suddenly ravaged by the plague. Byzantium did not need to put up a fight. Disease defeated the Venetian navy. Doge Vitale Michiel returned to Venice with the depleted fleet, bringing bad news and the plague with him. He was immediately murdered by an angry mob. The loan of 1172 was but one of many burdens to bear from this tragedy. Its principal would never be retired by the weakened republic. In time, although the state made steady interest payments, the debt evolved into a permanent fixture.

The first government bond ever issued was thus a result of fiscal weakness rather than strength; it was born from desperation and survived through the state's inability to repay capital. Nevertheless, it was a major financial innovation. It enabled the government to rapidly focus financial resources at a time of need and convert them into military assets. The failure of the expedition, not the conceptualizing of the loan as a permanent debt of the state, is what led to the longevity of the debt.

In 1262, the Venetian debt was formalized in a decree, the *Ligato Pecuniae*, which consolidated all earlier debts into a single fund that paid

5% interest on the face value of the loan in two annual installments. This fund came to be known as the Monte Vecchio. The Monte Vecchio had two key features: bond obligations could be transferred between investors, and the government could not retire the loans by repaying the principal. Transferability meant that a citizen forced to buy a prestiti could turn around and sell it to another. The payments would be henceforth paid to the next bondholder. The decision to restrict the government from retiring the prestiti by paying back the face value of the loan meant that the bonds would remain a financial asset forever, or until Venice itself repurchased them in the open market. What started as an expedient deferral of principal repayment became a permanent and evidently desirable feature of state debt. By Marco Polo's time—in fact right about the time Marco Polo was in China admiring the grandeur of the court of the Great Khan—Venetian prestiti had become formalized into loans that could be bought and sold in an active, competitive secondary market—the Rialto market.

Over the next several centuries Venice repeatedly turned to the Monte Vecchio in times of military need: the war with Ferrara (1310–1354), the third war with Genoa (1350–1354), the war of Chioggia against Genoa (1378–1381)—a war that demanded the loan of 41% of all individual capital in Venice and forced massive liquidations of real property[5]—and finally, the wars against Milan in the early 1400s. In 1454, the Monte Vecchio was closed out in favor of direct taxation to pursue a campaign against the Turks after the fall of Constantinople. However, in 1482, Venice began a Monte Nuovo to finance a war against Ferrara, resulting in two separate bond issues that traded side by side in the Rialto.

The prices of prestiti through time indicate how investors viewed Venice's prospects for continued payment of its debt. For the period of the loan consolidation in 1262 up to 1376, Venetian prestiti typically sold for 80–100% of face value. From 1376 to 1441, however, the average priced dropped to the 40–60% range—the republic was often in arrears on interest rate payments. Indeed, after that point, a seller was lucky to get 20% of face value. Payments due to investors in prestiti were sometimes determined by lottery—lucky winners received their overdue interest payments, while losers had to wait. Despite being the first to develop a government credit market, the pattern of prices for its debt suggests that the creditworthiness of Venice reached its peak circa 1340. The last glimmer of the Venetian debt was issued just before Napoleon conquered the republic in 1797. Remnants of the end of the republic's great financial innovation can still be found. I once bought at auction a coupon called a "*cedula*" issued by the Venetian Giro Bank in 1797, which apparently circulated like paper money and represented the final promise of Europe's longest-lived independent republic.

The striking feature of the Venetian money market of the thirteenth century was not the ubiquity of banks. After all, these had an ancient history in the Mediterranean. The institutionalization of state loans by means of the Ligato Pecuniae was the true innovation, for with it, the republic intentionally or unintentionally created a completely new income substitute. It was like nothing in antiquity or in other parts of the world. Although the foundations of the Venetian debt can be traced to the census contracts of the Middle Ages, the dispersion among its citizens was absolutely novel. Venetian citizens could take the economic value saved up from past labor or trade and convert it into future cash flows. In this way, it was possible to economically hedge against the depletion of earnings capacity as the body and mind grow old; it was possible to create a perpetual stream of benefits to endow a charity. It was also a way to pass along an asset that did not have to be managed. Venetian prestiti were attractive particularly because they were passive investment vehicles whose value depended only on the viability and honesty of the state, not on the capabilities of the owner.

USURY AND A REVOLUTION IN THOUGHT

In institutionalizing government loans, Venice would seem to have directly contradicted the well-known ecclesiastical proscription against usury. The mendicant orders of the Catholic Church were founded in the early thirteenth century: the Franciscans in 1206 and the Dominicans in 1216. Central to their teachings were an abhorrence of usury. In fact, it is tempting to see the emergence of these religious orders— which abjured wealth and the personal accumulation of capital, as an institutional response to the flourishing of finance and commerce in the centuries following 1000. Merchant capitalism in cities like Venice and its rivals created conditions for social mobility and threatened to upset the social order. A religious backlash is perhaps not surprising.

The heightened emphasis on the proscriptions against usury in the thirteenth century had legal and philosophical roots as well as religious ones. The philosophical roots are Aristotelian. According to Aristotle, whose works enjoyed a revival of scholarly interest in the late Middle Ages:

> The most hated sort [of money making], and with the greatest reason, is usury, which makes a gain out of money itself, and not from the natural use of it. For money was intended to be used in exchange, but not to increase at interest. And this term usury, which means the birth of money from money, is applied to the breeding of money because the offspring resembles the parent. Whereof of all modes of making money this is the most unnatural.[6]

In this passage, the greatest evil of finance is not the pain it causes to the borrower, but the suggestion that financiers have the hubris to challenge God in the creation of life. Their money begets money—it is a nonliving thing that has offspring, a kind of automaton; a monster created by humans transgressing on divine privilege. Money, which is "dead," should not be allowed to reproduce itself. This interpretation of finance as an unnatural phenomenon was taken up by the philosophers called Scholastics, who added another transgression to the list of the evils of finance: it represented the theft of time itself.[7] William of Auxerre in 1220 wrote "the usurer acts contrary to natural law, for he sells time, which is common to all creatures."[8] By charging periodic interest, financial contracts put a price on time, reducing the flow of existence to a stream of cash. Indeed, the perpetual loans of Venice spanned God's own time—infinite duration. Investors inevitably measured the passage of time by intervals between the payment of *paghe*.

The connection between money and time has been viewed by modern scholars as a revolution in thought, every bit as important as the revolution in commercial practice that accompanied it. Jacques Le Goff, the French historian and dean of medieval scholarship, argues that the scholastic attitude toward usury is evidence of a major transition in the way time itself was imagined. In Le Goff's view, merchant's time clashed with church's time, and the loan contract, or more generally, the parceling out of capital in the dimension of time, altered the way people experienced the world.[9] Natural time, the notion goes, is time measured by the sweat of the brow, agrarian work measured by the cycle of the seasons and the feast days of saints. When a farmer borrows, he or she equates labor with the money received from the lender—for it is the yield from labor that will repay the loan. Le Goff and other scholars see the clash between church and commercial society, most acutely embodied by finance, as the beginning of a social dynamic that freed Europeans from the serfdom of the Middle Ages and set them on a course toward capitalism. While recognizing the benefits of this evolution, Le Goff expresses ambiguity about the progress. He argues that finance is a fall from grace. Le Goff's sentiment is clear. The revolution that began in the Middle Ages may have gone too far by the twentieth century. Maybe there will come a time soon when culture shifts back away from the secular, empirical system of values—thesis, antithesis, synthesis!

In response to this evocation of the Middle Ages as a redemptive model for modern society, one must ask: Was time before markets and business a "better" time? Consider serfdom, a condition of permanent bondage that prevailed before the growth of urbanism and the re-emergence of trade in the Middle Ages. In a feudal framework, time is owned by the lord of the manor, and by the same token this lord's obligations to the crown were measured in days of military service. Substituting monetary obligation for labor obligation is arguably a major humanitarian advance. Reaching all the way back before Mesopotamian society; can we really say there was a golden age before finance? Never mind the subtle academic debate about the profane role of commerce and finance in modern society. Modern enthusiasm for this question suggests that the issues debated by philosophers and theologians in the Middle Ages and the Renaissance are alive and well today.

DEFINING TERMS

The medieval debate over finance was not confined to interpretation of church doctrine. It had legal foundations as well.

Just when financial tools were developing in northern Italy in the twelfth century, legal scholars were reviving Roman law—the Code of

Justinian was rediscovered. We saw earlier how the Code of Justinian represented the Roman legal tradition at the end of the empire rather than at the beginning. Ulrike Malmendier argues that, as such, it failed to describe early financial institutions, such as the societas publicanorum (see Chapter 7). The chief merit of the code in the Middle Ages is that it served as an institutional coordination mechanism for regularizing law across Europe. Its drawback was that it imposed an arbitrary, ancient, and restrictive framework on the emerging financial system.

Of particular importance to bond and loan financing is that the Code of Justinian contained rules against usury. Roman law defined a loan as a contract called "*mutuum*": a sum of money conferred to a borrower, which was then repaid to the lender in the same amount. The key feature is that ownership of the capital was transferred—the lender no longer shared in the ownership of the capital once it was lent. The repayment of a larger sum than the original amount was deemed unlawful. After the revival of the code, business contracts were compared to the model of mutuum to determine whether they were usurious and thus illegal. As a consequence, from the eleventh century on, Roman law as well as Scholastic philosophy and religious doctrine were critical of finance.

Differences of opinion were tolerated regarding the legitimacy of at least some interest yield on loan contracts. Interest was recognized as compensation for an alternative use of capital. "*Lucrum cessans*" referred to the return that could have been earned on money that would otherwise have been invested in a different asset. This concept justified a fair interest rate allowable as just compensation for a loan.

The medieval census contracts provided a clear model for the charging of fair interest on loaned capital. A census contract transferred the use of land to a "borrower" who pays rent until the land is returned to the owner. Some Scholastic thinkers might not have agreed with the lucrum cessans argument, but it was a clear model for comparing different streams of future payments—part of the emerging logical framework of finance.

Another important concept that emerged from the Scholastic debate was the notion of just compensation for risk. In 1234, Pope Gregory IX took up the question of usury when repayment is not certain. While acknowledging the existence of risk, he declared loans for risky merchant ventures to be usurious. Imagine the effect this declaration had on maritime trade.

Scholastic thinkers recognized the validity of a risk premium for equity investment but not for debt. For example, the Dominican Domingo Soto (1495–1560) argued forcefully that the risk of losing an investment—not just an equity investment—demanded legitimate compensation. Soto proposed that an insurance premium is a just reward for the risk assumed (*periculi susceptio*) due to an uncertain outcome. Without it, no one could be induced to invest in risky trade ventures. Soto also pointed out the social benefits of risk sharing through insurance, since it encouraged commercial enterprise and thus contributes to the common good. By extension, an investor risk premium is a legitimate compensation, regardless of who is the owner of the asset.

PRESTITI DEBATED

The Venetian prestiti became the focus of theological debate about usury. The first argument in their favor was that they were necessary for the maintenance of the state—a view supported by the late-fourteenth-century scholar Nicholas de Anglia. Another justification for the prestiti is that they were forced loans and thus not based on the desire by the bondholder to receive compensation. As long as the bondholder did not buy the loan in the secondary market, went the logic, it was not sinful. Of course, the liquidity provided by the Rialto market was one of the great attractions of prestiti. Nicholas argued for the virtuousness of the secondary sale: the seller took a loss, which amounted to a gift to the state, while the buyer stepped in to help someone in need of cash. Another argument for the legitimacy of prestiti is simply that everyone did it. Pietro d'Ancarano (d. 1415) noted that they were owned by members of the curia—how could they be impious? Pietro also made another argument: that the prestiti were not in fact loans, because the principal was never paid back. A mutuum contract implies a return of capital. If you don't have to give the money back, it's not a loan. As long as prestiti had no terminal date, they could not be deemed usurious. Strangely enough, the perpetual nature of the loan legitimized it.

Although views of Pietro and other scholars in favor of prestiti were not universally accepted, it mattered little to practice. The genie of public finance was out of the bottle. While proscriptions against usury would have considerable effect on the forms (but perhaps not the prevalence) of private finance through the Middle Ages and the Renaissance, they did not stop European cities and states from making frequent use of this financial innovation. Nor did they likely stem the demand for savings instruments by the European populace. However, what emerged from the debate were several key concepts. First was the notion of financial capital. The definition of mutuum required specification of capital as a transferable asset. Second was a notion of a risk premium. This concept remains today the basis for all modern asset valuation models. Third was the notion of alternative use of capital as a benchmark for return. This, too, later became a key asset valuation tool.

NEW CAPITAL, NEW PERSPECTIVE

The Venetian debt and the secondary market for it in the Rialto represented an important new financial technology for the state as well as for the individual. For the state, it represented a means to shift resources from the future to the present—to concentrate capital and apply it to military purpose. This shift meant that it could respond to strategic threats and opportunities. As a by-product, it also incentivized Venetian bondholders to make sure the state had the future capacity to meet those obligations. The fact that Venice was a self-governing republic for which the citizens had a say in the creation and maintenance of the debt meant that it was a joint venture in shifting money through time and ultimately depended on sharing responsibility for the survival and growth of state resources.

With this new capital also came a new perspective, a new way of thinking about the world: the redefinition and secularization of time itself. The financial architecture of the Rialto in Venice spread through the rest of Italy and ultimately through the money centers of Europe. With this spread came an acute awareness that time had a price; that, with the emergence of alternative forms of wealth and varieties of investment, money could be put to work. The strangely oversized clock on the San Giacomo in the Rialto was perhaps not an accident. It suggested that time was a crucial dimension to Italy's early financiers. In the next chapter we shall see the extent to which the new Italian financial architecture and commercial enterprise led to innovations in the mathematics of time and money, and ultimately to a radically different process of education that focused on quantification and economic decision-making.

FIBONACCI AND FINANCE

Leonardo of Pisa is better known today as Fibonacci—the mathematician most famous for finding a geometric progression that explains the structure of sunflower blossoms and nautilus shells, the golden section, and, by some accounts, the pattern of booms and busts in stock market prices. Fibonacci was a citizen of Pisa, one of Venice's rivals in Mediterranean trade. Pisa is not far from Florence. like Venice, it was a powerful trading city in the twelfth century—its famous leaning tower grew in height as its fortunes increased—its vast cathedral and baptistery rivaled that of Venice and even Florence in scale if not in artistic richness. Born in the twelfth century, Fibonacci's youth was spent in the Pisan colony of Bugia in North Africa, where his father was a government official. There the young man received a dramatically different kind of education. He was tutored in Arabic mathematics. While boys of his age in Italy might have learned calculation through the use of cumbersome Roman numerals—or through the use of the counting board and the abacus to do sums, fractions, and multiplication—Leonardo was introduced to the amazing technology of written algorithms using number symbols directly.

In his brief autobiography in the preface to *Liber Abaci*, he says that he traveled extensively, presumably as a merchant, and everywhere he went he sought mathematical knowledge. On his return to Pisa, he consolidated that knowledge in a remarkable book. The title *Liber Abaci* means roughly "book of calculating." It introduces the reader to the use of Arabic numerals and all the basic algorithms that employ them: multiplication, addition, subtraction, division, and fractions. Although not the very first book to introduce these tools to Europe, it was undoubtedly the most important. *Liber Abaci* is not an abstract mathematical treatise written for mathematicians. It is a manual for business. After introducing numbers and arithmetic, it then jumps into how to value

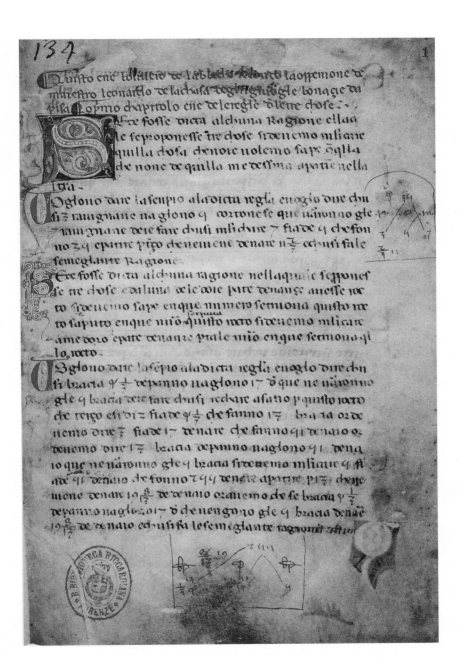

A page from Fibonacci's *Liber Abaci*, showing calculations for commodity pricing.

merchandise, bartering, how to calculate profits in a company, and, despite church laws against usury, it shows how to calculate interest rates. Only tacked on at the end is there a section on mathematical theory—a treatise on linear approximation, methods for finding square and cube roots, and techniques of solving binomials.

The *Liber Abaci* works through several examples to demonstrate how to apply these methods. The examples themselves are fascinating, because they are a window into the amazing vitality of Mediterranean trade at the turn of the eleventh century. Here is the kind of problem that the "New Math" of the Middle Ages was meant to solve:

> One has, near Sicily, a certain ship laden with 11 hundredweights and 47 rolls of cotton, and one wishes to convert them to packs; because 1⅓ hundredweights of cotton . . . is one pack. Then four hundredweights of cotton are 3 packs and four rolls of cotton are 3 rolls of a pack; you write down in the problem the 11 hundredweights and 47 rolls, and that is 1147 below the 4 rolls of cotton and you will multiply the 1147 by 3 and you divide by the 4; the quotient will be 860 and 1/4 rolls of a pack.[1]

Reading this passage, you can envision an Italian merchant in a trading galley of the twelfth century off the shores of Sicily, burdened with a load of cotton, planning how to sell it, and working to convert its value into quantities meaningful to Sicilian traders. The challenge of mind was not where to land the boat and who to contact to sell the goods. The challenge was how to convert quickly and surely from rolls to packs. Getting the conversion wrong will mean the loss of profit. Trading against Arab merchants trained in rapid commodity conversions forced Pisans to adapt to Arabic mathematics more surely than any academic treatise would have done.

The actual calculation in the above example uses "the Rule of Three," a form of cross-multiplication that solves for an unknown variable, given an equality relationship between two fractions. The Rule of Three can be traced back to earlier Arabic mathematical texts and from there farther to the East; to India and ultimately to China. Fibonacci did not invent the technique, but rather he learned it from his Arab tutor—or at least picked it up as a young mathematical tourist. In so doing, he re-connected Europe to the practical mathematical knowledge of Asia.

Most important of all, he introduced the numerals we call Arabic numbers. Arabic numbers were actually adapted by Islamic scholars from Indian numerals as were, undoubtedly, many of the techniques for using them for problem solving. Of course cross-multiplication implicit in the Rule of Three is one of the simplest operations of algebra—itself an Arabic term.

Leonardo of Pisa refers in his book to the Arabic mathematician al-Khwārizmi the eighth-century inventor of algebra. Although it uses algebraic techniques and pays service to al-Khwārizmi's *Algebra*, Leonardo's *Liber Abaci* differs in that it focuses on trade and commercial problems. Al-Khwārizmi applied his mathematical tools to legal issues—particularly problems of inheritance, such as how to divide up assets and liabilities among surviving family members. The *Liber Abaci* also has problems related to division of assets, but these are business assets rather than family assets.

Trade ventures in Leonardo's time were financed by contracts called "*commenda.*" These were the subject of extensive study and analysis by Robert Lopez, a Yale professor of an earlier generation, who saw in them the origins of modern commerce—perhaps even the origins of the modern corporation. Commenda contracts were actually more like partnerships in which the partners had different obligations. The *commendator* (or a group of commendators) invests capital while the *tractator* invests labor. In a standard contract, the commendator would invest in a merchant voyage, and on its return would receive three-quarters of the profits. Pisa's *Constitutum Usus* (1156) is the earliest surviving document defining the commenda contract. Fibonacci poses a problem that shows how such contracts were used as a means to divide the commendator profits among a company (or *societas*) of investors:

> Whenever ... any profit of an association is divided among its members we must show how the same is done according to the abovewritten method of negotiation. We then propose this of a certain company which has in its association 152 pounds, for which the profit is 56 pounds, and [it] is sought how much of the same profit each of its members must be paid in pounds. First, indeed, according to Pisan custom, we must put aside 1/4 of the abovewritten profit [apparently for the tractator] after this is dealt with there remains 42 pounds.[2]

Fibonacci then applies the Rule of Three to determine the profit per pound of investment and then shows how the profits to investors who commended different amount of capital can be determined. It is not unlike the partnership organized by Ea-nasir in Babylonian Ur in the second millennium BCE discussed in Chapter 3.

After working through various problems on company profits based on capital contributions, Fibonacci turns to banking and interest rate problems. Perhaps surprising in light of the usury debate in the thirteenth century, *Liber Abaci* contains a significant number of detailed interest rate problems. For example:

> A man placed 100 pounds at a certain [banking] house for 4 denarii per pound per month interest and he took back each year a payment of 30 pounds. One must compute in each year the 30 pounds reduction of capital and the profit on the said 30 pounds. It is sought how many years, months, days and hours he will hold money in the house.[3]

Notice what is required in this problem. The unknown in the equation is time, and the difficulty is that the investor withdraws a fixed amount each year from savings until the capital is depleted. In short, suppose you wished to live off of the interest on your nest egg. How long before your savings is depleted?

Fibonacci solves this challenging problem by brute force over three pages of calculation—the precise answer: 6 years, 8 days, and 5 hours. Whether or not bankers indeed parsed time and interest due down to the last hour, this problem is a perfect example of the secularization of time—the commodification of the sacred through the technology of finance condemned so vociferously by William of Auxerre. It suggests that innovations in banking manifested in the Rialto in Venice might not have been so unusual. Bankers' loans were evidently not only common but also of sufficient interest to warrant a number of problems in *Liber Abaci* as early as 1202. Alas, it would have been useful to know which "house" he referred to in the problem: The Templars (doubtful), a Lucchese or Florentine lender (possible), or a Venetian banker (again possible).

Although mathematically sophisticated, the ability to calculate interest rates on loans or even the term of a loan contract is not a factor that distinguished East from West. A problem in the *Suanshu shu*, the ancient Chinese mathematical text discussed in Chapter 8 in fact closely resembles this problem. Evidently even complex banking problems were also part of the shared knowledge of business mathematics of the medieval world by the turn of the twelfth century.

PRESENT VALUE

There is one problem in *Liber Abaci* that represents a watershed in financial history. It is titled "On a soldier receiving three hundred bezants for his fief." In the problem, a soldier receives an annuity from the king of 300 bezants [the coin of Byzantium] per year, paid quarterly. Fibonacci asks what would be the exact reduction in value if the king decided instead to defer the quarterly payments to a single payment at the end of the year. One might imagine just such a question arising in the Venetian Grand Council when contemplating the effects of deferring interest payments on their debt. Most importantly, the problem shows that money fiefs were in common use by the early thirteenth century as a way to compensate soldiers. It is also interesting that the fief was a retirement benefit, evidently granted for the life of the soldier. The problem is also important because the solution requires the notion of an alternative use of the money—the key concept that appeared in the usury debate. The problem specifies that the soldier could earn 2% per month on his investment, presumably by going to a banker.

From a mathematical perspective, the problem is a watershed in financial thought. Fibonacci solves it by valuing revenue forgone from an alternative investment stream—that is, what the soldier could get if he could earn interest on the cash each quarter by putting it in the bank. Forgoing this reduced the value of the fief considerably. The value of the 300-bezant fief is reduced to 259 and change.

Unlike even the complex banking problems, this problem is the earliest known case in which the present value of two cash flow streams are compared. Although I have searched earlier surviving works in mathematics, I can find no direct precedent for it in mathematical history. The method of "net present value" is the most important tool in modern finance.

Net present value can be used to guide a wide range of financial decisions—not only from the perspective of a government trying to reduce its expenses, but also from the perspective of a banker considering which loan to make: How much better is it to get payments quarterly as opposed to annually? Even today, this calculation fools many home buyers. Mortgage interest rates can be quoted based on daily, monthly, or annualized terms. The soldier's case shows how quarterly versus annual compounding makes a big difference. Fibonacci's *Liber Abaci* develops a framework for answering these and a vast array of other problems related to time and money.

Given its focus on commercial problems, bank loans, and present value, we might ask whether *Liber Abaci* was a salient factor in the "great divergence" in mathematics between East and West. Perhaps yes and perhaps no. Most of the techniques in the book, except the present value calculation, have an analog in the Chinese mathematical tradition—either slightly earlier or slightly later. A Chinese mathematician of the day could have solved every problem in the *Liber Abaci*—maybe even the problem of the soldier and his fief.

However, the classical Chinese mathematical texts before *Liber Abaci* have relatively few commercial problems. Thus, Leonardo represents mostly a difference in emphasis between Eastern and Western mathematics in the thirteenth century. The vast number and scope of commercial problems in the book clearly demonstrate the demand for the mathematical tools for business, a shift in the mathematical imagination toward practical problems of commerce. This secular orientation of leading mathematicians legitimized by Leonardo of Pisa would become much more important later in the Renaissance.

A BUSINESS EDUCATION

Strangely enough, despite being one of the most important works of mathematics in the European Middle Ages, a book that introduced widespread familiarity with Arabic numerals to the West, a book made famous for a ubiquitous geometric progression, and one that contains a wealth of information about thirteenth-century commerce in the Mediterranean, the first publication of the *Liber Abaci* in any modern language other than Italian occurred in 2002—800 years after it was written. Although pieces and examples from the book had earlier been translated, it was difficult for most scholars to appreciate its broad scope and design. For me, the experience of reading Larry Sigler's 2002 translation of *Liber Abaci* was extraordinary. I realized, as I read through each chapter, that Fibonacci had a distinctly familiar expository style. In many sections, he would introduce a simple problem, show how to use the techniques developed in a preceding section to solve it, and then move on through more complex examples. This approach is perfect for teaching—*Liber Abaci* was undoubtedly a textbook, constructed from a sequence of examples developed for education.

To describe it solely as a textbook does not completely do justice to its playful aspects. One whole section is devoted to curious mathematical puzzles. The famous geometric progression equation is really a puzzle about what happens when a pair of rabbits starts to breed unchecked—an echo of the Drehem tablet (see Chapter 2). The inclusion of recreational problems means that mathematicians were willing then, as now, to look at seemingly trivial events in everyday life and turn them into intellectual challenges. Parts of *Liber Abaci* are simply fun—something one could not say of later Scholastic philosophy. Perhaps this also made it a good book for teaching young students. It provides a means for engaging the reader. Leonardo of Pisa, who described his own early years as a student of mathematics, must himself have been a teacher.

Little is known about Fibonacci's life beyond his own brief autobiography in the opening chapter of the book. One public record of Fibonacci exists. The Pisan municipal archives document that Fibonacci was given a life annuity in 1241 (much like the soldier's fief!) in recognition of his teaching (*doctrinum*) and accounting, valuation, and calculating (*abbacandus estimationibus et rationibus*). This testament, brief though it may be, suggests that Fibonacci's teaching and advice had been of great public value.

Were his students the children of Pisan merchants? Did his knowhow give them an edge in their entrepreneurial ventures through the Mediterranean? My interpretation may, of course, be a stretch. "Doctrinum" could also mean learning, knowledge, or erudition. No public records of a school in Pisa exist to prove that Leonardo or anyone else was teaching business mathematics in the early thirteenth century, but then again, early records in general are scarce.

Professor Warren Van Egmond, historian of mathematics and an expert on early mathematics books, has made a study of the earliest known mathematics schools in medieval Italy.[4] A key feature of these early "reckoning schools" is that they were lay schools, not religious schools. Commercial education was secular. Business schools were separate from schools devoted to the humanities. He believes that organized reckoning schools postdate Fibonacci by a century. He cannot find any evidence of these schools in Italian cities before 1316, although by that time, mathematics teachers were numerous enough to have formed their own guild. Regardless of whether an older business school tradition existed, by the year 1338, as many as 1,000 youth in the city of Florence were attending abacus schools. Florence boasts some famous graduates of these schools—among them Niccolo Machiavelli and Leonardo da Vinci. Dante Alighieri sent his son to reckoning school.

QUANTIFICATION

Van Egmond's study suggests that, largely because of these reckoning schools, Florence became a major center of mathematical training and knowledge in the Renaissance. Florentine banking families were, for a time, the most powerful financiers in Renaissance Europe. Reckoning schools in the Renaissance must have played an important role in this success. In fact, historians have argued that the true revolution during the early Renaissance was not economic or even financial, but quantitative. If theologians and Scholastic thinkers in the late Middle Ages like William of Auxerre were worried that financial instruments would secularize life by the quantification of time itself, their concerns may have been well founded. The family archives of the great Italian banking families contain a wealth of numerical detail. Florentine households and businesses used careful records to track their financial wealth.

An Italian monk, friend of Leonardo da Vinci, mathematician, and the "father" of accounting, Lucca Pacioli published his most famous work of mathematics in 1494. Although much of the book was devoted to geometry, one section described the "Italian" technique of double-entry bookkeeping—a seemingly prosaic topic compared to the other subjects in his treatise. Yet this section immortalized Pacioli.

Pacioli based his bookkeeping method on a journal, a documentary record through time of the monetary inflows and outflows of the business. Each transaction is captured by two entries—a debit from one account and a credit to another. Debits and credits thus track the progress of the business through time, and they must balance each other when the accounts are periodically settled up—or else a mistake has been made. The genius of double-entry bookkeeping is that it was a means to reduce errors in documentation. But it also has a subtle effect. Once you begin to use it, you start to think of the world in terms of accounts. A household is not only a family, it is a sequence of expenses and periodic income. Even a soul can be envisioned as an account, with sins and penance needing to be totaled before passing on. The ledger becomes the quantitative essence of the organization—the numerical measure of its life.

Bookkeeping, long the foundation of administration in China—the redundant documentation of business transactions of an enterprise—became a revolutionary tool in Renaissance Europe. While the accounting revolution in China emerged from the need of the central government to control a vast, complex bureaucracy, these same techniques of enumeration and recording evolved in Europe as a means to calculate the progress of a business through time. From bullae to tablets to papyrus to bamboo slips to parchment and then to paper, the fundamental foundation of business and finance is the capacity to count, record, and thus verify economic value at a moment in time. The Scholastics rightly observed that processes defined how people viewed the world—that technology shaped reality as much as vice versa.

A FIBONACCI FUTURE

Fibonacci's *Liber Abaci* is important for historical, mathematical, and financial reasons. From a historian's perspective, it offers a rare, detailed picture of typical business problems current in the early thirteenth-century Mediterranean. It documents the variety of trade goods handled by Italian merchants and the various ports they visited. It also shows the developing tools of business, including the division of assets, sharing of profits, and putting money out to loan. Although Fibonacci was recognized for government service, the book is framed from the perspective of private enterprise—a perspective that has distinguished the West ever since.

From a mathematical perspective, *Liber Abaci* forever altered the way mathematicians work and reason. The introduction of Arabic numerals, ratios, and fractions freed them from counting boards and abacuses. It made paper (or parchment) and pen the tools of the mathematician. Fibonacci's financial methods reflect a process of reasoning that built from one solution to the next, from basic insight to increasingly complex solutions. This method of inquiry led him to an exquisitely precise measurement of the time value of money.

Most importantly, *Liber Abaci* extended the analytical powers of the human mind. The term for calculation is *"rationatabus"*—reasoning. The commercial arithmetic of *Liber Abaci* literally expanded the capacity for reason. It is difficult for the mind to juggle the relative value of multiple quantities and prices, particularly when they occur at different points in time. *Liber Abaci* provides the technology to do this. Just as spreadsheets and the Internet have narrowed the gap between Wall Street and Main Street, the new financial tools of the Middle Ages leveled the playing field of the marketplace. It is no wonder that *Liber Abaci* became the basic text for successive generations of Italian reckoning schools. Fibonacci created an educational tradition grounded in quantitative methods, not erudition and religion. In the final analysis, he changed the way Europeans learned, thought, and calculated.

Rather than embrace this new ethos, however, Europeans had to maintain not only the skills and knowledge of finance, but also a moral stance against it. Paying lip service to usury laws and condemning loans while teaching your children how to calculate the time value of money must have created problems. Although some Scholastics tried to reason their way around the implicit hypocrisy, financial development and the concomitant response of religious condemnation must have created problems in European society that were more psychological and existential rather than purely economic.

IMMORTAL BONDS

LEKDIJK BOVENDAMS

On July 1, 2003, a professor walked through the doors of the starkly modern headquarters of the water board of Utrecht, a utility company in charge of maintaining the dikes and canals around the city. The building is a sleek structure with a vast, sweeping glass facade; one of the kind of buildings that is remaking the architectural image of Europe from "old country" to "high-tech."

One of the company's age-old challenges is regulation of the flow of the river Lek; Utrecht sits at the juncture where the natural course of the river is diverted into human-made canals. The canal systems of the Netherlands are one of the great feats of human engineering; much of the Netherlands is the product of hydrological innovation and technology that began in the Middle Ages and continues today. The Dutch canal and dike system is not only a technological wonder but also a political and financial one. With a substantial part of the nation effectively below sea level, how does a nation—one that has not always even been a nation—respond to natural catastrophes like floods and dike ruptures? How does it get the capital to invest in large infrastructure projects whose costs far exceed any local underwriting capacity, and whose benefits extend in a complex geographical patchwork of municipalities that are threatened to varying degrees by dike failure?

Throughout Dutch history, by virtue of the crucial role they played in environmental security, the water companies like the firm in Utrecht, called "*Hoogheemraadschappen*," have had nearly extra-governmental power. Whether the country was run by the Spanish, French, or Dutch, the water companies maintained power of taxation and the ability to raise their own armies in times of need—armies to fight floods. Imagine Hoogheemraadschappen as a kind of separate, quasi-independent

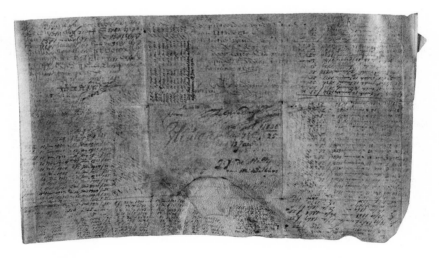

A perpetual 5% manuscript bond for 1,000 guilders issued by the Water Board of Lecdijk Bovendams in May 15, 1648. It was used to finance the repair of a dike in the river Lek, near Utrecht. It is a perpetual security that continues to pay interest.

lymphatic system in the political body of the Low Countries. Without their own capabilities, the great threat to the citizens would not be from their neighbors but from the ever-present risk of inundation. Throughout Dutch history, political disputes necessarily took second place to hydrology. The precursor to the Utrecht Hoogheemraadschappen was formed by treaty in 1323 between Holland and Utrecht. The bishop of Utrecht had allowed the dike of the Lek River to fall into disrepair, flooding not only Utrecht territory but also the neighboring lands of Count William of Holland, who responded by invading Utrecht and forcing an agreement on the bishop to maintain the integrity of the dike on the Lek in perpetuity.

The professor was not visiting today to discuss politics or hydrology or even the venerable history of the institution. He politely asked how to get to the accounting department. He was there to collect some money. Geert Rouwenhorst is my colleague at the Yale School of Management. He is an expert on international capital markets and on subtle techniques of stock and commodity trading to generate profits. He is also an expert in financial history. He carried with him an ancient, brownish parchment. Taking it out in front of the amazed accounting department of the Utrecht water board, he explained that they owed him twenty-six years of back interest.

The fading script recorded that, on May 15, 1648, Johan van Hogenhouck, the cameraer of Lekdijk Bovendams, received from Niclaes de Meijer 1,000 guilders. In return, he (or anyone else presenting the bond) would be paid 50 guilders of interest in two annual installments: November 15th and May 15th. The document was—is—a 1,000-guilder bond issued by the company in 1648—an important year in Dutch history, for it was the year of the signing of the treaty of Münster (part of the treaty of Westphalia), which ended eighty years of war with Spain and the Holy Roman Empire. It was a watershed event that marked the recognition by the Catholic powers of the Dutch republic's right to exist.

The parchment presented by Professor Rouwenhorst said nothing of this momentous event. It focused on an evidently simply agreement. It was issued by the Lekdijk Bovendams, an earlier predecessor of the modern Utrecht water board, which was responsible for maintaining a twenty-one-mile stretch of the dike of the Lek River, above the dam at Utrecht. The bond specifies precisely what the 1,000 guilders paid for—

the cribbing in the curve of the river near the town of Honswijck. The cribbing—long piers extending from the outside bank of the river turn—modulated the flow of the Lek and reduced the risk of a breach at that point. You can still see the modern replacements of the cribbing on the same curve in the river. The water company, the town of Honswijck, the cribbing—are all described in the document of 1648. All are there today.

When the Lekdijk Bovendams firm was incorporated into the Utrecht water board, all its responsibilities and obligations were carried with it, including the duty to continue to pay interest on its loans. What makes the document remarkable is not that it is a "fossil" from Holland's golden age, but that it is a living financial document, a perpetuity created more than 350 years ago that continues to accrue interest.

IMMORTALITY

Popular culture in America seems to have a fascination with vampires: movies, films, and popular novels feature these strange humanlike creatures. This fascination may reflect a general interest in gore, but it may also stem from the notion that a vampire lives indefinitely. In Anne Rice's novels, vampires bear witness to the passage of time. A vampire could have seen the building of the pyramids, the fall of Rome, the Napoleonic Wars, the invention of the airplane. A more benign version of perpetual life is envisioned in the book and 2002 film *Tuck Everlasting*, about a family that accidentally lives forever. Angus Tuck says "What we Tucks have, you can't call it living. We just . . . are. We're like rocks, stuck at the side of a stream."[1]

The Lekdijk Bovendams bond, like the Tucks, is a rock, stuck in the stream of Dutch history. For three and a half centuries, its owners (but who owns whom in this story?) have presented the document to the water board for payment. At first, perhaps, just to the home of Johan Hogenhouck, who dutifully counted out the semiannual payment and then noted the payment on the back of the document. Eventually, the empty space on the back of the bond filled up, and a paper document, called a "talon," was attached and notarized by the secretary of the Lekdijk Bovendams board to continue the record of payments. This happened in January 1944, at the height of the Second World War, when Anne Frank and her family still hid in the back rooms of their building in Amsterdam. The payments were first made in Carolus guilders; then Flemish pounds; then modern guilders; and finally, when professor Rouwenhorst showed up at the water board, in euros. Through it all, the money has flowed, the cribbing has been maintained, and the service on its ancient debt has held fast.

Is the ancient bond a vampire that is fated forever to suck the financial blood from the water boards in the future—to watch as generation on generation of buildings are built and the country transforms itself again and again, always mindful to maintain the basic hydrological infrastructure? Or is it simply, like Angus Tuck, a strange artifact that stands still as time sweeps by? The fact is, 50 guilders, translated into modern euros as €11.34 per year, is not much. The water board bonds—of which four from the seventeenth century are known for sure—are not such a financial drag. For a finance professor, the bond has yet another value. Whenever we teach students how to value a perpetuity, we are always asked if they are real—and if they are real, where are they? Finally we can show that they are not simply a convenient mathematical fiction!

What happened to all of the bonds from Venice, traded at the Rialto? What of the other perpetuities issued at first by rival Italian city-states? What of the later British consols, famous perpetuities issued in the eighteenth century? Some undoubtedly defaulted, some were restructured, and still others were repurchased by the issuers. In an open market, nothing stopped Venice from retiring her obligations at prevailing prices when resources were plentiful. Even the Lekdijk Bovendams could have been repurchased by the Utrecht water board when it came up for auction in 2003 and Yale University bought it. Then again, at the price Yale paid, it would not have been economically wise to do so.

The history of the bond since 2003 is also interesting. It was purchased for Yale's Beinecke Rare Book Library, which is one of the world's great archival libraries. It was hand-carried back to America on a plane and presented to the library. There the bond posed a serious problem. Apparently, Beinecke Library only accepts archival documents—things that are no longer functional instruments. The bond is a living tool, a piece of historical financial technology that still works. After all the trouble to find it, buy it at auction, authenticate it, and collect the interest, Beinecke could not take it. What to do? We eventually worked out a compromise. The bond itself would go into the collection, but the talon dating from 1944 would remain separate, at least until it got filled up. So periodically, someone at Yale can take it to Utrecht to collect the €11 of interest. The library cannot accept an immortal document.

LIFE ANNUITIES

The essence of a perpetual bond like the Venetian prestiti or the Lekdijk instrument is that its payments remain perfectly predictable through time, forever. Perpetuities are immortal. They transcend the scope of a single human life, they witness history. Indeed, their thrill is that they become part of a distant, dimly envisioned future. But one can imagine another species of financial instrument: a mortal bond, a bond tied to a human life.

At the same time that Italian cities were issuing perpetual securities, another form of financing flourished, one directly tied to the survival of its owner. These were an outgrowth of medieval census contracts, and life fiefs, like the one Fibonacci valued, but in modern times, they are called "annuities." A life annuity pays a fixed amount per year as long as the beneficiary is alive. It is like a perpetuity, only without the bequest. It inherits the buyer's mortality. An annuity thus should be cheaper to own, since it has a fixed life, but it is also a challenge to exactly value, because no one knows how long he or she will live.

Life annuities solved a really important problem. They guarantee that a person does not outlive their savings. Tying a payment stream to a person's life is an extremely efficient way to ensure against running out of money in old age. You buy neither too little nor too much future income. However, life annuities also raise another problem. How does the issuer calculate the value when the lifespan of the purchaser is unknown?

You might get lucky, and the buyer might die of plague right after buying the life annuity. Or you might end up paying and paying until the person lives to 100 years old or more. The risk of outliving your resources was shifted from the individual, but it did not disappear. It was shifted to the state. Place yourself in the shoes of the king who issued Fibonacci's soldier's fief. Suppose he issued a thousand of these; one for each of the soldiers who fought for him in a war. How much did this cost in present-value terms?

Annuities were known in the Greek and Roman world—indeed, they formed an essential part of the marriage contracts in Ptolemaic Egypt. Although they likely had private precedents, life annuities were issued by many of the northern European cities by the thirteenth century. The French towns of Douai and Calais issued life annuities by 1260;[2] Ghent used them by 1290. Researchers have found the practice extremely widespread: in Dordrecht, Bruges, Huy, and Amsterdam, to name only a few cities. By the sixteenth century, they had become the major form of public finance in the Low Countries—one study indicates that, by 1535, 60% of Amsterdam's annual budget went to make debt and annuity payments. By this time, if not long before, life annuities, along with government bonds, became widespread financial tools used by a broad spectrum of Europeans—not just the wealthy, but even those of moderate means. In this era, people could, in essence, buy social security contracts for themselves and their children. The state provided for their old age, certainly, but only in proportion to the investment they made.

Of course, Social Security in the United States has just this characteristic. On retirement or on reaching a certain age, annuitants receive a promise from the government to make periodic payments to them for as long as they survive, and in fact, for a married couple, this may extend to the lifespan of the surviving spouse. Social Security in the United States has the extra feature that the payments are wage-indexed, so retired people keep up with the steadily increasing quality of life and inflation. Thus, the concept of Social Security has its roots in the annuity contracts of Europe—and perhaps even deeper roots still. The modern problem of social security—how to value the long-term economic liabilities of the government when the payouts are many years in the future—is the very problem that sparked a whole new domain of mathematical science.

UNTIMELY DEATH

There is no clearer indication of the importance of life annuities to the economic existence of the Netherlands than the fact that, by the midseventeenth century, the head of state was called the "grand pensionary." The most famous of these grand pensionaries was Johan De Witt, who gained the post in 1653, the third year of the Lekdijk Bovendams payments. By most measures, De Witt was an extraordinarily successful head of state, negotiating an end to the first Anglo-Dutch War in 1654, building a strong Dutch navy, and furthering the cause of republicanism over the monarchy, represented by the family of William of Orange. Despite these accomplishments, in 1672 he was blamed for the attack on the Netherlands by the French and British. In that year, a plot was hatched against him and his brother by supporters of the Orangists. Cornelius De Witt was imprisoned on charges of conspiring to murder William III of Orange. Johan was lured to Cornelius's side in prison by an apparently fake letter. Both brothers were dragged from the prison into the streets, stabbed, torn apart, and partially eaten by an angry mob. William III of Orange praised and rewarded the conspirators.

What does the De Witt story have to do with finance? Much of the Netherlands' debt under his leadership took the form of life annuities, which were sold to young and old at equal prices. Johan De Witt quite rightly recognized that this made no sense at all. The stream of future payments for a child with long life expectancy should cost more than a stream of future payments tied to the life of an aging adult. It would be logical to charge a different price depending on the age of the individual. The question remained—what was the right price to charge?

De Witt attacked this question with mathematics and completed a pamphlet that worked out the basic features of the solution in 1671, the year before he was murdered. His work, *Value of Life Annuities in Proportion to Redeemable Annuities*, is a notoriously difficult publication to find, perhaps because of the confusion and dispersion of his and his brother's libraries after their deaths. It brings together the mathematics of the time value of money, much developed since Fibonacci's time, and the mathematics of probability—an infant but important science at the time of the book's writing. It tackled the most important fiscal problem for European governments of the age: how to balance revenues from issuing life annuities with the value of the future obligation to pay them.

De Witt recognized that the central challenge in the calculation of life annuity values was the probability of life expectancy—the need to estimate how long the cash flows would extend forward through time, on average, for annuitants of different ages. The problem was how to bring certainty to a quantity that was, by its very nature, uncertain.

De Witt sought to quantify the very risk that purchasers of annuities insured themselves against. To solve the problem, De Witt basically estimated survival probabilities according to age and then proposed an age-dependent pricing scale. It was a coarse simplification, but a significant step toward a solution. A more precise answer to the annuity valuation problem would actually emerge from something quite strange: games and play.

THE DISCOVERY OF CHANCE

The annuity contract was one of Europe's greatest contributions to humanity. By purchasing an annuity on a single life, or an annuity on a group of lives, citizens could shift the risk of longevity or untimely death from the family to the state. This allowed the state to pool together the risks of many families, which in turn made everyone better off. This innovation introduced a new problem, however. It was difficult for the state to understand the extent of the risk it assumed. Over the long run, how much would it cost to provide for the collective future of its annuitants, and what provisions must be made to pay off these complex annuity contracts in the future? The means to answer this problem lay in the new science of statistics and probability. The innovation in financial risk-sharing and the innovation in the means to understand it went hand in hand and became a salient difference between China and the West.

The mathematics of probability can be thought of as an organized approach to the unknown. Finance deals with the unknown future, and mathematical analysis of financial instruments led directly to the discovery of the laws of chance. Once the basic techniques of probability mathematics appeared in European culture, the genie of risk was out of the bottle. In this chapter, we trace the development of chance and the world that it ultimately created. Chance, of course, begins with gambling. Gambling has always been investment's evil twin—the active seeking of uncertainty rather than the avoidance of it. Even today, the archetypal dichotomy is strong. Investors are admired, speculators are vilified.

One of Italy's most illustrious doctors and astrologers, Girolamo Cardano (1501–1576) was a celebrity intellectual of the Renaissance. His autobiography is a colorful, highly personal, argumentative, and revealing work of a true polymath; the last in a series of more than 150 books

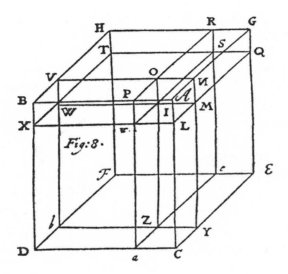

Edmond Halley's graphic representation of the mortality
probabilities for a tontine with three claimants.

that ranged over such diverse topics as mathematics, physics, astronomy, philosophy, diet, divination, and medicine. In it, he confesses a great regret:

> For many years—almost forty—I applied myself assiduously to gambling. It is not easy to say how greatly the status of my private affairs suffered, and with nothing to show for it . . . I say it with shame— every day, and with the loss at once of thought, of substance and of time.[1]

Cardano was a master student and strategist. His great contribution was to figure out the frequency with which certain number combinations would appear with the roll of one or more dice. He did this first by enumerating all possible outcomes, and then second, by counting the frequency with which these outcomes could appear, assuming that each side of each die is equally likely to appear on a given roll.[2] These frequencies helped Cardano decide with a high level of precision whether a given bet was a long shot or the odds were in his favor.

Before Cardano, gamblers may have known that the chance of rolling double sixes is slight, but they did not think of it mathematically as the result of multiplying 1/6 times 1/6 to get 1/36—or one in thirty-six times. Cardano's brilliant insight came from the simplicity of dice. With only six sides, it was possible to figure out all the different combinations of rolls and then count them up.

FROM DICE TO PEOPLE

After dice, mathematicians tried their hand at even more complex games of chance, such as wagering on sports events like predicting the outcome of a tennis match partway through. This latter problem is addressed by the Swiss mathematician Jacob Bernoulli in a letter to a friend on sets in tennis—or in the French, *jeu de paume*, in 1686. At the outset, he recognizes that the simplicity of enumerating all the outcomes of the role is not possible in games of skill and contests involving people rather than mechanical objects. However, he had a simple insight. If there is sufficient past history to study, it is possible to analyze complex games of skill involving unknown probabilities. Bernoulli's idea was that, even if you did not know the true probabilities of something happening, you could observe enough outcomes to be morally certain of the odds. For example, if you have a coin you know is lopsided, all you need to do is flip it many times to get an increasingly accurate idea of how much it favors heads versus tails.

Bernoulli argued that the mathematics of probability was humankind's way to deeper knowledge by cutting corners. We may not know whether a game will be won or lost by knowing what thoughts flash through the idea of a home-run slugger at the plate in the ninth inning of a tied baseball game, but if we study all the times the slugger was in that situation, we can calculate the odds of a game-winning home run and make a fair bet. For Bernoulli that's as close to omniscience as humankind can get.

Among all the great thinkers involved in the development of probability, Jacob Bernoulli is arguably the most important. He connected games of chance to real-world problems. Do you really have to know everything going on in the slugger's head to have moral certainty that he or she will hit that home run? Is moral certainty being 95% certain—99% certain? Bernoulli attacked the problem of moral certainty through the analogy of a silly game. It involved an urn.

An urn is filled with some white balls and some black balls. Do you need to count out every ball in the urn to be morally certain that the proportion of black to white is some fraction, say, 2:1? Bernoulli says no. If you are comfortable with being 99% certain that the fraction lies between 201/100 and 199/100, then he could tell you how many balls you have to check to have that level of certainty.

Does this make sense to you? If it takes a while to sink in, you are not alone. Bernoulli had to explain the concept twice—to the great mathematician Gottfried Leibnitz in a letter of 1704. Leibnitz is famous for having invented calculus, but he had a wide-ranging curiosity about the potential of mathematics to solve basic problems confronting humankind. This is why he and Bernoulli started a correspondence. Leibnitz was interested in the potential of statistically analyzing data to understand the laws of nature.

Bernoulli's argument is now called the "law of large numbers." In simple terms, it says that, as the number of cases you study increases, the estimated fraction of black to white in the urn converges closer and closer to the actual proportion in the urn. So even if the urn had 15 million balls in it, you would not need to count them all—or be their omniscient creator—you could tell with 99.9% certainty that the fraction of black to white is very close to 2:1. Still, this seems like a silly game and perhaps not obviously useful to any real problems. However, as Bernoulli explained to Leibnitz,

> If you now replace the urn with an old or young human body, which contains in itself germs [formitem] of diseases like the urn contains tokens, then you can determine in the same way by observations how much closer to death the former is than the latter.[3]

And in a later letter that year:

> The ratio between the number of deaths, even if the numbers are infinite, we can determine by a finite number of observations not exactly, but close enough for practice, approaching it more and more until the error is undetectable.[4]

For Bernoulli, drawing from an urn was only a model for understanding the probability of mortality in the young versus old. The law of large numbers—derived from the mathematical analysis of games of chance, allows one to predict with moral certainty the probability of death—and thus the life expectancy of both young and old. It could be used to solve the problem of life annuity prices—the political and economic problem undertaken by Johan De Witt just before his horrible death (Chapter 14).

In the Bernoulli–Leibnitz correspondence, they both withheld something from the other. Bernoulli would not show Leibnitz his proof of his marvelous proposition. Perhaps he feared Leibnitz would publish it before him. And Leibnitz withheld a book that Bernoulli pleaded repeatedly to obtain: De Witt's tract on annuities. Leibnitz toyed unmercifully with Bernoulli, excusing himself that he left it on his desk and can't find it now—promising it would be forthcoming. The pettiness of academic rivalry! Bernoulli thought (mistakenly) that De Witt had used real data based on mortality tables to value the Dutch annuities according to age and was hoping to get his hands on the data to apply his theory.

BASEL

Bernoulli was a professor at the University of Basel—still a vibrant intellectual center with a significant mathematics department. The university is on a hill overlooking the Rhine, but the Bernoulli family lived in a different part of town, just near the main market square, opposite the town hall of Basel. Jacob lived in a modest, narrow house on a tiny square. However, to get to work, Jacob would have walked through the market every day—confronted with the interesting problems of commerce as much as the heady problems of moral philosophy.

One of the oddest things about their correspondence is that Leibnitz did not share with Bernoulli the precious empirical data on life expectancy that he had obtained from another scholar with whom he corresponded. Caspar Naumann made a careful study of the city records of Breslaw in the 1690s. These records provided copious details about the births and deaths in the Silesian port city from 1687 to 1691—enough information to reliably estimate the life expectancy for various age groups. Instead of sharing this data with Bernoulli, Leibnitz forwarded it to the Royal Academy in London, where it piqued the interest of the astronomer, Edmund Halley. Halley used the Breslaw data to construct mortality tables, that is, frequencies of death by age group. He published his findings in 1693 in the *Transactions of the Royal Academy*.[5] Perhaps most importantly, Halley used statistical analysis to show that the government was selling their life annuities way too cheaply.

Life annuities in England during Halley's time cost the same for the young as for the old. Halley used the mortality tables to show that the government was playing a losing game when it sold an annuity to anyone younger than thirteen years old. Children, even with the high mortality of youth at the time, were more likely to live a long life, and the government would just have to keep paying and paying as they aged. A reasonably healthy thirteen-year-old could live another seventy years! Halley's analysis was of course ignored by the British government, which continued to price its annuities too low.

The implication of Halley's calculations is that governments were not benefiting financially from annuity sales. They were playing a losing game against their citizens. If a gambler keeps steadily losing at the craps table, surely she need not be a brilliant mathematician to figure out that the odds are against her. The mispricing of life annuities by France and Britain in the seventeenth and eighteenth centuries put into place a long-term fiscal problem. What's worse, this dramatic loss would be disguised by time. The losses would come in the distant future. As younger annuitants continued to live longer than expected, the governments would be paying out more than the benefits they received. For Americans listening to the Social Security debate today, this sounds familiar—a fiscal time bomb that would inevitably become a political time bomb.

Ironically, Basel today is best known as the nerve center of risk management for the global banking system. The Basel Accords are a set of standards for banking regulation. The Basel Committee on Banking Supervision comprises representatives from the central banks of twenty-seven countries who decide, in excruciating mathematical detail, how banks should measure their risk and decide how much capital they need to prevent insolvency. A key calculation the committee suggests is the measure of the amount of loss a bank can expect to incur in a given year. The fundamental tool used to give regulators confidence in the expected loss calculation is Jacob Bernoulli's law of large numbers. As the world tried to harmonize its rules to prevent the next global banking crisis, its tools—indeed its very way of conceptualizing the problem—owe a huge debt to the probability calculus of Jacob Bernoulli and the many other probabilists of his era who saw how to turn games of chance into a framework for analyzing risk.

ANNUITIES AND REVOLUTION

Around the turn of the seventeenth century, the gaunt figure of Abraham de Moivre seated in the bowed glass window of Slaughter's Coffeehouse in St. Martin's Lane, London, was a common sight. De Moivre always looked hungry, and indeed he often was. He rarely had cash, but that did not stop him from spending his day devouring books—plays and novels as well as treatises on mathematics and physics. He kept pages of Newton's *Principia* in his pockets, so he could read them at any spare moment. What cash he had came from math lessons he offered and small royalties from books he wrote. His most popular book, *A Doctrine of Chances, or a Method for Calculating the Probabilities of Events in Play,* was printed in 1718 and revised occasionally throughout his lifetime. The book was written in English and was a translation and extension of a treatise in Latin he had presented to the Royal Academy in 1709. Unlike Bernoulli's erudite works on probability, the publication in the vernacular made the work broadly accessible to the common person. His preface to *Doctrine of Chances* explains its purpose:

> The Doctrine of Chance may likewise be a help to cure a Kind of Superstition, which has been of long standing in the World, vz. that there is in Play such a thing as Luck, good or bad.[6]

The book systematically analyzed the various games of chance that amused Londoners of the day: dicing, lotteries, raffles, and card games. It is a peculiar irony that a man who had analytically mastered the most popular games of chance would lead a life of poverty. Perhaps he was averse to gambling because of his Calvinist faith. In any event, he likely tutored others in mathematics, the laws of probability, and in finance, and the London beaux who frequented the gambling tables undoubtedly considered his consulting services valuable. In all likelihood, so did financiers who traded in lottery tickets, and perhaps issuers and purchasers of life annuities, for whom the time value of money figured heavily.

One of de Moivre's most important contributions is a formula for a fixed stream of future payments over a fixed number of years. In 1724, he used his valuation method in *A Treatise of Annuities on Lives*. He gives credit to his friend Halley's earlier calculations, but also suggests that he is able to improve on them. De Moivre noted that the time value of money seriously complicates the calculations for correctly valuing life annuities. The age of the policyholder mattered even more than Halley supposed. He showed that annuity buyers at most age groups were, in effect, getting a price subsidy for purchasing financial security over their lives.

Consider the US Social Security system. When you reach retirement age, Social Security begins to pay you a life annuity. The major criticism of the Social Security system is that the present value of the payments made by US workers into the system when they are young does not cover the cost of the future payments they receive when they retire; people are living longer. This is precisely the issue faced by governments selling annuities in the seventeenth and eighteenth centuries. They were evidently not charging enough for the social security they provided. For the US Social Security system, as long as the population continues to grow, the income from payroll taxes can cover the payouts to annuitants. However, when this ratio changes, the system will become a drain on government resources. The implications of Halley's and de Moivre's calculations is that governments were not benefiting financially from annuity sales. Even after De Witt's, Halley's, and de Moivre's studies were written, governments did not change annuity prices to set the odds in their favor.

How could this be? Was the annuity system at that time envisioned like US Social Security, a way to provide widespread social insurance? Might the mispricing have been because lawmakers who set the prices of these annuities were themselves the major purchasers? Perhaps it was simply a problem that was too difficult to deal with. Or maybe governments were worried that if they priced annuities at something close to their real value no one would buy them.

FRENCH ANNUITIES

Throughout the eighteenth century, France increasingly financed itself through the issuance of life annuity contracts and tontines (i.e., annuities paid to the survivors of a group, rather than to a single individual). As already noted, these types of annuities depend crucially on understanding mortality tables and pricing the contracts accordingly. The tontines were extremely complex instruments, a bit like mortgage-backed securities of our day, except that the cash flows were based on government payments and parsed out to successive tranches of survivors.

A typical tontine from this era shows how this worked. It is a four-page printed document with a parchment insert—presumably because parchment can last longer than paper. It was issued in Paris to the family of Pierre l'hermitte de Chateauneuf (an infantry captain) and his wife Elisabeth Delalande. They purchased a contract on the head of their five-year-old daughter Suzanne Elisabeth L'hermitte de Chateauneuf. It cost 300 livres and paid 24 livres annually for as long as she lived. The day she died, one-quarter of the revenues would go to the crown, and three-quarters would go to the survivors in her age group; Suzanne was in the second subdivision, first class of a national tontine. As these young children passed away, the survivors would receive a greater and greater

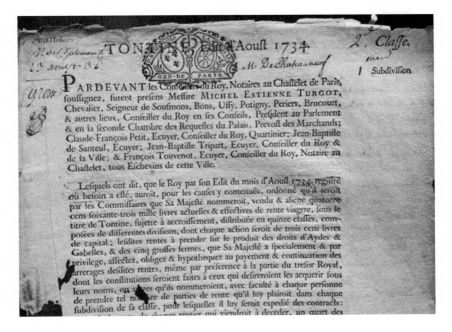

FIGURE 19. A French tontine from 1734.

share of the cash flow from the tontine. The tontine contract promises from the very start that the government guarantees the revenue to support the payments with salt and other commodity taxes—and promises that the rentes were exempt from seizure, revocation, or restructuring for any purpose whatsoever—including the needs of the king.

This looks like a great deal from a parent's point of view. You get 8% interest on your investment for as long as your child is alive, and if she lives to an old age, she will receive an ever increasing share of the income. If she survives 90% of the children in her age group in France, for example, she would be receiving her own 24 livres, plus three-quarters of the flows from her deceased cohort: 186 livres in total. Thus, 186 livres on 300 livres is a 62% yield!

From the government's point of view, over time, as it retired one-quarter of each tontine contract when a holder passed away, the rents paid to survivors gradually declined from 8% to 6% per year. Still, the survivors of the various tontines were a burden to the government, and in 1770, despite the many promises in the document, Abbe Terray, the

French controller general, restructured the tontine debts. He replaced all tontines with life annuities paying 10%—regardless of whether the holders were young or old.

If Suzanne Elisabeth were alive at age 40 in 1770, this took away a lot of the value of the tontine—she would never get the chance to retire with the promised 186 livres of income. Historian David Weir calculated that Terray's flat rate saved his government a lot of money on the tontines, but it cost a lot of money on the live annuities.[7] When the news broke that the government was issuing life annuities at a 10% yield—regardless of age—there was something of a financial gold rush. Speculators saw a wonderful opportunity.

The only thing worse than selling life annuities at the wrong price is selling them to clever people who know precisely how best to exploit the mistake to their advantage. By 1770, European financiers had all read the new research on probability and life annuity valuations, even if government officials had not. With each new French government issue of life annuities, financial engineers in Holland and Switzerland bought them up and then issued bonds collateralized by the annuity cash flow.

The securities issued by syndicates of Geneva-based bankers were among the most common. A Geneva investment syndicate would purchase French life annuities on the lives of thirty young girls at a time— trente demoiselles. The girls were from well-to-do families (some the daughters of the syndicators) and would typically have survived smallpox. Published life annuity tables at that time suggest that this age group was likely one for which the annuities were the most mispriced. The bonds issued against this portfolio of life annuities would pass through the annuity receipts from the French government each year to bondholders.

Weir and his coauthor François Velde dug into French financial data about tontines and found an interesting fact. In 1781, "three-quarters of the flat-rate [annuity] subscriptions were placed on young children."[8] Roughly 40–50% of these were arranged by bankers in Geneva. This suggests that the bankers were seriously exacerbating future expected losses. If the life annuities were sold to both young and old, at least some mispricing would be mitigated.

The historians have a slightly different interpretation, however. They showed that, as the French Revolution approached, France had to pay high rates for all of its borrowings—not just the annuities. Not only that, but with the restructuring of 1770, it was clear to the entire market that government promises could and would be broken. As much as anything, France on the eve of the revolution was simply a bad credit risk. Through tontines, life annuities, and other vehicles, it had borrowed to the limits of it taxation and revenue-generating powers. Cutting prices on life annuities and pumping them out to Genevan bankers to securitize and resell was a short-term financial fix that preceded an inevitable default.

One interpretation of French government finance in the eighteenth century is that the tontine and life annuity system—had it worked—solved two important problems at once: personal retirement and government finance. If everyone in France owned annuities or tontines, then they would all be provided for in old age. Life annuities insure beautifully against outliving your capacity to support yourself. Because of the law of large numbers, a government can take on this risk better than an individual can, and can collect the insurance premiums that individuals are willing to pay. As long as they are issued at a fair market price, life annuities and tontines should be a cheaper way to finance the government, as well as an excellent way to take care of people in their old age. Problems arise when the politics get in the way of fair pricing and when the government can't be trusted to pay off. Weir and Velde argue that the failure of trust was as much a factor in the French Revolution as the poor state of government finances. Life annuities represented a fundamental social contract between France and its citizens. When these contracts failed, the government followed suit.

SUMMING UP PROBABILITIES

Notice that, over the course of about a century, European mathematicians had done something extraordinary—and their accomplishments had real-world political consequences. First, they took a seemingly unhealthy interest in games of chance and turned it into a science. The crucial step in this transition was the recognition that games were controlled models of real-life situations. Mathematical insights into real situations might have stopped, however, at the point at which the complexity of real situations exceeded the analytical capacity of the mathematician. Bernoulli conceived of a means to attack even the most complex situations with probabilistic tools through the use of statistical data; history could be used to estimate probabilities, rather than having to enumerate all possible outcomes. If each moment in life were the result of the simultaneous roll of countless numbers of dice, Girolamo Cardano had given up attempts to forecast the net outcome. But De Witt, Halley, Bernoulli, and other probabilists around the turn of the eighteenth century discovered a new approach to the unknown. Statistics could get you pretty far along to moral certainty.

Their discoveries had unforeseen but dire financial implications and consequences. Although De Witt's contributions caused Dutch annuity issuers to control for age differences, Halley, de Moivre, and Bernoulli confronted France and Britain with undeniable evidence that their financing methods would lead to a future fiscal crisis. Indeed, by publishing their findings, they hastened and worsened the crises. Some countries were able to adjust their financing to match the mathematically fair prices—others could not. The cumulated debt from both borrowing and mispricing in France grew over the eighteenth century, and by the 1770s arbitrageurs in Geneva were making the problem even worse—making default all but inevitable. A potentially wonderful financial symbiosis between a deficit-running government and its annuity-reliant citizens fell to pieces with the French Revolution.

PROBABILITY IN CHINA

Was there a parallel development of probability theory and statistical analysis in Chinese mathematics during the seventeenth and eighteenth centuries? Joseph Needham's study of Chinese mathematics in *Science and Civilization in China* turns up some interesting possibilities. He identifies a figure in a Song dynasty text that resembles what is known today as "Pascal's Triangle"—a chart that enumerates all possible outcomes of a number of coin flips.[9] Interestingly, Needham notes that the Chinese figure was not for probability calculations but for algebra. It depicted the coefficients in an expansion of a sum of two terms taken to a higher power. It was called, according to Needham's translation, "the tabulation system for unlocking binomial coefficients."

Chinese mathematicians of the seventeenth and eighteenth centuries were most interested in algebra, geometry, trigonometry, and celestial mechanics—but evidently not probability theory. While China had games of chance, and Chinese mathematicians studied combinatorics, the dramatic discoveries in the mathematics of probability in Europe around the turn of the seventeenth century seem to have had little influence on the Chinese mathematical tradition. China effectively shut its doors to Western mathematics for the century from 1723 to 1839. This hiatus in contact meant that, not only did China fail to absorb advances in probability, it also did not learn about the calculus.

Mark Elvin, one of the leading thinkers about the great divergence between China and the West, is particularly puzzled by the absence of mathematical probability in China, or the adoption of the tools of probability from the West. He points out that gambling in China was just as pervasive as in Europe, and that China shared ancient Indian and Middle Eastern traditions of dice and board games.[10]

Perhaps most importantly, China had an ancient tradition of prediction based on random events, a tradition that began with Shang oracle-bone divination, continued in the Zhou dynasty with the *I Ching*, and from then on to the present. The *I Ching* divination system is implemented by random throws of coins or yarrow stalks. In fact, Leibnitz was interested in the *I Ching* figures, because they represent, in effect, all possible combinations of six flips of a fair coin.

Elvin documents many examples of probabilistic thinking and reason in Chinese history—some based on divination, others on gambling and games. In fact, Elvin finds a remarkable mathematical tract by Li Qingzhao [李清照] (1084–ca. 1151), a female Song poet who wrote widely admired, emotional, impressionistic verse. Like Cardano, she was a polymath—a book collector, antiquarian, and a devoted gamer.

Li invented a board game called "Horses Out!" which used three dice for a roll. In the game, she enumerated the different combinations that led to each outcome. However, she did not take the next, crucial step: working out probabilities from frequencies of outcomes. Elvin claims that this small but crucial leap evidently consistently eluded Li and other Chinese thinkers. Or, if the leap did take place, it was not documented in historical sources.

Perhaps professional gamblers in China knew how to calculate odds, but the knowledge never transitioned to higher mathematics or intellectual discourse. Why not? It could not be due to a lack of useful application of statistics in China. Economic statistics were a fundamental part of the government accounting system. Surely the law of large numbers might have been useful for estimating the net crop yield for a group of provinces, estimating the food needed for a standing army, understanding the attrition rates of horses brought from Mongolia, or a host of other situations requiring forecast and accurate allocation of resources.

It could have been an accident of history that China did not invent (or adopt) a mathematics of chance. Then again, the intimate relationship between the early probability theorists in Europe and the development of the capital markets suggest that finance may have been one of the motivating forces for the deep interest in probability and the adoption of these techniques from games.

The annuity valuation problem was noted by most probability theorists around the turn of the seventeenth century. Although it is clear that their methods had a major impact on financial innovation in the eighteenth century, perhaps the reverse is also true. Mathematicians were not only interested in solving problems of dice but also in solving problems like compound interest and the correct price of a government annuity. The two technologies evolved together—financial markets and financial thought.

CROSS-CHANNEL CONFLICT

In 1794, as the Reign of Terror raged, the Marquis de Condorcet penned one of the most optimistic tracts of the eighteenth century. He wrote hurriedly and in hiding, staying with his friend Madame Vernet in a back room at 14 Rue Servandoni near the present-day Luxembourg Gardens in Paris, evading an arrest warrant that would surely mean his death. Condorcet was a brilliant mathematician—a major contributor to the development of calculus. He had been lured into politics and economics by appointment as the inspector-general of the mint in Paris. He was one of the most enlightened of Enlightenment figures: an abolitionist, proponent of women's rights, an advocate of democracy, and a deep believer in the power of rational thought as the means to solve the problems of humankind. Despite these liberal views, he was in trouble for advocating imprisonment rather than the execution of Louis XVII. After completing his book, the marquise was caught escaping from Paris. *A Sketch for a Historical Picture of the Progress of the Human Spirit* was published posthumously in 1795 and has become one of the landmark works of the Enlightenment. It celebrates the progress of science as a means to knowledge and sketches a view of a future society in which many of the world's social problems are solved. Finance and probability play a major role in this vision. Notwithstanding the French government's debilitating defaults on tontines, Condorcet believed that the same financial architecture could be used to provide universal old age pensions:

> inequality, however, may be in great measure destroyed, by setting chance against chance, in securing to him who attains old age a support, arising from his savings, but augmented by those of other persons, who, making a similar addition to a common stock, may happen to die before they shall have occasion to recur to it . . . increased at the expence of those whom premature death may cut off before they arrive at that period. To the application of mathematics to the probabilities of life and the interest of money, are we indebted for the hint of these means, already employed with some degree of success, though they have not been carried to such extent, or employed in such variety of forms, as would render them truly beneficial, not merely to a few families, but to the whole mass of society, which would thereby be relieved from that periodical ruin observable in a number of families, the ever-slowing source of corruption and depravity.[11]

Condorcet proposed "setting chance against chance" to insure the chance that one person would live beyond their productive age against another chance that someone would die prematurely. In this way, he imagined using mathematics and probability as a path to a future in which the family was no longer exposed to ruin. He predicted that an ever increasing number of people would be able to live in a better world. In fact, he popularized the fundamental notion of progress.

(a)   (b)

FIGURE 20. (a) The Marquis de Condorcet and (b) Thomas Robert Malthus.

In 1798, Thomas Robert Malthus, a minister in Surrey who had studied mathematics at Jesus College, Cambridge, took public exception to
the rosy future portrayed by Condorcet. His book, *An Essay on the Principle of Population, as It Affects the Future Improvement of Society, with
Remarks on the Speculations of Mr. Godwin, M. Condorcet, and Other
Writers,* pointed out what he saw as fundamental flaws in the Marquis'
reasoning:

> By the application of calculations to the probabilities of life and the
> interest of money, he [Condorcet] proposes that a fund should be
> established which should assure to the old an assistance, produced,
> in part, by their own former savings, and, in part, by the savings of
> individuals who in making the same sacrifice die before they reap the
> benefit of it. . . . Such establishments and calculations may appear
> very promising upon paper, but when applied to real life they will be
> found to be absolutely nugatory. . . . Were every man sure of a com-
> fortable provision for his family, almost every man would have one,
> and were the rising generation free from the 'killing frost' of misery,
> population must rapidly increase.[12]

In Malthus's view, there were natural limits to the progress of humankind that are simple functions of biology. In good times, the population would expand and ultimately compete for limited resources; a social insurance system that eliminated the normal depredations suffered by humanity would tend to (1) reduce the death rate and further increase ruinous population growth and (2) eliminate the incentive to work, which would in turn slow the production of food and economic growth relative to population growth. He argued that the arithmetic of a social safety net based on a life annuity scheme was doomed to failure. A social security system, even one grounded in the modern mathematical methods of the eighteenth century that incorporated probabilities and the time value of money is a chimera—a plan for the future doomed to failure because of the natural propensity of humanity to reproduce.

With Condorcet and Malthus, the mathematics of probabilities and compound interest became the intellectual tools of moral philosophers exploring the possibilities and limitations of the human race. One dreamed of a state-run social security fund, the other claimed that it would destroy economic incentives. Without the development of the mathematics of chance and the European tradition of annuities and tontines, the dialectic between their views would never have occurred—or if it did, the framework of analysis would have been fundamentally different. Although the debate between Condorcet and Malthus was never consummated face to face, in the centuries that followed, it would frame one of the greatest challenges of the modern world—universal provision for an uncertain future.

So the creation of life annuities and the imagining of a future in which they could help everyone in society—not just those who could afford to buy them—led to the realization of another previously unimagined consequence: humanity would become the victim of its own success. The negative shadow of Thomas Malthus hovered over the shining hope of finance.

EFFICIENT MARKETS

The Enlightenment tradition of mathematical inquiry was stimulated by the financial markets and the variety of unusual securities traded in them and vice versa. In this chapter, we take a look forward in time. We deviate a bit from the historical timeline to follow the probability rabbit down the rabbit hole. In the nineteenth and early twentieth centuries—primarily in France—the continued inquiry in probability mathematics and the belief that training in probability was an essential part of an education led to some of the most important scientific models used to describe the physical world, as well as to a basic insight about the difficulty of beating the market.

In this chapter, we jump ahead and follow this story into modern times. We meet several interesting figures; the first is the Parisian broker and financial economist Jules Regnault, who developed the theory of efficient markets. The second is Henri Lefèvre, the accountant for the Rothschild bank in Paris who designed a way to calculate complex positions of stocks and bonds simultaneously. The third is Louis Bachelier, the French academic mathematician whose fascination with pricing options trading on the Paris Bourse led to the discovery of Brownian motion—an abstract model of how a system evolves through time.

Together, their insights led to virtually all the tools of modern financial engineering. The limitations of these tools ultimately exposed the potential for failure of even our most complex models. In particular, they led to the development of financial derivatives—financial tools referred to by investor Warren Buffett as "weapons of mass destruction,"[1] but which are also are widely recognized as the fundamental tools of insurance and risk mitigation. We shall see that the work of three of the giants of modern finance, Robert Merton, Fischer Black, and Myron Scholes, built directly on the insights and techniques of the French mathematical tradition—both in terms of its strength and also its weakness. This last

Nineteenth-century print of the Paris Bourse.

point is reserved for a discussion about a modern French mathematician, and my former Yale colleague, Benoit Mandelbrot.

RANDOM WALKS

Almost nothing is known about the nineteenth-century French stock-broker Jules Regnault (1834–1894). What we do know comes from the efforts of Franck Jovanovic, a lecturer in finance at Leicester University. Over the past decade, Jovanovic has studied the intellectual development of mathematical finance and traced a key logical foundation of modern quantitative methods to Jules Regnault, a successful broker on the Paris Bourse during the middle of the nineteenth century.[2]

In 1863, Regnault wrote a strikingly novel book, *Calcul des Chances et Philosophie de la Bourse*, arguing that it is impossible to profit by speculating in the market. This was quite an opinion from someone who made a living by brokering stocks and bonds! Regnault credits his insight to Jacob Bernoulli's "beautiful" theorem—that by averaging together a near-infinite series of random events, one converges arbitrarily close to the true tendency. Regnault saw the stock market as the embodiment of Bernoulli's famous urn—with thousands of individual opinions inside. Market prices are formed by drawing balls from the urn; each trade another draw. After hundreds of draws, the central tendency of the price would be revealed. As people trade, their opinions—both optimistic and pessimistic—all average out and push market prices to the "average" belief.

Because of this, Regnault argued, it is hard to make a profit. By the time you go to trade, the market price already reflects the collective wisdom and knowledge of all the speculators before you. Unless you know for sure that you have information that no one else, the chance that your trade will yield a profit or a loss is no better than 50:50. If this were not true, speculative forces would quickly push the price lower or higher to make it true. In short, the market becomes a fair game, with fair odds by virtue of its many, many active participants seeking to profit. No matter how sophisticated a trading scheme one devises to predict future price movement, Regnault argued, price changes will follow a random pattern.

Regnault also pointed out that, while the future price of a security is uncertain, the cost to trade it is not. Brokers get their fees. The only thing an investor knows for sure is that, with each trade you must pay a commission, and over time, this will lead to your ruin. Part of the book is devoted to a careful calculation of how long it will take a speculator to lose all his or her money.

Regnault developed his "fair game" theory of the market into a mathematical hypothesis. He noted that if his randomness theory were correct, then the range of values realized by a stock should increase according to a very specific pattern. Regnault calculated that the expected difference in a stock's price from one date to another should be proportional to the square root of the time between the dates.

He believed he had discovered something like a universal law of markets. If it were a "fair game," then variation in the price of a security in the market would grow according to a simple rule. To test his theory, Regnault collected bond prices over time and statistically analyzed them—it worked beautifully! While it may seem abstract, Regnault's rule is useful, because it allows an investor to calculate how much risk he or she is exposed to by holding a portfolio of stocks over a given time period. Indeed, this principle is at the heart of the rules used by international regulators to determine how much risk banks may take.

Regnault called the Bourse the "temple of modern times"—an apt description of the building in which he worked. The Paris Bourse is a massive neoclassical edifice designed in 1808 and constructed over the next two decades in the Place de Bourse. The building still stands. It resembles a grand palais wrapped by a Corinthian colonnade. Once inside, however, it opens to a trading floor beneath a four-story-high vault marvelously decorated with allegorical murals. Today the Paris Bourse has been acquired by Euronext, an electronic trading system that no longer requires floor brokers and the face-to-face interaction of market makers setting prices. Fortunately, Paris has preserved this glorious fragment of physical financial architecture, even though the technology of the market has moved on.

OPTION DIAGRAMS

Henri Lefèvre (1827–1885) is another pioneer in the development of mathematical models of the stock market. Franck Jovanovic has also made an in-depth study of his work.[3] Lefèvre focused on understanding the complex behavior of option prices. Recall that options on

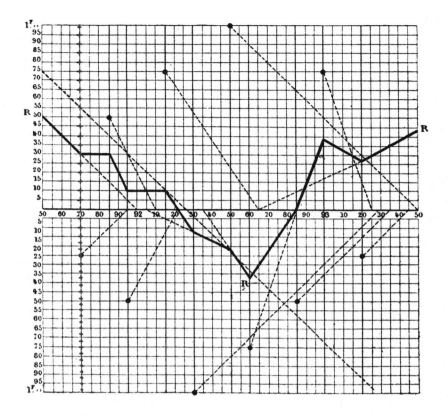

FIGURE 21. Complex option payoff diagram used by Henri Lefèvre to demonstrate the flexibility of his graphical method of representing options.

stocks were traded almost as early as stocks themselves. An option is a contract that gives you the right to buy a stock in the future at a price set today. An option to buy is termed a "call" option; the owner of the option has the right to call on the counterparty to deliver the stock in return for the agreed price—even if the stock has gone way up in value. A call option is a way of betting that a stock will go up without actually buying it.

A put option is the opposite. It gives you the right to sell a stock to someone—even if they don't want it—at a previously agreed-on price. You get to "put" the stock to the counterparty, and get your price, even if the market price has dropped way down. In Jules Regnault's world, puts and calls should be fairly priced for the same reasons as mentioned above: speculative activity will drive their values to a fair price. While puts and calls can be used for betting on stock price movements, they can also be used to reduce risk. For example, having a put allows you to hedge against a big drop in the price of a stock. This dual use has often made them the object of public criticism, but it also made them useful tools for risk management.

Lefèvre, like Regnault, was interested in the philosophy behind the market. He saw it as having great social value and as an engine of efficiency. His contribution was to create a very simple way to diagram the payoffs to options. For example, if you own a put and a call, then you can make money if the stock price goes up or down. Of course, the fair-game rule of the market implies that the price of buying these two options is equal to the profit you expect to get from them.

Lefèvre showed that this put-and-call position could be represented on graph paper—a Cartesian grid—as a V shape, with one arm representing the put and the other arm the call. As the stock prices changes along the *x*-axis, the value of the portfolio changes along the *y*-axis.

He then showed how to diagram even the most hopelessly complex set of option investments on a given stock (or bond or commodity) just by geometrically adding up the separate payoffs to each. He thus gave the world a rational diagram that decomposed some of the most complex securities ever devised—derivatives. No doubt his discovery was of great value to his employers, the Rothschilds!

This innovation was extremely important, because, among other things, it allowed option traders to quickly and precisely calculate their exposure to price movements in any security, and if need be, to adjust that risk by buying or selling more derivative contracts. This hedging goes on today at an enormous scale. Corporations that depend on raw materials and commodities as inputs to the production process use derivatives as a way to protect themselves against sudden shortages or sharp price changes. For example, airlines can use call options on the price of jet fuel to hedge against the risk that prices will increase. Nestle can use call options on cocoa futures to guarantee a supply even if the price goes up. But what makes options particularly attractive for speculation as well as hedging is that they are a cheap way of betting on price movements—you buy them for a fraction of the cost of the actual security and you only use them if the price moves in the direction you hope. If it does, the option can increase many times in value—doubling, tripling, quadrupling. This really gets one's gambling juices flowing.

Indeed, the greater the chance of a big move in the stock price, the more expensive is the option. Think of the call-and-put diagram discussed above. If the stock price moves around a lot, you are quite likely to make money from either the call or the put. When the price drops, the put option becomes more valuable. When the price rises, the call option becomes more valuable. You only do poorly if the stock price remains unchanged. The cost of a put plus a call should be high for very volatile stocks with a likelihood of going up or down a lot, but low for stocks that do not move much. For the same reason, options that are granted for a long period of time (e.g., two years rather than one month) should also be worth more money because of the rule Jules Regnault came up with: the expected price change (up or down) grows with time.

BROWNIAN MOTION

These general intuitions about what makes options more or less expensive can only get you so far. Toward the end of the nineteenth century, a French mathematician, Louis Bachelier (1870–1946), developed a mathematical technique for calculating the precise prices of options. As expected, it required as an input to the equation the riskiness of the stock—what Regnault had earlier called its "vibration." It also required the time period for which the option is granted (the "maturity" of the option).

Bachelier presented his book, *Théorie de la Spéculation*, as his doctoral thesis in mathematics at the Sorbonne in 1900. In working through the problem of option pricing, Bachelier had to devise a precise definition of how a stock price moved randomly through time. We now refer to this as Brownian motion. Interestingly, Albert Einstein developed a Brownian motion model in 1905, evidently later and independently from Bachelier.

Bachelier's answer to the option pricing problem turned out to be an equation beyond the knowledge of market participants at the time. This presented an interesting philosophical issue. If option prices conformed to a complex, nonlinear multivariate function that was undiscovered until 1900, how then did the invisible hand—the process of speculation—drive them toward efficiency?

Bachelier's thesis was not particularly well received. One of his examiners, Lucien Lévy, thought there was a mistake in Bachelier's analysis, a misfortune that consigned him to a provincial position outside the inner circle of top mathematicians of the day. Ironically, Lévy's son Paul became one of the giants of probability theory in the twentieth century.

Over the 115-plus years since Bachelier's thesis defense, his book came to be recognized as a classic of mathematical finance. It nearly, but not exactly, solved the problem of how to value an option—and thanks to Lefèvre, that means he came close to being able to value a complex portfolio of options, hedges, and speculations.

The option pricing problem would not be solved precisely until much later in the twentieth century. The scholars who did so, Myron Scholes, Fischer Black, and Robert Merton, recognized Bachelier's contribution. Scholes and Merton accepted the Nobel Prize in Economic Sciences in 1997 for their work on this important financial problem. Fischer Black had passed away before he could share in the award.

MODELS AND MODERN MARKETS

Scholes and Merton were professors of financial economics at the Massachusetts Institute of Technology in 1970, where they met the economist Fischer Black. Evidently none knew of Bachelier, and thus they had to retrace the mathematical logic of fair prices and random walks when they began work on the problem of option pricing in the late 1960s. Like Bachelier, they relied on a model of variation in prices—Brownian motion—although unlike Bachelier, they chose one that did not allow prices to become negative—a limitation of Bachelier's work.

The Black-Scholes formula, as it is now referred to, was mathematically sophisticated, but at its heart it contained a novel economic—as opposed to mathematical—insight. They discovered that the invisible hand setting option prices was risk-neutral. Option payoffs could be replicated risklessly, provided one could trade in an ideal, frictionless market in which stocks behaved according to Brownian motion. Later researchers[4] developed a simple framework called a "binomial model" that was able to match the payoff of a put or a call by trading just the stock and a bond through time. These solutions to the option pricing problem linked finance and physics together forever afterward. In fact, it turned out that the Black-Scholes option pricing model was the same as a problem in thermodynamics—a "heat" equation, in which molecules—not stock prices—were drifting randomly.

The foundation of the science of thermodynamics is entropy—the tendency toward disorder. Time only goes in one direction, and with it, the universe tends toward less organization, not more. The option pricing model is based on the principle of forecasting the range of future outcomes of the stock price by assuming it will follow a random walk that conforms to Regnault's square-root of time insight. However, the Black-Scholes formula gives a solution to the option price today by mathematically rolling time backward. It reverses entropy. In this, it echoes the most basic trait of finance—it uses mathematics to transcend time.

THERMODYNAMICS

The Black-Scholes formula was published in 1973, just around the time that the Chicago Board Option Exchange began to trade standardized option contracts. Like Bachelier's thesis, the path-breaking paper was not at first well received. The *Journal of Political Economy*, where it ultimately was published, needed serious urging from Chicago Professor Merton Miller to be convinced of its contribution. However, it not only created an entire field of financial research, it also gave Wall Street traders some extraordinary tools to use in their quest for profits. Black, Scholes, Merton, and the other financial economists who developed derivative pricing models based on probability calculus created a revolution on Wall Street. Among other things, they opened up new careers for physicists and mathematicians who suddenly realized that their familiarity with thermodynamic equations could land them high-paying jobs at investment banks. And just like the probabilists of the eighteenth century, this new generation of "quants," who applied mathematics to speculation, took the blame when markets crashed.

For example, Mark Rubenstein—of binomial option pricing fame— used his model in the 1980s to set up a way for investment funds to protect themselves against a market crash. Even if no put options existed, the binomial model provided a way to synthetically create them by a process of continuously trading stocks and bonds. The crash of 1987 in the US stock market exposed a major weakness in the model. For example, the Brownian motion process on which it was based assumed that the price never jumped. This seemingly innocuous assumption of continuity failed when markets went into freefall, dropping more than 22% over two days. In simple terms, this messed up the hedge. Investors who thought they had "portfolio insurance" discovered that they were only partly insured.

Market commentators were quick to blame Rubenstein and his colleagues for triggering the crash of 1987, claiming that their "programmed" trades caused a cascade. However, the crash was a global phenomenon, and portfolio protection methods were not widely used in non-US markets. This criticism raises a fascinating philosophical question. Could a model of the market have affected the market? If one participant is using a binomial technique to trade, could the application of that technique itself make the model wrong? I tend to think not. Wiser speculators looking for profit are always lurking, always ready to exploit prices that might be distorted by programmed trading.

The financial crisis of 2008 has been laid at the feet of investment bankers and financial engineers based on the theory that diabolical quants created complex financial securities doomed to fail, and then greedy bankers sold them. There are hints of a deeper theme of hubris on the part of the engineers, suggestions that they believed too much in their models. The story goes that a system built on mathematical formulas took finance higher and higher until their structural weaknesses were exposed and the entire edifice collapsed, leaving taxpayers around the world to clean up the mess.

Provocative money manager Nassim Taleb went so far in 2008 as to propose jail time for quants who used standard risk models. "We would like society to lock up quantitative risk managers before they cause more damage."[5] Respondents to his blog used even stronger language. Of course, Taleb was promoting his book *The Black Swan*, which argues that the standard probability models, based as they are on Bernoulli's original formulation, cannot account for the frequent occurrence of extreme events. A drop of 22% in a couple of days was not in Mark Rubenstein's game plan, because standard models used for option pricing effectively assume that the logarithm of stock prices are "normal"—that is, they conform to the standard bell-curve distribution.

In fact, the non-normality of security prices had been well known for decades prior to the crash of 2008—and for that matter the crash of 1987, as was the potential for extreme events. The "high priest" of non-normality before Nassim Taleb ever started to trade or write about extreme events was Benoit Mandelbrot, the creator of fractal geometry, a mathematician who both carried the mantle of French mathematical finance and who also believed he had discovered its fatal flaw.

Mandelbrot was a student of Paul Lévy's—the son of the man who gave Bachelier bad marks at his examination at the École Polytechnique in 1900. Lévy's research focused on "stochastic processes": mathematical models that describe the behavior of some variable through time. For example, we saw in Chapter 15 that Jules Regnault proposed and tested a stochastic process that varied randomly, which resulted in a rule about risk increasing with the square root of time. Likewise, Louis Bachelier more formally developed a random-walk stochastic process. Paul Lévy formalized these prior random walk models into a very general family of stochastic processes referred to as Lévy processes. Brownian motion was just one process in the family of Lévy processes—and perhaps the best behaved of them. Other stochastic processes have such things as discontinuous jumps and unusually large shocks (which might, for example, explain the crash of 1987, when the US stock market lost 22.6% of its value in a single day).

In the 1960s, Benoit Mandelbrot began to investigate whether Lévy processes described economic time series like cotton prices and stock prices. He found that the ones that generated jumps and extreme events better described financial markets. He developed a mathematics around these unusual Lévy processes that he called "fractal geometry." He argued that unusual events—Taleb's black swan—were in fact much more common phenomena than Brownian motion would suggest.

The crash of 1987 was not a surprise to him—he took it as a vindication of his theory. One of his major contributions to the literature on finance (published in 1966) was a proof that an efficient market implies that stock prices may not follow a random walk, but that they must be unpredictable. It was a nice refinement of Regnault's hypothesis articulated almost precisely a century prior.

Although Mandelbrot ultimately developed a fractal-based option-pricing model with two of his students that allowed for extreme events and a more general stochastic process, for various reasons Mandelbrot never saw it adopted in practice to any great extent. I suspect that this is because the solution, while potentially useful, is complicated and contradicts most other tools that quantitative financiers use. With Mandelbrot's models, it is all or nothing. You have to take a leap beyond the world of Brownian motion and throw out old friends like Bernoulli's law of large numbers. For most quants in practice (and professors studying the markets), the leap is too great, and the payoff in terms of understanding may not be sufficient. After all, Mandelbrot never promised that the timing of a giant crash could be predicted, just that it would likely happen.

Benoit Mandelbrot believed he had discovered a deep structure to the world in general and financial markets in particular. His insights, however, can be traced directly back to the special tradition of mathematical inquiry that has its roots in the Enlightenment. I think this is what most excited him about his work—thinking of it in historical context as a culmination of applications of probability to markets. Although not all quants are aware of it, when they use a stochastic process (like Brownian motion) to price a security or figure out a hedge, they are drawing from a very deep well of mathematical knowledge that would not have existed but for the emergence of financial markets in Europe. Yes, the models that modern quants have applied to markets can go wrong. Models are crude attempts to characterize a reality that is complex and continually evolving. Despite the crashes—or perhaps because of them—financial markets have continually challenged the best and brightest minds with puzzles that hold the promise of intellectual and pecuniary rewards. Perhaps it is the latter that is responsible for the emergence in Europe of a strikingly novel mathematical tradition to understand and place limits on uncertainty about the future.

The mathematical roots of modern quantitative finance and complex financial engineering can be traced more specifically to a strong French tradition that audaciously sought to model the investment process and market prices with the tools of probability. From Regnault to Lefèvre to Bachelier to Lévy to Black and Scholes and finally to Mandelbrot, we have seen how the notion of randomness was engineered and then re-engineered to help understand what the invisible hand managed to do without self-awareness.

In Chapter 17, we leave the world of mathematics to return to the world of geopolitics. As important as finance has been to the development of modern mathematical thought and the microstructure of risk management, the financial architecture in the modern era revolves around one distinctive economic unit—the corporation.

EUROPE, INC.

One of Europe's contributions to finance was the corporation: a business enterprise financed by shareholders. The question of the origins of the corporation is one of the oldest in the study of law and economics. While the roots of the corporation are still in dispute despite a century of research, its importance in the history of the modern world is not. In this chapter, I argue that the corporation had multiple roots inside (and outside) Europe. The earlier appearance of the share company in Roman Republican times was just one of many instances of the invention of the corporation. My claim is that the corporate form is an equilibrium that emerges under many different conditions and institutional circumstances. Just as we saw that banks evolved from institutions as disparate as Greek money brokers and medieval religious societies, in this chapter, I show that corporations had deep roots variously in feudal control of land rights and royal charters for merchant voyages. The key is that both of these paths of development evolved parallel solutions to the problem of raising capital, managing an enterprise, and providing liquidity to investors. The earliest corporations in Europe (at least since Roman times) appear in the western Mediterranean in the fourteenth century. Like the earliest negotiable debt instruments and the first bond market, their appearance owes much to the feudal legal tradition of transferable rights.

In 1407, Genoa took a radically new approach to public finance. The major creditors of the city created a separate financial institution, the Casa di San Giorgio, which assumed all of Genoa's outstanding debt and controlled major sources of the city's revenue. The Casa, in turn, issued shares (*luoghi*), which, like the Venetian prestiti (discussed in Chapter 12), could be traded in a secondary market. In simple terms, Genoa off-loaded her debt onto a private firm and also turned over key revenues—the customs receipts from overseas trade. The Casa di San Giorgio was managed like a company—indeed, it *was* a company. It had

Tolofa

A view of Toulouse from the *Nuremberg Chronicle*, 1493.
The arched structure at left had operated as a corporation for more than
a century when this picture was made.

a governance structure; the goal of making revenues exceed expenses; and a policy of declaring dividends (*paghe*), which depended on the company's success. The Casa di San Giorgio had its corporate headquarters near the Genoese harbor (a short walk, in fact, from the house of Christopher Columbus), it kept company records of assets, liabilities, income, and expenses—all the hallmarks of a business firm, except that it existed solely to lend money to the city of Genoa.

How did this novel institution come to be? Like Pisa and Venice, Genoa's first foray into debt was though private borrowing secured by revenues from government taxes. In effect, the government leased the right to collect tax revenues for a period of time to a lender. These leases were rooted in the law of medieval census contracts; rights to exploit property could be rented for periods of time. For example, one such arrangement hypothecated the revenues from the city's salt tax. This exchange apparently did not violate the usury laws, because, by analogy to the rent on land, the return on the lender's capital came from farming—tax farming. The fact that these contracts (*compere*) were divided into luoghi indicates that they were issued to consortiums of citizens who held them for investment purposes. Compere typically yielded 8% per year, although this varied with the risk and return of the various tax revenue streams. Michele Fratianni, a financial historian and professor of economics at Indiana University who has spent considerable time studying the innovative features of the Casa di San Giorgio, notes that luoghi in these separate compere were treated as liquid financial assets in the Genoese economy as early as the mid-twelfth century—they could be bought and sold.[1]

The Casa di San Giorgio consolidated all compere into a single portfolio by making a tender offer for the entire outstanding compere. Holders of luoghi in separate tax farm enterprises could exchange them for luoghi in the portfolio of ventures at a reduced yield: initially 7%. The alternative was reimbursement of the original investment. For most investors, the slight reduction in yield was more than compensated for by the reduction in risk due to diversification—and they would have faced loss of their current contracts in any case. The creation of the Casa di San Giorgio also attracted new investors from other cities. In 1420, the 7% fixed dividend was allowed to vary, and the transformation of the public debt to private equity was complete.

The true genius of the Casa di San Giorgio was that it turned Geno-ese debt holders into equity holders. They profited when the revenues of the city increased. Even more so than the Venetian prestiti, the Genoese luoghe sharply aligned the interests of citizens with those of the state. The issue of consolidated shares further broadened the base of investors, who literally bought into the fiscal management of Genoa and had an economic interest in its efficiency.

Innovation breeds further invention. The Casa di San Giorgio regularly declared dividends, but there was typically a lag between the declaration and the payment due to the timing of tax revenues. A speculative market developed on "dividend futures." Shareholders willing to take a discount could sell their promised future paghe in the Genoese money market, the amount of the discount reflecting the prevailing short-term time value of money—much like modern commercial paper or treasury bills. This market in paghe itself was an active one, and when it took place between two shareholders, the transaction was simplicity itself. The obligation to pay the next divi-dend was simply debited from the Casa account of one shareholder and credited to another. For shareholders, all financial transaction in luoghi and their paghe could be handled by account rather than by physical transfer. The Casa di San Giorgio effectively created a bank of account.

The Casa di San Giorgio was a semipublic institution, because it played a central role in the finance of the Genoese republic. However, it had many features of a modern corporation: a distinct legal entity, trans-ferable share ownership (although there were restrictions on transfer), and a governing body that declared dividends that varied depending on the revenues of the company. In some sense, the Casa di San Giorgio was as important as the state. A significant number of Genoese were investors, the dividends from the shares represented a financial asset, and the bank of San Giorgio created a convenient structure for holding and transferring wealth. The conversion of government debt to equity was a strikingly different model of public finance but was apparently as successful as Venice's development of long-term bonds. Indeed, both financial institutions thrived for centuries, despite—or perhaps because of—the intense rivalry between the two cities. Although the United States today has a national debt, it does not have an institution like the

Casa di San Giorgio. Could such an institution work in the modern world? Could a solution to the next international debt crisis involve the privatization of a national fisc?

The heyday of Genoa was the period when it controlled a significant proportion of the trade with the eastern Mediterranean. This peaked in the fourteenth and fifteenth centuries, but the Casa di San Giorgio continued as an institution long afterward, and the Genoese played an important role as merchants and financiers of the Spanish expansion into maritime trade. Not only was Columbus a Genoese, but some of the most important backers of Spanish ventures to the Canary Islands and then to the New World were Genoese living in Seville. Although Genoese fleets were no longer at the vanguard of trade in the sixteenth century, the city's financiers played a crucial part in Spain's maritime expansion—almost certainly because of their financial know-how and substantial accumulated capital. However, the Casa di San Giorgio was not the earliest example of the corporate form in the western Mediterranean world.

MOULINS DE TOULOUSE

Toulouse, a city in southwestern France has a venerable history. Roughly equidistant between the Atlantic and the Mediterranean, it began as a Celtic settlement, then flourished as a Roman city and was ultimately claimed by the Visigoths after the fall of the Roman Empire—a prize offered to the barbarian hordes if they would pass through Italy and continue west. As the capital of the Visigothic kingdom, Toulouse remained politically and culturally important through the early Middle Ages.

Toulouse in the eleventh and twelfth centuries was ruled by the counts of Toulouse as an independent heritable fiefdom encompassing half of southern France and parts of Spain. The counts gradually gave up local political control to a city council through a social contract that promised military support from the citizenry in return for self-governance. Thus, with the revival of European civilization after the year 1000, Toulouse shared many of the strengths of the trade-oriented Mediterranean city-states, including a strong merchant class, a tendency toward citizen rule, and openness toward religious freedom.

Toulouse differed in one key respect—its law. Although Roman law nearly disappeared in western Europe after the fall of the western Roman Empire, it was preserved in Toulouse by King Alaric II, who commissioned a codification of Roman legal traditions in 506 CE and applied the code throughout the Visigothic kingdom stretching from Gibraltar to the Loire. On this foundation developed a unique legal system that, while distantly based on ancient Roman code and Visigothic traditions, evolved into a flexible system of contracts and property rights that was particularly well suited to commerce and business. The law of Toulouse allowed widespread freedom for citizens to contract on financial obligations of all sorts. Toulouse contracts included money loans, loans in kind, loans of grain, loans assigned to others in payment of obligations, mortgages, leases, sub-leases, fiefs, baillies, and assets of all sorts held in partnership. Contracting parties ranged across the entire spectrum of Toulousain society, from the counts, to the churches, to the monasteries, to the local chapter of the Templars, to the city itself as a corporate entity represented by a town council, to the merchants, bankers, tradesmen, laborers, farmers, and to even minors. The contracts were not limited to Christians but included the Jewish community as well. In the same way that the Occitan language of Toulouse—the ancient language of the troubadours—is really only a distant cousin of modern French as both were based on Latin, so too was the Toulousain version of Roman law distinct from the Code of Justinian.

The Toulousain law was a system that accepted banking, lending, and the charging of interest, a system that defended the rights and claims of creditors even as the attacks on usury spread through other parts of Europe. As scholars at the University of Paris steeped in the Code of Justinian pondered the precise definition of *lucrum sesans* in the twelfth century, Toulouse did not even have a university or an academic tradition of legal scholarship. Instead it has a practical, functional legal technology characterized by clear, uncomplicated language.

On this novel legal base, Toulousain economy and society flourished, and Toulouse became an important stop on the European road to capitalism. As with Venice and the Italian city-states, Toulouse's political history during the twelfth and thirteenth centuries was intertwined with its financial history. However, financial development in Toulouse took a very different turn than in the northern Italian republics. Its evo-

FIGURE 22. View of the Bazacle mill on the Garonne River today.

lution is not bound up with maritime trade but with a very different enterprise: the milling of grain. If Genoa and Venice had the comparative advantage of access to the sea, Toulouse's advantage was access to the Garonne River.

A VISIT TO THE BAZACLE

The campus of the Toulouse School of Social Sciences stands just outside the bounds of the ancient city wall, fronting a picturesque canal. The school is renowned in Europe as a center for the study of corporate finance and capital markets. Just behind the school, at a spot on the Garonne called the Bazacle, stands a venerable old brick building that is now the Toulouse power plant. More than 700 years ago, however, the mill was the home of the Honor del Bazacle, Europe's oldest corporation. The Honor del Bazacle was formally incorporated in 1372, by merging twelve smaller mill companies that shared land near the Bazacle from at least the twelfth century. It survived as a public corporation until 1946, when it was nationalized as part of the French electricity company EDF. The Honor del Bazacle owes its foundation in equal parts to hydrology and law: the hydrology of the Garonne and the medieval property rights of Toulouse.

From at least the sixth century, European cities and towns used waterpower to turn their mills. The earliest mills were floating barges, anchored in the river stream, with vertical paddle wheels that could be raised and lowered to engage the current. Floating mills are mentioned in the historical records of Toulouse as early as the eleventh century, but they did not take to the shore until 1138.

ARCHIVES OF CAPITALISM

Remarkably, archival records dating to the Middle Ages have survived in Toulouse, documenting how its mills were financed. Millers raised money by pooling their capital and dividing the claims into partnership shares (*uchaux*)—each representing a one-eighth share in a mill. The mills generated profits by grinding grain and also by ancillary rights—including fishing. Uchaux could be bought and sold to anyone, not just millers. They paid off at harvest time in quantities of grain, of which the uchaux holder received a proportional share.

In the true spirit of capitalism, mill companies competed vigorously for prime anchoring locations in the stream. With as many as sixty mills jostling for position, occasional floods and nautical mishaps caused problems. Mills would come untethered and crash into one another, decimating the fleet. Some of these problems were solved by building mills on the riverbanks—at the Bazacle and at another advantageous site upstream. A system of dams (still visible at Bazacle) also helped use the current more efficiently. Both innovations required significant investment of capital and the involvement of civic authorities. Building on land required owning or leasing the property and getting requisite municipal permissions.

During the late twelfth and early thirteenth centuries, permission to develop land in Toulouse, including the Bazacle, was a feudal right granted by the count of Toulouse, one of his fief holders, or by the Catholic Church, which held its own land independently from the count's authority. These feudal rights were also intermediated by a town council. Placement of millraces, for example, required approval of "certain good men," who presumably represented the common interests of the town. Toulouse, like many of the Italian city-states in the twelfth century, operated in a quasi-democratic fashion. The powers of the count and, to some extent, the powers of the church were progressively challenged over the course of the eleventh and twelfth centuries by the self-governing body of townsfolk. This group included not only knights with feudal status, but also others called "burghers." The council was formalized in 1152 as a legislative body, which was a separate, subordinate power to the count.[2] The town council oversaw legal disputes and commercial practice, managed the police force, and organized military defense of the city. In 1188, an uprising against Count Raymond V enabled the council to further consolidate its civil power.

In 1138, four partners—one of whom was the prior of the nearby basilica called the Daurade—acquired the rights to develop three mills at Bazacle. It was a business company: a group of investors who pooled their capital, acquired development rights, built mills, ran them for profit, and divided the gains according to their respective shares. They obtained the rights by means of the age-old transfer of fief from the count of Toulouse.

It was probably not the first such company in Europe at the time. We have seen that partnership structures existed earlier in the Middle Ages—particularly in the Italian city-states, where trade ventures demanded large-scale investment capital. The importance of the company at Bazacle is that it became the first since the Roman Republic to develop many of the features of the modern joint-stock corporation.

In 1372, twelve mill companies operating at the Bazacle merged to form one big firm, the Honor del Bazacle. The shareholders in the smaller companies exchanged their uchaux for claims in the larger entity, and they drew up a detailed document determining how the company would operate. The firm held annual shareholder meetings and kept detailed accounts of operations, which were presented at the meetings. The Honor del Bazacle had limited liability shares that were fully transferable. The firm had a governing board of directors, professional managers, and employees, regular accounts of performance, dividends based on profit, even a sense of honor and mission of the organization. Courts treated it as a legal entity separate from the shareholders and managers. It could hold property and write contracts in its name.

Most astonishingly, in the high Middle Ages, a time we associate with serfdom, knights in armor, and royal privilege, the shares of the Bazacle mill company provided a steady source of income to a significant number of middle-class investors. The shares were not typically held by local gentry but instead were owned by moderately well-to-do citizens of Toulouse—lawyers, members of city government, bankers and even (although rarely) by millers. They were also held by religious institutions as a form of endowment. The shares were passed down from generation to generation, as well as bought, sold, and used as collateral for loans.

The genius of the Honor del Bazacle was threefold. As a financing vehicle, it brought together the considerable capital needed to build a large-scale enterprise. As an investment vehicle, it empowered a new economic class, a class of people who could live on the dividends of their investments rather than the sweat of their brow or the domain of royal privilege—a class later called the "bourgeoisie." And the firm was conceived at the outset as an ongoing enterprise, quite unlike trade ventures financed by partnerships. Its organizational form was suitable for a perpetually lived institution.

In 1953, Germain Sicard, the eminent historian of the French Middle Ages and a professor at the University of Toulouse, wrote a masterful study of the mills. The carefully researched work was truly interdisciplinary. It moved from hydrology to medieval politics, to the legal foundations of the firm to the operations, management, and governance of the organization, to a thoughtful evaluation of the role of the Toulouse company in society. Sicard was particularly interested in the relationship between the Toulouse firm and the modern corporation. In his study, he traced the prices paid for shares in the Bazacle firm, as well as its chief rival—the upstream firm called the Chateau company. Sicard was able to chart the fluctuating price of shares in the two firms over the century from 1350 through 1471. Not only did the mill history survive the Toulouse archives, but the archives also contain actual prices paid for its shares!

Long fascinated with the Bazacle company and Sicard's work, I teamed up David Le Bris (a finance professor at Bordeaux) and Sébastien Pouget (an economist at the Toulouse School of Economics). We wondered whether the records for the mill still existed for the period after 1471. Indeed they do! David found most of the account books, shareholder books, and annual reports of the company in the Toulouse archives and, over the course of two years he was able to reconstruct virtually the entire history of the prices and dividends of the firm. Perhaps the most exciting moment of this research was when we unfurled the eight-foot-long charter of the company formation from 1372. Here it was—the foundational document of the oldest known corporation, a detailed record of a corporate merger that happened more than six centuries ago. We could not read it, of course. It is written in a mixture of Latin and Occitan in Gothic script that requires special training to understand. Fortunately, the librarian at the archives is just such a specialist. She was able to point out some of the key passages in the document.

One remarkable feature of the charter document is that it is a private contract, not a royal decree. The document does not say something to the effect that the king grants this company the right to operate. Feudal law evidently had already conferred the right of joint ownership of a business. Rather, all of the features of the corporation were spelled out by mutual agreement among the parties.

Why was the document so long? Most early financial documents discussed in this book—from cuneiform loan transactions to Egyptian mortgages to early Dutch perpetual bonds—were fairly succinct records. Why would it take eight feet of tiny script to create a corporation? The feature distinguishing the corporation from a bond is that the bond is a promise of payment, but the corporation is an organization that is designed to operate autonomously, perhaps for several centuries. This document was the blueprint for an amazing machine, a special tool that first converted investor capital into a physical plant and then spelled out the rules by which this capital would be used and who would benefit from it. A blueprint might not be exactly the right analogy, however. The Honor del Bazacle charter is more like a complete set of rules for playing a game. These rules needed to ensure that no single player, either unintentionally or willfully, could ruin the game or cheat the other players. The rules also had to make sure that play was voluntary. The merger document was not coercive. Shareholders in the smaller firms were giving up their rights to own and operate properties that, in some cases, had been autonomous firms for centuries. The need to establish a fair exchange rate between the shares of each company and those of the merged firm was crucial. Thus, long passages in the document were devoted to a valuation of the shares in the individual mill companies that merged together. The essentially democratic process of jointly owning and operating the firm had to be spelled out to everyone's satisfaction. This must have been done right, for not only were the founding shareholders satisfied that their sharing and control rights were protected, but this satisfaction must also have extended to all future generations of shareholders. Each time an uchaux was sold, the price paid for it not only reflected the faith that the buyer had in grain milling, it also reflected the faith that he or she would continue to receive a fair share in a firm that was managed in their best interests. This meant, for example, that it would not be managed to minimize milling costs (though the citizens of Toulouse might have wished it), and it would not be managed to generate high salaries for the millers operating the business daily (thought the millers might have wished it). Rather the price reflected the belief that the rules of the game—the founding charter and its emanations—would protect their capital and ensure a fair return on the capital.

One of the things that a charter might or might not foresee is a complete disaster. For example, the company experienced a severe setback in 1427, when its mills caught fire, and in 1709, the mill dam was destroyed by a flood. In these circumstances, shareholders were called on to contribute money to rebuild. In some cases, they did not have the funds. This is where two useful features of the joint-stock company become apparent. Shareholders could not be compelled to pay an unlimited amount. Instead, they had the option of surrendering their shares to the company and walking away. This is called "limited liability" and is a distinguishing feature of the modern corporation. It puts a floor on the downside risk that an investor faces. As such, it makes people willing to risk their capital in uncertain ventures.

The catastrophe of 1709 is an interesting case. The mill was severely damaged and rendered inoperable, requiring expensive reconstruction. Some shareholders surrendered their uchaux rather than contribute. An enterprising engineer approached the firm with a deal. He promised that he could rebuild the mill; however, in return he wanted shares in the company. He then approached investors in Geneva who were willing to advance cash also in return for shares. The deal was struck, and new uchaux were issued to finance reconstruction. The rebuilt mill was as productive as ever. The entrepreneur was both a hydrological and a financial engineer, structuring a deal to revive the ancient firm.

Despite various such setbacks, the Honor del Bazacle outlasted all the governments in France before the twentieth century. It survived the 100 Years War and the French Revolution—indeed, it outlasted the Song, Yuan, and Ming dynasties of China. The survival was due to something more than solid construction—after all, the building and dams that constituted the mills were swept away more than once. What remained was its corporate form—its basic constitutional structure: a financial technology that proved amazingly robust through the centuries.

You might still find a share in the company—even today. I bought three of them over the Internet from a French dealer in stock memorabilia. These "living fossils" from the Société Toulousain du Bazacle date to the late nineteenth century. As corporate capitalism in France matured and stock markets developed, shares in the firm were ultimately traded on the Paris Bourse—the company was incorporated in the form of a *société anonyme*—a publicly held corporation. Despite its long history of joint-stock ownership, the company of Bazacle was ultimately nationalized by the French government in the twentieth century. The nationalized firm, the Toulouse Electric Company, still stands on the bend in the Garonne that for centuries conferred to the Bazacle milling company its unique natural advantage.

Now a public rather than private enterprise, the company of the Bazacle was remarkable as a milestone in the history of capitalism. But how exactly did such a modest enterprise exist for eight hundred years? How did it survive wars and political strife? More importantly, how did it survive expropriation by the state—at least until the twentieth century? We saw in Chinese history the constant temptation of the state to take over private enterprise, to seize, on moral grounds, the rents accruing to entrepreneurs. This did not happen in Toulouse until the twentieth century. Professor Sicard attributes the firm's survival to the widespread acceptance of specified contractual property rights. Even powerful counts who conceded the use of the riverbanks to common investors were held to contract by civil law. Whether this is due to the long tradition of the feudal contract, or the near pan-European recognition of Roman Law remains open to debate.

EUROPEAN COUNTERPOINT

The creation of such a private company would hardly seem revolutionary from our modern vantage point. After all, private firms like Archer Daniels Midland and Cargill (one public, the other privately held) supply a significant portion of the world's grain. But compare the Bazacle company to the salt monopoly of China, which flourished at the same time. At two ends of the Eurasian continent, radically different institutional forms were developing to finance the production of essential foodstuffs. In China, the government owned and controlled the production of salt. It issued rationing certificates that effectively controlled merchant profits. As we have seen in Chapter 9, these certificates themselves circulated as another form of money. The logic of a government-controlled monopoly for salt was twofold. First, it meant that control of essential foodstuffs was in the hands of a political authority with a political mandate. It allowed policymakers to decide when to increase or reduce production, depending on fluctuating needs. Second, profits accrued to the government that might otherwise have accrued to private investors.

How strange it might have seemed to a Chinese official of the Song dynasty were he to visit Toulouse. Here was a special, natural feature—a ford in a river that conferred a significant advantage for grain milling. Why wouldn't the government take the rents from that advantage? Why should individual citizens be allowed to profit? Why shouldn't the government lay claim to all such choice spots in the duchy or the kingdom and regulate the fees for milling and the quantity of grain milled? Wouldn't that also allow the government to respond effectively in times of need?

This fundamental question of government ownership versus private ownership—of nationalization versus privatization—is the central question of our time. Should the US government own shares in the top ten banks and top three automobile companies, and direct their operations for the public good? Should the banking system of India be privatized, or should it be directly accountable to the public interest? Does Airbus have a natural advantage (or disadvantage) as a government-owned enterprise? Are America's ports safer and better run in the hands of private investors as opposed to the hands of a foreign state? Should water rights in the American west be privately held and transferable? Should Russian oil companies be held by stockholders around the world and controlled by oligarchs with large capital stakes, or should they be nationalized so that the Russian government may take the profits? Why would one ever imagine that private ownership and management might be better for the public good—as opposed to simply better for the particular investors that happen to profit?

Beyond the issue of private versus public ownership is the question of whether it is feasible for the owners of a milling company to entirely delegate the responsibility for managing the enterprise. The genius and problem of the modern corporation is that it separates ownership and control. What prevents the managers from taking the lion's share of the profits from the mill and simply misreporting the results to shareholders? The classic agency problem addressed by China's thinkers—and China's accountants—appears again in the context of the publicly owned corporation. The survival of the Toulouse company depended on successfully solving this delegation, management, and oversight problem.

The Bazacle company is not well remembered today as the progenitor of the modern corporation. Indeed, it may not have been; although it is difficult to understand why not. Mills were everywhere in Europe in the late Middle Ages. The harnessing of water power was one of the most important technological advances of the period, and properly built mills required substantial capital investment. Other firms in southern France must have borrowed the idea of share capitalism, limited liability, and exchangeability from Toulouse—if indeed the situation were not vice versa. We know about Toulouse only through the accident of recorded history and the efforts of a dedicated scholar to analyze the evidence. In fact, when you look more closely at ventures in Europe during the Middle Ages, you begin to see hints of similar entities that may have been precursors to modern corporations. In Germany, there were mining firms which issued shares called "*Kuxen*." In Sweden, the venerable firm of Stora-Enso traces it lineage back to the thirteenth century as well, and its royal charter—still preserved to this day—dates from 1347.

It began as a cooperative mining venture divided into shares, perhaps something like the first mill companies of Toulouse. We saw that the Casa di Giorgio had many features of the modern corporation as well. It appears that the late Middle Ages in Europe was a lively period of experimentation in financing and different sorts of enterprise.

The inevitable conclusion to be drawn from tracing such sporadic appearances of medieval European milling and mining firms capitalized by share investment is that capitalism is an economic solution that crops up repeatedly in the historical record. Its lineage is neither linear nor unique. Rather, it is a naturally and commonly occurring "sport" in the economic biota. In fact, as we have seen, it cropped up in Republican Rome, only to fall victim to the imperial patronage system. This process of appearance and disappearance, of tenuous survival rather than instantaneous and overwhelming domination of an economy, suggests that share capitalism might in fact be a fragile thing, heavily dependent on the right environmental and political conditions to flourish. Capitalism is not teleological—despite Mao's observation about its inevitability in China. It can stop just as it can start. It is one of many equilibria.

CORPORATIONS
AND EXPLORATION

The historical origin of modern corporations in Europe is more typically traced to the overseas voyages of discovery launched by the English and the Dutch in the sixteenth and seventeenth centuries. Two
northern European trading enterprises, the English and Dutch East
India companies—created in 1600 and 1602, respectively—came to
dominate European trade with Asia over the next two centuries. The
two East India companies were at the same time corporations and colonial institutions, and the evolution from private enterprise to an instrument of the state is one of the defining themes in the history of
European finance.

We saw in China that the rewards to the private sector were subject
to the control and sometimes expropriation of the state. In the West, the
opposite also occurred. One may argue that, ultimately, the state came
to serve the interests of British and Dutch merchants engaged in global
trade. British and Dutch taxpayers ultimately paid for navies to defend
colonial empires that began as trading companies.

This chapter and those following will trace the means by which the
corporate form—more properly, the corporate form that emerged from
the early trading companies of northern Europe—embedded themselves in the economy of European society and then ultimately in the
dreams and aspirations of European culture. The financial architecture
of global trading enterprises in turn laid the foundation for the modern
economy.

One of the most surprising things about the history of the early overseas trading corporations is that they arose from some of the riskiest
ventures imaginable: travels around the Horn of Africa and voyages
through the Straits of Magellan, trips that took years and in which ships
were lost and people died. They operated without day-to-day or even

John White's illustration of the battle between Martin Frobisher's crew and native people of Frobisher Bay, 1577. Frobisher's Company of Cathay was formed to explore an eastern route to China.

month-to-month director oversight: there was virtually no news of the success or failure of the voyages until their return. We saw in Chapter 15 that European mathematics responded to the need to quantify, manage, and hedge risk in the investment markets. But how do you hedge against the uncertainty of whether you will bump into an unknown continent—or encounter a completely unknown culture—or discover spices and items of trade that you never knew about before?

Consider how different these companies were from the Honor del Bazacle, where investors could walk by their corporate assets every day. Toulouse shareholders of course knew there were risks of floods and fires, but these were at least probabilistically assessable, whereas trading ventures to the other side of the world—almost by definition—confronted the unknown. And yet, as we shall see, the joint-stock company corporate form, with tradable shares and separation between ownership and control, sufficed for both. The immediate question explored in this chapter is whether the corporate form made exploration possible, or whether the exigencies of exploration led to the independent development of the corporate form. Put another way, did financial innovation drive the Great Age of Discovery, or did the Great Age of Discovery drive financial innovation?

DISCOVERY OR FINANCE?

In the case of English discovery, most early voyages of exploration resulted from royal financial imperatives that provided entrepreneurial opportunity. The Elizabethan era brings to mind images of English power: the defeat of the Armada, the Virginia plantation, and the consolidation of the monarchy following the troublesome failure of Mary Queen of Scots. But English finances during Queen Elizabeth I's reign were weak. Lacking a domestic capital market, Elizabeth was repeatedly forced to borrow on the international money market: sending envoys to the bankers of Antwerp to secure lines of credit, hypothecating government tax revenues and crown assets, rolling over short-term loans, living from refinance to refinance at higher and higher rates of interest that reflected the very real possibility that England would default on its debts. English credit was simply awful—when new loans could be engineered, they came with high interest rates: 14% at a time when good credit, such as yields on shares in Genoa's Casa di San Giorgio, were as low as 3 or 4%. Unlike the city-states on the continent, English cities had no tradition of bond issuance, no broad base of domestic investors willing to buy and trade securities. The country's lag in financial development put England at a strategic disadvantage.

The government had few options. It could tax, it could borrow, and it could sell concessions and rights—and most of the concessions and rights that could be sold already had been. The monopoly on most foreign trade, for example, was long held by the Company of Merchant Adventurers. It functioned as a guild—not a share company, but rather an association of merchants who coordinated their efforts to obtain monopolistic trade concessions. Its members controlled the textile trade between England and the Low Countries and competed with the Germanic Hanseatic League for trade in other northern European ports. Even if Elizabeth restructured the trade concessions with the Merchant Adventurers, there were consequent risks to English international competitiveness.

The ancient presence of the English in Antwerp as merchants and borrowers is still visible. The University of Antwerp is partly housed in a building that once was a warehouse for the Antwerp branch of the Merchant Adventurers—its top floor arched with beautiful timbers from the sixteenth century. One of its governors, Thomas Gresham (1519–1579), worked in Antwerp at its apogee as a financial center. A short walk from the Merchant Adventurers' warehouse is a small courtyard, open to the air with a covered loggia on three sides. Above it stands a tower with a windowed lookout. The floors of the loggia are a checkerboard of marble. Their columns are slender gothic. This court was the Antwerp grain exchange—opened in 1460. The tower is reputed to have been a lookout post for scouts awaiting the arrival of ships—on first sight, the news could be shouted down to the floor traders. Gresham must have seen the way that traders took their posts at various stations around the court, quoting and trading merchant goods and commodities—perhaps even early bonds. One of his great projects was the creation of the Royal Exchange in London—a grand building patterned on the bourse of Antwerp. It is rare to be able to so explicitly trace the borrowing of a financial tool, for the Royal Exchange ultimately became the setting for British development of a stock market.

SEEKE OUT, DISCOVER, AND FINDE

There was an interesting loophole in the Merchant Adventurers trade monopoly. Elizabeth could authorize another company to trade with new lands and peoples, ports not currently frequented by English merchants. She could, if she wished, offer a monopoly on trade with unknown lands. If an Englishman could discover a hitherto unknown land, or a route to a port not currently controlled or challenged by the Merchant Adventurers, he would have a new monopoly. Her grandfather, Henry VII, first exercised this loophole. In 1496, he gave letters of patent to John Cabot, a citizen of Venice, authorizing Cabot to "seeke out, discover, and finde, whatsover isels, countreys, regions or provinces of the heathen and infidelles, whatsoever they be, and in what part of the world soever they be, which before this time have ben unknowen to all Christians."[1] Henry was promised one-fifth of the profits in exchange for this exclusive right. Cabot underwrote the cost of the expedition himself. On his first voyage, the Italian mariner planted the English flag in Newfoundland, which he suspected of being part of the Eurasian continent. His second voyage to the west was intended to establish a trading colony in Japan, with an eye to importing the spices of the East directly to England. Cabot and his ships were lost at sea, and with them all major efforts by the English crown to challenge the Spanish and Portuguese in the Asian trade.

In 1553, Elizabeth entertained a proposal to revive the dream of an alternative route to the Indies. The proposal came from a company called "The Mysterie and Companie of the Merchants Adventurers for the Discoverie of Regions, Dominions, Islands and Places Unknown." The Muscovy Company, as it is commonly termed, was founded to explore a northeastern route around Siberia to Cathay, but it essentially had the exclusive right to all unknown lands in the north. Sebastian Cabot, John Cabot's son, was one of the company's founders.

The Muscovy Company was officially chartered in 1555 and is widely considered to be the first modern, joint-stock company—the Toulouse mills long forgotten by most historians of the corporation. The company was structured as a self-perpetuating group of wealthy investors "one bodie and perpetuall fellowship and communaltie,"[2] who pooled their capital in return for shares in the venture. Some have speculated that this share ownership structure came from Sebastian Cabot's knowledge of Italian companies—and perhaps it even echoes the Casa di San Giorgio, for Genoese financiers were active in the Age of Discovery.[3]

THE PROBLEM OF SHARES

The shares held by the company's investors represented fractions of ownership, yet unlike modern stock shares, they also obliged the investors to put up extra capital when the company needed it. These "capital calls" represented an uneven burden on shareholders. Some could afford to chip in more money as needed, while others could not. The problem of capital calls led to the sale of shares. The investors who could not afford to stay in the game sold off their shares to previous or new investors who had the money to meet the capital calls. While not formally traded on an exchange, a secondary market for company shares evidently developed. Today, a modern company cannot require equity investors to pay in more to retain their stake. Instead, new shares are issued and sold to raise new working capital. Thus, the Muscovy Company had some features of the modern corporation but others it lacked—for example, limited liability.

While the similarities between the Muscovy Company and the corporate structure of the Honor del Bazacle are clearly evident, the differences are important. The financing for the Muscovy Company was venture capital with a capital V. To this day, the venture capitalist still only expects a small number of his or her many projects to pay off. Investment in the Muscovy Company was more like a lottery ticket than a meal ticket. Unlike the Honor del Bazacle, which had proved its economic validity over generations of profitable grain milling, the Muscovy Company was entirely speculative, born in the hope of future discovery and trade. It was, by its very nature, aspirational: appealing to the dream of future possibilities rather than founding itself on known value.

The English exploration firms represented a whole new form of risk and reward for investors. They were calculated gambles. Most would likely end in failure, but those adventures that succeeded might redraw the map of the world, fill the personal and government coffers with vast riches, even create—against all odds—an overseas global empire, ruled by a small European island on the northern edge of civilization.

The Muscovy Company failed to find a northern route to China, but it did open a profitable trade with Russia, expanding the market for English textiles and finding a source for vital mast timbers in the Siberian forests. Visitors to Moscow can still see the company headquarters a short walk from the Kremlin walls: a sturdy brick building overlooking the ancient wharves. The company profited handsomely in its early years. Some members of the company continued to dream of a northern passage, however. Among them was Michael Lok.

LOK AND FROBISHER:
FINANCIER AND PRIVATEER

Michael Lok (ca.1532–ca.1615) was a visionary businessman. The son of a well-connected British merchant, Lok spent his early career in the great financial centers of the world. He was apprenticed as a young man in the Low Countries; he traveled in Spain and Portugal; and he lived in Venice, where he plied the Levantine trade in silk and luxury goods. Lok's most significant appointment, however, was as London agent of the Muscovy Company.

Captain Martin Frobisher had served Michael Lok admirably in the past—among other things as a crew member of an ill-fated 1562 African expedition, which left Frobisher languishing for a time in a Portuguese prison. Frobisher was mostly, however, a pirate; at times a legitimate privateer, and at other times a hired mercenary—a rake in the Jack Sparrow mold. His adventures included being locked up in a British jail for appropriating an English cargo ship full of wine. Perhaps this afforded an opportunity to develop even greater plans. The freed Frobisher approached Lok and the Muscovy Company with an audacious plan to open up a Northwest passage to Cathay. The approval of the Muscovy Company was vital, as it retained the royal charter for northern exploration. The company was ultimately willing to turn its northern exploration rights over to a newly formed partnership, the Company of Cathay, organized by Michael Lok. The principal investors in the new company included Stephen Burough, lord treasurer of England, and Sir

Thomas Gresham, the founder of the Royal Exchange and famous for Gresham's law: "bad money drives out good." Although Lok was well connected, he could not quite raise all the funds required for the first Frobisher voyage, and thus covered the bulk of the expenses with a personal guarantee.

Setting sail in June 1576, Frobisher proceeded to high northern latitude, reaching Greenland in a little more than a month of sailing. Crossing to the east, he encountered another strait, which he hailed as the entrance to the long-sought northwest passage. Captain and crew sailed 150 miles north up the progressively narrowing route, which we now know is a long fjord with no outlet. Along the way, he kidnapped an Eskimo man from the throngs of curious natives who followed his boat and tried to bargain with him for the release of five of his crew who were lost when they struck out on their own to trade.

Headed once again south with their captive, the explorers landed at the entrance to the passage. This territory he named Loksland, in honor of his sponsor. The exploration of Loksland turned up almost nothing—with the exception of a friable black stone—a mineral with tiny bits of mica that glinted in the light. They sailed home in late August. Their native captive survived the passage but died soon thereafter.

Frobisher's report of a possible northwest passage, along with a highly suspicious assay of the black rock from Loksland suggesting it was gold ore, were enough to secure Frobisher and Lok a royal charter for a new company, patterned on the Muscovy Company, called the "Company of Cathay." Lok was the governor, and Frobisher was appointed "high admiral." This time, Queen Elizabeth herself subscribed to the company with 1,000 pounds. Lok as syndicator took a 20% cut of the 4,275 pounds total raised. Their mission—to head back to the New World with more boats and men to set up a colony and search for gold, and to probe ahead to find the northwest passage.

It is hard to imagine why anyone would think the Frobisher ore was valuable. It is a light iron pyrite with no gold content whatsoever. This was the same conclusion reached by two of the three Elizabethan assayers. Only a third assayer claimed it contained gold. Did the founders of the Company of Cathay find some way to fudge the third assay results? On the one hand, it helped them raise a considerable sum to continue their explorations. On the other hand, the penalty for lying to the queen would certainly have given pause to any thought of fraud. What would Jack Sparrow have done?

Frobisher's second and third voyages in 1577 and 1578 focused on collecting more of the black ore, and establishing a colony in the land the Queen dubbed "Meta Incognita." Frobisher set up the colony on a tiny spot near Loksland called Kodlunarn Island, where the black ore was particularly plentiful. As before, he encountered native peoples and fought skirmishes with them. The artist, John White, pictured one of these encounters in his painting of an Inuit man in his kayak in the foreground, and a standoff between English musketeers and bow-wielding natives in the background. It is a fair depiction of Kodlunarn Island and environs today: distant, glacier-rounded mountains in the foreground with the greenish tinge of Arctic summer vegetation, ice flows choking the bay, a native camp on the mainland opposite Kodlunarn, and steep sides of the island rising straight out of the water.

THE TEMPEST AND KODLUNARN ISLAND

As strange as Frobisher's lack of skepticism about the ore assay seems, it is also hard to believe that anyone would return to this desolate spot unless they truly believed they had discovered treasure. Kodlunarn is a small, oval-shaped tabletop of land sticking up out of the frigid waters— its only distinctive feature is a trench that the Elizabethan miners dug through the middle, following the seam of ore. Despite the passage of centuries, the foundations of their houses are easily identified. Not far away is a rough chute down which the ore must have been dumped and loaded into the ships—hundreds of tons of it, in fact. Across the strait of water on the mainland were Eskimos curious about their activities and not entirely friendly, given past encounters. Strange to think that on this spot were projected the highest aspirations of English exploration: riches equal to Spain, a northwest passage to China, a brand-new world controlled by the English crown. It seems like nothing but a Shakespearean dream from which the explorers and the investors would inevitably awake.

Indeed, a tempest in Frobisher Bay put an end to Frobisher's dreams of gold and the northwest passage. As his crew prepared to leave Kodlunarn island at the end of the summer of the third voyage, a sudden storm blew up, and their boats were "driven on rockes and Islandes of yce." One boat and many men were lost, others abandoned to winter on the island—out of reach of their comrades who were lucky enough to escape southward through the ice. The passage home without decent provisions caused more suffering. Of course, when they reached England, the suffering for the investors began. The expedition lost most of the company assets, Kodlunarn Island ore was worthless, and no passage to Cathay materialized. The ore was used "to repayre the high-wayes." Michael Lok spent the rest of his life dealing with the financial tempest caused by the failure of the company.

And what of Frobisher's ore? Was the assay after the first voyage a complete sham to gin up new capital for the second and third voyages? Were their dreams of gold foolhardy? Frobisher Bay is now a part of Nunavut, a separate Canadian territory created in 1999 and governed by the Inuit people. Iqaluit, its capital, is situated at the head of Frobisher Bay in Baffinland. Mineral exploration in Nunavut is big business. Nunavut has granted mineral exploration rights on Baffinland to a number of companies—the largest of which is Baffinland Iron, a publicly traded company that is developing a vast, high-grade iron mine just 200 miles or so north of Frobisher Bay. The small Canadian company estimates the reserves at about 650 million tons of 65% pure iron ore, enough to build an open-pit operation in this remote spot and solve the logistical problems of smelting or transporting the heavy ore by sea. Imagine a twenty-first-century miner flown up to Iqaluit following the footsteps of Frobisher's intrepid crew—and imagine the ghost of Michael Lok, fuming that his explorers failed to find this rare iron lode. The new miners are more likely to be Inuit, however. One of the attractions of development in the eastern Arctic is the possibility of industrial jobs for the people of Nunavut.

GOLD FEVER IN THE FAR NORTH

Queen Elizabeth I instructed Martin Frobisher to bring back gold from Meta Incognita. Is there any gold in Baffinland? Some investors think so. Commander Resources is a micro-cap stock, founded and managed by Canadian geologists and entrepreneurs. Its shares trade for about 20 cents each, and the entire company is worth about $14 million. Commander Resources' website displays a picture of a core sample taken in 2004 at a spot called Malrok—in the core are flakes of gold. Are these assays convincing enough to gin up further investment to keep the venture afloat?

How about jewels? True North Gems has located and mined a deposit of sapphires near the town of Kimmirut in Baffinland—they've named the stones Beluga Sapphires. Despite this discovery, however, their public income statements do not yet show profitable earnings. The value in the firm remains tied to its future potential. The discovery of a high-quality diamond in Baffinland suggests the geological potential to yield the most precious of all gems. DeBeers Canada has leased and explored vast tracts in the northern part of the island.

You can still invest in Martin Frobisher's vision—just buy shares in these small companies prospecting in Baffinland. The land Frobisher found has gold, diamonds, sapphires, and vast iron deposits. Will these deposits ever be commercially viable given the violent tempests, pack ice, and remoteness of northeastern Canada? Global warming might be a necessary input to profitability. At the very least we can say that dreams of vast riches in the Arctic still inspire investors.

Although the Company of Cathay was a bust as a business venture, other English companies dedicated to exploration survived and prospered. The company form provided a flexible business structure for channeling capital into business enterprise. Despite the disappointment of the Company of Cathay, England continued to charter companies of exploration and overseas trade: The Virginia Company most famously colonized America's mid-Atlantic coast, Hudson's Bay Company—still a thriving firm—successfully set up operations in what is now Canada, and most spectacularly of all, the East India Company, chartered in 1600, secured Britain's foothold in South Asian trade, and led to its colonial empire in India.

All of these companies started out as risky ventures. Some succeeded, while others failed. Investors put up money in the face of such grave uncertainties: the unknown quality of gold ore, the uncertainty of survival in the New World, the challenges of the Spanish in the Pacific, competition with the Portuguese and Dutch.

CORPORATE COUSINS

The Dutch East India Company, the Vereenigde Oost-Indische Compagnie (VOC), was created in 1602 in a manner somewhat similar to the founding of the Honor del Bazacle—as a merger among separate companies, in this case the various trading ventures sponsored by merchants in several Dutch cities. By uniting under one firm, the Dutch were following the example of the British East India Company that was founded in 1600. Both of these firms sought to compete with the Portuguese for access to the lucrative Asian spice trade—and they were successful at it. Over the next three centuries, the VOC claimed the lion's share of the Indonesian trade, while the British dominated trade with India and China. Spain and Portugal were first movers in the discovery of the New World and sea routes to Asia, and yet the Dutch and British rose to dominance.

A research team of legal, economics, and history professors in Europe is carefully studying the early history of the VOC. They argue that the eventual dominance of the Asian trade by the Dutch and British was due to the development of the corporation as the financing and governance framework of these enterprises. Giuseppe Dari-Martini, Oscar Gelderblom, Joost Jonker, and Enrico Perroti bring a range of perspectives to this problem. Joost Jonker and Oscar Gelderblom are leading scholars in the history of Dutch capital markets. Giuseppe Dari-Martini and Enrico Perroti are experts in law and economics.[4] Together they have delved into the archives of the VOC with the goal of understanding how and why the company developed into a firm with permanent capital, traded shares, and the separation of ownership and control.

Unlike the Bazacle company, the VOC was only chartered for ten years. This limited term derived from its origin as an overseas trade venture. Recall that the earliest known equity contracts were the Mesopotamian partnerships to trade with Dilmun (see Chapter 3). Investors contributed capital, and at the conclusion of the trip—if the voyagers returned—they divided up the profits. The capital was not permanent. In fact, the firm did not have limited liability or fully transferable shares.

Dari-Martini and his colleagues trace the origins of the VOC to profitable, one-off ventures to Asia sponsored by several of the provinces of the Dutch Republic in the years prior to 1600, with Amsterdam leading the way. The 1602 charter established a trade monopoly among six of the provinces that locked in investor capital for ten years and paid out a dividend only when the profits exceeded the amount of invested capital. In exchange for this long-term capital commitment, the shares were allowed to trade freely. The scholars argue that liquidity was a financial innovation that explicitly compensated for capital lockup. Tradability of VOC shares was not "borrowed" from the Bazacle or San Giorgio precedent but adopted as a local solution to the problem of attracting capital to a venture that would take years to reach fruition.

Like San Giorgio, but unlike the Honor del Bazacle, the VOC charter created a quasi-public institution. The Dutch Estates General certified the monopoly rights and extended the VOC governmental rights, including the right to enforce laws, make treaties, and wage war overseas.

The shares were fully subscribed, and they began to actively trade. Over a thousand investors subscribed for the Amsterdam issue alone.[5] The Amsterdam Exchange is generally recognized as the first stock market. In fact, over the course of the seventeenth century, Amsterdam was where the most sophisticated financial techniques for speculation evolved. Joseph De la Vega's *Confusion de Confusiones*, printed in 1688, chronicles the trading by bulls and bears betting on the movement of the VOC shares, the writing of put and call options, the short-selling of stock, and the clever means by which even small investors could speculate in fractions of shares. Investors traded with one another by issuing transfer receipts that were then used to change the ownership in the books of the company at a later date. Because of the time lag between the trade and the transfer of record, all sorts of interim speculation could—and did—occur.

Thus, even if the company had never developed all the features of the modern corporation, the creation of a stock market in Amsterdam to trade equities represents a major financial innovation.

The public market in the trade for VOC shares achieved many things. First, it gave investors tangible proof that, if they bought shares, they could sell them. This liquidity was worth a lot, because now equity claims were like the bond claims that had existed in Europe since the Venetian prestiti. Second, it tapped into the natural human tendency to gamble and speculate. De la Vega characterized some traders as naturally pessimistic and others naturally optimistic, and he saw a natural flow of trade among them over the fortunes of a company, which, after all, might not issue a dividend for years. The public issuance of VOC shares turned the Amsterdam Exchange into a barometer of opinion about the future of the spice trade. While Bazacle shares were fully tradable in the fifteenth century, and the Toulouse grain market was certainly the realm of speculation, as we saw in Chapter 17, the stock market as a frenzy of bulls and bears never quite materialized there. Perhaps it was the very uncertainty and risk of the VOC ventures with their potential for vast riches and threat of serious disaster that got the speculators' juices flowing.

It took the VOC—and its cousin, the British East India Company—several more years to complete the transition to modern corporations. Dari-Martini and colleagues attribute the step to limited liability to the need of the company to do interim finance by issuing debt. The VOC issued bonds as well as stocks, but only after it obtained permission to limit the liability of its partners. One of these bonds, yielding 6.25%, is in the financial history collection of the Beinecke Library at Yale—another treasure Professor Geert Rouwenhorst managed to track down and acquire for the university.

The transition to permanent capital came about through a major revision of the charter in 1612. The government intervened to extend the charter permanently, over the desires of shareholders, who wished to reap profits from the return on capital. Dari-Martini and colleagues noted that, by then, the government had a strong interest in the continuity of the company because of its representation and defense of the interest of the state—and as a practical matter, the firm had overseas assets that could not be easily valued and liquidated. Thus, while permanent capital was a natural feature of the Bazacle company by virtue of existing in *pariage*—a perpetual feudal claim—the shareholders of the VOC had to be coerced into this equilibrium. The British East India Company followed the example of the VOC much later in the eighteenth century.

Whether the corporate form was a superior model for overseas trade and ultimately colonial expansion is still debatable. The argument that the relative success of the British and Dutch was due to a superior financial technology is a plausible one. Like the Casa di San Giorgio, perhaps strategic decisions taken by a ruling body governed by merchants made for surer economic growth than control by a royal family with a variety of other goals (and a lack of funding to achieve them). However, anyone willing to mount an expedition to Baffinland in search of gold, or to spend good money on a share in a company whose boats had to travel around Africa and back to return with strangely flavored seeds that appealed to the palettes and purses of rich bourgeoisie would seem to be foolishly optimistic. The second birth of the corporation and the stock market seems anything but level headed.

A PROJECTING AGE

The vast reach and maritime power of England and the Netherlands were remarkable, given their small sizes. As we saw in Chapter 18, the expansion of both was inextricably tied to merchant voyages and ultimately to large, monopolistic trading companies that opened up and maintained trade routes to Asia. The birth of these empires began with individuals taking extraordinary personal and financial risks. The trading corporation in northern Europe developed as an institution to raise capital, share risks, and provide investor liquidity for projects demanding great patience to succeed.

Even when individual voyages failed, battles lost, and markets closed, the corporate form proved to be a robust paradigm—a set of rules for the game—that sustained investor interest and thus continuity of capital for years, generations, and centuries. For these two countries, corporations grew to be nearly as important as the state, and the interests of both became intertwined.

In this chapter, we visit the world of corporations and capital markets a century after their appearance in Britain and the Netherlands. We focus in depth on a moment in time when society became absolutely giddy with the new financial tool that trading companies had engendered. If corporations worked so well for exploration, discovery, and colonization, why not use them to do other things as well?

AN ESSAY UPON PROJECTS

In November 1687, at the height of the power of the Dutch Republic, the monarch William of Orange assembled a navy four times the size of the Spanish Armada and crossed the English Channel, landing in Devon. The flotilla was financed by a loan arranged by leading merchant bankers in Amsterdam. The invading army, composed of mercenaries

Engraving of the Royal Exchange in London, from the Dutch volume, *The Great Mirror of Folly*, 1720. In the center is a list of securities traded by brokers called, in Dutch, "wind merchants" for their trade in insubstantial paper.

from Germany, Scotland, Switzerland, and Scandinavia met little resistance. Indeed, they were welcomed by many. The Catholic King James II was so unpopular among his subjects that defections from the British navy and army to the Dutch side were widespread. Anti-Catholic riots broke out in several towns, and virtually all support for the English monarch evaporated by the end of the year. Even the landed gentry saw little benefit in putting up a fight. Hoping to keep William's hands off the last symbol of legal power, James II pitched the Great Seal of the British crown into the Thames and fled to France, leaving William and Mary to rule as joint monarchs. Although the near-bloodless invasion was welcomed by the largely Protestant English populace and the political transition was surprisingly smooth, the conquest of Britain by the Netherlands in 1688 had a deep and lasting impact on both nations. Political historians recognize it as an important step in reducing the power of the British monarch and stimulating the full transition to Parliamentary rule.

For financial historians, 1688 is a watershed that marked the ascendance of Great Britain as a global financial power. With the Dutch monarch came bankers and financiers who carried the financial "genetic code" of the Netherlands: an orientation toward open capital markets, an understanding of the use of bonds to fund government debt, lotteries to stimulate speculation, life-rents and annuities for the rentier class, and ultimately a central bank that could serve as an instrument of fiscal policy. The British added an exuberant creativity in the use of these tools—applying them in ways that society could barely imagine before 1688. The Glorious Revolution released the British financial imagination. Great Britain entered a new financial era, in the words of writer and entrepreneur Daniel Defoe, a "Projecting Age."

Few writers caught the new spirit of the British financial revolution as deftly as Defoe. Perhaps this is because he was a dreamer who embraced the new political order and the grand possibilities of finance, as well as the many ways that one could exploit both. As a young man, Defoe was among the throngs of Londoners who welcomed the new Protestant king on his triumphal visit to the city of London in 1689.[1] He may even have served the new king and queen personally in some capacity. For the next decade, Defoe tried his hand at a number of entrepreneurial ventures. A plunge into the marine insurance business turned disastrous when French pirates captured the ships he underwrote. He made a losing investment in a new kind of diving bell for his brother-in-law's salvage operations. Hoping to cash in on the upper-class British demand for perfume, he started a civet-cat farm on borrowed money. Defoe couldn't repay his debts and sold the cats to his mother-in-law, who then discovered that the livestock was not his to convey. These and other peccadillos brought him to court frequently after the Glorious Revolution and saddled him with crushing debt. He spent some time in London's Southwark debtors' prison before managing to discharge his obligations. He used connections to get occasional work as a promoter for private lotteries and as a tax collector. He eventually dreamed up a business that turned a profit: manufacturing ceramic roof tile in the Dutch style for the London building trade.

History does not remember Daniel Defoe as a businessman, however, but as an essayist, journalist, and novelist. He wrote *Robinson Crusoe*, published his own political review, and authored a number of pamphlets on politics, trade, finance, stock-jobbery, and the national debt. His first book was a series of proposals that explored the potential of the new age: *An Essay upon Projects*, printed in 1697.

The brief volume pondered the peculiar social change brought about by Britain's new capital markets at the end of the seventeenth century. It is worth quoting the author's introduction at length. He paints a striking picture of the new financial order.

> Necessity, which is allowed to be the mother of invention, has so violently agitated the wits of men at this time that it seems not at all improper, by way of distinction, to call it the Projecting Age. . . . There are, and that too many, fair pretenses of fine discoveries, new inventions, engines, and I know not what, which—being advanced in notion, and talked up to great things to be performed when such and such sums of money shall be advanced, and such and such engines are made—have raised the fancies of credulous people to such a height that, merely on the shadow of expectation, they have formed companies, chose committees, appointed officers, shares, and books, raised great stocks, and cried up an empty notion to that degree that people have been betrayed to part with their money for shares in a

new nothing; and when the inventors have carried on the jest till they have sold all their own interest, they leave the cloud to vanish of itself, and the poor purchasers to quarrel with one another, and go to law about settlements, transferrings, and some bone or other thrown among them by the subtlety of the author to lay the blame of the miscarriage upon themselves. Thus the shares at first begin to fall by degrees, and happy is he that sells in time; till, like brass money, it will go at last for nothing at all. So have I seen shares in joint—stocks, patents, engines, and undertakings, blown up by the air of great words, and the name of some man of credit concerned, to 100 pounds for a five—hundredth part or share (some more), and at last dwindle away till it has been stock—jobbed down to 12 pounds, 10 pounds, 9 pounds, 8 pounds a share, and at last no buyer (that is, in short, the fine new word for nothing—worth), and many families ruined by the purchase. If I should name linen manufactures, saltpetre—works, copper mines, diving engines, dipping, and the like, for instances of this, I should, I believe, do no wrong to truth, or to some persons too visibly guilty.[2]

Despite his condemnation of the hawking of hollow schemes and the stock-jobbing of shares, Defoe goes on in his book to propose a series of high-minded financial projects. His first visionary joint-stock project in the *Essay* was to vastly expand the British banking system. Why not raise a truly large sum of capital, he suggested, and create a huge national bank? This bank could perform commercial lending, write bills of exchange, underwrite large money transfers, and provide mortgages at 4% rates. The country needed capital! Expand the bank. Increase the number of directors, and open up branches throughout the British Isles. Bring capital to local centers of trade: Canterbury, Salisbury, Exeter, Bristol, Worcester, Shrewsbury, Manchester, Newcastle-upon-Tyne, Leeds, Halifax, York, Warwick, Birmingham, Oxford, Reading, Bedford, Norwich, and Colchester. All could benefit from a bank willing to lend on commerce. A bank like that could finance all sorts of new ventures directly. It could provide a conduit from savings to investment. It could overcome the shackles of local geography, facilitating trade among towns by taking deposits in one and issuing money in another.

Defoe followed the plan for a national banking system with a plan to create a national highway system, funded by Parliament through a tax and executed through contract with projectors who would undertake the construction of toll roads by appropriation of lands by eminent domain, and whose compensation for the service would be regulated by law. Defoe next offered a plan for a mutual insurance company to cover risks at sea, fire insurance, and title insurance—although curiously not life insurance or life-contingent annuities. He even proposed a national pension fund—amazingly like the US Social Security system, funded by beneficiary contributions that would then form a vast investment pool, which in turn would generate profits through lotteries and real estate investment. The plan could, in Defoe's words "banish beggary and poverty out of the kingdom." All was now possible in an age when money could be raised through new capital markets or appropriated by an enlightened and emboldened Parliament willing to further transform the financial system.

Defoe's *Essay upon Projects* sketched other ways to improve society: a bankruptcy code that eliminated debtors' prisons and provided orderly liquidation of assets and distribution to creditors. He went on to envision an academy for women, a learned society patterned on the French Academy, a merchant court that specialized in commercial disputes, and finally a fund for supporting merchant seamen. All in all, the book is a breathless, outrageous explosion of ideas to transform the human condition and commerce. It placed Defoe among the most visible editorialists and public commentators of his age. Defoe practically invented the role of the visionary journalist, although his voice was ultimately one of many in an age of new proposals and projects.

A TECHNOLOGY, NOT A TECHNIQUE

Defoe's Projecting Age asserted a new social order based on new institutions and technologies. As such, it was one of the first and brightest articulations of the way the new financial order could create vast accumulations of capital which, in turn could re-make society as a whole. The historian Francesca Bray makes a very useful distinction between techniques and technology. In her words, a technology is the technique exercised in its social context, and it is this social context that imparts meaning, both to the objects produced, and to the persons producing them . . . they serve to defuse conflict, at other times they provoke it. Technology . . . performs ideological work . . . that might stabilize as well as transform or develop a social order.[3]

The burgeoning new equity market of London on the verge of the eighteenth century was not only a new technique for raising capital but also a new technology in every sense of Bray's definition. It had the power to introduce a new social order and engender an extraordinary reimagining of social possibilities. Perhaps more troublesome—as Bray suggests—a new technology can provoke conflict due to a multiplicity of cultural interpretations.

Defoe himself rendered two such conflicting interpretations in one text—first decrying the markets and then using them to re-envision society. Defoe warned of the dangers of the new financial age: the emergence of dishonest intermediaries; the risk of market manipulation; and the potential to be fooled, tricked, gulled, trumped, and bankrupted by projectors with "mouths full of millions."

It is not that the financial techniques were so novel. After all, companies, stock markets, and speculators had been around for a long while when *Essay upon Projects* appeared. The true novelty was the assembling of these techniques by the creative imagination. Financial tools had begun to set in motion a feedback loop between investors and innovators. Defoe's *Essay* was already two stages down the road toward a financial revolution. Having witnessed what finance could do, he proposed to push it even further. The financial innovation of Defoe's age had to do with an intensification of techniques until they became a technology—which is inextricable from a new culture. This culture rested on the company as the central unit of enterprise, it involved an ever-widening public eager to invest and the development of intermediaries who promoted companies, bought and sold shares, wrote options, and made a market. It would take years for the legal and regulatory system to catch up to this new culture—to decide just what companies could and could not do; to clarify the roles of managers, owners, and board members; to comprehend what kind of property company shares represented; and to determine whether the government needed to exercise control or allow firms free hand. The years following Defoe's *Essay* would prove to be some of the most exciting in the history of finance.

MONEY DOWN

One way that companies were launched in the Projecting Age was through share subscriptions on a deferred payment plan. Although the book value of a share might be 100 pounds, a subscriber needed to put up only a small fraction (as little at 1%) to acquire the right to own it. On calendar intervals, the new company would call on the shareholder for capital until the share was fully "paid-in." Meanwhile, the subscription right was tradable. In other words, the company lent the subscriber nearly all the money to buy the share in the first place. If shareholders did not meet their capital calls, they faced forfeiture of their equity.

Buy a subscription for a pound, then sell it if the price goes up. If the company calls for a payment on the share and the price is still low, then hand the share back to the company. One pound lost, but a small price to pay for a chance at making a big profit if the business really took off. If the notion of buying a share on margin offered by the company seems like gambling, perhaps it was. Daily prices in the newspapers told you whether you were making or losing money—abstracting away from the fundamental business of the company and boiling it down to a single, fluctuating number. It was not too different from waiting to see whether your lottery number is called. Investing became a numbers game—it transformed investor consciousness from a long-term vision of return on capital to daily monitoring of the market to see whether you've won on your bet. No wonder it suddenly had such broad appeal. It was the seventeenth-century equivalent of day trading and margin accounts.

The first stock price list of new companies appeared in John Houghton's *Collections for Improvement of Husbandry and Trade* in 1691.[4] By 1694, Houghton was regularly listing fifty-two traded companies. For the big companies, he provided weekly price quotes for free. Interested subscribers had to pay to get quotes for the lesser firms. *Freke's Prices of Stocks &c.* offered another source of market news and Castaing's *Course of the Exchange* made a third.

Among the enterprises on Houghton's list were the company of copper miners in England; the company for casting and making guns and
ordnance in moulds of metal; the company for making imitation Russian
leather; a company for making a diving machine (not Defoe's!); a company
for making a draining pump (this was the ages of draining the fens of East
Anglia); the company for the Sucking-Worm Engine of Mr. John Lofting,
Merchant—a fire engine pump; the White Paper Makers; the Blue Paper
Company; the Society for Improving Native Manufactures so as to Keep
out the Wet (a glass company); a company for making "German Balls" to
preserve leather from damp; the Governor and Company for Smelting
Down Lead with Pit and Sea Coal; the Bank of England; the Million Bank;
the Orphans' Bank; a company for Greenland whaling; a Newfoundland-
bound cod fishing company; a pearl diving company; colonization companies for Pennsylvania, New Jersey, and Tobago; Southwark, City Conduits
and Hampstead waterworks companies; York Building Society; King's
and Queen's Corporation for Linen Manufacturing in Ireland; the Convex
Lights Company; the Newcastle Water Company—and more. Houghton's list leaves little doubt that a technological revolution was under way.
The fact that these were all investable ideas, with little money down, recalls
the sky-blue optimism of the Tech Bubble of 1990s almost exactly 300 years
later. Not only were scientists and engineers devising amazing new contrap-
tions that could change the world, you could actually own a share in them.

Broken down by industry, these new British firms included companies
for mining, salvage, fishing, forestry, agriculture, textile and mechanical
manufacturing, overseas trade, infrastructure, real estate, leasing, and
finance. Ever since 1623, when England enacted the Statute of Monopolies, an inventor had the exclusive right to profit from a novel invention. The new financial market after 1688 married capital with creativity
and intellectual property rights. Perhaps because they were engines of
innovation, joint-stock companies grew dramatically in importance relative to the rest of the economy. The historian William Robinson Scott
estimated that in 1695, they represented 1.3% of the national wealth of
Great Britain, but by the end of 1720, this had grown to 13%. By then,
the corporate system had emerged from a set of closely held companies
controlled by merchants relying on exclusive trade privileges to lightly
regulated pools of investment capital drawn from unrelated, enthusiastic
speculators who hoped that an idea or a patent might make them rich.

FIGURE 23. *The Bubbler's Mirrour or England's Folly.* A satirical British print from 1721 listing the many projects funded by issuance of stock in London's Exchange Alley.

The more people invested in these projects, the more liquid the shares and subscriptions became. Even when the initial subscriptions were limited to a few investors, as they sold their rights, the pool of owners and speculators continued to widen. Shares could turn over and over in the heated market of Exchange Alley, London's informal stock market. Prices jumped and crashed on rumors about whether the new company really had an innovative product or whether there was a market for its services.

Prices for companies really began to soar after 1692—some reached twice their book value, which was many times more than their paid-in capital. While launching ventures for the "improvement of Husbandry and Trade" was a means to increase the fortunes of British citizens in the long run, speculating in the shares of these ventures could increase individual fortunes very quickly. The sudden demand for shares in the 1690s quickened the practiced investor pulse, even as it drew many new speculators. The first crash in Britain came in 1697, when shares dropped from their highs of double book value to less than half of book value. The drop in prices unmasked the stock-jobber and the risk of speculation and led to Defoe's delightful diatribe. But the setback of 1697 was not the end of the Projecting Age—it was only the beginning. Like the Tech Bubble of the 1990s, it presaged even greater financial fireworks.

BUBBLING THE INDUSTRIAL REVOLUTION

The Industrial Revolution is generally viewed as beginning in England in the late eighteenth century and peaking in the mid-nineteenth century with the completion of an economic transformation to mechanized production processes and industrial specialization. However, William Robinson Scott in a massive, three-volume study, argued that the seeds of the Industrial Revolution were planted much earlier, in the Projecting Age that led up to the year 1720. Scanning the list of companies founded after the Glorious Revolution, it is difficult not to agree with him. All the ingredients were there: mechanization, innovation, property rights, and capital.

The puzzle of the Projecting Age is why the explosion of these new companies did not happen in the Netherlands. Amsterdam at the turn of the seventeenth century had all the financial sophistication of London and then some. The London market that emerged in the early seventeenth century was, in part, created by Dutch financiers in the wake of the Glorious Revolution. The basic structure and workings of the securities and the banking system were mostly adapted from Dutch precedents. In fact, the Dutch and other continental economies, with their development of bond markets, annuities, and other savings vehicles, proved how a market for investment paper could be driven by the capital supply. The Dutch made markets in the VOC and the Dutch West India Company (WIC) shares—why not in diving bell schemes, paper companies, and smelting works?

Perhaps the Glorious Revolution itself was the catalyst for the spirit of change. One might as well ask why the Tech Bubble of the late 1990s happened in the United States and not in Europe or Japan. All three markets had financial systems and active technological research programs. But clearly the real fever started in the United States, with talk of the transformative potential of the Internet, new models of marketing, new means of communication, the death of old technologies, and the convergence of "New Era" finance that relied on valuation by clicks and sales, not earnings and profits.

Yale economist and Nobel laureate Bob Shiller is, in some ways, a modern projector in the spirit of Daniel Defoe. He has proposed to use financial markets to help people deal with the big risks they face in their economic lives. Bob Shiller dreamed up (and patented) housing futures that could hedge against the decline in home equity. He proposed the creation of GDP-indexed products to hedge against unemployment. These products were met with mild interest in the boom years of the US economy, but, like other projectors before him, Bob Shiller may only have been ahead of his time. One of his ideas instantly caught the public's imagination, however. He became famous for his study of stock market bubbles and his forecast of the bursting of the Internet craze.

A scholar with a gentle, inquiring demeanor, Bob Shiller has always had an interest in the psychology of the stock market. We came to know each other over years of talking about everything from econometrics to the puzzle of investor behavior. At one point in his stellar academic career, Bob took a chance and wrote a trade book, *Irrational Exuberance*, based on his conviction that the Tech Bubble would burst. The book argued that bubbles are a psychological phenomenon that result from

a confluence of several factors: a plausible basis for speculation (for example, a new invention or idea) together with rumors or evidence that
others around you have made great profits from speculation—and then
reinforcement by the news media. He emphasized that these environmental conditions could change the mindset of even very sophisticated
investors and cause them to ignore rational probability assessments and
plain common sense.

The final ingredient in the development of a speculative bubble, in
Shiller's view, is a coordinating mechanism. Stocks can't all go up together unless investors are all buying together. Some big thing has to
seize the imagination, spark the bubble, and get the speculative juices
flowing. In the London markets, at the height of the Projecting Age, this
big thing was the South Sea Company.

ASIENTO

Daniel Defoe owed much to Robert Harley, Lord Oxford. In 1702,
Defoe's inflammatory pamphleteering landed him in Newgate Prison,
sentenced to three days at the pillory, a 130-pound fine, and jail until
the fine was paid. Harley convinced the queen to quietly pay the fine,
and Defoe became Harley's secret agent, propagandist, and economic
advisor.

Defoe emerged as a strong voice in the debate about the nation's pol-
itics and economics through an opinion journal he founded in 1704,
A Review of the State of the British Nation. The paper was strongly na-
tionalistic, particularly on the subject of foreign trade. As early as 1704,
Defoe proposed challenging the French and Spanish dominance of
South America and the Caribbean. Among other things, he argued for
seizing Canada from the French and founding a British colony in South
America.

In 1710, Robert Harley became chancellor of the Exchequer; in effect, the prime minister of Great Britain. Among his biggest challenges
was a huge national debt, the legacy of an extended war with France: the
War of the Spanish Succession. The country had more than 9 million
pounds of obligations—many of these short-term notes payable to war
veterans. Enter the London financiers John Blunt and George Caswall,
who proposed an ingenious solution to the debt problem. In a letter to

Harley in October 1710, they outlined a project that fit nicely with the views of Defoe about the lucrative South American trade. The similarities between their plan and Defoe's call to challenge Spain in the South Atlantic are so apparent that it is hard to doubt that Daniel Defoe had a hand in shaping the plan for the South Sea Company.

The proposal restructured the national debt and created a major financial firm under the control of Harley's Tory Party, which hitherto had been cut out of the directorships of the other major British financial giants of the day, the Bank of England and the East India Company. In essence, the idea was to exchange shares in the South Sea Company for outstanding British debts, including the antiquated tallies of the Exchequer, seaman's wages, army and navy debentures, and short-term bills of exchange. The government would then swap these debts for a fixed-rate 6% bond to the company which, in turn, would pass this dividend through to the shareholders of the company. The company would also enjoy the exclusive right to trade with the east coast of South America south of the Orinoco, and up the entire west coast, including Chile and Peru.[5]

The firm was approved by Parliament in May 1711 with Harley as the governor and a board largely composed of Tory directors. Its most important feature was its vast capitalization. By virtue of the colossal debt conversion of nearly 10 million pounds of face-value debt, the assets of the South Sea Company were larger than those of the East India Company and the Bank of England combined. Blunt and Caswall and a consortium of financiers made out well in the deal. They bought up 65,000 pounds of debt at huge discounts before the announcement of the project and then exchanged it at face value for South Sea shares.

In 1712, Defoe wrote *An Essay on the South-Sea Trade with an Enquiry into the Grounds and Reasons of the Present Dislike and Complaint against the Settlement of a South-Sea Company*. In his view, the true value of the company was that it allowed a British foothold in South America:

> We are to find out or discover some Place or Places in America, where we may fix and settle a British Colony, which by the treaty is to be our own; and is not this enough? Will not Trade fall in? Will not the Country produce to us as well as to the Spaniards? Are we less industrious than they; if we fix in a barren spot that's our fault; but

why not somewhere among the Gold, the Silver, the Drugs, the In-
dico, Cocoa, Cocheneal, and the like, as well as they. . . . This is what
we understand by a trade to the South-Seas (viz.) that we shall, under
the protection, in the name, and by the power of Her Majesty, seize,
take, and possess such port or place, or places, land, territory, country
or dominion, call it what you please, as we see fit in America . . . let
the King of Spain prevent it if he can.[6]

Defoe outrageously urged Parliament to use the South Sea Company as
a vehicle for seizing and colonizing South America, helping Britain to
the riches of the Spanish Atlantic empire.

In 1713, the Treaty of Utrecht concluded the costly War of the Spanish Succession, which pitted the Netherlands, Britain, and the Holy
Roman Empire against efforts to unify France and Spain under a single
monarch. As part of the settlement, the British, for the first time, received an *asiento* from Spain—permission to supply African slaves to
Spanish America. This included limited rights of mercantile trade, the
requirement to supply 4,800 African slaves per year for thirty years to
Spanish America (with the King of Spain receiving 10% of the profits on
the slave trade), and the right to establish factories—trading centers—
in South America with up to six Englishmen in each.[7]

The natural recipient for the asiento would have been the Royal African Company, which was chartered in 1660 and received a monopoly
on English trade with West Africa. The firm evidently branded its slaves
with the initials of the firm (or those of the Duke of York, its governor),
maintained a series of forts along the West African coast where it obtained prisoners, and traded actively in gold—hence the name for the
English gold coin, the guinea. The firm lost its monopoly in 1698 but
certainly had hopes of regaining parliamentary favor and with it, the
asiento.

Defoe turned his pen to the Royal African Company's aid in 1711 to
argue that British traders along the West African coast were free-riders
on the company's protection, and that the firm deserved financial relief.
The pamphlet made it clear that Defoe was not only an unapologetic
advocate of the slave trade but also that he did not regard the South Sea
Company and the Royal African Company as rivals so much as important institutions in Britain's Atlantic designs.

Despite the hopes of the Royal African Company, the asiento passed to the South Sea Company for a price of 7.5 million pounds.[8] The Spanish King Philip V received an allocation of 28% of new South Sea shares, the purchase of which the company financed by means of a million pesos' loan. Queen Anne's cut was 22.5%.

The costs were high, but clearly the British saw it as a vector into the lucrative South America trade. Although the principal business of the South Sea Company was slavery, Defoe—and perhaps his benefactor and governor of the company, Robert Harley—envisioned it as a means to extend Britain's commercial presence in the Atlantic. The asiento not only gave the transatlantic slave trade to the company, it provided cover to set up factories in South America that could become colonies. The award of the asiento must have been particularly painful to Britain's Dutch allies in the war. The Dutch West India Company (WIC) had colonies in Surinam and forts in West Africa, where they procured slaves. A significant part of the company's commerce was the slave trade. Now the British had a new company patterned on the Dutch model, and the right to take over the transatlantic trade in humanity. What's more, the British evidently coveted not only the Spanish settlements in South America, but apparently also the Dutch colonies in the New World.

The slave trade—or at least the licensed slave trade—had now become corporatized. The Projecting Age not only supplied capital to unfetter human mechanical ingenuity, it also supplied capital to support and expand one of the most egregious, systematic sins of humanity: freedom on the one hand and slavery on the other. The corporate structure not only gave entrepreneurs direct access to investor capital, it also provided a peculiarly efficient means to distribute profits, allocate control, and exploit political influence. What made the South Sea Company powerful was not its relative advantage in shipping and trade, but the degree to which it was an extension of the British government. It epitomized the opposite of the laissez-faire capitalist system that freed investors and entrepreneurs to buy and sell capital on a level playing field. Even as the Projecting Age made possible an explosion of new business plans and ideas, the corporation became an instrument of political favoritism and international negotiation. It is perhaps telling that the politicians settled on exploiting the most odious of all trades.

The year 1711 was only the beginning of the famous triangle trade that developed between Europe, Africa, and the Americas. Over the course of the eighteenth century, it became the major pattern of economic circulation in the Western world. Goods made in the factory towns of the industrial northwest of England were shipped to Africa in exchange for slaves; Africans were brought over on the infamous middle passage to Caribbean islands for systematic subjugation and sale to the mainland. Sugar, molasses, and other commodities bought with the profits of the slave trade were shipped back to Europe.

Joseph Inikori, a leading historian of the slave trade, argues that the intensification of the triangle trade contributed to the emergence of mechanical industrialization in Great Britain in the eighteenth century and that the great circular flow of goods and people following the Gulf Stream indirectly created modern Europe.[9] Perhaps so. An investor in the South Sea Company in 1711 might not have known that the venture would lead to trade that would transform the world economy. However, Daniel Defoe's jingoistic rhetoric that painted images of gold, silver, and South American plantations might have been sufficient to induce someone to swap their late-paying British government debt for a chance at a brand new enterprise founded and governed by none other than the prime minister himself, and one that possessed the asiento.

Bill Reese, a leading antiquarian book dealer with a keen eye for documents that changed history (he once bought and sold a Declaration of Independence) found a small leather-bound volume in a London sale some years ago. Inside were a set of documents in Spanish signed with a flourish, "Yo el Rey," granting the permission of the King of Spain (el Rey) for a ship to enter ports in Spanish territory. One of the documents also laid out in detail the specific conditions of the asiento. Most exciting was the binding. Impressed in gold on the outside cover were the initials SSC. It was the South Sea Company's own copy of the asiento. This little volume, which he showed me and let me handle, was the official permission for the company's slave trade—one of the most notorious documents in world history.

The South Sea Company was slow to get its slavery business off the ground. First there was a management shakeup. Harley's political fortunes waned to the point that he was impeached as lord treasurer in 1714, and the following year he was locked up in the Tower of London

for acts of treason. Although absolved and released after a two-year con-
finement, he had to step down as governor of the South Sea Company.
His place was taken by King George I. Political struggles with Spain,
including the short War of the Quadruple Alliance, caused a cessation
in the asiento from 1718 to 1722. Eventually, however, the company contracted with the Royal African Company to supply prisoners from their
string of forts along the coast of West Africa and also sent out ships to
procure slaves directly—perhaps with the notion that they could capture French or Portuguese slave ships and expropriate their cargo. The
firm then set up entrepôts in Jamaica and Barbados to receive the Africans who survived the middle passage. From there, healthy slaves were
re-exported to Portobello, Buenos Aires, and Cartagena. By one calculation the South Sea Company shipped 64,000 slaves to Spanish America over its lifetime. Defoe's plan for illicit trade in goods other than
human cargo also eventually came to fruition. By the late 1730s, Sevil-
lian merchants complained that the British had so thoroughly crowded
out the Latin American markets for textiles that they could sell nothing
at all in the New World.[10]

EXCHANGE ALLEY

Few people think of slavery when they think of the South Sea Company. It conjures up instead the South Sea Bubble—the great inflation
of share prices in 1720 that burst in spectacular fashion. Most economic
studies of the South Sea Bubble focus on the company's complex financial engineering in 1719 and 1720: a series of new share issues that were
eagerly snapped up by the British aristocracy, creating and destroying
vast fortunes. This disjunction between the company's business—slavery—and the strange behavior of its shares in 1720 may be partly an
accident of history's selective memory: our fascination with crashes
and blindness to the central role that slavery played in the eighteenth-
century world economy. However, it may also reflect the mentality of
the market at the time. Shares, the disembodied symbols of corporate
ownership, took on a physical reality and immediacy to London investors far greater than the distant human assets that provided future dividends. The market became the focus of investor attention—that market
was called "Exchange Alley."

London's Exchange Alley is where most of the projecting schemes were launched and where South Sea shares were traded. It is still worth a visit today. Walk up Cornhill Street from the Bank tube stop and turn into a passageway only 150 feet long that threads behind a few buildings. This unassuming little passage once occupied a particularly strategic location: a shortcut between the Royal Exchange Building, where markets were made in all sorts of commodities and securities, and the Post Office, where news of the value of these commodities and securities arrived. In effect, Exchange Alley made it possible to profit almost immediately on the news as it arrived by post. Open a letter, learn that boats from the Caribbean had arrived back safely, and buy some shares before anyone else heard the news. Not surprisingly, Lloyds Coffeehouse also moved close by the Post Office for the same reason. News of the world's seaways and weather disasters reached Lloyds first, and insurance brokers set new rates accordingly.

Two prominent coffeehouses opened directly onto this tiny lane: Galloway's and Jonathan's, both of which served as stock exchanges and places where subscriptions for new shares were taken. Jonathan's coffeehouse hosted a crowd of brokers who had been thrown out of the Royal Exchange for boisterousness—no doubt they continued this misbehavior in Exchange Alley. But their presence made a market.

A market is a place where buyers and sellers show up at the same time to trade. An empty market is a thin market with discontinuous prices, bids and no offers, and offers and no bids. The very definition of a successful market is a crowd. But the main thing that brings order to the market is price. Jonathan's posted prices for all the joint stock companies. Journalists like John Houghton, John Freke, and John Castaing sat in Jonathan's sipping coffee, recording prices, writing up the rumors, and then walking them over at the end of the day to be set and printed. It is hard to stand in the silence of Exchange Alley today and imagine the noisy crowd of stock-jobbers and speculators pushing their way in and out of the coffeehouses to trade shares; dropping around Lloyds to hear the latest news of Caribbean shipwrecks; buying lottery tickets in Cornhill; calling out bids and offers; running from a purchase to a prospective sale; and talking up or down new inventions, patents, and projects. It would have been hard for an aristocratic stock investor to maintain calm aloofness in an in-your-face chaotic world like Exchange Alley.

ANATOMY OF A BUBBLE

In late 1719, even though the slave trade had been slow to get off the ground and vexed by the temporary suspension of the asiento, the South Sea Company started a major buzz in Exchange Alley. The firm was offering a second subscription of shares to fund more than a million pounds of government debt, this time the government lottery debt of 1710. The value proposition of the new subscription was similar to the rationale for the formation of the company. Government debt-holders could exchange illiquid, hard-to-trade paper for dividend-paying stock in the South Sea Company and get the future expected profit from the transatlantic trade. The 1719 funding went well, and in 1720, the managers decided to take a giant leap forward and bid on funding a large portion of the 50 million pounds of outstanding British national debt.[11]

In early 1720, the publicly held British debt consisted of 15 million pounds in annuities of long and short duration that were not easily traded by the annuitants, and 16.5 million pounds of redeemable debt of various maturities in the hands of private borrowers. The South Sea Company bid for both. In the exchange, the annuitants and debt holders would get convenient, dividend-paying South Sea Company shares in exchange for their complicated and hard-to-transfer bonds and annuities. Their interest would be lower, but the shares would be liquid. On top of this, the South Sea Company proposed to pay the government a fee of 3 million to 7.5 million pounds to acquire it all. In the meantime, the company also took a series of subscriptions from the general public for cash purchase of shares. No need to own government debt to buy stock. Like other subscriptions at the time, you could effectively borrow money from the company to buy new shares.

The terms of the exchange between debt and equity were based on the market value of the shares. Thus, the higher the company stock price, the fewer shares had to be issued in exchange for the redeemable portion of the government debt, and the more money would be left over for the company to use as working capital. The South Sea Company did whatever it could to push up share values, including offering generous terms to subscribers. Ultimately 80–85% of the debt holders subscribed—evidently most were happy to become South Sea Company shareholders.

The South Seas Company stock price soared through the first half of the year, increasing from 116 pounds per share in November 1719 (on a face value of 100) to 310 at the end of March 1720, to 950 pounds per share at the end of June.[12] No matter how profitable the slave trade and other commerce in the Atlantic might prove to be in the future, it is hard to imagine any economic reason why the equity in the South Sea Company would suddenly move from 116 to 950 pounds in the space of eight months. Perhaps part of the explanation was political.

The South Sea Company was a creature of British politics from its inception. Its original value proposition was the ownership of trading concessions negotiated by Harley on behalf of the British people, which were then sold to a company he headed and in which the crowned heads of Spain and Britain invested. Its vast economic potential was thus due mainly to political favor. This was equally true in 1720. Investors were betting that politicians would cash in on their power to set the terms of the refinancing of government debt, because the high and mighty owned the majority of South Sea Company shares. Speculators were riding on the coattails of the well connected, whom they evidently trusted to cut a deal that would line their pockets. It was well known that the king and his family profited as the price of the company went up. The company also simply bribed some members of Parliament to get their endorsement of the South Sea conversion.

Market observers of the day warned that the numbers did not add up. MP Archibald Hutcheson circulated a sequence of studies through 1720 showing that the dividends paid by government debt bought by the company were insufficient to generate a reasonable pass-through dividend to shareholders. In other words, prices were too high to be explained by fundamentals—at least the fundamentals of the debt conversion.

Modern analysts have come to much the same conclusion. Economist Peter Garber made a study of the South Sea conversion and estimated that, when the company was trading at a price of 775 pounds per share, it was worth a total of 164 million pounds.[13] Of this, 107 million plausibly represented the value of the government debt held by the company, and 57 million was either due to irrational exuberance or to speculation about the future profitability of the firm's transatlantic enterprise. Given the great success of the funding, the company had gathered capital well in excess of that needed to buy the government debt. This "war chest" might be put to work earning high profits; either in the slave trade or in any other enterprise its parliamentary masters deemed attractive. But would it?

Was the bubble in South Sea shares caused by a sudden shift in expectations about the transatlantic trade? We know in hindsight that this trade became an immense business, although it was ultimately not the South Sea Company's main source of profit. We also know that the Royal African Company shares also bubbled in 1720, even though the company did not have a part in the debt refunding scheme. The Royal African Company made its own cash share offering in 1720, tapping into the burgeoning demand for shares despite not having the asiento.

The War of the Quadruple Alliance lasted from 1718 to February 1720 and pitted France, Britain, Austria, and the Netherlands against Spain. The main goal was to frustrate Spain's designs on Italy and the rest of the western Mediterranean, but a major secondary theater of the war was the Gulf Coast of America. French and Spanish troops squared off in Texas, Louisiana, and New Mexico, while the British hoped to capitalize on the war by control of Florida. These adventures in America made it clear that the countries involved believed the stakes were high. Had the French been able to take Texas and New Mexico from Spain, the French Mississippi Company would become the primary commercial enterprise controlling trade in the Gulf. British ownership of Florida would have likewise have been a strategic coup. While the treaty failed to deliver these hoped-for rights, the war highlighted to the investing public the economic potential of American trade. Other research has turned up lively discussions about the West Indies trade at the time— including speculation about a massive gold find in Jamaica. But was this enough to drive the prices in the South Sea Company and the Royal African Company sky high?

William Robinson Scott conjectured that the bubble may also have been driven by financial power itself. As prices swelled, it was evident to shareholders that the South Sea Company would be an immense fund of free capital. This pool of capital meant the South Sea Company could invest in any number of wide ranging, potentially money-making ventures beyond the transatlantic trade, and the rampant ingenuity of the Projecting Age offered abundant opportunity. The tragedy of the bubble in his view was not the crash in capital, but the constraints on access to capital imposed by regulators who clamped down on Exchange Alley just as it was beginning to function as a free capital market.

REGULATION TO CURB THE BUBBLE

At the height of the bubble, on June 9, 1720, Parliament passed the "Bubble Act," which, among other things, required all corporations to obtain a royal charter. It thus effectively forbade corporations from employing their capital on ventures other than for the purpose for which they were chartered—even the South Sea Company. The act chartered two marine insurance companies and forbade any future corporate competition in the insurance trade. The language of the act sounded suspiciously like the chiding tone of Defoe in his *Essay upon Projects*, and Hutcheson's constant lament about foolish speculation that prefaced each of his pamphlets knocking down the South Seas scheme. The act read like a direct attack on the stock-jobbers of Exchange Alley—a regulatory broadside at the exuberant issuance of new subscriptions. The act specifically threatened brokers from trading in unregistered stock. The promoter caught doing so would be subject "to such fines, penalties, punishments, whereunto persons convicted for common and publick nuisances are."[14] No one can say that, at the height of the first great stock market bubble, lawmakers did not try to douse the speculative flames. Unfortunately, the act may have succeeded all too well.

With the beginning of July, much of London society decamped to Bath for a summer of taking the waters and gambling at the card tables. The South Sea Company closed its transfer books for two months, although trading in shares for future delivery continued. Share prices drifted lower, dropping below 800. Larry Neal, the leading historian of the capital markets of the eighteenth century, believes that the roots of the crash lay in the details of when the company transfer books were closed, and what happened to investors when they reopened. He digitized the daily stock prices for the South Sea Company from John Castaing's price list, *Course of the Exchange*, and charted the daily path of prices. Neal noted that the bubble burst shortly after the books were reopened, and all the speculators who had traded through the summer had to pay up to their counterparties. Since prices had dropped a bit by that time, some traders backed out of their purchases, which added a new level of uncertainty to the market—a concern about counterparties and who would pay.[15]

Within a week, subscribers to the fourth cash subscription to South Sea shares had to come up with money—or lose their subscription rights. Many tried to withdraw their subscriptions in vain. Shares dropped like a rock, plummeting from 800 to 200 by October 1. Dutch and Swiss investors sold shares and took their money out of the country. Everyone who borrowed money to buy shares was in desperate trouble. Papers began to carry the sad news of speculator suicides.

Some scholars conjecture that Parliament passed the Bubble Act to protect the South Sea Company from competition for investment capital from the flurry of initial public offerings in Exchange Alley. Seen in this light, it was a move to enforce the old system of royal patents and privilege.

The confrontation between the government and the financial markets thus began with criticism that new companies were zeroing in on the business of legitimately chartered firms. It was further colored by language about the evils of stock-jobbing and the gullibility of the public with respect to new schemes. From this perspective, the democratically elected representatives were simply protecting investors and reasserting patent rights.

Another view of the Bubble Act is that it killed the capacity of the capital market to channel money to innovation. New issues dropped dramatically after the act. Companies just after its passage had to make sure they were not claiming limited liability—one of the rights of royal charter. But did it delay the Industrial Revolution, as William Robinson Scott theorized?

In the immediate aftermath of the crash, the government was mostly concerned with cleaning up the financial mess. South Sea Company directors were prosecuted for fraud. Their properties were confiscated and profits used to repay investors. But financial life went on. The stock market price lists like Castaing's kept publishing after 1720, and Larry Neal has shown that the London and Amsterdam markets continued to be integrated and active, if only in large company shares. But who knows what strange new inventions may have been forgone? Would British tinkers have dreamed up devices like mechanical looms and steam-powered locomotion if they had ready access to capital? Would an eighteenth-century chemist have invented dynamite? Perhaps one of the many diving bell schemers would have come up with the idea of a submarine, or maybe one of the economists of the day would have created a new way of insuring home equity investment. History only offers us one course—we have to imagine the alternatives.

The eighteenth century from that point on moved toward the transatlantic trade dominated by major chartered companies and by smaller entrepreneurs (some of them pirates) who operated in the gray area outside official sanctions. Economic development and the Industrial Revolution would eventually come to pass as a financial market based largely on banking, as opposed to stock issuance, evolved to support it. One can't help but wonder: Would an economy based on the free riot of corporations in the early eighteenth century—manufacturers, financial firms, mining companies, and the like—have written history differently? Was the intense triangle trade, based crucially on slavery, preordained, or did it result in part from pruning back economic competitors?

WHO WON AND WHO LOST?

Economic historians Peter Temin and Joachim Voth found a treasure trove of data about institutional speculation on South Sea shares during the bubble. It turned up right where you might expect it: in the records of one of the banks that managed money at the time.

Hoare's bank is a handsome building at 37 Fleet Street in London, about 200 yards from Temple Church, under the sign of the golden bottle, where it has been since 1690. It is a private bank that manages money for high net worth individuals. Hoare's was founded by Richard Hoare (1648–1714), who was one of the original directors of the South Sea Company. In 1720, it was headed by his son Henry Hoare, who, among other things, built the most magnificent of all English gardens, Stourhead. Hoare's opened its archives from the bubble period to Temin and Voth, who were able to trace the pattern of trades by one of the most well-connected institutions in the city at the time. Their conclusion? Hoare's bought low and sold high. Even if Henry Hoare believed the pessimistic analysis by Hutcheson and knew that the value of the stock was inflated, Hoare's rode the bubble up to the peak and then sold shares at the right times. Wealthy insiders took full advantage of the bubble.

How did that venerable bank survive the liquidity crisis that followed the crash? Many American bankers today would love to know the secret of its institutional longevity and resilience. Hoare's kept a lot of cash. Temin and Voth found Hoare's had 40% of its assets in cash in 1720; 15% in South Sea stock; some in silver, gold, diamonds, and pearls; and only a modest amount on loan. As Exchange Alley heated up before 1720, Hoare's kept more and more in cash, not less.[16]

What of Defoe? He was a great supporter of the South Sea refunding scheme in 1720. He was more sanguine than Hutcheson and responded to the MP's valuation with a calculation of his own. In a pamphlet of 1720, he declares the stock to be worth 400 pounds per share based solely on the purchase of government annuities. His view of the crash is that the collapse in share prices in September drove the stock well below its economic value. In true Defoe style, he wrote:

> And here it must be confessed with the greatest concern that unreasonable Jealousies, groundless fears, the most unaccountable Apprehensions, or rather an universal Infatuation, has so far seized on Mankind, as to run down the stock much below its Value, and beyond all expectation to the undoing of many, and the Loss of most . . . by purchasing vastly beyond what their abilities could make good . . . plunged into irretrievable ruin.[17]

Defoe correctly perceived that the true adverse effect of the bursting of South Sea bubble was a sudden contraction of credit and that the solution would require the concerted effort of government and people:

> A decay of credit must unavoidably end in a decay of substance. The farmer will find no Market to take the Produce and Effects of his labor, and consequently will be unable to pay his landlord. The Merchants will find no Demands for their Commodities, and the industrious manufacturer no Employment for his hands. As the poor will increase, the means of relieving them will lessen daily. . . . On the whole we are blessed with a wise and good prince, a faithful and able ministry and a parliament capable and disposed to concert such measures as tend to the common interest for all: let us join our endeavors

to their resolutions, to retrieve the difficulties we labour under; then will our credit soon revive, our trade flourish and we become a great, happy and powerful people to all succeeding generations.[18]

It is a message that speaks to us across time—as is particularly apt in light of the challenges to the financial system in the early twenty-first century.

A BUBBLE IN FRANCE

The most ambitious financial projector of his age—indeed of any age—was the Scotsman John Law. Like his contemporary Daniel Defoe, he spent time as a young man in Southwark prison, but not as a debtor. John Law killed a famous London dandy named Edward Wilson in a duel in Bloomsbury Square in 1694. Although Law admitted to the crime and received a stay of execution from the crown, Wilson's prominent social position and the influence of his grieving relatives made it impossible to receive a pardon. With the aid of highly placed benefactors, Law escaped Southwark and fled the country for Amsterdam, leaving his London social life behind.

Twenty-five years later, Law had become the richest person in Europe; the head of a vast corporate conglomerate that virtually privatized the entire fisc of France; and the central figure in the Mississippi Bubble, the event that sparked the international mania for stock speculation. One might say that he came to this extraordinary position by chance—although not by luck.

John Law was born into a well-to-do family and was the son of an Edinburgh goldsmith. Goldsmiths in the seventeenth century served as informal bankers, taking deposits of cash, such as silver specie, and issuing tickets to depositors called "goldsmith's notes," which circulated as paper money. Thus, Law had family roots in finance. As a young man, he was remembered for his talent in mathematics, his skill at tennis, his extraordinary good looks, and his outgoing, charming manner. Instead of entering his father's business in Edinburgh, as did his younger brother, Law indulged in the pleasures of cosmopolitan London. There he received a costly education. Law evidently spent and gambled his way through his inheritance with nothing to show for it but friends (and enemies) in high places. There is even a good chance he met Abraham de Moivre in Slaughter's Coffeehouse.

Portrait of financier John Law by Casimir Balthazar.

Following his escape from London, Law traveled among the major European cities, offering diversion and sport to high society, as well as dice and other wagering amusements. It was the ideal career for a suave, socially well-placed young man with a head for mathematics. Over the next fifteen years, he amassed a fortune from games of chance.

John Law is unquestionably the most interesting figure in the history of finance. Most historians use his early career at the gaming tables to add color to his personality or to cast him as a reckless charlatan. Even the most sympathetic writers about Law note a disconnect between the thoughtful, economic planner and daring policymaker he became, and the casino operator he was as a young man.

The exception to this perspective is Antoin Murphy, the author of an intellectual biography of John Law.[1] Murphy points out that Law was not a gambler per se, but someone who used the laws of chance to his advantage. Like the bankers who bought annuities on lives when they were undervalued by the government, Law's career as a gambler was actually built on the mastery of current mathematical knowledge about risk. When Law began his gaming operation, the key tracts on probability and games were accessible only with some difficulty. Girolamo Cardano's early work analyzing the probability of dice was likely to have been known only to serious students of mathematics. Still, the basic mathematical tools for analyzing games were in the air for those who sought them out: combinatorics and probability. According to a contemporary of Law's,

> No man understood calculation and numbers better than he; he was the first man in England that was at pains to find out why seven to four or ten; was two to one at hazard, seven to eight six to five, and so on in all the other chance of the dice which he bringing to demonstration, was received amongst the most eminent gamesters, and grew a noted man.[2]

RIDOTTO PUBBLICO

Any quest to understand John Law starts in Venice, at the Chiesa di San Moise—said by John Ruskin to be "Notable as one of the basest examples of the basest school of the Renaissance."[3] The elaborate, seventeenth-century baroque facade suggested to Ruskin a self-indulgent civilization in moral decline. San Moise is decorated with images glorifying the commercial success of its patrons.

When its facade was new in 1632, San Moise must have looked spectacular in the flickering, festive light of a Carnivale evening, when masked men in tri-corner hats, patrician robes, and powdered wigs, and ladies with haute coiffure and gowns as elaborate as San Moise's facade danced gaily in the piazza and played in the many *redotti*—Venice's special gambling parlors—until the early morning hours.

San Moise is a fitting resting place for John Law, who lies beneath a modest inscribed marble stone near the front entrance to the church. Just behind San Moise stands the Hotel Monaco, which, in Law's lifetime, was famous as the Ridotto Pubblico, a grand gambling hall for games of chance and other social entertainment. The Ridotto Pubblico overlooked the Grand Canal, with a high-ceilinged main room filled with card tables and smaller chambers for more intimate games. It is unlikely Law actually ran games in the Ridotto Pubblico, since the city permitted only licensed residents, generally paupers of noble blood, to staff the card tables and receive part of the house take. But he undoubtedly indulged, and in all likelihood ran his own high-class table in an exclusive venue somewhere nearby.

The Venice of John Law was no longer the financial center of Europe. It had long before been eclipsed by Amsterdam and London. It still had the aging financial architecture of the Rialto, with its banking system, and it was still an independent republic. However, the city had also reinvented itself as an international capital of art and entertainment. It was an essential stop on the Grand Tour, and increasingly the subject of the artist's eye. Central to Venice's allure was the Carnivale. In his memoirs, the writer Casanova captured the Carnivale's allure of sex and risk with his tales of gambling and seducing his way through the redotti and cassini of the city. It is the same mystique of naughtiness and possibility that draws people today to Las Vegas. Venice, like Las Vegas, encourages people to shed their inhibitions and indulge in fantasy. For Law to profit as a gamester and casino banker, he had to be a master of the imagination as well as a calculating mathematician, and Venice was a brilliant teacher.

An important innovation in gambling that emerged in seventeenth-century Venice was a game played against the house, or against one player who acted as the bank.[4] Instead of a card game in which all players are equal, house games put one player in control and effectively charged the others for this service. The most familiar modern example is Blackjack. In the eighteenth century, however, Bassette was the quintessential house game.[5] One player would set up as the bank with a large stake. Others would play against the bank at a slight statistical disadvantage. Despite a probabilistic advantage, however, Bassette could break the bank. Thus, it paid the banker to understand the odds.

John Law was evidently a master of Venetian-style bank games. He transplanted the magic of Venice's redotti to the various European cities to which he traveled—especially Paris, which seemed particularly enthralled by games of chance. Law ran his operation for the richest of the rich, and the high-stake games brought him high profits. He also seemed to embody the ideal to which other gamesters aspired: handsome, glib, lucky, and amorously successful. He scandalized European society by taking a beautiful, wealthy married woman as his mistress and then common-law wife—a feat even Casanova did not manage. Law was rumored to have made a fortune in the lottery; enough to buy a vast estate outside of Genoa. By the age of thirty, the Scotsman had made back his lost inheritance many times over. Had he then simply retired—or even continued his life as a successful gambler—history might remember him as one of Europe's great bonvivants and perhaps as an outstanding example of an applied mathematician. However, John Law had pretensions to much, much more.

DEAD TREASURE

Sometime in the early 1990s, Antoin Murphy found himself looking at a manuscript of a hitherto unknown economic treatise titled *Essay on a Land Bank*. Although its provenance was unknown, it came up in the antiquarian book trade and was shown to Murphy due to his reputation as a top economic historian. He identified it as Law's earliest known work as an economist. It was an extraordinary document that showed the first step in Law's intellectual evolution.

In the essay, Law proposed the creation of a bank in England backed by land rather than specie. The reason? Silver fluctuated in value due to variation in supply. The supply of land was fixed, and this made it a better form of money. Land banks had been proposed before, and indeed, Parliament had authorized the incorporation of a National Land Bank in 1696, whereby money would be raised from shareholders to extend mortgages to landowners. The bank would then issue banknotes—competing with the Bank of England to supply paper money to the English economy. The argument put forward by the Tory backers of the project was, in part, that access to mortgages at cheap rates would be a general stimulus to the economy, since money and credit were its lifeblood.[6]

The logic sounds compelling. The wealth locked up in property could be brought to life by borrowing against it. As the pamphleteer Davenant put it at the time: "the twenty Million trusted upon Land Security is now noe better than a Dead Treasure, which formerly was a quick Stock in continuall Motion and transferrable from hand to hand."[7] Davenant waxes wonderfully on credit and how it depends on the elusive quality of trust:

> Of all beings that have existence only in ye minds of men, nothing is more Fantasticall, and Nice than Credit. Tis never to be forced; it hangs upon opinion. It depends upon our passions of hope and fear. It comes many times unsought for, and often goes away without reason, and when once lost, is hardly to be recovered.[8]

The National Land Bank failed to attract sufficient subscribers. Moneyed Whigs saw it as an attack on the primary position of the Bank of England, which they controlled. Plus, the terms of the subscription rights were evidently not economically attractive. The financial project to redefine wealth in terms of property did not fly.

Despite this earlier failed attempt at a land bank by others, John Law took the concept a bold step further. Rather than write mortgages, why not have a bank that actually held land? Land could be contributed by subscribers as capital to the bank in standardized units of value. Notes would then be issued by the bank and would be redeemable in these standardized units. The notes would be a rival paper money—in his view a better and more stable money: "Land pledged is a more certain value than silver pledged and the lands being pledged to the full value of the notes given out, these land notes will be preferred to Bank notes or goldsmith's notes."[9]

Law envisioned paper money as a security backed by real estate held by a bank as a financial intermediary. The fixed supply of land and the transparency of the assets would reduce uncertainty about the institution and its notes—instilling confidence in the use of paper as currency. The currency was convertible back into land. When land was dear, the notes would thus circulate at a high value relative to other goods. In economic terms, land would become the "numeraire" good, and silver, which played no important role in the economy other than as a unit of account, would wane in significance. In effect, if grocers would accept paper bills from John Law's land bank, they would be quoting the price of carrots and celery in standardized units of property—almost an algebraic sleight of hand that would eliminate the dependency of the economy on a precious metal to which Spain largely controlled access through its mines in the New World. Alas, English power brokers were evidently not enthusiastic about Law's plan, and it also went nowhere.

The following year, John Law floated a larger and more elaborately argued scheme to the Scottish Parliament, hoping for a different outcome. This plan was accompanied by a public essay, *Money and Trade*, which was printed and distributed by a firm owned by his aunt. Antoin Murphy argues that *Money and Trade* qualifies John Law as one of the most important political economists of his age due to its sophisticated analysis of the crucial role of money and credit play in the economy. In Law's view, trade depended on credit, the availability of which depended on the quantity of money in the economy. Mandating low interest rates would only drive lenders out of the markets. Instead, the interest rate could be efficiently modulated by the money supply:

> Some think if Interest were lower'd by Law, Trade would increase, Merchants being able to Employ more Money and Trade Cheaper. Such a Law would have many Inconveniencies, and it is much to be doubted, whether it would have any good Effect [However] if lowness of Interest were the Consequence of a greater Quantity of Money, the Stock applyed to Trade would be greater, and Merchants would Trade Cheaper, from the easiness of borrowing and the lower interest of Money, without any Inconveniencies attending it.[10]

The main instrument by which the money supply could be regulated is through a banking system that could extend credit through fractional reserves to meet the demand for money due to trade:

> Banks where the money is pledg'd equal to the credit given, are sure ... [but] so far as they lend they add to the money which brings a Profit to the Country by employing more People and extending Trade. ... But the Bank is less sure.[11]

Thus, John Law's big insight in *Money and Trade* was a quantity theory of money based on aggregate demand and the notion that the optimal quantity of money is directly related to the productive capacity of the economy.[12] Too little money would constrain the economy, and too much would lead to inflation or bank failure. Better to use monetary instruments like banknotes to get the economy operating at optimal capacity, rather than to rely on the haphazard availability of a metallic numeraire or heavy-handed restraint on interest rates.

This is the essential principle underlying the decisions by the US Federal Reserve Bank today, using news about inflation and the changes in GDP and unemployment as the essential inputs into the decision about how to set discount rates and hence how much money to release into the economy. Of course, Law's quantity theory of money also has echoes back to the *Guanzi*—the knives and spades being the ditches through which the lifeblood of the economy runs (see Chapter 8). Despite Law's erudite treatise, Scotland likewise passed on the creation of a land bank. With the joining of Scotland and England in 1706, Law was forced once again to flee to the continent and continue his new career as economist and bank projector.

JOHN LAW, BANKER

John Law finally got his chance at a bank in 1716. Like Britain, France was economically exhausted from the ruinous War of the Spanish Succession. Law managed to convince the Regent Philippe, Duc d'Orleans, of the benefits of using a bank as an instrument of monetary policy. Law opened the bank in his home in the Place Vendôme. Like the Bank of England and the South Sea Company, the Banque Générale was capitalized by state loans, as well as with Law's own fortune. To get it off the ground and to inspire public confidence, it received deposits from the Regent and a number of highly placed members of the nobility. It issued banknotes against these deposits and performed other banking services as envisioned by Law's plan. It made commercial loans by discounting merchant's bills, and it wrote bills of exchange that facilitated international commerce. The Banque Générale began to prove itself after a year of operation in the reduction of interest rates paid by merchants. It also began to function as a state bank, receiving tax revenues for the government by payment in banknotes.[13] It became the Banque Royale in 1718, and its banknotes became government issue. The bank moved out of his home to an official location. John Law became the finance minister of France.

In the meantime, Law created another company, patterned on the South Sea model but imagined in much grander terms. In 1717, the Companie d'Occident (commonly called the "Mississippi Company") offered a public subscription for shares through the conversion of state debts. This is the same equity for debt swap that launched the South Sea Company, and it served the same purpose: to reduce government debt service and to exploit the future riches of the Americas. It also had the same appeal to investors. They currently possessed discounted and illiquid government loans and quickly saw the advantage of exchanging them for uniform shares in a company that not only received debt payments directly from the crown but also had the promise of a big future payoff in the New World. The company held the rights to the entire Louisiana Territory.[14]

The Louisiana Territory had not yet been mapped in 1720. That was left to Lewis and Clark in 1803, following its acquisition by the young United States. However, few questioned its long-term economic potential. The tiny settlement of New Orleans was situated at the mouth of one of the world's largest continuously navigable rivers that linked the northern fur trade of French Canada to a southern port. Although the plantation system had not yet been actively implemented in Louisiana, the rich alluvial soil held promise for intensive agricultural exploitation. For shareholders valuing future cash flow, the 800 million square miles of North America must have seemed like a pretty good long-term gamble.

Law's vision quickly surpassed the model of the South Sea Company. He saw the potential to absorb all overseas trading rights of France into one firm through mergers and acquisition. The success of his conversion of the debt in 1717 was followed by share offerings with attached rights issues in 1719, giving him a vast capital base. His firm quickly absorbed the Senegal Company, the Indies Company, and the China Company— French equivalents of the Royal African and the East India Companies. In so doing, Law had a virtual monopoly on all long-distance French commerce. He also acquired the tobacco monopoly, the royal mint, and the General Farms—France's tax collection agency. This new, giant conglomerate then tendered for the entirety of the French national debt at favorable terms to the state. It swallowed the entire French debt following the War of the Spanish Succession, bringing down the interest rate to manageable scale by inspiring investors with the long-term promise of an equity return.

Within a few amazing years, John Law had achieved a remarkable feat. Using the new financial engineering of Exchange Alley and his own economic analysis of the role of money in the economy, he had effectively privatized the financial operations of France and put them into the hands of the public through the issuance of public shares of stock. He had replaced a depleted currency based on scarce silver specie with fiat money that could respond to market demand. He had created a corporate governance structure that had the potential to respond strategically to France's competitors in the rush to globalization. He had also created a world that depended fundamentally on the financial market.

MERES ET FILLES

Law's share issues were cleverly designed. The shares issued in June 1719 were offered on an installment plan of 10% paid in capital per month, thus attracting investors of lower means and broadening the capital market clientele.[15] The Banque Royale loaned money against company shares, thus serving as what today would be called a "repo" facility, which ensured liquidity to investors. Law posted prices the firm would pay for its shares on the door of the bank. In addition, to further inspire confidence in the issuance of shares in the company, Law offered to buy in shares with his personal fortune—putting his money where his mouth was.[16]

Finally, Law came up with a clever structure for issuing shares with associated rights offerings. Subscribers to the first issue received a right to purchase shares on a 4:1 ratio in the next subscription at preferential terms, and the rights could be exercised with a modest payment. Shares issued in the first subscription came to be known as the *mères* and those of the second subscription the *filles* because of this offering. There was yet a third offering in 1719 for shares called *grand-filles*. These series of issues and the extraordinary measures Law took to support their price attracted enormous interest. Not only did he expand the investor clientele domestically, but he also attracted international speculation. Dutch newspapers carried daily stories of the events in Paris and the quoted prices. Law created a system that quickly drew capital into France from abroad.[17] The joint events of the South Sea Company flotation and the Mississippi Company flotation had, within the course of a few months, transformed vast sums of illiquid government debt into equity shares, simultaneously lowering the cost to the government, broadening the base of investor demands for shares, and virtually inventing a new currency based on claims on companies rather than on promises of specie. Both firms did this by appealing to the public willingness to gamble on the future prospects for New World riches, and expectations that the companies, favored by the rich and powerful, would be fostered and promoted by Parliament and the crown.

Much of the trading in France took place in Rue Quinquepoix, a narrow street behind the modern Center Pompidou on the right bank. The contemporary accounts of the Parisian mania for share speculation read much like the descriptions of Exchange Alley. Law managed to create a buzz—an infectious enthusiasm for speculation that fed into a growing demand for Mississippi Company shares. And of course, the rising share prices created some instant millionaires (a term perhaps coined in the Mississippi Bubble), feeding a casino atmosphere. Prices rose from 400 livres in August 1719 to 1,000 in September, faltered a bit until the end of the year, and then spiked dramatically to 1,800 by December 1719. With this last, dramatic rise in prices, the owners of rights from the *mères* made huge profits. Derivative instruments were traded on the shares, such as call options and contracts for future delivery. The

Mississippi Bubble had jump started a sophisticated financial market in Paris virtually overnight.

In February 1720, Law merged the Company and the Bank into one great firm. Antoin Murphy argues that Law had this grand design in mind from the start—that he saw the potential of pooling the biggest French trading companies into a single firm under one master—a sort of Genoese model on a grand scale. Murphy also theorizes that Law envisioned a further, radical extension of that system, which would replace all specie and even banknotes with shares in the company. Indeed in March 1720, Law fixed an "exchange rate" between shares and banknotes at 9,000 livres, essentially turning the shares into money.[18]

Although Law "privatized" France and put the control of the fisc in the hands of shareholders, his plan was a far cry from a laissez-faire capitalist vision. Law instead planned a monolithic company under his personal control. It was not necessarily a sinister vision—after all, his theories had shown that central control of monetary policy could be of great benefit to the economy. It might not have even been a totalitarian one. The plan, if fully realized, would have been an alternative form of democracy—a shareholder democracy—in which investors participated in the future economic gains to government grants and rights—as well as in the exploration and exploitation of French-controlled territories around the world held by the company. It would have been a one share–one vote model, as opposed to a one person–one vote model.

What was missing from the Mississippi Bubble, in contrast to the South Sea Bubble, was the wellspring of innovation. France had its projectors, with plans for public works and trading companies, but there seems to be no evidence that any other shares were seriously traded in the Rue Quinquepoix. Law apparently had no successful competitors for the public appetite for share investing. The creation of a share market appears to have been a means to an end—a method for building the Mississippi Company out of investor cash, rather than an institution used to channel resources to innovation.

MAKING MONEY

While the company was issuing shares through 1719, the Banque Royale was printing money. In a series of proclamations, the government worked to replace specie money with banknotes. Beginning in January 1720, it issued a series of proclamations to prevent the cross-border transport of specie and enacted draconian prohibitions against the production and display of objects of precious stones and metals.[19] The government next sought to prevent the hoarding of specie. These moves were part of Law's long-sought goal of weaning the economy away from reliance on gold and silver. His logic, from today's vantage point, was correct. Fiat money gave the government greater control over the money supply, which in turn allowed active monetary policy. Asking an entire nation to trust enough to give up its savings—money that is perfectly good just across the border—was asking too much. The real danger in a fiat money economy is the printing press. The public must have faith that the government will limit the supply of banknotes. Antoin Murphy points out that this was the fatal flaw in Law's system. His guaranteed conversion price in early 1720 between shares and cash meant that he had to print money for redeeming those shares. As a result, the fall in demand for shares—or even an adverse difference between the Rue Quinquepoix price and the bank price—triggered conversion and thus inflation. Paradoxically, the guaranteed share price took control of the money supply out of the hands of the policymakers.[20]

The fall came in late May 1720, following a proclamation that the guaranteed price for the shares of the company would be reduced according to a schedule that would take them from 8,000 livres to 5,000 livres by the end of 1720, as well as other measures to support the currency. The proclamation was recognition that the cost of supporting the share price, in terms of inflation, was too dear. It was not well received by the public.

DECORATIVE FINANCIAL ARCHITECTURE

John Law and Giovanni Antonio Pellegrini were kindred spirits. Pellegrini was a cosmopolitan artist, a Venetian-born muralist who worked in the Netherlands, Germany, and Great Britain. He would be classified today as a Baroque or even a Rococo decorative painter. He was particularly skilled at trompe l'oeil ceilings: skies filled with flowing allegorical figures that were painted with sharply forced perspective to create the illusion of great heights. Law might have seen his work in the Duke of

Portland's St. Albans House had he chanced to return surreptitiously to London in the early eighteenth century. He might also have known it from the Golden room in Mauritzhuis in the Hague. More than likely, however, Law has seen Pellegrini's oculus at the Scuola Grande de San Rocco in Venice, a dizzying, swirling fantasy featuring Charity carrying the torch of faith.

Like all allegorical paintings, Pellegrini's were meant to be decoded. Abstract concepts are given human form and are then brought together into an imagined interaction, in which spatial relationships carry the essential grammar of the visual language. Needless to say, the style was not John Ruskin's favorite. What Ruskin saw as a manifestation of weakening morals can also be interpreted as art seeking to comprehend an increasingly complex world, in which secular themes were competing with religious ones for public contemplation.

Law charged Pellegrini with the complex task of visually depicting the essence of his scheme. Working in 1719 and 1720, even as the grand hall of the Banque was alive every day with the breathless events transforming the French economy, Pellegrini painted a canvas of such vast scale—42 meters by 9 meters, that it must have challenged comprehension. Art historian and economist Darius Spieth has written about the giant ceiling mural and has translated a description of the central figures in the ceiling. It is worth quoting at length—it is Law's own higher vision, filtered through the eye and hand of an artist who sought to understand and then capture the idealism of his patron:

> A portrait of the king, sustained on the one side by Religion, and by a hero representing Mgr. the Regent on the other. . . . Above Religion a winged armed Genius takes Commerce by the hand, followed by Wealth, Security, and Credit. At the feet of the Genius, a child holds a bow, symbol for Invention; towards the right, slightly below the Genius, one can see Arithmetic holding in her hands a paper with calculations. She is accompanied by Industry, characterized by body armor and the sword she holds in her hand. . . . Above all of these figures, at the highest point in the ceiling, Jupiter is seated in the clouds; Juno is a little bit off to the side. They send out Abundance to distribute her riches. To the left of Wealth is the River Seine embracing the Mississippi River. . . . Winged Happiness floats above these

rivers in the clouds, holding in her hands a flame of fire. Tranquility is next to her, holding, in a completely relaxed pose, a sheaf of wheat. On the banks of the Seine, one discovers a wagon with a team of two horses, on which workers load the merchandise discharged from the vessels arriving from Louisiana; there are also other types of vessels carrying Mississippi princes. . . . Above the entryway, the Bourse is represented as a portico, grouped around which one sees the representatives of diverse nations distinguishable by their dress, as they engage together in trade.[21]

The mural introduced new gods and goddesses: Commerce, Wealth, Security, Credit, Invention, Industry, Arithmetic, and Abundance. It personified the Mississippi as grand provender of the riches of America, although evidently as a result of its embracement by the Seine. It sought to place these new concepts and new geographies in the context of the classical, religious, and political orders, but like Pellegrini's other works, these relationships must have been fluid, energetic, and dramatic.

How could the logic of John Law's *Money and Trade* translate into scenery, deities, and drapery? How could economic arguments built one atop the other ever make sense as a huge, decorative cartoon? Yet, the appeal of art—the appeal of the allegory—is that it is a different logical system, a system of archetypes: good and evil, heroism and betrayal, beauty and ugliness. The valence of the figures in Pellegrini's masterwork left little doubt about which archetypes Law wanted to conjure up for Banque Royale patrons. They represented almost too much goodness to be true.

And who, after all, was the winged and armed Genius in the painting, with Invention and Arithmetic at his feet? Did Law have the ultimate hubris to include himself in the pantheon of the new gods of the market?

Imagine John Law and his ministers under this immense ceiling on May 22, 1720, after having instituted the proclamation that decreased the price of shares, in effect publicly admitting that the system would not hold. They were hoping for what we in the 1990s called a "soft landing." They kept the doors to the bank closed all morning, as shareholders rushed to redeem. They finally opened the doors and let the crowds in, buying as many shares and old notes as they could with the banknotes on hand. It was not enough, however. Over the next few days, riots broke out in the Rue Vivienne. Stones started to rain on the doors and through the windows of the bank, strewing broken glass over the floor. Although the proclamation would be recalled, Law's fate was sealed. Shares plunged, and his dream of a system built on fiat money and a privatized fisc was finished. France went back to its earlier financial architecture based on rentes and life annuities, and rapidly sought to expunge any memory of the John Law episode. The offices of the Banque Royal were gutted in 1724, the mural unceremoniously destroyed.

ACCORDING TO HOYLE

On July 13, 1720, the town council of Rotterdam met to consider a business proposal put to them by Edmond Hoyle and Gerard Roeters, two projectors from the city of London. Mr. Hoyle was an Englishman with no Dutch, perhaps more of a mathematician than a salesman. Mr. Roeters, however, came from a well-known Amsterdam merchant family with ties to the royal family. He did all the talking. Rotterdam was in danger of slipping further behind its competitors, he argued. Right now, the city was a vigorous commercial center and had much to be proud of. It held one of the six seats in the VOC and thus shared in the lucrative Asian trade, although it had less of a share than its big sister, Amsterdam. In contrast, its stock exchange, founded in 1595, was older than Amsterdam's. Rotterdam boasted a number of successful bankers, a lively shipping trade, and a full range of financial services, including insurance.

Nevertheless, Roeters argued, financial innovations taking place at this very moment in London threatened the competitive viability of Rotterdam. One innovation in particular loomed large. London financiers had just launched two insurance companies using vast pools of public capital floated by share subscriptions in the coffeehouses of the city. The Royal Exchange Assurance and the London Assurance Companies, using a combination of political influence and outright bribery, the previous month had convinced the king to grant them exclusive corporate rights to all maritime insurance in Britain. The companies had already been writing insurance policies on voyages and drawing away Dutch business. As a result, Roeters claimed, the old models of shipping insurance were doomed.

Up until then, maritime insurance in Holland was handled on an exchange, where buyers and sellers of policies could meet and come to terms. Prices of risks were quoted in standardized terms. Risks at sea

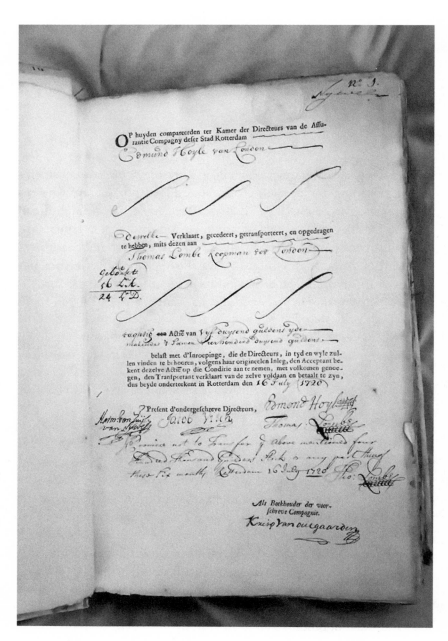

Transfer book for the Stad Rotterdam company, showing Edmond Hoyle's sale of his stake in the new firm. His shares went to Thomas Lombe, one of the first entrepreneurs in the Industrial Revolution.

were bought and sold like other commodities. If a claim was disputed, a local insurance council, the Kamer van Assurantie, made up of the leading underwriters, would hear arguments, weigh evidence, and rule fairly. Insurance underwriters of the day risked their personal capital for a modest premium—1–2% of the value of the cargo and ship to nearby ports, and up to 8% for risky gambles such as transatlantic expeditions. For this, they were on the hook to cover the losses. Insurance thus required deep pockets and mutual trust. The insurer had to trust that the captain did not intend to wreck his boat to get the claim, and the policyholder had to trust that the insurer had the wealth to make good on a claim if necessary. This last condition meant that only verifiably wealthy insurers would attract customers—and even then their capacity for underwriting was limited by their personal capital. Although occasionally groups of investors might partner in insuring a large expedition, risk sharing under current practice was limited. It was a system as old as Demosthenes.

Insurance is a business of understanding and diversifying away risk. Few were as canny as the Dutch and English underwriters at calculating risks at sea—or the risk of a dishonest captain contemplating insurance fraud. However, scale trumps calculation. If you make an insurance company big enough and underwrite projects that are uncorrelated enough, any single claim is small relative to the size of the firm. This simple maxim was a direct implication of the newly discovered law of large numbers (see Chapter 15).

The two English companies threatened to overwhelm the traditional insurance market by raising a capital base that could insure hundreds of voyages at a time. In effect, their capital base was unlimited, since they could issue shares to as many individual investors as they wanted as the business scaled up. Dutch dominance, Roeters claimed, could rapidly come to an end unless the civic leaders in Rotterdam were prepared to act now.

Hoyle and Roeters proposed a Rotterdam company that would compete with the English insurance behemoths, as well as with local rivals—the Amsterdam insurance brokers and underwriters. The good news for Rotterdam investors was that the British king had just signed into law the Bubble Act. Hence other British insurance corporations could not be formed or enjoy limited liability and access to public share subscriptions.

To this day, this explains why Lloyds of London operated for most of its history with investor capital exposed to unlimited liability. But British law did not extend to the Netherlands, and a new company in Holland could thus effectively enjoy the protection of the Bubble Act in limiting further British competition.

Under the Rotterdam proposal, the capital would come from the pockets of the city's leading citizens—perhaps members of the council—who subscribed in the firm. Subscribers did not have to pay the full price of a share—they had to put 10% down and would pay the rest in time installments. These subscribers in turn could sell their rights on the stock exchange—potentially at great profit.

Rotterdam citizens already knew how this offering worked. The newspapers in Holland carried regular news of the great fortunes made in speculation in British joint-stock offerings in 1720. The papers had even begun quoting prices of Royal Exchange Assurance and London Assurance—a sure sign that Dutch capital was already interested in funding these innovative new companies. Hoyle and Roeters were there today to present the good city of Rotterdam an opportunity to stem the exodus of Dutch investment capital; to take a leadership role in the new financial order; to compete with Amsterdam insurance brokers by pooling local capital; and finally, to make a tidy speculative profit.

The city council deliberations were not recorded; however, there was likely some disagreement. The same kind of project had been put to Amsterdam just a month before and was rejected. Evidently, one reason for the rejection was that it threatened the existing insurance trade with a powerful monopoly that could set prices. It did not help that the proposed directors knew little about the insurance trade and thus would do a poor job at management oversight—and finally that the scheme put the crucial maritime insurance industry in Amsterdam at the mercy of the "Wind Negotie," the speculative trading in shares that would cause the value of the firm to fluctuate with the fads and fashions of the market.

In the end, however, Hoyle and Roeters' proposal won the day. What Amsterdam had soberly rejected the month before Rotterdam now embraced. The projectors had their company with 388 subscribers. The subscriptions traded on the exchange, fortunes were made, and the new company opened its books and started writing insurance policies. Hoyle quietly cashed out within a fortnight. His profits evidently allowed him to pursue his true passion. He spent the rest of his life mastering the mathematics of card games. Some years later, he began to write books on how to win at the card tables using probability calculus, perhaps giving away the secrets that helped him best his opponents over the years. Anyone who has ever used the phrase "according to Hoyle" pays him homage. Before he became the arbiter of the rules of parlor games, Hoyle was a schemer, a projector, a probabilist—a man of his age—a financier.

What happened to the investors? Many of them, like Hoyle, sold at a profit as shares in the company were quickly bid up on the Rotterdam and the Amsterdam exchanges in August to more than 90% over the subscription price. A few speculators nearly doubled their money in a month. The company quickly made a second issue of shares to take advantage of investor enthusiasm. Other cities in the Netherlands immediately followed Rotterdam's lead, launching similar insurance and trading companies: Gouda, Delft, the Hague, Utrecht, Schiedam, Naarden, Weesp, Muyden, Medelblik, Enkhuysen, Edam, Hoorn, Munnickendam, Purmerent, Alkmaar, Zwol, Middleburgh, Ter Veer, Dortrecht, Vlardingen, Briele, and Maasland all issued shares that traded on one or more of the exchanges in Rotterdam, Amsterdam, or Delft.

Hoyle and Roeters had unleashed a frenzy of initial public offerings and speculation in "New Age" companies throughout Holland, but the frenzy was short lived. By late November, the shares of the Rotterdam company had dropped to a modest 17% premium, and shares in most of the other companies went even lower. Speculators who bought at the top saw their shares cut to a quarter of the value—a 75% decrease in three months. Was this because the projects were foolish ventures? Certainly time has shown that the concept of a publicly traded insurance company was robust. There were other *windhandel* companies that survived and prospered. The Middleburg Company became a major force in transatlantic trade later in the eighteenth century—sharing some of the Dutch culpability for slave trading in the era of the triangle trade (see Chapter 18), as well as some of the credit for financially innovative securitizations that evolved in the Netherlands to lay off the risk of the New World plantation system.

A DISCOVERY IN THE HAGUE

The standard story of investor irrationality does not quite seem to explain the events of 1720. For example, the survival and prosperity of the Rotterdam company suggests it was not such a crazy scheme. In fact, it immediately began to write policies with the capital it raised and turned a regular profit of about 5% per year through 1780, with only three losing years out of sixty. The company also used its large capital base to discount bills of exchange and to make mercantile loans using commodities as capital. It broadened its underwriting lines to include fire and life insurance. The Maatschappij Assurantie, Discontering en Beleening der Stad Rotterdam outlasted its two British rivals founded in the same year, and over the centuries competed successfully with Lloyds, the British insurer. While Amsterdam stuck to its old ways of matching private underwriters with policyholders, "Stad Rotterdam," as it is called in modern times, became a dominant institution in insurance underwriting in continental Europe and grew to become one of the great financial institutions in the world.

If an investor in 1720 had even a glimpse of this long, successful future, then taking up Hoyle and Roeters' proposal was not irrationally exuberant but eminently sensible. Maybe Rotterdam was an exception that proved the rule, but maybe not. What happened to the other insurance companies in that year: the London Assurance, Royal Exchange Assurance, and all the new Dutch firms? Oddly enough, despite at least one hundred years of scholarly hunting, no records of the first Dutch stock market bubble had yet come to light. If the Dutch market got excited about the seemingly staid insurance trade, maybe the key to understanding the bubble of 1720 in Great Britain was connected to the insurance trade as well. The first step in following this thread was to find the data.

Rik Frehen is a finance professor at the University of Tilburg and, as it turns out, a skilled reader of old Dutch. He and I and Geert Rouwenhorst became interested in the causes of the 1720 bubble. To explore the role of the Dutch insurance trade in the global financial bubble of 1720, Rik systematically explored every archive in every major city in the Netherlands, looking at each run of eighteenth-century newspapers and gathering all available record books of all Dutch companies formed in 1720. He found what he was looking for in the Hague: a run of the *Leydse Courant* beginning in 1719. Printed on a sturdy two-sided broadsheet three times a week, the *Leydse Courant* reported the financial and political news of the world—including stock prices.

Perhaps the most exciting discovery of all from the *Leydse Courant* was a series of prices for the VOC and WIC. Although it was long known that these firms were traded actively in 1720, no one knew whether they had bubbled up like the French and British shares. The *Leydse Courant* provided empirical evidence of the third leg of the 1720 bubble. Working with his father, a skilled photographer, Rik carefully documented each page of the newspaper and began to analyze the data.

Meanwhile, it seemed odd that the Dutch papers would have prices for British companies like Royal Exchange, London Assurance, Royal African, and York Buildings but these were not to be found in the existing South Sea Company research sources. That problem was also soon solved. With the help of Larry Neal, who had scans of British stock pricelists, we were able to fill out the records for the remaining British firms. We now could tell whether there was a bubble in insurance companies in London—and if so, when and how it happened.

THE TRANSATLANTIC THEORY

These new price series first allowed the three of us to test the hypothesis about transatlantic trade as a major driver of the bubble. If the transatlantic trade was the target of speculation, then we should expect that both the Royal African Company and the WIC stocks would also go up with those of the Mississippi Company and the South Sea Company. The share prices told a striking story. Both the Royal African Company and the Dutch West India Company bubbled as high in 1720 as the South Seas Company—up by 700%. In contrast, the VOC and the British East India Company grew by comparatively modest proportions over the same period. From another source we were able to confirm that other companies in London related to the transatlantic trade also bubbled.[1]

Yes, there was a general stock market bubble in 1720, but the transatlantic trade companies were among the biggest gainers, while the Asian trade companies and the staid Bank of England were among the smallest gainers. Our conclusion: Defoe's vision of challenging Spanish hegemony in the transatlantic trade must have been an important motivating force in the South Sea Bubble, but evidently not the only one.

WHY INSURANCE?

But what about the insurance companies? Our charts for the Royal Exchange and London Assurance showed huge bubbles—far greater than for the South Sea Company. Even though the Rotterdam company issued shares late in the year, it, too, shot up before the crash kicked in. Maybe these dynamics reflected shifts in the specific prospects about insurance firms.

Publicly traded insurance companies were not novel ideas in 1720. From 1716 on, London entrepreneurs had been trying to get government permission to start a company that pooled public capital. In 1718, a solicitor named Case Billingsley nearly succeeded with a petition for a royal charter for an insurance company with a million pounds of capital. The arguments sounded much like those advanced by Hoyle and Roeters—with the addition of another angle that only a solicitor might think advantageous: a single insuring entity could be taken to court with less trouble, whereas a consortium of lenders would be difficult and costly to track down, ergo the former exhibits legal efficiency.[2] The attorney general and solicitor general turned down the petition after much deliberation and perhaps bribes paid by existing underwriters. Billingsley and company had also bought out the dormant Mines Royal company, thinking that they could perhaps stretch this unrelated charter to cover their new trade. The attorney general said no.

Many of those involved in the Billingsley proposal were also behind the Royal Exchange Assurance Company, which appeared a year later with a powerful political backer: Lord Onslow, member of the House of Lords and former speaker of the House of Commons. The new company sold subscriptions in 1719 and was referred to in the early price lists as Onslow's Insurance. It later became Royal Exchange Assurance. The precursors to the Royal Exchange Company and the London Assurance Company (called variously "Ram and Colebrook" or the "New Insurance Company") presented a new petition late 1719—now with stronger political advocates. Another committee on insurance was formed in

January, a parliamentary committee was formed in March, and hopes were raised for some possibility of success.

Our data showed that stock prices for both firms had doubled by March 1, undoubtedly on the renewed hope of the petition's success. However, a preliminary negative report by the attorney general drove prices lower. In mid-May, prices jumped by a factor of five. Word had evidently spread of a deal with the king to support the petition.

The final, signed Bubble Act went far beyond the original aspiration of Billingsley and company. It gave the two firms a complete monopoly on marine insurance and outlawed any other companies to compete with them. The only loophole was for individual underwriters, who could still conduct business as usual. They just could not form tradable companies with pooled capital. The Bubble Act thus culminated a long struggle against an entrenched insurance trade. The hard-fought (and sometimes underhanded) battle to create a public company to write insurance had finally been won. The stakes were potentially enormous. It was not unreasonable to expect the two firms to capture all shipping insurance business for Great Britain and perhaps for a substantial amount of Dutch shipping as well.

Consider how investor expectations shifted over one miraculous year. The probability of a chartered firm getting a monopoly on all maritime insurance in Britain went from near zero in late 1719 to very slight in March 1720, to a certainty in June 1720. Any sudden burst of exuberance about public insurance stocks in the second quarter of 1720 was understandable and entirely justifiable. Investors had every reason to expect that the two firms together would, in effect, become the sole national insurers for all overseas British trade, including of course, the trade in the Atlantic.

There was an Achilles' heel, however. To secure the king's favor, the companies had to promise to pay the monarch 600,000 pounds in installments one, three, five, and ten months after the granting of the charter. The first installments by both companies were easily raised from the proceeds of the sale of subscriptions, and they both anticipated further sales in the summer. In fact, another share offering was planned for early September, just before another major payment to the king was due. In addition, to keep pace with the required future payments, they both also planned to rapidly expand their lines into fire and life insurance, hoping to capture substantially all British insurance business. This meant taking the risk of over stepping the bounds of their charters.

REGULATION OF COMPANIES

Notwithstanding the Bubble Act passed in June, many companies, chartered and unchartered, had plunged right ahead into a great variety of businesses in 1720. Among these, the York Building Society was the most brazen. It was chartered in 1665 to supply waterworks to London; like the first Billingsley insurance company, the hope was that this would provide a reasonable cover under which it might pursue other profitable opportunities. These now included the purchase of confiscated estates in Scotland and a plan to sell life annuities. In other words, they planned to follow whatever profitable opportunities might arise under the guise of a limited liability corporation.

On August 18, the attorney general announced his intention to enforce the Bubble Act constraints on companies and named the York Building Society as a major transgressor.[3] Also directly named, the insurance companies were at risk of prosecution for overstepping their charters by selling fire insurance. They pled their case to Parliament but received no immediate relief to raise further capital.[4]

On August 19, London Assurance experienced another shock. The *Leydse Courant* noted the news in London on that date: twelve British ships from Jamaica were lost.[5] The paper reported that the company had insured them for a total of 72,000 pounds. The next payment to the crown was due on September 22 for 50,000 pounds. To top it off, the home of one of the company directors was burglarized and considerable property was lost.

On August 18, York Buildings, Royal Exchange, London Assurance, and the Royal African Company all began a rapid decline. Three days later—the travel time between London and Amsterdam—the WIC shares began a near free-fall. The fact that the enforcement of the Bubble Act triggered the crash in London strongly suggests that some of the preceding rise in prices was due to expectations about the potential to deploy corporate capital freely into other profitable opportunities—whether they be as closely related as fire insurance and marine insurance, or as unrelated as real estate and life annuities. Companies had begun to spread their wings and compete against one another for business, using their war chests of capital raised from recent share issues. The attorney general clipped their wings.

The year 1720 was thus more than a turbulent year of investor exuberance. It was a moment in history that defined the corporate enterprise. On one hand, it witnessed the creation of a national behemoth that swallowed the national debt. Yet on the other hand, with the creation of the insurance companies, risk sharing was revolutionized through financial innovation. A series of regulatory actions in 1720 responded to aggressive company actions by the insurance firms and other even more creative enterprises. These firms at first emboldened investors with the hope that corporations would have broad freedoms. These freedoms, in turn, could have expanded growth opportunities laterally across industries as opposed to vertically in a single subindustry. When the rulings favorable to the new insurance companies were promulgated, in late spring of 1720, it encouraged speculation that other companies might also be extended new liberties. With the writ of August 18, these hopes were dashed.

The insurance firms, not the South Sea Company, turned out to be the true bellwethers of the shifting political winds with respect to the power of the corporation in 1720, as they fell in and out of favor. Their price drop after August 18 triggered a widespread financial collapse.

It is difficult to argue that the ups and downs of the markets in 1720 were too extreme to have been justified by fundamentals. The fundamentals themselves were radically changing on virtually a weekly basis, as the British government alternately widened and then constrained the legal and regulatory environment in which firms could operate. The various governmental committees, studies, inquiries, and decisions about the markets were at least as important as basic economic factors. It was a moment in history when the rules of the game were in important flux, because the power of the new financial technology was becoming more and more evident. It had already evidently transformed the political economy of France and was on the verge of transforming Britain.

The year 1720 was the culmination of a process that began in the 1690s with Defoe's audacious vision of finance as a tool that society could use to transform itself for the better even while resisting its corrupting moral influence. The Bubble Act was the perfect expression of this Janus-like attitude toward financial technology. It permitted two companies that were unquestionably better able to manage risks at sea but it did so in language that was sharply critical of speculation, or "stock-jobbing." People wanted the gift that the financial mind could provide without the rude and sometimes merciless marketplace that made it possible.

DUTCH INTERPRETATION

It is through the eyes of the Dutch imitators of the British bubble companies that one can truly understand which financial innovations captured the public imagination in 1720. The eloquent arguments for the Rotterdam company of course stress the importance of a new institution for risk sharing. However, more than twenty-five new companies were founded in the Netherlands immediately following Rotterdam's move. Subscriptions for these companies traded on the exchanges beginning in the late summer and continued through the end of the year. The curious fact about all of these companies is that they were not founded to pursue singular businesses. All of them stated an intent to pursue multiple lines of business.

The financial technology they adapted from Britain was not only the notion of a public insurance firm but also the notion of a company that could do many different things at once—an unconstrained corporation that could pursue commerce, banking, insurance, fishery, manufacturing—whatever it deemed appropriate and profitable. Before 1720, the Dutch stock market comprised two chartered international trading firms that held essentially non-overlapping monopoly rights. Suddenly there was an explosion of new companies proposing to pursue a course that would lead them inevitably into competition, perhaps in several industries at once. It is as if the genetic code for a new kind of virus had escaped from Exchange Alley and had begun to multiply and migrate around the world. The old version of the code engendered the chartered mercantilist companies from the first Great Age of Discovery. But the mutations that occurred after the Glorious Revolution emboldened companies to skirt regulation, to plunge into new schemes, and to compete against one another. When individual governments tried to rein them in, the virus jumped borders and bred in other markets. It did not stop in Holland. An insurance company was launched in Hamburg in July, and it fueled the same fears of rampant speculation.[6] The windhandel trade of 1720 gave the world something of enduring value, however. Together with its two British cousins, the Royal Exchange Assurance and the London Assurance companies, it created a new model for pooling risks at sea and tapping public capital to cover those risks. Until the twenty-first century dreamed up new risks for insurance companies to take on—credit default swaps and complex mortgage-backed securities—the corporate model of the insurance trade would prove socially and economically useful.

THE ART OF INVESTOR FOLLY

The lessons of the great crash extend well beyond financial architecture. Despite the transformations of the corporation that took place in 1720, the crash is most often remembered as an episode in human folly. *Het Groote Tafereel der Dwaasheid* is the title of a book printed in Amsterdam after the great crash. The title can be translated as *The Great Mirror of Folly* and recalls Erasmus's satirical essay *In Praise of Folly*. Like the philosopher's comic work, the book uses humor and allegory to devastating effect. Published anonymously, it is more of a large folio of assorted printed documents and pictures than a reasoned essay. It portrays the way the Amsterdam society of 1720 viewed the capital markets.

The book begins with the prospectuses of the Dutch companies formed in the wake of Stad Rotterdam in 1720. Each prospectus tells of the plans for the firm, its financing, and its governance. Following these dry documents, which only a financial economist could love, are a series of humorous plays and poems written about the great crash, brought to life by comic characters like the greedy fool, the clever stock-jobber, and puzzling archetypes with names like Harlequin and Bombario—superhuman personalities that steal humans' reason and cause them to buy worthless paper.

After the plays comes the artwork. *The Great Mirror of Folly* contains dozens of satirical engravings of the stock market crash—allegorical scenes involving the personification of fame, fortune, and folly; the crowded stock markets of Amsterdam and Paris; the suffering and depredations of investors who gambled and lost—a great, entertaining, theatrical pageant of images that, page after page, brings home the human dimension of financial disaster.

On one page, John Law floats on a cloud like a god, while a stock broker furiously pumps a bellows to keep a balloon-trussed cat afloat—an allusion to propping up the Mississippi Company share prices. Law wears a windmill on his head—the wind being the metaphor for the insubstantiality of his financial system. The print lists the offending financial contracts: time-dated script, raw shares, subscriptions, loans, lottery prizes, and double interest. A box full of these contracts has a hole in it and rats have gotten to them.

Another page, titled "Monument consacré à la postérité en mémoire de la folie de la XX année du XVIII siècle," depicts a grand parade of crazed investors following a cart driven by Folly toward three doors: the poorhouse, the hospital, and the insane asylum. It is emerging from the Quinquepoix Coffeehouse, where a John Law figure can be seen in the background. The cart is pulled by personifications of the major trading and financial companies of the day: the South Sea Company, the East India Company, the Mississippi Company, the Bank of England, the Dutch West India Company, and the Royal Assurance Company. The cart rolls on wheels with spokes representing each of the new Dutch trading and insurance firms—the image of the wheel echoing the wheel of fortune. The caption explains that the prices of shares rise and fall as the cart moves. Floating above the cart is the goddess of Fortune, spreading shares intermingled with serpents.

Beneath the wheel of the cart is an accountant with the books of a corporation; the responsible businessman crushed by the madness of the speculative orgy. Vignettes in the crowd are equally entertaining. One depicts the attempt to sell shares in the Amsterdam scheme. Another represents loan dealing. Despite these isolated details, however, the crowd itself is a unified force in the picture—the obvious implication being that the financial crisis derived from the madness of the mob, the tendency of people to get swept up and lose their reason.

Several of the prints in the book hearken back to earlier Dutch art. For example, borrowing freely from Peter Brueghel and Hierony-

FIGURE 24. Engraving from *The Great Mirror of Folly*, 1720, depicting the global market bubble on its path from the coffeehouse, pulled by the six great companies.

mus Bosch, *The Great Mirror of Folly* artists portrayed loony investors having the stone of folly extracted from their feverish brains, or as fools doomed to perpetually drift in lunatic reverie. One print of the Dutch tulip mania of the 1630s is simply reproduced in the volume to draw the direct analogy between the episode of bulb speculation and the great financial crash. The bulb print is a figure of a giant, empty cap—suggesting the loss of the head and mind to speculative passions.

John Law's history as a gambler was not overlooked in the scathing satire. One *Great Mirror of Folly* image is a page of playing cards, printed in black and red ink. John Law is the king, and Mrs. Law is the queen of each suit. A similar deck of South Sea playing cards was produced in Britain. The message is clear: gaming was the root of the financial disaster. The projectors who created the disaster were gamesters, and gambling was the conceptual foundation of financial innovation.

SERMON ON THE MARKET

The amazing images in *The Great Mirror of Folly* go on and on. In picture after picture, Dutch, French, and perhaps British artists, inspired by the financial markets of 1720, used all their tricks—allegory, humor, caricature, and sly allusions to make sense of the shocking collapse of what had seemed but a few months before to be the dawn of a new financial order. Darius Spieth argues that these prints are the counterpoint to the John Law mural on the ceiling of his Banque Royale in Paris (see Chapter 20). His idea is compelling. The book is a topsy-turvy version of an uplifting allegorical composition. The Law mural was elitist; the Folly prints are populist. The former was a unified vision; the latter a fragmented series of critiques. Pellegrini appealed to lofty sentiments; the Folly prints are scatological. And yet they use the same allegorical vocabulary and grammar. Abstractions are embodied as figures interacting with one another—and with society—in subtly structured, dynamic compositions. In the baroque mural, the sky and swirling clouds allude to a celestial realm—the dynamic world of the gods. In the *Folly* prints, the clouds refer to the wind-trade, the insubstantial paper economy created by John Law.

Both works of art—high and low—are didactic. Pellegrini's mural explained the Mississippi system and its advantages; *The Great Mirror of Folly* was a warning to future generations. The warning was mostly about human behavior. Lacking the psychological models of the modern era, the creators of the book used the models of the eighteenth century—myth and allegory—to depict a psyche pulled in different directions by different modes of thought. The book is arguably the beginning of research in behavioral finance. It recognized that the market embodied the collective aspirations and fears of its participants, and that it had a peculiar power to force its own logic on investors.

It is tempting to simply accept the wisdom of *The Great Mirror of Folly*'s account of the failure of financial markets. Certainly in the wake of the subprime crisis of 2008, it seems a fitting characterization. However, the limitations of the analysis of the book lay in the language of allegory. Just as John Law could never represent the subtleties of monetary policies with floating, draped deities, the allegorical language of the *Folly* artists could never represent the complexity of innovations,

instruments, markets, contracts, and information flows that the newly
emerged stock markets of London, Paris, and Amsterdam represented.
The reason the images are so powerful and convincing is their appeal to
archetypes. The language of allegory is more deeply embedded in consciousness than the logic of mathematics and markets. When faced with
the apparent failure of the mathematical mind—represented most perfectly by the rational John Law and his system—society turned back to
an older language to make sense of the collapse.

We are at risk of repeating this mistake today. Since the most recent
crash, securitization of mortgages is dismissed as a hopelessly complex
financial innovation that failed, and society has turned the modern
crisis into a simplistic morality play with leading financiers as villains.
These archetypes are dangerous because of their universal appeal to the
subconscious, particularly in democratic societies in which elected officials need to communicate to the electorate. It seems almost as though
the ancient part of the brain, the part that thinks in myths and stories,
has harbored a long grudge against the rational mind and, jealous of its
increasing control over human behavior, it has seized on the failures of
reason.

It is not surprising that the cultural dialectic over finance in 1720
engendered such dramatic imagery. After all, it was a year of humanity
versus company. Investors in 1720 were inspired by an abstraction—a
trope—an entity (not a person) imbued with various rights and privileges. Some generations before, Thomas Hobbes had described the commonwealth as just such an abstraction: the citizens ruled by a king as a
leviathan. Corporations were new beasts that seemed to evolve more
quickly than rules and laws could constrain them. How large would
they grow? What parts of the economy would they secure for themselves? For example, could they really dare to take over the entire insurance trade?

John Law's company virtually swallowed France before overextend-
ing itself. Next, British companies sought to throw off their regulatory
shackles to pursue profits, regardless of mandate, cheered on and financially supported by throngs of investors whose expectations about the
future of unfettered corporate profits doubled, tripled, and quadrupled. Dutch companies then sprang up like dozens of new heads on the
hydra, each seeking to extend themselves into previously unexploited

businesses. But at each point, corporate growth was checked by reversals in public sentiment. Because they fed on fresh capital, they were easily starved into submission. The war ended in a truce rather than in defeat. The crash exposed the fundamental weakness of the corporation: it could swell to frightening proportion on investor enthusiasm, but such scale is not easily sustained. The awesome energy of the company was likewise revealed, however. It transcended the power of the single human. It could draw from the latent capital reserves in an economy and expand to vast scale. Corporations allocated capital in ways never before seen. They were the new leviathans: beasts beyond human scale to be harnessed by regulation and law and channeled to the public and private good.

CONSEQUENCES

Faced with this transformation, Europe recoiled from the great equity bubble of 1720, and financial technology took a different course of development in the decades that followed. The Bubble Act sharply curtailed the creation and trading of joint-stock companies in Great Britain. But in the Netherlands, public trading in stocks other than those of the VOC and WIC simply dried up. Even the shares in successful firms like Stad Rotterdam were no longer liquid. Trading was virtually nil until the end of the eighteenth century, and the recovery of the market seems not to begin in earnest until the 1820s. The Netherlands went through a dead century of equity finance. Only a handful of companies were chartered during the eighteenth century. In France, the shares in the Mississippi Company continued to trade, but only just. There were no significant flotations of firms to the public. The extraordinary irony of the Industrial Revolution is that it got started despite equity aversion and regulatory constraints in Britain and France in the eighteenth and early nineteenth centuries.

What replaced the public equities market? In eighteenth-century Britain and France, infrastructure projects like turnpikes and canals were sometimes financed by limited partnership companies organized by wealthy investors. These limited partnerships did not seek government charter for limited liability and access to public capital markets, but they nevertheless managed to pool capital for worthy projects. In

France, for example, the iron industry was indirectly funded by landed gentry, who were not otherwise permitted to engage in manufacturing and trade. Smelters required hot fires; hot fires depended on charcoal; charcoal is made from timber, and in the Ancien Régime, the aristocracy owned the forests. Likewise, metallurgy depended on coal mines to supply fuel.

Consider, for example, the Compagnie des fosses à Charbon de Monsieur Le Marquis de Traisnel, a coal mining operation in the town of Aniche, near the Belgian border. The company operations began in 1773 and eventually grew to become a major mining operation—mining coal until the early twentieth century and employing more than 10,000 miners. A share issued in the company in 1781 (before the French Revolution) has the coat of arms of the marquis, and proclaims that its owner, Monsieur de Monepevreuil, had the right to participate proportionally in the company profits, under the conditions that he submit to the debts of the firm and that he not alienate his shares without the consent of the company. In other words, limited liability and the transfer of shares were not in the deal. In the eighteenth century, at least in some places, the technology of the corporation took a step backward. Coal mines got funded and the metallurgy—so central to the construction of machines and engines that drove the Industrial Revolution in the nineteenth century—developed in the eighteenth century. But the financial tools that enabled the broader public to participate in the profits of economic growth and the access to larger pools of capital that a fully developed equity market would have provided did not materialize. The Fosses a Charbon de Monsieur Le Marquise de Traisnel was a closed company, and equity investing in the wake of the bubble of 1720 went back to being an insider's game.

SECURITIZATION AND DEBT

If the equity markets took a step back after the bubble of 1720, the fixed income markets took a step forward. The eighteenth century in Europe and America was a period of extraordinary financial innovation that took a turn away from equities—at least until nearly the end of the century—and instead focused on a financial architecture built on credit. By the end of the eighteenth century, paper money had made a comeback in many different forms, and financiers had developed ways of collateralizing paper money and complicated bonds of all sorts. These sophisticated financial innovations provided a means to transform illiquid assets to liquid securities.

This may sound a bit technical, but as we shall see, the drive for secure loan collateral played a part in the American colonial economy and the American Revolution. We have seen how John Law unleashed the genie of fiat money and inflation with disastrous consequences (see Chapter 20). The argument in this chapter is that the very insubstantiality of paper currency—and paper bonds—caused investors to demand hard collateral to back their investments. The new technology involved the pooling of assets in trust and the issuance of securities against this pool. Securitization is nothing more than a repackaging and reselling of an asset. The repackaging might involve pooling flows from several assets, restructuring of the flows through time—perhaps to smooth out future payouts—or even dividing the flows in some way that might make them more attractive to investors. The story begins, not surprisingly, in the Netherlands.

DUTCH MUTUAL FUNDS

Dutch financial engineers of the eighteenth century used the underlying structure of the pooled life annuity to create the first diversified investment funds. In the 1770s, around the time of the American Revolu-

Wheat Row, the first brick houses built in Washington, DC. They date to 1794, when James Greenleaf and his partners financed the purchase of lots in Washington by issuing bonds in the Netherlands backed by title to property. Their enterprise failed.

tion, Dutch investment bankers began to market investments that were funds—something like the trente demoiselles bond (see Chapter 15)—only instead of life annuity contracts on little girls, these funds held bonds issued by many different countries and different sorts of enterprises.

For example, in his search for the beginnings of the modern mutual fund, Geert Rouwenhorst has studied a negotiable security (*negotiatie*) called "Eendraght Maakt Magt," which was floated in Amsterdam in 1774 by the banking firm of Abraham Van Ketwich. This was an extraordinary, innovative financial security. It comprised the debt of a wide range of enterprises: Danish and Viennese banks; Danish and Holstein tolls; bonds issued by Russia, Sweden, Brunswick, and Mecklenburg; the postal services of Saxony and the peat-extraction enterprises of Brabant; Spanish and French canals; British colonies; mortgage loans to plantations in the Dutch colonies of Essequebo and Berbice; and loans to the Danish American Islands. These holdings were a mixture of international sovereign, municipal, and enterprise debt—strikingly international in its orientation.

Some of the components in the Eendraght Maakt Magt were not simple bonds. The plantation loans in the Dutch colonies, for example, were secured by mortgages on plantations in Surinam and included their slaves. The loan revenues were derived from forward contracts on the underlying commodities produced by the plantation, which presumably could be sold at a price profitable enough to ensure the yield on the loan. Similarly, the revenues from tolls, canals, and postal services that backed other loans in the portfolio also ensured a steady flow of income to cover the payout promised to Eendraght Maakt Magt investors: the 1774 offering prospectus promised an annualized 4% yield. The investors holding Eendraght Maakt Magt negotiaties would share equally in the cumulated cash flow from the underlying portfolio of debt. The title of the negotiatie succinctly expressed the concept—Strength in Many. Four percent seems a low yield for a portfolio tipped as it was toward emerging market debt. The yield on the underlying loans was significantly higher than this rate. The extra income the trust received from the cash flow of the underlying securities was "restructured" to change the way negotiatie investors were compensated. On a regular basis, some of the cash flows from the underlying bonds were diverted from dividend payments to redeem a fraction of the outstanding negotiatie, which were chosen by lottery. If your bond was one of the lucky winners, it was retired at a 20% premium over its face value. Also, the bonds in sequence next to your bond would have their dividend rate increased from 4% to 6%. And people think modern financial products are complicated!

Despite the amazing variety of underlying debt securities and complexity of the cash flow to investors by lottery, the concept of the 1774 Eendraght Maakt Magt negotiatie was simple. Bernoulli's law of large numbers ensured a 4% yield, despite the higher risk of the underlying securities. Bad luck could cause any of the underlying bonds to die early. A failed sugar harvest in South America could cut the revenues from the plantation loans. Russia could default on its debt. The Danish-American islands could change hands, and debts could be declared null and void. However, if you held enough of these potentially mortal securities, the law of large numbers rendered the defaulted bonds in the portfolio predictable. After all, what are the chances that all of these negative scenarios could happen at once?

This is just the painful question that the world asked in 2008, when American subprime borrowers began to default in unusually high numbers on their mortgages. Structured investment vehicles, issued by clever financial engineers in the early twenty-first century, used precisely the same concepts as Abraham Van Ketwich used 240 years ago. A bundle of potentially risky bonds, collateralized with flows from loans of various sorts (such as home mortgages, car loans, and credit card receivables) were pooled together in trusts—just like the eighteenth-century Dutch negotiatie—and then bonds were issued against the assets in these trusts.

These twenty-first-century bonds were structured, meaning that the cash flows from the underlying assets flowed to different purposes. For example, the first dollars in a structured investment vehicle went to pay off investors who bought a premium tranche. Once the premium tranche investors were fully or partially repaid, the next tranche would begin receiving cash flows. And on and on; a cascading waterfall of cash thrown off by debtors each month as they sat down to pay their credit card bills, home mortgages, car loans, and student loans; the cash bucket—minded by investment bankers as trustees—filling up and then spilling into different pools to pay different investors (maybe even some of the same investors who were writing the checks). After all, asset-backed securities were then widely held by mutual funds, money market funds, and pension funds, which in turn were invested in by ordinary savers.

The principle of securitization has remained the same since the eighteenth century. If you pool enough risky debt together, and the risk of default is sufficiently uncorrelated, then you can structure part of the resulting cash flow into a safer security. An asset-backed security also has the extra benefit of a claim on an underlying real asset. It is not like the holder of a mortgage-backed security must simply rely on the earnest promises of a homeowner. If the homeowner fails to pay, you can foreclose. What, then, could go wrong?

Abraham Van Ketwich and a number of other Dutch bankers also negotiated the structure to securitize the early debt of the United States. They bought the high-yielding bonds of the young nation in hopes that the Revolution would succeed. Dutch investors made out well when the debt of the United States was reorganized by Alexander Hamilton and the young nation made good on its financial commitments.

LAND BANKS

The securitization of land grew out of the financial imagination of the eighteenth century. Remember that John Law not only floated a sophisticated plan for a land bank, but ultimately his Mississippi Company also gave shareholders a stake in the largest securitized tract of all, the Trans-Mississippi West. The Dutch plantation loans backed by land, slaves, and commodity forward contracts were more complex versions of this New World investment—only structured as debt not equity. As we shall see, these were merely precursors to a transatlantic phenomenon that took off in the decades following the Mississippi Bubble and culminated in the aftermath of the French Revolution.

The American adventure with real estate securitization began with land banks. While the idea of a land bank remained mostly theoretical in Europe, it became a reality in North America during the eighteenth century. The Atlantic triangle trade left Americans chronically short of cash. This lack of currency turned the American colonies into financial laboratories. The first paper money in America appeared in 1690. It was a bond issued by Massachusetts to pay for an expedition against French Canada. Later, the famous printer Benjamin Franklin became one of the most vocal advocates of a paper currency system to address the chronic problem of money shortage. In fact he developed a special printing process using organic forms and subtle misspellings to combat the ever-present problem of counterfeiting that plagued paper currencies.

Money without collateral of some sort—whether coercion, commodity value, or specie convertibility—is inflationary. To counteract this, the colonies took up the idea of land banks. These were colonial land offices that collateralized money with the one asset that the New World had in abundance: land. The Massachusetts General Court established a public land bank in 1714, and all other colonies rapidly followed suit.[1] Generally these banks were public institutions that made loans on property by issuing paper currency. Private banks sprang up to do the same sort of financing: a corporation in Hartford was formed and issued bills in 1733, and one in New Hampshire in 1735—both issuing their own currency. Public or private, however, the land served as collateral on the loans and the banknotes that entered into public circulation. A private land bank was launched in Massachusetts by a group of citizens in 1741 to make twenty-year mortgages on properties at 3% interest to "mechanics" and people of modest means of up to 100 pounds.[2] Among the founders of the bank was Samuel Adams's father. The loans were made by giving borrowers paper money printed by the bank. The collateral was the land that the bank held mortgage to. Repayment of the principal would be made in the "value of thereof in manufactures of the Province"—in other words, payment in goods.

The bank infused much-needed cash into the economy, so that the people of Massachusetts had money to buy goods—and also to invest in projects that would lead to economic growth. In addition, the paper money could circulate as reliable tender, because it represented a promise from an organization with considerable assets: promises of payment in goods from borrowers, and in the event they failed to pay, with land they held title to.

Adam Smith, writing a generation later, faulted American paper money in *The Wealth of Nations* because it bore no interest. Smith could not understand why a zero-interest rate note was accepted as legal tender, although he admitted that the currency of Pennsylvania was well managed and traded above its par value in British sterling.[3] In contrast, the Massachusetts currency dropped to 20% of British currency value.[4]

Some of this discount may have had to do with self-dealing and fraud. To work properly, the collateral of a land bank had to be valued fairly. Otherwise you would have the same problem that cropped up in the Song dynasty when the reserves of the note issuers were less than the value needed to redeem the currency (see Chapter 9). Valuation could be a subjective and potentially corrupt process. Even if the rules required loan to value ratios of one-half, the market value is inherently difficult to ascertain; particularly for vacant, undeveloped property. The potential for over lending loomed.

In 1741, spurred by the Massachusetts controversy and concerned with a looming financial crisis, Parliament clamped down on American paper money and wound up the colonial land banks. It did so by extending the Bubble Act to cover the American colonies. Among many who suffered was Samuel Adams's father. He and the other directors were liable for the debts of the company. His anti-British sentiments may have been passed on to his son. In some places, however, American financial engineers got around the prohibition. In 1766, Maryland replaced its notes with a new security that could be redeemed for sterling—when presented in Britain!

FOUNDING FATHERS

The Bubble Act was extended to the colonies in 1741 to restrict financial engineering, but despite this regulatory restriction, American entrepreneurs pushed the financial envelope, particularly in land investments. America was one of the few exceptions to the global retreat from using stocks to finance business. Indeed, of the many divisive issues that led to the American Revolution—from taxation without representation to the restrictions on American trade—one of the sharpest disagreements between the crown and the American colonies centered on the role of land development, particularly expansion into the Western territories, where the West in the eighteenth century was land west of the Allegheny Mountains. Schemes to populate the Western territories were organized as partnerships, companies, and chartered corporations, and these firms lobbied hard to promote their interests with the British crown.

Land speculation was a common thread that connected many of the leaders of the American Revolution. The Ohio Company was created by a group of wealthy Virginians, including George Washington's father and two of his brothers. It was chartered by the crown in 1748 and allotted 200,000 acres in the Ohio Valley. George Washington made his name as commander of the Virginia regiment in the French and Indian War at the Battle of Duquesne, the site of present-day Pittsburgh but also the site of the grant to the Ohio Company. The French claim to the land was not only a challenge to British control, it was also a challenge to the land claims of prominent Virginia land speculators. They and other investors interested in the development of the West were not pleased that, at the conclusion of the war, the Parliamentary Proclamation of 1763 reserved lands west of the Allegheny Mountains for native tribes.

The Ohio Company was only one of many firms set up to speculate on lands in the West. The Loyal Company of Virginia, founded in 1749, involved Peter Jefferson, the future president's father. Its charter was not renewed after the French and Indian War due to the Proclamation of 1763. The Virginians were not the only colonists interested in western lands. The Illinois and Wabash Companies were launched in 1773 to buy and develop Native American lands and involved prominent Philadelphia merchants. The Vandalia Company claimed land in what is now West Virginia. Its directors included Benjamin Franklin and his son. Disputes between the Virginians and Pennsylvanians over claims in the west were acrimonious, but both groups could at least agree that the British policy of discouraging westward expansion stood in their path.

George Washington was one the most active participants in early American land companies. According to historian Barbara Rasmussen, his holdings included shares in "The Walpole Grant, Mississippi Company, Military Company of Adventurers and the Dismal Swamp Company,"[5] totaling more than 62,000 acres.

The basic business proposition of these land companies was to acquire large, fertile tracts of land, divide them into lots, develop basic infrastructure, and then sell them to American and foreign settlers. In fact the Ohio Company grant explicitly required the land to be settled within a certain time period. This was not so easily accomplished, given ownership disputes with Native Americans, lack of hard currency to invest in development, and lack of cash on the settler side to acquire the property. Financing was a necessary ingredient—settlers in the Ohio tract would need financing terms using property as collateral. Credit was the only thing that could make the land company plans work. Restrictions on land banks were also effectively restrictions on mortgage credit in the colonies, and restrictions on western expansion undermined the hopes on which the early American land companies were built. It is not difficult to understand how the Washingtons,

Adamses, Jeffersons, and Franklins would be tempted to support independence. Independent American colonies would be free to pursue a policy of western land development, mortgage banking, and optimal monetary policy. Finance, closely tied to collateralized lending and land speculation through incorporated companies, was an important driver behind the push to independence. After the revolution, the freedom from the Bubble Act and the Proclamation of 1763 unfettered American finance.

The American Revolution was financed partially by Dutch and French investors. We saw above that a group of Dutch bankers arranged loans for the young United States by securitizing pools of American debt; buying the bonds of the young United States issued in America and overseas, pooling them into mutual funds, and selling them to Dutch investors. These Dutch investors were betting on a new, young country. In France, the king supported the colonial revolt, even as his subjects noted with admiration the American struggle for freedom from monarchy. American independence inspired both the French and the Dutch, leading to the Dutch Patriot Revolt in 1782, the French Revolution in 1787, and the founding of the Dutch Batavian Republic in 1795 that chased William of Orange from the country. These new Republics also took inspiration from American finance. In France, this imitation took the form of collateralization of money with land. In the Netherlands, it took the form of land speculation. New World financial ingenuity was adopted by the Old. America served as a testing grounds for some of the ideas and techniques that Europe largely had rejected in the wake of the bubble of 1720. The idea of land banks, paper money, and private corporations as units of business development bubbled up in the American colonies that chafed under any regulation and control by Parliament. American-enhanced financial technology reached back across the Atlantic, along with the urge for revolution. There were some unintended consequences.

REIGN OF TERROR

In France, the theory of a land bank—of paper currency collateralized by property—became a bloody reality during the Reign of Terror. Despite the long shadow of John Law and France's aversion to financial engineering after the Mississippi Bubble, the revolutionary Jacobin government had few means of financial support and no convincing basis for issuing fiat money. It turned instead to asset-backed securities. Money backed by property.

The French government seized the property of the Catholic Church and then began to pay its bills in paper vouchers (assignats), which could be used in public auctions to purchase the nationalized church properties. In some ways, the assignats were a realization of John Law's earlier vision of a currency based on property rather than on gold or silver reserves (see Chapter 20). They failed for the same reason Law's earlier experiment collapsed: an overactive printing press. There were too many assignats chasing too few properties. Robespierre desperately fought that balance by guillotining the gentry and adding their estates to the "biens nationaux," the national property account which backed the assignats. It was not enough. Despite financial restructurings, France's second attempt at a paper currency was no more successful than the first.

The iconic image of the Reign of Terror is Jacques-Louis David's painting *Death of Marat*, an image of the assassinated revolutionary slumped in his bath. The picture is actually as much about the finance of the French Revolution as it is about the death of one of its leaders. In Marat's dying hand is a petition from his assassin, Charlotte Corday, whose aristocratic family suffered at Jacobin hands. Immediately below this document is a letter penned by Marat to an impoverished widow of the revolution, together with an assignat—a personal financial sacrifice by Marat. The documents tell the story of financial transubstantiation; the seizure of goods from the aristocracy on the one hand and its passage into the hands of the working class on the other. To the viewers of the painting in 1793, the irony of the assignat would have been clear. The document allowed the widow to make a claim on the seized property of Corday and those of her class. A hero of the revolution had died in battle, but the battlefield was the abstract domain of finance. With the dying visage of a revolutionary clutching paperwork instead of a sword, David managed to equate securitization with the sublime.[6] The issuance of property-backed notes caused a speculative frenzy in France as investors bought up the notes and managed

(a)

FIGURE 25. (a) *Death of Marat*, by Jacques-Louis David.

to acquire properties at great discounts. The revolution redistributed property, but the redistribution was from the church and gentry to clever property speculators who understood how to take advantage of a securitized currency system gone wild.

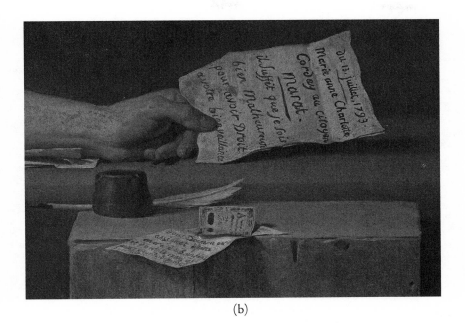

(b)

FIGURE 25 (*continued*). (b) detail of his letter and French Assignats.

DUTCH LAND SPECULATION

We saw earlier that one of the key innovations in securitization of land
in the New World was the Dutch plantation loan. Those bonds were
collateralized by commodity contracts for sugar and cocoa produced
in the Surinam plantations, and also by the Surinam properties themselves. Theophile Cazenove was a Dutch entrepreneur who tried his
hand at a number of ventures, including Surinam. His first foray into
international trade was a Russia venture that went bust in 1770, despite
connections through Russian in-laws. He then took a chance at the Surinam trade—operating a plantation in Berbice. However, in 1789, he
was hired by a group of Dutch bankers—the same group who financed
the American debt—to scout out investment opportunities in the new
United States. He settled in Philadelphia.

Cazenove found kindred spirits in Philadelphia after the Revolution. Americans, free of the Bubble Act, were launching corporations to
build infrastructure, such as canals and turnpikes, and even to promote

industry. Westward expansion and settlement was back on track. Cazenove met land speculators with all sorts of companies and schemes. He invested in the James River Company, a firm nominally headed by George Washington to develop commercial traffic in southern Virginia. Cazenove also bought a substantial block of shares in the Pennsylvania Population Company, a firm with large tracts of land in the region of Erie—the far northwestern part of Pennsylvania.

The Pennsylvania Population Company land came from grants set aside for veterans of the Revolutionary War. In true American fashion, soldiers were paid with Depreciation certificates that gave them rights to claim and settle western property—a variation on the assignat technology. Those who did not want to settle in the west could of course sell their land-backed Depreciation certificates. One of the biggest buyers was John Nicholson, comptroller-general of the Commonwealth of Pennsylvania and prior commissioner in charge of the Depreciation certificate program. Nicholson organized a group of investors, including Cazenove and Robert Morris. Morris served as the first superintendent of the Treasury for the United States and essentially ran the finances of the American Revolution. He was also one of America's richest men and its greatest land speculator.

Nicholson's methods were not entirely honest. He used false claims and phony names to amass a huge position in western land claims. Since his official duties involved adjudicating disputed claims on Depreciation certificates, he wielded great power and was impeached for abusing it. Despite impeachment, he held on to his acquisitions, and they became the assets of the Pennsylvania Population Company. Selling shares to Dutch speculators was a means to monetize his land grab.

Cazenove's clients formed the Holland Land Company in Amsterdam in 1792 as a company roughly similar to the early American land companies. It was thus a share partnership among investors with the intent to buy and develop western lands. That year, Cazenove acquired for them 3.3 million acres in New York's Genesee River Valley from Robert Morris. Because of the strong interest the Dutch investing public had in American securities, the Holland Land Company consortium was able to finance this purchase with the issuance of a bond—actually a negotiatie for 3 million guilders in January 1793, backed by 1 million acres of Genesee Valley land as collateral. The actual negotiatie was a complicated structure.

Not only did the investors get claim to the undeveloped land, but they also were promised interest payments derived from a portfolio of US government bonds held for them in trust. This was something like the early mutual funds, but instead of holding liquid securities, one part of the assets underlying the Holland Land Company negotiaties was undeveloped forest in western New York state. Why in the world would anyone ever invest in that?

To explain how the land would eventually begin to generate profits, one of the partners of the Holland Land Company, Pieter Stadnitski, published a detailed set of calculations that predicted great waves of settlement to the western lands (despite potential conflict with Native American nations). The plan was to promote the American dream not only to Americans but to French, Dutch, and Germans who would emigrate from Europe to set up a new life on the American frontier. These settlers would purchase property on credit extended by the company and over ten years or so, the firm would be raking in profits, as settlers paid off their loans and built farms and towns that in turn attracted more settlers. Stadnitski was, of course, wildly off the mark.

The Holland Land Company negotiaties plunged in value with the political turmoil of the Batavian Republic (when France essentially annexed the Netherlands). However, they recovered somewhat, based at first on the income derived from the US bonds as backing for interest payments. Eventually the company had to come back to investors with a new deal: they offered an exchange of bonds for a share in the equity of the firm. No matter how cleverly structured the negotiatie was, a long-term project like the development and population of the western wilderness did not quite fit the profile of bond investment. Oddly enough, although the project seemed wildly optimistic and doomed from the first—a speculative venture by a consortium of idealistic Dutch merchants who had never seen America and who trusted their investment to a twice-failed entrepreneur teamed up with one of the most unsavory crooks of American revolutionary history—the investors accepted the terms of the offer. And over the next five decades, the slow but steady development—aided of course by the Erie Canal—turned out to be highly profitable. Large swaths of New York state owe their early settlement to the enterprising vision of Dutch financiers and their crazy faith in the future of a young nation. Not all investments in American lands turned out as well.

CAPITAL BUBBLE

American history is filled with real estate developers whose speculative reach exceeded their financial grasp. Much of America's westward expansion was organized around land companies formed by investors and speculators. Wheat Row in Washington, DC, is a beautifully preserved federalist building from 1794. When it was built, it was something like a model home: a series of row houses that shows how the mature city would look once the vacant lots were filled in. It was finished while the White House and Capitol buildings themselves were still under construction. Located on Fourth Street in the southeast section of the city, it is virtually all that remains of the plans of James Greenleaf, the land speculator whose rash purchase of undeveloped land in the District of Columbia helped jump-start the creation of the new capital. His vision also led to the rise and fall of the United States' greatest real estate company—a crisis that mortgaged the new city even before it was built.

Greenleaf was a Bostonian financier who moved to Amsterdam during the American Revolution and helped negotiate Dutch loans for the young United States. Abandoning his Dutch wife and returning to America, he began to speculate in land. The catalyst for his most ambitious scheme was the government decision to move its capital to a marsh on the banks of the Potomac River. The Residence Act of 1790 established the District of Columbia, moved the permanent capital of the new nation from New York, and touched off a land grab. Imagine the amazing opportunity! An entire capital city would be built: not just government offices but everything that went with it: houses, hotels, stores, streets, and bridges. If you got in first, how could you lose?

In 1793 and 1794, James Greenleaf borrowed in the Dutch capital markets to buy up vacant land in the new capital. He partnered in this venture with Robert Morris and John Nicholson. The triumvirate acquired 10,000 lots in the District of Columbia and arranged a further Dutch loan for the construction of public buildings. The property became the collateral for publicly issued and traded loans in negotiatie very similar to those of the Holland Land Company. However, the Greenleaf negotiaties did not do as well as hoped. Only about 20% of them were sold, and thus, from its very inception, the company formed to develop the new US capital was painfully and impossibly in deep debt.

Desperate for cash, Greenleaf, Nicholson, and Morris turned to is-suing stock in a new company. They formed the North American Land Company in February 1795 by pooling their properties. The plan was to raise equity capital in Europe and America and to forge ahead with building Washington. Greenleaf, Morris, and Nicholson each contrib-uted huge swaths of undeveloped properties from New York state to Georgia. All had been buying wilderness lands in the West, convinced that the country would inevitably expand beyond the Appalachians. The North American Land Company began with 4 million acres.

Unfortunately, the one thing the company lacked was income. The floatation of shares yielded less capital than hoped. European interest in stocks—as in bonds—was particularly weak due to the outbreak of war following the French Revolution. Greenleaf wisely sold his shares back to the company in July in exchange for promissory notes on acquired building plots in Washington. Their vast, leveraged empire of American raw land teetered. Bills went unpaid. All three entrepreneurs hid out from creditors and spent time in debtor's prison. In fact, the spectacle of Robert Morris bankrupt so soon after his service in the American Rev-olution was a colossal, national shock. Among other things, it brought about passage of the first comprehensive bankruptcy law in the United States.[7]

Greenleaf, Morris, and Nicholson were right about the westward course of empire and their conviction that Washington, DC, would grow to become a great city. They simply miscalculated the time it took for their dreams to come true and the expense of holding on to them. Like John Law, they held real assets that centuries later would be worth a fortune. The time value of money is important. Their vision to use finance to transform the landscape—to create a new kind of city—was a peculiarly American one. As the United States marched westward across the continent through the nineteenth century, it experimented with new architectures and ways of financing them: sod houses, balloon-frame houses, beautiful beaux-arts city designs; grids on the plains like Chicago, and grids on the hills like San Francisco. This rapid transfor-mation of the continent was financed by real estate speculation.

To the European eye, parallels to the great stock market bubble of 1720 were impossible to miss. The French economist Michael Cheva-lier was dispatched by his government in 1834 to study the American economic system. His observations on American real estate speculation are worth quoting at length:

> Everybody is speculating, and everything has become an object of speculation. The most daring enterprises find encouragement; all projects find subscribers. From Maine to the Red River, the whole country has become an immense rue Quincampoix. Thus far everyone has made money, as is always the case when speculation is in the ascendant. . . . The amateurs in land at the north, dispute with each other the acquisition of the valuable timber-lands of that region; at the southern extremity, the Mississippi swamps, and the Alabama and the Red River cotton lands, are the subject of competition, and in the West, the corn fields and pastures of Illinois and Michigan. The unparalleled growth of some new towns has turned the heads of the nation, and there is a general rush upon all points advantageously situated; as if, before ten years, three or four Londons, as many Parises, and a dozen Liverpools, were about to display their streets and edifices, their quays crowded with warehouses, and their harbours bristling with masts, in the American wilderness.[8]

Chevalier's observations ring as true in the twenty-first century as they did in the nineteenth century.

REFLECTIONS ON EUROPEAN INNOVATION

The financial innovation of the eighteenth century in Europe set it on a distinct course from China. The century began with innovations of probabilistic thinking and mathematics. Its first great bubble involved the discovery of paper money and the use of corporations in myriad creative directions. The eighteenth century also unleashed the wild force of speculation, upsetting the social order and creating a moral backlash against financial markets and financial thinking. It engendered serious attempts at regulating and controlling the forces of finance. In Britain, this included constraining companies, markets, banks, and even mortgage finance.

After the bubble, Dutch finance led the way in developing increasingly sophisticated financial instruments for an investing public that sought relatively safe returns from bonds. Merchants in Amsterdam and other major Dutch cities devised methods for financing their commodity trade. The plantation loan system began as a means to finance transatlantic commodity trade, but the merchants who led the way in this financial innovation ultimately developed into the world's first investment bankers. Although they continued merchant trade, they discovered that the underwriting and issuance of asset-backed securities was extremely profitable.

The American Revolution played a key part in the development of a new transatlantic financial system. We saw how Americans sidestepped the regulatory backlash in Europe against equity markets and paper money. The chronic lack of hard currency in the colonies meant that some financial engineering was crucial—a key insight of John Law. America was currency poor but land rich, and this inexorably led to the use of property as collateral—as the underlying source of value—in the financial system. The early American land companies took up where the bubble companies of 1720 left off. The various companies that leading colonial families set up to settle the Ohio valley were echoes of the same kind of firms that bubbled up in 1720 with dreams of riches flowing from the New World. After the American Revolution, not only did US companies set out to realize these dreams but so did companies set up by Dutch merchant bankers.

It is particularly interesting that the same investment bankers who made fortunes securitizing the debt of the young United States leaped into land speculation, and doubly interesting that their astute management of the Holland Land Company was a great success. They avoided the calamity of Robert Morris, James Greenleaf, and John Nicholson, despite having dealings with all three. Somehow the canny Dutch bankers managed to mostly sidestep the Washington, DC, fiasco, which came about because the American partners foolishly bought the property before they secured their financing. The Amsterdam house that did underwrite the Washington loans suffered serious reputational harm. In this way it recalls the recent mortgage crisis that brought down the more incautious US banks.

The eighteenth-century experiments with paper money that bounced back and forth across the Atlantic were some of the most creative in financial history. Among other things, they elucidated the great potential for asset-backed money. They demonstrated how a bank can be thought of as an institutional structure for transforming loans into currency. It is particularly interesting to contrast the colonial American land banks that issued money by making mortgages to the invention of paper money in China, which can be thought of as early fractional reserve savings institutions that took deposits and wrote claims against them. This contrast demonstrates just how financial technology can develop from different imperatives but arrive at quite similar solutions. The idea of issuing assignats and Depreciation certificates with claims on property makes the notion of the dollar bill backed by gold or silver seem remarkably tame.

When I think of the eighteenth-century merchants, investors, businesspeople, and citizens trying to navigate the complexities of a new financial world, I am certain that—even with all of my modern financial training, I would have been overwhelmed with the problem of understanding insurance contracts, negotiaties, stocks, mutual funds, land certificates, plantation loans and assortment of paper monies, bills of exchange, securities offerings, and all the other amazing products that flourished in that extraordinary century. I see the development of the financial mind in this period—and the development of mathematical tools to extend that mind—as an absolute necessity. By the end of that century, finance had become a system of intermediation between present and future that took many different forms. It used both future government revenues and profits from entrepreneurial ventures and vehicles for transferring value to the present. It also pushed to solve the basic paradox of fiat money—that there was no "there" there. An absolute state can decree a medium of exchange, but a weak state needs to back this up with assets. Countries in chronic debt, colonies and revolutionary governments short of cash—these polities resorted to the transmutation of illiquid assets like land into liquid assets like publicly tradable debt and paper money.

THE EMERGENCE
OF GLOBAL MARKETS

GLOBAL CONFLICTS

This part of the book narrates the final act in a story in which the technology of finance has so far played both hero and villain—or more aptly perhaps, a protagonist uncertain of moral valence. In the modern era, the problems and possibilities inherent in finance led to a dramatic conflict over the direction of civilization itself. In Part I we saw from the earliest urban city-states that finance enabled the emergence of complex political organizations—but not without the costs inherent in contracting about an uncertain future. Default on a loan, for instance, could lead to enslavement. In this structure lay the seeds of global conflict and political rupture.

In Part III, with the first appearance of financial instruments and financial thinking in Europe in the Middle Ages, we saw a reaction that led to proscriptions against usury and the defining of financial technology as inherently immoral. We then saw the emergence of financial ways of thinking—from mathematical techniques for analyzing uncertainty to projectors' dreams about the potential of corporations to do everything from risk sharing to colonizing the world. In Part IV we will see the reassertion of earlier amoral characterizations of finance and a seductive argument against the fundamental principles that support financial technology, including private property and entrepreneurial freedom. This reinvigorated dialectic over the role of finance in society comes to a crescendo in the early twentieth century and literally breaks the world in two.

The ultimate implication of the discovery in Venice of municipal bonds led, over the centuries, to situations in which the bonds of one nation could be held by citizens of another. Colonialization was a consequence of this financial structure. When the borrower is a nation-

Bond issued to finance the construction of the Suez Canal.

state and the lenders are bondholders from countries with big, modern armies, this creates a major problem. In this part we shall explore how this problem defined relationships among nation-states in the modern era. In particular, we will see how nations like Great Britain used debt and the power of its capital markets as an instrument to weaken sovereign control. The reparations claims we saw in the dispute between Umma and Lagash in the third millennium BCE appear again and again in the nineteenth and twentieth centuries.

The world ultimately managed to address some of the worst issues raised by sovereign debt. The modern international institutions of the International Monetary Fund and the World Bank, for example, were designed in part to defuse the political problems caused by finance. They attempt to eliminate military enforcement of sovereign debt contracts by nation-states. The process of political negotiation within the Eurozone is a prime example. The modern story of global debt is a major theme of Part IV.

GLOBALIZATION OF EQUITY

A second major theme in this final part of the book is the opening up of investment to all levels of society. The year 1720 released a strange genius. It revealed the amazing power of the stock market to capture the imagination and open the wallet. As investment markets emerged all over the world in the nineteenth century, they allowed more and more people to save and speculate—to plan for their economic future and to trade on hopes and dreams of instant riches.

This new configuration of social assets had a number of consequences, institutional as well as intellectual. The opening of investment markets spurred a quest by investors for greater returns and greater diversification—and this led inexorably to cross-border investing. European capital worked its way to every corner of the globe chasing returns, but it also spread risk, resulting in the globalization of equity.

We shall trace the process of stock market investing and the cultural response as it spread around the world. We look at Britain, Russia, China, and the United States as different case studies in equity market development in the modern era.

John Maynard Keynes famously asserted that the fundamental driver of economic growth is animal spirits—of the kind we saw in abundance in 1720. We shall see the pattern of hope and despair—or even anger—about the financial markets play out again and again in this part. A rush of optimism about investing in new markets and new technologies can just as suddenly reverse. When stock values crash, people lose faith in markets, and the ability to tap investor wallets ebbs with stock prices. The key lesson is that belief in the power of the stock market is vital to sustaining it.

One of the most important financial developments in the modern era is the science of diversification, a discovery that came from the mathematics of probability. The science of diversification makes some important predictions about the behavior of the world's investors once global markets are broadly accessible to them. It predicts that all assets in the world will be held in equal proportion by all of its investors. That is, given a frictionless investment market, a family in France will hold essentially the same stocks as a giant pension fund in California. And that this portfolio would hold a little bit of every stock—actually every security—in the world. Theory says that, as a global society, we would share equally in the benefits of finance. It was not until the modern era that smaller investors could begin to hold such well-diversified investment portfolios. How the theory developed—and how investors have moved toward holding this strange, egalitarian portfolio—is another key theme in this part of the book.

Finally, I will argue that globalization of equity investing leads to cross-border conflicts of interest. It enflames nationalistic passions. It erodes domestic political influence and control over corporations. These conflicts between equity investors and the nation-state are real and have yet to satisfactorily resolved. The final portion of this part explores the future of such conflicts, and I offer some conjectures about how we might solve them.

MARX AND MARKETS

All fixed, fast frozen relations, with their train of ancient and venerable prejudices and opinions, are swept away, all new-formed ones become antiquated before they can ossify. All that is solid melts into air, all that is holy is profaned, and man is at last compelled to face with sober senses his real condition of life and his relations with his kind.[1]

Thus Karl Marx and Friedrich Engels described capitalism's relentless rush to innovation that effaced traditional society. Their book *The Communist Manifesto* was printed in 1848 and challenged capitalism to a fight. It spelled out what was wrong with the world and how to fix it. The root of society's problems in their view: money, savings, and investors.

JUST A BOOK

It is difficult to imagine the shock that Jenny Marx felt when she saw her new home at 28 Dean Street in London's Soho district. Today the address is occupied by a cheery restaurant and surrounded by upscale shops and bars. In 1849, Soho was a dismal slum. The daughter of a Prussian baron, Jenny knew that marriage to her stormy, intellectual husband Karl Marx would make life difficult. Marx was expelled from Prussia despite his wife's prominent social position. In fact, her brother was the head of the state security service. It was clear, however, that Karl Marx was dangerous. He championed the short-lived 1848 revolt in Paris and fled to Belgium when it was put down. He moved on to Cologne to edit a radical paper, where he was put on trial twice—the last time for sedition. Ejected from Prussia and France, Britain was one of the few countries that would take him in. Although the Marx family was

Building in Chelsea, London, where Karl Marx lived and wrote *Das Kapital*.

financially supported by the industrialist/Communist Friedrich Engels, their meager resources left them little choice but to take a third-floor flat in Soho. Life for Jenny did not get much better—their son died from tuberculosis, she had to constantly negotiate with creditors, they had barely any furniture and even that was at constant risk of seizure. But it was here that one of the most important books of the modern world took shape. Marx conceived and wrote much of *Das Kapital* in this tiny flat. The location had one huge benefit. Dean Street is a short walk from the British Library, where Marx had access to unparalleled research resources on the history of capitalism. At once the crucible of European capitalism and the home of its greatest critic, London engendered the dialectic that shaped the modern world.

Das Kapital is a vast book that took years to write and was finished in stages. After eight years in Soho, Marx and Jenny moved out of the slums closer to Engels's home in Primrose Hill, but the bitterness of their early years added an extra edge to Marx's social criticism. In some ways *Das Kapital* is a lifelong labor of hate: an attack on an economic system that, in his view, enabled the investor class to victimize the working class. Its first volume appeared in 1867. The second and third volumes were published posthumously in 1894, with Friedrich Engels as editor and publisher.

While criticism of market forces, banks, stock markets, lending, and investment existed long before Karl Marx, the novelty of *Das Kapital* is that it redefines capitalism in its own terms and predicts its doom. He argued that the seeds of capitalism's future failure lay in the business cycle. Eventually, a great recession in the industrialized economies would stir the proletariat to seize the means of production from the capitalists. In the meantime, capitalism would relentlessly and systematically drain the life blood of the working class.

KAPITAL IN A NUTSHELL

In Marx's world, the value of everything is a function of the labor expended to create it. Marx adapted this view from the work of David Ricardo—a brilliant and influential political economist of the early nineteenth century who proposed a theory of value based on human input to the production process. In Marx's reformulation of Ricardian theory, money is bad, because it conceals the amount of labor required for the production of a given commodity. Arbitrageurs who profitably buy and sell commodities exploit money's distorting role. Corporate dividends are derived from paying meager subsistence wages to laborers and then turning around and selling goods at higher money prices that no longer reflect their labor value. Capitalists control the means of production and use it to generate and hoard surplus labor. Mechanization and productivity gains generate higher profits and result in layoffs, which in turn lead to a reserve of cheap labor. Unemployment drives down demand, however, and profits suffer. This cycle of productivity gain and unemployment leads to periodic crises in the capitalist economy. At some point, the cycle will break down, and workers will control the means of production and thus be able to retain for themselves the surplus value of their own labor. With apologies to Marx and a century of Marxist scholarship, that's the book in a nutshell.

Generations of scholars have debated *Das Kapital* and pointed out key weaknesses in its argument—particularly with respect to the labor theory of value. The logical limitations of the book hardly matter—its influence on history is indisputable.

Financial technology, beginning with the invention of money and the first Italian bond issues, was fundamental to Marx's argument:

> The system of public credit, i.e., of national debts, whose origin we discover in Genoa and Venice as early as the middle ages, took possession of Europe generally during the manufacturing period. . . . But further, apart from the class of lazy annuitants thus created, and from the improvised wealth of the financiers, middlemen between the government and the nation—as also apart from the tax-farmers, merchants, private manufacturers, to whom a good part of every national loan renders the service of a capital fallen from heaven—the national debt has given rise to joint-stock companies, to dealings in negotiable effects of all kinds, and to agiotage, in a word to stock-exchange gambling and the modern bankocracy.[2]

In Marx's reading of history, the government debt of Venice and Genoa led to the development of the public corporation and ultimately to the modern capital markets. To him this was a bad thing—his prose is laden with the same moral condemnation used by medieval Scholastics.

Bondholders, in Marx's view, were "lazy annuitants." This distinction between capitalists and workers may seem to be painfully theoretical and turgid, but strangely enough, it would ultimately justify revolutions in many countries in the world and separate East from West for nearly fifty years of the twentieth century. At least for a moment in the history of Western thought, a crucial argument about social equity turned on the details of financial history.

Das Kapital articulates a comprehensive model interpreting every aspect of society. In modern academic terms, it is the ultimate *hermeneutical* text: it provides a way of reading history, politics, economics, interpersonal relations—even the family. It does so by stereotyping people into class roles and then imputing to them the incentives of the class. Marx uses the latent archetypes of the European tradition—the allegorical figures we saw in *Het Groote Tafereel*, for example (see Chapter 21)—but he develops them further. Take for example, his portrait of the saver:

> The hoarder, therefore, makes a sacrifice of the lusts of the flesh to his gold fetish. He acts in earnest up to the Gospel of abstention. On the other hand, he can withdraw from circulation no more than what he has thrown into it in the shape of commodities. The more he produces, the more he is able to sell. Hard work, saving, and avarice are, therefore, his three cardinal virtues, and to sell much and buy little the sum of his political economy. . . . [A]ntagonism between the quantitative limits of money and its qualitative boundlessness, continually acts as a spur to the hoarder in his Sisyphus-like labour of accumulating.[3]

Marx's hoarder is the archetypal miser, but he is also embellished into a fetishist whose repressed libidinal desires are transferred to money.

In another time, *Das Kapital* might have been written as an epic poem (Dante's *Inferno*), a novel (Thomas More's *Utopia*), or a satire (Erasmus's *In Praise of Folly*). Of these, *Das Kapital* comes closest to the *Inferno* in depicting a world of the damned: of trapped souls, like the hoarder, forced by the capitalist system to labor perpetually and purposelessly. Marx, in *Das Kapital*, is a spirit guide into the depths of the living hell of the modern industrial state. His goal is to expose the evils and flaws of society. Frighteningly, *Das Kapital* does not lead the way out of the inferno; it merely predicts its ultimate demise. It poses the problem but does not outline a solution.

If *Das Kapital* portrays Hell, *The Communist Manifesto* points the way to redemption. Marx and Engels took as their inspiration the French Revolution, embracing the necessity for a violent overthrow of the ruling class. To that end, they articulate the goals of the Communist party:

> The immediate aim of the Communists is the same as that of all other proletarian parties: Formation of the proletariat into a class, overthrow of the bourgeois supremacy, conquest of political power by the proletariat.[4]

Once that is accomplished, the Communists will establish a new, classless society. They will seize all private land; tax heavily and progressively; eliminate inheritance; confiscate property from emigrants and resisters; nationalize banking, credit, communication, transportation, production, and agriculture; conscript everyone into industrial armies to share manual labor equally; move people out of cities to the countryside; eliminate child labor; and establish free schools that are integrated into industrial production. It is hard to believe that such a radical plan could ever be implemented. Then again, as a child of the Cold War, I lived during a time when the these policies were the law of the land, at least hypothetically, in the Soviet Union and the People's Republic of China.

NEWS OF THE WORLD

Among history's greatest ironies is that, despite his acid view of capitalists, Engels worked much of his life in the family manufacturing firm in Manchester. Even more surprising, even though Karl Marx dismissed "agiotage" and stock exchange gambling, he himself was a keen speculator and observer of the markets—trading avidly and profitably in US bonds and British stocks on the London Exchange, and boasting to his uncle of the killing he made in the markets. In addition, both men worked as professional journalists for the *New York Daily Tribune*, Marx with a byline, Engels occasionally ghostwriting for him. Thus, while penning history's greatest indictment of capitalism, Marx fed New York investors with news and analysis of European politics and economics throughout the 1850s and early 1860s.

Marx's *Tribune* articles contain some of his most interesting analysis. Reportage demanded empirical evidence and reasoned interpretation, and yet it also gave him latitude to editorialize on current trends. Marx speaks out in a strong, moral voice against many injustices: the conditions of the working class, the British opium trade in China, the mistreatment of the insane, American slavery, and the colonization of India. He applauds the emerging labor union movement and the success of Giuseppe Garibaldi in unifying Italy in a populist revolt. His prose is terse, witty, and convincing. When I read these lively columns I can almost forgive him.

Marx in his *Tribune* articles portrays a world of global linkages and geo-political dynamics. In the 1860s, the world financial markets had developed to the point that Marx could buy and sell bonds issued in markets thousands of miles overseas. He could comment on the daily fluctuation in interest rates on the colonial debt of India. Marx the journalist was at the center of the new financial universe: a market that stretched around the globe. The international events of 1720 with their cross-border flows, capital issuances, and speculation on world events were a minor dress rehearsal for the nineteenth-century financial world.

In the high Victorian era, more people in London were reading the business news than the commentaries and manifestos of Marx and Engels—and business news was increasingly quantitative. The financial markets in London were generating vast amounts of information. *The Economist* magazine—a London business journal devoted to the philosophy of free trade—published a monthly list of stock and bond prices that ran to more than fifty pages of small print. A perusal of the December 1869 issue of *The Economist*'s price list, *The Investor's Monthly Manual*, provides a window into the world of Karl Marx's fetishist/ hoarder—a figure he called "our friend, Moneybags."

Imagine our friend Moneybags spending a shilling and four pence on Saturday, New Year's Day, of 1870 to find out how his various investments were progressing. Perhaps he buys it from a printer in London's Fleet Street, or farther afield in Birmingham, Manchester, Hull, or Edinburgh. Personally, I like to think of Moneybags as the aging Friedrich Engels, stepping out for a brief walk in Regents Park and stopping by a newsstand before returning to his comfortable house overlooking the gardens—after all, Engels retired around 1870 to live on his investments and continue the Communist struggle, finishing Marx's great project.

Opening up the paper, it strikes you that the *Investor's Monthly Manual* is a far cry from *Castaing's Course of the Exchange* 150 years before: it quotes thousands of prices for securities from all over the world. Turning to section one, Moneybags could trace more than 204 government bonds from thirty-four different countries or colonies. In January 1870, however, government bonds were just a part of the world investment portfolio.

Moneybags could peruse more than 700 railway securities—bonds, stocks, and preferred shares that financed rail networks on every continent save Antarctica. Railroad investments equaled 1.1 billion pounds. Banks and other companies—including the new wave of intercontinental telegraph enterprises—accounted for another 53 million pounds. The dreams of Defoe and other visionaries who imagined the stock market as a vast pool of capital deployed for the betterment of society had finally come to fruition.

LABOR THEORY OF INVESTMENT VALUE

Think, for a moment, how Marx and Engels would interpret these massive numbers generated by capital markets. By 1870, the London Exchange quoted prices on roughly 3.6 billion pounds of financial assets, equivalent at the time to about two British pounds for each person on earth. Translated into units of labor, Karl Marx's preferred measure of value, the sum was even more staggering. A common laborer in London in the 1860s earned 20 shillings a week, or 52 pounds per year.[5] Assuming that a working life lasted for fifty years, the capital on the London Exchange was equal to 1.4 million working lifetimes of labor.

By 1870, Marx might have reckoned that the London capital market had distilled the working lives of a vast population of workers, first draining value through wage slavery, then transforming it into excess profit, and finally storing it as intangible paper capital priced daily on the exchange. Marx might have argued that these prices were an illusion—the numbers in the *Investor's Monthly Manual* were not real. The reality, in Marx's terms, was the labor that went into them. As our friend Moneybags contemplated the purchase of shares in a Vienna tramway company or the great Russian Railway on New Year's Day, 1870, was he a villain who lived by the exploitation of generations of laborers, or an investor willing to risk his economic future on modernization of the global infrastructure? Neither? Both?

Suppose we now think of the 3.6 billion pounds as the net savings that the British and other world investors held back from consumption up to 1870. Imagine that the capital came from their own labor, not the exploitation of others. It represents a vast transfer of labor value through time. The stored up capital could support 1.4 million people for fifty years at a London day laborer's rate. The population of Great Britain itself was roughly 20 million in 1870 so the financial market amounted to 180 pounds per person.

These numbers are a bit deceptive, since these same stocks and bonds also traded in other capital markets, such as Amsterdam, Paris, Berlin, and Brussels, and the total population of Europe was about 300 million in 1870. Yet by any measure, the technology of the London capital market was intermediating a vast amount of stored human energy between past and future. The countries and corporations that issued the bonds and stocks in effect promised the current value of this stored capital and more to the security holders. The investors expected to be able to spend this and more as they moved through their lives. Capital was not stolen labor but a vast reserve against the risk of an uncertain future. The London Stock Exchange in 1870 was a giant economic lever with the fulcrum planted in the present, balancing past savings and future promises.

MARKETS EVERYWHERE

Capital markets during the Victorian era had spread across the globe in a few short decades: faster than the spread of any religion. Between 1880 and 1910, more than half the world's markets were launched. Nowhere was change more evident than in the florescence of stock exchanges themselves. Suddenly, every nation needed a fountain of capital. Virtually every major capital city built a stock exchange building. It was a nineteenth-century symbol of modernity and progress, a new institutional structure that took its place beside the royal palace, the legislature building, and the palace of justice. Exchanges around the world altered the configuration of nineteenth-century cities; created new districts; and decorated themselves with pediments, columns, and new gods.

While many of these countries built exchanges, London was still the place where stocks and bonds were most often floated and traded. For example, although the New York Stock Exchange dates back to 1792, many American railroads in the 1880s sold the lion's share of their stocks and bonds in London. US western expansion was, in part, financed by British investors. The reason was simple. London was where the money was.

UNIVERSAL STOCK EXCHANGE

At the end of Pall Mall in the heart of London stands an imposing edifice that, a century ago, housed the Universal Stock Exchange, Ltd., a financial company catering to London investors speculating in the world's financial markets. The Universal Stock Exchange offered two advantages over the Stock Exchange of London. First, it took orders by telegraph—in effect it was an electronic exchange. Second, it was designed for cheap speculation. The Exchange gave traders three months to actually settle transactions. Instead of delivering shares or paying up within the customary two-week grace period, you could trade the share many times over without incurring settlement costs. Think of the Universal Stock Exchange as the forerunner of the modern on-line day trading platform—Karl Marx's worst nightmare.

Henry Lowenfeld, the genius behind the Universal Stock Exchange, is not remembered today as a giant of modern finance. After emigrating from Poland, he made a fortune in the brewery business, selling nonalcoholic ales during the height of the temperance movement. He later became a successful London theater entrepreneur. In 1889, Lowenfeld turned his talents as a businessman and keen observer of social trends to the vogue for securities market speculation. As he plunged into the brokerage business, however, Lowenfeld had a brilliant insight that inevitably induced people to buy more investments. He was convinced that the more different securities an investor bought, the safer his or her investment portfolio would be. He pioneered the modern science of diversification.

In 1909, Lowenfeld wrote the book *Investment: An Exact Science*, in which he proposed the theory of the Geographical Distribution of Capital, according to which a portfolio should be divided among securities from several different economic zones around the world: North America, South America, Africa, Northern Europe, Southern Europe, Russia,

China, and India. He noted that bonds from a given region tended to move together. For example, no matter how many British securities one held in the portfolio, they were all subject to the same common influence. In short, don't put all of your eggs in one basket:

> The Safety of Capital is obtained by dividing it (1) equally among a number of sound stocks (2) of identical quality, but (3) every stock [i.e., bond][6] must be subject to an entirely different market or trade influence . . . by market influence we mean the influence created by the general investment conditions obtaining on the Stock Exchange in which the stock is mainly dealt in.[7]

Lowenfeld proved his theory using graphs of price trends of securities traded on the Universal Stock Exchange from 1895 to 1906. His graphs showed how each country's bonds marched to a separate tune over the period: when one country went down, the others did not necessarily follow. Never mind the global crash of 1720. Lowenfeld concentrated on the recent past, the period of intense growth in the world markets. These data, once collected and studied, showed him that spreading investments internationally made the overall portfolio less risky. As a result, he reasoned, a truly diversified portfolio had to be spread over the entire world. And investors needed a convenient exchange to build such an ideal, modern diversified portfolio.

Lowenfeld constructed a beautiful example using only railway securities. Bonds from one industry in a single country are usually highly correlated, but the Lowenfeld portfolio invested equally in ten railroad bonds from around the world: British, Canadian, German, Sardinian, Indian, Egyptian, American, Mexican, Argentinean, and Spanish; all with about the same yield. The portfolio thus had the same expected return as a single railway bond, but combining international bonds together dramatically reduced volatility. Lowenfeld the magician pulled a rabbit from a hat. Into the hat goes a bunch of exotic securities from all over the globe. Out of it comes a surprisingly stable investment. Although scholars later in the twentieth century would formalize and generalize this discovery, Lowenfeld had hit on a great idea that, among other things, promoted the export of capital from London around the world. Paradoxically, he proved that investing in seemingly risky ventures around the globe was actually a safe thing to do.

GEOGRAPHICALLY DISTRIBUTED INVESTMENTS° PRODUCING 4 PER CENT. PER ANN.

Value £	Chart Shewing Movement of Value.	Geographical Division.	Quantities and Names of Stocks.	Table Shewing Annual Income.									
	1897 1898 1899 1900 1901 1902 1903 1904 1905 1906			1897	1898	1899	1900	1901	1902	1903	1904	1905	1906
1150		BRITISH.	① £1,000 India 3½% Stk.	£ 35	£ 35	£ 35	£ 35	£ 35	£ 35	£ 35	£ 35	£ 35	£ 35
1100		BRITISH COLONIES.	② £900 Canadian Pacific Rly. 4% Perp. Debs.	36	36	36	36	36	36	36	36	36	36
1050		EUROPE, NORTH.	③ £1,000 Russian 4% Cons. R. Rd. Bonds, Ser. I.	40	40	40	40	40	40	40	40	40	40
1000		EUROPE, SOUTH.	④ £1,000 Italian 5% Rentes†	40	40	40	40	40	40	40	40	40	40
950		ASIA.	⑤ £1,000 Japan 5% 1895–6	50	50	50	50	50	50	50	50	50	50
900		AFRICA.	⑥ £900 Cape Town 4% 1943	36	36	36	36	36	36	36	36	36	36
850		AMERICA, NORTH.	⑦ £1,100 Denver & Rio Grande 4% 1st Mtg. G. Bonds	44	44	44	44	44	44	44	44	44	44
800		AMERICA, CENTRAL.	⑧ £800 Mexican Railway 6% Debs.	48	48	48	48	48	48	48	48	48	48
750		AMERICA, SOUTH.	⑨ £900 Great Western Brazil Rly. 6% Perm. Debs.	54	54	54	54	54	54	54	54	54	54
		INTER-NATIONAL.	⑩ £900 International Invest. Trust 4% Perp. Debs...	36	36	36	36	36	36	36	36	36	36
£	10,185 10,096 10,146 10,021 9,965 10,176 10,022 9,882 10,196 10,165	Capital—Total Annual Values—Income £		419	419	419	419	419	419	419	419	419	419

* NOTE.—Geographical Division of Capital necessitates an equal division over similar stocks, every one of which is subject to a different trade influence. In the above Chart the conditions of similarity in quality and difference in trade influence only have been complied with, the Capital division is quite uneven. If an even Capital division had been adopted all zig-zag price lines would of necessity have started from the same point, and this would have made the Chart quite undecipherable. For this reason the above is not a perfect investment list from a practical point of view.
† Italian Tax of 20% deducted.

FIGURE 26. Chart from *Investment, an Exact Science*, by Henry Lowenfeld, showing the price movements of global bonds and how the movements cancel each other out to produce an even price path and coupon stream.

A LIVING PORTFOLIO

Lowenfeld's analysis was strikingly innovative, and his Universal Stock Exchange provided an efficient vehicle for investing in global markets. In some ways he was only advocating an investment approach that had long been practiced in the Netherlands and Great Britain. Recall from Chapter 22 that the Dutch mutual funds were created in the eighteenth century to diversify across international bond investments. The same concept was introduced in Great Britain by the Foreign and Colonial Government Trust (F&C) in 1868 as a securities holding company. Founded by well-connected Conservative Party solicitor Phillip Rose, the F&C held a portfolio of mostly high-yielding international bonds: Egyptian, Italian, Peruvian, Spanish, Russian, Austrian, Turkish, Danubian, Australian, Nova Scotian, US, Brazilian, and Portuguese; with yields ranging from 5% (New South Wales) to 15% (Turkey).[8] Any single one of these bonds might have gone bust (in fact some did) but bundled together, they provided ample insurance against loss. The financial historian Ben Chabot, who has collected and analyzed an extraordinary amount of data about the British market in the nineteenth century, took a close look at the performance of the first British investment funds and concluded that, while they generally lagged the market as a whole, they provided stability, and better still, broad diversification for ordinary investors.[9]

Stable indeed. The F&C is still around today, managing billions of pounds of investor assets—a survivor of two world wars, the Great Depression, and of course the financial crisis of 2008. The firm's portfolio is a living thing—long since changed to focus on equities rather than fixed income. However, the essential feature that made it work from the start is that it held people's money in trust, spread it across securities, passed through dividends, and allowed investors to cash out by selling shares. Formed a year after the first volume of *Das Kapital* appeared in print, F&C removed as much as possible the element of speculative risk from investing. Rather than trying to pick winners and losers in the world markets, funds like the F&C allowed people to earn the average; and in a booming world economy, as Henry Lowenfeld's statistical analysis showed, the average was often good enough.

In counterpoint to Karl Marx, Lowenfeld wrote about the public securities market as a huge benefit to society, a means by which ordinary savers could participate in global expansion and economic growth, a way of freeing up capital for socially productive investment. He advocated investing by all members of society, especially the working class. The more money invested in the capital markets, the greater would be the growth of industry and the more employment for the workers. And ultimately, with judicious diversification, the creation of a nest egg for future retirement would be made possible. For Marx, financial capitalism was an instrument of doom for the working class; for Lowenfeld, it was a means to security. It did, however, have unintended political consequences.

HOBSON'S IMPERIALISM

In this chapter, we examine how corporate finance and the political ecology around it set the stage for global conflicts and revolutions in the modern era. It begins with the British liberal tradition of self-criticism. The chief spokesman against British overseas investment before the First

World War was the economic writer John A. Hobson. Hobson today is recognized as an important economist and political observer, but in his lifetime he was marginalized by the academic community as a Marxist ideologue. Today we might call Hobson a "public intellectual," a popular commentator on world events. Hobson's 1902 book *Imperialism: A Study* is his masterwork. It took up the banner of Karl Marx and argued that European nations had embarked on a disastrous course of world colonization driven by a capitalistic quest for profits. At great military and economic expense Europe had extended its political control over much of the rest of the world. The driver was excess capital acquired through capitalistic savings, and the desire to minimize investor risk:

> Investors who have put their money in foreign lands, upon terms which take full account of risks connected with the political conditions of the country, desire to use the resources of their Government to minimise these risks, and so to enhance the capital value and the interest of their private investments. The investing and speculative classes in general also desire that Great Britain should take other foreign areas under her flag in order to secure new areas for profitable investment and speculation.[10]

In Hobson's view, wealthy investors—perhaps even the managers of the Foreign and Colonial Government Trust—inevitably pushed the government to protect their overseas investments.

An immediate drawback of Hobson's argument, however, is that for every buyer there is a seller. Although European investors were pushing their governments to look after their foreign investments, the stocks and bonds issued by emerging market nations were voluntary. Governments and companies around the world floated loans on the London Exchange of their own volition. A vast number of the securities traded in London paid for modernization, new technology, and infrastructure. The railroads, canals, tramways, and electrical grids in North America, Russia, South America, China, and Africa were built with European investor money. Imperialism and development were two sides of the same coin. Finance was a great international equalizer. Ethiopia, for example, could have railways every bit as good as Scotland's, provided it had access to capital markets. All investors wanted was a fair return on capital and some assurance that the loans would be paid back.

One such assurance was collateral. For example, if bondholders financed the construction of a railway in China, they felt that they should get that railway back if the government defaulted on loan payments. Governments understood this need for assurance and often pledged property rights or tax revenues from government monopolies on such things as salt and tobacco. The question is, did governments have the right to makes such pledges? Could a profligate ruler borrow against the nation's assets and then default, leaving the assets in the hands of foreigners? Sovereign default raised the fundamental questions of political legitimacy.

IN DEBT TO *AIDA*

Verdi's *Aida* is still the most lavish opera ever conceived. Commissioned by Ismail Pasha, the Ottoman-appointed ruler of Egypt, it opened in Cairo in 1871 and dazzled an audience of international diplomats. Its magnificent staging with Egyptian monumental motifs is still a crowd pleaser more than 140 years after its premier—I'll never forget seeing the giant props for *Aida* being assembled in the great Roman amphitheater of Verona; a double anachronism. Although unbelievably costly, *Aida* achieved what Ismail sought: international recognition of Egypt as a modern nation-state and closer cultural ties between his country and Europe.

Ismail Pasha was one of the most aggressive foreign borrowers on the international debt markets. He became the khedive of Egypt, an Ottoman protectorate, in 1863 and began immediately to modernize his nation by building infrastructure and adapting to Western culture and tastes. His most famous proclamation:

> My country is no longer in Africa; we are now part of Europe. It is therefore natural for us to abandon our former ways and to adopt a new system adapted to our social conditions.[11]

His most spectacular success was the opening of the Suez Canal in 1869—as much a feat of finance as hydrology. The capital for the project was raised by the private firm Compagnie universelle du canal maritime de Suez, founded in 1858 by the brilliant diplomat and projector Ferdinand de Lesseps. The company negotiated a deal with Ismail's predecessor that exchanged shares in the firm for a long-term operating concession. The details of this deal reveal the basic tension of European overseas investment and Hobsonian imperialism.

The Suez company was actually an Egyptian corporation that, by agreement with the Egyptian government, was subject to French company law.[12] Egyptian legal infrastructure at that time was insufficient to define and protect shareholder rights. The enormous capital needed could not be raised without a trustworthy corporate code. The deal also involved a territorial concession. While the canal remained Egyptian, the company had full rights to develop and manage the property. In effect the firm acquired a long-term land lease cutting through Egypt. The board of directors and top management of the Suez company resided in France and from there oversaw the Egyptian operations.

Theoretically, despite French governance of an Egyptian firm, the Suez company remained effectively under the khedive's control. In Egypt's name he retained 44% of the shares and received 15% of the future revenues of the canal. This complicated structure seemingly preserved Egyptian territorial integrity while attracting global investment capital.

By 1875, Ismail's indebtedness became an international problem. He evidently miscalculated the benefits of modernization and territorial expansion. Unable to make payments to foreign bondholders, he was forced to sell his shares in the Suez company to Great Britain. The acquisition, engineered by Benjamin Disraeli, brought the canal under British control—even though this political control took the form of British ownership in an Egyptian corporation administered under French company law. Hoping to recover their investment, foreign debt holder associations pushed for direct control of the khedive's finances, which he relinquished in 1878. A few short years after the triumph of *Aida*, Ismail turned the administration of Egypt over to an Anglo-French consortium. A later division of control resulted in the French obtaining Libya in exchange for Egypt going to Britain.

Egyptians were incensed at this foreign control, particularly since the revenues from the canal were minimal and the benefits from modernization were slight. With the financial takeover, the major revenue-generating asset of the nation was in British hands, leaving Egyptians with no fiscal control. While long ruled from afar by the Ottomans, the country bristled at a European takeover.

In 1882, Colonel Ahmed Urabi led a democratic revolt to overturn the British occupation. His popular rallying cry was democracy. The Ottoman-appointed Ismail had burdened the Egyptian people with an impossible international debt. Egyptian citizens had no voice in the matter, and yet they were responsible for its repayment. Foreign managers of Egyptian finances now sought only to extract money to repay foreign debtholders.

The Urabi revolt started in Alexandria in June with attacks on foreigners and spread throughout Egypt. British gunboats bombarded the port city, eventually defeating the rebellion at the battle of Tel el-Kebir. What began as a sovereign debt crisis turned inexorably into imperialism; the catalyst, of course, being the control of the strategically vital Suez Canal.

The fall of Egypt into debt, even as it was furiously modernizing itself with foreign capital, was a warning to all nations. One moment Ismail Pasha was entertaining European dignitaries in the Cairo Opera house, the next he was stripped of his wealth and power by the same. Even worse, his subjects were made to pay for his excess. It was the same story of debt and servitude played out since ancient times. In the modern version, however, national sovereignty was at stake. The colonization of the world in the seventeenth and eighteenth centuries was the result of national protection of international trade by the great trading nations Britain, Spain, the Netherlands, Portugal, and France. In contrast, the mechanism by which sovereignty was relinquished in the nineteenth century increasingly took the form of contractual default. The defense of investor rights justified the erosion of sovereignty. Financial contracting had reached a critical point in history—it now played a major role in rearranging political control.

Strangely enough, even though John A. Hobson pointed out the fundamental conflict of interest between money-center investors and the developing world, he held that imperialism was a great pacifier. In a series of essays on investment written for Lowenfeld's pet journal, the *Financial Review of Reviews*, Hobson reasoned that the complex web of interdependent international financial markets and institutions guaranteed that no major country would even consider attacking another.[13] In his view, if Germany were to attack Great Britain, the interest of German savers would be hurt as much as those of Great Britain. No country that exported its capital could afford to rupture its financial ties with another. The global markets were, in effect, a pact of mutually ensured financial destruction. Although revolts like Egypt's might break out on the periphery of the financial world, the center must hold. If the colonies and quasi-colonies of the European powers occasionally fought the harness of imperialism, the ultimate state of the world must tend toward pacifism enforced by interested investors and the nations that served them. How remarkably wrong he was.

CHINA'S FINANCIERS

The Egyptian experience was replicated in other countries—one of these was China. China's encounter with European finance is a complex and interesting story that underscores some of the best and worst features of capitalism. Although China endured gradual financial colonialism through the nineteenth century, Chinese officials and entrepreneurs also rapidly adopted state-of-the-art tools of finance and developed them to their own purposes. Thus by the early twentieth century, Shanghai was a major financial center with important banks and stock markets that funded both private enterprise and China's key infrastructure development projects. Chinese investors, like investors in the rest of the world, caught the bug of speculation. The markets boomed with the prospects of new businesses like the rubber trade and crashed with shocks to the banking and financial systems. The Chinese markets served an expanding based of individual investors. Chinese entrepreneurs managed their way through a multicultural world of foreign competition, wars, and the complexities of an eroding nation-state to lead China into the modern world economy. By 1905, Chinese officials had adopted corporate governance and a sophisticated corporate legal code that formed the basis for the transition to successful private corporate ownership. However, China's Communist Revolution in 1949 reinterpreted this success story in stark terms as colonial exploitation by the capitalistic West. There is a germ of truth in their revisionist history. China's financial modernization resulted from the weakening of the central government and erosion of sovereignty. It also began with a dangerous drug.

ADDICTION IS A VALUE PROPOSITION

The opium trade is one of the most shameful episodes in the history of finance. By the late eighteenth century, the British East India Company

Offices of China Merchants Steamship Navigation Company, at the Bund in Shanghai. The company, launched in 1872, was China's first publicly held and traded corporation.

had a well-developed trade network that imported opium from India into China. It served a key purpose for the firm. It was a natural exchange commodity to balance the British export of Chinese tea. Payments for tea in hard currency—silver—could be offset by sales of opium in the British trade port of Canton. The dangers of this trade were well recognized by Chinese rulers. Despite various attempts at embargo, by the 1830s it represented one of the most important traded commodities in the world. Smoking opium in China was legal but destructive. The profits to investors in the British East India Company made the opium trade attractive, and the Chinese government profited from the arrangement as well. In 1834, the British East India Company lost its monopoly, and the opium trade was open to competition. The opium trade fell to a handful of competitive merchant firms, among them the partnerships of Jardine, Matheson and Company, Russell and Company, and Dent and Company.

The last of these, Dent and Company, made a fortune buying opium in Calcutta and importing it to Canton, despite increasing Chinese insistence that the British end the opium trade. In 1839, the governor of Canton, Lin Zexu [林則徐], was tasked with reasserting Chinese authority and stopping the opium trade. He starting by imprisoning Lancelot Dent and seizing and destroying the firm's store of opium. Lin went on to force all the foreign merchants to turn over their opium stores: 2.6 million pounds in total. Disagreement over compensation for the seized opium sparked the First Opium War.

Despite sympathetic voices in Parliament supporting China's right to end the scourge of opium and an outraged global press that recognized the naked self-interest of British trade, commercial interests and diplomatic might won out. British gunboats forced China to open her ports to the opium trade. The treaty of Nanking, signed in 1842, gave British merchants trading rights in five treaty ports: Canton, Amoy, Foochow, Ningpo, and Shanghai.[1] Once restricted to just Canton, now British traders could move their lucrative tea and opium trade to several ports along the Chinese coast.

THE GREAT CONVERGENCE

Although the opium trade was the proximate cause of the First Opium War, a deeper issue was the right of China as a sovereign nation to control its borders and hold foreign merchants accountable to its laws. The First Opium War represented a critical erosion of Chinese sovereignty. The Second Opium War (1856–1860) went a step further, culminating in the looting and near-complete destruction of the Old Summer Palace in Beijing. It completed a process of forcing China to allow foreign trade and accommodate a system of extraterritorial rights by foreign commercial interests.

An additional result of the Opium Wars was the ceding, by long-term lease, of Hong Kong to the British and a reparations settlement from China to Britain and her allied participants—first for the price of the burned opium and second for the cost of pursuing the wars. The reparations for the First Opium War were 21 million dollars over a three-year period at 5% accrued interest. The collection of the tribute was overseen by a British official controlling the tariffs collected at the treaty ports—in effect, removing Chinese sovereignty over an important portion of government revenues. The oversight of maritime customs at the treaty ports later became an important institutional feature of Chinese finance.

This structure was of course a boon to China trade, particularly for the British firms but also for American entrepreneurs, who staked their claims in the treaty ports as well. It became a vector for Western business practices and financial technology into China. Although China by the late nineteenth century had a number of financial institutions—including a native banking system and a smattering of share companies that financed enterprises, such as salt mining and agriculture—these were not limited liability firms nor were their shares traded on stock exchanges. It essentially took a foreign incursion to plant the seeds of modern finance in Chinese markets. However, when it began to grow, it grew in its own distinct way.

Although the Chinese ethos of crowding out private enterprise and government control of business had a long history, by the First Opium War, Britain's own rules against public share issuance were still in place. Under British law deriving from the Bubble Act of 1720, the free incorporation of a limited liability company by British subjects was still sharply constrained. Firms had gotten around this stricture in Britain by forming share associations without limited liability, but the freedom to set up corporations as we know them today was not available. The few companies that did so had to negotiate terms with Parliament. This weak structure in the early nineteenth-century British equity finance made the launching of a major corporation in British-governed Shanghai a remarkable project.

In 1865, a group of Hong Kong merchants and British officials, including John Dent of Dent and Company; Arthur Sassoon of Sassoon and Sons; and Thomas Sutherland, the superintendent of the Hong Kong docks and chair of the Peninsular and Oriental Steamship Company, launched the Hong Kong Shanghai Banking Company, now known as HSBC. The firm was granted corporate status in 1866—only a decade after Britain had finally relaxed the controls on domestic enterprises to operate as limited liability corporations. This long-awaited freedom occurred by means of a series of parliamentary acts culminating in the Joint Stock Companies Act of 1856. The Hong Kong Shanghai Banking Company—situated as it was in a British-controlled treaty port halfway around the world—still required special permission, which it ultimately obtained. It floated its shares in Hong Kong first and then did a second offering six months later in Shanghai.

Well connected from the beginning, HSBC became not only a major merchant bank financing China trade but also the repository of the Chinese maritime customs revenues. Based on these, it extended loans to the Chinese government based on future customs revenues. In a sense, HSBC managed the Chinese government's transition to the modern methods of deficit government spending. Loans against maritime customs receipts were arranged repeatedly in the early days of HSBC. For example, in 1866, the governor of Fukien, Tso Tsung-t'ang, borrowed against them to put down a rebellion. In 1877, HSBC underwrote the Chinese government's first international financing with a 5 million tael (a Chinese silver currency unit) loan.[2] This was the final step in Chinese government's reconnection with Western-style sovereign debt, after the great financial divergence that began with the Venetian prestiti (see Chapter 10).

Notwithstanding the taint of its founders' hand in the opium trade, HSBC played a crucial role as repository, intermediary, and underwriter throughout the process of China's adoption of modern finance. Thus in China—as in Europe—it turned out to be a weakened government's needs for finance that led to the adoption of bond issuance.

A global institution founded in Shanghai under the auspices newly revamped British company law emerged as a key catalyst for the adoption of a new financial technology. Ultimately, a series of international loans, many of which were arranged by HSBC and floated in London, Belgium, Paris, Saint Petersburg, and other European capitals, financed the development of China's major railroads and infrastructure in the late nineteenth and early twentieth centuries. The process of securing these loans with customs revenues and other specified taxes gave international investors comfort about the likelihood of repayment. They also eventually became a sticking point with the Chinese people.

ENTREPRENEURS AND THE CHINESE WAY

The first Western firms in Canton—the only port open prior to the First Opium War—were required to use officially sanctioned Chinese intermediaries. This requirement was eliminated in 1843, but the practice continued. Trading firms were locally managed to a significant extent by Chinese administrators, referred to historically as compradors. Compradors were the Chinese agents of the trading firms, but they also served as intermediaries who took a cut on the exchange of the commodities trade: opium, silk, tea, and cotton. As key employees of foreign firms, they enjoyed extraterritorial rights, and their intermediary position gave them opportunities to trade on their own accounts. With the opening up of additional treaty ports, the comprador system also expanded, and Cantonese merchants were well placed. A key feature of the comprador is that he interfaced with Chinese domestic enterprises, the network of connections based on trust, guarantees, and the extended family.[3] By the same token, the firm's comprador vouched to this network for the trustworthiness of the Western company. Failure to deliver by either side represented a liability to the comprador, and for this he was typically well compensated.

A number of compradors became extremely wealthy; however, most importantly, they acquired financial know-how. Compradors were expert in not only two (or more) languages but were also expert in the two financial systems. Their arbitrage between East and West extended to more than intermediating commodities and manufactured goods; they intermediated financial technology. This intermediation took the form of participation in banking and the launching of China's own stock exchange.

One Cantonese family in particular played a key role in introducing new financial techniques. Xu Rongcun [許榮村] (1822–1873) was the lead comprador for Dent and Company. He made as fortune as a very young man in the silk trade but is most famous for sponsoring the exhibition of Chinese silk in the London World Expo of 1852. Thus, while he served Dent, he was also a successful entrepreneur in his own right. Xu brought his nephew, Xu Run [徐潤] (1838–1911) into Dent. Xu Run took over from his uncle as head comprador in the Shanghai office of Dent and Company in 1861, leaving in 1868 to develop his own businesses—among these was a vast, highly leveraged property empire in Shanghai.

Xu Run was Dent's Shanghai comprador when Dent and Company officials organized the flotation of shares in the Hong Kong Shanghai Banking Corporation in 1865—first in Hong Kong and then six months later in Shanghai. Thus, not only was Xu Run deeply knowledgeable about Dent's merchant trade, he was also quite likely involved in HSBC's public offering in Shanghai. As such, he would have seen firsthand how a corporation was created and shares were floated.

Chinese compradors were actively investing in many of the companies launched in treaty ports in the nineteenth century. In a curious echo of the financial innovations in 1720, some of these were insurance and shipping firms. Chinese merchants invested significant capital in the Union Insurance Company of Macao (1835), the Canton Insurance Company (1836), Yangtze Insurance Association (1862), North-China Insurance Company (1863), and four additional insurance companies prior to 1871.[4] W. A. Thomas, historian of the Shanghai Exchange, estimates that Chinese investors—merchants and compradors—represented as much as 40–50% of investor capital in the companies launched in Shanghai from the 1860s on. Thus, not only did the introduction of the public corporation to China provide a new means to finance enterprise (particularly in the shipping and marine insurance sectors), it also was a means for Chinese investors to diversify their holdings. To the extent that Chinese merchants had a major stake in firms that were set up and managed by foreigners, the distribution of equity stakes in these firms aligned the interests of Chinese and British traders in these enterprises. A Chinese merchant with a significant stake in an insurance or shipping company would be more likely to send business its way. As British business expanded rapidly with the opening of the treaty ports, Chinese merchants were among the capitalists financing the expansion. Historian Yen-p'ing Hao [郝延平] argues that compradors not only supplied much of the expertise, but also much of the entrepreneurial capital for development of businesses in treaty ports in the late nineteenth century.[5]

SELF-STRENGTHENING

As China opened up economically to international trade, Chinese officials and merchants became keenly aware of the rapid technological advances taking place in the world—from the modernization of transportation systems to advances in weaponry and defense. China's "Self-Strengthening Movement" was an effort by Chinese leaders to adopt these new technologies and use them to build a powerful, independent Chinese nation that did not have to rely on foreign know-how for its growth. Among the leading lights of the Self-Strengthening Movement was Li Hongzhang [李鸿章], the governor of a large area of southeastern China—Kiansu. The key ingredients of the movement were the acquisition of knowledge and technological expertise, and the adoption of Western-style financing to equalize China's access to capital for development. Li helped a number of Chinese students study overseas, and his foresight bore fruit. One of these was Yale graduate Yung Wing [容闳], a former employee of Dent and Company.

In 1867, Yung Wing returned to China and brought with him the idea of using public corporations to develop China's key industries. He had seen how the capital market in the United States channeled funds to build major infrastructure, such as canals and railroads. Why not use the same methods to raise capital for such projects in China?

Yung Wing's idea was to start with a crucial transportation link: shipping. His vision came to fruition in 1872 with the founding of the China Merchants Steamship Navigation Company in Shanghai.[6] Up to this time, China's merchant trade was heavily dependent on foreign-held shipping companies, such as the British-owned Peninsular and Oriental Steamship Company. Even though Chinese compradors were investors in many of these firms, they recognized foreign ownership as a key national vulnerability.

Yung Wing's former classmate, Tong King-sing [唐景星], was the comprador for Jardine's in Shanghai, but he resigned that post to become the general manager of the China Merchants Steamship Navigation Company. Li Hongzhang recruited other leading businessmen as sponsors—chief among them, Xu Run. Xu Run essentially operated as the main promoter and underwriter of the shares of the company, buying on his own account and encouraging other Shanghai merchants to follow his lead. At one point he was directly or indirectly responsible for raising half the capital of the firm.

Xu's experience must have been useful. He saw how HSBC was able to garner a central role in Chinese finance by including powerful foreign merchant firms among its founders. In a sense, HSBC was a financial tool for its major shareholders. The same principle could make the China Merchants Steamship Navigation Company powerful as well. If the major Shanghai merchants both held shares in the firm and exclusively used its services, then their transportation fees would effectively be paid back out to them in dividends.

A novel feature of the company was the proviso that shares could only be owned by Chinese nationals. The aim of the venture was to adopt Western means of financing to modernize China's infrastructure. Similar Chinese-only companies were launched to fund mines, mills, arsenals, and a telegraph company. Thus, in a kind of "big bang," China formed a suite of Western-inspired corporations to lead its modernization and take back control of its development from the West. In addition, it put its own spin on the process. China Merchants Steamship Navigation Company was organized and governed in a distinctive Chinese manner.

It and the other domestic Chinese joint-stock companies were structured under the *guandu shangban* [官督商辦] system ("Official Supervision and Merchant Management"), which explicitly reserved a board role for government officials. This joint government-merchant structure was borrowed from the organization of the Chinese salt monopoly, for which merchants provided capital, and government officials controlled production quotas.[7] This structure reflected the age-old ideal of an enlightened official governing a profit-making business to ensure that public interests were properly represented. Of course, we have seen the deeper roots of this kind of joint public-private structure earlier in Chinese history (see Chapter 9). It can rightly be regarded as a financial innovation—a new re-configuration of corporate governance that sought to reconcile the traditional Chinese governmental control and value extraction with modern corporate forms. The question is whether this new experiment would succeed.

A couple of problems emerged. First, the guandu shangban structure requires an enlightened, as opposed to a self-interested, government official. When this condition is not met, the structure is ripe for exploitation. For example, the government official appointed to oversee the privatization of the China Merchants Steamship Navigation Company in 1895 acquired a significant stake in the firm as a result.[8] Second, the government set a high bar for dividend payouts. The firms distributed profits as opposed to retaining them, and the government share in these was substantial. It drained the resources of the company and eroded its long-term viability.

Li himself recognized the potential problems of heavy-handed government control. In its early years, he was able to shield the firm from intervention, but ultimately the government exerted control, and the result was mismanagement, misuse of funds, and a poor return to shareholders.[9] Indeed, the government's hand in the pot made it difficult to attract investors. The handful of domestic enterprises founded in the 1870s along with the China Merchants Steamship Navigation Company continued to trade, but the share market failed to immediately unlock the flood of private capital that could stimulate Chinese development and build firms to rival Western incorporated enterprises operating in China.

While Li Hongzhang was a visionary who recognized the potential for funding enterprise through joint-stock companies, the firms he sponsored survived more because of his personal patronage and the quasi-monopoly they enjoyed rather than their capacity for attracting investment. When he stepped down as governor, he was no longer able to defend his favored firms from competition.

China's first experiment with corporate capitalism was based on a model of official patronage that had benefits and drawbacks. Powerful officials could exhort merchants to fund the enterprises— and could offer governmental benefits of various sorts in return for capital investment. However, this structure was not robust to succession.

Over the course of the nineteenth century, China worked through the development of its own financial institutional structure for domestic companies. In the 1880s for example, the government tried out a *guangshang heban* [官商合辦] structure, which gave more autonomy to the merchants and private investors, but it did not entirely work. The catalyst for the development of China's stock markets was actually the loss to Japan in the Sino-Japanese War and the Treaty of Shimonoseki, which allowed foreigners not only to trade in Chinese treaty ports but also to set up and own manufacturing enterprises in China. After the treaty, the government had to extend the same rights to domestic Chinese entrepreneurs.

As a result, there was a boom in the founding of private enterprises after 1895. Between 1895 and 1916, for example, thirty-five new cotton mills, eighty new weaving mills, and thirty-five new mining companies were founded. The number of guangshang heban enterprises was meager in comparison.

Elisabeth Köll is a Chinese historian at Harvard Business School whose approach to understanding the emergence of early corporations in China is to dig into the details of how these companies actually worked. One of her research projects is an analysis of a major textile company, Dasheng Cotton Mills [大生紗廠], formed in 1895 in the wake of the treaty of Nanjing. It began as a government-sponsored initiative near the city of Nantong northwest of Shanghai.[10] Zhang Jian [張謇], a progressive government reformer, launched the firm on the public-private model. The firm enjoyed the strong support of the governor-general of Jiangsu province Zhang Zhidong [張之洞], another progressive politician; however, he did not directly participate in the firm's governance. The crucial transformation of Chinese companies from guandu shangban to private enterprise on the Western corporate model ultimately minimized Zhang Zhidong's role. Dasheng Cotton Mills operated very much on a Western corporate model. It issued shares, it held annual shareholder meetings, and its books were audited. It registered under the company act in 1905 and was recognized as a limited liability company in 1907.

Although it weaned itself away from government control and patronage, Dasheng was not exactly a model of shareholder democracy. Although Zhang Jian and his family owned a minority of the shares, they essentially controlled the firm. Elisabeth Köll found active shareholder resistance to the Zhang family's use of corporate resources. Shareholders complained at meetings about the use of company funds to support the Tong school of the Zhang family clan, about management compensation, and also about the lack of independence of the auditors, who were chosen from among firm management. The fact that the board provided a forum for this discussion and the minutes dutifully recorded this dissent suggests that shareholder democracy had begun to take root. Alas, board reform curtailed the voices of some of the most outspoken shareholders.

Interestingly enough, the Dasheng company survives to the present day. Although it was nationalized, it is currently a limited liability company called Jiangsu Dasheng [江蘇大生] Group Company, a highly successful textile manufacturer. On its website it pays tribute to its founder, Zhang Jian.

RAILWAYS AND REVOLUTION

Another boom in share issuance occurred after 1904, when China officially adopted its corporate law based on Western models. A host of Chinese railway companies were launched to compete with foreign firms, which were able to issue stocks and bonds on the international capital markets. Partial inspiration for these firms also came from Chinese observations of railway finance in Europe. Ma Jianzhong [馬建忠] was an overseas Chinese student a generation after Yung Wing, who graduated from the École Libre des Sciences Politiques. In 1876, he wrote back to his sponsors about the power of the Paris bond market:

> It seems that these countries can draw on a source as vast and copious as a wellspring or river. By what means do they bring about such a situation? They ensure firstly that they gain the people's trust, secondly that they have a clear method of borrowing, and thirdly that they repay the loans within a fixed time period.[11]

The China Railway Rights Recovery Movement during 1894–1911 raised national fervor for domestic control over its rapidly growing rail networks. Before this movement, most Chinese railways were financed, built, and controlled by non-Chinese firms. The imperial government negotiated rail concessions to French, Belgian, German, Russian, British, and American companies, allowing them to run track through vast stretches of China, enjoying such things as extraterritorial rights and independence from Chinese courts.

Chinese entrepreneurs figured that they could launch companies to compete for these same concessions. The domestic railway firms raised strong nationalistic sentiments, and some speculative fervor among Chinese investors, but ultimately most failed due to lack of both capital and expertise.

For example, a railway company was formed in 1905 by merchants and officials to link the two major provincial capitals in the Chinese region known then as Huguang [湖廣], an area encompassing parts of modern Hunan [湖南], and Hubei [湖北]. The consortium of investors had successfully lobbied the imperial government to cancel the development rights of a J.P. Morgan–sponsored venture that had failed to meet its deadlines. The Chinese project met with considerable investor enthusiasm. The *North China Herald* reported that:

> Not only are the monied classes rushing to buy shares but the poorest of the poor who are supposed to have no cash to spare and hardly enough to keep body and soul together are buying up more and more shares.[12]

The Railway Rights Recovery Movement drove the dream of self-financed industrial growth down to a grassroots level in China. The notion of Chinese shareholder empowerment was not simply something that a few big merchants in the treaty ports dreamed of. The railway rights movement spread it across the country. The railways symbolized not just a new technology for linking a vast country, but also a means of regaining Chinese control over its own development—by unlocking the hidden power of China's own capital reserves. These reserves were the savings of ordinary Chinese, who were persuaded that self-financing was empowerment.

But the domestic firms were hastily formed and not typically well managed. Although some of them attracted the best and brightest—like the Yale-educated engineer Zhan Tian, who successfully constructed China's first domestically funded railway from Beijing to Zhangjiakou [張家口]—many fell prey to corruption and lack of managerial and technical expertise.

Not surprisingly, these new railway companies also did not enjoy the complete support of the imperial government, which preferred to horse-trade development rights with global financial companies like J.P. Morgan and saw less benefit from granting rights to develop trans-provincial railway lines to local firms.

In 1911, ostensibly because of the lack of progress in construction (but also likely due to external pressure from international financial interests), the imperial government nationalized all domestic railway companies. It essentially shut down the Railway Rights Recovery Movement. It then issued the Huguang Railway loan organized by a J.P. Morgan syndicate to finance a foreign-managed Huguang Railway. The loan was secured by a host of taxes on interprovincial tariffs as well as salt and rice taxes. In effect, the loan took back a major concession from domestic investors—the concession that was so eagerly subscribed by rich and poor alike in 1905—and handed it to foreigners and collateralized it with taxes on the people.

The response was immediate. The people of Chengdu [成都] in Sichuan [四川] marched on the official residence of the viceroys, protesting railway nationalization. Sentries fired into the crowd, killing thirty-two people. The people in Sichuan refused to pay taxes and levies. The government sent in the army. The general and the provincial viceroys were both killed. Sichuan declared independence in September 1911, and by October, the Prince Regent Chun [醇親王] had abdicated in the name of the child-emperor. The imperial government was replaced by the Republic of China.

Zhang Zhidong and Zhang Jian both played important roles in the revolution. Zhang Zhidong was the commander of the troops who sided with the rebels against the imperial army in 1911, and Zhang Jian was appointed minister of enterprise in the new government formed in 1913. Thus the first Chinese revolution had an interesting Dasheng connection. Fault lines of loyalties ran along disputes between local versus imperial control of China's economic and commercial development.

Of the many examples of finance as a disruptive technology, this is one of the most striking. While the civil unrest in China that led to the overthrow of the imperial government cannot be solely attributed to the dispute over railway concessions and the public reaction to the onerous Huguang Railway loan, the dramatic shift in financial architecture and the dramatic power shift from local to global control were certainly important catalysts. China had rapidly adopted the financial tool of joint-stock financing and with it came a powerful realignment of allegiance and a change in expectations among an ever-widening set of participants in the equity market. An unintended consequence of China's experiment with shareholder democracy, and the funding of new physical technologies, was that it was not easily controlled either by the guandu shangban organization, or by imperial granting and withdrawing of concessions. Chinese people had literally bought in to a financial arrangement that many had hoped would allow them to participate in the rapid transformation of their nation.

Through the comprador system and the travels of Chinese students overseas sent specifically to learn about modernization—both financial and technical—China quickly absorbed the lessons of corporate capitalism over the course of only forty years or so. Chinese merchants and officials rapidly learned to float shares, launch banks, build railroads, and access global markets for government bonds. They did this despite the foreign exploitation that began the Opium Wars, and imposed reparations, extraterritorial concessions, and treaties that eroded sovereign control of its borders and its trade.

It is tempting to interpret this narrative as evidence consistent with the hypothesis that financial innovation is a consequence of political weakness and not strength. However, a more conservative view is simply that China's rapid period of financial innovation in the nineteenth and the early twentieth centuries had surprising and unintended consequences. In this respect, the Chinese revolution of 1911 has more similarities to the American Revolution of the eighteenth century than one might at first expect. In the American case, local officials had their own ideas about economic development and chafed under the control of a central government. In America, taxes, land companies, and constraints on foreign trade were the catalysts. In China, heavy-handed imperial control of development played a major part.

THE SHANGHAI STOCK MARKET

What happened to the Chinese markets after the formation of the new republic? There were signs of weakness and strength. Yuan Shikai [袁世凱], the president of the Republic of China, did not restore the domestic rights of local railroads. Instead the financially strapped government was forced immediately to borrow on foreign capital markets to fund its recovery. The China Reorganization Loan of 1913 was floated by a consortium of Great Britain, Germany, France, and Russia. The United States refused to participate on principle. The loan extracted even more extreme concessions from the new Chinese government—in effect, it promised not to defend itself from the funding nations.

After the revolution, China was wracked by political instability in a time known as "the Warlord Period." It defaulted on many of its sovereign debts in 1921, although those backed by the maritime customs revenues continued to pay. By 1939, virtually all Chinese debt was in default. One might think that Chinese finance was moribund by this point. Not so. By 1939, Shanghai was one of the great financial centers of the world. Its banks were a major source of merchant financing. Much of Shanghai's world-famous Bund—a majestic wall of grand financial edifices facing the city waterfront, was built in the early twentieth century. And China's stock market thrived. Despite political and economic turmoil, the commercial and financial infrastructure of China boomed.

Recall that HSBC was financed by the floatation of shares in 1865, and China's domestic-only market for shares was launched in 1872 with the creation of the China Merchants Steamship Navigation Company. From that point on, both domestic and foreign shares traded vigorously and were listed in both the English-language and the Chinese-language newspapers.

By 1870, for example, the *North China Herald* quoted prices on thirty-one companies, six banks (including HSBC), seven shipping companies, three dock companies, three gas companies, five marine insurance companies, three fire insurance companies, two bridge companies, a racquet club, and a "recreation fund." By 1913, the year of the Reorganization Loan, the number of quoted firms had grown to 109. In that same year, the New York newspapers only regularly quoted sixty-six firms—although the British stock list was far, far greater. Up to 1939, when the Japanese occupation curtailed normal market operations, the Shanghai exchange was a major equity market. Virtually all the firms it quoted were companies doing business in Shanghai and East Asia: banks, property companies, docks, utilities, Shanghai manufacturing firms, and rubber companies.

China's domestic-only stock market—the brainchild of Li Hongzhang, Xu Run, and other Chinese modernizers—followed a slightly different path. We know a lot more about the course of these early shares thanks to Li Zhou, a former Yale student who collected considerable new price data from the Shanghai newspaper *Shenbao* [申報] for 1882–1887 and for 1908–1912.

In 1882, a decade after Xu Run helped launch the China Merchants Steamship Navigation Company, shares in thirty-three domestic Chinese firms actively traded in Shanghai, including companies involved in mining, insurance, commodities, utilities, manufacturing, and transportation and a property company. Most traded at a premium to par, meaning they were priced at about the level of their original issuance. Some, like the mining and transportation sector, were priced a third to a half higher, meaning that the prices had grown substantially in the first decade, even with high dividend payouts to investors and the relatively inefficient guandu shangban governance structure.

In 1883, a financial crisis brought the market down. The crisis began with the unsettling fear of war and the collapse of a silk company just after the new year. Chinese banks had lent money on shares and had also made loans to land speculators—Xu Run being one of the most prominent. By October 1883, many Chinese banks failed, and the foreign banks, which had formerly extended credit to the domestic Chinese firms, withdrew their loans. It was a classic financial crisis—not unlike that of 2008—which began with bank loans collateralized by property and securities. When share prices collapsed, the financial scaffolding holding up the rest of the system fell with it. Xu Run recounts the collapse in his autobiography in great detail. He lost a million taels of silver and had to liquidate his property portfolio at steep discounts. He also lists what he lost in stocks: nearly half a million in the China Merchants Steamship Navigation Company, plus mines, mills, glassworks, a dairy, a sugar refinery company, and three land development firms. He went from being the richest man in Shanghai to being its most dramatic bankrupt.

By January 1885, most domestic companies were selling at less than half their par value, and by the end of the year, only a handful were actually quoted. It is a pattern we saw with the great crash in 1720. The crash not only brought down prices, but it also eroded interest in stocks in general. Liquidity for the domestic shares dried up. The leading proponent of the market, Xu Run—whose fabulous wealth had no doubt inspired the dreams of many Chinese speculators hoping to profit from the success of the Self-Strengthening Movement—was ruined.

But for the outcome of the crash of 1883, Xu Run would likely have been remembered as the J. P. Morgan of Shanghai. Like Morgan, he was a major financier, and his prestige and influence is what sold shares in many of the domestic companies in the first place. In fact, J. P. Morgan faced a crisis very much Xu Run's in 1907. With the stock market plunging, Morgan famously told his brokers to go out and buy, and as a result, total collapse was averted. Morgan became the hero of Wall Street. But suppose Morgan's gambit had failed? Perhaps the New York market would itself have failed and dried up. Perhaps the difference between the two financiers—and the two stock markets—is simply luck.

The domestic Chinese market did not actually disappear after 1883. Indeed, as we saw, it picked back up in 1905, although none of the domestic railway companies so enthusiastically launched actually made it to price quotations in *Shenbao*. Besides the China Merchants Steamship Navigation Company and the Kaiping [開平] mines, the list had grown to include financial infrastructure. The Imperial Bank of China was a publicly traded firm, for example, and HSBC was quoted—despite being a foreign-registered company. Although there were nominal barriers to Chinese trade, by the twentieth century, Chinese and foreign-listed firms were both quoted in *Shenbao* and in the *North China Herald*. By 1935, the main market in Shanghai still maintained a handful of the Chinese-only companies, but for the most part, the foreign-registered and domestic markets were essentially integrated into one.

As an interesting aside, the existence of Chinese-only firms caused a legal backlash against Chinese investors in foreign-registered companies. A dispute in 1897, arising from a capital call on Chinese shareholders in the China Trust Bank, highlighted an ambiguity in the prior treaties governing Chinese investment in "foreign" businesses. Shanghai's magistrate interpreted the Chinese domestic shares as evidence for legal exclusion of foreign nationals from partnership with Chinese—and vice versa. He consequently withdrew legal protection for Chinese investors in non-Chinese firms—leaving them without protection under Chinese law; a problem that had to be rectified by treaty in 1902.[13]

In a few short years, China had not only advanced to the vanguard in capital market innovation, it had done so through its own form of technological experimentation. It had moved from a financial structure organized around the opium trade and dominated by a few powerful foreign merchant banks to a major world capital market that financed not only exports but also manufacturing and development. The comprador class was one major vector for this rapid absorption and redefinition of Western financial tools. While the Chinese imperial government and the Republican government that followed were financially weakened by the exploitation that began with the Opium Wars, the compromises in the form of opening trade imposed by Western nations paradoxically empowered a merchant and financial class in China in unexpected ways.

China's emergence into the modern global world in the late nineteenth and early twentieth centuries reinforces a lesson we have now seen repeated throughout financial history. Financial technology can diffuse rapidly and adapt to existing circumstances, but even as it opens new possibilities, it can be disruptive. The parallels between China's domestic stock market boom and the bubble of 1720 suggest a pattern. Stock markets are wonderful mechanisms for unlocking a broader base of capital. The common individual can open the newspaper and see the potential for sharing in new and profitable enterprises. Joint-stock companies can capture the imagination and open the wallet. In the Chinese case, the railway rights movement in particular tapped into a hope that Chinese investors—even those of modest means—could share in the rapid technological self-development of their country. The markets became a means for redefinition of a nation from one of a fallen, semi-colonial empire humiliated by the British into an entrepreneurial nation that seized its own destiny, defined corporations on its own terms, and used its own vast wellspring of internal capital to move itself forward. Despite China's long history of centralized government and control, it owed these advances to the energy of its reformers—a collection of politicians and merchants who learned well the tools of modern finance and who found the heavy yoke of the imperial government intolerable.

Shanghai of the 1920s and 1930s captured that spirit of transition—it embodied the notion of modernity and global cultural and economic integration. China could absorb and remake on its own terms the best of what the world offered: modern banks, stock markets, skyscrapers, consumer products, transportation and communication systems, educational institutions, arts, and culture. Its role as a financial capital played an important part of this bold cultural expression. However, the connection between finance and social change also played a role in China's next redefinition: the Communist Revolution of 1949. The ultimate rejection of capitalism and individualism followed the path of an international backlash against free markets.

THE RUSSIAN BEAR

In this chapter, we turn to another country that was a major focus of European investment during the late nineteenth century: one that also embraced creative techniques of government funding, welcomed foreign bondholder and stockholders, and used external capital to build its infrastructure and develop its industry. And yet this country ultimately rejected modern finance—or at least the financial technique of capitalism—and led the entire world down a completely different ideological path. The Russian Revolution not only rejected foreign ownership and concessions, it also turned to an economic theory that rejected the very principles on which these investments were based.

THE SAINT PETERSBURG STOCK EXCHANGE

The architecture of Saint Petersburg still embodies the idealist vision of its creator, Peter the Great. It is Russia's entrance to the sea and portal to maritime trade, a city spread across islands, some accessible by bridges, others—like the magnificent summer palace of Catherine the Great—best reached by boat. There are times of the year when the city has the feel of Paris and the Seine, with its great municipal structures like the Hermitage and the Russian National Museum arrayed around beautiful promenades.

The prerevolutionary stock exchange in Saint Petersburg is a brilliant white neoclassical edifice situated on a choice waterfront spot. While the history of the early New York Stock Exchange is well studied, few researchers have paid attention to its counterpart in Saint Petersburg, even though finance played a central role in Russian economic development throughout the nineteenth century. Like other European countries, Russia experimented with creating companies in the years circa 1720. Its first documented share-financed enterprise

The Saint Petersburg Stock Exchange Building, designed by French architect Thomas de Thomon and built between 1805 and 1810.

dates to 1704, and by the 1830s, trading in stocks raised the fear of excess speculation. Speculative booms occurred in 1869 and in 1893—the latter driven by the relaxation of rules about credit on shares. Thus, the history of the Russian market in some ways parallels the development of the US stock market.

In the nineteenth century, the Saint Petersburg Exchange was a microcosm of the London market—roughly comparable in size and number of listings to the New York Stock Exchange. Although trading began decades earlier, the ministry yearbook tally starts in 1869 with forty-six stocks, one of which is the Rossisko-Amerikanskaia kompania, the Russian-American Company that once colonized Alaska. Founded in 1799 by royal charter to pursue the fur trade in North America, the company built a series of forts along the Pacific coast of North America as far south as California. When Russia sold Alaska to the United States in 1867, the Russian-American Company no longer operated in America, although it survived as an exchange-listed trading company on the Saint Petersburg Exchange. Along with the Russian-American Company, the other early listed firms on the Saint Petersburg Exchange pursued finance, insurance, shipping, railroads, trade, manufacturing, and utilities. The list grew to 635 by February 1917—a substantial market by any account.

The tale told by the numbers is interesting. Russian stocks outstripped the American market by nearly 100% over the period 1869–1917, although the Russian market was much more volatile. Saint Petersburg stocks crashed during the Russo-Japanese War and the 1905 Revolution, only to recover dramatically in 1910. If anything, the data from the Russian capital markets paints a rosy picture of financial development and prosperity up to the First World War. Russia had a stock market. It was actively used to raise the capital needed to develop modern infrastructure. It was also a vehicle for individual investors, who could diversify across a number of industries.

Russian debt markets were also innovative and active. The government issued a clever form of bond that appealed to both savers and gamblers: on the one hand, it was a savings vehicle paying regular interest; on the other hand, the Russian bonds of 1864 had detachable lottery tickets that appealed to the speculator.[1] A separate market for these tickets emerged, and the national lottery drawings in Russia were major events in which some lucky ticketholders would prove that winning was not an impossible dream.

Despite these sophisticated internal financial markets, most Russian companies—like those of America—raised capital on foreign exchanges. In fact, few emerging nations in the nineteenth and the early twentieth centuries, used the capital markets as aggressively as Russia did. It floated vast amounts of sovereign debt on the Paris Bourse—by virtue of a political alliance intended for that purpose. British investors got involved in Russian investment as well, particularly in financing operating mines through private companies. The Trans-Siberian Railway, the electrification of Saint Petersburg, the tapping of the Baku oil fields—all of these were financed by European investor money. By 1917, roughly half of Russian assets were owned by foreigners. Default on these claims carried with it the implicit threat of foreign asset seizure and perhaps challenges to sovereignty. The examples of China and Egypt—both large, modernizing, and to some extent cosmopolitan nations—could not be ignored.

FINANCE AND THE FINLAND STATION

Vladimir Lenin, a lifelong opponent of Tsarist rule, triumphantly arrived at the Finland station in Saint Petersburg on April 3, 1917, after years of political exile. The revolution he long championed was finally under way. Russians had deposed the tsar in the midst of the First World War. On April 3, Lenin brought with him a manuscript written while in exile in Zurich. His work, *Imperialism: The Highest Stage of Capitalism*, depicted the Great War as the final clash of the great powers as they sought to carve up the globe into respective markets. In the spirit of Marx, Lenin envisioned this ultimate global battle as the end of capitalism itself; the transformative financial crisis predicted by Marx in *Das Kapital* that would reunite workers and the means of production to take back the accumulated labor value stored in the portfolios of the world's moneybags.

Imperialism, he argued, was the transition of competitive capitalism to monopoly capitalism, in which the means of production are finally controlled by a handful of powerful global financial giants who have divided the world into spheres of interest and thus reduced costly competition. At the outset, Lenin made it clear that his book was inspired by Hobson's *Imperialism*—taking the 1902 treatise as an inspiration but throwing out Hobson's bourgeoisie pacifism and replacing it with the iconoclastic vision of Marx's end of capitalism. Lenin's *Imperialism* is strident, brief, and lacking in the extended philosophical discourse of Marx. He relies instead on data. Throughout the short book, Lenin culls a wealth of data from Hobson and other turn-of-the-century economists about the rise of global banking consortiums; the ever-increasing issuance of stocks and shares on the worlds' exchanges; and the massive export of capital from Britain, France, and Germany to Asia, Africa, and America. Some data are likely derived from counting up numbers in the *Investment Monthly Manual*—using the capitalist publication itself to document the dramatic increase in the scale of global finance.

He dazzles his readers with the vast sums invested in financial securities. He pictures a world of accelerating flux, overrun in a few short decades by a financial oligarchy that controls the world's banks and industry through a matrix of trusts and cartels. The rapidly developing capital markets, in Lenin's view, were the tools of these capitalist combines, allowing the oligarchs to suddenly tap vast pools of capital for their acquisitions. The financial oligarchs of Lenin's time had changed the rules and altered the normal expectations about business and competition. Here is his critique of Standard Oil, for example:

> When a big enterprise assumes gigantic proportions, and . . . directs all the consecutive stages of processing the material right up to the manufacture of numerous varieties of finished articles; when these products are distributed according to a single plan among tens and hundreds of millions of consumers (the marketing of oil in America and Germany by the American oil trust)—then it becomes evident that we have socialisation of production, and not mere "interlocking", that private economic and private property relations constitute a shell . . . which may remain in a state of decay for a fairly long period (if, at the worst, the cure of the opportunist abscess is protracted), but which will inevitably be removed.[2]

The irony of the modern Russian state reassembling monolithic corporate oil and gas companies with international market power through wheeling and dealing in the capital markets is probably un-appreciated today.

NO ONE LIKES MONOPOLIES

Some of Lenin's book rings true to a modern reader. The anticompetitive monopolies he attacked were later reined in by US antitrust law. Standard Oil was broken up into separate companies to defeat the effective control of large sectors of the economy by a giant company.

Lenin reserved his greatest criticism for the railroads and the banks that financed them. He documented the same extraordinary growth of railroad capital we noted earlier in the *Investor's Monthly Manual* (see Chapter 23). They had grown in scale to rival even sovereign debt:

> Railways are a summation of the basic capitalist industries, coal, iron and steel; a summation and the most striking index of the development of world trade and bourgeois-democratic civilisation. . . . The building of railways seems to be a simple, natural, democratic, cultural and civilising enterprise; that is what it is in the opinion of the bourgeois professors who are paid to depict capitalist slavery in bright colours, and in the opinion of petty-bourgeois philistines. But as a matter of fact the capitalist threads, which in thousands of different intercrossings bind these enterprises with private property in the means of production in general, have converted this railway construction into an instrument for oppressing a thousand million people (in the colonies and semicolonies), that is, more than half the population of the globe that inhabits the dependent countries, as well as the wage-slaves of capital in the "civilised" countries.
>
> Capitalism has grown into a world system of colonial oppression and of the financial strangulation of the overwhelming majority of the population of the world by a handful of "advanced" countries. And this "booty" is shared between two or three powerful world plunderers armed to the teeth (America, Great Britain, Japan), who are drawing the whole world into their war over the division of their booty.[3]

The inclusion of Japan in the list of imperialistic powers is significant. Russia lost the Russo-Japanese War in 1905, sparking a revolt on the streets of Saint Petersburg and Moscow that the tsar brutally suppressed. Lenin's Russian readers would have understood imperialism as a force directed at their country, threatening their independence. To blame were not native Russians but foreign shareholders and bondholders. Although Russia itself participated in carving up China into spheres of influence after the Boxer Rebellion, the lessons learned from its neighbor's loss of sovereignty also were clear. In an imperialistic world, political barriers were being replaced by economic domains. If half of Russian industrial assets were owned by foreigners and Russia could not pay its debts, what would happen? Would Germany take the Baku oil fields, France take the railroads, Japan take the Russian East, and Great Britain take the mines?

Lenin returned to Russia in the midst of the First World War and immediately advocated peace with Germany—the country that had given him safe passage from Zurich. The Bolsheviks were a minority party following the February Revolution, but by October they had seized control. Under Lenin's leadership, Russia made peace with Germany by ceding the Baltic states, Belarus, Ukraine, Georgia, Armenia, and Azerbaijan. Peace, however, would be a long time coming.

The Russian civil war extended the conflict from 1917 to 1923. The Great Powers sided with the White Russian Army against the Bolshevik government. In 1919, American and British forces advanced from Archangel in the north, Japan seized Vladivostok in the east, France briefly held Odessa in the south; all eventually were pushed back but at great cost. The Bolsheviks improbably won the civil war and the war against the Great Powers. They repudiated all of Russia's foreign debt and nationalized all Russian industry. British and French investors were left holding worthless claims to Russian infrastructure, oil fields, and factories. The new state did not even recognize individual property rights, let alone the claims of foreign capitalists. By 1923, Lenin could finally begin to remake Russia as the model Marxist state. His death in 1924 left the task to his successor, Josef Stalin.

The Bolshevik Revolution created the world's first Communist state—the polar antithesis of capitalism. The USSR became a laboratory for a nation without financiers, shareholders, investors, and savers. It enshrined the rhetoric of Karl Marx that placed the proletariat in control. However, Russians still had to eat. The state had to finance itself and assume the monumental task of central planning. The capitalists of the world could not believe Russia would truly do without.

They found it difficult to believe that such extreme views of capitalism could actually prevail. For example, in December 1917, Leslie Urquhart, a director of the Kyshtim Mining Corporation, sought to assuage the fears of the firm's shareholders:

> As to the question of how the vital interests—that of the ownership of our properties—are likely to be affected by the happenings in Russia, I would say as definitely as I possibly can that the statements of the absurd Bolshevik usurpers as to the repudiation of contracts should not be taken seriously; they are the ravings of crazy men. . . . [A]re all of these people going to give up their heredity and private ownership rights in order to satisfy the socialistic ravings of madmen and the greed of the landless proletariat of the towns? . . . I have a passionate certainty of conviction that all this chaos and anarchy in but the cleansing fire which will get rid of all that is rotten and make Russia purer and greater (hear, hear).[4]

The firm's shares continued to trade through 1918 despite expropriation of the copper mines by the Bolshevik government. Perhaps Urquart was among those urging the British government to send in the troops to support the White Russian Army. This time, though, it didn't work.

YOU CAN'T EAT MONEY

Having repudiated its foreign debt and fought off the attempts by the world's leading investor nations to reverse the October Revolution, Russia still needed to raise money. In the Yale collection of historical financial documents is a printed bill, about twice the size of a modern dollar. On the front of the bill is a picture of a farmer sowing a field. The inscription on the bill identifies it as a short-term loan from 1923: an obligation of the government. Oddly enough, it does not promise payment in rubles but instead it can be redeemed for one sack of rye flour. Karl Marx would have been proud. The young Soviet government had bravely dispensed with the object of money fetishism—the veil that concealed true value and encouraged capitalist monetary accumulation. Instead, the idealistic Bolsheviks introduced a more fundamental source of value as a medium of investment and exchange. Lest Russians imagine that the grain itself held the value, the romantic pastoral image of the farmer sowing the grain pictured the labor theory of value. The commodity was worth the amount of honest labor used in planting and harvesting it. What is not clear from the document is whether the bill represented fiat money or whether it was truly redeemable. If it were actually a short-term note used to redeem a sack of rye, there is missing information. The bill does not state when and where the sack can be collected. Perhaps it really was a manifestation of the labor theory of value. Alternatively, it could have been a manifestation of the weakness of the young Soviet state. Russia was in the throes of hyperinflation in the early 1920s as the needs of the state outstripped its resources. Perhaps the rye bond was an inflation-protected currency. Then again, who knows how many sacks of rye the government had to deliver on such promises—or indeed, whether they ever did. The fact that you can buy one of these bills today for less than $50 suggests that many of them were left unredeemed.

SEEDS OF OBJECTIVISM

Alisa Zinov'yevna Rosenbaum was born in 1905 in Saint Petersburg. Her father was a pharmacist whose handsome red-brick Aptek stood at a prominent intersection not far from the city center—still now a pharmacy. Alisa's family lived upstairs from the store and had an excellent view of the events of 1917 as they unfolded in the streets of the capital. As a twelve-year-old, she saw the violence and chaos of revolution. She fled with her family to Crimea after the Bolsheviks took over the family store; eventually returning to her native city in 1921 as a young woman. She witnessed the transformation of Russia from a relatively free market to a collective, centrally planned economy. Her own apartment in the 1920s was close to Nevsky Prospect, a short tram ride away from Saint Petersburg State University, where she studied history and political theory.[5] Some courses, such as "Historical Materialism," were heavily influenced by Marxist theory. Others, such as "Medieval History," "Modern History," and "The History of Medieval Trade," reflected the prerevolutionary interests of the Russian academy in the history of economics and finance.

In 1926, the intellectual young woman moved to the United States and determined to become a screenwriter. She adopted the American name Ayn Rand. She was eventually moderately successful as a screenwriter, but her true claim to fame came through her political novels. *Atlas Shrugged* is widely regarded as one of the most influential books of the twentieth century. Published in 1957 at the height of the Cold War, it stridently rejects Soviet-style collectivism and instead proposes "Objectivism"—a libertarian philosophy championing laissez-faire capitalism and self-interested rational economic action. *Atlas Shrugged* pits the economic elite—the entrepreneurs and self-made CEOs of a future United States—against a system of political favoritism that rewards mediocrity, a system in which business decisions are made in the back rooms of Washington, DC.

Rand spins out a tale of moral, social, and technological decay caused by well-intentioned collectivism—an obvious reflection of the failure of Russian society and economy she witnessed in Saint Petersburg as a young woman. In *Atlas Shrugged*, the market fails, the elites retreat to a mountain hideaway, and the state-run railroads fall apart. *Atlas Shrugged* has become the foundation on which much of modern US libertarian thought is based. While potentially deeply appealing to advocates of free-market solutions, Rand's thought suffers from many of the same deficiencies as the writings of Marx, Engels, Hobson, and Lenin. It is primarily a critique of the system, full of inspiring rhetoric but ultimately short on practical, political solutions. Indeed Rand portrays politics as the enemy of principle. Karl Marx would likely agree with her on this point, and Lenin's political implementation of an ideal Marxist state through totalitarianism betrayed Marxist ideals, placing the means of production in the hands of the party, not the proletariat.

Although Rand would certainly have rejected the idea, her books are clearly one link in an ongoing dialectic between advocates and critics of financial markets. Without markets, there would be no Marx. Without Marx there would be no Lenin; without Lenin, there would be no Ayn Rand. Each uses a different style of argument, but each is almost unnaturally persuasive. It can only be so because each managed to tap deep, enduring, and conflicting social schemas.

In the early twentieth century, Russia became the battleground over the modern financial system. However improbable, during the fog of an unprecedented world war, a revolutionary party seized power over a nation of more than 100 million people and fought off the Great Powers. Rejecting a long tradition of financial innovation and reliance on global capital markets, Russia instead villainized capitalism and formed itself in the image of the *Communist Manifesto*; a slim volume short on practical detail, written by two armchair revolutionaries and elaborated by them in a massive work of cultural criticism, penned in London, the bastion of laissez-faire capitalism. The strange schism of the twentieth century would not soon heal.

One might have expected that the world would divide itself along lines of religious intolerance. After all, the Crusades are still the rallying cry in parts of the Islamic world. But the notion that the theory of finance—in particular, a disagreement over the role of investors in society—could rip the world in two is difficult to conceive of ex ante. We now know that the world took two different paths. China followed Russia in a Marxist-Leninist revolution in 1949 after a similarly destructive world conflict and civil war. So did Cuba, North Korea, and Vietnam. I grew up as a child fearing the sound of bomb shelter alarms that would signal nuclear attack—echoes of the historical split between East and West over economics and the financial system.

Henry Lowenfeld had only been partially correct when he claimed that a portfolio of securities from around the world would provide a stable return. His theories were based on statistical analysis of the markets in a rare, golden age of capitalism before the rupture of the First World War, the Russian Revolution, the Second World War, Lenin, and Mao. The geographically distributed portfolio would have suffered from Bolshevik and Maoist expropriations, Japanese and German market crashes in the wake of the Second World War, and the loss of assets in Eastern Europe as the iron curtain split Europe in two. Global diversification looked like a good idea unless the whole world suffered a crisis at the same time.

KEYNES TO THE RESCUE

The Bolshevik Revolution was not the only consequence of the First World War. Beaten back by Allies and the Russian army, Germany was stripped of its colonial possessions, its merchant marine, its access to the sea, large swaths of productive territory, and then saddled with an unpayable debt. This debt finally brought into sharp focus some of the dangers of an international financial system built around sovereign borrowing.

Cambridge economist John Maynard Keynes participated in the negotiations at the conclusion of the war as part of Great Britain's team. He served as the official representative of the British Treasury Office at the Paris Peace Conference in 1919, resigning in June of that year in protest over the onerous terms of the treaty.

Keynes wrote a popular account of the deal-making that resulted in the Treaty of Versailles called *The Economic Consequences of the Peace*. In his view, the treaty was a continuation of the war by economic means. Despite the horrible toll in British lives taken by the Great War, Keynes pleads in the book for Allied mercy. Germans would simply starve— they could not afford to pay their war bills and import enough food to sustain existence. Such conditions would have dire political consequences. The Allies handed Germany a bill for the Great War of 269 billion gold marks. By my calculations, the reparations amounted to about 2 trillion liters of barley—about half of the bill submitted to Umma by Lagash (see Chapter 2). The trajectory from Lagash and Umma to the Treaty of Versailles stretches from the origins of financial indebtedness to the full-blown modern financial technology of the debt subjugation of nation-states.

The Economic Consequences of the Peace is full of humanity, philosophy, finance, and gossip. For a world curious about how the Treaty of Versailles came about, Keynes's exposé is titillating. He sketches dev-

John Maynard Keynes in 1908, by Gwendolen Raverat.

astating portraits of the world's leaders. In Keynes's view, Woodrow Wilson's failure to impose a realistic settlement stemmed from his stiff, "Presbyterian" demeanor and insensitivity to the machinations of his counterparties. Lloyd George is cast as a demon with preternatural craft and subtlety. He tricks the plodding Wilson at every turn. The French president Georges Clemenceau is portrayed as an aloof, intransigent, and implacable enemy of the German state. Together the three become a modern incarnation of *Macbeth*'s witches.

While the book entertained readers with fly-on-the-wall accounts of the negotiation, at heart, Keynes laid both the war and the failure of the peace negotiations on the shortcomings of capitalism and the psychology of modern society. In this he echoed Marx, Hobson, and Lenin. In his view, modern investment markets had enabled humanity to unnaturally store up capital for the future in a vast pool controlled by a ruling class:

> Society was so framed as to throw a great part of the increased income into the control of the class least likely to consume it. The new rich of the nineteenth century were not brought up to large expenditures, and preferred the power which investment gave them to the pleasures of immediate consumption. In fact, it was precisely the inequality of the distribution of wealth which made possible those vast accumulations of fixed wealth and of capital improvements which distinguished that age from all others. Herein lay, in fact, the main justification of the Capitalist System.[1]

To Keynes, the "double bluff" of the capitalist system was inherently unstable. His biggest complaint was the stinginess of the ruling class—their psychological fixation on saving up money. Keynes's antagonism toward deferred gratification—toward moving economic value from the present into the future—is what made him acutely critical of the peace treaty.

He saw the war as a turning point toward a new financial order. It showed the working classes just what they were missing, and it made the capitalist class realize their savings were worthless when facing an extremely uncertain future. He argued that the psychology of both classes would turn toward consumption and quality of life in the here and now. In his view, spending some of the stored up capital of capitalism was the path toward a better future. Keynes's book became famous for its terrible but prescient prediction. The knock-on disasters that emerged in the aftermath of the First World War included hyperinflation, Fascism, and a totalitarian Marxist state in neighboring Russia.

Critics of the book have pointed out that the German economy actually recovered better than Keynes predicted and that the reparations payments were ultimately substantially reduced.[2] No matter—the basic problem of the political implications of sovereign debt was clearly highlighted to a global readership—cast in the Marxist rhetoric of the day.

In this chapter, we explore not only the contributions Keynes made to the reshaping of finance after the First World War but also his role as a financial thinker and strategist. He is one of the most important figures in the modern history of finance, because he stands at the nexus of three great, intersecting themes: the problem of sovereign debt, the importance of emotion and markets, and the headlong rush to invest in the stock market.

THE PROBLEM OF SOVEREIGN DEBT

As a young economist, Keynes brought international attention to the Hobsonian problem of international debt. Many years later, after the Second World War, he helped create financial institutions that solved—or at least attempted to mitigate—this fundamental failure of financial markets. The agreement resulting from negotiations among twenty-nine allied countries at Breton Woods, New Hampshire, in July 1944, established for the first time an international financial architecture. The conference had echoes of a "World Economic Conference" proposed by Keynes in his 1933 article "The Means to Prosperity," in which the goal of such a conference would be the establishment of common world currency and an institutional structure for managing it. Eleven years later, at Bretton Woods, Keynes was on hand to represent British interests as well as his global vision. He proposed a plan that essentially interposed an international institutional framework between debtor nations and their creditors.

While the final plan was not strictly the one offered by Keynes, it shared with it the basic structure. The key components of the system, the International Monetary Fund (IMF) and the International Bank for

Reconstruction and Development (later, the World Bank), provided a new means for the international community of nations to deal with sovereign debt. The IMF was designed to address the disjunctions in the international balance of payments; roughly speaking, to help countries with excessive debt in foreign currencies by lending to them while guiding them back toward a balance of payments. The IMF was a new means of collective bargaining with a state having currency problems. Countries paid into a pool against which any nation with payment imbalances could draw.

A crucial feature of the IMF is that it dispensed with the old notion of collateral for sovereign debt. No longer, for example, would a region like the Ruhr be held as security to force payments. No longer would import duties or canal revenues be seized by another country for direct debt service. Instead, the IMF set macroeconomic benchmarks as conditions for future loans and required structural adjustments to an economy that got itself into serious debt. These ranged from austerity measures to currency devaluation, to increased exports and trade liberalization, to introduction of free market policies and privatization: a toolkit of solutions designed by macroeconomists, as opposed to self-interested bondholders or bank lenders.

Countries with these IMF-imposed conditions sometimes complain about the hardships they impose and the failure of the prescription. Look, for example, at the IMF bailouts of Greece in recent times. Austerity conditions imposed by the IMF and the European Union did not turn the Greek economy around, but instead were associated with deeper unemployment and hardship. Compare, however, the modern Greek debt default to the restructuring of Greek debts in 1898. After losing a war with Turkey over the island of Crete, Greece—then as now—was unable to make payments on its international debt. Instead of dealing with an IMF, the Greek government instead negotiated with French, German, and British bondholder committees. The resulting bailout turned over control of Greek finances to an international commission—much like the British exercise of control over Egypt in 1878 (see Chapter 23). The commission took revenues directly for bondholder repayment—incidentally diverting them from the Turkish reparations imposed after the loss of the war. At least with an IMF, the integrity and sovereignty of the nation is preserved. While Keynes may not have been the only architect of this new structure, he was certainly a major force for it—and his conviction that it was the right thing to do stemmed from his early experience with the Paris negotiations in 1919. Modern Greece owes Keynes at least a little bit of thanks for laying the foundation of a messy bailout, but one that at least preserves its integrity as a nation.

THE WORLD BANK

The second major institution created at Bretton Woods was a bank designed to finance growth. As we saw above, the global financial markets essentially created the world's infrastructure. Regulating investor access to collateral, while desirable from a political perspective, affects the willingness to lend. In the wake of new rules about international lending, how would big projects get financed? The International Bank for Reconstruction and Development—which later became the World Bank—was set up to fill this potential funding gap. The World Bank makes loans to developing countries and provides assistance for a number of noble goals: poverty alleviation, health improvement, and education.

In postcolonial times, the World Bank takes on the role formerly held by colonial nations: funneling capital, expertise, and legal and educational institutions into developing countries through debt financing.

Does the world need a World Bank? This issue has become a major topic of discussion and research in recent years. It has been crystallized by the mounting evidence that the World Bank has been relatively ineffective at accomplishing its central mission in developing countries. William Easterly, professor at New York University and former economist at the World Bank, has argued that the World Bank has simply spun its wheels—poured massive amounts of money into impoverished countries and walked away with little to show for it. Easterly and his colleagues found a disconnect between foreign aid, investment, and economic growth.[3] World Bank loans are essentially a form of aid, because they are made at low rates and the enforcement of repayment is lax. In Africa, where a considerable number of loans and aid dollars have been directed, the relationship between foreign aid and per capita growth has actually been negative over the past several decades. As well intentioned as the World Bank may be and as dedicated and idealistic as its employees are, as a top-down institution for financing positive change in the world, it has very few success stories.

Easterly and others have argued that the failure of the institutions has its roots in the Keynesian presumption that a top-down regulatory structure—as opposed to the invisible hand of the marketplace—is more effective in allocating resources to projects. Easterly's argument is simple. Alignment of incentives to promote growth works a lot better than a control-and-command approach. Keynes, of course, posited a central role for government in solving the disjunctions caused by unchecked financial globalization and bad savings habits. His legacy is a financial architecture designed to blunt the potential for colonial exploitation by disintermediating lenders and sovereign borrowers—replacing that relationship with a collective institutional financial organization. Did Bretton Woods save the world from a revival of imperialism? Did it bring more nations into the fold of prosperity? Whether it did or not, it undeniably altered the way that nations interact with one another and with the capital markets.

By introducing the IMF and World Bank as lenders of last resort, it blunted the sharp needs for nations to negotiate terms that reduced sovereignty. One can always argue that this moved the world away from a free market for financial contracts and thus reduced capital market efficiency. So did Solon's proclamation that Athenians could not contract on their personal freedom.

Even if Keynes had never written another book, his legacy as a true financial innovator would still be preserved in the Bretton Woods Agreement. It has served the world well over the decades that followed. Like many government-based solutions, it is imperfect, inefficient, subject to different kinds of abuse, and often the object of criticism by both its benefactors and beneficiaries. Still, as we have seen with other such institutional technologies, they may start out with one purpose but gradually adapt to meet the needs of an evolving economic situation. With any luck, the IMF and World Bank will remain flexible enough to follow the same course.

THE IMPORTANCE OF EMOTION

Keynes did write another book—several in fact. None had as great an impact on economic thought as his magnum opus. Published in 1935, in the depths of the Great Depression, *The General Theory of Employ-*

ment, Interest and Money attempted to explain how the economy could be trapped in a seemingly endless depression. The germ of the idea can be found in the *Economic Consequences of the Peace* (that hoarding is the source of economic problems). When employment rates drop and future prospects look dim, people save more and consume less, which leads to still lower employment. Keynes reasoned that government action could alter this equilibrium: lower interest rates could stimulate investment, and, in extreme circumstances like the Great Depression, government work projects that increased employment could stimulate demand and hence production and employment. The government could jolt the economy out of its moribund state.

Perhaps the most famous part of the book is his theory that market psychology plays a key role in changing the equilibrium. Keynes observed that the market is driven by animal spirits. For Keynes, this spontaneous, mutual hope—even if driven by irrationality or at least overly optimistic dreams of the future, became a major feature of a new economics. He posited that humankind's "animal spirits" are a fundamental and desirable force. Without them, people will save too much, consumption drops, production declines, salaries go down, and people decide they have to save more. Progress is based on excessive optimism:

> Business men play a mixed game of skill and chance, the average results of which to the players are not known by those who take a hand. If human nature felt no temptation to take a chance, no satisfaction (profit apart) in constructing a factory, a railway, a mine or a farm, there might not be much investment merely as a result of cold calculation . . . it is probable that the actual average results of investments, even during periods of progress and prosperity, have disappointed the hopes which prompted them . . . a large proportion of our positive activities depend on spontaneous optimism rather than on a mathematical expectation, whether moral or hedonistic or economic.[4]

In other words, if all investment were based on rational assessment of net present value, nothing new would ever be built. Technological progress proceeds on the folly of the gambling businessperson. Who knows how much Keynes knew about John Law. But recall that the bubble of 1720 was based on dreams and hopes of new technologies and new companies that harnessed the spirit—and capital—of the crowd. It is almost as if the increased density of speculation in that remarkable year revealed a latent, novel force of nature that suddenly enabled capital markets to overcome financial inertia—setting in motion all sorts of new possibilities.

Keynes not only recognized this as a powerful potential force in the economy, he also believed that the government could harness this force and use it to change the macroeconomic equilibrium. He had the insight that economic policy could manage public expectations. Change people's view of the future, and they would open their wallets and spend in the present. Market sentiment could be holding back the economy because of irrational fears, but managed correctly, it could become a force for great good.

Rather than attacking recessions by eliminating booms, his proposal was to have the government step in as a bubble reached its peak and stop the downward spiral through stimulus and management of sentiment. His plan was to maintain the economy in a perpetual state of quasi-boom. Right when the yields on investment start to drop, share prices fall, speculators have to liquidate their positions, and factory orders start to dry up, Keynes had the clever notion that the government could hold out a carrot at the end of a stick to keep the donkey moving forward—lifting its eyes up to the prize rather than dwelling on its exhausted condition.

Of course, investors played a role in maintaining this quasi-boom, but only for a while. If the economy were properly managed, investors were only a temporary expedient. Once interest rates dropped and full employment became the norm, the moneybags, the hoarders, the capitalists who lived by exploitation of the working class would become unnecessary:

> the euthanasia of the rentier, of the functionless investor, will be nothing sudden, merely a gradual but prolonged continuance of what we have seen recently in Great Britain, and will need no revolution. . . . But even so, it will still be possible for communal saving through the agency of the State to be maintained at a level which will allow the growth of capital up to the point where it ceases to be scarce.[5]

Keynes predicted that individual investing would ultimately give way to communal savings. The state would manage our savings to the point of plentitude. Meanwhile, until that day, Keynes was an exuberant and quite successful speculator and rentier in his own right.

THE HEADLONG RUSH TO THE STOCK MARKET

I want to manage a railway or organise a Trust, or at least swindle the investing public; it is so easy and fascinating to master the principles of these things.[6]

J. M. KEYNES, 1905

A confident young Keynes thus confided to his friend Lytton Strachey in a letter in 1905 while an undergraduate at Cambridge. Keynes intended right from the start to make money as a projector and speculator. Reading Keynes the economist, it is easy to presume that he took a dim view of the free market system. However, in his personal life, he embraced it exuberantly.

Even as he was revolutionizing macroeconomics and plotting a new course for global financial architecture, Keynes launched an investment trust, speculated vigorously in stocks and commodities, and moved the institutional investing world back toward the stock market. The story of Keynes the financier and investor has only recently come to light, thanks to the efforts of David Chambers. David is a professor at Cambridge University—a place where the legacy of John Maynard Keynes looms large.

Keynes was not only one of Cambridge's most famous economists, he also managed some of its endowment. In a period in which professors regularly stepped up to administrative service, Keynes served as a bursar to King's College during a turbulent period in world financial history. During the years 1921–1946, Keynes was in charge of the King's College investment portfolio. It was a time over which Keynes's own ideas about investment, savings, and animal spirits evolved.

Chambers, himself a former financier before going back to an academic career, was curious about how the investment portfolio reflected Keynes's own intellectual development and vice versa. Were Keynes's views on market sentiment driven by his personal experience trying to time the ups and downs of the 1920s and 1930s? Did he have personal experience in assessing the prospects of technological innovation? Was Keynes a rentier who hoarded money and clipped the coupons of bonds, or a speculator who optimistically bought stocks in new enterprise, despite the uncertainty about their prospects—and about his own capacity to evaluate the true risks?

Together with Elroy Dimson of London Business School, a longtime friend and mentor, David dove into the King's College archives to reconstruct the history of Keynes's investments. What they found was that, as with everything else in his life, Keynes was an iconoclast in his investment behavior. He deviated immediately from a centuries' old tradition of Cambridge college endowment management by turning away from real estate and fixed income toward stocks. Even in his stock portfolio he took chances—focusing on a few stocks rather than diversifying broadly. The strategy paid off. Over the whole period, Keynes's portfolio handily beat an equal-weighted portfolio of UK stocks. He was a true pioneer in what became a rush to switch from bond investing to stock investing.

The *General Theory* contains some insight into Keynes's investment policies. Keynes praised investment in long-term, productive enterprises. Withdrawing money from the bond markets and investing in entrepreneurial projects was consistent with this philosophy. He felt that speculation, if it became the predominant reason for investment in the markets, discouraged sustained enterprise. Nevertheless, his investing relied on both. Chambers and Dimson observed that, before the mid-1930s, Keynes tried to time the ebb and flow of the market. Perhaps he believed he was smart enough to predict animal spirits. We saw earlier that the efficient market theory suggests that this is not possible.

In fact, Keynes the thinker was subtly dismissive of efficient market theory. Not only did he emphasize that market sentiment could push prices away from fundamental values, he also did not believe in the statistical foundation of Jules Regnault's random walk theory. Keynes's most academic book is *A Treatise on Probability*, written when he returned to Cambridge after the Paris negotiations. The book argues that the statistician should not automatically assume that there is a central tendency in the data. Recall from Chapter 16 Regnault's example of many people looking at the same security and the resulting efficient market price. Keynes cautions that such a mechanism might not apply in markets. For example, all the people may not be looking at the same security, or some of them might have better insight than others. He argues that, when you look at market information, you need to dig deeper to understand how the data are generated. Conditions matter. An astute analyst therefore may be able to discern trends when others presume that the market follows a random walk.

Alas, Keynes's market timing did not work out so well. In particular, he failed to foresee the crash of 1929. The twists and turns of the market in the 1930s ultimately caused him to change his philosophy. He became a fundamental investor—looking for companies with reliable fundamentals and long-term earnings prospects. He focused on a relatively few favorites: mining companies, a shipping firm, an automobile company. This strategy worked well.

KEYNES VERSUS MARX

Keynes is nearly as important as Karl Marx in creating new and seductive interpretations of capital markets. Both have defined entire schools of economic thought. Both changed the world.

From my perspective, their persuasive power stems as much from their literary talents as their economic logic. They both play on deep stereotypes—particularly the vision of savers as miserly hoarders. These stereotypes resonated in the public imagination, because both authors wrote at a time of great uncertainly and public anxiety about the future of the modern world. People needed not only a logical analysis of the economics of the time, but also a tale that appealed to the subconscious—an explanation that suited both sides of the brain.

For Marx, the social dislocation of industrialization and the emergence of the new phenomenon of a global capital market, with a new world order of winners and losers, resonated with his fiery, accusatory rhetoric and radical proposals for restructuring the economy into a collective enterprise.

Keynes was only slightly more subtle in his criticism. As a young man, he wrote a self-righteous manifesto that attacked the financial warfare of modern times. As a mature economist, his magnum opus appeared at the depths of the Great Depression and attacked classical economics as a failed paradigm. He challenged rational optimization and re-introduced the age-old specter of human nature—the sprites and demons and manias of *The Great Mirror of Folly*. Those images still resonate.

Unlike Marx, Keynes offered salvation from the current condition. For Marx, salvation lay in revolution. Keynes's *General Theory* gave a prominent role to central government in reversing economic doldrums. In that sense, it is deeply optimistic. The ups and downs that plague the modern economy—the problems created by credit cycles and inefficient investment decisions—can be managed by government through interest rate policy and even the direct provision of employment. A Keynesian future promises all of the highs and none of the lows. It breaks the moral calculus of crashes as penance for excess. No wonder it remains the centerpiece of discussions around economic policies in the wake of the Great Recession.

KEYNES AND AMERICA

Keynes began his career in an era when London was the financial capital of the world, and over his career, he witnessed a major shift toward the New World. The negotiations after the First World War took place in Paris and featured the British, French, and American leaders. This was the entry of the United States into the theater of world power. Bretton Woods took place in America, and it is commonly agreed that the major dynamics in negotiating a new financial architecture pitted Keynes against the American, Harry Dexter White of the US Treasury. At this point, Keynes was fighting for Britain's financial relevance. His nation could no longer set the terms of the settlement as it could when London was the nexus of the world's capital. Keynes took the American eclipse of Britain hard but certainly recognized the emergence of a new chapter in financial history. He was interested in what this new American world was like and, typically, he had strong opinions.

THE NEW FINANCIAL WORLD

Americans are apt to be unduly interested in discovering what average opinion believes average opinion to be; and this national weakness finds its nemesis in the stock market. It is rare, one is told, for an American to invest, as many Englishmen still do, "for income"; and he will not readily purchase an investment except in the hope of capital appreciation. This is only another way of saying that, when he purchases an investment, the American is attaching his hopes, not so much to its prospective yield, as to a favourable change in the conventional basis of valuation, i.e. that he is, in the above sense, a speculator. Speculators may do no harm as bubbles on a steady stream of enterprise. But the position is serious when enterprise becomes the bubble on a whirlpool of speculation. When the capital development of a country becomes a by-product of the activities of a casino, the job is likely to be ill-done. The measure of success attained by Wall Street, regarded as an institution of which the proper social purpose is to direct new investment into the most profitable channels in terms of future yield, cannot be claimed as one of the outstanding triumphs of laissez-faire capitalism—which is not surprising, if I am right in thinking that the best brains of Wall Street have been in fact directed towards a different object.[1]

J. M. KEYNES, *THE GENERAL THEORY*

AMERICAN WAY

The seminar room was classic Harvard: paneled walls; a coffered ceiling; and a long, beautiful table. Professors and graduate students wandered into the room to take their seats following the accustomed pecking order that reserves prime spots for senior professors and chairs along

Georgia O'Keeffe's *Radiator Building, at Night,* painted in 1927. Skyscrapers in
the 1920s were financed with new investment instruments, and Americans
were thrilled with the high-flying stock market.

the wall for doctoral students. Into the room strode a young historian who seated herself at the head of the table. She unfolded a sheaf of papers, waited for the room to still itself, and then took a hand grenade out of her satchel. Without a word she set it upright in front of her. It was not clear to the audience whether they should smile or simply bolt. Regardless, Julia Ott succeeded in getting their attention.[2] Her seminar that day at Harvard Business School was a lesson in how Americans adopted stock market investing. The hand grenade was from the First World War. It was a reminder that much of American attitudes toward investing emerged in the wake of the Great War.

As post-war Russia in the 1920s marched toward a Marxist state, Americans moved vigorously in the opposite direction with a distinctive American kind of idealism and fervor. The subject of Julia Ott's lecture—and the subject of her extensive dissertation—was the profound shift in the American mind about the issue of stock market investing. While Europeans, particularly the British, had long relied on capital markets as a means of savings and investment, investing by American households increased significantly only during the First World War. The US government issued savings bonds to finance the American war effort, and these were purchased, in part, as a matter of patriotic duty. As the US government retired this debt, investors sought financial substitutes, and brokers sought additional product.

Julia Ott is now a historian at the New School of Social Research in New York and an expert on the conversion of America to the cult of equity in the early twentieth century—in her words, a "shareholder democracy." Retail investing was pushed, not pulled, particularly at the outset. While Russians were being trained in the 1920s to reject the bourgeois idea of money and savings, Americans were introduced to a sophisticated new world of capital markets by brokers and bankers who saw retail investing as a new profitable area of marketing. The zeitgeist of market speculation had finally crossed the Atlantic.

Although the New York Stock Exchange has operated since 1792 and the nineteenth century is replete with colorful stories of Wall Street speculators and railroad magnates, the United States was a net importer of capital until the twentieth century. Once the power of the common investor was harnessed, however, the country rapidly became a global financial force. Americans were cognizant of how British capital markets underwrote British imperialism in the Victorian era and saw themselves as the natural inheritors of that mantle. However, imperialism was never the driving force in retail investing.

Julia Ott points out that investment in American companies in the 1920s became a means for self-improvement, self-reliance, and personal empowerment. For the price of a share, an investor became a voting partner in a giant company and a stakeholder in its future. These themes did not emerge spontaneously in American society; rather, they were carefully nurtured by Wall Street—particularly through the promotional activities of the New York Stock Exchange. Julia Ott's research in the archives of the exchange turned up a vast amount of material about how the idea of a shareholder democracy was managed—not only through speeches and publicity releases, but also through such populist media as financial cartoons that distilled the complexities of financial operations for ordinary people and appealed to aspirations of family security and self-improvement.

In contrast to the popular pre-war notion of a Wall Street dominated by insiders like Daniel Drew, Cornelius Vanderbilt, and J. P. Morgan, the New York Stock Exchange in the 1920s emphasized fairness. In the "New Era" of stock market investing, the small American investor was no longer a victim of market manipulation by insiders—the New York Stock Exchange promoted itself as the seal of approval for a square investment deal. If common stocks once were synonymous with speculation and back-room trickery, they were now transformed, via a period of patriotic fervor and sudden familiarity with brokers and investment portfolios, into a major new "appliance" in the American household. America was late to the development of a retail investor market, but once it got a taste, investing suddenly became a national pastime.

STOCKS VERSUS BONDS

Keynes was right. Stocks captivated the American imagination in the 1920s in a fundamentally different manner from the British investor movement of the Victorian era. Most of Henry Lowenfeld's studies of global diversification in London used bonds to illustrate a sound investment policy. The Foreign and Colonial Government Trust was fashioned to capture high average bond yields, not capital appreciation of shares. Keynes was an exceptional early advocate of equities as the future of finance, but he was a bit ahead of his time in Britain. But in America, tastes turned sharply toward equities. Americans still bought bonds, but people grew increasingly wary of them. One thing made bonds less safe in the modern era: they carried the risk of inflation.

The hyperinflation in Germany after the First World War horrified the world. From 1921 to 1924, prices in Germany rose more than a trillion times over: currency reform in 1924 involved lopping off twelve zeros from the bills in circulation. Money was literally not worth the paper it was printed on. The crazy spiral of zeros upon zeros, images of people carrying cartloads of cash into stores and papering their walls with bills—these images threatened the fundamental belief in government. The world realized that, with the failure of the gold standard, no currency was truly safe, no country was truly immune.

Yale economist Irving Fisher went so far as to postulate that ordinary people could not even perceive the terrible effects of currency devaluation. In a curious, perhaps unconscious echo of Marxist "money fetishism," Fisher coined the phrase "money illusion" to describe the human tendency to believe that the "nominal" value of currency was somehow fixed and reliable. He argued instead that people needed to be convinced to use "real" value: the value after accounting for inflation. In Fisher's view, people got hung up on the monetary prices as reference points for the value of goods and ignored the extent to which this was determined by the quantity of money in circulation. His prescription to savers: stay away from money and bonds. Future dollars might be worthless. Better buy real things—like real companies. Shares in American corporations promised not only a dividend cash flow but also a stake in tangible corporate assets whose monetary value would automatically rise when the government printed money. Like Keynes, Fisher was a progressive who believed that economists could help solve the world's problems. He introduced mathematical methods of economics to America and is famous for his macroeconomic theories about the quantity theory of money and debt-deflation market cycles.

Fisher's contribution to financial economics was particularly important. He took the mathematics of present value (first formalized by Fibonacci!) and applied it to investment decisions. In Fisher's analysis, corporate managers acting in the best interests of shareholders should choose projects with the highest positive net present value that takes into account not only the time value of money but also the risk of the project. Generations of Yale graduates who took his courses in finance learned to apply this rational decision criterion. Fisher's net present value equation is the workhorse of all modern financial analysis today.

Fisher's study of corporations and his analysis of the effects of inflation led him to strongly advocate stock investing as opposed to bond investing. It was advice he took himself, moving much of his personal wealth—and the savings of his well-to-do wife and her family—into equities.

FUND A AND FUND B

Edgar Lawrence Smith worked on Wall Street as a bond analyst in the early 1920s. Interested in the stock market craze, he ran a test to see whether an investor who held stocks would have done better than an investor who held bonds over the long term. This was a quite different study than Henry Lowenfeld's of decades earlier. He was not interested in global investing or in risk per se but rather in return. Which did better—stocks or bonds?

Smith's experiment was simple. He checked whether the actual cash flows from investing from the 1830s to the 1920s in corporate stocks would have covered the payouts to bondholders. He found that over the long term, stocks practically always beat bonds. He also argued that equities should be able to make a steady dividend payout that grew proportionally as a percentage of market values. He published the study *Common Stocks as Long Term Investments* in December 1924.

The book immediately became a hit. Smith turned the traditional idea of safe investing on its head: bonds, which were once considered conservative and safe, were now deemed extremely risky. He and his book ushered in a new era of finance that would define its followers as bold, modern, and clever; active not passive; and direct participants in modern American industrial growth and technological innovation. Out with the railroads bonds, in with the aviation companies!

In Smith's careful empirical analysis, replete with graphs and figures, American investors found a convincing argument for revolutionizing the way they saved for the future. Benjamin Graham and David Dodd, fundamental value investors of the 1930s, scoffed that *Common Stocks as Long Term Investments* was "destined to become the official 'textbook' of the new-era stock market."[3] John Maynard Keynes reviewed it positively in 1925. Irving Fisher was even more enthusiastic, arguing that Smith had started a trend that fundamentally altered the relative demand for stocks and bonds.

Edgar Smith launched the Investors Management Company shortly before the publication of his landmark study. It offered its services on a strictly fee basis—eliminating some of the extreme conflicts of interest held by other firms. Unlike big Wall Street companies, Investors Management Company did not underwrite securities and then park the failures in their investment trusts.

The firm offered two products: Fund A and Fund B. Both allowed investors to hold a diversified portfolio of common stock, formed chiefly according to the principles outlined in his book. Fund A planned to pay out 5% per year in dividends, which was the rate Smith figured was a sustainable yield based on historical analysis. Fund B allowed investors to plow back all dividends by reinvesting in more common stock shares. Smith not only demonstrated that stocks were a superior long-term investment; by launching his investment funds, he also offered Americans a vehicle to capitalize on his research. Although the Investors Management Company Funds A and B were not the very first mutual funds in America, they were very prominent and immediately attracted imitators.

Just as suddenly as Americans became infatuated with buying stocks, they fell in love with investment trusts. The simple idea of pooling investor money and buying a diversified portfolio of securities is a great one and is certainly not new. After all, the Dutch invented mutual funds every bit as sophisticated. The British model for American funds—including the famous Foreign and Colonial Government Trust—was widely acknowledged in the 1920s. Trusts were even referred to as a "British" style of investing. The American wrinkle was the emphasis on equity. Irving Fisher was also a big fan of investment trusts:

the risks that . . . attach to [common stock] may be reduced, or insured against, by diversification . . . investment trusts and investment
council tend to diminish the risk to the common stock investor. This
new movement has created a new demand for such stocks and raised
their prices, at the same time it has tended to decrease the demand
for, and to lower the price of, bonds.[4]

Notice what this statement predicted. Fisher reasoned that, as small
investors began to use diversified investment trusts as vehicles to hold
stocks, the risk of their portfolios would go down. Historically, the risk
of holding just one stock is about twice the risk of holding a portfolio of
stocks. If you can buy a portfolio as easily as a single share in one company, then you can double your stock market investment while keeping
the same level of risk.

Fisher predicted that, because of this diversification effect, small
investors would dump bonds and buy stocks. This would push stock
prices up, and the market would reach a "permanently high plateau." In
the optimistic world of the 1920s, Fisher foresaw a new financial order
based on stocks and investment trusts. Investors big and small would
hold investment trusts that offered broad, diversified stock market
portfolios. They would provide a sustained demand for shares in America's corporations.

Unfortunately, Fisher made his prediction in the summer of 1929,
and the American public never forgot it. Not only did Irving Fisher lose
his own life savings, but he lost his in-laws' savings as well—and he was
devastated to have encouraged a nation of small investors to invest with
him in the market.

Yale University bailed him out by buying his grand house on Prospect Street in New Haven and renting it back to him until he passed
away in 1947. The cloud of his market forecast followed him to the
grave. Indeed, it followed him beyond it. I was born in New Haven, and
as a child I played in the front yard of Irving Fisher's mansion, which
had been converted to a school after he passed away. No one ever told
me it was the home of America's greatest economist. A little more than
a decade after his death, New Haven regarded Irving Fisher as best
forgotten.

A MACHINE THAT MAKES THE LAND PAY

"I like to see a man standing at the foot of a skyscraper," he said.
"It makes him no bigger than an ant—isn't that the correct
bromide for the occasion? The God-damn fools! It's man who
made it—the whole incredible mass of stone and steel. It doesn't
dwarf him, it makes him greater than the structure."[5]

AYN RAND, *THE FOUNTAINHEAD*

To Ayn Rand, nothing embodied American individualism so much as
the skyscraper. The grand symbol of America created by the extraordinary force of a single visionary who overcomes convention and mediocrity to leave a mark on the world. In the 1920s, while the Soviets built
grim, constructivist housing blocks in Moscow for privileged party
members, Americans built Manhattan. The skyscraper was a new architectural order: the extension of the grid of the American city upward
to the sky. Skyscrapers and jazz heralded the American century. "Not
only is the skyscraper a symbol of the American spirit—restless, centrifugal, perilously poised—but it is the only truly original development in
the field of architecture to which we can lay unchallenged claim," wrote
critic Charles Bragdon in 1925.[6] The Manhattan that took shape in the
1920s amazed the world.

In 1929, Georgia O'Keeffe set up her easel and paint box close to the
window of her thirtieth-floor apartment at the Shelton Hotel, looking
south. She had a peculiar canvas that was twice as high as it was wide—a
vertical field, perhaps to echo the vertical window. O'Keeffe did not
bother sketching out the scene on canvas before beginning. Rather she
tried to feel it; her eye soared through the forest of New York skyscrapers. Evening fell. She picked her nearest neighbor as a focal point, the
Berkley Hotel. The Berkley became her way of retelling the history of
architecture. The golden pagoda on the top began the tale: elemental
building, roof, door, and walls. It sat precariously atop a crenulated castle with a single rose window—the archetype of gothic design, a passing
reference to cathedrals and Notre Dame. Beyond these forms lay the
future: a great glowing avenue with shining headlights stretching limit-
lessly southward to the horizon. It became the modern counterpoint to

antiquity—its angularity pulling and tugging at the Berkley, tipping it left into the graceful spire of another skyscraper, perhaps the Chrysler building. To the right she imagined an architecture that had not yet even been created: an unadorned grid of windows; a digital surface, a concept that would not be realized until the 1950s, but to her, perhaps, the ultimate expression of a new American art form.

O'Keeffe and husband, the photographer and gallery owner Alfred Stieglitz, were Manhattan Cliff Dwellers. They embraced the new vertical city. O'Keeffe used her 49th Street views to inspire a distinctive new style of painting: elemental, unadorned, and yet strangely luscious and sensual. Her paintings of skyscrapers executed from 1924 to 1929 captured the sense of novelty and boldness but above all else, they searched for a new American archetype, some primal form or theme that would release her art from the academic constraints of decorative Beaux Arts style.

The Shelton suited her well. It was the type of building that could have been designed by Ayn Rand's Howard Roark: "The structures were austere and simple, until one looked at them and realized what work, what complexity of method, what tension of thought had achieved the simplicity. . . . The buildings were not Classical, they were not Gothic, they were not Renaissance. They were only Howard Roark."[7] The Shelton is today a shockingly undecorated building, defined by its stark utilitarian form. Indeed, it was the first major building to conform to the design code requiring tall New York buildings to step back from the street; New Yorkers worried that cheek to jowl towers would shut out light. They forced architects to use setbacks. O'Keeffe celebrated the Shelton's sharp setbacks in her paintings: it was both the subject of her art and the home for her new, vertical, high-tech order.

Her masterpiece was *Radiator Building, at Night* a painting of Raymond Hood's greatest building, which still stands on Bryant Park, a striking, set-back tower with luscious black facing and a magnificent crown. It was built to advertise the American Radiator Company (later the American Standard Company), which supplied plumbing and fixtures to the building trades. The skyscraper punctuated an amazing century of American real estate innovation. This peculiarly American style of building represented a key inflection point—a moment when cities began to grow up, not out. The first skyscrapers appeared in New York (1870) and Chicago (1891), and by the 1920s, they had entirely transformed urban architecture. Steel frame construction freed the walls of the building from the responsibility to bear the load of the upper floors, thinning the skin of the building and eliminating the limits of vertical growth. Tensile metal replaced masonry; elevators became the new circulatory system of the goliath. Eventually integrated systems of heating, cooling, and illumination completed the redefinition of the American office building and the reshaping of American cities.

FINANCING MODERNITY

Skyscrapers also demanded a "new-age" technology for raising capital. Almost all of them were built on borrowed money through a new kind of bond that securitized the mortgages used to construct the buildings. Instead of a bank holding the mortgage on a property, American real estate financiers figured out how to borrow directly from retail investors. There was at least one kind of bond that American investors fell in love with in the 1920s: skyscraper bonds.

It worked like this. A developer would form a corporation to build a building, borrowing a significant part of the capital for construction. A mortgage company would underwrite the debt, issuing bonds to small investors through a retail sales force—a legacy of the war bond distribution system. The mortgage company bought the bonds it could not sell, leaving it exposed to the potential default by the borrower; however, the bulk of the exposure to the real estate market belonged to individual investors, who bought these bonds in denominations as small as 100 dollars.

For investors too cautious to fling themselves into the bubbling equity market of the 1920s, skyscraper bonds seemed a perfect balance between prudence and modernity. After all, how could a bondholder lose if the developer defaulted? The lenders would own the property: a big, public, physical asset that could be resold. The assets of the company seemed completely transparent: you could walk downtown and see the actual building that backed your bond. They were also investments in the new technology of American cities: an architecture that transformed the American metropolis into a three-dimensional matrix, soon to be connected by cross-walks, airplanes, and dirigibles.

More than a thousand of these new mortgage bonds were issued with more than 4 billion dollars in face value. More buildings taller than 200 feet were built in New York between 1922 and 1931 than in any other period before or since. In 1925, an eighth of the national income was derived from building construction.[8] The reach upward was made possible by the invention of the elevator, the development of steel-frame construction, and the demand for dense, location-specific business operations. Skyscrapers made possible the multiplication of prime city locations many times over—indeed, they gave these choice spots an iconic sculptural identity. Great buildings like the gothic-inspired Woolworth Building, designed by Cass Gilbert, were advertisements for themselves. They established a new metric for executive prestige: giddy heights; glorious views; and architecture that, for all its symbolism and iconography, ultimately was, in Gilbert's own words, "a machine that makes the land pay."[9] And did it.

Each new skyscraper was a vast layer-cake of floors for rent. As business boomed in cities like New York, Chicago, and Detroit, tenants took out long-term leases on floors in these new steel and stone machines. Each building was thus a bundle of long-term future cash flows promised by leaseholders. Mortgage-backed securities packaged and transformed these flows into bond coupons, which were then clipped and claimed by investors. Skyscraper mortgage bonds transformed the new-style rents on the sky into monetary assets.

Of course, skyscraper bonds did not appear out of thin air. While mortgage securitization had a long history before the 1920s, S. W. Straus & Co., of Chicago claimed to have developed and perfected single-building mortgage securitization in 1909.[10] Straus began as a Midwestern mortgage bond company, but it became the leading issuer of skyscraper bonds. At its peak in the 1920s, the market for skyscraper bonds was dominated by three companies: the S. W. Straus & Co., the American Bond & Mortgage Company of New York, and G. L. Miller & Co. also of New York. The bond houses played a central role in the securitization process. Not only did they construct the bond issue by designing the terms of the securities, the payment schedules, coupon rates, and collateral requirements, they also marketed the bonds to the public and serviced the debt. They collected the rents from the borrowers and paid the bond coupons to investors. Safety was their hallmark. The Straus Company, for instance, prominently advertised a continuous history of mortgage bond issuance of more than thirty-two years.

The crash of 2008 made me curious about the history of commercial mortgage-backed securities in America, and I had a vague idea that a public market for commercial mortgage securities existed in the 1920s—in fact, I had bought a few of these early bonds on eBay as curiosities. These Internet finds piqued my academic interest. I just knew that today, bond issues to build buildings are considered a new innovation. Twenty years ago, if I wanted to buy a bond backed by, say, the John Hancock Center in Chicago, I could not do it. Only in recent times have financial engineers revived the securitization market for skyscraper finance. What happened to this huge financial market for single building bonds in the 1920s? How could a market like that just disappear for generations?

Oddly enough, the American mortgage bond market was a victim of its own success. Hints of the weakness of this new age mortgage financing appeared well before the 1920s. In 1911, Harry S. Black, the president of a major New Jersey development company, noted:

> The skyscraper problem in lower New York is attracting more attention. . . . The difficulties which have been encountered by many large office structures below the City Hall in showing a fair return of their investment, in addition to the strong competition occasioned by the many new buildings within the last year or two have demonstrated that so far as office buildings, theaters and hotel were concerned, New York is overbuilt.[11]

These pre-war financial problems abated, and office building construction resumed with a boom in the 1920s. The sheer volume of new bond issues—many in small denominations to attract retail investors of modest means—shocked even real estate industry leaders. Lee Thompson Smith, president of the National Association of Building Owners and Managers, complained in 1926 of outright speculation in the office market and of a bubble driven by bond issuers rather than fundamental demand:

> Buildings are being put up entirely through the endeavors of bond houses to sell bonds, whether the buildings are needed or not . . . over production is caused by speculative builders who borrow the full cost of construction regardless of return. They then sell the

building at a profit and proceed to erect another somewhere else....
I condemn the scheme of financing the whole cost of building enterprises by bond houses with their thin margin of ownership equity. It
is unscientific, loaded with danger and riding for a fall.[12]

Smith, of course, was right. The tail was indeed wagging the dog. An
extraordinary example of this was the sale of the G. L. Miller Company
in July of 1926 to a consortium controlled largely by the Brotherhood
of Locomotive Engineers.[13] The reason for labor's involvement? The
potential to sell real estate bonds directly to union membership. The
popular demand for mortgage bonds was so great that the bond houses
themselves were perceived as money machines.

On August 6, 1926, a strange thing happened. The Miller Company
undertook a bond issue for the 571 Park Avenue Corporation and, despite an apparently successful sale of securities, it failed to pass along the
proceeds to the development company. Instead it declared bankruptcy.
The Miller Company had been using issuance proceeds to cover, among
other things, payments to bondholders of earlier issues. As James
Grant, financial historian, commentator on bonds markets, and author
of *Money of the Mind* noted, "the Miller enterprise was a kind of Ponzi
scheme."[14] Part of the common lore of the 1920s is the great Florida
Land Bubble that burst in 1925. We still chuckle to this day when someone brings up buying swampland in Florida. It is worth considering that
perhaps skyscrapers built in Manhattan were the real bubble, driven by
a demand for bonds that backed them rather than by a demand for the
amazing new machines to make the land pay.

The Straus Company survived until 1932. It turns out that it, too,
had eventually resorted to robbing Peter to pay Paul. Even after numerous bond failures, however, Straus had gotten itself placed in an
outrageous position of representing the interests of mortgage bondholders in their claims to foreclose on properties of borrowers in default. Straus itself held equity positions in the building companies and
thus had a direct conflict of interest when it sought to work out a deal
that would benefit the borrowers at the expense of the lenders. The
firm's behavior was so egregious that it sparked one of the first major
fraud investigations by the newly constituted Securities and Exchange
Commission (SEC).

If the collapse of building values and the widespread defaults did not destroy the market for mortgage bonds, the complete erosion of trust must finally have done it. Millions of small investors had bought bonds from Straus and Miller and other companies on faith. They believed in the unblemished track record and in the value of the collateral. When these companies failed, they pulled down with them any faith that the legal system could protect investor interests. The SEC investigation culminated in a report issued in 1936 titled *Committees for the Holders of Real Estate Bonds*. It starkly highlighted the many and various ways by which mortgage investors had been tricked and cheated.[15]

For example, take the Majestic Apartments on Central Park West, a grand art deco edifice designed by architect-developer Irwin S. Chanin in 1930, situated between 72nd and 73rd Streets and financed by a bond issue by the S. W. Straus Company in June 1930. Straus underwrote $9.4 million in 6% bonds. Despite motivating its sales force with a contest, by October, more than $2 million went unsold. An SEC deposition of the Straus New York chief at the time revealed what happened to unsold construction bonds. They were repackaged as short-term notes backing an issue by Straus; now dubbed "Straus-Manhattans." Putting old wine in new bottles did the trick—the bonds were pumped out to a market unaware that the security on their short-term debt was an unbuilt property that would not actually pay out for some time. Majestic debt defaulted in December 1931, and Straus-Manhattans followed suit in 1933.

The SEC report detailed example after example of how Straus and other major firms looked after their own interests rather than those of their investors. When the dust settled after the investigation, the SEC concluded that fundamental flaws existed in the bankruptcy process that left publicly issued security holders exposed to exploitation. They added the specter of institutional failure to economic collapse.

O'Keeffe's own interest in the skyscraper also passed with the great crash. After 1929, she abandon the skyscraper for her signature cow skull and flower paintings and became better known as a western artist; a sage who preferred the simplicity of the American Southwest to the buzz of urban life. Then again, maybe she recognized that the American love affair with the skyscraper had ended, at least temporarily, in tragedy.

THE WRECKAGE OF 1929

The Crash of 1929 and the Great Depression seemed for many to be proof of the failure of capitalism—or at least the failure of unregulated markets. Keynes saw it as the result of Americans' propensity for excess speculation. John Kenneth Galbraith—one of the most entertaining analysts of the Crash of 1929—saw it as the consequence of cynical Wall Street hucksters preying on the hopes and dreams of small investors and the irrational spirit of speculation. The Great Depression that followed has been blamed on the bubble of the 1920s and the financial fallout of the stock market decline.

Wall Street stocks in the 1920s certainly did boom with the unprecedented American enthusiasm for equities—fueled in part by brokers, investment trusts, and dreams of speculative profits. They crashed on October 28, 1929 (Black Monday), dropping by nearly 13% in a single day—a little more than a month after stock prices on the London Stock Exchange had collapsed. People who bought stocks on borrowed money were ruined. Banks that held stocks as collateral were in trouble. The crash was followed by roughly a decade of extreme turbulence in the stock market that turned on its head the earlier economic prediction of stocks as safe and bonds as risky.

Not everyone lost faith in the market. *Fortune* magazine launched its fabulously expensive inaugural issue in January 1930, with a cover depicting—without a trace of irony—the wheel of fortune, a motif with echoes of *The Great Mirror of Folly*. My grandfather—and many other investors whose expectations had formed in the optimism of the 1920s—held fast to stocks and even bought more. But others looked for signs that the 1920s were nothing more than an irrational bubble that burst; a moment of speculative mania with no rational foundation.

Recently an economist at Harvard Business School, Tom Nicholas, figured out an interesting way to test whether stock prices in the 1920s were based on rational assessment of future promise. Tom studies technological innovation. He theorized that the boom in stocks prices in the 1920s was due to the extraordinary technological change in that period and the high value investors placed on innovation. Were stocks booming because of the invention of the radio, the widespread adoption of the automobile, the emergence of public air travel, and myriad other changes to modern life? In a period when old technology was losing and new technology was winning, perhaps investors placed a premium on companies that were ahead of the curve. That is also, of course, the story of the Tech Bubble of the 1990s. New economy stocks shot up in the expectation that they would become dominant companies.

Nicholas tested his theory in an interesting way.[16] He took all the patents by American companies in the 1920s and then looked decades into the future to see which patents turned out to be valuable. He calls this "knowledge capital." Nicholas found that firms with the most knowledge capital were much more valuable in the 1920s. The market in the 1920s treated innovation as a major factor in pricing. This was particularly strong in the last great run-up to the crash, from March 1929 to September 1929. Firms with no patents seriously lagged those with knowledge capital. It was also true across all industries—not just high-tech ones. Investors in the 1920s saw the world at a major turning point in many areas, and they valued companies with the knowledge capital to take advantage of this change.

Nicholas also found that, while firms after the crash continued to invest in research and development, investors did not value knowledge capital in the same way from 1932 to 1939. His conclusion: investors in the 1920s were driving up the prices of firms that, ex post we know had more knowledge capital. The steep rise in the 1920s reflected the importance of innovation in a world of change. Investors at that time literally placed great stock in the future. Were they wrong to do so? The Dow Jones index went from $63.90 in 1921 to a peak of $381.17 in 1929 and then dropped to $41.22 in 1932. How could the valuation of knowledge capital change so abruptly?

Perhaps Keynes had it right. Perhaps investors anticipated the financial and economic troubles that followed. Patents are only designs for future technology. They only pay off when things are actually built and then sold. They are not about products that people are already used to, like tobacco. Their value will fluctuate considerably with prospects for future consumption. For example, a company in the 1920s may have patented a brilliant new process for making color photographs. During times of high consumption, this might lead to rapid product development and marketing to a world looking for the latest new gadget. However, in a world where unemployment looms and people are thinking about savings and safety rather than buying new stuff, the company will likely have to put off product development for years. Their patents remain good, but their economic value drops with the hopes that they would bring revenues any time soon.

Irving Fisher's net present value criterion would tell you that an unanticipated event that suddenly makes companies shelve all their most innovative new projects will undoubtedly cause stock prices to drop. Delaying a profitable project by ten years will cause its present value to drop by roughly half. If the project is a risky one—and most innovations are—a delay of ten years could cause the value to drop by 80%. Perhaps the fall in share prices in the early 1930s reflected the realization that those marvelous patents, so valuable when people had money in their pockets, would take a very, very long time to yield future dividends.

A contrary view—proposed by Bradford DeLong and Andrei Shleifer, both deep thinkers about markets, is that the euphoria of investors about the market pushed valuation way beyond its fundamental economic worth.[17] Delong and Shleifer tested this idea by gathering prices of investment funds trading in the 1920s and looking at the prices of the stocks they held. What the professors found was that investors typically paid a premium of 60% just to get the pool of stocks. They could have "rolled their own" for a much cheaper price. The conclusion: if investment trusts were overvalued, then anything and everything selling on the stock market must have been overpriced as well. Investor sentiment—not rational investing—was behind the market of the 1920s.

Edgar Lawrence Smith's investment fund outlived the fame of its author. His name went from being literally a household word in the 1920s to a relatively obscure footnote in financial history, despite the major role he played in highlighting the benefits of equity investing. Smith continued his research interest in the markets, however. When I was studying a curious thing called the "weather effect"—the peculiar tendency of stock markets to go up on sunny days—I found Smith's 1939 treatise *Tides in the Affairs of Men*. The book argues that weather volatility and stock market volatility are tied together, and they both are driven by sunspots. Smith was convinced that the weather predicted the Crash of 1929. I'm not so sure he was right about that one.

TESTING PREDICTIONS

One major effect of the Crash of 1929 was a loss of American faith in the cult of equities in general and Wall Street in particular. Irving Fisher was not the only forecaster embarrassed by the sudden reversal of the market. We saw earlier that the crash shook Keynes's iron faith in his own methods. Another investor who was similarly affected was Alfred Cowles, the heir to a Chicago newspaper fortune. Cowles met Irving Fisher at a tuberculosis sanatorium in Colorado Springs, and they spent time talking about the crash. Cowles was an investment advisor who had been managing his family's considerable portfolio in the 1920s and like many in his situation, he lost in 1929. Cowles wondered why the assembled wisdom of Wall Street had failed to warn investors of the impending catastrophe. Maybe the Wall Street analysts knew nothing more than their customers.

Cowles set about testing this idea with data. First, he collected all the various stock recommendations that the big brokerage houses had sent out through the 1920s and early 1930s. He compared these recommendations to a random selection of securities, using historical stock price and dividend information. His conclusion was devastating to the prediction profession. Stock market forecasters couldn't forecast. You were better off with a dartboard.[18] Although we know that Jules Regnault came to the same conclusion nearly a century earlier, investors in 1929 like Alfred Cowles learned the hard way. Later researchers looking at modern analysts' predictions and modern mutual fund performance generally find the same results. There is no evidence that professionals as a group add value (after taking their fee), and yes, compared to the typical mutual fund, you are typically just as well off with a no-fee dartboard—although a low-cost, well-diversified stock portfolio is an even better way to go.

Alfred Cowles tested the random walk model of stock markets as well. Again with no awareness of his predecessor Jules Regnault (or the subtleties of the equations for Brownian motion), Cowles looked at stock market returns over various holding periods to see whether they followed predictable trends. The answer was yes and no. There seemed to be some momentum in market price moves. For investment horizons up to three years, past trends appeared to persist, rather than reverse themselves, but the trading expenses necessary to profit from them would likely cancel out any gains.

There was one forecasting method that got the crash right, however: the Dow Theory. The Dow Theory is a cyclical model of stock market trends attributed to the founder of the *Wall Street Journal* and creator of the Dow Jones Industrial Average Charles Henry Dow. As explained and interpreted by later followers, the theory breaks the movement of the market into three parts: primary trends that last more than a year, secondary trends lasting months or weeks that can diverge from the primary trend, and tertiary movements that are daily "noise." The theory sought to identify the primary trend by using stock price movements based on the Dow industrial and Dow transportation indexes. The joint movement of the industrial and transportation indexes upward or downward was thought to be a signal of a primary trend and worthy of a buy or sell signal. The theory is not implausible—indeed, mathematicians have used this basic intuition of combining waves of different frequencies to model all sorts of natural phenomena. However, it contradicts the original insight that an efficient market is unpredictable.

In the late summer of 1929, William Peter Hamilton, the *Wall Street Journal* editorialist who used the Dow Theory to predict a bull or bear market, was decidedly bearish. He called the market decline, and followers of the Dow Theory were spared. This must have been particularly interesting to Cowles, because the Dow Theory was not some obscure hypothesis—it was widely followed by readers of the most important financial magazine of the day. Cowles invested a considerable effort to see whether there was something to the theory.

Cowles collected all of Hamilton's predictions over his career from 1907 to December 1929 (when he passed away) and tested to see whether the forecaster just got lucky with one great call. Cowles concluded that the Dow Theory would have done no better than simply passively holding a portfolio of stocks and came to the nihilistic conclusion that not even the best and brightest could have predicted the market crash. Cold comfort to his friend Irving Fisher, of course. However, his conclusions did not make a big splash. More people alive today have heard more about the Dow Theory than about Alfred Cowles.

But Alfred Cowles did have a profound impact on the future of academic research in finance, both as a researcher and as a benefactor. His greatest contribution to modern finance was his focus on data and statistics. To test his theories, Cowles created a complete database of US stocks and their dividends that started in 1872. This was so demanding that he was not able to use the human calculators of his day—clerks who did arithmetic calculation before the advent of electronic computing. He instead used the new technology of punch-cards to construct his stock market indexes.

Cowles—in an interesting parallel to Jules Regnault—was a practitioner who nevertheless had a deep love and extraordinary intuition for statistics. His tests about market forecasters and time-series patterns in the stock market index became landmark research papers in the empirical study of the efficiency of the stock market. Cowles carried the torch of Regnault's random walk theory into modern times and developed a number of new methods to empirically test it. As a benefactor, however, Cowles has had even more influence. He endowed a research center for the study of markets—called the Cowles Commission for Research in Economics, which is now housed at Yale University. The foundation published a number of his first studies but also brought together leading scholars interested it the role of markets in society. A unifying factor in their research came from Cowles's personal passion for wedding mathematical and statistical tools with a deep curiosity about the markets.

Alas, it turns out that Cowles was wrong about the Dow Theory. A replication of Cowles's work that takes into account risk as well as return would actually have added 4% per year to an investor's portfolio by following his recommendations.

Didn't Jules Regnault's random walk theory say that's not possible? Yes perhaps, but we found that there was some basis for the forecasting ability. Delving deeper into the pattern of Hamilton's Dow-based predictions, my colleagues Alok Kumar of the University of Miami and Stephen Brown of New York University discovered that the Dow forecasts were based on past market trends. Using some tricks like neural network algorithms, we reconstructed the rules implicit in the Dow Theory. It was a market momentum strategy.

Not surprisingly, the Dow Theory predicted a bear market when prices had dropped in recent weeks. Several other price patterns were involved in bull or bear forecasts, making the Dow Theory a bit more complex, and of course Hamilton likely did not use a sophisticated "quant" model. Nevertheless, there was something to it, even in the years after the Dow forecasts stopped. Although Hamilton died at the end of 1929, taking the secret of the Dow Theory with him, our model of the theory generated excellent simulated performance over the following seventy years or so.

Did this shake my faith in the random walk hypothesis? Yes, maybe a little bit. As we have seen earlier, much of the edifice of high-tech modern finance is built on a foundation of unpredictability. It is as if all the pieces almost fit nicely together, but the gaps between them leave open possibilities for research and also perhaps hope for the world of speculators.

MIND OVER MARKET

The Dow Theory inspired generations of analysts looking for hidden structure in stock market trends. In March 1949, the sociologist Alfred Winslow Jones did a survey of a newly emerging field of technical stock market forecasting for *Fortune* magazine. With the sure-thing of an ever-rising market apparently gone forever, investors looked for expert advice on how to profit anyway from stocks. Jones noted the rise of newsletters based not on fundamental valuations of stocks, but on charts and statistical measures like volume of trade, ratios of advancing to declining stocks, measures of investor sentiment, and of course of past trends in the market. He wrote:

> In the past ten years, however, the market has been notoriously out of gear with the underlying fundamentals, hence the older methods of judging the market has been of little help. Moreover the competition in making money in the stock market is a good deal keener than in the roaring twenties; consequently there is a demand for new methods of calling the turn.[19]

This new field of technical analysis studied by Jones was almost certainly a response to the memory of the sudden Crash of 1929 and the hope of some rational method for forecasting the next market crisis.

Technical analysis was predicated on a belief that statistics could discover some hidden truth in the apparently random movement of the market. This quest for moral certainty with math hearkened back to Jacob Bernoulli himself.

The schism between believers in the efficient market theory and the predictability of the stock market with systems like the Dow Theory divided the investment world into believers and nonbelievers in value versus technical investing. In his article, Jones noted that one value-investor journalist directed "a steady, fine spray of ridicule at the technicians and lumping them with spiritualists, Ouija-board operators, astrologers, sunspot followers and cycle theorists."[20]

An alternative response to the shock of the Crash of 1929 was fundamental research. If the bubble and crash were due to market euphoria and then dashed expectations, the natural conclusion is that stock prices can deviate far from fundamental value. One way to deal with market swings is to look for mispricing of individual securities. Benjamin Graham and David Dodd published their book *Security Analysis* in 1934. The enormous success of Benjamin Graham's most famous student, Warren Buffett, has added to the widespread interest in *Security Analysis* over the years, but the appeal of the book in the depths of the Great Depression must certainly have been the premise that, while market prices fluctuate, the intrinsic value of a company can be uncovered through careful, thorough, and astute research. The book provides methods for probing beyond the accounting statements and reported earnings of a firm to understand its economic fundamentals, and to make reasoned forecasts about its future earning power. *Security Analysis* did not promise easy money; analysis was a discipline to be learned through careful study. It required mastering not only quantitative methods but also developing superior qualitative judgment.

Like many inspiring books, it taps into powerful archetypes. *Security Analysis* constructs a bold, independent persona, an investor with the courage of his or her convictions, who stands strong against the

fickle winds of the market. Graham and Dodd's security analyst is not
a mere speculator willing to risk loss, but rather a principled investor
who makes few but carefully considered commitments and then sticks
to them. This investor seems closest in character to Ayn Rand's Howard
Roark in *The Fountainhead*: a person of brilliant insight and uncom-
promising integrity who sees the world about him switching from one
style to another while he holds firm to the work he has done. Graham
and Dodd's security analyst was a perfect hero for new, turbulent, and
frightening times.

THE LEGACY OF THE 1920S AND THE CRASH

The arc of American enthusiasm for stock market investing in the 1920s
was driven by several factors: the spirit of self-reliance, the historical
evidence that stocks beat bonds, the marketing of stocks by Wall Street
to fill in the product gap left by war bonds, the shift in risk offered by diversified portfolios to smaller investors, and perhaps the technological
acceleration that placed a premium on knowledge capital mixed with
the euphoria of speculation.

In some ways the American fascination with stocks was no different from what happened in Britain, China, or Russia with the global
rediscovery of equity investing. One key difference is that the US stock
market emerged at about the same time America was becoming an
important world power. The spirit of enterprise, shareholder democracy, and corporate capitalism became part of America's self-image.
The stock market crash of 1929 not only called stocks into question as
an investment, but also eroded the confidence Americans had in the
financial structure itself. In the depths of the Great Depression, the
US government addressed this crisis of confidence by establishing the
SEC specifically to rebuild faith in the fairness of financial markets. But
the fact that stocks could change value so quickly raised doubts about
whether the market was really an appropriate vehicle for long-term savings after all. With these doubts in the air, a long time passed before
Americans rationally revisited the question of whether stocks were a
good investment.

The skyscraper craze also diminished after the crash, although some
of our most beautiful buildings were designed and built in the 1930s.

FIGURE 27. Detail of Josep Maria Sert's mural for the lobby of
Rockefeller Center, New York.

Rockefeller Center, with its grand Radio City Music Hall and soaring
RCA (now GE) tower, were planned in 1928 but only finally completed
in 1932. The turn of the times was embodied by the dust-up over
the murals for the RCA lobby. The Rockefellers commissioned the
Mexican muralist Diego Rivera, whose ambitious painting *Man at the
Crossroads* depicted social transformation in the twentieth century. It
was a humanistic view, centered on a proletarian-scientist controlling
the scientific nexus of the modernity: mechanization, biology, astronomy. To the side, Rivera portrayed two views of society; one view was
a smoke-filled room of elites playing cards and drinking cocktails. The
other view pictured Lenin, Trotsky, and a nursing mother. The implicit
question asked by Diego Rivera: which vision of the future do you
choose?

The Rockefellers had the mural painted over and replaced with one
by Josep Maria Sert—a friend of Salvador Dalí and a powerful muralist in his own right. He created an admirable interior in classic Beaux
Arts style, replete with muscular laborers building the magnificent skyscraper—the cathedrals of Manhattan. Airplanes swirled into the tun-

nel of the heavens. It pays its respects to globalization, mechanization, and the American working man. Nevertheless, it lacks the glowing optimism of the 1920s. Its sepia tones are somber. Its dynamic sweeps and trompe l'oeils are frightening. Its swirls and vistas seem to fight against the curved but stolid rectilinearity of the art deco lobby design. When you walk into the GE building today, you still feel as though you are trapped in a terrifying dream of humanity cast down into a purgatory of construction, having neither reached up to heaven nor fallen down into hell. It catches the spirit of the 1930s rather well.

RE-ENGINEERING
THE FUTURE

While the Crash of 1929 alerted Americans to the uncertainty of financial markets, the Great Depression underscored the enormous risks of the macroeconomy. These risks called for financial solutions. The widespread unemployment and poverty in the 1930s made it clear that America faced a desperate crisis of savings and social insurance. Private insurance, personal savings vehicles of various types, federal, state, municipal, and corporate pension plans all existed in America before the depression, but the economic crisis revealed their fragility and exposure to a systemic shock. America in the early twentieth century placed hope in corporations, but the recession caused many to fail, taking jobs and pension plans down with them. What could replace corporations as providers for current and future needs? Government.

As governor of New York in 1930, Franklin Roosevelt introduced a state pension plan. He brought this concept to his presidency as a major element of the New Deal. In this chapter, we look at the transformation of American finance during the 1930s. As with many of the financial innovations discussed in this book, the changes that took place addressed important problems with new methods but led to later difficulties. The financial architecture created in the 1930s is still with us, and the country still wrestles with the institutional issues it engendered. It is one of the most dynamic and interesting periods in the history of finance, and its legacy is still very much a part of the modern financial framework.

SOCIAL SECURITY

Everyone has begun to realize something must be done for our
old people who work out their lives, feed and clothe children
and are left penniless in their declining years. They should be

Frances Perkins, economist and architect of the US Social Security system.
Cornell School of Industrial and Labor Relations, Ithaca, N.Y.

made to look forward to their mature years for comfort rather
than fear. We propose that, at the age of 60, every person should
begin to draw a pension from our Government.

HUEY LONG, 1935 SENATE RECORD[1]

"Share our wealth," proclaimed Huey Long, the charismatic populist
senator from Louisiana. His plan was to redistribute the wealth of Wall
Street millionaires to the people. A centerpiece of his program was a
guaranteed retirement pension for everyone with an income under
$10,000 per year; paid for not by worker contributions but by taxes
on the rich. Long saw the government as an equalizer and provider.
In contrast, Franklin Roosevelt envisioned a pension plan that workers self-financed—a government-run savings program that was funded
by contributions. In the debate over Social Security in June 1935, Long
grandstanded in the Senate, accusing Roosevelt of scuttling the pension
plan by failing to contribute the $3 billion needed to fully pay for it. In
the end, however, Long voted for the bill, and Social Security became
law.

Social Security was originally envisioned to provide life annuities
upon retirement for low-income workers, but it was soon modified to
be a program available to nearly everyone who worked. The US Social
Security system has some unusual features, which can be traced to the
particular attitudes of Americans in the 1930s about individual responsibility versus collective insurance. The sparks from the clash of Roosevelt
and Long over how to create a pension program resulted in a uniquely
American outcome.

Social Security pays a monthly benefit from retirement to death
based on the average of your highest thirty-five years of earnings—non-
working years count as zero. The benefit is adjusted through time for
changes in the cost of living. The system is mandatory. Workers must
pay in part of their wages to Social Security; it is essentially financed
by a tax on earnings. Social Security is actually something you might
like to buy in the private markets but would either find it impossible
or very expensive: a life annuity that is inflation-protected; guaranteed
by the strongest nation in the world, and backed by its taxpayers. It's an
amazing benefit.

The configuration of Social Security had a lot to do with the 1920s ethos of financial self-determination. The safety-net feature of Social Security clashed with the American spirit of individualism. The savings-plan feature, however, appealed to American notions of personal investment. This dual nature is what made it palatable to both the haves and the have-nots. By the 1930s, many Western European nations had adopted social safety net plans. The American approach was different, because it had to accommodate a different vision of the role of finance in society.

The problem then—as now—was how to pay for it. The original conception was to set up a fund with worker contributions and use this as an endowment to cover future withdrawals. At the time, however, this seemed almost preposterous. How would you invest the millions and billions coming in from wage earners? Would you buy stocks? Who would select them? Who would have control over this vast pool of wealth? *Fortune* magazine, analyzing the various proposals for Social Security at the time, estimated that the size of the fund in 1940 would have to be $75 billion—calling the establishment of such a reserve "financial idiocy of the first water . . . it would be virtually impossible to invest any such sum."[2] Huey Long of course would simply confiscate it from the investments of America's multimillionaires.

After some debate about the relative benefits of maintaining a fund versus simply treating the contributions and disbursements as income and obligations of the federal government, the latter won out. Social Security became a pay-as-you-go operation. Investor contributions to the system go into the Treasury's coffers, and monthly retiree payments come out. The Social Security contributions do not just sit in a bank, however. They are used to purchase US government bonds; the government invests your payroll taxes in its own securities. The bonds are a bit of accounting sleight of hand—placeholders for the government's long-term guarantees. They are not exactly an investment fund—although they could be treated like one if the government chose to sell them off and buy other assets.

Much of the discussion about Social Security from the outset focused on whether it would go bankrupt. The driving force behind the bill was the firebrand Secretary of Labor Frances Perkins—one of the key architects of the New Deal. She placed the implementation in the hands of a committee of economists. Edwin Witte, the executive director, was an economics professor at Wisconsin. Other academics included Wisconsin Professor John Commons, Professor Barbara Armstrong of the University of California, and J. Douglas Brown of Princeton.[3] This brain trust set up the basic structure and made the calculations about the near- and long-term financial viability of the plan. Of course the numbers did not exactly work out.

The March 1935 issue of *Fortune* highlighted the fundamental financial problems confronting the committee. It was not in any true sense an insurance plan, because it did not provide a pool of assets that could support future payouts. The *Fortune* article cited the shrinking ratio of workers to retirees, declining birth rates, and increasing life expectancy as factors that would inevitably lead to underfunding of the program by 1980—forty-five years after its creation:

> The whole plan realistically comes down to this . . . its final guarantee of performance is the general taxing power of the government. In essence the law declares that any man [sic] fulfilling the conditions named shall have an enforceable *claim against the government.*[4]

The designers went into the plan in full knowledge that future taxpayers would ultimately be on the hook for the system.

Pension historian Sylvester Scheiber argues that FDR did not intend a pay-as-you-go system at the outset, but that the political process made a kick-the-can-down-the-road solution inevitable. He points out that the designers knew full well that Social Security payments would consume a huge fraction of the federal budget in the late twentieth century, but that this problem just took a back seat to the more immediate imperatives of the New Deal.

We argue today about leaving a terrible legacy of debt to our grandchildren. No one blames our grandparents for doing precisely this with their eyes wide open to the consequences of ignoring modern demographic trends. My grandfather's generation stuck me with the Social Security deficit—although it also left me with the peace of mind that my aging parents and other relatives would be at least minimally cared for.

Social Security was an extraordinary financial innovation—and it was designed to go broke—or at least to use tax revenues to incentivize future lawmakers to revise its structure to maintain its viability in the future as liabilities of the plan exceeded promised government allocations. The creation of the Social Security system in 1935 exquisitely highlights the lessons of financial history. Recall how European governments financed themselves by issuing mispriced life annuities in the eighteenth century. How could actuarial mathematics, so crucial to the viability of the future nation-state, have been ignored? The design of US Social Security in the twentieth century suggest that the mispricing then, as now, was perhaps not due to the ignorance of the long-term costs, but rather to the political framework that gives higher weight to short-term dispute resolution.

FINANCIAL SOCIAL ENGINEERING

Such a major innovation as a government-guaranteed retirement life annuity to all American workers surely must have a profound impact on behavior. How does it affect savings rates, risk taking, personal initiative, family structure, employment decisions, and a host of other factors tied to long-term planning for the economic future? That is difficult to say. If a tax on my wages is buying an inflation-indexed life annuity, I'll be less likely to buy inflation-indexed bonds on my own. Indeed, I might simply save less, because I know there is a stream of Social Security payments waiting from me when I turn 65. Linking the payments to work-years and wages incentivizes employment and striving for higher wages. However, the existence of a minimum Social Security payment despite only working the bare minimum number of years may lead some people to a lifetime of slacking off after a few years of effort. Simply insuring retirement also incentivizes retirement. A worker with no pension will cling to a job as long as possible. Social Security was seen as a way to free up jobs for new—potentially more efficient—workers. Giving a safety net to a single person eliminates the need to fall back on family support in old age. One would expect fewer intergenerational households after Social Security. One might expect fewer children when the government, as opposed to offspring, is the principal form of social insurance.

Lives fill out the form that financial architecture creates. Rules established by the creators of Social Security not only change economic behavior, they also change the way we live and how we structure our families. Of course, it is difficult to test the effects of Social Security on society, because we don't have an alternative universe to compare it to. This does not mean, however, that economists cannot make predictions. Some researchers are currently at work on how Social Security may affect behavior and how different forms of savings have different potential effects.

Deborah Lucas is one of the leading financial economists of her generation and is deeply dedicated to national service. A professor at the Massachusetts Institute of Technology, she has served in the Office of Management and Budget, using her financial engineering skills to figure out how much the various guarantees made by the US government actually cost taxpayers. One of her projects is studying the effect of Social Security on people and financial markets. In various studies with coauthors John Heaton of Chicago and Stephen Zeldes of Columbia, Deborah uses theoretical models to look at what happens to savings rates, the choice to invest in stocks versus bonds, and what happens to security prices. Theory is a bit like using stick figures to represent human beings. There are situations in which a simplified representation can capture the essentials. But when details matter a lot, it is hard to know whether your theory is a reasonable representation of reality.

With this caveat, their theory suggests that investors with a government life annuity will reduce non-Social Security savings—some a lot and others just a little. Markets allow savers to "unwind" the Social Security plan, should they choose to do so. Another interesting thing that Lucas and colleagues found is that the original fear expressed in *Fortune* regarding the impossibility of investing Social Security inflows was probably overblown. It does not make much difference to asset prices whether the stocks and bonds are held by the government or private individuals. However, the deeper question of whether the companies will operate better under government ownership is another issue.

REBUILDING TRUSTS

Even while the New Deal was creating a government pension system to address the immense uncertainties about the future, it also was shoring up the private sector vehicles for savings. The modern mutual fund company was one of the greatest legacies of the New Deal. When Edgar Lawrence Smith launched his Investment Trust in 1925, he virtually had to design the structure from scratch: who governed it, how conflicts could be mitigated between manager and client, how investors could buy in and cash out—and many other practical issues. As investment trusts caught on, Wall Street figured out all sorts of clever variations on the basic theme, sometimes taking a good idea to dangerous extremes.

The most notorious investment company was the Goldman Sachs Trading Corporation in 1928. It was an extraordinary feat of complex financial engineering involving a pyramid of several companies, which ultimately gave Goldman controlling interest in a highly leveraged fund vehicle, which, on top of everything else, sold in early 1929 at a premium well above the market value of the assets in the portfolio. It made excellent fodder for Senate hearings following the crash:

> SENATOR (JAMES J.) COUZENS: Did Goldman, Sachs and Company organize the Goldman Sachs Trading Corporation?
> MR. SACHS: Yes, sir.
> SENATOR COUZENS: And it sold its stock to the public?
> MR. SACHS: A portion of it. The firms invested originally in ten per cent of the entire issue for the sum of ten million dollars.
> SENATOR COUZENS: And the other ninety per cent was sold to the public?
> MR. SACHS: Yes, sir.
> SENATOR COUZENS: And what is the price of the stock now?
> MR. SACHS: Approximately one and three quarters.[5]

Goldman Sachs Trading Corporation figures prominently in John Kenneth Galbraith's highly entertaining account, *The Great Stock Market Crash of 1929*—an ideal companion to *Het Groote Tafereel* and written in much the same spirit.

According to Galbraith, in the Crash of 1929, Goldman's fund plummeted from $104 issue price per share to $1.75 per share. One wonders what bonus the CEO of Goldman Sachs made at the end of the following year. By turning the spotlight on the Goldman Sachs Trading Corporation, Galbraith implicitly blamed part of the stock market bubble on the emergence of investment trusts. However, Galbraith highlighted a fundamental problem as true in 2008 as it was in 1928. Financial innovation pushes boundaries—sometimes at the expense of customers, clients, and investors. In a period of rapid financial innovation, risks are not always easy to assess—or worse, they are easy to conceal from investors by those who do understand them. The overleveraged and self-dealing investment trusts of the 1920s highlighted by high-profile Senate hearings and sensational stories of Wall Street financial engineering gave a black eye to all funds.

The SEC was charged with fixing the problem of "trust in the trusts." The commission began by standardizing their structure and governance. One of the problems identified in Senate hearing in 1932 was that the same companies that were underwriting stock issues were also selling funds that held these stocks. If, for example, a bank had trouble selling a new stock issue to the public, it could stick the dog into one of its funds. The SEC divided securities underwriters from the investment trust managers. To address the Goldman-style pyramiding of control, it prevented funds from holding shares in other funds. The Investment Company Act and Investment Advisers Act of 1940 also limited the leverage, compensation, insider control, and types of securities allowed to investment funds marketed to the general public. The leverage and control issues further protected against a repeat of the Goldman Sachs debacle.

Funds were set up as companies that held diversified portfolios of stocks and bonds and allowed investors to buy and sell shares in the pool. They had a governance structure independent of the firm that actually managed the money. They could not (at first) charge anything except a flat fee for services. These basic, plain-vanilla vehicles were simplified, stripped-down versions of the various products marketed at the height of the boom in 1928 and 1929, when more trusts were launched than new corporations.

One of the measures of the success of the American mutual fund legacy is how the funds actually performed for customers over the long term. For example, what happened to Edgar Lawrence Smith's Investors Management Company? That fund is actually alive today, and you can trace its daily fluctuations from 1932 to the present. The sponsoring company, American Funds, still maintains the daily record of prices and dividends. Reinvesting dividends (and not having to pay taxes), each dollar invested in the fund in 1932 would have grown to $2,747 by 2010; an annual, compound rate of return of about 10.7%. This is just about what an investment in a broad index of large US stocks would have earned—10.9%. You might not have beaten the market, but you would have made a great return over nearly eighty years, just as Edgar Lawrence Smith predicted. Those eight decades included four major US wars (Second World War, Korean War, Vietnam War, and the Gulf Wars), and they included most of the Great Depression and the Great Recession. They included periods of loose and tight economic policy, Republican and Democratic administrations, periods of double-digit inflation, and wild bubbles and crashes.

The American equity trusts that were created in the 1920s and regulated into mutual funds in the 1930s lived up to their promise of providing a sound vehicle for long-term investment growth across several generations. Although the legacy fund of Edgar Lawrence Smith's Investors Management Company is a "living fossil" that traces its lineage back deep into financial history, its great track record is a testament to the Darwinian theory of the survival of the fittest. The mutual fund structure today has a few more bells and whistles than the funds vetted by the SEC using the 1940 Investment Company Act, but all of us currently have an opportunity to take advantage of a financial tool that has admirably stood the test of time. While one always hopes that fund companies will offer the same thing just a bit cheaper, the fact is that the investment structure—with its transparency and simplicity—has become a model for the world.

By the way, the 1940 Investment Company Act did not make other forms of investment products illegal—it just made them hard to sell to the retail investor. For those investment managers who chafed at the restrictions of the 1940 act, they were free to manage nonretail money. As long as they did not solicit more than a few investors, they could do what they wanted. Interestingly, by exempting certain investment pools from the retail market, the act also created the modern hedge fund industry. The SEC ring-fenced retail investing, cleaned it up, and standardized it. It might be argued that this sanitization drove out some good ideas and some good managers; however, the hoped-for net effect was to bring Americans back to financial markets.

Thus, by the 1940s, the American financial system had been significantly re-organized. The effect on savings was mostly positive. A government safety net and a life annuity plan backed by a government guarantee were set up for a large fraction of workers. This did not replace individual investment choice, although it may have crowded it out a bit at the margins. Regulators used the crisis of the Crash of 1929 to streamline and standardize diversified investment vehicles and to break down some of the cozy relationships among financial institutions that were perceived to be detrimental to investor well-being. Even if the basic premise of trust in financial markets as an insurance mechanism against an uncertain future was shaken by the 1930s, a foundation was laid for a new, post-crisis financial world.

POST-WAR THEORY

In 1952, Harry Markowitz was invited to join the fellowship of the Cowles Foundation, then housed at the University of Chicago. Markowitz was a student interested in economics and a field of applied mathematics called "operations research," an outgrowth of the pioneering wartime effort to use mathematics to solve operational problems, such as strategically managing bombing runs and naval convoys. Operations researchers later found they could apply these techniques to a broad variety of fields: manufacturing, transportation, and even social and strategic interactions were analyzable by mathematical methods.

Markowitz had the idea that mathematics might be used to solve one of the most important of all financial problems: choosing the optimal investment portfolio. According to Markowitz,

> When it was time to choose a topic for my dissertation, a chance conversation suggested the possibility of applying mathematical methods to the stock market. I asked Professor Marschak what he thought. He thought it reasonable, and explained that Alfred Cowles himself had been interested in such applications. He sent me to Professor Marshall Ketchum who provided a reading list as a guide to the financial theory and practice of the day.[1]

Markowitz developed this idea into an extraordinary model that changed the world of investments in the twentieth century. In mid-century, even as Wall Street had turned mostly away from simple, diversified portfolio investing toward a variety of forecasting methods and fundamental security analysis, the seeds of mathematics and statistics planted in American finance by Cowles and Fisher began to grow and lead to a new financial revolution. In this chapter, we look at how the Markowitz model and a model that followed close upon it, the Capital Asset Pricing Model (CAPM), which revived a global framework

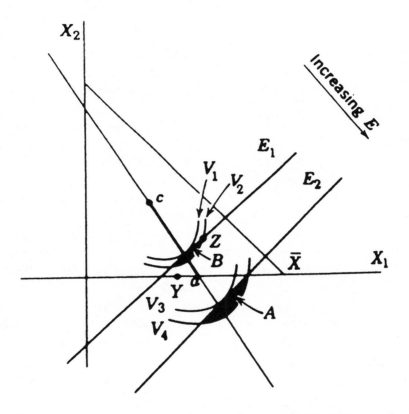

Harry Markowitz developed a mathematical method to choose an optimal investment portfolio. This is a picture of a Markowitz "optimizer" in practice. The curve shows a set of portfolios made up of stocks and bonds. Each portfolio has a level of expected return.

for investing and introduced new, unforeseen conflicts between finance and nation-states.

INVESTMENT AND EXACT SCIENCE

Harry Markowitz essentially applied statistical methods to the earlier insight of Henry Lowenfeld and Irving Fisher. He wrote down an exact formula for optimally diversifying across stocks. While Lowenfeld had suggested an equally balanced portfolio across the assets of different countries and Fisher had recommended a well-diversified investment trust, Markowitz asked how to achieve the best, most diversified solution.

The answer to this problem depended on how stocks moved together. Choosing stocks that are not correlated with one another improves the diversification of the portfolio and lowers the risk. By measuring the co-movement of each asset with every other asset and then also calculating its risk and return, Markowitz showed that it was possible to identify the portfolio with the lowest possible risk.

When stocks drop in a crash, bonds sometimes go up—this opposite behavior means that one asset "insures" against the risk of the other. The Markowitz model takes the basic intuition of not putting all your eggs in one basket and tells you just exactly how to best spread your risk across baskets. It tells you, for example, whether you are better off with 60% bonds and 40% stocks as opposed to say, a 50/50 mix. Markowitz took the guesswork out of portfolio composition and replaced it with a certain answer.

What is remarkable about Markowitz's method is that he completely disregarded the tenets of fundamental investing and deep research. He assumed that this information was already impounded in the prices and expected returns of the stocks. The only information a Markowitz-type investor needed was statistical: the expected return for the stock, the volatility of the stock (Regnault's "vibration"), and the correlation, or co-movement of each stock with every other one. He turned investment management from a profession based on deep research on companies into a mathematical exercise.

The Cowles research program moved to Yale in the 1950s, and Markowitz spent time in 1958 and 1959 writing up his thesis on investing into a book, *Portfolio Selection*, published in 1959 as Cowles Foundation Monograph 16. The style of the book was radically different from Graham and Dodd's influential text about fundamental investing and reflects the profound change in the tools of finance that had occurred since the 1930s.

The abstract scientist, armed with computer programs and linear algebra, eclipsed the heroic, loner, fundamental analyst. The new financial hero of the atomic age could show the path to optimality. As computers got bigger and bigger in the decades following the book's publication, it became feasible for managers of pension funds, college endowments, and other large pools of savings to use the Markowitz model. Of course, like all mathematical models, the application relies on the quality of the inputs and reliability of the assumptions. With these caveats—and later methods developed to deal with them—the Markowitz model has become the primary tool used by virtually all institutional portfolio managers in the world. Surprisingly, Harry Markowitz did not copyright or patent his optimizer. In fact, he gave it away to the world as an appendix to his book.

THE PERFECT PORTFOLIO

Bill Sharpe entered the economics profession just as the striking results of Markowitz's portfolio optimization model were introduced, and he wrote his dissertation, working closely with Markowitz while at the Rand Institute in Santa Monica—the mecca for operations research in the years after the Second World War. Sharpe's thesis essentially explored the logical implications of a world in which all investors optimized their investment portfolio. Suppose the Markowitz model came into universal use—what would happen to stock prices? People would care, first and foremost, about how assets comoved. The less stocks moved together, the more they insured against risk. People would use a stock's inherent tendency of co-movement as the basis for completely diversifying their portfolios.

This index of co-movement is now called "beta." When a modern investor looks at whether a stock will add risk to the portfolio, he or she looks at the beta. High-beta stocks add more risk than low-beta stocks.

Even more interesting than the beta measure, Sharpe discovered that ultimately, all investors converged on a single portfolio of risky assets. His theory predicted a one-size-fits-all portfolio. In Sharpe's theoretical world, everyone, rich or poor, all over the world holds shares in an investment trust that, in turn, holds all the companies in the world. We all delegate our investment decisions to a vast mutual fund manager who just holds everything. We don't share this wealth equally, however. My personal slice of that company is much smaller than say, Warren Buffett's. We all eat the same pie, only Buffett's slice is larger.

Of course, because the CAPM is an idealized model, it only makes predictions about a world that does not exactly exist. However, when conditions move closer to the assumptions of the CAPM, the model implies that people will move their choices closer to a broad, diversified portfolio. This is evidently what happened in the London market in the late nineteenth century, when investors had access to the world's assets. Following Lowenfeld's maxim to diversify internationally, as a group, London's investors in the golden age of globalization appear to have held assets in near-optimal proportion, as given by a Markowitz model.[2]

The CAPM is not only an elegant—though abstract—theory, but it is actually widely used for many things in finance. The prediction it makes about equilibrium rates of expected return for high-beta stocks and low-beta stocks is used in corporate decision-making and risk analysis. The prediction about the universal demand for holding a capital-weighted portfolio of assets led to the development of a new type of investment product, an index fund.

INDEXATION

The development of passive index-based investing came about from the convergence of two streams of academic research in the 1970s. The first is the CAPM result about the market portfolio. Sharpe's model was a marketer's dream, because it predicts immediate, widespread demand for a very simple product. The second was a re-consideration of the case for equity investment.

In the 1970s, with Edgar Lawrence Smith mostly forgotten, two young Chicago professors, Roger Ibbotson and Rex Sinquefield, decided to return to the basic question of whether stocks were a good long-term investment. They used a database from the Chicago Center for Research in Security Prices called "CRSP." They also collected data on US government bonds not previously studied by Smith or other analysts from the 1920s and 1930s and set about measuring the equity premium—the amount by which stock returns exceeded bond returns. Their finding? Stocks outperformed short-term US debt by about 6% per year over the period 1926 to 1976. Their sample fortuitously was completely independent of Edgar Lawrence Smith's study and included not only the Great Depression and the Second World War but also the horrendous stagflation of the early 1970s, when US share prices in real terms dropped by as much as 50%.

Ibbotson and Sinquefield not only documented the long-term positive performance of equities, they also made a bold prediction. They forecast the future performance of stocks, bonds, treasury bills, and inflation for the twenty-five-year period from 1976 to 2000 based on the historical experience. Although they were leaning against the winds of market skeptics in the 1970s, their predictions were surprisingly accurate—indeed, by 2000, stocks were a bit over the Ibbotson-Sinquefield predictions. Even today, despite a miserable decade in which equities have been flat, the predictions in 1976 are right on the mark. History turned out to be a pretty good predictor of the long-term rate of return to investing in stocks.

In an interesting parallel to the 1920s, the 1970s also saw the launch of a new kind of investment fund: a mutual fund indexed to the Standard and Poor (S&P) 500. William Sharpe worked with Wells Fargo in San Francisco to develop low-cost index products that echoed his CAPM market portfolio. On the East Coast, the Vanguard company offered its Market Index Trust in 1976 to match (not beat) the market with very low management fees. It was based on the principle of capturing the equity risk premium and relied on the long-term historical evidence of S&P 500 returns as a motivation. By indexing, you could earn the same long-term return measured and predicted by the Ibbotson-Sinquefield studies. It made long-term planning and investment really simple. Choose a cheap, generic brand and avoid the risk of picking a lousy manager. It was a simple, brilliant financial product based on the efficient market theory and the CAPM.

To the horror of much of the investment management community, over the next thirty-five years, the Vanguard Market Index Trust regularly beat the majority of equity mutual funds each year, even though their managers were unquestionably smart, experienced, well-educated, dedicated professionals whose compensation depended on doing well. It didn't seem to matter much. Long-term, investors were better off investing in the index fund than with active managers. Like Gary Kasparov being beaten by Deep Blue, a low-cost, mechanical rule of holding US equities in proportion to their company size turns out to eventually perform better than most managers. Even though by chance some active managers may beat the market in the long term, it is hard to figure out in advance who will outperform. Why does the indexation policy grind its competitors into dust? Simple: low fees and low trading costs. Active managers are expensive. They do a lot of research; they gather and digest information. They maintain staffs of analysts covering the prospects for various industries. They monitor economic developments that might affect the value of their securities.

In contrast, index funds simply hold everything. They are so diversified that even if there were some bad stocks in the portfolio, these do not have a proportionally large effect. By weighting by the size of the company, there is no need to buy and sell stocks to rebalance the portfolio. It does so automatically as prices for individual securities go up and down. Why doesn't everyone index? Perhaps this is due to an irrepressible, unwarranted, deeply seated hope to do better (i.e., human nature).

There is a bit of a downside to indexing, however. As Wells Fargo, Vanguard, and then other investment companies promoted the virtues of indexing, the pool of money invested in a "benchmark" portfolio of the S&P 500 grew to larger and larger proportions. Paradoxically, stocks in the index are actually overvalued. When one goes on to the S&P 500 index, its price goes up—not because the company has better earnings prospects, but simply because everyone wants to hold stocks that are in the index. This "index effect" is minor, however, and is a relatively innocuous, if unintended, consequence of a generally positive financial innovation.

Thus, by the mid-1970s, America had finally rediscovered the virtues of stock market investing and the attractiveness of an inexpensive, well-diversified investment portfolio. The fact that it took fifty years for this basic investment style to come back into vogue is telling. Crashes have great power to change public opinion. The crash of 1720 reversed the course of finance in Europe in the eighteenth century. The Crash of 1929 shook investors' belief in diversified market investing. It can take decades to re-learn or reconstruct a technology. And even with the slow return to well-diversified, low-cost investing, hope of beating the market continues to spring eternal.

A GLOBAL FINANCIAL FUTURE

In the twenty-first century, the dreams of Marquis Condorcet and many other prognosticators about a future made better by finance are coming closer to reality. The world has made progress in building an architecture of savings for the future. The World Bank has a think tank of researchers who track the increasing coverage of pension systems in every country in the world. Its 2012 report on international pension provisions would have thrilled Condorcet. Virtually every country has some sort of pension system organized by the government that provides support for retirees. In many of these, pensions are funded by the contributions of workers as envisioned by the marquis. The study shows of course that there is a lot of progress still to be made. High-income countries provide a plan for up to 85% of the labor force. In sub-Saharan Africa, this fraction is only about 10%. Pension expenditures as a percentage of GDP for high-income countries is about 7.5%—rich nations spend a lot to support their retirees.

Other dreams of the financial future have also come to fruition. Irving Fisher imagined a world where small investors all diversified by holding mutual funds. Another World Bank study tracked the development of the mutual fund industry in the late 1990s and found an extraordinary rate of growth. For developed countries particularly, mutual fund assets represented a nontrivial percentage of GDP.[3] They stood at $5.5 trillion in total assets in 1998, for example. Quite a recovery from the catastrophe of 1929. Even the CAPM is coming closer to reality. Professors Utpal Bhattacharya and Neal Galpin conducted a study in 2011 to track the prevalence of value-weighted investment portfolios around the world. They found that over the past thirty years, the trend toward the theoretical ideal has been pronounced—particularly in developed countries.[4]

Remember Keynes's prediction that a state investment fund would eventually supplant the individual investor? In some countries, this prediction is becoming a reality through the vehicle of sovereign wealth funds. Sovereign funds started in natural-resource-rich countries that generated government revenue from oil extraction. The Gulf states like Kuwait and Dubai needed vehicles for turning their oil into financial wealth, planning for a time when the oil would run out. A second wave of sovereign funds emerged in countries seeking to profitably invest their central bank reserves. Was Keynes right? Is this the future of world finance?

NORWAY

The discovery of oil off the Norwegian coast in the late twentieth century completely altered the country's economy. Oil—and lots of it—became a major factor. The discovery of petroleum in the North Sea was a windfall that in some sense challenged Norwegian society: how to preserve traditional values in the face of a flood of income?

The Norwegian Parliament—the Storting—made a remarkable decision. It created a national savings fund called the Norwegian Pension Fund Global, designed for the benefit of future generations of Norwegians. The fund would only spend a small fraction of its assets each year and let the remainder accrue interest and dividends from global financial investments. Keynes might not have approved of this abstemious approach, but it is in keeping with Norway's traditional values.

Is the Norwegian policy of investing in a portfolio of stocks and bonds a good idea? That is a profound question of political economy. Should a global investment portfolio be a part of the ideal state? What would John Law say? What would Karl Marx say?

In the twenty-first century, the American cult of equity has gone global. Stock investing has morphed into a national political strategy as opposed to an individual portfolio choice. The really important issue for Norway is not whether the global investment markets are efficient at the margin but whether transforming geological assets into financial assets makes sense.

A NEW ARCHITECTURE

Sovereign wealth funds represent a striking new financial innovation that might well realign world economy and diplomacy. Perhaps this is why other countries are getting into the act. Although the trend has been led by the petroleum-producing states, other countries have lately decided to create sovereign wealth funds. Singapore, Korea, China, and Russia have multibillion-dollar funds. Although some of the money for these funds comes from sales of natural resources and taxation, some of it comes from US dollar reserves traditionally held by nations to pay their bills. In the same way that a household might keep some money in a checking account and put the rest in an investment account, countries with sovereign funds are trading off liquidity for long-term asset growth. This trade-off makes some sense, but it raises some interesting new issues.

Why not hand the money back to taxpayers? In a transparent democracy like Norway, there is considerable trust in the political process. Nevertheless, there remains an agency problem. Countries with sovereign funds have broad variation in democratic processes and political transparency. Even in the United States, political favoritism and influence peddling around large state pension funds is rife. A government fund inevitably means a government contract for managing the assets of the fund. If the United States created its own sovereign fund, who would we ask to manage it? What would the salary of the chief investment officer be?

A more basic issue is the polarity between government versus household responsibility. The American enthusiasm for equity was based on a sense of self-sufficiency and independence. Owning shares and taking responsibility for your personal retirement went hand in hand in the 1920s, when stock and fund investing expanded to the ordinary citizen. A natural American view would be to tell the government to give the money back to the taxpayers and let them decide what to do with it. The periodic debates about Social Security in the United States divide along this fault line: individual investor accounts versus a government fund. Individual accounts would allow citizens to decide how much financial risk to take, or whether to consume their assets sooner rather than later. A government investment fund would relieve people from the burden of making those investment choices, but is essentially paternalistic. Paternalism versus individualism is a theme that runs throughout financial history. Fiefs, annuities, government bonds, corporate shares, mutual funds, and public capital markets all have individual investment decisions at their root. The institutionalization of savings, beginning with the emergence of state-owned pension funds and now sovereign funds, drives a wedge between savers and financial markets.

DELEGATED DECIDING

The good thing about institutionalizing investment is that it saves people from themselves. We know that most investors think they are good at stock selection, but they are not. We know that indexing is the smart thing to do for the vast majority of investors, but human nature stands in the way of rational choice. Richard Thaler, professor at the University of Chicago, is one of the leading lights of behavioral finance. He and Shlomo Benartzi of the University of California in Los Angeles did a study of investor decisions about pension fund options.[5] They found a disappointing pattern. People seemed not to understand the difference between stocks and bonds. They tended to divide their portfolio equally across the choices presented in their 401(k) plans, regardless of whether there were more bond funds or stock funds. The implications of this study and similar experiments testing investor skill at basic asset allocation are that people might not be able to manage their own investments. The future might be better for the average person if someone else decided for them. Walking down this logical path leads to a paternalistic state that disempowers the individual. This is contrary to American values and the early theme of a shareholder democracy. Or could we just push people a little bit in the right direction without taking the decision-making power from them? Thaler and Benartzi suggested establishing programs that have a default allocation or savings contribution percentage that is good for the average person. One could always override the default, but the no-decision decision is designed to be good for you. Richard Thaler and another co-author of his, Cass Sunstein, coined a term for this: a "nudge."[6]

Do you want the government thinking for you—nudging and cajoling you to save or put 50% of your savings into equities? I guess I wouldn't mind too much, given that the government already sets all kinds of norms and standards based on welfare considerations. How do you feel about the IRS withholding payroll taxes? Would you rather be given the option of setting aside your taxes each week from your salary and then writing a check for the total tax balance due on April 15? In the future, the balance between individual investment freedom and responsibility on the one hand and government-mandated or influenced savings behavior on the other will become central to personal finance. Perhaps sovereign wealth funds will replace personal savings, and the government will use them to fund post-retirement income. It might be the future of Social Security.

WHO WILL OWN COMPANIES?

A striking fact about sovereign funds is that as they grow, they will inevitably become the largest shareholders of every single publicly traded company in the world. Even at the current scale, Norway itself owns something like 2% of every corporation in Europe. The day will soon come when the boards of directors of every public company report primarily to a handful of sovereign fund managers. This concentration of ownership in the hands of national funds has pluses and minuses. When ownership is concentrated, corporate managers are on a short leash. A few powerful shareholders can easily kick out a dishonest or incompetent CEO. That is more difficult to accomplish when ownership is broadly diffused.

However, national interests sometime conflict with good corporate business decisions. For example, when the US government became a major shareholder in General Motors during the 2008 financial crisis, the prospect that the firm would outsource production overseas, even if it were profitable, dimmed. Imagine a discussion among sovereign fund representatives from China, Korea, and Russia at a Honda Motors Company board meeting over where to locate the next high-tech manufacturing plant! How about a BP board meeting packed with sovereign fund investors from the Emirates? The world has been sharply attuned to issues of foreign ownership and control of domestic corporations. In 2007, there was a great gasp when Dubai sought to buy a company that operated several US ports. The British shuddered at the thought of US ownership of their favorite sweets provider, Cadbury.

The French were up in arms about Pepsi's interest in yogurt manufacturer Dannon.

What is there to worry about? The current debate about foreign ownership of companies has contrasted the argument that sovereign funds have the same interests as any other shareholder (profit maximization) versus the suggestion that foreign owners will use their stake to further national interests. I believe that profit maximization will dominate most board decisions by sovereign funds, but that the potential for the exercise of rights in the national interest is also present and of potential concern. The reason for this is governance. States have a fiduciary duty to their citizens, not to other shareholders in a company. In certain circumstances, they will face trade-offs between profit maximization and national interest, and it is only right that they serve their citizens first. A question for every country is whether a sovereign fund will become a diplomatic necessity in the future. Can the United States live without a sovereign fund? Without a major financial stake in world corporations will the United States literally not have a seat at the table when major concerns, such as how corporations can fight global warming, come up?

Perhaps this is making too big a deal about the importance of corporate governance. After all, corporations were developed to allow investors to delegate management responsibility—we would mostly expect delegation to dominate. However, democracies appear to be particularly susceptible to the potential for political influence as politicians running for office may promise to influence corporate policy in favor of voters.

DON'T FORGET MALTHUS

If the growth of pensions, mutual funds, and sovereign funds has at least partially fulfilled the hopes and dreams of Marquis Condorcet penned in hiding in 1794, there are many signs that the Reverend Malthus was also partially correct. The same World Bank report that painted a glowing picture of the spread of pension systems around the globe also warned of an increasing inability to pay for them.

Malthusian demographic trends were blunted in the twentieth century by a decrease in fertility, despite a growing abundance of resources. Either through national policy (e.g., China) or individual choice (e.g., the United States), families had fewer children in the twentieth century than predicted by the famous eighteenth-century curmudgeon. And yet the demographics of modern times are devastating for models of financing retirement. The story of US Social Security is repeated with minor variations around the globe. With increasing life expectancy and decreasing fertility, the ratio of workers to retirees is reaching intolerable levels. This measure—the dependency ratio—is currently about 20% in the United States and 12% worldwide, according to the World Bank. By 2050, this ratio will rise to about 33% for developed countries: three workers for one retiree.

This shifting balance between workers and retirees affects all sorts of things. For example, if their pensions are already fully funded, then an increasing amount of the world's capital will be owned or promised to the aging population and invested for their benefit. One can imagine disputes between the haves and the have-nots—where the elderly are the haves and the young people are those without the capital. More likely, however, is a scenario in which the assets backing the huge pension obligations are simply government promises. We saw how the US Social Security system defaulted to a pay-as-you-go structure in the 1930s and how the French life annuity system in the 1770s had to partially default because the promises were untenable. History is almost certainly a template for the future. Perhaps Malthus was devastatingly correct in his prediction that the niceties of mathematics and probability forecasts just cannot make the schemes for retirement savings and social security add up. Finance in the end just might not work. The most basic of financial operations, the contract promising money in the future for money now, was invented in Mesopotamia 5,000 years ago and has been used ever since. But it might not be feasible at the global scale as a mechanism for managing retirement. Although much attention over the past decade has focused on the financial crisis of 2008 and restructuring the institutional architecture, the most fundamental challenge of facing the world is the finance—and politics—of savings.

In the United States, the future of financial failure is now. The bankruptcy of the city of Detroit in recent years brought the conflict between retirees and workers into sharp relief. Retired municipal workers—police, firemen, teachers, and sanitation workers—were confronted with the possibility that the city could default on its promises at a time when they needed the money the most. It might be unwise to forget the French Revolution. Breaking the social compact between government and citizens around the most basic of savings vehicles could cause irreparable damage to the political system as a whole. What might seem to be a financial restructuring of debt has deeper implications— and stirs up many different emotions—for people who are beneficiaries, and for younger people who are contemplating their relationship to government.

CONCLUSION

This book has been a broad inquiry into the development of finance as a technology and why it matters. From the first chapters it should be clear that roots of financial techniques are ancient and widespread. They are embedded not only in the economics of culture, but in its social and intellectual structures as well. The joint development of financial tools and complex society was a process of give and take on many levels. Discoveries of various financial solutions led to some of civilization's most important achievements: writing, the mathematics of probability, mechanisms for savings and investment, and the harmonization of global relations. Financial technology also created serious problems. The invention of debt was connected to slavery, reparations payments, imperialism, and financial crises. A long-term historical perspective on this duality in the nature of finance is important. At a minimum, it can guide our thinking about the design of financial institutions in the future.

Another argument in the book is that financial thinking is difficult. Although many of the complex techniques used by financiers today can be traced back a millennium or more, finance has often been regarded as foreign or contrary to tradition. Crashes and bubbles seem to always take people by surprise. Tools like options, futures, bonds, and mutual funds, and institutions like money markets, corporations, and banks seem to many of us impossibly complex. I argue that this is due at least in part to the relatively recent development of financial thinking and its reliance on specialized analytical tools—from the complex legal arguments of Demosthenes to the advanced mathematics of modern portfolio theory.

Like any technology, as finance became more sophisticated, it demanded increased specialization to understand and implement. By the same token, when finance failed, it had major economic implications for everyone—not just financiers. In times of financial crises, society has tended to express a collective nostalgia for a pre-financial world. However, the many examples in this book demonstrate that civilization has always depended on financial tools to move value through time and restructure myriad economic risks. Occasionally such thinkers as Karl Marx have dreamed of eradicating financial institutions like money or corporations. Despite the visceral appeal of such suggestions, rolling back the clock on financial tools would mean reversion to a way of life before the first cities and large-scale nation-states.

Another argument in the book is that there are different ways to solve financial problems. Chinese financial history provides the opportunity to study comparative development; particularly how political context can determine technical solutions. The development of money and coinage in China, for example, followed a pathway quite distinct from that in the Greek and Roman worlds. Yet ultimately there was a convergence in both East and West of money as a key tool of the state.

Cross-cultural comparison also shows the extent to which the corporation—in some sense the most important unit of enterprise in the modern global economy—is an unusual phenomenon. Chinese civilization flourished for millennia without the corporate form. This may or may not explain the differential industrial development in the late eighteenth and early nineteenth centuries between Europe and China—the Needham problem discussed in Chapter 10. However, the rapid adoption and repurposing of the corporate structure in late-nineteenth-century China shows a self-conscious flexibility and ingenuity—a clear understanding that finance is a tool that could be learned and adapted to solving China's problems. The history of the corporation over the long durée suggests that it is a very stable equilibrium—a kind of complex economic "game" that can be applied to many different kinds of enterprises and allows for many different players. I suspect it will be robust enough to survive even as the global financial system moves toward large-scale collective investments like sovereign funds.

In the larger context of global financial development, Europe's intense reliance on capital markets sets it apart. I argue that the roots of this distinct tradition lie in the fragmentation and weakness of medieval European states. A broader implication of this is that perhaps the global financial market system is a substitute for strong, centralized political organization with an organized bureaucracy. Financial markets and governments today coexist and complement each other, but at times they collide. Financial history provides a framework for understanding this dynamic.

History is interesting in its own right, but it is also important as a measure of the present and a guide for the future. As the world moves toward a collective global civilization with a greater proportion of its population participating in complex society, financial tools need to keep up. The lessons from our collective financial past take on more relevance. History has shown us financial mechanisms for risk sharing and intertemporal transfers and how variations in these tools can be adapted to different kinds of societies. We are free to repurpose past successes and learn from past failures about what to avoid. The experience of five millennia of financial innovation, however, suggests that finance and civilization will forever be intertwined.

NOTES

INTRODUCTION

1. Goetzmann, William H. 2009. *Beyond the Revolution: A History of American Thought from Paine to Pragmatism*. New York: Basic Books, p. xii.

CHAPTER 1

1. Jacobsen, Thorkild. 1976. *The Treasures of Darkness: A History of Mesopotamian Religion*, vol. 326. New Haven, CT: Yale University Press, p. 196.

2. For the historical background of its discovery and translation, see Foster, Benjamin R. (trans.). 2001. *The Epic of Gilgamesh*. New York: W. W. Norton and Company.

3. Schmandt-Besserat, Denise. 1992. *From Counting to Cuneiform*, vol. 1. Austin: University of Texas Press.

4. Aubet, María Eugenia. 2013. *Commerce and Colonization in the Ancient Near East*. Cambridge: Cambridge University Press.

5. Leiberman, Stephen J. 1980. "Of clay pebbles, hollow clay balls, and writing: A Sumerian view." *American Journal of Archaeology* 84(3): 339–358.

6. Englund, Robert. 1988. "Administrative timekeeping in ancient Mesopotamia." *Journal of the Economic and Social History of the Orient* 31: 121–185.

7. Englund, Robert. 2004. "Proto-cuneiform Account Books and Journals," in Michael Hudson and Cornelia Wunsch (eds.), *Creating Economic Order*. International Scholars Conference on Ancient Near Eastern Economies, vol. 4. Bethesda, MD: CDL Press, pp. 32–33.

CHAPTER 2

1. See Van De Mieroop, Marc. 2005. "The Invention of Interest: Sumerian Loans," in William Goetzmann and K. Geert Rouwenhorst (eds.), *The Origins of Value: The Financial Innovations That Created Modern Capital Markets*. Oxford: Oxford University Press, pp. 17–30, p. 19.

2. Van De Mieroop (2005), p. 29.

3. See Nissen, Hans J., Peter Damerow, and Robert K. Englund. 1993. *Archaic Bookkeeping*. Chicago: University of Chicago Press, p. 97.

4. See Van De Mieroop (2005), p. 20.

5. See Garfinkle, Steven J. 2004. "Shepherds, merchants, and credit: Some observations on lending practices in Ur III Mesopotamia." *Journal of the Economic and Social History of the Orient* 47: 1–30. Garfinkle, Steven J. 2012. *Entrepreneurs and Enterprise in Early Mesopotamia: A Study of Three Archives from the Third Dynasty of Ur.* Bethesda, MD: CDL Press. Van De Mieroop, Marc. 1986. "Tūram-ilī: An Ur III Merchant." *Journal of Cuneiform Studies* 38(1): 1–80.

CHAPTER 3

1. For details of this ancient financial district, see Chapter 5 in Van De Mieroop, Marc. 1992. *Society and Enterprise in Old Babylonian Ur.* Berlin: Dietrich Reimer Verlag, pp. 121–167.

2. Darling, M. L. 1925. *The Punjab Peasant in Prosperity and Debt.* London: Oxford University Press.

3. Goddeeris, Anne. 2002. *Economy and Society in Northern Babylonia in the Early Old Babylonian Period (ca. 2000–1800 BC).* Leuvin, Belgium: Peeters.

4. Goddeeris (2002), p. 153.

5. See Van De Mieroop, Marc. 2014. "Silver as a Financial Tool in Ancient Egypt and Mesopotamia," in Peter Bernholz and Roland Vaubel (eds.), *Explaining Monetary and Financial Innovation: A Historical Analysis.* Financial and Monetary Policy Studies, vol. 39. Cham, Switzerland: Springer International Publishing, pp. 17–29.

6. See Aubet, María Eugenia. 2013. *Commerce and Colonization in the Ancient Near East.* Cambridge: Cambridge University Press. Veenhof, Klaas R. 2010. "Ancient Assur: The city, its traders, and its commercial network." *Journal of the Economic and Social History of the Orient* 53: 39–82.

7. Larsen, Mogens Trolle. 1977. "Partnerships in the old Assyrian trade." *Iraq* 39(1): 119–145.

8. See Veenhof, K. R., and J. Eidem. 2008. *Mesopotamia: The Old Assyrian Period.* Saint Paul, MN: Academic Press Fribourg, p. 267.

9. Eidem, Jesper 2003. "Apum: A Kingdom on the Old Assyrian Route," in Klaas. R. Veenhof and Jesper Eidem (eds.), *Mesopotamia, The Old Assyrian Period.* Orbis Biblicus et Orientalis, vol. 160/5. Saint Paul, MN: Academic Press Fribourg, pp. 265–352.

CHAPTER 4

1. Stolper, Matthew W. 1985. *Entrepreneurs and Empire: the Murašû Archive, the Murašû Firm, and Persian Rule in Babylonia.* Istanbul: Nederlands Historisch-Archaeologisch Instituut te Istanbul.

2. Slotsky, Alice Louise. 1997. *The Bourse of Babylon: Market Quotations in the Astronomical Diaries of Babylonia.* Bethesda, MD: CDL Press, p. 7. See also an economist's perspective: Temin, Peter. 2002. "Price behavior in ancient Babylon." *Explorations in Economic History* 39(1): 46–60.

3. Slotsky (1997), p. 19.

4. Van der Spek, R. J., Jan Luiten van Zanden, and Bas van Leeuwen (eds.). 2014. *A History of Market Performance: From Ancient Babylonia to the Modern World*, vol. 68. London: Routledge.

5. See Jursa, Michael. 2014. "Market Performance and Market Integration in Babylonia in the 'Long sixth century' B.C.," in R. J. Van der Spek, Jan Luiten van Zanden, and Bas van Leeuwen (eds.), *A History of Market Performance: From Ancient Babylonia to the Modern World*, vol. 68. London: Routledge.

6. Huis, Joost, Reinhart Pirngruber, and Bas Van Leeuwen. 2014. "Climate, War and Economic Development: The Case of second century BC Babylon," in R. J. Van der Spek, Jan Luiten van Zanden, and Bas van Leeuwen (eds.), *A History of Market Performance: From Ancient Babylonia to the Modern World*, vol. 68. London: Routledge.

CHAPTER 5

1. Fleck, Robert K., and F. Andrew Hanssen. 2012. "On the benefits and costs of legal expertise: Adjudication in ancient Athens." *Review of Law & Economics* 8(2): 367–399.

2. Figueira, Thomas. 1986. "*Sitopolai* and *Sitophylakes* in Lysias' 'Against the Grain Dealers': Governmental intervention in the Athenian economy." *Phoenix* 40: 149–171.

3. Dunham, Wayne R. 2008. "Cold case files: The Athenian grain merchants, 386 BC." *Cato Journal* 28: 495.

4. Lysias. *Oration XXII*. Available at: http://www.gutenberg.org/cache/epub/6969/pg6969.html.

5. Moreno, Alfonso. 2007. *Feeding the Democracy: The Athenian Grain Supply in the Fifth and Fourth Centuries BC*. Oxford: Oxford University Press, p. 32.

6. The Dnieper river, in what is now Ukraine.

7. Demosthenes. 2004. "35 Against Lacritus," in *Demosthenes, Speeches 27–38*, Douglas M. Macdowell (trans.). Austin: University of Texas Press, p. 137, paragraphs 10–14.

8. Demosthenes (2004), p. 144.

9. Cohen, Edward E. 1997b. *Athenian Economy and Society: A Banking Perspective*. Princeton, NJ: Princeton University Press.

10. Garland, Robert. 1987. *The Piraeus from the Fifth to the First Century B.C.* Ithaca, NY: Cornell University Press, p. 92.

11. Cohen (1997b), p. 9.

12. Millett, Paul. 2002. *Lending and Borrowing in Ancient Athens*. Cambridge: Cambridge University Press, p. 199 and ff.

13. Millett (2002), p. 64.

14. Cohen (1997b), p. 123. Demosthenes. 2004. *Demosthenes, Speeches 27–38*, Douglas M. Macdowell (trans.). Austin: University of Texas Press, p. 21.

15. Demosthenes. 1939. "Against Aphobus," in *Demosthenes with an English Translation by A. T. Murray*. London: William Heinemann, speech 27, paragraph 9. Available at: http://data.perseus.org/citations/urn:cts:greekLit:tlg0014.tlg027.perseus-eng1:9. For currency conversion: 1 talent = 60 minas = 6,000 drachmas.

16. Aeschylus. 1926. *Aeschylus, with an English Translation by Herbert Weir Smyth*, vol. 1: *Persians*. Cambridge, MA. Harvard University Press, lines 234–239. Available at: http://data.perseus.org/citations/urn:cts:greekLit:tlg0085.tlg002.perseus-eng1:232-248.

17. Davis, Gil. 2014. "Mining money in Late Archaic Athens." *Historia* 63(3): 257–277. See also: Sverdrup, H., and Peter Schlyter. 2013. "Modeling the Survival of Athenian Owl Tetradrachms Struck in the Period from 561–42 BC from Then to the Present," in *Proceedings of the 30th International Conference of the System Dynamics Society*, vol. 5. St. Gallen, Switzerland: Systems Dynamics Society, pp. 4024–4043.

18. Xenophon. 1892. *The Works of Xenophon*, H. G. Daykins (trans.). London: Macmillan and Co., p. 331.

19. Aperghis, G. G. 1998. "A reassessment of the Laurion Mining lease records." *Bulletin of the Institute of Classical Studies* 42(1): 1–20.

20. Papazarkadas, N. 2012. "Poletai," in *The Encyclopedia of Ancient History*. http://onlinelibrary.wiley.com/doi/10.1002/9781444338386.wbeah04267/full.

21. Camp, John McKesson. 2007. "Excavations in the Athenian Agora: 2002–2007." *Hesperia* 76(4): 627–663.

CHAPTER 6

1. Van Wees, Hans. 2013. *Ships and Silver, Taxes and Tribute: A Fiscal History of Archaic Athens*. London: IB Tauris.

2. Quoted in Seaford, Richard. 2004. *Money and the Early Greek Mind: Homer, Philosophy, Tragedy*. Cambridge: Cambridge University Press, p. 204.

3. Plato. 1967. *Plato in Twelve Volumes*, Vol. 3 translated by W.R.M. Lamb. Cambridge, MA: Harvard University Press; London: William Heinemann Ltd. Gorg. 515.

4. Sverdrup, H., and Peter Schlyter. 2013. "Modeling the Survival of Athenian Owl Tetradrachms Struck in the Period from 561–42 BC from Then to the Present," in *Proceedings of the 30th International Conference of the System Dynamics Society*, vol. 5. St. Gallen, Switzerland: Systems Dynamics Society, pp. 4024–4043.

5. Thucydides. 1910. *The Peloponnesian War*, Richard Crawley (trans.). London and New York: J. M. Dent and E. P. Dutton, 2.13.2–4.

6. Schaps, David M. 2004. *The Invention of Coinage and the Monetization of Ancient Greece*. Ann Arbor: University of Michigan Press, p. 93.

7. Schaps (2004), p. 5.

8. Schaps (2004).

9. Bresson, Alain. 2006. "The origin of Lydian and Greek coinage: Cost and quantity." *Historical Research* 5: 149–159.

CHAPTER 7

1. Rathbone, Dominic, and Peter Temin. 2008. "Financial Intermediation in First-Century AD Rome and Eighteenth-Century England," in Koenraad Verboven, Katelijn Vandorpe, and Véronique Chankowski (eds.), *Pistoi dia tèn technèn. Bankers, Loans and Archives in the Ancient World*. Leuven, Belgium: Peeters.

2. Tacitus, *Annals*, Book 6, Chapters 16 and 17.

3. Verboven, Koenraad. 54–44 BCE. "Financial or monetary crisis?". Edipuglia, 2003.

4. Rosenstein, Nathan. "Aristocrats and agriculture in the Middle and Late Republic." *Journal of Roman Studies* 98 (2008): 1–26.

5. Tacitus, *Annals*, Book 6, Chapter 17. A sestertius was a Roman coin and unit of account worth a quarter of a denarius.

6. Rodewald, Cosmo. 1976. *Money in the Age of Tiberius*. Manchester, UK: Manchester University Press, p. 11.

7. Harris, William V. (ed.). 2008. *The Monetary Systems of the Greeks and Romans*. Oxford: Oxford University Press, p. 188.

8. Dio's account of the bailout differs a bit. He says Tiberius "gave the public treasury twenty-five million [sc. denarii, the equivalent of 100 million sesterces] to enable senators to make loans to applicants." See Rodewald (1976), p. 2.

9. Von Reden, Sitta. 2007. *Money in Ptolemaic Egypt: From the Macedonian Conquest to the End of the Third Century BC*. Cambridge: Cambridge University Press, p. 284 and ff.

10. Schmitz, Leonhard. 1875. "Argentarii," in William Smith (ed.), *A Dictionary of Greek and Roman Antiquities*. London: John Murray, pp. 130–132. Available at: http://penelope.uchicago.edu/Thayer/E/Roman/Texts/secondary/SMIGRA*/Argentarii.html.

11. S.J.B.Barnish. 1985. "The wealth of Julius Argentarius." *Byzantion* 55: 5–38.

12. Temin, Peter. 2013. *The Roman Market Economy*. Princeton, NJ: Princeton University Press, p. 182.

13. Seneca. "On Taking One's Own Life," in *Epistulae Morales*, R. M. Gummere (trans.). Cambridge, MA: Harvard University Press, epistle 77.

14. Jones, David Francis. 2006. *The Bankers of Puteoli: Finance, Trade and Industry in the Roman World*. Stroud, UK: Tempus.

15. Jones (2006), pp. 97–99 gives a complete account of these tablets and his reconstruction of the respective roles played by the signatories.

16. Casson, Lionel. 1980. "The role of the state in Rome's grain trade." *Memoirs of the American Academy in Rome* 36: 21–33.

17. Andreau, Jean. 1999. *Banking and Business in the Roman World*. Cambridge: Cambridge University Press, p. 75.

18. Temin, Peter. 2006. "The economy of the early Roman Empire." *Journal of Economic Perspectives* 20(1): 133–151.

19. For a discussion of the role of slavery in Roman business, see Bruce W. Frier and Dennis P. Kehoe. 2007. "Law and economic institutions," in Walter Scheidel, Ian Morris, and Richard Saller (eds.), *The Cambridge Economic History of the Greco-Roman World*. Cambridge: Cambridge University Press, pp. 113–143.

20. Hansmann, Henry, Reinier Kraakman, and Richard Squire. 2006. "Law and the rise of the firm." *Harvard Law Review* 119(5): 1333–1403.

21. Malmendier, Ulrike. 2005. "Roman Shares," in William N. Goetzmann and K. Geert Rouwenhorst (eds.), *The Origins of Value: The Financial Innovations That Created Modern Capital Markets*. Oxford: Oxford University Press, p. 38.

22. Cicero, M. Tullius. 1891. "Against Publius Vatinius," in *The Orations of Marcus Tullius Cicero*, C. D. Yonge (trans.). London: George Bell & Sons, part 29.

23. Badian, Ernst. 1972. *Publicans and Sinners: Private Enterprise in the Service of the Roman Republic*. Ithaca, NY: Cornell University Press, p. 103.

24. Verboven, Koenraad. 2003. "54–44 BCE. Financial or Monetary Crisis?" In E. L. Cascio (ed.), *Credito e Moneta nel Mondo Romano*. Bari, Italy: Edipuglia, pp. 49–68, p. 57.

25. Kay, Philip. 2014. *Rome's Economic Revolution*. Oxford: Oxford University Press, p. 15.

26. Kay (2014).

27. Harris, William V. 2006. "A revisionist view of Roman money." *Journal of Roman Studies* 96: 1–24.

28. Harl, Kenneth W. 1996. *Coinage in the Roman Economy, 300 BC to AD 700*. Baltimore: Johns Hopkins University Press, p. 125 and ff.

29. Harl (1996), p. 130.

30. Rubin, Jared. 2009. "Social insurance, commitment, and the origin of law: Interest bans in early Christianity." *Journal of Law and Economics* 52(4): 761–786.

31. Silver, Morris. 2011. "Finding the Roman Empire's disappeared deposit bankers." *Historia* 60(3): 301–327.

32. Davis Jr., R. A., A. T. Welty, J. Borrego, J. A. Morales, J. G. Pendon, and J. G. Ryan. 2000. "Rio Tinto estuary (Spain): 5000 years of pollution." *Environmental Geology* 39(10): 1107–1116.

33. Rosman, Kevin J. R., Warrick Chisholm, Sungmin Hong, Jean-Pierre Candelone, and Claude F. Boutron. 1997. "Lead from Carthaginian and Roman Spanish mines isotopically identified in Greenland ice dated from 600 BC to 300 AD." *Environmental Science & Technology* 31(12): 3413–3416.

PART II

1. Mao, Tse-Tung. 1965. *Selected Works of Mao Tse-Tung*, vol. 2. Oxford: Pergamon Press, p. 309.

CHAPTER 8

1. Chou, Hung-hsiang [翔周鴻]. 1970. "Fu-X ladies of the Shang Dynasty." *Monumenta Serica* 29: 346–390.

2. Translation modified from David S. Nivison. 1996. "'Virtue' in Bone and Bronze," in *The Ways of Confucianism: Investigations in Chinese Philosophy*, edited with an introduction by Bryan W. Van Norden. La Salle, IL: Open Court Press.

3. Watson, Burton (trans.), 1971. *Records of the Grand Historian of China. Ttranslated from the Shih chi of Ssu-ma Ch'ien.* New York: Columbia University Press, p. 344.

4. Watson (1971), p. 435.

5. Watson (1971), p. 436.

6. Watson (1971), p. 436.

7. Peng, Xinwei, and Edward H. Kaplan. 1994. *A Monetary History of China*, vol. 1. Bellingham: Western Washington University, p. 95.

8. Peng and Kaplan (1994), p. 96.

9. Peng and Kaplan (1994), p. 96.

10. Peng and Kaplan (1994), p. 95.

11. Peng and Kaplan (1994), p. 100. Peng's translation from *Strategems of the Warring States, Strategems of Qi.*

12. This and the problem following are from The *Suàn shù shū*. C. Cullen (trans.). 2007. *Historia Mathematica* 34(1): 10–44.

CHAPTER 9

1. Ebrey, Patricia Buckley (ed.). 2009. *Chinese Civilization: A Sourcebook*. New York: Simon and Schuster, p. 36.

2. Biot, Edouard. 1851. *Le Tcheou-li: ou rites des Tcheou.* Paris: Imprimerie nationale. Translation of the beginning passage of Book 1 by Matthew Landry, unpublished manuscript.

3. Hansen, Valerie, and Ana Mata-Fink. 2005. "Records from a Seventh Century Pawn Shop," in William N. Goetzmann and K. Geert Rouwenhorst (eds.), *The Origins of Value: The Financial Innovations That Created Modern Capital Markets.* Oxford: Oxford University Press, pp. 56–64.

4. Goetzmann, William N., and K. Geert Rouwenhorst. 2005. *The Origins of Value: The Financial Innovations That Created Modern Capital Markets.* Oxford: Oxford University Press, p. 62.

5. Elman, Benjamin A. 2013. *Civil Examinations and Meritocracy in Late Imperial China.* Cambridge, MA: Harvard University Press, p. 176.

6. Von Glahn, Richard, "The Origins of Paper Money in China," in William N. Goetzmann and K. Geert Rouwenhorst (eds.), *The Origins of Value: The Finan-*

cial Innovations That Created Modern Capital Markets. Oxford: Oxford University Press, pp. 65–90.

7. For an excellent account of the role of government enterprise in the Song, see Smith, Paul J. 1991. *Taxing Heaven's Storehouse: Horses, Bureaucrats, and the Destruction of the Sichuan Tea Industry, 1074–1224*. Harvard-Yenching Institute Monograph Series, vol. 32. Cambridge, MA: Council on East Asian Studies and Harvard University Press.

8. Polo, Marco. 1920. *Marco Polo; Notes and Addenda to Sir Henry Yule's Edition, Containing the Results of Recent Research and Discovery, by Henri Cordier*. London: John Murray. Project Gutenberg. Chapter 24. Available at: http://www.gutenberg.org/ebooks/10636.

CHAPTER 10

1. Lin, Justin Yifu. 1995. "The Needham Puzzle: Why the Industrial Revolution did not originate in China." *Economic Development and Cultural Change* 43(2): 269–292.

2. Zelin, Madeleine. 2005. *The Merchants of Zigong: Industrial Entrepreneurship in Early Modern China*. New York: Columbia University Press.

3. Pomeranz, Kenneth. 1997. "'Traditional' Chinese business forms revisited: Family, firm, and financing in the history of the Yutang Company of Jining, 1779–1956." *Late Imperial China* 18(1): 1–38.

4. Allen, Robert C. 2005. "Capital Accumulation, Technological Change, and the Distribution of Income during the British Industrial Revolution." Discussion Paper. Department of Economics, University of Oxford.

CHAPTER 11

1. Delisle, M. Leopold. 1888. "Mémoires sur les Operations Financieres des Templiers." *Mémoires de l'Institute National de France*. Academie des Inscriptions Belles-Lettres, Paris 33: 11.

2. Delisle (1888), p. 47.

3. Delisle (1888), p. 48.

4. Forey, A. J. 1973. *The Templars in the Corona de Aragon*. Oxford: Oxford University Press, p. 22.

5. Delisle (1888), p. 87.

6. Forey (1973), p. 113.

7. Forey (1973), p. 115.

8. Bisson, Thomas. 1984. *Fiscal Accounts of Catalonia under the Early Count Kings*. Berkeley: University of California Press, p. 82.

9. Bisson (1984), vol. 2, p. 211.

10. Bisson (1984), vol. 2, p. 222.

11. Bisson (1984), vol. 2, p. 222.

12. See Munro, John H. 2003. "The Medieval origins of the financial revolution: Usury, rentes and negotiability." *International History Review* 25(3): 505–562.

CHAPTER 12

1. Ruskin, John. 1867. *The Stones of Venice*. New York: J. Wiley & Son, vol. 1, p. 17.

2. See Norwich, John Julius. 1982. *A History of Venice*. New York: Alfred A. Knopf, pp. 104–106.

3. Mueller, Reinhold C., and Frederic Chapin Lane. 1997. *The Venetian Money Market: Banks, Panics, and the Public Debt, 1200–1500*. Baltimore: Johns Hopkins University Press, vol. 2, p. 461.

4. Mueller and Lane (1997), vol. 2, p. 466.

5. Reinhold Mueller notes that charities were prevented from using real estate as an asset to support perpetual endowments, because too many properties were passing into "dead" hands. Financial assets were thus an ideal substitute.

6. The research of historian John H. Munro of the University of Toronto focuses on the intellectual foundations of financial revolution of the Middle Ages and the philosophical framework of public and private loan contracts. This quote is taken from his article. It appeared originally in Benjamin Jowett (trans. and ed.) 1885. *The Politics of Aristotle: Translated into English, Volume I: Introduction and Translation*. Oxford: Oxford University Press, p. 19: *Politics*, Book I.10, 1258, p. 5.

7. Goetzmann, William N., and K. Geert Rouwenhorst (eds.). 2005. *The Origins of Value: The Financial Innovations that Created Modern Capital Markets*. Oxford: Oxford University Press, p. 5.

8. Cited in Munro, John H. 2003. "The Medieval origins of the financial revolution: Usury, rentes and negotiability." *International History Review* 25(3): 505–562.

9. Le Goff, Jacques. 2004. *From Heaven to Earth: The Shift in Values between the 12th and the 13th Century in the Christian West*. A. H. Heinecken Prize for History Lecture Series. Amsterdam: Royal Netherlands Academy of Arts and Sciences.

CHAPTER 13

1. Goetzmann, William, and K. Geert Rouwenhorst (eds.). 2005. *The Origins of Value: The Financial Innovations that Created Modern Capital Markets*. Oxford: Oxford University Press, p. 131.

2. Goetzmann and Rouwenhorst (2005), p. 134.

3. Goetzmann and Rouwenhorst (2005), p. 135.

4. Van Egmond, Warren. 1980. *Practical Mathematics in the Italian Renaissance: A Catalog of Italian Abbacus Manuscripts and Printed Books to 1600*. Monografia n 4, Annali dell'Istituto e Museo di Storia della Scienza di Firenze Firenze 1 (1980). Florence: Istituto e museo di storia della scienza.

CHAPTER 14

1. Lieber, Jeffrey, and James V. Hart. "Tuck Everlasting," a screenplay adapted from a book by Natalie Babbit. Quote identified from the Internet site http://www.whysanity.net/monos/tuck.html.

2. The story of risk has been told eloquently by others—particularly by Peter Bernstein, the noted Wall Street investor, journal editor, and writer. Peter's book clearly shows that the mathematician's desire to understand games led to a set of unique mathematical tools: Bernstein, Peter. 1998. *Against the Gods: The Remarkable Story of Risk.* New York: John Wiley & Sons.

CHAPTER 15

1. Cardano, Girolamo. 2002. *The Book of My Life,* Jean Stoner (trans.). New York: New York Review of Books, p. 50.

2. Kavanagh argues convincingly that gambling was deeply influential in the evolution of intellectual culture in Europe. Kavanagh, Thomas. 2005. *Dice, Cards, Wheels: A Different History of French Culture.* University Park: University of Pennsylvania Press.

3. Bernoulli, letter to Liebnitz, April 20, 1704, in Bernoulli, Jacob, and Edith Dudley Sylla. 2006. *The Art of Conjecturing, Together with Letter to a Friend on Sets in Court Tennis.* Baltimore: Johns Hopkins University Press, p. 40.

4. Bernoulli and Sylla (2006), p. 44.

5. Halley, Edmund. 1693. "An estimate of the degrees of mortality of mankind, drawn from curious tables of the births and funerals at the city of Breslaw, with an attempt to ascertain the price of annuities upon lives." *Philosophical Transactions London* 17: 596–610. Available at: http://www.pierre-marteau.com/editions/1693-mortality/halley-text.html.

6. De Moivre, Abraham. 1756. *The Doctrine of Chances: Or, a Method of Calculating the Probabilities of Events in a Play,* third edition. London: Millar, p. viii. Reprinted in 1967, New York: Chelsea Publishing.

7. Velde, François, and David Weir. 1992. "The financial market and government debt policy in France, 1746–1793." *Journal of Economic History* 52(1): 1–39.

8. Velde and Weir (1992).

9. Needham, J., and L. Wang. 1959. *Science and Civilisation in China,* vol. 3. Cambridge: Cambridge University Press, p. 133 and ff.

10. Elvin, Mark. 2005. "Why Premodern China—Probably—Did Not Develop Probabilistic Thinking." Working paper, Australian National University.

11. From the final chapter of M. de Condorcet and Marie-Jean-Antoine-Nicolas Caritat. 1796. *Condorcet's Outlines of an Historical View of the Progress of the Human Mind, Being a Posthumous Work of the Late M. de Condorcet.* (Translated from the French). Philadelphia: M. Carey.

12. Malthus, T. R., Donald Winch, and Patricia James. 1992. *Malthus: An Essay on the Principle of Population*. Cambridge: Cambridge University Press, p. 47.

CHAPTER 16

1. Annual Report of Berkshire Hathaway, Inc., 2002, Chairman's Letter, p.15.
2. Jovanovic, Franck. 2001. "Does God practice a random walk? The 'financial physics' of a 19th-century forerunner, Jules Regnault (avec Philippe Le Gall)." *European Journal of the History of Economic Thought* 8(3): 323–362.
3. Jovanovic, Franck. 2006. "Economic instruments and theory in the construction of Henri Lefèvre's science of the stock market." *Pioneers of Financial Economics* 1: 169–190.
4. William Sharpe, John Cox, Stephen Ross, and Mark Rubenstein.
5. This is Money. 2008. "Nassim Taleb and the Secret of the Black Swan," *Daily Mail*, November 3. Available at: http://www.thisismoney.co.uk/markets/article.html?in_article_id=456175&in_page_id=3#ixzz161dvBHe7.

CHAPTER 17

1. Fratianni, Michele. 2006. "Government debt, reputation and creditors' protections: The tale of San Giorgio." *Review of Finance* 10(4): 487–506.
2. Mundy, John. 1954. *Liberty and Political Power in Toulouse 1050–1230*. New York: Columbia University Press, p. 60.

CHAPTER 18

1. Scott, William Robert. 1995. *Joint Stock Companies to 1720*. Bristol: Theomes Press, p. 19. Original edition 1910–1912.
2. Scott (1995), p. 18.
3. Tyson, Peter. 2006. "Future of the Passage." Available at: http://www.pbs.org/wgbh/nova/arctic/passage.html.
4. Dari-Martini, Guiseppi, Oscar Gelderblom, Joost Jonker, and Enrico Perroti. 2013. "The Emergence of the Corporate Form." Amsterdam Law School Legal Studies Research Paper 2013–11.
5. See Neal, Larry. 2005. "Venture Shares in the Dutch East India Company," in William N. Goetzmann and K. Geert Rouwenhorst (eds.), *The Origins of Value: The Financial Innovations That Created Modern Capital Markets*. Oxford: Oxford University Press, p. 167.

CHAPTER 19

1. Richetti, John J. 2005. *The Life of Daniel Defoe: A Critical Biography*. Oxford: Blackwell, p. 11.

2. Defoe, Daniel. 1697. "Author's Introduction," in *An Essay upon Projects*. London: Printed by R. R. for Tho. Cockerill. Available at: http://etext.library.adelaide.edu.au/d/defoe/daniel/d31es/part3.html.

3. Francesca Bray. 1999. "Towards a Critical History of Non-Western Technology," in Timothy Brook and Gregory Blue (eds.), *China and Historical Capitalism*. Cambridge: Cambridge University Press, p. 167.

4. Scott, William Robert. 1995. *Joint Stock Companies to 1720*. Bristol: Theomes Press, Bristol, vol. 1, p. 395. Original edition 1910–1912.

5. For details of the founding of the South Sea Company, see Dale, Richard. 2004. *The First Crash*. Princeton, NJ: Princeton University Press, p. 46 and ff. Carruthers, Bruce. 1996. *City of Capital. Politics and Markets in the English Financial Revolution*. Princeton, NJ: Princeton University Press, p. 152 and ff.

6. Defoe, Daniel. 1712. *An Essay on the South-Sea Trade with an Enquiry into the Grounds and Reasons of the Present Dislike and Complaint against the Settlement of a South-Sea Company*. London: J. Baker.

7. Dale (2004), p. 49.

8. Thomas, Hugh. 1997. *The Slave Trade*. New York: Simon and Schuster, p. 235.

9. Inikori, Joseph E. 2002. *Africans and the Industrial Revolution in England*. Cambridge: Cambridge University Press.

10. Thomas (1997), p. 246.

11. See Temin, Peter, and Hans-Joachim Voth. 2003. "Riding the South Sea Bubble." MIT Working Paper, Cambridge, MA.

12. Neal, Larry. 1993. *The Rise of Financial Capitalism: International Capital Markets in the Age of Reason*. Cambridge: Cambridge University Press, p. 235.

13. Garber, Peter M. 1990. "Famous first bubbles." *Journal of Economic Perspectives* 4(2): 35–54.

14. Banner, Stuart. 1998. *Anglo-American Securities Regulation*. Cambridge: Cambridge University Press, p. 76.

15. Neal (1993).

16. Temin, Peter, and Joachim Voth. 2006. "Banking as an emerging technology: Hoare's Bank, 1702–1742." *Financial History Review* 13(2): 149–178.

17. Defoe, Daniel. 1720. *The South-Sea Scheme Examin'd: And the Reasonableness Thereof Demonstrated. By a Hearty Well-Wisher to Publick Credit*, third edition. London: J. Roberts, p. 8.

18. Defoe (1720), p. 13.

CHAPTER 20

1. Murphy, Antoine. 1997. *John Law: Economic Theorist and Policy-Maker*. Oxford: Oxford University Press.

2. Quoted in Murphy (1997), p. 38.

3. Ruskin, John. 1867. *The Stones of Venice*, vol. 1. New York: John Wiley & Sons, p. 328.

4. Like many financial innovations, this one also likely has an Eastern precedent. House gambling profits were limited by law in ancient India—implying that house games were common long before they appeared in Venice.

5. Schwartz, David. 2006. *Roll the Bones: The History of Gambling*. East Rutherford, NJ: Gotham Books, p. 94.

6. An interpretation advanced nicely by Ludovic Desmed. 2005. "Money in the 'Body Politick': The analysis of trade and circulation in the writings of seventeenth-century political arithmeticians." *History of Political Economy* 37: 1, to whom I am also indebted for the following quotes.

7. Davenant, Charles. 1942. *Two Manuscripts by Charles Davenant: (A) a Memorial Concerning the Coyn of England (B) a Memorial Concerning Credit*. Baltimore: Johns Hopkins University Press, p. 213. First published in 1696. Quoted in Desmed (2005), p. 1.

8. Davenant (1942), p. 75.

9. Murphy (1997), p. 60, quoting Law.

10. Law, John. 1750. *Money and Trade Considered: With a Proposal for Supplying the Nation with Money*. Edinburgh: R. & A. Foulis, p. 35. First published in 1705.

11. Law (1750), p. 50.

12. Murphy, Antoine. 2005. "John Law: Innovating Theorist and Policy Maker," in William Goetzmann and Geert Rouwenhorst (eds.), *The Origins of Value: The Financial Innovations That Created Modern Capital Markets*. Oxford: Oxford University Press, 2005, pp. 225–238.

13. Murphy (2005), p. 163.

14. Murphy (2005), p. 167.

15. Neal, Larry. 1993. *The Rise of Financial Capitalism: International Capital Markets in the Age of Reason*. Cambridge: Cambridge University Press, p. 75.

16. Murphy (2005), p. 189.

17. Neal (1993), p. 67.

18. Murphy (2005), p. 228.

19. Murphy (2005), p. 221.

20. Murphy (2005), p. 320.

21. Spieth, Darius. 2013. "The French Context of Het Groote Tafereel der dwaasheid, John Law, Rococo Culture, and the Riches of the New World," in William N. Goetzmann, Catherine Labio, K. Geert Rouwenhorst, and Timothy Young (eds.), *The Great Mirror of Folly: Finance, Culture, and the Great Crash of 1720*. New Haven, CT: Yale University Press, p. 231.

CHAPTER 21

1. Interestingly enough, the source is a print from 1721 titled "The Bubbler's Mirror."

2. Martin, Fredrick. 1876. *The History of Lloyds and of Marine Insurance in Great Britain*. London: Macmillan and Company, p. 90 and ff.

3. *London Gazette* no. 5879, August 20–23, 1720.

4. Frehen, Rik G. P., William N. Goetzmann, and K. Geert Rouwenhorst. 2013. "New evidence on the first financial bubble." *Journal of Financial Economics* 108(3): 585–607.

5. An interesting detail is that scholarship long had the date for this loss at sea wrong—mistakenly attributing it to October 1720. See, for example Martin (1876), p. 101, citing Postlethwayt, Malachy, Jacques Savary des Brûlons, Emanuel Bowen, Thomas Kitchin, Charles Mosley, and Richard William Seale. 1766. *The Universal Dictionary of Trade and Commerce*. London: Printed for H. Woodfall, A. Millar, J. and R. Tonson, et al.

6. Sombart, Werner. 2001. *The Jews and Modern Capitalism*, M. Epstein (trans.). Kitchener, Ont.: Batoche, p. 68. Originally published in 1911.

CHAPTER 22

1. Thayer, Theodore. 1953. "The land-bank system in the American colonies." *Journal of Economic History* 13(2): 145–159.

2. Sumner, William G. 1896. *A History of Banking in All the Leading Nations: The United States*, vol. 1. New York: Journal of Commerce and Commercial Bulletin, p. 10.

3. Smith, Adam. 1921. *An Inquiry into the Nature and Causes of the Wealth of Nations*, vol. 2. London: J. M. Dent & Sons, p. 423.

4. Thayer (1953).

5. Rasmussen, Barbara. 1994. *Absentee Landowning and Exploitation in West Virginia: 1760–1920*. Lexington: University Press of Kentucky, p. 28.

6. Spieth, Darius A. 2006. "The Corsets Assignat in David's 'Death of Marat.'" *Source: Notes in the History of Art* 30: 22–28.

7. See Mann, Bruce H. 2002. *Republic of Debtors: Bankruptcy in the Age of American Independence*. Cambridge, MA: Harvard University Press, p. 203. For an excellent account of early American land speculation, see Sakowski, A. M. 1932. *The Great American Land Bubble*. New York: Harper and Brothers.

8. Chevalier, Michael. 1839. *Society, Manners and Politics in the United States; Being a Series of Letters on North America*. Translated from the third Paris edition. Boston: Weeks, Jordan and Company, pp. 305–306.

CHAPTER 23

1. Marx, Karl, and Friedrich Engels. 1906. *Manifesto of the Communist Party*. Chicago: Charles H. Kerr and Company, p. 17.

2. Marx, Karl, 2007. *Capital: A Critique of Political Economy—The Process of Capitalist Production*. New York: Cosimo, p. 827.

3. Marx, Karl. 1921. *Capital: The Process of Capitalist Production*, Samuel Moore and Edward Aveling (trans.), Frederick Engels (ed.). Revised and amplified according to the fourth German ed. by Ernest Untermann. Chicago: Charles H. Kerr, p. 150.

4. Marx and Engels (1906), p. 33.

5. Porter, Dale H. 1998. *The Thames Embankment: Environment, Technology, and Society in Victorian London.* Akron, OH: University of Akron Press.

6. The British term for a debt instrument is "stock" and for an equity instrument is "share." This is confusing for Americans used to calling equities "stocks."

7. Lowenfeld, Henry. 1909. *Investment: An Exact Science.* London: Financial Review of Reviews, pp. 11–12.

8. Hutson, Elaine. 2005. "The early managed fund industry: Investment trusts in 19th-century Britain." *International Review of Financial Analysis* 14: 439–454.

9. Chabot, Benjamin, and Christopher Kurz. 2011. "Trust Me with Your Money: English Investors and the Precursor of the Modern Mutual Fund." Available at: http://citeseerx.ist.psu.edu/viewdoc/summary?doi=10.1.1.195.459

10. Hobson, J. H. 1902. *Imperialism: A Study.* London: Cosimo, p. 63.

11. Scham, Sandra A. 2013. The Making and Unmaking of European Cairo. *Journal of Eastern Mediterranean Archaeology and Heritage Studies* (1)4: 313–318.

12. Piquet, Caroline. 2004. "The Suez Company's concession in Egypt, 1854–1956: Modern infrastructure and local economic development." *Enterprise and Society* 5(1): 107–127.

13. Cain, P. J. 2002. *Hobson and Imperialism: Radicalism, New Liberalism, and Finance, 1887–1938.* New York: Oxford University Press.

CHAPTER 24

1. The modern Romanizations of the names of these cities are: Guangdong, Xiamen, Fuzhou, and Ningbo, respectively.

2. See Goetzmann, William N., Andrey Ukhov, and Ning Zhu. 2007. "China and the world financial markets 1870–1939: Modern lessons from historical globalization." *Economic History Review* 60(2): 267–312.

3. See Pui Tak Lee. 1991. "Business Networks and Patterns of Cantonese Compradors and Merchants in Nineteenth-Century Hong Kong," *Journal of the Royal Asiatic Society Hong Kong Branch* 31: 1–39.

4. Thomas, W. A. 2001. *Western Capitalism in China.* Burlington, VT: Ashgate, p. 88.

5. Hao, Yen-p'ing. 1970. *The Comprador in Nineteenth-Century China: Bridge between East and West.* Cambridge, MA: Harvard University Press.

6. Now the China Merchant's Group, a major Hong Kong conglomerate.

7. See Goetzmann, William N. and Elisabeth Köll. 2005. "The History of Corporate Ownership in China," in Randall Morck (ed.), *A History of Corporate Governance around the World: Family Business Groups to Professional Managers.* Chicago: University of Chicago Press, p. 157 and ff.

8. Goetzmann and Köll (2005), p. 158.

9. See C. K. Lai. 1992. "The Qing State and Merchant Enterprise: The China Merchant's Company, 1872–1902," in J. K. Leonard and J. R. Watt (eds.), *To Achieve Security and Wealth: The Qing Imperial State and the Economy, 1644–1911*. East Asia Program. Ithaca, NY: Cornell University Press, pp. 139–155.

10. This account is taken from Goetzmann and Köll (2005).

11. Bailey, Paul. 2013. *Strengthen the Country and Enrich the People: The Reform Writings of Ma Jianzhong*. London: Routledge, p. 74.

12. Lee, En-han. 1977. *China's Quest for Railway Autonomy, 1904–1911: A Study of the Chinese Railway Rights Recovery Movement*. Athens, OH: Ohio University Press, p. 104.

13. Thomas (2001), p. 89.

CHAPTER 25

1. Ukhov, Andrey. 2003. Financial Innovation and Russian Government Debt before 1918. Yale ICF Working Paper 03–20, May 5.

2. Lenin, V. I. 1963. *Imperialism, the Highest Stage of Capitalism*. Lenin's Selected Works, vol. 1. Moscow: Progress Publishers. Originally published in 1917. Available at: https://www.marxists.org/archive/lenin/works/1916/imp-hsc/.

3. Lenin, V. I. 1917. *Imperialism, the Highest Stage of Capitalism*, Preface to the French and German editions. Available at: https://www.marxists.org/archive/lenin/works/1916/imp-hsc/pref02.htm.

4. *Times*. 1917. "COMPANY MEETINGS. Kyshtim Corporation (Limited). Mineral Resources of the Estates. Metallurgical and Commercial Industries," December 15, p. 12.

5. See Sciabarra, Chris Matthew. 1995. *Ayn Rand: The Russian Radical*. University Park: Pennsylvania State University Press.

CHAPTER 26

1. Keynes, John Maynard. 1920. *The Economic Consequences of the Peace*. New York: Harcourt, Brace and Howe.

2. See Guinnane, Timothy. 2005. "German Debt in the Twentieth Century," in William Goetzmann and K. Geert Rouwenhorst (eds.), *The Origins of Value: The Financial Innovations That Created Modern Capital Markets*. Oxford: Oxford University Press, pp. 327–341.

3. Easterly, William. 2003. "Can foreign aid buy growth?" *Journal of Economic Perspectives* 17(3): 23–48.

4. Keynes, John Maynard. 2006. *General Theory of Employment, Interest and Money*. London: Atlantic Books.

5. Keynes (2006).

6. Quoted in Chambers, David, and Elroy Dimson. 2013. "John Maynard Keynes, investment innovator." *Journal of Economic Perspectives* 27(3): 213–228.

CHAPTER 27

1. Chambers, David, and Elroy Dimson. 2013. "John Maynard Keynes, investment innovator." *Journal of Economic Perspectives* 27(3): 213–228.

2. Ott, Julia C. 2011. *When Wall Street Met Main Street*. Cambridge, MA: Harvard University Press.

3. Graham, Benjamin, David J. Dodd, and Sidney Cottle. 1962. *Security Analysis: Principles and Techniques*. New York: McGraw-Hill, p. 409 note.

4. Fisher, Irving. 1930. *The Theory of Interest*. New York: Macmillan, pp. 220–221.

5. Rand, Ayn. 2005. *The Fountainhead*. London: Penguin.

6. Chave, Anna C. 1991. "'Who Will Paint New York?': 'The World's New Art Center' and the skyscraper paintings of Georgia O'Keeffe." *American Art* 5(1/2): 87–107.

7. Rand (2005).

8. Shultz, Earle, and Walter Simmons. 1959. *Offices in the Sky*. Indianapolis, IN: Bobbs-Merrill, p. 143.

9. Gilbert, Cass. 1900. "The financial importance of rapid building." *Engineering Record* 41: 624.

10. Grant, James. 1992. *Money of the Mind*. New York: Farrar, Straus and Giroux, p. 159.

11. Quoted in Shultz and Simmons (1959), p. 73.

12. Shultz and Simmons (1959), pp. 143–144.

13. Grant (1992), p. 164.

14. Grant (1992), p. 165.

15. *Report on Protective Committees of the Securities and Exchange Commission.* 1936. Part III, *Committee for the Holders of Real Estate Bonds*. Washington, DC: US Government Printing Office, p. 67 and ff.

16. See Nicholas, Tom. 2008. "Does innovation cause stock market runups? Evidence from the great crash." *American Economic Review* 98(4): 1370–1396.

17. De Long, J. Bradford, and Andrei Shleifer. 1990. *The Bubble of 1929: Evidence from Closed-End Funds*. No. w3523. Cambridge, MA: National Bureau of Economic Research.

18. The following paper was read before a joint meeting of the Econometric Society and the American Statistical Association, Cincinnati, Ohio, December 31, 1932. It was reprinted in Cowles, Alfred. 1933. "Can Stock Market Forecasters Forecast?" *Econometrica* 1(3): 309–324.

19. Jones, Alfred Winslow. 1949. "Fashions in forecasting," *Fortune*, March, pp. 88–91.

20. Jones (1949).

CHAPTER 28

1. Senator Huey P. Long, addressing the 73rd Congress, on February 5, 1934. Congressional Record, v. 78, pt. 3. Quoted in "Social Security History," on Social Security, Official Social Security Website. Available at: http://www.ssa.gov/history/longsen.html.

2. *Fortune.* 1935. "Social Security by any other name," March, pp. 86–87.

3. For an excellent account of the origins of the social security system, see Scheiber, Sylvester J. 2012. *The Predictable Surprise: The Unraveling of the U.S. Retirement System.* Oxford: Oxford University Press.

4. *Fortune* (1935).

5. Senate Hearings of Stock Exchange Practices, 1932, quoted in Galbraith, John Kenneth. 1997. *The Great Stock Market Crash of 1929.* Boston: Houghton Mifflin Harcourt, pp. 64–65.

CHAPTER 29

1. Marowitz, Harry. 1991. "Autobiography," in Tore Frängsmyr (ed.), *Les Prix Nobel. The Nobel Prizes 1990.* Stockholm: Nobel Foundation.

2. See Goetzmann, William N., and Andrey D. Ukhov. 2006. "British investment overseas 1870–1913: A modern portfolio theory approach." *Review of Finance* 10(2): 261–300.

3. Klapper, Leora, Víctor Sulla, and Dimitri Vittas. 2004. "The development of mutual funds around the world." *Emerging Markets Review* 5(1): 1–38.

4. Bhattacharya, Utpal, and Neal Galpin. 2011. "The global rise of the value-weighted portfolio." *Journal of Financial and Quantitative Analysis* 46(3): 737.

5. Benartzi, Shlomo, and Richard H. Thaler. 2001. "Naive diversification strategies in defined contribution saving plans." *American Economic Review* 91(1): 79–98

6. Thaler, Richard H. and Cass R. Sustein. 2008. *Nudge: Improving Decisions About Health, Wealth and Happiness.* New Haven: Yale University Press.

BIBLIOGRAPHY

Aeschylus. 1926. *Aeschylus, with an English Translation by Herbert Weir Smyth*, vol. 1: *Persians*. Cambridge, MA. Harvard University Press.

Allen, Robert C. 2005. "Capital Accumulation, Technological Change, and the Distribution of Income during the British Industrial Revolution." Discussion Paper. Department of Economics, University of Oxford.

———. 2009. *The British Industrial Revolution in Global Perspective*. Cambridge: Cambridge University Press.

Andreadēs, Andreas Michaēl. 1933. *A History of Greek Public Finance*, vol. 1. Cambridge, MA: Harvard University Press.

Andreau, Jean. 1999. *Banking and Business in the Roman World*. Cambridge: Cambridge University Press.

Angela, Alberto. 2009. *A Day in the Life of Ancient Rome*. New York: Europa Editions.

Aperghis, G. G. 1998. "A reassessment of the Laurion mining lease records." *Bulletin of the Institute of Classical Studies* 42(1): 1–20.

Archibald, Zosia, John K. Davies, and Vincent Gabrielsen (eds.). 2011. *The Economies of Hellenistic Societies, Third to First Centuries BC*. Oxford: Oxford University Press.

Archibald, Zosia Halina. 2013. *Ancient Economies of the Northern Aegean: Fifth to First Centuries BC*. Oxford: Oxford University Press.

Aubet, María Eugenia. 2013. *Commerce and Colonization in the Ancient Near East*. Cambridge: Cambridge University Press.

Badian, Ernst. 1972. *Publicans and Sinners: Private Enterprise in the Service of the Roman Republic*. Ithaca, NY: Cornell University Press.

Bailey, Paul. 2013. *Strengthen the Country and Enrich the People: The Reform Writings of Ma Jianzhong*. London: Routledge.

Banner, Stuart. 1998. *Anglo-American Securities Regulation*. Cambridge: Cambridge University Press.

Barnish, S.J.B. 1985. "The wealth of Julius Argentarius." *Byzantion* 55: 5–38.

Benartzi, Shlomo, and Richard H. Thaler. 2001. "Naive diversification strategies in defined contribution saving plans." *American Economic Review* (Evanston) 91(1): 79–98.

Bernoulli, Jacob, and Edith Dudley Sylla. 2006. *The Art of Conjecturing, Together with Letter to a Friend on Sets in Court Tennis*. Baltimore: Johns Hopkins University Press.

Bernstein, Peter L. 1998. *Against the Gods: The Remarkable Story of Risk*. New York: John Wiley & Sons.

Bhattacharya, Utpal, and Neal Galpin. 2011. "The global rise of the value-weighted portfolio." *Journal of Financial and Quantitative Analysis* 46(3): 737.

Biot, E. 1851. *Le Tcheou-li: Ou rites des Tcheou*. Paris: Imprimerie nationale.

Bisson, Thomas. 1984. *Fiscal Accounts of Catalonia under the Early Count Kings*. Berkeley: University of California Press.

Bowman, Alan, and Andrew Wilson. 2009. *Quantifying the Roman Economy*. Oxford Studies in the Roman Economy 1. Oxford: Oxford University Press.

Bray, Francesca. 1999. "Towards a Critical History of Non-Western Technology," in Timothy Brook and Gregory Blue (eds.), *China and Historical Capitalism*. Cambridge: Cambridge University Press, p. 167.

Bresson, Alain. 2006. "The origin of Lydian and Greek coinage: Cost and quantity." *Historical Research* 5: 149–159.

Cain, P. J. 2002. *Hobson and Imperialism: Radicalism, New Liberalism, and Finance, 1887–1938*. New York: Oxford University Press.

Camp, John McKessen. 2007. "Excavations in the Athenian Agora: 2002–2007." *Hesperia* 76(4): 627–663.

Cardano, Girolamo. 2002. *The Book of My Life*, Jean Stoner (trans.). New York: New York Review of Books.

Carruthers, Bruce G. 1996. *City of Capital: Politics and Markets in the English Financial Revolution*. Princeton, NJ: Princeton University Press.

Casson, Lionel. 1980. "The Role of the State in Rome's Grain Trade." *Memoirs of the American Academy in Rome* 36: 21–33.

Chabot, B., and C. Kurz. 2011. "Trust Me with Your Money: English Investors and the Precursor of the Modern Mutual Fund." Available at: http://citeseerx.ist .psu.edu/viewdoc/summary?doi=10.1.1.195.459.

Chambers, David, and Elroy Dimson. 2013. "John Maynard Keynes, investment innovator." *Journal of Economic Perspectives* 27(3): 213–228.

Chancellor, Edward. 2000. *Devil Take the Hindmost: A History of Financial Speculation*. New York: Plume.

Chave, Anna C. 1991. "'Who Will Paint New York?': 'The World's New Art Center' and the skyscraper paintings of Georgia O'Keeffe." *American Art* 5(1/2): 87–107.

Chevalier, Michael. 1839. *Society, Manners and Politics in the United States; Being a Series of Letters on North America*. Tranlated from the third Paris edition. Boston: Weeks, Jordan and Company.

Chou, Hung-hsiang [翔周鴻]. 1970. "Fu-X ladies of the Shang Dynasty." *Monumenta Serica* 29: 346–390.

Cicero, M. Tullius. 1891. *The Orations of Marcus Tullius Cicero*, C. D. Yonge (trans.). London: George Bell & Sons.

Clark, Gregory. 2007. *A Farewell to Alms: A Brief Economic History of the World*. Princeton, NJ: Princeton University Press.

Cohen, Edward E. 1997a. *Ancient Athenian Maritime Courts*. Princeton, NJ: Princeton University Press.

———. 1997b. *Athenian Economy and Society: A Banking Perspective*. Princeton, NJ: Princeton University Press.

Condie, Bill. 2008. "Nassim Taleb and the Secret of the Black Swan," *London Evening Standard*, October 27, p. 1.

Condorcet, M. de., and Marie-Jean-Antoine-Nicolas Caritat. 1796. *Condorcet's Outlines of an Historical View of the Progress of the Human Mind, Being a Posthumous Work of the Late M. de Condorcet*. (Translated from the French). Philadelphia: M. Carey.

Cowles, Alfred. 1933. "Can stock market forecasters forecast?" *Econometrica* 1(3): 309–324.

Dale, Richard. 2004. *The First Crash: Lessons from the South Sea Bubble*. Princeton, NJ: Princeton University Press.

Dari-Martini, Guiseppi, Oscar Gelderblom, Joost Jonker, and Enrico Perroti. 2013. "The Emergence of the Corporate Form." Amsterdam Law School Legal Studies Research Paper 2013–11.

Darling, M. L. 1925. *The Punjab Peasant in Prosperity and Debt*. London: Oxford University Press.

Davenant, Charles. 1942. *Two Manuscripts by Charles Davenant: A Memorial Concerning the Coyn of England (B) a Memorial Concerning Credit*. Baltimore: Johns Hopkins University Press. First published in 1696.

Davis, Gil. 2014. "Mining money in Late Archaic Athens." *Historia* 63(3): 257–277.

Davis Jr., R. A., A. T. Weltry, J. Borrego, J. A. Morales, J. G. Pendon, and J. G. Ryan. 2000. "Rio Tinto estuary (Spain): 5000 years of pollution." *Environmental Geology* 39(10): 1107–1116.

Davis, William Stearns. 1910. *The Influence of Wealth in Imperial Rome*. New York: Macmillan.

Defoe, Daniel. 1697. "Author's Introduction," in *An Essay upon Projects*. London: Printed by R. R. for Tho. Cockerill. Available at: http://etext.library.adelaide.edu.au/d/defoe/daniel/d31es/part3.html.

———. 1704. *A Review of the State of the British Nation*. June 14. London: Defoe.

———. 1712. *An Essay on the South-Sea Trade with an Enquiry into the Grounds and Reasons of the present Dislike and Complaint against the Settlement of a South-Sea Company*. London: J. Baker.

———. 1720. *The South-Sea Scheme Examin'd: And the Reasonableness Thereof Demonstrated. By a Hearty Well-Wisher to Publick Credit*, third edition. London: J. Roberts.

Delisle, M. Leopold. 1888. "Memoires sur les Operations Financieres des Templiers." *Mémoires de l'Institute National de France*. Academie des Inscriptions Belles-Lettres, Paris 33: 11.

De Long, J. Bradford, and Andrei Shleifer. 1990. *The Bubble of 1929: Evidence from Closed-End Funds*. No. w3523. Cambridge, MA: National Bureau of Economic Research.

De Moivre, Abraham. 1756. *The Doctrine of Chances: Or, a Method of Calculating the Probabilities of Events in a Play*, third edition. London: Millar. Reprinted in 1967, New York: Chelsea Publishing.

Demosthenes. 2003. *Demosthenes: Speeches 50–59*, Douglas M. Macdowell (trans.). Austin: University of Texas Press.

———. 2004. "35 Against Lacritus," in *Demosthenes, Speeches 27–38*, Douglas M. Macdowell (trans.). Austin: University of Texas Press, pp. 137–144.

Desmed, Ludovic. 2005. "Money in the 'Body Politick': The analysis of trade and circulation in the writings of seventeenth-century political arithmeticians." *History of Political Economy* 37(1): 1.

Duncan-Jones, Richard. 1998. *Money and Government in the Roman Empire*. Cambridge: Cambridge University Press.

Dunham, Wayne R. 2008. "Cold case files: The Athenian grain merchants, 386 BC." *Cato Journal* 28: 495.

Easterly, William. 2003. "Can foreign aid buy growth?" *Journal of Economic Perspectives* 17(3): 23–48.

Ebrey, Patricia Buckley (ed.). 2009. *Chinese Civilization: A Sourcebook*. New York: Simon and Schuster.

Eidem, Jesper. 2008. "Apum: A Kingdom on the Old Assyrian Route," in Klaas R. Veenhof and Jesper Eidem (eds.), *Mesopotamia, The Old Assyrian Period*. Orbis Biblicus et Orientalis, vol. 160/5. Saint Paul, MN: Academic Press Fribourg, pp. 265–352.

Elman, Benjamin A. 2013. *Civil Examinations and Meritocracy in Late Imperial China*. Cambridge, MA: Harvard University Press.

Elvin, Mark. 2005. "Why Premodern China—Probably—Did Not Develop Probabilistic Thinking." Working paper, Australian National University.

Englund, Robert. 1988. "Administrative timekeeping in ancient Mesopotamia." *Journal of the Economic and Social History of the Orient* 31: 121–185.

———. 2004. "Proto-cuneiform Account Books and Journals," in Michael Hudson and Cornelia Wunsch (eds.), *Creating Economic Order*. International Scholars Conference on Ancient Near Eastern Economies, vol. 4. Bethesda, MD: CDL Press, pp. 32–33.

Ferguson, Niall. 2002. *The Cash Nexus: Money and Power in the Modern World, 1700–2000*. New York: Basic Books.

Figueira, Thomas J. 1986. "*Sitopolai* and *Sitophylakes* in Lysias' 'Against the Grain Dealers': Governmental intervention in the Athenian economy." *Phoenix* 40: 149–171.

Fisher, Irving. 1930. *The Theory of Interest*. New York: Macmillan.

Fleck, Robert K., and F. Andrew Hanssen. 2012. "On the benefits and costs of legal expertise: Adjudication in ancient Athens." *Review of Law & Economics* 8(2): 367–399.

Forey, A. J. 1973. *The Templars in the Corona de Aragon*. Oxford: Oxford University Press.

Fortune. 1935. "Social Security by any other name," March, pp. 86–87.

Foster, Benjamin R. (trans.). 2001. *The Epic of Gilgamesh.* New York: W. W. Norton and Company.

Fratianni, Michele. 2006. "Government debt, reputation and creditors' protections: The tale of San Giorgio." *Review of Finance* 10(4): 487–506.

Frehen, Rik G. P., William N. Goetzmann, and K. Geert Rouwenhorst. 2013. "New evidence on the first financial bubble." *Journal of Financial Economics* 108(3): 585–607.

Frier, Bruce W., and Dennis P. Kehoe. 2007. "Law and Economic Institutions," in Walter Scheidel, Ian Morris, and Richard Saller (eds.), *The Cambridge Economic History of the Greco-Roman World.* Cambridge: Cambridge University Press, pp. 113–143.

Galbraith, John Kenneth. 2009. *The Great Stock Market Crash of 1929.* Boston: Houghton Mifflin Harcourt.

Garber, Peter M. 1990. "Famous first bubbles." *Journal of Economic Perspectives* 4(2): 35–54.

Garfinkle, Steven J. 2004. "Shepherds, merchants, and credit: Some observations on lending practices in Ur III Mesopotamia." *Journal of the Economic and Social History of the Orient* 47(1): 1–30.

———. 2012. *Entrepreneurs and Enterprise in Early Mesopotamia: A Study of Three Archives from the Third Dynasty of Ur.* Bethesda, MD: CDL Press.

Garland, Robert. 1987. *The Piraeus from the Fifth to the First Century B.C.* Ithaca, NY: Cornell University Press.

Gilbert, Cass. 1900. "The financial importance of rapid building." *Engineering Record* 41: 624.

Goddeeris, Anne. 2002. *Economy and Society in Northern Babylonia in the Early Old Babylonian Period (ca. 2000–1800 BC).* Leuven, Belgium: Peeters.

Goetzmann, William H. 2009. *Beyond the Revolution: A History of American Thought from Paine to Pragmatism.* New York: Basic Books.

Goetzmann, William N., and K. Geert Rouwenhorst (eds.). 2005. *The Origins of Value: The Financial Innovations That Created Modern Capital Markets.* Oxford: Oxford University Press.

Goetzmann, William N., and Elisabeth Köll. 2005. "The History of Corporate Ownership in China: State Patronage, Company Legislation, and the Issue of Control," in Randall K. Morck (ed.), *A History of Corporate Governance around the World: Family Business Groups to Professional Managers.* Chicago: University of Chicago Press, pp. 149–184.

Goetzmann, William N., and Andrey D. Ukhov. 2006. "British investment overseas 1870–1913: A modern portfolio theory approach." *Review of Finance* 10(2): 261–300.

Goetzmann, William N., Andrey Ukhov, and Ning Zhu. 2007. "China and the world financial markets 1870–1939: Modern lessons from historical globalization." *Economic History Review* 60(2): 267–312.

Goetzmann, William N., Catherine Labio, K. Geert Rouwenhorst, and Timothy Young (eds.). 2013. *The Great Mirror of Folly: Finance, Culture, and the Great Crash of 1720*. New Haven, CT: Yale University Press.

Grant, James. 1992. *Money of the Mind*. New York: Farrar, Straus and Giroux.

Guinnane, Timothy. 2005. "German Debt in the Twentieth Century," in William N. Goetzmann and K. Geert Rouwenhorst (eds.), *The Origins of Value: The Financial Innovations That Created Modern Capital Markets*. Oxford: Oxford University Press, pp. 327–341.

Hadden, Peter. 1994. *On the Shoulders of Merchants: Exchange and the Mathematical Conception of Nature in Early Modern Europe*. Albany: State University of New York Press.

Halley, Edmund. 1693. "An estimate of the degrees of mortality of mankind, drawn from curious tables of the births and funerals at the city of Breslaw, with an attempt to ascertain the price of annuities upon lives." *Philosophical Transactions* London 17: 596–610. Available at: http://www.pierre-marteau.com/editions/1693-mortality/halley-text.html.

Hansen, Valerie, and Ana Mata-Fink. 2005. "Records from a Seventh Century Pawn Shop," in William N. Goetzmann and K. Geert Rouwenhorst (eds.), *The Origins of Value: The Financial Innovations That Created Modern Capital Markets*. Oxford: Oxford University Press, pp. 56–64.

Hansmann, Henry, Reinier Kraakman, and Richard Squire. 2006. "Law and the rise of the firm." *Harvard Law Review* 119(5): 1333–1403.

Hao, Yen-p'ing. 1970. *The Comprador in Nineteenth Century China: Bridge between East and West*, vol. 45. Cambridge, MA: Harvard University Press.

Harl, Kenneth W. 1996. *Coinage in the Roman Economy, 300 BC to AD 700*. Baltimore: Johns Hopkins University Press.

Harris, William V. 2006. "A revisionist view of Roman money." *Journal of Roman Studies* 96: 1–24.

Harris, William V. (ed.). 2008. *The Monetary Systems of the Greeks and Romans*. Oxford: Oxford University Press.

Hobson, J. H. 1902. *Imperialism: A Study*. London: Cosimo.

Huis, Joost, Reinhart Pirngruber, and Bas Van Leeuwen. 2014. "Climate, War and Economic Development: The Case of Second Century BC Babylon," in R. J. Van der Spek, Jan Luiten van Zanden, and Bas van Leeuwen (eds.), *A History of Market Performance: From Ancient Babylonia to the Modern World*, vol. 68. London: Routledge.

Hutson, Elaine. 2005. "The early managed fund industry: Investment trusts in 19th century Britain." *International Review of Financial Analysis* 14: 439–454.

Inikori, Joseph E. 2002. *Africans and the Industrial Revolution in England*. Cambridge: Cambridge University Press.

Jacobsen, Thorkild. 1976. *The Treasures of Darkness: A History of Mesopotamian Religion*. New Haven, CT: Yale University Press.

Jones, Alfred Winslow. 1949. "Fashions in forecasting," *Fortune*, March, pp. 88–91.

Jones, David Francis. 2006. *The Bankers of Puteoli: Finance, Trade and Industry in the Roman World*. Stroud, UK: Tempus.

Jovanovic, Franck. 2001. "Does God practice a random walk? The 'financial physics' of a 19th-century forerunner, Jules Regnault (avec Philippe Le Gall)." *European Journal of the History of Economic Thought* 8(3): 323–362.

———. 2006. "Economic instruments and theory in the construction of Henri Lefèvre's science of the stock market." *Pioneers of Financial Economics* 1: 169–190.

Jowett, Benjamin (trans. and ed.). 1885. *The Politics of Aristotle: Translated into English*, 2 vols. Oxford: Oxford University Press.

Jursa, Michael. 2014. "Market Performance and Market Integration in Babylonia in the 'Long Sixth Century' B.C.," in R. J. Van der Spek, Jan Luiten van Zanden, and Bas van Leeuwen (eds.), *A History of Market Performance: From Ancient Babylonia to the Modern World*, vol. 68. London: Routledge.

Kavanagh, Thomas. 2005. *Dice, Cards, Wheels: A Different History of French Culture*. University Park: University of Pennsylvania Press.

Kay, Philip. 2014. *Rome's Economic Revolution*. Oxford: Oxford University Press.

Keynes, John Maynard. 1920. *The Economic Consequences of the Peace*. New York: Harcourt, Brace and Howe.

———. 2006. *General Theory of Employment, Interest and Money*. London: Atlantic Books.

Klapper, Leora, Víctor Sulla, and Dimitri Vittas. 2004. "The development of mutual funds around the world." *Emerging Markets Review* 5(1): 1–38.

Kuran, Timur. 2011. *The Long Divergence: How Islamic Law Held Back the Middle East*. Princeton, NJ: Princeton University Press.

Lai, C. K. 1992. "The Qing State and Merchant Enterprise: The China Merchant's Company, 1872–1902," in J. K. Leonard and J. R. Watt (eds.), *To Achieve Security and Wealth: The Qing Imperial State and the Economy, 1644–1911*. East Asia Program. Ithaca, NY: Cornell University Press, pp. 139–155.

Larsen, Mogens Trolle. 1977. "Partnerships in the old Assyrian trade." *Iraq* 39(1): 119–145.

Law, John. 1750. *Money and Trade Considered: With a Proposal for Supplying the Nation with Money*. Edinburgh: R. & A. Foulis. First published in 1705.

Lee, En-han. 1977. *China's Quest for Railway Autonomy, 1904–1911: A Study of the Chinese Railway Rights Recovery Movement*. Singapore: Singapore University Press.

Lee, Pui Tak. 1991. "Business networks and patterns of Cantonese compradors and merchants in nineteenth-century Hong Kong." *Journal of the Royal Asiatic Society Hong Kong Branch* 31: 1–39.

Le Goff, Jacques. 2004. *From Heaven to Earth: The Shift in Values between the 12th and the 13th Century in the Christian West*. A. H. Heinecken Prize for History Lecture Series. Amsterdam: Royal Netherlands Academy of Arts and Sciences.

Leiberman, Stephen J. 1980. "Of clay pebbles, hollow clay balls, and writing: A Sumerian view." *American Journal of Archaeology* 84(3): 339–358.

Lenin, V. I. 1963. *Imperialism, the Highest Stage of Capitalism*. Lenin's Selected Works, vol. 1. Moscow: Progress Publishers. Originally published in 1917. Available at: https://www.marxists.org/archive/lenin/works/1916/imp-hsc/.

Lin, Justin Yifu. 1995. "The Needham Puzzle: Why the Industrial Revolution did not originate in China." *Economic Development and Cultural Change* 43(2): 269–292.

London Gazette. 1720. no. 5879 August 20–23.

Lowenfeld, Henry. 1909. *Investment: An Exact Science*. London: Financial Review of Reviews.

Luzzatto, Gino. 1963. *Il Debito Publico della Repubblica di Venezia*. Milan: Instituto Editoriale Cisalpino.

Lysias. *Oration XXII*. Available at: http://www.gutenberg.org/cache/epub/6969/pg6969.html.

Malmendier, Ulrike. 2005. "Roman Shares," in William N. Goetzmann and K. Geert Rouwenhorst (eds.), *The Origins of Value: The Financial Innovations That Created Modern Capital Markets*. Oxford: Oxford University Press, pp. 31–42.

Malthus, T. R., Donald Winch, and Patricia James. 1992. *Malthus: An Essay on the Principle of Population*. Cambridge: Cambridge University Press.

Mann, Bruce H. 2002. *Republic of Debtors: Bankruptcy in the Age of American Independence*. Cambridge, MA: Harvard University Press.

Manning, Joseph Gilbert. 2003. *Land and Power in Ptolemaic Egypt*. Cambridge: Cambridge University Press.

Manning, Joseph Gilbert, and Ian Morris (eds.). 2007. *The Ancient Economy: Evidence and Models*. Redwood City, CA: Stanford University Press.

Marowitz, Harry. 1991. "Autobiography," in Tore Frängsmyr (ed.), *Les Prix Nobel. The Nobel Prizes 1990*. Stockholm: Nobel Foundation.

Martin, Fredrick. 1876. *The History of Lloyd's and of Marine Insurance in Great Britain*. London: Macmillan and Company.

Marx, Karl. 2007. *Capital: A Critique of Political Economy–The Process of Capitalist Production*. New York: Cosimo.

———.1921. *Capital: The Process of Capitalist Production*, Samuel Moore and Edward Aveling (trans.), Frederick Engels (ed.). Revised and amplified according to the fourth German ed. by Ernest Untermann. Chicago: Charles H. Kerr.

Marx, Karl, and Friedrich Engels. 1906. *Manifesto of the Communist Party*. Chicago: Charles H. Kerr and Company.

Meadows, Andrew, and Kirsty Shipton. 2004. *Money and Its Uses in the Ancient Greek World*. Oxford: Oxford University Press.

Millett, Paul. 2002. *Lending and Borrowing in Ancient Athens*. Cambridge: Cambridge University Press.

Moreno, Alfonso. 2007. *Feeding the Democracy: The Athenian Grain Supply in the Fifth and Fourth Centuries BC*. Oxford: Oxford University Press.

Mueller, Reinhold C., and Frederic Chapin Lane. 1997. *The Venetian Money Market: Banks, Panics, and the Public Debt, 1200–1500*. Money and Banking in Medieval and Renaissance Venice, vol. 2. Baltimore: Johns Hopkins University Press.

Mundy, John. 1954. *Liberty and Political Power in Toulouse 1050–1230*. New York: Columbia University Press.

Munro, John H. 2003. "The Medieval origins of the financial revolution: Usury, rentes and negotiability." *International History Review* 25(3): 505–562.

Murphy, Antoine. 1997. *John Law: Economic Theorist and Policy-Maker*. Oxford: Oxford University Press.

———. 2005. "John Law: Innovating Theorist and Policy Maker," in William N. Goetzmann and K. Geert Rouwenhorst (eds.), *The Origins of Value: The Financial Innovations That Created Modern Capital Markets*. Oxford: Oxford University Press, pp. 225–238.

Neal, Larry. 1993. *The Rise of Financial Capitalism in the Age of Reason*. Cambridge: Cambridge University Press.

———. 2005. "Venture Shares of the Dutch East India Company," in William N. Goetzmann and K. Geert Rouwenhorst (eds.), *The Origins of Value: The Financial Innovations That Created Modern Capital Markets*. Oxford: Oxford University Press, pp. 165–175.

Neal, Larry, and Jeffrey Williamson. 2014. *The Cambridge History of Capitalism*, vol. 1. Cambridge: Cambridge University Press.

Needham, J., and L. Wang. 1959. *Science and Civilisation in China*, vol. 3. Cambridge: Cambridge University Press.

Nicholas, Tom. 2008. "Does innovation cause stock market runups? Evidence from the Great Crash." *American Economic Review* 98(4): 1370–1396.

Nissen, Hans J., Peter Damerow, and Robert K. Englund. 1993. *Archaic Bookkeeping*. Chicago: University of Chicago Press.

Nivison, David S. 1996. "'Virtue' in Bone and Bronze," in *The Ways of Confucianism: Investigations in Chinese Philosophy*, edited with an introduction by Bryan W. Van Norden. La Salle, IL: Open Court Press.

Norwich, John Julius. 1982. *A History of Venice*. New York: Alfred A. Knopf.

Ott, Julia C. 2011. *When Wall Street Met Main Street*. Cambridge, MA: Harvard University Press.

Papazarkadas, N. 2012. "Poletai," in *The Encyclopedia of Ancient History*. Available at: http://onlinelibrary.wiley.com/doi/10.1002/9781444338386.wbeah04267/full.

Parkins, Helen, and Christopher Smith (eds.). 2005. *Trade, Traders and the Ancient City*. London: Routledge.

Peng, Xinwei, and Edward H. Kaplan. 1994. *A Monetary History of China*, vol. 1. Bellingham, WA: Western Washington University.

Piquet, Caroline. 2004. "The Suez Company's concession in Egypt, 1854–1956: Modern infrastructure and local economic development." *Enterprise and Society* 5(1): 107–127.

Plato. 1967. *Plato in Twelve Volumes*, vol. 3, W.R.M. Lamb (trans.). London: William Heinemann.

Polo, Marco. 1920. *Marco Polo; Notes and Addenda to Sir Henry Yule's Edition, Containing the Results of Recent Research and Discovery, by Henri Cordier*. London:

John Murray. Project Gutenberg. Chapter 24. Available at: http://www.guten-berg.org/ebooks/10636.

Pomeranz, Kenneth. 1997. "'Traditional' Chinese business forms revisited: Fam-ily, firm, and financing in the history of the Yutang Company of Jining, 1779–1956." *Late Imperial China* 18(1): 1–38.

Porter, Dale H. 1998. *The Thames Embankment: Environment, Technology, and Soci-ety in Victorian London*. Akron, OH: University of Akron Press.

Postlethwayt, Malachy, Jacques Savary des Brûlons, Emanuel Bowen, Thomas Kitchin, Charles Mosley, and Richard William Seale. 1766. *The Universal Dictionary of Trade and Commerce*. London: Printed for H. Woodfall, A. Millar, J. and R. Tonson, et al.

Rand, Ayn. 2005. *The Fountainhead*. London: Penguin.

Rasmussen, Barbara. 1994. *Absentee Landowning and Exploitation in West Virginia: 1760–1920*. Lexington: University Press of Kentucky.

Rathbone, Dominic, and Peter Temin. 2008. "Financial Intermediation in First-Century AD Rome and Eighteenth-Century England," in Koenraad Verboven, Katelijn Vandorpe, and Véronique Chankowski (eds.), *Pistoi dia tèn technèn. Bankers, Loans and Archives in the Ancient World*. Leuven, Belgium: Peeters.

Regnault, Jules. 1863. *Calcul des Chances et Philosophie de la Bourse*. Paris: Mallet-Bachelier [et] Castel.

Richetti, John J. 2005. *The Life of Daniel Defoe: A Critical Biography*. Oxford: Blackwell.

Rodewald, Cosmo. 1976. *Money in the Age of Tiberius*. Manchester, UK: Manchester University Press.

Rosenstein, Nathan. 2008. "Aristocrats and agriculture in the Middle and Late Re-public." *Journal of Roman Studies* 98: 1–26.

Rosenthal, Jean-Laurent, and Roy Bin Wong. 2011. *Before and Beyond Divergence*. Cambridge, MA: Harvard University Press.

Rosman, Kevin J. R., Warrick Chisholm, Sungmin Hong, Jean-Pierre Candelone, and Claude F. Boutron. 1997. "Lead from Carthaginian and Roman Spanish mines isotopically identified in Greenland ice dated from 600 BC to 300 AD." *Environmental Science & Technology* 31(12): 3413–3416.

Rostovtzeff, Michael Ivanovitch. 1926. *The Social & Economic History of the Roman Empire*, vol. 1. New York: Biblio and Tannen.

Rubin, Jared. 2009. "Social insurance, commitment, and the origin of law: Interest bans in early Christianity." *Journal of Law and Economics* 52(4): 761–786.

Ruskin, John. 1867. *The Stones of Venice*, vol. 1. New York: John Wiley & Sons.

Sakowski, A. M. 1932. *The Great American Land Bubble*. New York: Harper and Brothers.

Schaps, David M. 2004. *The Invention of Coinage and the Monetization of Ancient Greece*. Ann Arbor: University of Michigan Press.

———. 2006. "The Invention of Coinage in Lydia, in India, and in China." Paper presented at Session 30 of the XIV International Economic History Congress, Helsinki, August 21–25, 2006.

Scheiber, Sylvester J. 2012. *The Predictable Surprise: The Unraveling of the U.S. Retirement System*. Oxford: Oxford University Press.

Scheidel, Walter (ed.). 2009. *Rome and China: Comparative Perspectives on Ancient World Empires*. Oxford: Oxford University Press.

Scheidel, Walter, Ian Morris, and Richard P. Saller (eds.). 2007. *The Cambridge Economic History of the Greco-Roman World*. Cambridge: Cambridge University Press.

Schmandt-Besserat, Denise. 1992. *From Counting to Cuneiform*, vol. 1. Austin: University of Texas Press.

Schmitz, Leonhard. 1875. "Argentarii," in William Smith (ed.), *A Dictionary of Greek and Roman Antiquities*. London: John Murray, pp. 130–132. Available at: http://penelope.uchicago.edu/Thayer/E/Roman/Texts/secondary/SMIGRA*/Argentarii.html.

Schneider, Robert Alan. 1989. *Public Life in Toulouse, 1463–1789: From Municipal Republic to Cosmopolitan City*. Ithaca, NY: Cornell University Press.

Schwartz, David. 2006. *Roll the Bones: The History of Gambling*. East Rutherford, NJ: Gotham Books.

Sciabarra, Chris Matthew. 1995. *Ayn Rand: The Russian Radical*. University Park: Pennsylvania State University Press.

Scott, William Robert. 1995. *Joint Stock Companies to 1720*. Bristol: Theomes Press. Original edition 1910–1912.

Seaford, Richard. 2004. *Money and the Early Greek Mind: Homer, Philosophy, Tragedy*. Cambridge: Cambridge University Press.

Seneca. 1920. "On Taking One's Own Life," in *Epistulae Morales*, R. M. Gummere (trans.). Cambridge, MA: Harvard University Press, epistle 77.

Shultz, Earle, and Walter Simmons. 1959. *Offices in the Sky*. Indianapolis, IN: Bobbs-Merrill.

Silver, Morris. 1995. *Economic Structures of Antiquity*. Contributions in Economics and Economic History 159. Westport: Greenwood Press.

———. 2011. "Finding the Roman Empire's disappeared deposit bankers." *Historia* 60(3): 301–327.

Slotsky, Alice Louise. 1997. *The Bourse of Babylon: Market Quotations in the Astronomical Diaries of Babylonia*. Bethesda, MD: CDL Press.

Smith, Adam. 1921. *An Inquiry into the Nature and Causes of the Wealth of Nations*, vol. 2. London: J. M. Dent & Sons.

Smith, Paul J. 1991. *Taxing Heaven's Storehouse: Horses, Bureaucrats, and the Destruction of the Sichuan Tea Industry, 1074–1224*. Harvard-Yenching Institute Monograph Series, vol. 32. Cambridge, MA: Council on East Asian Studies and Harvard University Press.

Sombart, Werner. 2001. *The Jews and Modern Capitalism*, M. Epstein (trans.). Kitchener, Ont.: Batoche. Originally published in 1911.

Sosin, Joshua D. 2000. "Perpetual Endowments in the Hellenistic world: A Case-Study in Economic Rationalism." Dissertation, Duke University, Durham, NC.

Spieth, Darius. 2006. "The Corsets Assignat in David's 'Death of Marat.'" *Source: Notes in the History of Art* 30: 22–28.

———. 2013. "The French Context of Het Groote Tafereel der dwaasheid, John Law, Rococo Culture, and the Riches of the New World," in William N. Goetzmann, Catherine Labio, K. Geert Rouwenhorst, and Timothy Young (eds.), *The Great Mirror of Folly: Finance, Culture, and the Great Crash of 1720*. New Haven, CT: Yale University Press, p. 231.

Stasavage, David. 2011. *States of Credit: Size, Power, and the Development of European Polities*. Princeton, NJ: Princeton University Press.

Stolper, Matthew W. 1985. *Entrepreneurs and Empire: The Murašû Archive, the Murašû Firm, and Persian Rule in Babylonia*. Istanbul: Nederlands Historisch-Archaeologisch Instituut te Istanbul.

The United States, vol. 1. New York: Journal of Commerce and Commercial Bulletin.

Sverdrup, H., and Peter Schlyter. 2013. "Modeling the Survival of Athenian Owl Tetradrachms Struck in the Period from 561–42 BC from Then to the Present," in *Proceedings of the 30th International Conference of the System Dynamics Society*, vol. 5. St. Gallen, Switzerland: Systems Dynamics Society, pp. 4024–4043.

Temin, Peter. 2002. "Price behavior in ancient Babylon." *Explorations in Economic History* 39(1): 46–60.

———. 2006. "The economy of the early Roman Empire." *Journal of Economic Perspectives* 20(1): 133–151.

———. 2013. *The Roman Market Economy*. Princeton, NJ: Princeton University Press.

Temin, Peter, and Hans-Joachim Voth. 2003. "Riding the South Sea Bubble." MIT Working Paper, Cambridge, MA.

———. 2006. "Banking as an emerging technology: Hoare's Bank, 1702–1742." *Financial History Review* 13(2): 149–178.

Thayer, Theodore. 1953. "The Land-Bank system in the American colonies." *Journal of Economic History* 13(2): 145–159.

Thomas, Hugh. 1997. *The Slave Trade*. New York: Simon and Schuster.

Thomas, W. A. 2001. *Western Capitalism in China*. Burlington, VT: Ashgate.

Thucydides. 1910. *The Peloponnesian War*, Richard Crawley (trans.). London and New York: J. M. Dent and E. P. Dutton.

Times. 1917. "COMPANY MEETINGS. Kyshtim Corporation (Limited). Mineral Resources of the Estates. Metallurgical and Commercial Industries," December 15, p. 12.

Tyson, Peter. 2006. "Future of the Passage." Available at: http://www.pbs.org/wgbh/nova/arctic/passage.html.

Ukhov, Andrey. 2003. Financial Innovation and Russian Government Debt before 1918. Yale ICF Working Paper 03–20, May 5.

Van De Mieroop, Marc. 1986. "Tūram-ilī: An Ur III merchant." *Journal of Cuneiform Studies* 38(1): 1–80.

———. 1992. *Society and Enterprise in Old Babylonian Ur*. Berlin: Dietrich Reimer Verlag.

———. 1997. *The Ancient Mesopotamian City*. Oxford: Oxford University Press.

———. 2005. "The Invention of Interest: Sumerian Loans," in William N. Goetzmann and K. Geert Rouwenhorst (eds.), *The Origins of Value: The Financial Innovations That Created Modern Capital Markets*. Oxford: Oxford University Press, pp. 17–30.

———. 2014. "Silver as a Financial Tool in Ancient Egypt and Mesopotamia," in Peter Bernholz and Roland Vaubel (eds.), *Explaining Monetary and Financial Innovation: A Historical Analysis*. Financial and Monetary Policy Studies vol. 39. Cham, Switzerland: Springer International, pp. 17–29.

Van der Spek, Robartus J. 1997. "New evidence from the Babylonian astronomical diaries concerning Seleucid and Arsacid history." *Archiv für Orientforschung* 1997: 167–175.

Van der Spek, Robartus J., Jan Luiten van Zanden, and Bas van Leeuwen (eds.). 2014. *A History of Market Performance: From Ancient Babylonia to the Modern World*, vol. 68. London: Routledge.

Van Egmond, Warren. 1980. *Practical Mathematics in the Italian Renaissance: A Catalog of Italian Abbacus Manuscripts and Printed Books to 1600*. Monografia 4, Annali dell'Istituto e Museo di Storia della Scienza di Firenze. Florence: Istituto e Museo di Storia della Scienza.

Van Wees, Hans. 2013. *Ships and Silver, Taxes and Tribute: A Fiscal History of Archaic Athens*. London: IB Tauris.

Veenhof, Klaas R. 2010. "Ancient Assur: The city, its traders, and its commercial network." *Journal of the Economic and Social History of the Orient* 53: 39–82.

Veenhof, Klaas R., and Jesper Eidem (eds.). 2008. *Mesopotamia: The Old Assyrian Period*. Orbis Biblicus et Orientalis, vol. 160/5. Saint Paul, MN: Academic Press Fribourg.

Veenhof, Klaas R., K. R. Veenhof, and Jesper Eidem. 2008. *Mesopotamia: Annäherungen*. Saint Paul, MN: Academic Press Fribourg.

Velde, François, and David Weir. 1992. "The financial market and government debt policy in France, 1746–1793." *Journal of Economic History* 52(1): 1–39.

Verboven, Koenraad. 2003. "54–44 BCE. Financial or Monetary Crisis?" In E. L. Cascio (ed.), *Credito e Moneta nel Mondo Romano*. Bari, Italy: Edipuglia, pp. 49–68.

Verboven, Koenraad, Katelijn Vandorpe, and Véronique Chankowski. 2008. *Pistoi dia tèn technèn. Bankers, Loans and Archives in the Ancient World*. Leuven, Belgium: Peeters.

Von Glahn, Richard. 2005. "The Origins of Paper Money in China," in William N. Goetzmann and K. Geert Rouwenhorst (eds.), *The Origins of Value: The Financial Innovations That Created Modern Capital Markets*. Oxford: Oxford University Press, pp. 65–90.

Von Reden, Sitta. 2007. *Money in Ptolemaic Egypt: From the Macedonian Conquest to the End of the Third Centrury BC*. Cambridge: Cambridge University Press.

Watson, Burton (trans.). 1971. *Records of the Grand Historian of China. Translated from the Shih chi of Ssu-ma Ch'ie*. New York: Columbia University Press.

Xenophon. 1892. *The Works of Xenophon*, H. G. Daykins (trans.). London: Macmillan and Company.

Zelin, Madeleine. 2005. *The Merchants of Zigong: Industrial Entrepreneurship in Early Modern China*. New York: Columbia University Press.

ILLUSTRATION CREDITS

CHAPTER 14.   Beinecke Rare Book and Manuscript Library, Yale University.

CHAPTER 15.   From Halley's *An Estimate of the Degrees of Mortality of Mankind* (1693). Philosophical Transactions of the Royal Society of London 17 (1693), 596-610 and 654-656. Reprinted, edited with an introduction by L.J. Reid, Baltimore, MD: The Johns Hopkins Press 1942.

FIGURE 20.   (a) https://commons.wikimedia.org/wiki/File:Nicolas_de _Condorcet.PNG; (b) https://commons.wikimedia.org/wiki/File: Thomas_Robert_Malthus_Wellcome_L0069037_-crop.jpg.

CHAPTER 16.   http://www.antique-prints.de/shop/catalog.php?list=KAT32&seg=2.

FIGURE 21.   Franck Jovanovic. 2006. "Economic instruments and theory in the construction of Henri Lefèvre's science of the stock market." *Pioneers of Financial Economics* 1: 169–190.

CHAPTER 20.   University of Cambridge Digital Library.

CHAPTER 18.   "The search for the North West Passage" by Ann Savors (page 6). The British Museum.

CHAPTER 19.   Courtesy of The Lewis Walpole Library, Yale University.

FIGURE 23.   Courtesy of The Lewis Walpole Library, Yale University.

CHAPTER 20.   http://en.wikipedia.org/wiki/John_Law_%28economist%29#/ media/File:John_Law-Casimir_Balthazar_mg_8450.jpg.

FIGURE 24.   Courtesy of The Lewis Walpole Library, Yale University.

CHAPTER 22.   https://commons.wikimedia.org/wiki/File:Wheat_Row_-_ Washington,_D.C..jpg.

FIGURE 25.   1886: bequeathed by Jules David-Chassagnol, Paris; 1893: acquired by Royal Museums of Fine Arts of Belgium. http://commons .wikimedia.org/wiki/File:Jacques-Louis_David_-_Marat_ assassinated_-_Google_Art_Project_2.jpg.

FIGURE 26.   Henry Lowenfeld, *Investment, an Exact Science*.

CHAPTER 24.   Swire Chin.

CHAPTER 25.   © Valeriya|Dreamstime.com-Portico of the Old Saint Petersburg Stock Exchange (Bourse) Photo.

CHAPTER 26.   National Portrait Gallery, London.

CHAPTER 27.   Alfred Stieglitz Collection, co-owned by Fisk University, Nashville, Tennessee, and Crystal Bridges Museum of American Art, Bentonville, Arkansas. Photograph by Edward C. Robison III.

FIGURE 27.   (c) Ann Parry/Ann-Parry.com.

CHAPTER 28.   Kheel Center, Cornell University. Photographer: Alan J. Bearden, ca. 1963.

CHAPTER 29.   Markowitz, *Portfolio Selection: Efficient Diversification of Investments*, John Wiley & Sons Ltd.

The following illustrations are from the author's private collection:

PARTS   I and IV

CHAPTERS   7, 8, 11, 12, 21, and 23

FIGURES   2, 14, 15, 17, 19, and 22

INDEX